Contemporary Readings in
Criminology

D1434526

litan

Contemporary Readings in
Criminology

Gennifer Furst
William Paterson University

Editor

Contemporary
CRS
Readings Series

SAGE

Los Angeles • London • New Delhi • Singapore • Washington DC

For information:

SAGE Publications, Inc.
2455 Teller Road
Thousand Oaks, California 91320
E-mail: order@sagepub.com

SAGE Publications Ltd.
1 Oliver's Yard
55 City Road
London EC1Y 1SP
United Kingdom

SAGE Publications India Pvt. Ltd.
B 1/I 1 Mohan Cooperative Industrial Area
Mathura Road, New Delhi 110 044
India

SAGE Publications Asia-Pacific Pte. Ltd.
33 Pekin Street #02-01
Far East Square
Singapore 048763

Printed in the United States of America.

Library of Congress Cataloging-in-Publication Data

Contemporary readings in criminology / edited by Gennifer Furst.
        p. cm.
Includes index.
ISBN 978-1-4129-5662-8 (pbk.)
    1. Criminology. I. Furst, Gennifer.

HV6025.C625 2009
364—dc22   2008036646

This book is printed on acid-free paper.

08 09 10 11 12 10 9 8 7 6 5 4 3 2 1

Acquisitions Editor:	Jerry Westby
Editorial Assistant:	Eve Oettinger
Production Editor:	Karen Wiley
Copy Editor:	Heather Jefferson
Typesetter:	C&M Digitals (P) Ltd.
Proofreader:	Kevin Gleason
Indexer:	Jean Casalegno
Cover Designer:	Candice Harman
Marketing Manager:	Jennifer Reed Banando

CONTENTS

Advancements in mapping technology have prompted researchers to focus on the environmental characteristics related to crime. In this article, Potchak, McGloin, and Zgoba draw on insights from rational choice theory to examine the effect of criminal effort—operationalized as distance traveled to a criminal opportunity—on auto theft incidents in Newark, New Jersey, during the year 2000. Mapping software (a) allowed the measurement of distance traveled between offender residences and points of theft and (b) provided a visual display.

Hummer analyzes data collected by the Bureau of Justice Statistics, which administered a questionnaire to larger (enrollment more than 2,500 students) colleges and universities throughout the United States. The primary focus of the original Bureau of Justice study was to assess the organization and functions of campus public safety departments. The survey also collected data on a number of variables that indicate the principles of situational crime prevention, as well as data on serious (Part I) offending.

Some authors claim that cybercrime *is not qualitatively different from* terrestrial crime, *and can be analyzed and explained using established theories of crime causation. One such approach, oft cited, is the "routine activity theory" developed by Marcus Felson and others. In this article Yar explores the extent to which the theory's concepts can be used to explain crimes committed in a "virtual" environment. The author concludes that, although some of the theory's core concepts can indeed be applied to cybercrime, there remain important differences between "virtual" and "terrestrial" worlds that limit the theory's usefulness. These differences give qualified support to the suggestion that cybercrime does indeed represent the emergence of a new and distinctive form of crime.*

III. POSITIVISM   57

To form a clear view of the origins of criminology and present-day practices in criminal justice, Rafter argues that criminologists need to recognize phrenology as one of their ancestors. Although phrenology is dismissed as a "pseudo-science" and mocked as "bumpology," it in fact constituted an important early science of the mind and the theories that phrenologists generated in the fields today called criminology, criminal jurisprudence and penology influenced those fields long after the phrenological map of the brain had been forgotten. Coming to terms with phrenology requires rejecting simple distinctions between science *and* pseudo-science.

In this article Plomin and Asbury argue that rather than nature versus nurture, we should approach criminology from a nature and nurture model. Research has found evidence of substantial genetic influence on many behavioral traits, as well as established the importance of environmental influences. Because much of human behavior is a result of the interaction between genes and the environment, genetic research needs to incorporate measures of the environment, and environmental research will be enhanced by collecting DNA.

This article discusses advantages of randomized experiments and the key issues raised by their use. Farrington focuses on the use of randomized experiments by the California Youth

Authority, the U.S. National Institute of Justice, and the British Home Office, although other experiments are also discussed. He concludes that feast and famine periods are influenced by key individuals. He recommends that policy makers, practitioners, funders, the mass media, and the general public need better education in research quality so that they can tell the difference between good and poor evaluation studies. They might then demand better evaluations using randomized experiments.

Control. Data from the 2001 National Household Survey of Drug Abuse are used to determine the relative effects of peers (social learning), strain (general strain theory), and favorable attitudes toward risk-taking (self control). Analysis of the data according to gender suggests that males are more likely to be chronic users, and that psychological strain, social learning, and low self control are significant factors associated with chronic use.

Section B: Disorganization

Largely absent from the research are examinations exploring the role of neighborhood context on police use-of-force practices. Using data collected as part of a systematic social observation study of police in Indianapolis, Indiana and St. Petersburg, Florida, Terrill and Reisig examine the influence of neighborhood context on the level of force police exercise during police-suspect encounters. The authors find police officers are significantly more likely to use higher levels of force when suspects are encountered in disadvantaged neighborhoods and those with higher homicide rates. The results reaffirm Smith's 1986 conclusion that police officers "act differently in different neighborhood contexts."

Community-level factors such as disadvantage, disorder, and disorganization have been linked to a variety of antisocial and illicit activities. Although crime and deviance tend to concentrate in areas with these characteristics, not all residents of disorganized neighborhoods participate in proscribed activities. In this study, Patchin, Huebner, McCluskey, Varano, and Bynum examine the relationship between exposure to community violence and involvement in assaultive behavior and weapon carrying among a sample of at-risk youth. Findings demonstrate that youth who witnessed more violence in their neighborhoods are more likely to self-report assaultive behavior and weapon carrying.

Section C: Subculture

The extent to which subcultural theories of deviance are still relevant to understanding recreational drug use, given the relatively widespread nature of drug use among today's youth, is not known. Gurley examines the social and subcultural use of the popular drug ecstasy (MDMA) through semi-structured interviewing and observation conducted in Australia. The data suggest that ecstasy use results from social involvement in a subculture of drug use. It is argued that subcultural theories of deviance provide an important understanding of ecstasy use in today's society.

The subculture of violence thesis suggests that African Americans are disproportionately likely to respond to minor transgressions with lethal force because of a culturally defined need to protect one's reputation and a normative aversion to legal forms of dispute resolution. Using data on over 950 non-justifiable homicides from police files, Hannon tests this hypothesis by examining race-specific patterns of victim participation (i.e., the victim's role in initiating the homicide). If, as the theory suggests, African Americans are more likely to respond to minor affronts with lethal violence than Whites, then African American homicide incidents should have more victim participation, particularly in the form of minor acts of provocation. The results of the current analysis do not support this hypothesis and are inconsistent with the notion that a unique subculture of violence among African Americans explains their disproportionately high levels of homicide victimization and offending.

VI. SOCIAL PROCESS PERSPECTIVE   147

Section A: Social Learning

Tammy Castle & Christopher Mensley, (2002), *International Journal of Offender Therapy and Comparative Criminology*, 46, 453–465

Scholars have studied the motivation and causality behind serial murder by researching biological, psychological, and sociological variables. However, the study of serial murder continues to be an exploratory rather than explanatory research topic. In this article, Castle and Hensley examine the possible link between serial killers and military service. Citing previous research using social learning theory for the study of murder, this article explores how potential serial killers learn to reinforce violence, aggression, and murder in military boot camps. As with other variables considered in serial killer research, military experience alone cannot account for all cases of serial murder.

Allison T. Chappell & Alex R. Piquero, (2004), *Deviant Behavior*, 25, 89–108

Although numerous studies have attempted to understand the causes of various forms of police misconduct, there is still no clear theoretical explanation of police misbehavior. According to Akers' social learning theory, peer associations, attitudes, reinforcement, and modeling are predictors of delinquency and crime in general. With this article Chappell and Piquero seek to determine if the theory can account for police deviance. Data from a random sample of Philadelphia police officers are used to examine how officer attitudes and perceptions of peer behavior are related to citizen complaints of police misconduct. Findings suggest that social learning theory provides a useful explanation of police misconduct.

Section B: Labeling and Reintegrative Shaming

Patricia Funk, (2004), *European Economic Review*, 48, 715–728

Stigma affects convicted offenders if employers reduce their wage. Current research considers this kind of informal sanctioning an effective means for reducing crime. In this article, Funk first shows that increasing stigma may even enhance crime. While stigma enhances deterrence of an unconvicted offender, it may drive a stigmatized ex-convict towards recidivism. Secondly, the author offers a solution to guarantee stigma's effectiveness: harsh(er) punishment for repeat offenders is required. Finally, stigmatization policies in the United States, Switzerland and Spain are compared.

Xiaoming Chen, (2002), *International Journal of Offender Therapy and Comparative Criminology*, 46, 45–63

In this article, Chen examines the philosophy and functions of social control in Chinese society where control mechanisms are grounded in a macro-control system which is not found in typical Western countries. The article also considers the implications of labeling theory and reintegrative shaming theory, as they are elaborated in the West, and tests their sensitivity to cross-cultural differences. The evidence presented here tends to support reintegrative shaming theory rather than labeling theory.

Section C: Social Control/Bond

John R. Hepburn & Marie L. Griffin, (2004), *Criminal Justice Review, 29*, 46–75

Recent studies of the effect of social bonds on offenders' adjustment to probation have produced mixed results, with some suggestion that successful adjustment is the result of the deterrent effects of probation supervision rather than the stabilizing effects of social bonds. In this article, Hepburn and Griffin study child molesters entering probation–an offender population with maximum physical and social estrangement from society. The authors use measures of employment and of the quality of social relationships with family and friends to test the hypothesis that social bonds will significantly affect successful adjustment to probation supervision. They find support for the hypothesis that positive social bonds enhance offenders' positive adjustment to supervision. Employment and support of family and friends were also found to affect offenders' ability to successfully adjust to the problems of community reentry.

Douglas Longshore, Eunice Chang, Shih-chao Hsieh, and Nena Messina, (2004),
Crime and Delinquency, 50, 542–564

With longitudinal data from a sample of adult male drug offenders, Longshore, Chang, Hsieh, and Messina test four aspects of social bonding (attachment, involvement, religious commitment, and moral belief) and association with substance-using peers as outcomes of low self-control and drug use. Low self-control was negatively related to social bonds and positively related to drug use and association with substance-abusing peers. The results support the utility of integrating self-control and social bonding perspectives on deviance.

Section D: Self-Control

L. Thomas Winfree, Jr., Terrance J. Taylor, Ni He, & Finn-Aage Esbensen, (2006),
Crime and Delinquency, 52, 253–286

Gottfredson and Hirschi claimed, as part of their general theory of crime, that a child's criminal propensity, level of self-control, is fairly fixed by age 10. Low self-control children exhibit greater delinquency and analogous behaviors than children with high levels of self-control. They see self-control levels as unchangeable over the lifecourse. In this article Winfree, Taylor, He, and Esbensen explore self-control levels, self-reported illegal behavior, and supporting attitudes exhibited by a panel of youths from six cities at five points in time. Some of the findings substantiated Gottfredson and Hirschi's claims (e.g., claims linking self-control, sex, and race or ethnicity); however, other findings are at odds with their theory (e.g., the unchanging nature of self-control). The authors review the implications of these findings for self-control theory.

VII. LIFE COURSE THEORY   217

Brent B. Benda, Nancy J. Toombs, & Mark Peacock, (2006), *Journal of
Criminal Justice, 34*, 27–38

This study of 784 inmates in a boot camp in a southern state was designed to determine what elements from life-course theory distinguished between graduates, dropouts, and dismissals from the program in this facility. Analysis showed that several social bonds–such as employment, income, marital status–and personal assets, like self-efficacy, differentiated graduates from dropouts and dismissals from that program. In contrast, selling drugs, illegal income, and carrying a weapon were also associated with graduation. Lack of self-control, drug use, and peer association differentiated dropouts from graduates, whereas history of being abused, emotional problems, and suicidel attempts distinguished dismissals from graduates. The implications of these findings for further research and current decision-making are discussed.

Marilyn Brown, (2006), *Critical Criminology, 14,* 137–158

This paper develops what some researchers call the "pathways" approach to explaining women's criminality. The perspective argues that women's offending is an outgrowth of histories of violence, trauma, and addiction—conditioned by race, culture, gender inequality, and class. In this article, Brown expands the perspective on crime across the life course for females, providing a more detailed analysis of the nature of intimate relationships and developmental turning points for women. While men's assumption of adult responsibilities such as marriage and childrearing may be turning points away from delinquency and crime, the matter is more complex for some women. Brown also finds that women of Native Hawaiian ancestry have more negative experiences with education, employment, and poorer outcomes on parole compared to women without Hawaiian ancestry, thus contributing to the literature on the relationship between ethnicity, social structure, and offending over the life course.

Nickie D. Phillips & Staci Strobl, (2006), *Crime, Media, Culture, 2,* 304–331

The current study utilizes a cultural criminological approach to examine paradigms of justice portrayed in American comic books. Based on a review of the literature, Phillips and Strobl hypothesize that the dominant crimes depicted in comic books are violent street crimes and that the portrayed responses to these crimes are executed outside the rule of law by an avenging protagonist. Based on a content analysis of 20 contemporary best-selling comic books, themes of organized crime, often involving complex transnational networks, are more prevalent than street crimes, contrary to the authors' hypothesis. However, the response to crime remains focused on vigilante methods and on the restoration of a constructed utopia-like community that embraces the rule of law.

Moira Peelo, (2006), *Crime, Media, Culture, 2,* 159–175

In this article, Peelo identifies ways in which newspapers invite readers to identify with victims and victimhood as a route to engaging them in "human interest" stories; the reader is placed as witness. The author raises questions about the functions of pubic narratives, particularly in expressing public or social emotion, in an era in which public responses to crime are part of a highly politicized crime agenda.

Karim Ismaili, (2006), *Criminal Justice Policy Review, 17,* 255–269

As the criminological subfield of crime policy leads more criminologists to engage in policy analysis, understanding the policy-making environment in all of its complexity becomes more central to criminology. In this article, Ismaili presents a contextual approach to examine the criminal justice policy-making environment; the approach emphasizes the complexity inherent to policy contexts. For research on the policy process to advance, contextually sensitive methods of policy inquiry must be formulated to illuminate the social reality of criminal justice policy.

TOPICS GUIDE

Adolescent/teen delinquency: article 16

Campus crime: article 5

Car theft: article 4

Comparative (cross-cultural): article 3, 12, 20, 21, 26, 36, 37

Crime policy: article 33, 34

Criminology history: article 1, 7, 9

Cultural criminology: article 29, 30

Cyber crime: article 6

Drugs/alcohol: article 13, 16

Female delinquency/crime: article 2, 13, 26, 38

Labeling: article 20, 21,

Life course theory: article 25, 26

Nature/nurture: article 8

Police: article 14, 19, 32, 34, 38

Property crime: article 34, 35

Psychopathology: article 10, 11

Public order crime: 38, 39

Routine activities theory: article 4, 5, 6

Self control: article 23, 24

Sex offenders: article 22

Social disorganization: article 14, 15

Social learning: article 18, 19

Social control/bond: article 22, 23

Strain: article 12, 13

Subculture: article 16, 17

Terrorism: article 11

Victimization: article 2, 3, 17, 28

Violent crime: article 31, 32, 33

White-collar/organized crime: article 36, 37

ADVISORY BOARD

David E. Krahl, PhD—University of Tampa

Tammy Castle—James Madison University

Ashley G. Blackburn, PhD—University of North Texas

David J. Thomas, PhD—Florida Gulf Coast University

Melissa A. Logue—Saint Joseph's University

Bruce Bikle—California State University at Sacramento

Jennifer Schwartz—Washington State University

E. Britt Patterson—Shippensburg University

Mark E. Correia—San Jose State University

Dr. Ida Dupont—Pace University

Steven Downing—College of Mount St. Joseph

Gordon M. Robinson—Springfield College

Martha L. Shockey-Eckles, PhD—Saint Louis University

Robert Garot—John Jay College of Criminal Justice

Leana Allen Bouffard—Washington State Universiy

James G. Foley—Texas College

PREFACE

The chapters included in this volume were chosen for reflecting the interests of undergraduate students in criminology. Because research and methodology can seem overwhelming and arcane to students, this compilation introduces students to criminological research and methodology using chapters that are accessible and examine explanations for criminality via contemporary topics. The organization of this volume is based on what is found in most criminology textbooks, generally according to the historical development of the field.

The volume begins with Part I (Introduction), starting with chapter 1, "The State of the Field of Criminology," which summarizes the state of the field of criminology today. Then, chapter 2, "The Relationship Between Child Sexual Abuse and Female Delinquency and Crime," demonstrates the cycle of violence, which is important to consider as we begin to examine what influences and causes criminality. Chapter 3, "A Comparison of Help Seeking Between Latino and Non-Latino Victims of Intimate Partner Violence," considers cross-cultural differences in domestic violence victims' help-seeking behavior.

Part II, Classical Criminology (Choice Theory), examines research regarding classical criminology and its modern form, choice theory, as applied to three crimes of interest to many undergraduates. Chapter 4, "A Spatial Analysis of Criminal Effort," discusses car theft. Chapter 5, "Serious Criminality at U.S. Colleges and Universities," examines crime committed on college campuses. Chapter 6, "The Novelty of 'Cybercrime'," explores crime using the Internet. Part III, Positivism, considers the legitimacy of phrenology, early science's attempt at data-driven theory development in chapter 7, "The Murderous Dutch Fiddler: Criminology, History, and the Problem of Phrenology." Then, in chapter 8, "Nature *and* Nurture: Genetic and Environmental Influences on Behavior," an alternative to the nature versus nurture debate regarding the causes of behavior is presented—a nature and nurture approach. The limited but significant findings to come from true experiments in the field of criminology are reviewed in chapter 9, "A Short History of Randomized Experiments in Criminology."

In Part IV, Psychological theories of criminality are presented prior to the several branches of sociological theories that comprise the majority of the volume. Psychopathy, the cluster of psychological symptoms most commonly associated with criminality, is applied to the unique topic of tattooing among incarcerated people in chapter 10, "Psychopathology and Tattooing Among Prisoners." Then, psychopathy and terrorism are examined in chapter 11, "The Terrorist Mind: Typologies, Psychopathologies, and Practical Guidelines for Investigation."

The first branch of sociological theories is presented in Part V, Social Structure Perspective. Strain is examined cross-culturally in chapter 12, "Life Strain, Coping, and Delinquency in the People's Republic of China," and its role in marijuana use is considered in chapter 13, "Marijuana Use as a Coping Response to Psychological Strain," which also examines race, gender, and ethnic differences. Disorganization, an ecological approach, is examined for its effect on police use of force during interactions with the public in chapter 14, "Neighborhood Context and Police Use of Force." Chapter 15, "Exposure to Community Violence and Childhood Delinquency," considers the overlap of social disorganization and social learning approaches. Finally, subcultural theories are presented, first as applied to ecstasy use in chapter 16, "A Subcultural Study of Recreational Ecstasy Use," and then as an explanation for homicide in chapter 17, "Race, Victim-Precipitated Homicide, and the Subculture of Violence Thesis."

The second branch of sociological theories is presented in Part VI, Social Process Perspective. The effects of social learning on serial killing are examined in chapter 18, "Serial Killers With Military Experience: Applying Learning Theory to Serial Murder." The theory is applied to police misconduct in chapter 19, "Applying Social Learning Theory to Police Misconduct." Labeling, and its modern application as reintegrative shaming, is presented in chapter 20, "On the Effective Use of Stigma as a Crime-Deterrent," which examines the duality of stigma—it prevents some from offending, but makes others more likely to offend. Chapter 21, "Social Control in China: Applications of the Labeling Theory and the Reintegrative Shaming Theory," a comparative examination, explores how labeling and reintegrative shaming are used as social control in China. Chapter 22, "The Effect of Social Bonds on Successful Adjustment to Probation," examines social bonds as they influence the connections to work and family/friends of successful probation among child molesters. The strengths of self-control and social bond theories are joined in a combined control perspective on deviance in chapter 23, "Self-Control and Social Bonds." The final subtopic in Part VI, self-control, is examined in chapter 24, "Self-Control and Variability Over Time," which considers longitudinal data regarding changes in self-control over the life course.

Part VII examines contemporary Life Course Theory, first applied to success in boot camp in chapter 25, "Distinguishing Graduates From Dropouts and Dismissals: Who Fails Boot Camp?" In chapter 26, "Gender, Ethnicity, and Offending Over the Life Course: Women's Pathways to Prison in the Aloha State," the approach is applied to the criminality of females of Hawaiian ancestry.

Critical theories of crime are represented in Part VIII by chapters examining Cultural Criminology. Chapter 27, "Cultural Criminology and Kryptonite: Apocalyptic and Retributive Constructions of Crime and Justice in Comic Books," presents an analysis of constructions of crime and justice in comic books. Chapter 28, "Framing Homicide Narratives in Newspapers: Mediated Witness and the Construction of Virtual Victimhood," provides a critical assessment of how homicides are framed or written about in newspapers.

In Part IX, Crime Policy, chapter 29, "Contextualizing the Criminal Justice Policymaking Process," explores the link between policymaking and theories explaining crime. Part X considers the Future of Criminology in chapter 30, "Criminalizing War: Criminology as Ceasefire," which outlines a new criminology of war.

After discussing explanations for crimes, the volume concludes with Part XI, Crime Typologies, which introduces various types of crimes. The typology is presented using chapters from more popular sources such as newspapers. Four major types of crime are included: violent crime and terrorism, property crime, white-collar and organized crime, and public order crime.

PART I

INTRODUCTION

The three chapters included in this introductory section were chosen to highlight several basic principles of criminology and victimology, a subarea of the field often presented to students at the start of a criminology course. In *The State of the Field of Criminology*, Chris Eskridge (chap. 1) describes contemporary criminology as a science that is not yet mature. He suggests a global, interdisciplinary approach to the field that considers the role of politics and increasingly relies on evidence-based research for program and policy development. As we begin to examine criminality, it is important to recognize the cycle of violence, which Jane Siegel and Linda Williams (chap. 2) establish in *The Relationship Between Child Sexual Abuse and Female Delinquency and Crime: A Prospective Study*. Using a longitudinal research design, the authors examine the criminal offenses committed by a sample of females who were treated for sexual abuse as children in the 1970s. They find victimization from child sexual abuse and other serious family problems increased the likelihood of having engaged in crime. In *A Comparison of Help Seeking Between Latino and Non-Latino Victims of Intimate Partner Violence*, Eben Ingram (chap. 3) examines the prevalence of intimate partner violence and help seeking in a large sample (more than 12,000) of randomly chosen participants. Ingram finds differences in help seeking through formal and informal channels across ethnic groups.

CHAPTER 1

The State of the Field of Criminology

Brief Essay

Chris W. Eskridge
University of Nebraska

Preface

I wish to utilize a bit of editorial license as the general editor of this chapter and . . . examine the state of the field of criminology in the following article. This piece has not been refereed, although I have sought and received feedback from more than a dozen colleagues. I sincerely thank all who took the time and effort to read and comment. In the end, of course, I take the responsibility for the notions and concepts outlined, and consequently I will not note the reviewers' names, lest they be accused of guilt via association. . . .

Introduction

It is useful at times to pause and examine, to assess where we are, and to consider where it is that we need to go. Academic criminology has perhaps a greater need than most disciplines to engage in such introspection given its rather convoluted history. We trace our intellectual roots to those who would classify themselves as philosophers (Beccaria), physicians (Lombroso), lawyers (Blackstone), sociologists (Durkheim), psychologists (Garafalo), and practitioner politicians (Vollmer). Yet like the proverbial elephant in Aesop's fable, criminology is all of these, yet none of these in their entirety. At the dawn of the 21st century, criminology has morphed into something different, something quite unique that tends to incorporate virtually all other disciplines in some fashion or another. Criminology is also a dose of contemporary social and political reality, from which a wellspring of new ideas and notions flow endlessly. The purpose of this chapter is to examine the state of the field of criminology and propose a model for future growth and development.

REDUCTION OF CRIME

I would suggest initially that I ascribe to the principles laid out by Emile Durkheim a century ago. . . . I ascribe specifically to his constant dictum—there will always be behavior that society defines as deviant, unacceptable, criminal. In an aggregate, longitudinal context, we cannot reduce the extent of crime. It is omnipresent. Occasionally, I hear a politician speak to the need of embarking on one policy or another so as to "eliminate" crime. We cannot eliminate crime anymore than a physician can eliminate death. Like a physician, however, criminologists can develop preventative and curative responses that can affect positively the problems at hand.

. . . Within the distinctive socioeconomic portfolio of each individual community or nation, we need to be about the business of identifying and incorporating various preventative and curative programs and responses that will minimize the impact of crime and deviance. This is what criminology is about. It is not about eliminating crime in the aggregate, but rather minimizing the

Source: "The State of the Field of Criminology: Brief Essay." Eskridge, C. W., (2005), *Journal of Contemporary Criminal Justice, 21*, 296–308. Reprinted by permission of Sage Publications, Inc.

impact of crime—reducing the severity of the impact of crime. From an aggregate, longitudinal context, the extent of crime may remain constant; however, the seriousness of the nature of crime can be reduced.

For example, it is quite apparent to me that if handgun controls were instituted in the United States, there would be fewer murders. Fewer murders you might ask? That is a reduction in crime. To the contrary, the scenarios would play out like this: Two people would get into an argument; however, because there is no gun available, they would grab a knife or club. They could still kill; however, a knife or club has a decidedly lower killing capability quotient, and the victim would be more likely to live. Result: murder down, aggravated assault up, extent of crime the same, and nature of seriousness decreased. This is what modern criminology should be about: finding programs and policies and procedures that can reduce the severity of the nature of crime.

REDUCING THE SEVERITY OF CRIME

How do we reduce the severity of crime? A comprehensive U.S. Congress-sponsored study concluded that we simply do not know. . . . Some programs and policies seem successful, whereas others are clearly dismal failures; however, we are not sure why on either count. We have not been able to crack the cause-and-effect barrier with any degree of surety. However, what we have concluded is that there is a procedural model that we must now embrace that will put us on the path to eventually be able to answer the question. That model has three components:

- expand criminology and/or criminal justice education in universities throughout the world, and particularly the developing and transitional nations
- embrace an interdisciplinary perspective in academic criminology and/or criminal justice
- incorporate systematic, evidence-based evaluation within academic and political criminology.

Criminal Justice Education

We need to bring criminology and/or criminal justice education into universities throughout the world. It is my proposition that, in time, this strategic plan will, among other benefits, reduce the scope and extent of crime and corruption in every nation. This, in turn, will yield an enhanced opportunity for all, and particularly the developing nations, to secure external investment, realize increased economic stability, and eventually participate to a greater degree in the global economy. . . .

This notion is of some significance because we will not even begin to adequately address the world's crime problems until the developing and transitional nations are able to participate in the market economy as full partners. They are not full partners at present; however, developing criminal justice programs can, among other things, help them move in that direction.

Let me couple these initial observations with another that is, to some extent, a blinding flash of the obvious—the Western concept of the rule of law, democratic traditions, and the professional development of and the communal legitimization of institutions of public order have not been firmly established in most transitional and developing nations. Because of, in large part, this factor, these nations have particularly struggled to adequately address their crime and corruption problem, which in turn has contributed to their difficulty in becoming fully integrated into the Western world's market economy and, ultimately, to their disproportionate contribution to the crime problem worldwide. The problem is that social democracy and contemporary capitalism cannot be easily grafted onto many traditional societies. It is my proposition that criminal justice education can help reverse this trend.

Specifically, there are three positive impacts that will accrue for nations that embrace criminal justice education:

1. Over time, graduates from university criminal justice programs will gradually begin to fill justice system positions within their respective countries, which will slowly and steadily help to further professionalize justice operations within each country.

2. Most who take university classes in criminal justice will not seek employment in the justice system per se, but will move on to careers in other areas, such as business, engineering, nursing, and so on. They become the body politic, and their exposure to the principles and concepts outlined in their criminology and/or criminal justice classes will have increased their understanding as to the proper role and function of the justice system and its personnel. Subsequently, this more attuned and aware general populace will hold justice system personnel to a higher standard. . . .

3. Justice officials also will be able to respond more positively to increased public demand because of, perhaps, the most important aspect of all: By

embracing criminal justice education, nations will benefit from an enhanced research capability. The faculty and students of the university criminal justice programs will engage in research activities that will produce a more complete knowledge base and shed further light on the ways and means of improving justice system practices, programs, and policies. Armed with these new tools and a more refined knowledge-based justice system, personnel will be in a better position to perform their duties in accordance with heightened public demand.

In summary, criminology and/or criminal justice education will, over time, produce thousands, tens of thousands, and even hundreds of thousands of informed citizens who will hold justice officials more accountable and who will demand a higher standard of performance. In addition, criminology and/or criminal justice education will produce thousands of justice officials with the academic background to be able to respond professionally and who can turn to locally developed and locally relevant research undertaken by local university criminologists (students and faculty) to help them. . . .

An Interdisciplinary Academic Model

We need to continue to embrace an interdisciplinary perspective within academic criminology and criminal justice. The hard sciences and medicine were two of the great success stories of the 20th century. Conspicuously absent in this great leap, however, were the social and behavioral sciences. . . . Compared with the hard sciences and medicine, the traditional disciplines of sociology, psychology, anthropology, economics, history, and political science are comatose, if not altogether dead. The primary reason . . . is intellectual incest.

. . . PhDs in the social sciences . . . anoint their own. Sociologists train sociologists, psychologists teach psychologists, and political scientists prepare political scientists, and the result is inevitably some measure of academic atrophy in these fields. . . .

Although there are a few social science research think tanks, there is nothing in the social and behavioral sciences that even comes close to paralleling National Aeronautics and Space Administration, the Center for Disease Control, or the Mayo Clinic. Cross-disciplinary consultations are the rule of the day in the hard sciences and medicine. The old barriers in the hard sciences are being torn down daily with stupefying results. The social and behavioral sciences have simply not even begun to

keep pace with the rate of development and progress in the hard sciences. However, there have been some contributions of merit coming from the soft sciences in this past century. . . .

I would suggest that much of the momentum behind the rather rapid rise of criminal justice as a field of study in the United States has been its cross-disciplinary diversity. A marginal field of study in the 1960s and 1970s, criminal justice exploded onto the academic scene in the 1990s, in part, because of not only the emergence of crime as a fundamental matter on the mind of the body politic, but also, in large part, academic diversity and to its multidisciplinary character. It is not unusual to see criminal justice faculty members' degrees in history, psychology, sociology, public administration, law, political science, urban studies, and criminology and criminal justice.

There is a need to continue to cling to the multidisciplinary model that has fueled this rather abrupt contemporary rise of criminal justice in the world of academe. Such a proposal has two distinct advantages:

1. Students will have their educational experience enhanced because of this academic cross-breeding. They will interact with faculty and students from other disciplines and see things from a broader perspective. The nature of education suggests the need to break out, to examine and explore from new perspectives and new horizons. A narrowly focused degree in the social science and/or liberal arts tradition is an oxymoron. . . .

2. This proposal will serve to increase the nature and scope of the interaction among faculty members from different fields of study, with a resulting increase in productivity as a result of this cross-fertilization. It also will strengthen ties among academic departments on campus. There is, in fact, a need to break down the walls of disciplinary sterility that infect so many academic institutions, and this proposal will go far to achieve that end. A side effect will be multidepartmental grant proposals and a general aura of collaborative research and writing. . . . [T]he hard sciences have already moved in this direction, particularly the medical field; a single author piece in a medical journal is as passé as a prescription for laudanum. . . . No one individual can possibly be expected to absorb and assimilate all relevant material in the vast and exploding entity we call the *body of knowledge*. An interdisciplinary criminal justice program recognizes this reality and serves as an aggressive and robust response to the realities of modern social science.

Evidence-Based Criminology

What do we know about reducing the severity of crime? What works—specifically what operational programs and policies reduce the severity of crime in a relatively consistent and uniform fashion? What specific programs and policies can improve our cities and neighborhoods in a justice and equity context? As already noted in this chapter and by others . . . , we are not certain; we lack specificity and causal understanding, and what we do implement has generally not been systematically evaluated.

We criminologists are somewhat akin to physicians of the 18th century. We have a few ideas, we are making progress; however, we have yet to attain the status of a mature, evidence-based, and evidence-driven science. We lack consistent, proven diagnostic instruments; we lack a definitive body of knowledge; and we lack generally consistent treatment modalities. . . . We are using relatively crude instruments, as did the physicians of the 1700s, and we largely respond to the crime problem using crude, homespun, untested remedies, as did the physicians of the 18th century. . . . Medicine, of course, is still developing and does not possess all the answers. However, it does have numerous proven diagnostic instruments, a solid body of knowledge, a cause-and-effect and/or epistemological understanding, and a wide variety of effective, disease-specific, and patient-specific treatment modalities. . . .

Perhaps the primary weakness in the would-be science of criminology is the lack of a basic epistemological understanding. A criminological Louis Pasteur has yet to appear to push our field into a new paradigm of scientific inquiry. In addition, what is implemented is generally because of more political value, rather than scientific merit. In the final analysis, academic criminology is generally polluted by political criminology because public policy tends to be a pinch of science (and often bad science at that) and a pound of ideology. I would suggest that much of what passes for knowledge in criminology today is myth; it is not backed with systematic evaluation. That which is implemented (or shunned) is not based on sound inquiry, but generally on the omnipresent query of all politicians: "Is this a politically palatable program or policy?"

My field, our field, the would-be science of criminology, is polluted by power and politics, which often renders carefully crafted evaluations useless in a pragmatic context. We can speak of scientific criminology; however, it has a Siamese twin, political criminology. It is incumbent on us as criminologists to engage not only in the science of criminology, but also in political criminology, if we ever expect to see our findings have any practical value. . . .

This account highlights the need of scientific criminologists to recognize that there are actually two fields that need to be surmounted if impact is to be achieved: scientific criminology and political criminology. As quantitatively sound as it is, removing handguns from the American public is just not going to happen despite that such a policy would definitively result in fewer murders. As quantitatively sound as it is, the horribly unbalanced social inequality quotient is not going to be addressed in the United States despite that this is clearly a precipitating factor when it comes to crime issues. There is no political capital for seriously addressing either notion in the United States. They are not politically palatable themes. There are political truths, and there are scientific truths. Our role as criminologists is not only to uncover scientific truths, but also to engage in activities that create an environment where those scientific truths can be implemented.

Finally, we should recognize that there are some programs that do seem to work (affect positively crime and streamline justice system operations) and that at least now are somewhat politically acceptable: Project Head Start, community policing, the ADAM project, neighborhood justice centers and/or dispute resolution centers, and hot-spot or ROP patrolling. These and other programs and ideas seem to work well in a generally uniform fashion across various jurisdictions and regions in the United States; however, it remains to be seen whether they are transferable to other countries and cultures. Only by engaging in systematic evaluation will we know for sure.

Conclusions

I have tried to highlight several points in this chapter:

- We cannot eliminate crime, but can reduce its severity and, thus, minimize its negative impact.
- To reduce the severity of crime, we must adopt a model that:
  a. advances criminology and/or criminal justice education on a global scale, particularly in the transitional and developing nations;
  b. embraces an interdisciplinary perspective in academic criminology and/or criminal justice; and
  c. incorporates systematic, evidence-based program and policy evaluation.

We are not a mature science at this point, and we are not certain how to systematically reduce the severity of crime. We have some ideas, and we are making progress; however, we are not there yet. We lack instruments, a definitive body of knowledge, an understanding of cause and effect, and a series of generally consistent treatment modalities. In this context, we are somewhat akin to physicians of the 18th century.

Because political criminology often rears its head and supercedes scientific criminology, to reduce the severity of crime, we must become effective political as well as scientific criminologists.

I would again temper this discussion with the thought that the model I propose (widespread interdisciplinary criminal justice education, systematic evaluation, and political efficacy) emerges as quite inconsequential when examined in the context of the complex and dynamic socioeconomic-political world. As noted at the outset of this chapter, any number of Armageddon-like events (worldwide famine, detonation of weapons of mass destruction in urban areas, significant reduction in access to energy resources, etc.) would obviously have a much greater influence on the global crime and deviance factor than any model I may propose. Yet as criminologists, we can, in our own way, and in our own sphere, offer much. "The chief duty of society is justice," wrote the American statesman Alexander Hamilton some 200 years ago. By clinging to this proposed model, we can improve the environments in which we live, and, as a result, justice and equity will be more frequent visitors to our homes, our neighborhoods, our nations, and our world.

Questions

1. According to Eskridge, why are criminologists of today like physicians in the late 1700s?

2. Eskridge argues "that politics pollutes this field." What does he mean?

CHAPTER 2

The Relationship Between Child Sexual Abuse and Female Delinquency and Crime

A Prospective Study

Jane A. Siegel

Center for Children and Childhood Studies, Rutgers University

Linda M. Williams

National Violence Against Women Prevention Research Center,
Wellesley Centers for Women, Wellesley College

In recent years, women and girls have accounted for a growing proportion of people arrested and convicted for serious offenses . . . , a trend that underscores the need for better understanding of the etiology of female crime and delinquency. Several scholars have posited that explanations of female offending must take into account the victimization that women experience as both children and adults, and research suggests that child sexual abuse may indeed play a central role in some girls' pathway to delinquency and subsequent crime. For instance, studies of female delinquents . . . report that approximately half (48–53%) have been sexually abused, and the proportion of women prisoners who report having a history of childhood sexual victimization is two to three times greater than women in the general public. . . . The literature on the relationship between sexual abuse and female crime, together with that on the effects of child sexual abuse, provides evidence that helps explain why such victimization may be an important etiological factor for various behaviors—such as running away, drug abuse, prostitution, and even violence—that can lead to criminal justice involvement.

Accounts of female offenders' life histories have led to the hypothesis that sexual abuse triggers a woman's criminal career by leading her to run away as a means of escaping the abuse she is experiencing at home. . . . Running away may result in arrest and incarceration, but also can lead to other forms of offending: Once on the streets, the runaway may turn to prostitution and stealing to survive. . . . Indeed, several retrospective investigations find that substantial proportions of prostitutes have a history of childhood sexual abuse . . . , although more recent research . . . reports no significant difference in the proportion of adolescent prostitutes who have been sexually abused when compared to demographically similar nonprostitutes. McCarthy and Hagan . . . also found that a history of sexual abuse was not a significant predictor of prostitution once situational variables such as unemployment were controlled for in their study of homeless youth and adolescents living at home. However, sexual abuse was found to be a statistically significant predictor of running away, as it has been in other studies . . . , and at least one study of male and female runaways has found that only females identified sexual abuse as the reason that they ran away. . . . Some evidence indicates that sexually abused runaways also appeared to be at greater risk of engaging in prostitution . . . or sex work . . . when compared with nonabused runaways

Source: "The relationship between child sexual abuse and female delinquency and crime: A prospective study." Siegel, J. A. & Williams, L. M. (2003), in *Journal of Research in Crime and Delinquency, 40,* 71–94. Reprinted by permission of Sage Publications, Inc.

and that female runaways who were sexually abused were at greater risk of engaging in other forms of delinquency, although males were not.... Widom and Ames..., however, reported that none of the sexual abuse victims in their prospective study who had an adult arrest for prostitution had previously been arrested for running away as a juvenile.

As with running away and prostitution, another offense category in which differences between abuse victims and others might be expected is drug offenses because research has generally shown that both adolescents and adults with substance abuse problems report significantly higher rates of child sexual abuse victimization than others.... Studies of female prisoners... and a cohort of abused children... have concluded that there was a relationship between maltreatment in general and drug abuse or arrests for drug offenses.

The relationship between violent offenses and child sexual abuse has received less attention than the other forms of crime discussed earlier, but prior research on the behavioral consequences of child sexual abuse and evidence from life histories of female offenders suggest that there is reason to investigate the relationship between violent offending and a history of sexual abuse. Several studies have reported that children who are sexually abused are significantly more physically aggressive than children who are not..., and a meta-analysis of studies of the effects of child sexual abuse found that such victimization accounted for 43% of the variance in measures of aggression when comparing abused and nonabused children....

Histories of sexual abuse also have figured in the backgrounds of aggressive women observed in qualitative studies. Baskin and Sommers's... life history interviews with 170 violent female felons revealed that 36% reported having been sexually abused by a member of their immediate family and 26% by a member of their extended family. The histories recounted in Artz's... ethnographic study of violent girls in Canada likewise revealed backgrounds that include sexual abuse at home. Self-reports obtained from interviews of adult survivors of child sexual abuse in the present sample revealed extensive reports of physically aggressive behavior....

Despite these findings based on self-reports, evidence of a relationship between child sexual abuse and violent offending is weaker than that for other types of offenses when the dependent measure is official arrests. Retrospective studies of adjudicated delinquents indicate that those who were sexually abused do not have a significantly greater likelihood of arrest... or of rearrest ... for violent offenses, and at least one prospective

study of maltreated children... also reported that sexual abuse victims were no more likely than nonabused children to be arrested for a violent crime. Widom's... analysis of violent arrests in a prospective study produced similar results when she examined arrest records for her entire sample of abused and nonabused children. When the analysis was restricted to those subjects who did have matched controls, however, sexual abuse was a statistically significant risk factor for violent offending. In a subsequent reanalysis of Widom's data, McCord... compared the records of female victims and their paired nonvictim controls to determine which of the two had a record of more offending. She found that the proportion of cases where the sexual abuse victim had a more serious record of violent offending than her match was twice what it was for the opposite combination (8% vs. 4%).

However persuasive the foregoing is, prior research on the role of victimization in criminal behavior does have limitations. Virtually all such research has been based on retrospective reports of child sexual abuse. With few exceptions..., histories of abuse were established through self-reports, which may be subject to recall bias or forgetting and, without further validation, risk producing prevalence estimates that are of questionable validity.... Furthermore, life histories and other studies of female offenders show that child sexual abuse is only one form of victimization they experience.... Many also have been physically abused, neglected, and exposed to violence at home and in their communities, experiences that also have been linked to criminal behavior and aggression.... Others have noted that abuse often arises in families characterized by multiple problems. Thus, when examining the relationship between child sexual abuse and subsequent delinquency and crime, other family background factors should be controlled to determine the impact of the sexual abuse net of exposure to other forms of family violence and neglect.

This study, which uses a sample of women sexually abused as children in the 1970s, permits us to address the question of whether sexual abuse victims are at increased risk of arrest relative to other girls and, if so, what the magnitude of that risk is net of other serious family problems. It also examines whether the two groups engage in different types of offenses. The current study includes a larger sample of sexually abused girls than prior prospective studies and, unlike other prospective studies, includes cases that were documented by medical personnel, but did not result in official action by child protective services because the abuse was reported prior to the enactment of legislatively mandated reporting to child protective services. It is expected that the sexually abused girls will be more likely to have juvenile and adult arrest histories than a matched comparison sample of nonabused girls and that they will be more likely to have been arrested for running away, drug offenses, and violent offenses.

Method

Sample

The sample consists of 411 women, including 206 victims of reported child sexual abuse and a matched comparison group of 205 women with no recorded child sexual abuse history.

In the 1970s, all reported victims of sexual abuse in a major northeastern city were brought to the emergency room of a municipal hospital for medical treatment and collection of forensic evidence. From 1973 to 1975, a sample of 206 girls ranging in age from younger than 1 to 12 years old ($M = 8.3$ years) were examined, and they and/or their family members were interviewed as part of a National Institute of Mental Health study of the consequences of the sexual assault. . . . The sexually abused girls were predominantly African American (83.5%), and most came from low-income families, with 56% known to have been receiving public assistance at the time of the abuse. Given the city's policy in effect at that time, which mandated that all reported victims of sexual assault be brought to this particular hospital, girls from a wider range of socioeconomic backgrounds might have been expected in the sample of abused girls because there is little evidence that socioeconomic status is associated with risk of sexual victimization. . . . However, families from more affluent backgrounds in the city at that time may have been less likely to have revealed abuse to or come into contact with official agencies due to a decision to take their children instead to a private physician for treatment.

Details of the sexual abuse were recorded at the time the incident was reported and documented in both hospital medical records and research interview forms. The abuse experienced by the 206 girls ranged from touching and fondling to intercourse, with penetration occurring in 67% of the cases. All of the perpetrators in these cases were males. One third of the girls were victimized by a member of their immediate or extended family, whereas in the rest of the cases, the offender was classified as either an acquaintance, a friend, or a peer (39%) or a stranger or a "relative stranger" (i.e., someone she may have seen before but not known) (28%). Although this distribution may seem to include fewer girls victimized by a family member than expected, it is likely that such victimizations would be less frequently reported to the authorities and thus underrepresented in this hospital sample. However, this distribution is more comparable to data on the distribution of child sexual abuse in the general population than the distribution of types of cases in child protective services samples, suggesting that the range of child sexual abuse cases in this sample is more representative of community samples than is a sample of children who had contact with child protective services.

The comparison group of girls was selected from the emergency room records of the same hospital where the victims were examined. Using the hospital's pediatric emergency room archives, records were examined to identify a girl who matched each victim on race, age (within 1 year), and the date they were seen in the emergency room (within 1 year). All records were screened for any report of child sexual abuse because the city policy mandating that all reported victims of sexual abuse be brought to this hospital meant that the emergency room archives would contain documentation of such reports. Girls for whom there was a report of child sexual abuse, who lived outside of the city, or whose records indicated that they were mentally retarded were ineligible for inclusion in the comparison group. Girls selected as matches were seen in the emergency room for a variety of reasons, ranging from respiratory or intestinal illnesses to accidental injuries, such as cuts, dog bites, or a broken bone.

. . . To assess the comparability of the victim and comparison groups on family-of-origin income levels, we compared median family income for the census tract of residence for each girl based on her race using data from the 1970 U.S. census for the city. A t test comparing the median household incomes of the two groups revealed no statistically significant differences, $t(409) = -1.62, P = .11$.

Using the method described earlier, a match was found for all but one of the victims, resulting in a total sample of 411 girls. Although this procedure ensured that cases of *reported* child sexual abuse were excluded from the comparison group, some women within the comparison group undoubtedly did suffer unreported sexual abuse during their childhood given the prevalence estimates of unreported childhood victimization of females in the general population. The effect of their inclusion in the comparison group, however, would be to make estimates of differences between the abused subjects and their matched counterparts more, not less, conservative because any differences found might have been greater if the unreported victims in the comparison group were excluded from the analysis and the victims were compared only to those not victimized.

DATA COLLECTION

Criminal histories. In 1995, some 20 years after the women were seen in the hospital, official histories of arrests for the entire sample of 411 women were searched for through the city's courts, which maintain records of all arrests and court dispositions. Records of delinquency for the entire period of the girls' childhood and adolescence were obtained from the city's family court, which has jurisdiction over both delinquency and dependency matters. With the exception of running away, status offenses were not routinely recorded at the family court because most were adjudicated in the city's municipal court, and those records were unavailable for the entire period of interest. No status offenses except running away were included in this analysis.

We used the family court's computerized records to collect information on the five most serious charges against an individual for each arrest, as well as the disposition of the case. Any dependency hearings involving the child also were included in the computerized records and coded for use in these analyses. None of the dependency hearings resulted from the sexual abuse the victims experienced.

Adult criminal histories were obtained by a search of the city's computerized court histories, which contain records of all arrests and dispositions in the city. Prior to the search of the criminal records, more than 700 marriage license applications issued to women with the same names as women in this sample were examined in the city's marriage license bureau to determine whether any had in fact been issued to one of the participants. Eighty-five of the applications proved to be for women in this sample. The search of the court records was then carried out by checking for a woman's maiden and married names where both were known. For each woman with an arrest record identified through the search, a copy of the complete court history was obtained; arrests were coded in the same manner as noted previously for juvenile arrests.

MEASURES

Dependent variables. For juvenile outcomes, dichotomous variables (0 = no, 1 = yes) measure whether a person had ever been arrested for any offense, arrested for a violent or property offense, or arrested for running away (three separate variables). For adult outcomes, dichotomous variables measured whether she was ever arrested and ever arrested for a violent, property, or drug offense (three separate variables). Although arrests for prostitution were recorded as well, so few women were arrested for that offense that analyses for that offense category are not reported here. . . .

Because data had not been collected on the family background characteristics of the comparison group, complex models could not be tested to determine the independent effect of victimization status on offending patterns among the victims when compared with their matches net of other potentially influential variables. Absent such data, having a dependency hearing is used as an indicator of family violence or dysfunction for both groups. At a minimum, dependency hearings indicate that a girl was living in a family where supervision was inadequate or, at worst, where physical abuse or neglect was occurring. Whatever the specific reason for the hearing, dependency can be viewed as a potential risk factor on its own for delinquency. Therefore, a dichotomous (0 = no, 1 = yes) variable measuring whether a girl had a dependency hearing was used as a control variable in multivariate analyses.

In view of the literature hypothesizing that many female runaways are fleeing sexually abusive situations at home, a four-category variable reflecting the relationship between the victim and offender was used to determine whether incest victims were at increased risk of arrest for running away as juveniles (0 = stranger, 1 = acquaintance/peer/friend, 2 = extended family, 3 = nuclear family).

Analysis. Analyses were performed separately for delinquent and adult outcomes to see whether sexual abuse status would have the same effect on criminality at different stages of a woman's life. Tests of association between sexual abuse status and the delinquent and criminal outcomes among the full sample were carried out at the bivariate level through McNemar's test. . . . In this method, the significance of the association is based on a comparison of the distribution of pairs of subjects and their matches instead of individuals. If the factor on which the pairs differ is unrelated to the outcome, then the outcomes theoretically should be the same for both people forming the pair. Thus, when a subject has no arrest record, neither should her match. . . .

Results

BIVARIATE RELATIONSHIPS

For descriptive purposes, Table 2.1 shows percentages of the entire sample and each of the two groups who were arrested as juveniles and adults for various offenses. As juveniles, a larger proportion of victims of child sexual abuse than matches were arrested in every category, and the abused girls also were more likely to have had a dependency hearing. The child sexual abuse victims were more commonly arrested for violent offenses (13.6%) than for property offenses (9.2%). However, girls in the comparison group were arrested in equal proportions for violent and property offenses (6.3% in each category). All but one of the girls arrested for running away were in the sexually abused group. The victim–offender relationship was significantly associated with running away: 13.2% of the 53 girls victimized by a stranger or relative stranger were arrested for running away, compared with none of the 63 girls victimized by a family member, $\chi^2 = 9.186$, $P = .027$. Among the 69 girls in the sample who were arrested, abuse victims were significantly more likely to have been adjudicated delinquent (31.7% vs. 7.1%), $\chi^2 = 5.901$, $P = .015$. In addition, all of the girls who were sent to a juvenile institution ($n = 7$) were abuse victims, $\chi^2 = 7.087$, $P = .008$.

Nearly twice as many victims (20.4%) as matches (10.7%) were arrested as adults, and the rate for violent offenses was more than two times greater (9.3% vs. 4.4%). The largest difference in adult offending, however, is in arrests for drug offenses, in which 7.8% of the victims were arrested, whereas only 1.5% of the comparison group was. Larger percentages of victims than matches were arrested for property offenses and prostitution as well. The abused women were arrested for violent offenses as often as they were for property offenses, whereas the matches were arrested more often for the latter. In adulthood, neither conviction nor incarceration was significantly associated with abuse status.

The results of the McNemar tests for the various offense categories are shown in Table 2.2. In every arrest category, the number of cases in which a victim was arrested and her match did not exceed the number for which the reverse is true. However, an arrest for a violent offense was the only category where the differences were statistically significant for both juvenile and adult arrests. In addition, cases where a victimized girl had an arrest for running away, but her match did not, were significantly more common than the reverse. The number of pairs ($n = 33$) in which an abuse victim also had a dependency hearing, but her match did not, was three times greater than the number in which a match had a dependency hearing, but the abuse victim did not ($n = 11$),

Table 2.1   Juvenile and Adult Arrests and Court Outcomes, by Child Sexual Abuse Status (%)

Outcome	Overall (N = 411)	Victims (n = 206)	Matches (n = 205)
Juvenile			
Any arrest	16.8	19.9	13.7
Violent offense	10.0	13.6	6.3
Property offense	7.8	9.2	6.3
Runaway	2.9	5.3	.5
Dependency hearing	12.4	18.0	6.8
Adult			
Any arrest	15.6	20.4	10.7
Violent offense	6.8	9.3	4.4
Property offense	7.3	9.3	5.4
Drug offense	4.6	7.8	1.5
Prostitution	2.0	2.4	1.5

Table 2.2　　　Distribution of Pairs of Victims (V) and Matches (M) With Dissimilar Arrest Histories and Court Outcomes

| Offense | Number of Pairs | | | |
	V Yes, M No[a]	M Yes, V No	McNemar's χ^2	P
Juvenile				
Any arrest	36	23	2.441	.118
Violent offense	27	12	5.026	.025
Property offense	16	10	—[b]	.164[b]
Runaway	11	1	—[b]	.003[b]
Adult				
Any arrest	39	19	6.224	.013
Violent offense	19	9	—[b]	.045[b]
Property offense	19	11	—[b]	.100[b]
Drug offense	15	3	—[b]	.004[b]
Prostitution	5	3	—[b]	.363[b]

[a] "Yes" indicates that a subject had an arrest for a given offense category, and "No" indicates that she did not. Pairs with similar outcomes (V Yes, M Yes; V No, M No) are not shown.

[b] Significance is based on one-tailed binomial test due to cells with 10 or fewer cases. Therefore, chi-square values are not shown. In the case of adult property offenses, the cells with counts of fewer than 10 cases occurred where the outcomes were similar and thus are not shown.

$\chi^2 = 10.023$, $P = .002$. Statistically significant differences occurred in the categories of adult arrests in general and for adult drug offenses, for which there were two and five times as many pairs, respectively, where the victim was arrested, but her match was not.

Role of dependency status in delinquency and adult criminality. If dependency was associated with an increased risk of delinquency or crime, the differences observed between those sexually abused and the comparison group may have been attributable to the higher rates of dependency among the former because they were significantly more likely than the comparison group to have had a dependency hearing. Bivariate analysis showed that girls who came before the court for dependency hearings in fact were more likely to have a juvenile arrest record and also were more likely to be arrested for all categories of offenses as juveniles, except drug offenses. . . . Arrest rates for those who had dependency hearings were even higher than those for the sexual abuse group. Nearly 4 out of 10 (39.2%) of the dependent girls were arrested as juveniles, and 1 in 5 (19.6%) was arrested for a violent offense. The strongest relationship between dependency and any arrest category was for running away: Not surprisingly, all of the runaways had dependency hearings, and nearly 1 out of 4 of the dependent girls was arrested for running away.

Although a larger percentage of dependent girls were arrested as adults for all types of offenses except drug offenses than those who had not had a dependency hearing, the only category in which the association between dependency and an adult arrest outcome is statistically significant is arrests in general, for which the percentage of dependent girls with adult arrests (27.5%) was approximately twice what it was for those who did not have a dependency hearing (13.9%). The strength of this association, however, was weak ($\tau = .015$). . . .

Discussion

The findings from this study with respect to the prevalence of arrests among victims of child sexual abuse are consistent with other prospective research . . . , in that most of the girls who were sexually abused, like their nonabused peers, did not have an official record of delinquency or adult criminality. In fact, contrary to expectations, victimization status was not associated with juvenile arrests in general. The hypothesized relationship was confirmed, however, for adult offending: Sexual abuse victims were significantly more likely to have been arrested as adults than their matched counterparts even after controlling for a childhood history characterized by family problems serious enough to have resulted in a dependency hearing.

Expectations about the participation of those known to have suffered sexual abuse in childhood and the matched comparison group in different types of offending were, for the most part, confirmed. In keeping with the findings of earlier research . . . , we found that sexually abused girls were more likely to become runaways than were their matched comparisons, although this relationship appears to have been associated with the increased likelihood that those who were sexually abused also were significantly more likely to have been declared dependents of the court. Although it had been hypothesized that they also would have been more likely to have been arrested for drug offenses as juveniles, in fact equal and, notably, small numbers of victims and matches were arrested as juveniles for such offenses. In adulthood, however, the child sexual assault victims were more likely to be arrested for drug offenses. Contrary to several other studies . . . , we found that the sexual abuse victims in this sample also were significantly more likely to have been arrested for violent crimes throughout their lives.

The offense categories, in which abuse victims were at greater risk as juveniles and adults, represent distinct types of behavior. Although violent offenses are associated with aggression, running away has been referred to as an "escape" offense. . . . Drug offenses also may be symptomatic of escape or avoidance behavior. Both escape and aggression, however, may simply be different ways of responding to the same problem. The aggressiveness inherent in violent offenses may be an attempt to reassert a sense of power believed to have been lost as a result of the victimization . . . or simply a misplaced expression of anger. . . .

The pattern of arrests for violent and property offenses for the victims in this sample was decidedly "unfeminine." Although girls are most commonly arrested for property crimes and status offenses, such as running away, and women typically are arrested for larceny and other property crimes . . . , the number of victims in this sample arrested as juveniles for violent crimes was nearly one and a half times greater than the number arrested for property crimes. As adults, equal numbers were arrested for each type of crime. This ratio of arrests is much more similar to that for men than for women reported in the UCR. . . .

A partial explanation for the victims' higher participation in violent crime than that found in national arrest statistics may be found in the demographic composition of this sample, which is not representative of the general population. Low-income, inner-city African-American women, who constitute 86% of this sample, have higher rates of arrest for violent offenses

than other women, comparable in some cases to rates to White men. . . .

If higher violent crime arrest rates for African-American females were the sole explanation of differences between the pattern of offenses for abuse victims when compared to national data for females, then the matched comparison group should display similar divergence from the typical female patterns. However, the pattern of arrests for the comparison women was distinctly different from that for the victims. As juveniles, women within the comparison group were as likely to be arrested for property offenses as for violent offenses. As adults, a slightly larger percentage of comparison women were arrested for property crimes than for violent crimes. Therefore, the overrepresentation of African-American women in this sample cannot completely explain the observed differences in their rates of arrest when compared to national data. The findings suggest a need to further explore the role of child sexual abuse in the violent offending of African-American women. These findings also point to a need for additional investigation into the violent arrest patterns of female survivors of sexual abuse to determine whether these results would be replicated for other samples of low-income, inner-city African-American women and for samples representative of a broader spectrum of abuse victims particularly because similar patterns among sexual abuse victims have not been found in other prospective studies. . . .

Studies of community samples have consistently shown an association between drug abuse and a history of childhood sexual victimization. Estimates of the prevalence of substance abuse among female survivors in such surveys range from 14% to 31%, compared with 3% to 12% of nonabused females. . . . Given the consistency of this finding, it was somewhat surprising to find that the abused victims in this study were no more likely than the nonabused matches to be arrested for drug offenses as juveniles, although they were as adults. Nevertheless, these findings are consistent with Ireland and Widom's . . . analysis of drug offending, which uncovered a similar pattern, wherein the females in their sample of maltreated children were significantly more likely than the matched controls to be arrested for a drug and/or alcohol offense as adults, but not as juveniles. In their analyses, this relationship was not specific to sexual abuse, but to maltreatment in general.

One possible explanation of the difference between juvenile and adult arrests for drug offenses could be related to the period during which the majority of the women in this sample were at risk of juvenile arrest because it preceded the increased efforts directed at enforcement of drug laws that began in the 1980s. That, in turn, could have meant that the probability of an arrest for a drug offense was relatively low. Furthermore, a considerable amount of research indicates that criminal activity precedes serious drug use . . . , which could indicate that involvement with drugs becomes serious enough to result in an arrest only as a woman ages and that a girl could incur a juvenile record without any evidence of drug offending.

In view of findings about the temporal ordering of drug use and criminal behavior, the increased risk of substance abuse among sexually abused women may not represent a mediating factor in the link between child abuse and crime, but it may prove to have a moderator effect that would explain differences in the type and severity of offending behavior found between the two groups of women in this study. Further investigation of this relationship is warranted.

Running away has frequently been conceptualized as an attempt by an abuse victim to escape from an abusive environment, whether maltreatment takes the form of physical, emotional, or sexual abuse, and empirical findings indicate that many runaways indeed do have histories of abuse. . . . Once on the street, runaways may be at greater risk of involvement in more serious forms of behavior . . . , be introduced to drugs, or resort to prostitution either as a survival technique or because of exploitation by others they meet on the street. These hypothetical sequences cannot be confirmed from available arrest data. However, if the first part of the sequence were true for these women, it would be expected that victims of incest would have a greater likelihood of arrest for running away. In this sample, that is not the case. In fact, none of the women abused by a member of her nuclear or extended family was arrested for running away. Instead, nearly two thirds (63.6%) of the runaways were abused by a stranger, whereas the balance was abused by an acquaintance.

The difficulty in understanding the full meaning or impact of arrests for running away in this sample is compounded by the fact that all of the runaways had dependency hearings. For some women, the dependency hearing may have resulted in placement in a foster home. In such cases, their arrests for running away may have resulted from attempts to run from abusive environments in their foster homes. Thus, the running away would have been precipitated by the removal from her family that resulted from the dependency hearing. However, it also is possible that a girl's running-away behavior prompted a dependency hearing because a report that a child has run away could alert the court to a family problem that then becomes the subject of a hearing.

The fact that all of the runaways had dependency hearings and all but one were sexually abused makes it extremely difficult to determine the independent contribution of sexual victimization to the risk of running away in this sample. Future investigations of the role that running away plays as a pathway to delinquency for girls should be undertaken using longitudinal designs that can take into account both the precipitating reasons for running away and the sequencing of delinquent acts. In addition, a sampling procedure that identified a larger number of girls who were being abused by a family member than was the case in this sample would facilitate a more in-depth exploration of the relationship among abuse, running away, and delinquency.

The findings about the role of dependency hearings, which reflect some type of family breakdown, underscore the importance of other family variables in understanding the factors that affect the likelihood of delinquency. Having a dependency hearing showed stronger associations with virtually all forms of delinquent behavior than did sexual abuse status, although the abuse was still a significant risk factor in violent offending, controlling for having had a dependency hearing.

The finding that the victims were more likely than the matched comparison girls to have had a dependency hearing and to have been arrested for certain offenses suggests the possibility that "child maltreatment and juvenile misconduct are products of a common family environment." . . . Inasmuch as none of the dependency hearings resulted from the specific sexual victimization incident reported during the first phase of this research, the fact that the abuse victims were significantly more likely to have been the subject of a dependency hearing than the girls in the comparison group suggests that some underlying family dynamic may have played a role in the risk of victimization for some.

Although the findings of the current research add to the growing literature about the relationship between sexual abuse of girls and delinquency, some limitations should be noted. As mentioned earlier, the demographic composition of this sample is not representative of the general population, which limits the generalizability of these findings. Due to their greater probability of being a subject of a dependency hearing, the victims in this sample were more likely than the comparison group to have been involved with the formal system of child protection, which could in turn have led to a greater likelihood that the sexual abuse they experienced would be reported. Thus, they may not be representative of the population of girls who experience sexual abuse. Similarly, their greater involvement with the social service system may have subjected them to more police surveillance, but absent first-hand observation, there is no way to confirm or disprove this hypothetical situation. In addition, although reliance on official arrest histories enabled us to analyze differences in more serious delinquent offenses, the limitations on the availability of some court records prohibited analysis of any differences in status offending other than running away. . . .

An additional concern is related to the possibility of differential rates of mortality between the victims of child sexual abuse and those not victimized, which in turn would affect the number of women susceptible to arrest. Two diverging hypotheses could be posited. First, if those in the comparison group were seen in the emergency room for serious illnesses, then they might have been at higher risk of early mortality. However, virtually all of the girls were seen for relatively minor injuries, such as cuts or dog bites, or for ordinary childhood illnesses, such as stomachaches, sore throats, or ear infections. Their records suggested, in fact, that their families used the emergency room for their primary medical care rather than going to a doctor. Yet a plausible argument could be made that the victims of child sexual abuse would be at higher risk of premature mortality because their victimization put them at risk for behaviors such as drug abuse or prostitution, which could have serious adverse health consequences leading to early mortality. Future analyses should examine mortality rates in the two groups.

Despite these limitations, the research does contribute important information about a group (i.e. low-income, inner-city, predominately African-American women) that, although overrepresented in the both the juvenile and adult justice systems, has been relatively underrepresented in the research on the relationship between abuse and delinquency. The fact that a majority of the girls who suffered abuse in this sample were not arrested as juveniles or adults should of course be taken as an encouraging finding that points to the need to explore in more depth those factors that may insulate victims from the negative consequences of abuse. Nonetheless, the child sexual abuse victims' histories of arrests for more serious (i.e., violent) offenses than their nonabused counterparts is a troubling outcome, one that underscores the need to find ways to mitigate the adverse consequences of abuse.

Questions

1. How do Siegel and Williams operationally define *victim of child sexual abuse*?

2. What do the authors find is the association between child sexual abuse and juvenile and adult patterns of criminal offending?

(

CHAPTER 3

A Comparison of Help Seeking Between Latino and Non-Latino Victims of Intimate Partner Violence

Eben M. Ingram

Centers for Disease Control and Prevention, Atlanta, GA

Although intimate partner violence (IPV), with its physical and emotional consequences for society, victims, and families, is a major public health problem in the United States . . . , research has been limited in certain arenas. One arena is in dealing with the experience of IPV within various ethnic minority communities. . . . A review of the family violence literature of the past 20 years has found only a small number of studies focusing on ethnic minority populations. . . . Thus, knowledge of IPV across ethnic groups is limited. Evidence of the potentially limited relevance of this knowledge of IPV across different ethnic groups is seen in some studies that report that Latino and non-Hispanic White American families may not differ significantly in their risk for IPV . . . and others that report risk levels that are nearly equivalent between Latinos and other racial and ethnic groups. . . . Other researchers have found Latino families to be at greater risk for IPV than non-Hispanic White families . . . , demonstrating some of the highest rates of violence toward spouses. . . . However, research accounting for sociodemographic factors such as urban residence, age, and family income found these differences between Latino and non-Hispanic Whites to dissipate. . . . For instance, the Kaufman Kantor et al. . . . national study found Latino families to be at greater risk of wife assault than their non-Hispanic White American counterparts, and the difference in violence risk was accounted for by the effects of age, economic factors, and attitudes toward violence. Neff, Holamon, and Schluter . . . also found that differences in the amount of

violence between Mexican American and non-Hispanic White American families disappeared when the effects of economic resources were accounted for. Therefore, these studies raise the question of whether there are actual differences in the prevalence and incidence of IPV between Latinos and other groups.

In addition to questions about the actual extent of IPV among Latinos, information about the extent and nature of help-seeking behavior also is lacking. As a result of the few studies of help-seeking behavior, the general finding has been that Latino women underutilize IPV services and thus may be less willing than non-Hispanic White American women to seek help for IPV. . . . Using shelter samples, researchers found that, when compared with non-Hispanic White Americans, Latinas were less likely to utilize informal sources of help such as friends and family and other sources of help than professional caregivers. Furthermore, Latinas have been reported to be less likely to use formal sources, such as services provided by social services agencies, than their non-Hispanic White counterparts. . . . In the few studies addressing Latinos, they generally have been characterized as underutilizing IPV-related services. . . .

As in the case with IPV victimization, there also is the need to identify factors that determine help-seeking behavior in Latinos and the factors that account for the differences in help-seeking activities between Latinos and non-Latinos. For instance, sociodemographic factors have been shown to be predictors of medical and mental health services utilization . . . , yet few studies

Source: "A Comparison of Help Seeking Between Latino and Non-Latino Victims of Intimate Partner Violence" by Ingram, E. M., (2007), in *Violence Against Women, 13,* 159–171. Reprinted by permission of Sage Publications, Inc.

have evaluated these factors as predictors of help seeking among Latinos. . . . Thus, a clear understanding of the factors that influence Latinos to seek help is necessary for the development of IPV and culturally appropriate interventions and policies.

This chapter seeks to address this gap in knowledge by using a population-based sample to examine the relationship among sociodemographic and community factors such as gender, age, income, marital status, immigration status, length of residence in the United States, and education for Latinos and non-Latinos in terms of IPV victimization and help-seeking activities. Also addressed are factors such as awareness of community resources, experiences with IPV screening, and attitudinal factors such as support for IPV.

Method

This is a secondary analysis of data from a random digit dial (RDD) telephone survey conducted January through March 2003 as a postintervention assessment of the impact of coordinated community responses (CCRs) to IPV. Ten nonrandomly selected sites and 10 comparison sites matched on sociodemographic characteristics were surveyed. The 20 sites were located across the different regions of the United States. Overall, 600 adults from each of the 20 sites participated in the survey ($N = 12,039$; 75.3% of contacted eligible households).

Within the communities surveyed, the RDD survey was conducted to determine knowledge, attitudes, and beliefs about IPV; behaviors such as use of services and response to victims; and prevalence and past-year experience of IPV in these communities. . . .

Measures

ETHNICITY

Respondents' ethnicity was determined by the response to a two-part question asking about their racial and ethnic backgrounds. Respondents who identified themselves to be Hispanic or Latino were coded as Latinos, and those who identified themselves as not Hispanic or Latino were coded as non-Latinos. Ethnic status was dichotomously coded (0 = non-Latino, 1 = Latino).

IMMIGRATION STATUS

Immigrant status was determined by participants' responses to a question asking how long they had lived in this country. Response options . . . varied from less than 1 year to more than 5 years and "all my life." Immigration status was dichotomously coded (0 = nonimmigrant, 1 = immigrant). In addition, length of time in the United States was dichotomously coded (0 = less than 5 years, 1 = 5 or more years).

IPV

A modified version of the Conflicts Tactics Scale . . . was used to assess IPV. The scale is composed of 16 items (with yes–no response categories), with which both annual and lifetime occurrence of IPV were captured. An affirmative answer to any item in the scale resulted in classifying the respondents as having experienced IPV at some point in their life. IPV was dichotomously coded (0 = no experience of IPV, 1 = have experienced IPV). IPV occurring in the past year was assessed identically to lifetime IPV experience.

Acceptability of IPV was assessed by a question (with yes–no response categories) asserting that "there are times when slapping your partner is OK." Respondents also were asked about their awareness and use of existing IPV services and whether anyone had ever asked about their experiences with IPV. In terms of the latter, respondents were asked whether they had been asked by a doctor, an advocate at a health center, an advocate at a police station or court, someone at work or school, a clergy person (a pastor, priest, or rabbi), a police officer, a friend, or a family member if they were "afraid of or hurt by an intimate partner." Respondents were asked to respond with yes or no to each of these categories. Awareness of existing IPV services was assessed by reading respondents a list of local organizations providing IPV services and asking whether they had heard about each of the organizations (yes–no).

HELPING-SEEKING BEHAVIORS

Help seeking by victims of IPV was assessed by asking respondents whether they had ever personally contacted organizations in their community, sought a restraining order (formal support), or talked with someone to get help or information about IPV (informal support). If participants answered any of these questions in the affirmative, they were classified as having sought some form of help. Help seeking was dichotomously coded (0 = no, 1 = yes). Respondents also were asked what services they received from each organization they contacted. As an index of informal help seeking, IPV victims were asked whether they talked to anyone about their victimization and, if so, whom they told.

Analytic Strategy

Chi-square tests were used to compare Latinos to non-Latinos across IPV prevalence, incidence, related cultural factors, and help-seeking factors. Comparisons also were made among Latinos examining the influence of immigration status on IPV victimization and help-seeking activities.

Results

The majority of respondents in the sample (N = 12,039) were non-Hispanic White (70.3%) and were middle aged (M = 47.5 years), and respondents had an average of 13.6 years of education. . . . Slightly more than half were female (52.0%) and married (45.5%) at the time of the interview, and the respondents lived in a household with an average annual income of $43,747.

Just more than 16.4% of the sample identified themselves as Latino. More than half of Latinos were immigrants to the United States (52.6%), and most of the non-Latinos were lifelong residents (90.5%).

Table 3.1 shows the analysis of prevalence and incidence of IPV, witnessing violence as a child in the home, and acceptance of IPV. Overall, 57.2% of respondents reported experiencing any type of intimate partner aggression during their lifetime and 16.2% in the past year. Latinos reported a lower percentage of lifetime experience of IPV than non-Latinos, but a slightly higher percentage of past-year victimization. Also, more Latinos than non-Latinos witnessed IPV in the home as a child. Although the vast majority of Latinos and non-Latinos do not support IPV, significantly more Latinos believe that there are times when slapping one's partner is OK. Among Latinos, more nonimmigrants (56.5%) than immigrants (43.5%) reported IPV victimization (c^2 = 66.75, df = 1, P < .0001). With more than 90% of non-Latinos being lifelong residents, immigrant status among non-Latinos was not related to IPV victimization.

. . . [T]he difference between Latinos and non-Latinos in help seeking was not significant. There was, however, a significant difference between Latinos and non-Latinos in knowledge of community resources for IPV and in the extent to which IPV victims were asked about their IPV experiences by a service professional. Thus, significantly more non-Latinos than Latinos reported having been asked whether they were afraid or

Table 3.1 Chi-Square Analysis of Intimate Partner Violence (IPV) Experiences and Attitude Toward Acceptance of IPV

IPV Experience and Attitude About IPV	Latinos[a]		Non-Latinos[b]		x^2	P
	n	%	n	%		
Experienced any form of IPV during lifetime	999	50.6	5,841	58.5	41.81	.0001
Experienced any form of IPV in the past 12 months	369	18.7	1,571	15.7	10.65	.001
Witnessed violence in the home as a child	699	35.5	2,912	29.2	30.17	.0001
Agree that there are times when slapping one's partner is OK	122	6.4	418	4.3	15.98	.0001

[a] n = 1,973.

[b] n = 9,982.

hurt by an intimate partner. In addition, among Latino IPV victims, more nonimmigrants (14.7%) than immigrants (6.9%) contacted a formal service agency for IPV services ($c^2 = 14.95$, $df = 1$, $P < .0001$). With more than 90% of non-Latinos being lifelong residents, immigrant status among non-Latinos was not related to help-seeking activities.

Analysis of who the victims approached when they told someone about their victimization indicated that the overall pattern of informal help seeking was similar for both groups. . . . Both groups most frequently approached friends and family. Latino victims told a family member, a friend or acquaintance, a health care worker, the police, and the clergy, in that order. Non-Latinos' help seeking followed a similar pattern. They talked to a friend, a family member, a health care worker, an acquaintance, the clergy, and the police. The differences between the two groups were that more Latinos told a family member (31.5%) than did non-Latinos (25.4% . . .), more non-Latinos (11.0%) than Latinos (7.9%) told health care workers . . . , and more non-Latinos (12.6%) than Latinos (9.6%) told the clergy. . . .

Furthermore, both Latinos and non-Latinos also sought similar types of services. There were no differences between Latinos and non-Latinos in requests for information, use of court advocacy, support group participation, health care, financial assistance, child care, and job training or assistance in getting a job. The only significant difference between Latinos and non-Latinos in the types of services sought was that more non-Latinos (14.2%) than Latinos (10.2%) reported seeking access to shelters . . . , which is consistent with the IPV literature.

Discussion

. . . Although fewer Latinos experienced a lifetime prevalence of IPV than non-Latinos, more Latinos reported experiencing IPV in the past year. They also reported witnessing more violence in their homes as children. Unlike findings frequently reported in the literature, where the reported rate for Latinos is 23% . . . , Latinos in this survey reported lifetime IPV at a much higher level. The higher level of lifetime IPV might be a result of the nonrandom sample of the communities surveyed or could be explained by the way IPV was measured. The survey used a measure of IPV consisting of a modified version of the Conflict Tactics Scale . . . , where each item in the scale refers to a form of IPV and an affirmative response to any item results in the categorization of IPV perpetration or victimization. Thus, this focus on asking

the respondents whether they ever experienced a specific act avoids some of the definitional issues associated with whether a specific act constitutes IPV that may be a source of measurement problems. . . . Furthermore, the presence in the survey of the specific violent act item may prompt better and more accurate recall and thus result in reports of greater occurrences of IPV.

Latinos tend to be characterized as underutilizing formal and informal sources of help. . . . For both groups, the most frequent informal activity in seeking assistance was to talk to someone about the abuse, most commonly family and friends. This response to IPV is consistent with a strong cultural-based identification with and an attachment to the family that characterizes a number of cultural groups. For Latinos, "familism" is considered one of the most important cultural values. . . . Therefore, the willingness to tell family members about the IPV victimization found in this study and others . . . suggests that the apparent underutilization of informal resources by Latinas, reported in the literature in comparisons of White non-Latino and Latino women . . . , may be because of problems in the informal support network resulting from the impact of immigration and other cultural factors. For instance, the immigration process may lead to fragmentation of the extended family on which Latinos tend to rely. . . . Other belief systems, such as codes of behavior that underscore the concepts of maleness and femaleness (*machismo* and *marianismo*, respectively) and avoidance of personal conflict, have been cited as influencing Latinos' decisions to disclose their abuse to others. . . .

In this study, the only significant difference between Latinos and non-Latinos in self-reported utilization of formal services was that non-Latinos indicated seeking access to shelters more frequently than did Latinos. These self-reports of services utilized are consistent with findings reported in the IPV literature examining the utilization of services provided by caregiving agencies. To account for differences in the willingness to utilize formal services such as the criminal justice system and mental health services, immigrant status has frequently been cited in the IPV literature as a contributing factor, and in this study being an immigrant was found to have an impact on help-seeking activities by Latinos. . . . Other factors, such as language barriers and lack of familiarity with the availability of services, have been found to be among the most frequently reported problems in seeking services. Moreover, research has reported that when Latinas who did not seek assistance were compared to Latinas who did, those who sought assistance were more acculturated, as defined by language use. . . .

Overall, it can be concluded from the findings in this study that Latinos report seeking help for IPV victimization at a level similar to that of others in the general population. Similar to research reported in the help-seeking literature . . . , these findings also suggest that victims frequently tend to reach out within their families for help. Consequently, family services for abused women could focus on the development of interventions that enhance family support and provide direct services to family members. . . . This would specifically help those populations who rely heavily on the family network for support and direction in addressing IPV.

Research cites language, lack of transportation, lack of money or resources, fear of spouse or boyfriend, and lack of knowledge of where to go for assistance as the major barriers to getting needed IPV services. . . . In many instances, these factors may amount to institutional barriers because agencies may lack translators, may require travel over large geographic distances from Latino communities, and may have prohibitive fee structures . . . , which make it particularly difficult for underserved populations to access their services.

Furthermore, community partnerships and interventions that focus on the resources that abused Latinos need, whether immigrant or not, are essential. These interventions should be linguistically and culturally appropriate and take into consideration factors facing abuse victims in general and cultural minorities specifically. Thus, an approach providing interventions taking into consideration the many factors confronting abuse victims would likely be more productive in addressing the complex and multifaceted problem of IPV. Attention should be paid to victims' need for sound educational information about available resources and the characteristics of these resources and the needs they meet. Objectives of intervention programs should be to develop mechanisms to increase the utilization of these resources and increase the skills and competence (specifically, cultural competence) of social service providers to identify and respond to Latinos at risk for IPV. Outcome research should be utilized to test the efficacy of population-based interventions to reduce violence and identify violence-related

issues and help seeking that are most likely to benefit Latinos and other abuse victims.

These findings and our interpretations should be considered in the context of the methodological limitations in the study. First, our measure of impact is based on an RDD telephone survey, and, as in all self-reports, recall and social desirability may be problems. In addition, awareness campaigns such as those conducted in CCR communities could have sensitized the population, increasing their willingness to self-report or improving their recall of exposure to IPV. Second, sample selection and size also may be issues. These communities were not randomly selected. However, they were located in different regions of the United States and included both urban and rural communities and different ethnic and racial populations, and thus they might be considered representative of communities in the United States. Moreover, in a separate analysis by community, no differences were found in sociodemographic and IPV profiles between the different communities. Third, reliable analyses of racial and ethnic differences within the comparison groups were not possible because details of ethnic membership within the Latino group were not available because of the design of the RDD survey. Furthermore, the possibility of meaningful cultural differences between the different Latino ethnicities also may have affected outcomes by obscuring the response characteristics of the different groups. Despite these and other possible limitations, findings reported here add to the limited body of research examining ethnic and racial characteristics of the help-seeking process.

Questions

1. Overall, what does Ingram conclude from the findings in this study regarding differences among Latinos and non-Latinos in terms of rates of help seeking for IPV victimization?

2. What are some recommendations for reducing barriers to help seeking among Latino IPV victims?

PART II

CLASSICAL CRIMINOLOGY

Dating to the 1700s, the founding ideas of the field of criminology were set forth in the principles of classical criminology, which argued that humans are rational and crime results when benefits outweigh the costs or risks. Choice theory was resurrected in the form of routine activities theory in the 1970s and has gained recent popularity with the development of crime-mapping techniques. In *A Spatial Analysis of Criminal Effort: Auto Theft in Newark, New Jersey*, Marissa Potchak, Jean McGloin, and Kristen Zgoba (chap. 4) examine the effect of criminal effort, measured as the distance traveled to commit a criminal act, on the pattern of car thefts in Newark, New Jersey's largest city. The decision-making process of offenders is considered from the perspective of situational crime prevention strategies by Don Hummer (chap. 5) in *Serious Criminality at U.S. Colleges and Universities: An Application of the Situational Perspective*. Using data obtained from surveying a large sample of schools, he examines the effectiveness of crime-prevention techniques developed from the situational perspective at reducing incidences of serious crime on campus. Crime committed over the Internet, a most contemporary form of criminal activity that some argue is different from traditional crime, is examined for support of routine activity theory by Majid Yar (chap. 6) in *The Novelty of "Cybercrime."* Finding limited support for the theory, the author suggests that cybercrime may, in fact, represent a unique form of crime.

CHAPTER 4

A Spatial Analysis of Criminal Effort

Auto Theft in Newark, New Jersey

Marissa C. Potchak

Jean M. McGloin

Kristen M. Zgoba

Rutgers University

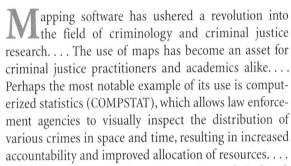apping software has ushered a revolution into the field of criminology and criminal justice research. . . . The use of maps has become an asset for criminal justice practitioners and academics alike. . . . Perhaps the most notable example of its use is computerized statistics (COMPSTAT), which allows law enforcement agencies to visually inspect the distribution of various crimes in space and time, resulting in increased accountability and improved allocation of resources. . . .

Although mapping is an impressive analytical tool, Eck . . . argued that researchers must be wary of solely focusing on the data to the exclusion of theory. Using maps in an informed and effective manner hinges on our ability to embed them in a theoretical context. . . . Both researchers and practitioners must remember that mapping is another form of data analysis, one that must be appropriate to the data and to the corresponding theory . . . . The practice of mapping atheoretically actually impedes data analysis. Without a theoretical premise, one cannot understand the meaning of the data or whether they were selected and analyzed appropriately.

Driven by this concern, early perspectives on environmental criminology began to emerge . . . alongside the analysis of "hot spots" of crime. . . . Much of this literature, which focuses on the spatial and temporal distributions of crime, shares a common theme in that offender decision making should be structured, to a certain extent, by the opportunities for crime shaped by the physical environment. . . .

Although some of this literature focuses on deterrence, other portions attempt to understand the offender's decision process in the context of the surrounding environment. . . . Specifically, Cornish and Clarke . . . stated in their rational choice theory that a utilitarian cognitive process precedes and informs an offender's decision of whether to commit a particular crime at a particular time and place. The factors that inform this decision—namely, the associated risks, benefits, and costs—have primarily been discussed in an abstract sense. These factors are generally examined only empirically in studies assessing individuals' perceptions of potential costs and benefits associated with their perceived likelihood of committing particular criminal acts. . . . Less empirical attention has been paid to articulating or evaluating the latent variables that enter into the decision process with more specificity. The present study seeks to fill this gap in the research literature by addressing the role of effort in an offender's decision-making process. Specifically, this chapter uses recent advancements in mapping technology to explore the hypothesis that offenders will travel to the closest opportunity to commit auto theft.

Source: "A spatial analysis of criminal effort: Auto theft in Newark, New Jersey." by Potchak, M. C., McGloin, J. M., & Zgoba, K. M., (2002), in *Criminal Justice Policy Review, 13,* 257–285. Reprinted by permission of Sage Publications, Inc.

Theoretical Background

EFFORT

Effort defined here is the use of energy to do something. This chapter assumes that criminal effort is not merely a way to characterize the criminal behavior or act (i.e., the act of stabbing someone to death requires more exertion than the act of stealing office supplies), but that it is a salient part of the criminal decision process. The previous sentence carries with it two important assumptions. First, it assumes that a criminal makes a decision to commit such an act—that she or he is not completely ushered into such behavior through external forces. Second, it assumes that the decision is a product of a cognitive process in which various factors enter into and are considered in that decision. In other words, some form of a reasoning process determines the decision the offender makes of whether to offend and in which criminal act to engage. Therefore, this premise of criminal effort fits within the context of rational choice theory....

Rational choice theory ... speaks indirectly to the use of effort by an offender when determining whether to commit a crime. Rational choice assumes there is a decision process in which the offender calculates the risks, costs, and benefits of committing a particular crime in a particular time and place.... The theory takes a utilitarian perspective, stating that if the balance results in a positive anticipated consequence, then the individual engages in the act. If the anticipated consequence of the criminal act is negative, then the individual refrains from such action.

Effort in the context of the reasoning decision process can be either high or low in cost. Consider the example of a premeditated bank robbery versus a purse snatching. A premeditated bank robber would exert much more physical and psychological energy in the planning and commission of a crime in comparison to someone who snatches a purse on the sidewalk. The rational choice perspective implies that effort is important to the decision process preceding a criminal act, in that minimal effort would be supportive of committing a crime, whereas high effort would not.

This focus on effort is not a claim that it is the only or even the most important factor in the reasoning decision process. The decision process is complex and is based on multiple factors that likely influence one another. For empirical clarity, however, this chapter focuses on effort in isolation of other factors. After all, it is appropriate to first understand this factor before considering it in relation to other variables.

Situational crime prevention is the first theory that makes direct reference to effort.... Specifically, Clarke ... proposed four strategies of crime prevention: (a) increasing perceived risks, (b) reducing anticipated rewards, (c) removing excuses, and (d) increasing perceived effort. If effort were not an important part of the decision-making process, then increasing perceived effort would not be a technique used to reduce or prevent crime.... This conception of effort, as presented by situational crime prevention theorists, refers to guardians increasing the effort needed by the offender to obtain the target.

DISTANCE

Empirical work has demonstrated that offenders commit crimes close to home.... The rationale is that it takes time, money, and effort to travel and overcome large distances.... "Such a phenomenon, the reduction of activity or interaction as distance increases, has been repeatedly observed in spatial behavior of all types and can be generically referred to as 'distance decay.'" ... [T]here is a small concentric area around the offender's home where crime will not occur at such a high rate.... This is due to a high risk of apprehension because the offender is known in the area immediately surrounding the residence.

Although some studies address the idea that the average crime trip is short, others focus on finding evidence for the actual distribution described by the distance decay function. As for the former notion, Rossmo ... reviewed multiple studies that reported the mean distance traveled by the offenders from home to the place where they committed a variety of crimes. Almost all of the reported studies found that the average crime trip was less than 2 miles....

OPPORTUNITY

To look only at distance when conceiving of effort is not sufficient because the distance traveled to a crime is inherently linked to opportunity.... For crime to occur, opportunity must be present. If opportunity were uniformly distributed, one could look at distance in isolation of this factor ... ; however, opportunity is neither uniformly distributed in time nor space....

According to routine activities theory ... , opportunity exists when there is a convergence of a suitable target, a motivated offender, and a lack of a capable guardian. These three factors converge in time and space according to the routine activities of individuals as they go about their daily lives. Opportunity is therefore a necessary, although not sufficient, cause of crime.

Finally, it is worth noting that Cohen and Felson . . . stated that opportunity is crime-specific. In other words, if the opportunity exists for a particular type of crime, it will be that type of crime that occurs. Accordingly, if opportunity is an important element of effort, one must be sure to specify a particular type of crime when exploring this construct.

Hypothesis

This chapter argues that effort is a combination of distance and relevant opportunity. In other words, Effort = f (Distance + Opportunity), where effort and opportunity are crime specific. Will an offender minimize such effort in accordance with rational choice theory? The corresponding hypothesis states that offenders will travel to the closest relevant opportunity to commit auto theft. . . .

METHOD

DATA

The geographic data used for the construction of the four layers of the opportunity structure were not originally collected for the specific purpose of this exploratory study. . . . Because the units of analysis are not identical across the layers of the opportunity structure we are creating, they carry the unfortunate consequence of eliminating traditional confirmatory statistical techniques adapted for spatial data. . . . Although some may consider this problematic, certain scholars are beginning to voice concerns over some of the problems associated with relying on significance-testing procedures for understanding underlying social processes. . . . A complementary, emerging methodological trend in social science research is to use the graphic display of data as an analytic tool in and of itself. . . . As Maltz . . . noted, "The fundamental idea is to develop methods of displaying data that permit the reviewer to see relationships within the data." . . . Accordingly, this exploratory analysis of the spatial dynamics of auto theft uses cartographic technology to generate such visual displays so that a clearer picture of criminal opportunity for these offenses can emerge.

The crime dataset consists of auto theft incidents in Newark, New Jersey, for the year 2000. Variables from the police reports include theft location; recovery location; make, model, and color of the car; year of the car; and offender residence (if an offender was arrested). . . .

The initial dataset included 5,459 incidents of car theft in Newark for the year 2000. However, the data to be analyzed had to include the address of the offender (thus requiring an arrest) to calculate the distance between this point and the point of theft. In addition, the mapping software had data available only on the city of Newark, requiring the offender's address to be in Newark. These two facts dictated the selection of a purposeful sample of the 228 cases in which an offender residing in Newark was arrested for the theft of the automobile in Newark. . . . Although this sample is not large, it is appropriate for the exploratory nature of the study because the analysis is a first step in both addressing a gap in the literature and using mapping software to investigate an offender's cognitive process.

OPERATIONALIZING DISTANCE

To effectively determine the distance the offenders traveled from home to commit auto theft, it was necessary to link these two points. "Point-to-point distance" calculations . . . linked the offender residence and point of theft for each unique case and calculated the Euclidian distance between these two points in space.

OPERATIONALIZING OPPORTUNITY

The concept of opportunity is one of the most complex constructs presented here. The opportunity structure consists of four maps layered over one another to form a pseudodensity map, indicating the areas with differential opportunity. A coding scheme consisted of four grid layers, which were then summed for an overall opportunity structure. The four layers are land use, public housing, major roadways, and Penn Station, which are discussed in detail in the following sections. It is important to note that data on a temporal distribution of opportunity to commit auto theft and on the full citywide distribution of parking lots (an important variable when discussing opportunity to commit auto theft) were unavailable.

LAND USE

Although Newark is an urban environment, there are a variety of land uses throughout the city, including agriculture, water or wetlands, parks, athletic fields, cemeteries, transportation, residential areas, commercial areas, and barren lands. Such variety in terms of land use speaks to a similar diversity in terms of opportunity to commit auto theft.

Data were taken from a land survey that was conducted by the New Jersey Department of Environmental Protection. . . . The authors treated this layer as if it were an ordinal variable, with values ranging from 0 to 3. Zero represented little to low opportunity, whereas 3 represented high opportunity to commit auto theft. The sliding scale accounted for activity, street parking, and parking lots.

- 0: Land that had been coded as agricultural, water, wetlands, cemetery, industrial, transportation, and "other urban" was given a value of 0 due to the limited vehicular activity in these areas. Although most of these categories are self-explanatory, two require some elaboration for clarity. Transportation includes major highways, airports (which are outside the Newark Police jurisdiction), bus and truck terminals, railroad facilities, ports, telephone lines, utility plants, and communication facilities. "Other urban" refers to underdeveloped, open land.
- 1.0: Athletic fields and places of recreation received a value of 1 because activity is sporadic and seasonal. In other words, there are times when many cars are present (e.g., for a softball game), but this is not a consistent phenomenon.
- 1.5: "Mixed urban" refers to a number of possible combinations of previous types of land use. According to the land use and land classification system . . . , this category contains land that cannot be placed in individual categories. Mixed urban subcategories include areas that are primarily residential, primarily commercial, primarily industrial, primarily transportation, or a heterogeneous mixture. . . . Because mixed urban could therefore refer to land types that had values that ranged from 0 to 3, such areas were given a value of 1.5 or the midpoint of the scale. . . .
- 2.0: Residential areas received a value of 2 because they have both activity and street parking. The presence of cars is likely because activity is typically constant. . . .
- 3.0: Commercial areas received a value of 3 due to high activity, street parking, and the presence of parking lots. These areas are open to constant traffic during both times of day and year. Accordingly, most streets in the commercial district are lined with cars, and most lots are consistently full. . . .

After coding the entirety of Newark according to the aforementioned scale, the authors' conception of opportunity for auto theft by land use is demonstrated in Figure. 4.1.

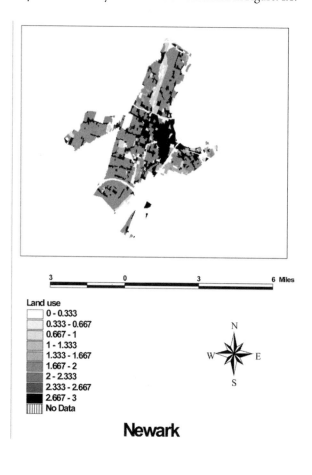

Figure 4.1   Map of Land Use Coded for Opportunity to Commit Auto Theft

PUBLIC HOUSING

There is a literature that speaks to increased opportunity for crime in public housing complexes. . . . Recognizing the fact that public housing units have received attention in the literature as structures that provide, or at least support, opportunities to commit crime, the authors visited public housing projects in Newark. These residential areas not only had street parking, but all of the public housing units also had parking lots (sometimes more than one) surrounding the units. Therefore, such areas provided more opportunity for auto theft than other typical residential areas. Accordingly, a data layer was created to account for such structures.

Because the data points referred to the public housing buildings, small buffers were first created around these points to capture the surrounding parking lots. Areas contained within the buffer zones were given a value of 1, whereas areas outside these zones received a value of 0. The reason that public housing unit areas received a value of 1, rather than a higher value, is because these areas were coded as residential in the previous land-use layer. If they received an additional value greater than 1, then that would be equivalent to stating that area provided greater opportunity for auto theft than commercial areas. Such an assertion would not be accurate. Commercial areas received a value of 3 because they contained high activity, street parking, and parking lots. . . .

After assigning the appropriate values, the data were converted to a grid, which was converted to a map. Figure 4.2 illustrates the resulting map, the second data layer to be considered in the overall opportunity structure. . . .

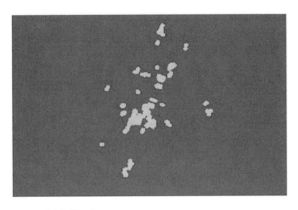

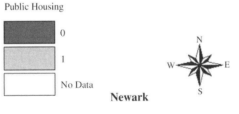

Figure 4.2   Map of Public Housing Coded for Opportunity to Commit Auto Theft

MAJOR ROADWAYS

As mentioned in the land-use section, areas coded as transportation, which included roadways, received a value of 0. To be satisfied with this and to ignore the role of major roadways would be to ignore the fact that relevant

literature has suggested that they are extremely important when considering the opportunity to commit crime.

For example, Beavon, Brantingham, and Brantingham . . . argued that property crimes occur in areas that are known to have attractive targets. Consequently, street networks that are well traveled play an important role in creating criminal opportunity. They provide the means by which one goes about his or her routine activities and therefore play a primary role in the construction of that person's awareness space. . . . Beavon et al. . . . defined a criminal's awareness space as a knowledge base or a cognitive map that one acquires of his or her environment through the routine activities of his or her daily life. It is within this awareness space that an offender commits crime. . . .

To place this in the larger theoretical context of routine activities theory . . . , major roadways provide one way for motivated offenders to come into contact with, or at least to become aware of, suitable targets. Accordingly, the opportunity to commit crime, in this case auto theft, should be higher around well-traveled roadways. . . .

Major roadways (initially given a value of 0 in the land-use layer) were given a value of 2, accounting for both activity and street parking. All other areas in Newark received a value of 0. Once such assignments were made, these data were converted to a grid, which was displayed in a map. Figure 4.3 is the resulting map of this data layer.

PENN STATION

Recent studies on the Newark subway systems, the Port Authority Terminal in New York City, and the Washington, DC, Metro have been conducted . . . , and in each case the public transportation facilities and systems were reported as generators of crime. P. L. Brantingham and Brantingham . . . called such locations "crime generators" because they bring potential offenders and victims together, although it is for reasons unrelated to crime.

A boundary of 2,300 feet in Manhattan distance was created around Penn Station, an area that was previously given a 0 in the land-use section. This is different than a simple buffer because it encompasses walking distance, rather than a distinct radius. This walking distance was created to incorporate commuter activity and the cars that are parked around Penn

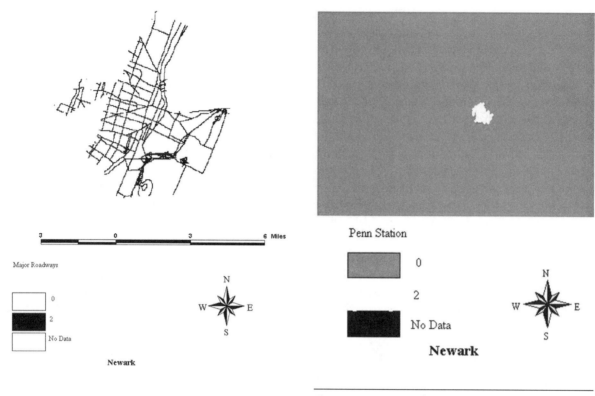

Figure 4.3   Map of Major Roadways Coded for
Opportunity to Commit Auto Theft

Figure 4.4   Map of Penn Station Coded for Opportunity
to Commit Auto Theft

Station when commuters leave their vehicles and take trains into New York City. Accordingly, cells that fell within the 2,300-feet walking distance of Penn Station received a value of 2 for activity and street parking. The remainder of areas received a value of 0, representing no increase or decrease in opportunity for automobile theft. This data column was converted to a grid, which was then displayed in a map. Figure 4.4 is the resulting map.

Analysis

To analyze the data, both mapping and statistical techniques were employed. A spatial analysis was appropriate because both the concept and the data are environmental in nature. Mapping provides a clear and accurate representation of the point of the theft, as well as the offender's residence because these two events are fixed locations in space and time. Conversely, a crime such as an assault, which may start on one block and continue

for a few blocks, would be difficult to capture using such an analytic technique.

DISTANCE

As stated, the distance between offenders' residences and their respective points of auto theft was calculated. These data were analyzed to investigate whether support was found for the distance decay function posed by P. J. Brantingham and Brantingham. . . . Using statistical software, both the mean distance and the distribution of the distances traveled were calculated to achieve this goal.

OPPORTUNITY

The opportunity structure layers were summed using the map calculator in ArcView, a mapping software program. The resulting map was then smoothed using the mean to obtain a more accurate representation of opportunity. To clarify, imagine two adjoining

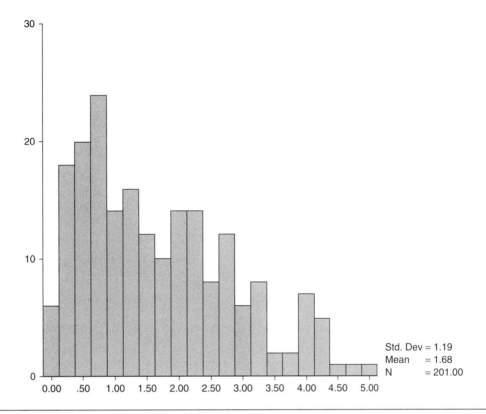

Std. Dev = 1.19
Mean   = 1.68
N   = 201.00

Figure 4.5   Distance Traveled From the Point of Residence to the Point of Theft

blocks. Based on the operationalization of opportunity, one has received a value of 6, whereas one has received a value of 0. In reality, however, these areas likely influence one another so that the values may be somewhat inaccurate. Smoothing the opportunity structure by the mean therefore captures the influence adjoining areas have on one another. . . .

<u>EFFORT</u>

To analyze effort as it has been operationalized here, it was necessary to develop an indicator of distance against or relative to the overall opportunity structure. Accordingly, we attached the distance value calculated earlier to its respective point of residence. This theme was displayed as points, which represented the offenders' residences. The shape of the points represented the distance that offenders had traveled to the respective points of auto theft. These shaped points were then placed on the map of the overall opportunity structure. This allowed visual inspection of the distance an offender traveled from home to commit auto theft relative to the surrounding relevant opportunity structure, thus allowing an exploration of the hypothesis that offenders will travel to the closest opportunity to commit auto theft.

Results

DISTANCE RESULTS

The results supported the notion of the distance decay function. Figure 4.5 is the distribution of the distances the offenders traveled from the point of residence to the point of theft. . . . Note still that the closest points to the offenders' home bases have a low relative rate of offending. Furthermore, the mean distance traveled is 1.68 miles, which falls under the prediction of Rossmo . . . that the offender will travel less than 2 miles from his or her residence to commit crimes.

OPPORTUNITY RESULTS

Figure 4.6 represents the final overall opportunity structure to commit auto theft. To repeat, this map is a summation of the four data layers: land use, public housing, roadways, and Penn Station. Opportunity values range from 0 to 6.33 (smoothed by the grand mean). Areas with a 0 (light gray) indicate no opportunity based on the scheme. Black areas (5.63–6.333) indicate a high opportunity for auto theft. To determine whether this opportunity structure had any merit or validity, a density map of all 5,459 points of theft for the year 2000 was created.

Although the maps are not identical, Figure 4.7 illustrates that theft is prevalent (dark spots on the right map) in the corresponding areas of high opportunity (dark areas on the left map) as it has been operationalized here. This lends validity to the conception and measurement of opportunity for auto theft.

EFFORT RESULTS

Figure 4.8 illustrates the effort map, which consists of various points layered over the opportunity structure. The points show where the offender lives, and the shape indicates how far she or he traveled to commit the auto theft. More specifically, the shape of the point suggests how large of a radius around the offender's residence she or he traveled to commit auto theft.

The north section has a number of areas that provide an opportunity to commit auto theft, illustrated by

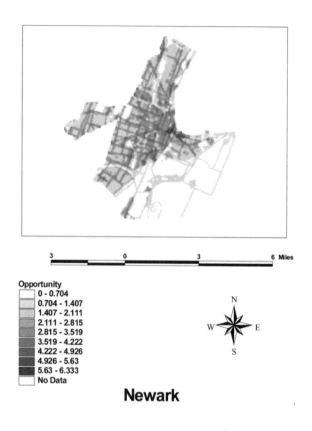

Figure 4.6   Smoothed Opportunity Structure for Auto Theft in Newark

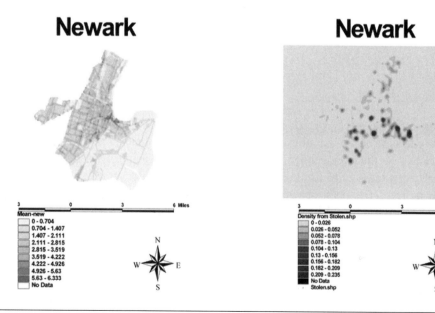

Figure 4.7   Comparison of the Opportunity Structure to a Density Map of Auto Theft Incidents in Newark

the dark-colored portions of the map. There are several triangle- and square-shaped points (approximately 0 to 1.5 miles traveled) in this district, almost all of which fall in or close to the dark portions of the opportunity structure. This would indicate that the offenders traveled within 1½ miles from the point of residence, likely going to the closest opportunities. This supports the hypothesis put forth by the authors. There are, however, a few points in this area that suggest some offenders traveled between 3 and 4 miles from their points of residence. Such offenders would therefore have committed auto theft outside of the north district, thus bypassing closer opportunities.

Within the commercial area and Ironbound, the vast majority of residential points also indicate short distances traveled to the point of auto theft. This finding is consistent with the hypothesis that the offenders are likely traveling to the closest opportunity—the dark core in the center of the commercial district that extends somewhat into the Ironbound. . . .

Overall, most data points lend support to the hypothesis under consideration, in that most offenders have traveled to close opportunities rather than opportunities farther away. Even so, a few data points run con-

trary to our hypothesis, raising the question of why this may be the case. This is addressed in the "Discussion" section.

Discussion

Working under the assumption that the measurement model of effort is appropriate and accurate, the analyses in this chapter suggest that effort is an important variable in the decision process that precedes the commission of a crime. In other words, when a person is considering and weighing the costs, benefits, and risks of committing a particular crime at a particular place and time . . . , she or he likely considers the distance that she or he will need to travel to the corresponding points of opportunity and tries to minimize that distance.

. . . [T]he findings lend further credence to the utilitarian premise of rational choice theory. . . . This is quite significant because there is a tendency to speak abstractly of the factors that influence this decision process. This study specified a particular factor thought to be important to the cognitive process, determined an analytic manner appropriate to access this variable, and accordingly conducted an empirical exploration of that premise.

One must also think critically about the data points that appear to run contrary to the chapter's hypothesis. Why is it that in some clusters of residences, most offenders abide by the hypothesis and travel to the closer opportunities to commit auto theft, but a few travel much farther? One possible answer is that these offenders are bypassing close opportunities in favor of greater opportunities that are farther away. In other words, there may be a higher number of targets or targets may be more suitable in certain areas. As stated earlier, effort is one factor among many related to the criminal decision-making process. Another such factor is the anticipated reward that will be contingent on committing a crime at a particular place and time. . . . For certain individuals, the anticipated reward may be a more important variable in the decision process than effort, resulting in traveling a larger distance. The anticipated reward contingent on committing auto theft in these areas may therefore be higher than that in the closer opportunities. The map in Figure 4.8 lends some support to this premise. The majority of points that appear to run contrary to our hypothesis translate into a traveling distance radius that includes the commercial area, which contains the greatest opportunity to

Figure 4.8   Distance Traveled From Points of Residence to Points of Theft Relative to the Opportunity Structure

commit auto theft. These few points may represent offenders who are committing specialized forms of auto theft. In such cases, these offenders may bypass general auto theft opportunities for those in which the suitable target, specific to their particular motive, exists. These offenders would be abiding by the hypothesis because they are going to the closest relevant opportunity. Therefore, both possible explanations suggest that those data points that appear to run contrary to the hypothesis may actually be tapping into the complexity involved in the criminal decision process.

POLICY IMPLICATIONS

In a series of papers, Rossmo . . . developed a mathematical model that predicts the likely residence of a serial offender based on the environmental distribution of the incidents. This model has been quite useful to police and other law enforcement agencies because it helps to determine the appropriate search radius during the course of an investigation.

The findings from this study are also useful to law enforcement agencies, although in a subtly different way because the structure of our investigation differed from that of Rossmo. . . . First, this chapter not only considered distance, but also considered distance relative to relevant opportunity, which is not uniformly distributed in time or space. Therefore, any construction of search radii would have to incorporate the surrounding opportunity structure. Second, the analyses originated distance calculations from the point of residence, not the point of crime. This difference is subtle, but important, because these findings cannot be used to predict an offender's residence based on the point of auto theft. Instead, these findings would be useful when the Newark Police Department (or some other similar city) knows of an offender or group of offenders who they suspect will commit auto theft, such as a gang that derives its funds from the sale of stolen cars and auto parts.

FUTURE CONSIDERATIONS

First and perhaps most obviously, future work should venture outside of Newark, New Jersey. Newark is a racially and ethnically heterogeneous, densely populated city. It provides a multitude of opportunities to commit auto theft, and it has a large number of offenders to take great advantage of them. Conducting an exploration of criminal effort in a different locale would begin to answer the question of how generalizable these findings are.

Second, the concept of guardianship is important to the construction of an opportunity structure, yet it is relatively difficult to measure compared with other constructs. Future research projects should explore the possibility of including police substations, police patrol, security systems, and residents as a means of operationalizing guardianship. Although this would be possible theoretically, practically it would pose a problem. To clarify, how does a researcher measure absence? In all likelihood, its presence would have to be coded as a negative number in the opportunity structure.

Finally, it would be beneficial to consider how differing levels of opportunity would affect the general hypothesis under investigation. What if a moderate level of opportunity exists 1 mile from the offender's residence, but a high level of opportunity exists 3 miles from the offender's residence? Where should the offender travel? Although going to the first site would minimize the effort, going to the other site would maximize the reward. It would be helpful to think about how the other factors important to the criminal decision process (in this situation, the level of anticipated reward) interact with effort to influence the distance traveled relative to opportunity.

The beginning of this chapter argued that considering effort in isolation from these other factors was necessary for empirical clarity. At this point, however, it would be informative and beneficial to re-embed the findings on effort into the complex decision process and to consider their relative role. Nevertheless, this work represents a solid first step toward understanding a latent construct that is important in an offender's decision-making process. In addition, this chapter illustrates that mapping is an effective analytical tool for exploring these constructs.

Questions

1. Describe how Potchak, McGloin, and Zgoba define criminal effort.

2. What three factors are required for a crime to occur, according to routine activities theory?

CHAPTER 5

Serious Criminality at U.S. Colleges and Universities

An Application of the Situational Perspective

Don Hummer

University of Massachusetts–Lowell

Concern about the safety of campus constituents and preventing criminal activity at institutions of higher learning have become a hot topic in the academic press as well as among university administrators throughout the United States. As violent criminal victimization rates increased nationally throughout the 1980s and early 1990s, the campus environment ceased to enjoy the traditional immunity that it had in the past. . . .

The reasons that college and university campuses in the United States have been slow to come to grips with crime and violence are varied; however, most observers agree that, to some extent, administrators, parents, employees, and students simply did not want to acknowledge that problems existed in places that should perhaps be resistant to such social malaise. Although it has been documented that postsecondary institutions have had instances of crime and deviance throughout the centuries . . . , some schools have seen crime rates become a serious and sizable problem within only the past decade or so. . . .

Although the rise in crime to parallel the larger society had been evident to campus administrators and law enforcement personnel for several decades . . . , the general public was not privy to such information until the federal statute known as The Student Right-to-Know and Campus Security Act of 1990 (also the Crime Awareness and Campus Security Act of 1990, the Campus Crime and Security Act of 1990) mandated colleges and universities that receive federal funds, or as a condition of participating in federal student aid

programs, to annually compile and publish instances of violent and property crime occurring within their borders. . . .

Furthermore, although the tenets of the Campus Crime and Security Act of 1990 do not require them to do so, many colleges and universities voluntarily report crime statistics to the FBI for inclusion in the *Uniform Crime Reports*. . . . In summary, those interested parties wishing to utilize such information have been able to obtain it since the Campus Crime and Security Act of 1990 became effective in 1992. . . .

Situational Crime Prevention as Integrated Theory

Clarke . . . presented a compelling argument concerning the weaknesses of applying sociological-based theories of deviance to practical crime prevention situations. Many of these positivist theories focus on "dispositional" aspects of criminal behavior, which develop at a young age in the offender and/or emerge over time. Techniques that could prevent the aspects from emerging are most certainly outside the sphere of influence of any criminal justice systemic body. The utility of trying to explain the root causes or contributors of deviant behavior, whether from a positivist or critical perspective, is indeed a laudable task; however, the application of the results of such research has not proven beneficial to the practitioner.

Source: "Serious criminality at U.S. colleges and universities: An application of the situational perspective." By Don Hummer (2004), in *Criminal Justice Policy Review, 15,* 391–417. Reprinted by permission of Sage Publications, Inc.

The attractiveness of situational crime prevention, particularly for practitioners and agencies that are responsible for ensuring a certain area is safe for those who venture into it, is rooted in the versatility of the approach. More specifically, by incorporating the tenets of the theories incorporated by the situational approach (rational choice, environmental criminology, and routine activities theory), a more sophisticated and effective strategy of crime prevention can be implemented. Crime prevention through environmental design (CPTED), which at present is extremely popular and widely utilized by crime prevention specialists, is essentially a hybrid of the three theoretical strains discussed earlier and is directly linked to the idea of "defensible space." Relating this concept directly to the college or university campus setting, the components of situational crime prevention can be incorporated to work cooperatively in efforts to prevent victimization. The physical design of the campus may reduce the need for additional guardians, given that facilities planning can incorporate "natural" guardianship . . . , which also raises the costs for potential offenders. Not to be overlooked is the idea that constituents can do their part, in conjunction with campus law enforcement, to reduce their attractiveness as a potential crime target. . . .

An integrated situational crime prevention theory incorporates certain assumptions about the nature of humans, their thought processes, cues that provoke behaviors, and factors that make criminal opportunity seem less attractive to the potential offender. Clarke . . . reasoned that the subjective state and thought processes that play a part in the decision to commit a crime will be most influenced by immediate situational variables, thus the perceived opportunity to offend may be as much of a trigger in taking a criminal act through to fruition as any life circumstances or psychological variables that serve as the basis of much criminological thought. Felson . . . argued that, because security, or the protection of oneself, family, and possessions from predators, is one of our basic human needs, it is illogical to argue that crime prevention is abstracted from social scientific theory. He went on to posit that the notion of security as "locks, bolts, and badges" is a relatively recent definition, and that security should look to its roots as a basic need for conceptualization purposes. . . . If one also includes the ideas inherent in CPTED, this integrated approach outlines specific techniques and strategies for security specialists, architects, and planners to consider, thus moving situational crime prevention from an esoteric, theoretical idea to a concrete plan of implementation for policymakers.

THE SITUATIONAL PERSPECTIVE AND CAMPUS CRIME

The nature of most Part I index crime on college and university campuses facilitates the application of situational crime prevention as a theoretical framework for examinations of serious criminality. Postsecondary institutions have become increasingly concerned with deterring would-be offenders and eliminating the infinite opportunities for criminal behavior available to the potential offender. However, because the development of the perspective and the empirical research into campus crime are in their infancy, the situational perspective has not, as an integrated theory, been applied to any systematic analyses of serious on-campus crime. Scholars who have previously done research into campus crime highlighted its opportunistic nature and stated their belief that those individuals who engage in such acts can effectively be dissuaded. . . . Because situational crime prevention focuses on the factors conducive to offending, it is logical to apply the perspective to campus crime as a method of explaining and to aid in eradicating these behaviors.

Method

To ascertain the nature and scope of protective services at larger U.S. colleges and universities, the Bureau of Justice Statistics (BJS) surveyed 4-year institutions of higher education with 2,500 or more students during 1995. . . . The survey was administered under the auspices of the BJS Law Enforcement Management and Administrative Statistics (LEMAS) program. . . .

Public safety departments at 680 college and university campuses were included in the study population. Of these campuses, 581 (85%) schools returned the questionnaire with all or most questions answered, including 91% of the agencies at public institutions and 76% of those at private institutions. . . . Almost all safety departments responded at least in part. About three fourths of these agencies employed sworn police officers with arrest powers equivalent to municipal policing agencies, while the other fourth relied primarily on nonsworn security personnel. . . . For reasons of convenience, the term *campus public safety* is utilized to describe both groups irrespective of whether the officers are sworn peace officers or nonsworn security personnel.

DEPENDENT VARIABLES

The measurable outcomes of the LEMAS questionnaire are crime statistics, similar to the *Uniform Crime*

Report, collected by campus public safety agencies and subsequently kept on file at the schools for public inspection on request. In the current study, gross numbers of Part I index crimes (felony offenses that include murder/manslaughter, forcible sex offenses, robbery, aggravated assault, burglary, larceny/theft, motor vehicle theft, and arson) occurring on campus were reported for 1994, the latest year for which complete data were available when the questionnaire was administered in late 1995 by the BJS.

Most researchers realize that gross numbers of crimes occurring in a particular jurisdiction are contingent on a number of factors. Most obvious, the number of students enrolled at the institution directly affects the actual number of offenses reported to campus public safety. When presenting the overall numbers of crimes for comparative purposes, the FBI standardizes gross index crime statistics utilizing U.S. Census Bureau population data. . . . Because crime rates in the larger society are standardized using permanent residents as a base, rates on campus should be calculated similarly for comparative purposes. Therefore, dependent measures of campus criminality become: Total Part I Index Crimes/ Number of Enrolled Students, Part I Violent Offenses/ Number of Enrolled Students, and Part I Property Crimes/Number of Enrolled Students. Collectively, these measures are referred to as "the extent of serious criminality on campus."

INDEPENDENT VARIABLES

The key independent variables in the current research are the same as the variables that scholars examining the overall effectiveness and organizational structure of state and municipal law enforcement agencies make use of given that the survey instrument is identical to those utilized in research on police departments and their crime prevention initiatives. Therefore, comparisons may be made between campus law enforcement agencies and those agencies that serve the population at large in terms of personnel and crime prevention initiatives. The independent variables that are to be included can be subdivided under four distinct subheadings: characteristics of the institutions surveyed, campus safety department selection and training criteria, campus safety department structure and functions, and crime prevention strategies. . . .

Characteristics of the institutions surveyed. Environmental criminologists hold that factors associated with the physical structure of a location or facility are key to preventing or encouraging criminal acts to take place. Of course, putting the necessary components into place to achieve defensible space becomes a more difficult endeavor when the space to be defended is large in terms of physical area. Furthermore, the task is made even more complex when the types and number of facilities on campus is great. . . .

In addition to the variables collected by BJS using the LEMAS questionnaire administered to college and university public safety agencies, additional data were collected on the nature of the campus environment, as well as the state of criminal justice programming at schools in the sample; the latter of the two is included for exploratory purposes. Information on the campus environment was collected because of the differing nature of crime in, and the policing of, urban, suburban, and rural environments. . . . Information on this variable was gathered from the College Entrance Examination Board's (1997) *The College Handbook, 1998*. This source was chosen because it provides information on the nature of the campus environment and does not simply characterize a campus solely based on the size of the community in which it is located. Following are the College Entrance Examination Board's (1997) definitions of *urban, suburban*, and *rural campuses*:

> *Urban Campuses*: Can be as different as the cities in which they are located. They include some of the nation's oldest colleges, with historic buildings and park-like quadrangles, as well as colleges located in a single high-rise building with no traditional campus at all. What most urban campuses share is ready access to the extended cultural life of the city— museums, theaters, professional sports, concerts, and so on.

> *Suburban Campuses*: Can be quite varied, ranging from converted shopping malls to traditional, ivy-covered buildings. Suburban campuses are, by definition, located near cities; students who have transportation into the city can take advantage of a diversity of cultural events.

> *Rural Campuses*: Generally some distance from metropolitan areas, and students must rely almost entirely on the social and cultural events offered on campus. The "sense of community" may be increased because the college is more self-contained than in larger communities. . . .

These definitions of the nature of the campus environment are preferred because they take into account the individual physical characteristics of the campus and do not simply rely solely on the latest census statistics for classification. Therefore, a campus that is technically within the borders of a major city may still be classified as suburban if the campus has defined boundaries or is primarily residential in nature. Conversely, a campus may be classified as urban according to the previous definition even if the community in which it is located is classified as a minor metropolitan area or even a large town. It is thought that the nature of the school's environment may be correlated with the extent of crime prevention policies and, subsequently, with the reported crime rate at the institution.

The College Entrance Examination Board's . . . *The College Handbook, 1998* also was used to collect data regarding the nature of the criminal justice program at each of the 680 institutions. Specifically, this guidebook was used to determine whether a school had a separate baccalaureate program in criminal justice. Those colleges and universities that had no criminal justice program or that offered a criminal justice concentration in another discipline were coded as not offering a bachelor's degree in criminal justice, whereas those who specifically reported having an undergraduate major in criminal justice were so coded. . . . This independent variable is included for experimental purposes. Personal experience has demonstrated to the author that schools with reputable criminal justice programs tend to work closely with campus police departments on numerous issues. Logically, this interaction may help build a safer campus environment.

Campus safety department selection and training criteria. The passage of the Campus Crime and Security Act of 1990 significantly altered the way that safety personnel at American colleges and universities are selected and trained. This professionalization of campus public safety departments in the United States has been well documented. . . . However, the past decade has witnessed the most dramatic changes in campus safety personnel, as selected officers now come from the same pool of candidates as large municipal departments and state police forces. No longer is campus law enforcement seen as simply an entry-level stepping stone in which the officer gains valuable experience and then moves on to "real" police work.

Selection and training criteria for the largest institutions are measured thoroughly by the LEMAS survey. A candidate's aptitude was screened by a battery of tests, including level of education and the results of oral, written, physical agility, and psychological testing. Also looked at is whether institutions perform medical examinations and drug screens on applicants as well as thorough background and criminal records checks. When hired, the number of hours of classroom and field training a recruit must complete also is included as an independent variable indicative of professionalism within campus public safety departments.

Campus safety department structure and functions. The dataset utilized for the current research was born out of the idea that, because many schools are choosing to employ sworn law enforcement officers in place of traditional private security guards to protect their campuses and many of these departments are separate entities recognized by municipal departments near the institutions, there should be a comprehensive analysis of the structure and functions of these departments. Because the survey instrument was nearly identical to that given to municipal law enforcement departments, items pertaining to structure, function, and role of these campus departments model those of other policing agencies. For the following analyses, certain variables were selected as indicators of the theoretical tenants of situational crime prevention and as gauges of proactive order-maintenance activity at the participating institutions.

One variable unique to campus public safety departments is that of outsourcing. Some schools, especially those smaller institutions and/or those in areas with lower crime rates, will contract out to either local or state law enforcement agencies or contract security companies to provide routine patrol for campus property. Most often this practice is seen as a savings in revenue and may informally help enhance school–community relations by supplying revenue to the local municipality. Similarly, criminality at institutions whose campus safety departments possess arrest powers within their respective jurisdictions will be compared with those institutions whose departments are without such powers. This variable, arrest power, is a demarcation between those institutions utilizing sworn officers (either in house or contracted) and those using private security contractors because private security officers normally possess only the same arrest powers as the average citizen.

An area that has become a central focus for colleges and universities is that of dealing with the flow of illicit narcotics on campus. As is the case in larger society, the underground economy of the drug trade flourishes in an environment where individuals are receptive to the idea of experimenting with controlled substances and have the resources to support such experimentation. The postsecondary institution certainly typifies this description, and thus the personal use and distribution of narcotics on campus is a major concern for public safety chiefs and administrators alike. Many schools with fully sworn officers are responsible for the enforcement of narcotics laws on campus, and some participate in multiagency drug task forces on campus and in the surrounding communities. These two items are included to determine whether the enforcement of drug laws is significantly related to overall crime rates on campus. . . .

Crime prevention strategies. The LEMAS questionnaire also contained a number of items that enabled an analysis of the relationship between crime statistics and crime prevention initiatives presently in place at the institutions included in the sample. A few of the items that fall under this heading have been so designated with some degree of subjectivity. For example, the item pertaining to the arming of campus public safety officers may not strike some as a crime prevention technique. However, if one views the arming of officers as aiding guardianship as in routine activities theory or as upping the potential costs inherent in a given criminal act as in rational choice, then providing side arms to officers may be viewed as another, perhaps logical, preventative strategy employed by postsecondary institutions to ensure constituent safety.

Other items, such as the presence of an emergency blue light system, an emergency 911 system, and the various programs offered by institutions and administered by the public safety department clearly fall under the heading of crime prevention. This subset of independent variables is representative of the routine activities segment of situational crime prevention and demonstrates that colleges and universities are best able to affect the guardianship element of routine activities theory. However, some of these crime prevention program strategies, such as date rape prevention and self-defense training, also help students reduce their target suitability. Thus, the two facets of routine activities over which institutions have at least some sphere of influence are indicated by this grouping of independent variables.

Analysis and Results

EXTENT OF SERIOUS CRIMINALITY

The LEMAS survey collects information on *UCR* Part I offenses occurring on and reported to campus public safety departments. As previously noted, prior research has indicated that relatively minor offenses, such as alcohol violations and vandalism, are the most prevalent offenses that officers deal with on campus and that campus crime rates are generally significantly lower than those in the surrounding community. . . . However, these studies acknowledge that the gross numbers and rates of more serious crimes seem to be increasing at a faster rate proportionate to the surrounding community, thus warranting an investigation of the factors influencing Part I offending nationwide at larger colleges and universities.

Table 5.1 presents the gross number of Part I crimes reported by the participating schools, the average (mean number of offenses per institution), the rate of the various Part I offenses using mean enrollment as a standard, and the rate of Part I offenses using mean resident population of the campus as a standard. The mean number of students enrolled at the institutions surveyed is 10,783, and the average number of on-campus residents is 2,538. Using these figures, two different rates of serious criminality may be calculated for comparative purposes. The table clearly indicates that the nation's colleges and universities were not battling an extraordinary amount of serious violent crime in 1994. Of these campuses, 607 responding institutions reported only 16 homicides during the calendar year, and only 1 institution had more than 1 homicide occur on campus (1 institution reported 2 homicides). Furthermore, when a murder rate is calculated using either student enrollment or resident population as a standard, this figure indicates almost zero risk of homicide while on campus, either as an enrolled student or resident of campus housing. The most prevalent type of serious violent offending reported to campus safety department is aggravated assault. Unfortunately, the *UCR* does not disaggregate domestic assaults, stranger-on-stranger assaults, and so on from the more general category, thus we are unable to determine, from these data, context of these assaults. Regardless, schools in the study averaged about only four aggravated assaults on campus. This figure translates into rates of less than one assault per student enrolled or campus resident (.229 and .974, respectively).

As expected, the rates of Part I property offenses were correspondingly higher than those for violent crime on campus. Larceny/theft continues to be the most often reported offense to campus safety departments. In 1994, for instance, 124,681 such crimes were reported. More interesting, only 563 schools reported the number of overall larcenies to BJS in the survey. This could perhaps reflect a reluctance on the part of campus police chiefs to divulge the true number of thefts their agency receives because such information is not required to be tabulated as stipulated by the Campus

Table 5.1   Part I Offenses and Rates of Offending at Participating Institutions, 1994

Offense	No. of Crimes Reported (Mean no. per campus)	No. Crimes Enrollment (M = 10,783)	No. Crimes Resident Population (M = 2,538)
Murder/manslaughter (n = 607)	16 (.03)	.001	.006
Forcible sex offenses (n = 608)	831 (1.37)	.077	.327
Robery (n = 606)	1,213 (2.00)	.112	.478
Aggravated assault (n = 609)	2,471 (4.06)	.229	.974
Burglary (n = 611)	17,370 (28.43)	1.61	6.84
Larceny/theft (n = 563	124,681 (221.46)	11.56	49.13
Motor vehicle theft (n = 606)	5,017 (8.28)	.465	1.98
Arson (n = 550)	784 (1.43)	.073	.309
All violent offenses	4,531 (7.48)	.420	1.79
All property offenses	147,852 (268.82)	13.71	58.26
All Part I offenses	152,383 (277.06)	14.13	60.04

Crime and Security Act of 1990. Of course, another possible explanation is that the requested information was not readily available. Either of these explanations may account for the response rate for this particular offense being significantly lower than for the other seven Part I offenses (563 vs. 606 to 611).

The mean number of larceny offenses was slightly higher than 221, and the corresponding rates totaled just more than 11 per enrolled student and just over 49 per campus resident. Schools reported raw offense numbers for the other Part I property offenses (burglary, motor vehicle theft, and arson) to be significantly lower than those for larceny. In fact, the calculated rates for the remaining three property offenses seem to be comparable to the rates of serious violent criminality, although the rates of burglary and motor vehicle theft were slightly higher.

Taken together, the total number of violent offenses occurring on the participating campuses in 1994 was 4,531, with a mean rate of about 7½ serious violent offenses per school. This translates to a rate of .420 violent offenses per enrolled student and 1.79 violent offenses per campus resident. The total number of serious property crimes occurring at the institutions in 1994 was 147,852, approximately 32 times greater than the total number of serious violent crimes. Campuses averaged almost 269 serious property crimes in 1994, a rate of 13.71 per enrolled student and 58.26 per resident. In summary, the schools reported 152,383 total index crimes for 1994, an average of slightly more than 277 per campus.

These rates were calculated using the most conservative reporting figure for each of the four serious violent crimes. For example, 607 institutions reported the number of homicides occurring on campus. This was the lowest number of institutions reporting for any of the four violent crimes, thus this number was used as the divisor in calculating total violent crime rates. Similarly, the most conservative estimate was used to calculate property crime rates as well. . . . Of course, using the most conservative figure slightly inflates the overall crime rates; however, given the difference in the number of schools reporting figures for each crime, it is perhaps the most valid method of calculation. . . .

[B]ecause the LEMAS survey administered by BJS was not a formal request for crime data in compliance with the Campus Crime and Security Act of 1990, some institutions in the current dataset also failed to supply requested data, therefore direct comparisons for a handful of institutions was not feasible. What follows . . . is a comparison of index crime, violent crime, and property crime rates for those institutions supplying complete data for the BJS LEMAS questionnaire and to the FBI, which was subsequently used by Bromley. . . . All rates are standardized by dividing the raw number of offenses per 1,000 enrolled students. Total index crime rates were rounded to the nearest whole number by Bromley . . . , and for comparative purposes, the calculated total index crime rate for 1994 also was rounded in the same manner. Rates for violent index crimes and property index crimes remained as calculated to the hundredths decimal in Bromley's . . . study and the current research. . . .

Although overall crime rates appear to have decreased, it seems that neither the level of violence nor the amount of property offenses has decreased sufficiently enough, as subgroupings, to have registered as an overall significant decline within categories. Therefore, the results . . . must be read with caution because it would most certainly be premature to suggest that the amount of serious crime at these colleges and universities is decreasing. As mentioned previously, the purpose of this research is not to determine which factors correlate with levels of crime at individual institutions. . . .

Furthermore, because it is normal for crime rates to fluctuate on a yearly basis, and in different directions depending on which indicator is chosen to measure criminality, it is difficult to ascertain which factors (demographics, impact of crime prevention, policing tactics, etc.) are responsible for the rising and falling of crime rates over time. . . . Last, a precipitous drop or increase in the levels of serious crime would not be expected given that the time lag in between measurements is a relatively scant 2 to 3 years. Even supposing a radical shift in institutional philosophy (e.g., proactive law enforcement or design initiatives to prevent criminality) regarding criminal activity on campus, the results of such initiatives would not likely be reflected in actual crime statistics over such a short period of time.

REGRESSION ANALYSES

The . . . analyses that follow are intended as a preliminary test of the situational perspective's predictive power concerning crime figures and rates at larger colleges and universities in the United States. . . .

Regarding the subset of independent variables measuring characteristics of the institutions, there is a strong association between the number of buildings found at a school and total crime rates; that is, the more buildings, the higher the overall crime rate and the greater the incidence of Part I property offenses. This finding seems to illustrate the notion of defensible space being a problem for institutions, especially considering that the most prevalent types of crimes being committed at these schools are property offenses. Most surprising perhaps is the fairly strong relationship between the nature of criminal justice programming and serious crime because schools with undergraduate and graduate programs in criminal justice appear to have less overall on-campus criminality. Again, because of the lack of previous empirical work surrounding this issue, conclusions drawn from this result should be seen only as speculative in

nature. However, this result does support the idea that having a group of criminal justice scholars and students of the discipline in residence may have an ameliorating influence on serious campus criminality.

Another significant finding concerns the selection and training criteria for new campus public safety officers. Institutions that utilize a number of criteria when interviewing recruits from an applicant pool are more likely to have more total index and property index crimes. This result also may reflect the notion that schools with rising crime rates and/or more qualitatively serious crimes occurring in the recent past may implement new, innovative strategies to combat this problem, such as more carefully screening officers. Professionalizing the campus public safety department through rigorous hiring standards is another method that many institutions have adopted. This argument is furthered with the relationship between officer education level and property crime rates; those schools with less educated campus safety officers also tend to have higher property crime rates, although none of the results from this section of the regression model are particularly strong.

Proponents of professionalism will further be supported by the result that indicates that high numbers of violent index crimes are significantly associated with campuses that outsource for their protective services. The finding that schools which contract out to law enforcement and private security agencies are more likely to see higher rates of violent crime bolsters the position that only a professional, in-house public safety agency is familiar with the problems specific to the campus being served. Similarly, those schools with campus safety officers possessing arrest powers also have lower total and property crime rates. Taken together, this appears to be convincing evidence for a professional, well-educated, municipal-style police department for larger educational institutions, perhaps mirroring the municipal departments in which the institution is located.

For the public safety department to be truly proactive and preventive in nature, it must be part of the campus network in much the same way that neighborhood community police officers are in tune with the goings on in their beat. Although it is perhaps a generalization, outside contractors most likely do not have the personal stake in the well-being of the campus in a way that an in-house department would have. Therefore, although both types of services could respond to calls for service, only the in-house department has the capacity to be proactive. This means that crime prevention and the implementation of strategies aimed at lessening the probability of victimization require significant expenditures of time and resources that contract providers may be unwilling or unable to supply.

The last section of the full regression model taps specific crime prevention activities at major colleges and universities. Surprisingly, few of these variables are significantly related to either total, violent, or property crime rates. The only exceptions are moderate relationships between blue light telephone systems, general crime prevention education programs, and violent crime rates. Those institutions without strategically placed emergency blue light phones have higher rates of violent crime, whereas schools with more crime prevention education programs also have higher rates of violence. This latter effect most likely reflects an institutional response to higher incidences of violence. Because the data for this research were collected shortly after the Student Right-to-Know and Security Act went into effect, policies and procedures resultant from institutions revamping their security practices, the time lag is probably insufficient for any significant effects to become evident.

Discussion and Policy Considerations

Critics of situational crime prevention are quick to point out the theoretical and empirical shortcomings of the perspective, and the results of this research would seem to add fuel to the fire. The formulation of the perspective is denounced for being a reactionary, ex post facto framework regarding criminal behavior. Naysayers point out what they believe to be a gross indifference to the conditions and factors within the social framework that breed individuals who, for whatever reason, are inclined to commit acts of serious criminality. Furthermore, it is said that if society continues to focus on protecting the law abiding from the lawbreakers, those who do not perpetrate criminal acts are forced to cloister themselves behind protective barriers of whatever sort (either physical or psychological), worsening the social structural and environmental factors that are thought to influence serious criminality. In a sense, society would retreat behind its crime prevention barriers leaving the "barbarians at the gate."

Although it is certainly true that the situational perspective does little to explain or influence the genesis of criminality among groups or individuals, it is as necessary to have reactionary theoretical perspectives as it is necessary to have a criminal justice system designed to react to instances of wrongdoing. The current research depicted the needs and responses of one particular social

institution, the university, in protecting its specific constituency from criminal acts committed by constituents and outsiders on campus property. To be sure, persons affiliated with postsecondary institutions would most certainly relish a revolutionary idea or ideas that would make prolific steps forward in eradicating unlawful behavior in American society. However, these institutions certainly do not have the luxury of waiting for such a remedy to be found. Furthermore, the Student Right-to-Know and Campus Security Act of 1990 forced the hand of administrators at postsecondary institutions to look at the crime problems at their schools with prevention as the best alternative. In doing so, the situational perspective is perhaps the most useful tool available to colleges and universities in terms of criminological theory.

The results presented in the previous section were not to be expected given the theoretical framework and the prior empirical work concerning campus criminality. Ordinary least squares regression analysis indicates that the most predictive factor concerning crime rates is the physical size of the institution in terms of number of buildings and the overall professionalism of the campus public safety department, which provides increased guardianship for the institution as a whole. It would be erroneous, given the exploratory nature of the data, to make overarching generalizations about campus crime or the success of responses to campus criminality at this point. These results could be viewed more as a gathering of baseline data (or a starting point for longitudinal analyses) than any valid empirical evidence against the situational perspective. To reiterate, given the changes that campus safety departments have undergone due to the Campus Crime and Security Act of 1990, it is wholly possible, and perhaps probable, that the crime prevention programs presented in the prior analyses are responses to crime rates and have thus been implemented after rates of criminality already peaked.

With the results viewed in this light, instituting precautionary strategies that are in keeping with the situational perspective can do nothing but benefit institutions of higher learning. First, there is no way of knowing how much overall serious criminality is deterred by the various situational tactics that have been put into operation by the schools included in this analysis. The nature of preventive measures allows us to assume that at least some criminal behavior is deterred, or at least displaced off campus, which, to the thinking of the institution, is just as productive. Therefore, logically speaking, these preventive measures, even if only slightly successful in preventing criminal offenses, are bettering the campus environment.

Second, in keeping with the currently popular community-oriented policing paradigm, situational tenets are a natural stratagem for reducing general fear and improving the working relationship between campus law enforcement and university constituents. By taking the first preventive steps, institutions set a definitive example for encouraging all in the campus community to take responsibility for their own personal safety. Third, through the incorporation of situational crime prevention techniques, institutions help protect themselves from potential liability under the Campus Crime and Security Act of 1990 by having a systematic set of prevention strategies in place to ensure constituent safety. At the least, this gives the appearance that a school is doing everything possible to afford a secure learning environment. These efforts can easily be demonstrated with a coherent, rational crime prevention plan.

Implementing the situational crime prevention approach need not be an involved, expensive undertaking. Recognizing the lean nature of most university budgets at this particular juncture, a number of the tactics tested in the current research could be implemented using existing institutional resources or investing a modest dollar figure. For example, specific patrols of officers to known trouble spots, installation of emergency blue light telephones, or conducting more in-depth interviews and background checks on potential new officers are all policies with evidence of effectiveness that come with a relatively inexpensive price tag. In the long run, the justification of expenditures for safety and security is a rather straightforward one when balanced against the possible public relations and financial repercussions of not providing a safe environment for the pursuit of higher education.

Questions

1. Describe the three theories incorporated by the situational approach presented by Hummer.

2. Describe how each of the four independent variables is related to the dependent variables.

CHAPTER 6

The Novelty of "Cybercrime"

An Assessment in Light of Routine Activity Theory

Majid Yar
University of Kent, UK

Introduction

It has become more or less obligatory to begin any discussion of "cybercrime" by referring to the most dramatic criminological quandary it raises—namely, does it denote the emergence of a "new" form of crime and/or criminality? Would such novelty require us to dispense with (or at least modify, supplement, or extend) the existing array of theories and explanatory concepts that criminologists have at their disposal? Unsurprisingly, answers to such questions appear in positive, negative, and indeterminate registers. Some commentators have suggested that the advent of "virtual crimes" marks the establishment of a new and distinctive social environment (often dubbed "cyberspace," in contrast to "real space") with its own ontological and epistemological structures, interactional forms, roles and rules, limits and possibilities. In this alternate social space, new and distinctive forms of criminal endeavor emerge, necessitating the development of a correspondingly innovative criminological vocabulary. . . . Skeptics, in contrast, see cybercrime, at best, as a case of familiar criminal activities pursued with some new tools and techniques. . . . If this were the case, then cybercrime could still be fruitfully explained, analyzed, and understood in terms of established criminological classifications and etiological schema. Grabosky . . . nominates in particular Cohen and Felson's routine activity theory (RAT) as one such criminological approach, thereby seeking to demonstrate

"that 'virtual criminality' is basically the same as the terrestrial crime with which we are familiar." . . . [T]here has yet to appear any sustained *theoretical* reflection on whether and to what extent RAT might serve to illuminate "cybercrimes" in their continuity or discontinuity with those "terrestrial crimes" that occur in what Pease . . . memorably dubs "meatspace." The present chapter aims to do just that in the hope of shedding some further light on whether some of our received, "terrestrially grounded" criminology can, in fact, give us adequate service in coming to grips with an array of ostensibly "new" crimes.

This chapter is structured as follows. I begin by briefly addressing some of the definitional and classificatory issues raised by attempts to delimit cybercrime as a distinctive form of criminal endeavor. I then explicate the formulation of routine activity theory that is utilized in the chapter, and I offer some general reflections on some of the pressing issues typically raised vis-à-vis the theory's explanatory ambit (in particular, its relation to dispositional or motivational criminologies and the vexed problem of the "rationality" or otherwise of offenders' choices to engage in law-breaking behavior). In the third section, I examine cybercrime in relation to the general ecological presuppositions of RAT, focusing specifically on whether the theory's explanatory dependence on *spatial* and *temporal convergence* is transposable to crimes commissioned in online or virtual environments. . . . In conclusion, I offer some comments

Source: "The novelty of 'cybercrime': An assessment in light of routine activity theory," by Yar, M. (2005), in *European Journal of Criminology, 2,* 407–427. Reprinted by permission of Sage Publications, Ltd.

on the extent to which cybercrimes might be deemed continuous with terrestrial crimes. Substantively, I suggest that, although the core concepts of RAT are, to a significant degree, transposable (or at least adaptable) to crimes in virtual environments, there remain some qualitative differences between virtual and terrestrial worlds that make a simple, wholesale application of its analytical framework problematic.

Cybercrime: Definitions and Classifications

A primary problem for the analysis of cybercrime is the absence of a consistent current definition even among those law enforcement agencies charged with tackling it. . . . [T]he term has no specific referent in law, yet it has come to enjoy considerable currency in political, criminal justice, media, public, and academic discourse. Consequently, the term might best be seen to signify a *range* of illicit activities whose common denominator is the central role played by networks of information and communication technology (ICT) in their commission. A working definition along these lines is offered by Thomas and Loader . . . , who conceptualize cybercrime as those "computer-mediated activities which are either illegal or considered illicit by certain parties and which can be conducted through global electronic networks." The specificity of cybercrime is therefore held to reside in the newly instituted interactional environment in which it takes place, namely the virtual space (often dubbed "cyberspace") generated by the interconnection of computers into a worldwide network of information exchange, primarily the Internet. . . .

Within the prior definition, it is possible to further classify cybercrime along a number of different lines. One commonplace approach is to distinguish between computer-assisted crimes (those crimes that predate the Internet, but take on a new life in cyberspace; e.g. fraud, theft, money laundering, sexual harassment, hate speech, and pornography) and computer-focused crimes (those crimes that have emerged in tandem with the establishment of the Internet and could not exist apart from it; e.g., hacking, viral attacks, and website defacement). . . . On this classification, the primary dimension along which cybercrime can be subdivided is the manner in which the technology plays a role (i.e., whether it is a contingent [computer-assisted] or necessary [computer-focused] element in the commission of the offense).

Although this distinction may be sociotechnically helpful, it has a limited criminological utility. Hence, one alternative is to mobilize existing categories derived from criminal law into which their cyber-counterparts can be transposed. Thus, Wall . . . subdivides cybercrime into four established legal categories:

1. Cyber-*trespass*—crossing boundaries into other people's property and/or causing damage (e.g., hacking, defacement, viruses).

2. Cyber-*deceptions* and *thefts*—stealing (money, property; e.g., credit card fraud, intellectual property violations) (a.k.a. "piracy").

3. Cyber-*pornography*—activities that breach laws on obscenity and decency.

4. Cyber-*violence*—doing psychological harm to, or inciting physical harm against, others, thereby breaching laws pertaining to the protection of the person (e.g., hate speech, stalking).

This classification is certainly helpful in relating cybercrime to existing conceptions of proscribed and harmful acts, but it does little in the way of isolating what might be qualitatively *different* or *new* about such offences and their commission when considered from a perspective that looks beyond a limited legalistic framework. . . . [T]heorists of the new informational networks suggest that cyberspace makes possible near-instantaneous encounters and interactions between spatially distant actors, creating possibilities for ever-new forms of association and exchange. . . . Criminologically, this seemingly renders us vulnerable to an array of potentially predatory others who have us within instantaneous reach, unconstrained by the normal barriers of physical distance.

Moreover, the ability of the potential offender to target individuals and property is seemingly amplified by the inherent features of the new communication medium—computer-mediated communication (CMC) enables a single individual to reach, interact with, and affect thousands of individuals simultaneously. Thus, the technology acts as a force multiplier, enabling individuals with minimal resources (so-called empowered small agents) to generate potentially huge negative effects (mass distribution of e-mail scams and distribution of viral codes being two examples). Further, great emphasis is placed on the ways in which the Internet enables the manipulation and reinvention of social identity—cyberspace interactions afford individuals the capacity to reinvent themselves, adopting new virtual personae potentially far removed from their real-world identities. . . . From a criminological perspective, this is viewed as a powerful tool for the unscrupulous to perpetrate offences while maintaining anonymity through disguise . . . and a formidable challenge to those seeking to track down offenders.

From the previous discussion, we can surmise that it is the supposedly novel sociointeractional features of the cyberspace environment (primarily the collapse of spatial-temporal barriers, many-to-many connectivity, and the anonymity and plasticity of online identity) that make possible new forms and patterns of illicit activity. It is in this alleged discontinuity from the sociointeractional organization of terrestrial crimes that the criminological challenge of cybercrime is held to reside. . . .

Delimiting the Routine Activity Approach: Situational Explanation, Rationality, and the Motivated Actor

Birkbeck and LaFree . . . suggest that the criminological specificity of RAT can be located via Sutherland's . . . distinction between "dispositional" and "situational" explanations of crime and deviance. Dispositional theories aim to answer the question of criminality, seeking some causal mechanism (variously social, economic, cultural, psychological, or biological) that might account for why *some* individuals or groups come to possess an inclination toward law- and rule-breaking behavior. . . .

In contrast, situational theories (including various opportunity and social control approaches) eschew dispositional explanations largely on the grounds of their apparent explanatory failures—they appear recurrently unsuccessful in adequately accounting for trends and patterns of offending in terms of their nominated causes. . . . Routine activity theorists "take criminal inclination as given" . . . , supposing that there is no shortage of motivations available to all social actors for committing law-breaking acts. They do not deny that motivations can be incited by social, economic, and other structural factors, but they insist that any such incitements do not furnish a *sufficient* condition for actually following through inclinations into law-breaking activity. . . . Rather, the *social situations* in which actors find themselves crucially mediate decisions about whether they will act on their inclinations (whatever their origins). Consequently, routine activity theorists choose to "examine the manner in which the spatiotemporal organization of social activities helps people translate their criminal inclinations into action." . . . Social situations in which offending becomes a viable option

are created by the routine activities of other social actors; in other words, the routine organizational features of everyday life create the conditions in which persons and property become available as targets for successful predation at the hands of those so motivated. . . . If this is the case, then the emergence of cybercrime invites us to inquire into the routine organization of *online* activities, with the aim of discerning whether and how this "helps people translate their criminal inclinations into action." More broadly, it invites us to inquire as to whether the analytical schema developed by RAT—in which are postulated key variables that make up the criminogenic social situation (what Felson . . . calls "the chemistry for crime")—can be successfully transposed to cyberspatial contexts, given the apparent discontinuities of such spaces vis-à-vis real-world settings.

. . . As with many other theoretical approaches, RAT does not comprise a single, self-subsistent set of explanatory concepts. Rather, it can take a number of different forms, utilizing a variable conceptual apparatus and levels of analysis depending on the specific orientations of the criminologists who develop and mobilize it. . . . Moreover, the work of a single contributor does not remain static over time, but typically undergoes revision and development. Thus, for example, Felson has elaborated and refined his original chemistry for crime over a 25-year period by introducing additional mediating variables into what is an ever-more complex framework. Here I discuss RAT in something like its original formulation. This statement of the theory hypothesizes that "criminal acts require the convergence in space and time of *likely offenders*, *suitable targets*, and the *absence of capable guardians*." . . . This definition has the virtue of including the "central core of three concepts," . . . which appear as constant features of all routine activity models.

A second issue relates to the theory's controversial attachment to presuppositions about the rational character of actors' choices to engage in (or desist from) illegal activity. Routine activity approaches are generally held to be consistent with the view that actors are free to choose their courses of action, and do so on the basis of anticipatory calculation of the utility or rewards they can expect to flow from the chosen course. . . . One common objection raised in light of this commitment is the theory's potential inability to encompass crimes emanating from non-instrumental motives. Thus, for example, Miethe et al. . . . and Bennett . . . conclude that, although routine activity theory exhibits considerable explanatory power in relation to property offences (those oriented to material and economic gain), it is considerably weaker in respect of expressive crimes, such as interpersonal violence. Similar objections can be raised from outside routine activity analysis, for example by proponents of cultural criminology who highlight the neglect of emotional and affective seductions that individuals experience when engaged in criminal and deviant activity.... I would suggest, however, that the basic difficulty here arises not so much from the attribution to actors of "rationality" per se, but from taking such rationality to be necessarily of a limited, economic kind.... It may be a mistake to view affective dispositions as inherently devoid of rationality; rather, as Archer ... argues, emotions can better be seen as responses to, and commentaries upon, situations that we encounter as part of our practical engagements with real-world situations.... For the remainder of this chapter, I follow routine activity theorists in taking motivations as given, without, however, conceding that such motivations must necessarily be reducible to instrumental calculations of economic or material utility.

Convergence in Space and Time: The Ecology and Topology of Cyberspace

At heart, routine activity theory is an *ecological* approach to crime causation, and as such the spatial (and temporal) localization of persons, objects and activities is a core presupposition of its explanatory schema. The ability of its etiological formula (offender + target – guardian = crime) to explain and/or anticipate patterns of offending depends upon these elements converging in space and time. Routine activities, which create variable opportunity structures for successful predation, always occur in particular locations at particular times, and the spatiotemporal accessibility of targets for potential offenders is crucial in determining the possibility and likelihood of an offence being committed. As Felson ... puts it: "The organization of time and space is central. It ... helps explain how crime occurs and what to do about it." ... Thus, at a general level, the theory requires that targets, offenders, and guardians be located in particular places, that measurable relations of spatial proximity and distance pertain between those targets and potential offenders, and that social activities be temporally ordered according to rhythms, such that each of these agents is either typically present or absent at particular times. Consequently, the transposability of RAT to virtual environments requires that cyberspace exhibit a *spatiotemporal ontology* congruent with that of the physical world (i.e., that place, proximity, distance, and temporal order

be identifiable features of cyberspace). I reflect on the spatial and temporal ontology of cyberspace in turn.

SPATIALITY

Discourses of cyberspace and online activity are replete with references to space and place. There are purported to exist portals, sites complete with back doors, chat rooms, lobbies, classrooms, and cafes, all linked together via superhighways, with mail carrying communications between one location and another.... Such talk suggests that cyberspace possesses a recognizable geography more-or-less continuous with the familiar spatial organization of the physical world to which we are accustomed. However, it has been suggested that such ways of talking are little more than handy metaphors that provide a convenient way for us to conceptualize an environment that in reality is inherently discontinuous with the nonvirtual world of physical objects, locations and coordinates.... The virtual environment is seen as one in which there is zero distance between its points ..., such that entities and events cannot be meaningfully located in terms of spatial contiguity, proximity and separation. Everyone, everywhere and everything are always and eternally just a click way. Consequently, geographical rules that act as a friction or barrier to social action and interaction are broken.... If this is true, then the viability of RAT as an etiological model for virtual crimes begins to look decidedly shaky, given the model's aforementioned dependence on spatial convergence and separation, proximity and distance, to explain the probability of offending....

Positions that claim there is no recognizable spatial topology in cyberspace may be seen to draw upon an absolute and untenable separation of virtual and nonvirtual environments—they see these as two ontologically distinct orders or experiential universes. However, there are good reasons to believe that such a separation is overdrawn and that the relationships between these domains are characterized by similarity and dissimilarity, convergence and divergence. I elaborate two distinctive ways in which cyberspace may be seen to retain a spatial geometry that remains connected to that of the real world.

First, cyberspace may be best conceived not so much as a virtual reality, but rather as a real virtuality, a sociotechnically generated interactional environment rooted in the real world of political, economic, social, and cultural relations.... Cyberspace stands with one foot firmly planted in the real world and, as a consequence, carries nonvirtual spatialities over into its organization. This connection between virtual and nonvirtual spatialities is apparent along a number of dimensions. For instance, the virtual environments (websites, chatrooms, portals, mail systems, etc.) that comprise the virtual environment are physically rooted and produced in real space. The distribution of capacity to generate such environments follows the geography of existing economic relations and hierarchies. Thus, for example, 50% of Internet domains originate in the United States, which also accounts for 83% of the total web pages viewed by Internet users. . . . Moreover, access to the virtual environment follows existing lines of social inclusion and exclusion, with Internet use being closely correlated to existing cleavages of income, education, gender, ethnicity, age, and disability. . . . Consequently, presence and absence in the virtual world translate real-world marginalities, which are profoundly spatialized (First World and Third World, urban and rural, middle-class suburb and urban ghetto, gated community and high-rise estate). In short, the online density of both potential offenders and potential targets is not neutral with respect to existing social ecologies, but translates them via the differential distribution of the resources and skills needed to be present and active in cyberspace.

A second way in which cyberspace may exhibit a spatial topology refers to the purely internal organization of the information networks that it comprises. It was noted above that many commentators see the Internet and related technologically generated environments as heralding the death of distance and the collapse of spatial orderings, such that all points are equally accessible from any starting point. . . . However, reflection on network organization reveals that not all places are equidistant—proximity and distance have meaning when negotiating cyberspace. This will be familiar to all students and scholars who attempt to locate information, organizations and individuals via the Internet. Just because one knows, suspects or is told that a particular entity has a virtual presence on the Net, finding that entity may require widely varying expenditures of time and effort. Those domains (e.g., websites) with a higher density of connections to other domains (e.g., via hyperlinks) are more easily arrived at than those with relatively few. . . . Arriving at a particular location may require one to traverse a large number of intermediate sites, thereby rendering that location relatively distant from one's point of departure; conversely, the destination may be only a click away. Thus, the distribution of entities in terms of the axis proximity–distance, and the possibility of both convergence and divergence of such entities, can be seen to have at least some purchase in cyberspace.

Despite these continuities, it should also become clear that there exist qualitative differences between the spatial organization of nonvirtual and virtual worlds. Most significantly, they exhibit significantly different degrees of stability and instability in their geometries. Nonvirtual spatialities are relatively stable and perdurable. Granted, they can undergo significant shifts over time: patterns of land use can and do change . . . ; the sociodemographic configuration of locales is also subject to change . . . ; the proximity of places is elastic in light of developing transport infrastructures; and so on. However, given that nonvirtual spatial orderings are materialized in durable physical artefacts (buildings, roads, bridges, and walls), and their social occupation and uses are patterned and institutionalized, change in their organization is likely to be incremental rather than wholesale. It is this very stability in sociospatial orderings that permits ecological perspectives such as RAT to correlate factors such as residential propinquity with predation rates and patterns. In contrast, virtual spatialities are characterized by extreme volatility and plasticity in their configurations. It was noted above that virtual proximity and distance may be seen as the product of variable network geometries and connection densities. Yet these connections are volatile and easily transmuted—little resistance is offered by virtual architectures and topologies. Thus, the distance or separation between two sites or locales can shift instantly by virtue of the simple addition of a hyperlink that provides a direct and instant path from one to the other. Similarly, virtual places and entities appear and disappear in the cyber environment with startling regularity—the average lifespan for a web page is just a couple of months . . . ; actors instantaneously appear and disappear from the environment as they log in or out of the network. Consequently, the sociospatial organization of the virtual world is built on shifting sands. This quality presents considerable difficulty for the application of routine activity analysis to cyberspace, given its presuppositions that (a) places have a relatively fixed presence and location, and (b) the presence of actors in locations is amenable to anticipation in light of regularized patterns of activity.

Temporality

The ability to locate actors and entities in particular spaces/places *at particular times* is a basic presupposition of RAT. The explanatory power of the theory depends on routine activities exhibiting a clear temporal sequence and order (a *rhythm*, or regular periodicity with which events occur, and a *timing*, in which different activities are coordinated "such as the coordination of an offender's rhythms with those of a victim"...). It is this temporal ordering of activities that enables potential offenders to anticipate when and where a target may be converged upon....

The temporal structures of cyberspace, I would argue, are largely devoid of the clear temporal ordering of real-world routine activities. Cyberspace, as a *global* interactional environment, is populated by actors living in different real-world time zones, and so is populated 24/7. Moreover, online activities span workplace and home, labor and leisure, and cannot be confined to particular, clearly delimited temporal windows (although there may be peaks and troughs in gross levels of network activity, as relatively more people in the most heavily connected time zones make use of the Internet . . .). Consequently, there are no *particular* points in time at which actors can be anticipated to be *generally* present or absent from the environment. From an RAT perspective, this means that rhythm and timing as structuring properties of routine activities become problematic—for offenders, for potential targets and for guardians. Given the disordered nature of virtual spatiotemporalities, identifying patterns of convergence between the criminogenic elements becomes especially difficult.

Thus far, I have largely focused on the question of cyberspatial convergence between the entities identified as necessary for the commission of an offence. Now I turn to consider the properties of those entities themselves, in order to reflect upon the relative continuity or discontinuity between their virtual and nonvirtual forms. As already mentioned, the first of these elements, the motivated offender, is assumed rather than analyzed by RAT. Therefore, I do not consider the offender further, but take the existence of motivated offenders in cyberspace as a given. Instead, I follow RAT in focusing on the other two elements of the criminogenic formula—namely, suitable targets and capable guardians.

Targets in Cyberspace: VIVA la Différence?

For routine activity theory, the suitability of a target (human or otherwise) for predation can be estimated according to its four-fold constituent properties—value, inertia, visibility, and accessibility, usually rendered in the acronym VIVA....

VALUE

The valuation of targets is a complicated matter even when comparing "like with like" (e.g., property theft). This complexity is a function of the various purposes the offender may have in mind for the target once appropriated—whether it is for personal pleasure, for sale, for use in the commission of a further offence or other noncriminal activity, and so on. Equally, the target will vary according to the shifting valuations attached socially and economically to particular goods at particular times—factors such as scarcity and fashion will play a role in setting the value placed upon the target by offenders and others. . . . Most cybercrime targets are *informational* in nature, given that all entities that exist and move in cyberspace are forms of digital code. Prime targets of this kind include the various forms of intellectual property, such as music, motion pictures, images, computer software, trade and state secrets, and so on. In general terms, it may well be that, in the context of an information economy . . . , increasing value is attached to such informational goods, thereby making them increasingly valued as potential targets. The picture becomes more complex when the range of targets is extended—property may be targeted not for theft but for trespass or criminal damage (a cybercriminal case in point being hacking, where computer systems are invaded and websites are defaced, or malware distribution, where computer systems are damaged by viruses, Trojan horses, and worms . . .); the target may be an individual who is stalked and abused; or members of a group may be subjected to similar victimization because of their social, ethnic, religious, sexual, or other characteristics; the target may be an illicit product that is traded for pleasure or profit (such as child pornography). Broadly speaking, we can conclude that the targets of cybercrime, like those of terrestrial crime, vary widely and attract different valuations, and that such valuations are likely to impact on the suitability of the target when viewed from the standpoint of a potential offender....

INERTIA

The term *inertia* refers to the physical properties of objects or persons that might offer varying degrees of resistance to effective predation: A large and heavy object is relatively difficult to remove, and a large and heavy person is relatively difficult to assault.... Therefore, there is (at least for terrestrial crimes against property and persons) an inverse relationship between inertia and suitability, such that the greater the inertial resistance the lower the suitability of the target, and vice versa. The operability of the inertial criteria in cyberspace, however, appears more problematic, since the targets of cybercrime do not possess physical properties of volume and mass.... This apparent weightlessness ... seemingly deprives property in cyberspace of any inherent resistance to its removal. Information can be downloaded nearly instantaneously; indeed, it can be infinitely replicated thereby multiplying the offence many-fold (the obvious example here being media piracy ...). However, further reflection shows that even informational goods retain inertial properties to some degree. First, the volume of data (e.g., file size) impacts upon the portability of the target—something that will be familiar to anyone who has experienced the frustration of downloading large documents using a telephone dial-up connection. Secondly, the technological specification of the tools (the computer system) used by the information thief will place limits on the appropriation of large informational targets; successful theft will require, for example, that the computer used has sufficient storage capacity (e.g., hard drive space or other medium) to which the target can be copied. Thus, although informational targets offer *relatively* little inertial resistance, their weightlessness is not absolute.

VISIBILITY

RAT postulates a positive correlation between target visibility and suitability: "the potential offender must know of the existence of the target." ... Property and persons that are more visible are more likely to become targets. Conceptualizing visibility in cyberspace presents a difficult issue. Given that the social raison d'etre of technologies such as the Internet is to invite and facilitate communication and interaction, visibility is a ubiquitous feature of virtually present entities. The Internet is an *inherently* public medium.... Moreover, because the internal topology of cyberspace is largely unlimited by barriers of *physical* distance, this renders virtually present entities *globally* visible, hence advertising their existence to the largest possible pool of motivated offenders.

ACCESSIBILITY

The term *accessibility* denotes the "ability of an offender to get to the target and then get away from the scene of a crime." ... Again, the greater the target's accessibility, the greater its suitability, and vice versa.

Thus, Beavon et al. ... identify the number of physical routes through which a target is accessible as a significant variable in the distribution of property crimes.... However, given that traversal of cyberspace is nonlinear, and it is possible to jump from any one point to any other point within the space, it is difficult to conceive targets as differentiated according to the likelihood of accessibility to a potential offender in this manner.... It is, of course, possible that an offender may be noticed during the commission of the offence (e.g., by an Intrusion Detection System) and subsequently trailed back to his or her home location via electronic-tracing techniques. However, such tracing measures can be circumvented with a number of readily available tools, such as anonymous remailers, encryption devices, and the use of third-party servers and systems from which to launch the commission of an offense ...; this brings us back to the problem of *anonymity*, noted earlier. The one dimension in which accessibility between nonvirtual and virtual targets might most closely converge is that of security devices that prevent unauthorized access. Cohen and Felson ... note the significance of "attached or locked features of property inhibiting its illegal removal." The cyberspatial equivalents of such features include passwords and other authentication measures that restrict access to sites where vulnerable targets are stored (e.g., directories containing proprietary information). Such safeguards can, of course, be circumvented with tools such as password sniffers, crackers, and decryption tools ..., but these can be conceived as the virtual counterparts of lock-picks, glass cutters, and crowbars.

In summary, it can be seen from the above that the component subvariables comprising target suitability exhibit varying degrees of transposability to virtual settings. The greatest convergence appears in respect of target value.... However, the remaining three subvariables exhibit considerable divergence between real and virtual settings. In the case of inertia, the difference arises from the distinctive *ontological properties* of entities that exist in the two domains—they are physical in the case of the real world and nonphysical (informational) in the case of the virtual. In respect of the other two subvariables (visibility and accessibility), divergences between the real and the virtual arise from the structural features of the environments themselves; as previously discussed, features such as distance, location, and movement differ markedly between the two domains, and these configurations will affect the nature of visibility and accessibility within the respective environments.

Are There "Capable Guardians" in Cyberspace?

"Capable guardianship" furnishes the third key etiological variable for crime causation postulated by routine activity theory. Guardianship refers to "the capability of persons and objects to prevent crime from occurring." . . . Guardians effect such prevention "either by their physical presence alone or by some form of direct action." . . . Although direct intervention may well occur, routine activity theorists see the simple presence of a guardian in proximity to the potential target as a crucial deterrent. . . . Such guardians may be formal (e.g., the police), but RAT generally places greater emphasis on the significance of 'informal' agents such as homeowners, neighbors, pedestrians, and other ordinary citizens going about their routine activities. . . . In addition to such social guardians, the theory also views physical security measures as effecting guardianship—instances include barriers, locks, alarms, and lighting on the street and within the home. . . . Taken together, the absence or presence of guardians at the point at which potential offenders and suitable targets converge in time and space is seen as critical in determining the likelihood of an offence taking place. . . .

How, then, does the concept of guardianship transpose itself into the virtual environment? The efficacy of the concept as a discriminating variable between criminogenic and noncriminogenic situations rests on the guardian's copresence with the potential target at the time when the motivated offender converges on it. In terms of formal social guardianship, maintaining such copresence is well nigh impossible, given the ease of offender mobility and the temporal irregularity of cyberspatial activities (it would require a ubiquitous, round-the-clock police presence on the Internet). However, in this respect at least, the challenge to formal guardianship presented by cyberspace is only a more intensified version of the policing problem in the terrestrial world; as Felson . . . notes, the police "are very unlikely to be on the spot when a crime occurs." In cyberspace, as in the terrestrial world, it is often only when private and informal attempts at effective guardianship fail that the assistance of formal agencies is sought. . . . The cyberspatial world, like the terrestrial, is characterized by a range of such private and informal social guardians: These range from in-house network administrators and systems security staff who watch over their electronic charges, through trade organizations oriented to self-regulation, to ordinary online citizens who exercise a range of informal social controls over each other's behavior (such as the practice of flaming those who breach social norms on offensive behavior in chatrooms . . .). In addition to such social guardians, cyberspace is replete with physical or technological guardians, automated agents that exercise perpetual vigilance. These range from firewalls, intrusion detection systems, and virus scanning software . . . , to state e-communication monitoring projects such as the U.S. government's Carnivore and ECHELON systems. . . . In summary, it would appear that RAT's concept of capable guardianship is transposable to cyberspace even if the structural properties of the environment (such as its variable spatial and temporal topology) amplify the limitations upon establishing guardianship already apparent in the terrestrial world.

Conclusion

The impetus for this chapter was provided by the dispute over whether cybercrime should be considered as a new and distinctive form of criminal activity, one demanding the development of a new criminological vocabulary and conceptual apparatus. I chose to pursue this question by examining if and to what extent existing etiologies of crime could be transposed to virtual settings. I have focused on the routine activity approach because this perspective has been repeatedly nominated as a theory capable of adaptation to cyberspace; if such adaptability (of the theory's core concepts and analytic framework) could be established, this would support the claim of *continuity* between terrestrial and virtual crimes, thereby refuting the novelty thesis. If not, this would suggest *discontinuity* between crimes in virtual and nonvirtual settings, thereby giving weight to claims that cybercrime is something criminologically new. I conclude that there are both significant continuities and discontinuities in the configuration of terrestrial and virtual crimes.

With respect to the central core of three concepts, I have suggested that motivated offenders can be treated as largely homologous between terrestrial and virtual settings. The construction of suitable targets is more complex, with similarities in respect of value but significant differences in respect of inertia, visibility, and accessibility. The concept of "capable guardianship" appears to find its fit in cyberspace, albeit in a manner that exacerbates the possibilities of instituting such guardianship effectively. However, these differences can be viewed as ones of *degree* rather than *kind*, requiring that the concepts be adapted rather than rejected wholesale.

A more fundamental difference appears when we try to bring these concepts together in an etiological schema. The central difficulty arises, I have suggested, from the distinctive *spatiotemporal ontologies* of virtual and nonvirtual environments: Whereas people, objects, and activities can be clearly located within relatively fixed and ordered spatiotemporal configurations in the real world, such orderings appear to destabilize in the virtual world. In other words, the routine activity theory holds that the "organization of time and space is central" for criminological explanation . . . , yet the cyberspatial environment is chronically spatiotemporally *disorganized*. The inability to transpose RAT's postulation of "convergence in space and time" into cyberspace thereby renders problematic its straightforward explanatory application to the genesis of cybercrimes. . . . Routine activity theory (and, indeed, other ecologically oriented theories of crime causation) thus appears of limited utility in an environment that defies many of our taken-for-granted assumptions about how the sociointeractional setting of routine activities is configured.

Questions

1. Discuss the various ways in which cybercrime is defined.

2. Explain what Yar means by the acronym *VIVA*.

PART III

POSITIVISM

Positivism refers to both the early biological theories of the field and the use of the scientific method to obtain empirical research data in criminology. The chapters included in this part reflect the dual meanings of positivism. In *The Murderous Dutch Fiddler: Criminology, History and the Problem of Phrenology*, Nicole Rafter (chap. 7) argues that, rather than dismissing phrenology as pseudoscience, its role as one of the field's founding ideas should be acknowledged. Although regarded as laughable today, phrenology and the concepts it served to inspire should be recognized for its place in the history of science in criminology. Although criminological theories may appear to swing like a pendulum between the concepts of nature versus nurture, contemporary science argues for explanations that incorporate both nature and nurture. In *Nature and Nurture: Genetic and Environmental Influences on Behavior*, Robert Plomin and Kathryn Asbury (chap. 8) describe what genetics research has taught us about behavior and explore the future of the work, specifically the promise of DNA. Regarding true or randomized experiments as representing the highest quality of social science research, David Farrington (chap. 9) describes how criminology has both rejected and embraced the approach in *A Short History of Randomized Experiments in Criminology: A Meager Feast*. He argues that if the public were more knowledgeable about what makes valid and reliable research, there would be an increased call for producing and relying on knowledge garnered from randomized experiments.

CHAPTER 7

The Murderous Dutch Fiddler

Criminology, History, and the Problem of Phrenology

Nicole Rafter
Northeastern University

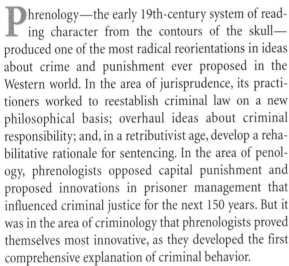

Phrenology—the early 19th-century system of reading character from the contours of the skull—produced one of the most radical reorientations in ideas about crime and punishment ever proposed in the Western world. In the area of jurisprudence, its practitioners worked to reestablish criminal law on a new philosophical basis; overhaul ideas about criminal responsibility; and, in a retributivist age, develop a rehabilitative rationale for sentencing. In the area of penology, phrenologists opposed capital punishment and proposed innovations in prisoner management that influenced criminal justice for the next 150 years. But it was in the area of criminology that phrenologists proved themselves most innovative, as they developed the first comprehensive explanation of criminal behavior.

On the basis of their understanding of the brain as an aggregation of independent organs or faculties, phrenologists could explain every form of criminal behavior, from petty theft to wife-beating to homicide. They had guidelines for distinguishing between sane and insane criminals; they introduced the idea that people vary in their propensity to crime; and they could account for differences in crime rates by age, nationality, race, and sex. Phrenologists could even explain the behavior of criminals whom we today would call serial killers and psychopaths, as in this case from one of phrenology's basic texts:

> At the beginning of the last century several murders were committed in Holland, on the frontiers of the province of Cleves. For a long time the murderer remained unknown; but at last an old fiddler, who was accustomed to play on the violin at country weddings, was suspected in consequence of some expressions of his children. Led before the justice, he confessed thirty-four murders, and he asserted that he had committed them without any cause of enmity, and without any intention of robbing, but only because he was extremely delighted with bloodshed. . . .

At a time when most people would have explained the Dutch fiddler's behavior in terms of sin, phrenologists attributed it to innate biological defect. Their criminological ambition and scope—their desire to develop a science of criminal behavior—excited progressive thinkers on both sides of the Atlantic.

Phrenologists' writings on criminal jurisprudence, penology, and criminology were part of a much broader, all-encompassing biosocial system that aimed at scientifically explaining not only criminal behavior, but all human behavior (and a great deal of animal behavior as well). Their system rested on five fundamental assumptions:

1. The brain is the organ of the mind.

2. The brain is an aggregation of about 30 separate organs or faculties, such as Combativeness, Covetiveness, and Destructiveness, which function independently.

3. The more active an organ, the larger its size.

Source: "The murderous Dutch fiddler: Criminology, history, and the problem of phrenology," by Rafter, N., (2005), in *Theoretical Criminology, 9*, 65–96. Reprinted by permission of Sage Publications, Ltd.

4. The relative size of the organs can be estimated by inspecting the contours of the skull.

5. The relative size of the organs can be increased or decreased through exercise and self-discipline.

These fundamental ideas, all but the last of them formulated in about 1800 by the Viennese physician Franz Joseph Gall, became the basis of an international movement to develop a science of phrenology and spread its gospel. The movement fell into two stages: a scientific phase, from about 1800 to 1830, when the phrenological system was developed, mainly by physicians and psychiatrists; and an overlapping popularizing stage, from about 1820 to 1850, during which phrenology became a fad, complete with marketers, clubs, and hucksters. But the timing and duration of these phases differed by place. Although phrenology underwent little development after the 1840s, its ideas segued into the theory of degeneration that underpinned concepts of deviance into the 1920s. Moreover, some phrenological societies remained active into the 20th century.

Like other early students of social behavior, phrenologists adopted the previously developed methods of the natural sciences, assuming that the social world could be studied using the same procedures. They collected data, formulated hypotheses, and made positivist assumptions about the possibility of direct, objective apprehension of social phenomena. During its scientific phase, phrenology intersected with a range of other scientific endeavors, including anatomy, anthropology, physiology, psychology, and psychiatry, and it used a range of scientific procedures, including empirical observation, induction, and deduction. (Some phrenologists also claimed to use the experimental method, but their failure to experiment rigorously proved to be their scientific Achilles' heel.) Phrenology constituted an ambitious and complex effort to break with older metaphysical and theological explanations of behavior and replace them with an empirical science.

Today, phrenology is remembered primarily for the popular culture of its second stage: the manufacture of inkwells and caneheads shaped like phrenological skulls, with the organs marked out for study; the calling in of phrenological experts to examine the heads of job applicants; and the quackery of itinerant practitioners of *bumpology*. It has been dismissed as a medical cult, discredited science, dead science, pathological science, and pseudoscience. These refusals to take phrenology seriously as an early scientific discourse place criminologists in an awkward position. Phrenology constituted an

important episode in the history of criminology and criminal justice, but to recall that history is to risk seeming ridiculous. The problem becomes: How can criminologists relate to this apparently embarrassing forerunner?

Criminologists have essentially three choices when confronted with phrenology:

1. *Ignore it.* Traditionally, historians of criminology and criminal justice have chosen this route. It is difficult to find an extended discussion of phrenology in any standard history of criminology or criminal justice other than Fink . . . and Savitz et al. . . . Histories of phrenology sometimes include a chapter on penology, but even they slight what phrenologists said about the causes of crime. It may well be that historians of phrenology have simply been unaware of the doctrine's significance in the evolution of criminology. More difficult to explain is the marginalization of phrenology by historians of criminology and criminal justice. Although historians of insanity have thoroughly explored the phrenological model of mental disturbance and its impact on the development of neuroscience and treatment of the mentally ill, for crime-and-justice historians, the rule has been to ignore it.

2. *Make it "relevant."* This approach would involve mining phrenological doctrine for material resembling today's research on the role of brain dysfunction in criminal behavior and then treating phrenology as a precursor science. Given phrenology's disrepute, it is unlikely that any present-day PET scanner of criminals' brains would claim phrenological ancestry. However, an example of this approach can be found in an article on the ways in which phrenology anticipated later ideas in American psychology. . . . The trouble with this kind of approach is that it reduces the past to anticipations of the present, denying it value in its own right. Equally misguided would be any effort, such as that cited by Shapin . . . , to fold phrenology into a sociology of error or mistake. Phrenology was indeed erroneous, but it was neither an error nor a mistake; it was an early science of the mind, and to reduce it to something else is no more respectful of the past than the first alternative of ignoring it entirely.

3. *Come to terms with it.* This approach would acknowledge phrenology as an episode in the history of criminology and criminal justice, evaluate its influence and significance, and attempt to establish some sort of relationship with it.

Aside from the two exceptions cited previously, the third approach seems not to have been tried. This chapter aims at implementing it.

Our attitudes toward phrenology depend on our conception of the criminological enterprise and ultimately on how we define science. If we conceive of criminology as an independent and free-floating subject, a set of truths about crime that it is the job of criminologists using scientific methods to discover, then we must agree that phrenologists failed, and we can safely ignore them. The history of criminology will become a chronicle of the stockpiling of currently acceptable scientific techniques and knowledge.... If, however, we conceive of criminology and other sciences as discourses formulated in time and space, shaped by their social contexts and scientists' own backgrounds, then we can open the historical door to phrenology. We can view it as a discourse on the human brain that greatly advanced understandings of mind–behavior relationships ... that advocated scientific methods, but failed in some respects to meet the scientific criteria of its own day, and that formed the first coherent explanation of criminality. . . .

The primary and secondary literatures on phrenology are vast. For this study, I concentrated on English-language sources of both types. Because phrenology was mainly generated in Great Britain and the United States and had its greatest impact in these countries, I was confident that in omitting other-language materials I did not overlook key phrenological proposals relative to crime and justice. Within the domain of English-language sources, my emphasis fell on Great Britain, where I conducted my research. . . . The primary literature can be difficult to interpret when one deals with materials that are rife with phrenological concepts and were endorsed by phrenologists, but that avoided using phrenological terminology, sometimes for political reasons. When I draw on materials of this type, I make note of my inferences. My aim is not to produce a comprehensive study of the influence of phrenology on criminology, jurisprudence, and penology, but rather to identify phrenology's major achievements in these areas, discuss distinctions between good and bad science, and argue for more work on the history of criminology as scientific knowledge.

In what follows, I establish the sociopolitical context in which phrenology emerged and then summarize the doctrine, emphasizing those aspects relevant to criminology and criminal justice. Next come sections on phrenologists' explanations of crime, their criminal jurisprudence, and their penology. A summary of phrenology's achievements in the areas of criminology and social control is followed by brief remarks on reasons for the doctrine's eventual failure. I then turn to the bad science issue, arguing that if criminology welcomes its apparently disreputable forerunners into its history, it will be able more accurately to understand both its own identity and the nature of its scientific enterprise.

Phrenology: Context and Substance

Phrenology emerged out of the Enlightenment drive to replace metaphysical and theological explanations with scientific accounts of natural and social phenomena. "One fact is to me more positive and decisive than a thousand metaphysical opinions," declared Johann Gaspar Spurzheim, one of phrenology's founders, in a phrase much admired by his followers.... Whereas churchmen interpreted the world in terms of divine creation and insisted on religious authority, in the late 18th and early 19th centuries, laymen were growing interested in less authoritarian, more rational approaches to understanding. The new emphasis on observation and human reasoning as sources of knowledge was reinforced by democratic revolutions in North America and France—vivid demonstrations of the possibility of breaking free of older systems. With democracy came the ideal of universal education and the bold notion that any educated person might at least dabble in the study of natural phenomena. Phrenology grew out of the Enlightenment's enthusiasm for scientific explanation and its democratic impulses. Insanity and criminality, previously interpreted as signs of sin, now seemed as if they might be comprehensible in scientific terms. At the same time, the fall of authoritarian regimes, their gradual replacement by bourgeois industrial societies, and the growing distaste for older, retributivist punishments of the body created a demand for new methods of social ordering and discipline. . . . This, roughly, was the situation in about 1800, when phrenology made its first appearance.

Two more specific developments lay in phrenology's immediate background: the science of physiognomy and the theory of moral insanity. The Swiss theologian who founded physiognomy, Johann Caspar Lavater (1741–1801), explained that "Physiognomy is the science or knowledge of the correspondence between the external and internal man, the visible superficies and the invisible contents." . . . He elaborated his theory of reading people's character from their faces in his *Essays on Physiognomy*, a work first issued in German . . . , but published in English on both sides of the Atlantic by 1795. The *Essays*, with their drawings of heads and claims to scientific psychology, enjoyed remarkable success, appearing in more than 150 editions by 1850. . . .

Particularly popular were illustrated pocketbook versions that readers could use to gauge the character of new acquaintances and passers-by. (For example, Lavater taught that long foreheads indicate comprehension; short ones, volatility; and "perfect perpendicularity . . . , want of understanding." . . .) Physiognomy, like its successor science of phrenology, illustrates the early 19th-century hunger for a science of human psychology. Both fields began with the assumption that outer appearances must reflect inner states. But the differences between the two are also instructive. Although Lavater hoped that physiognomy would become a full-fledged science, he did not attempt rigorous study; his assertions are based more on appeals to common sense ("everyone knows," "no one can deny" . . .) than on systematic data collection, and he did not attempt to *explain* the correlations he observed. . . .

The other immediate forerunner of phrenology was the late 18th- and early 19th-century theory of moral insanity, formulated by the first generation of psychiatrists to explain uncontrollable, undeterrable criminality. . . . The earliest remarks on what became known as moral insanity appear in an essay of 1786 by Dr. Benjamin Rush . . . of Philadelphia; Rush conceives of the mind as a congeries of independent "faculties," thus presaging the phrenological conception of the brain as a series of autonomous organs. . . . Rush in America, Philippe Pinel in France, and James Cowles Prichard in England developed the theory of moral insanity to explain criminal behavior that seemed insane, but was committed by people who, like Spurzheim's Dutch fiddler, suffered from neither delusions nor hallucinations. They explained moral insanity as a state of partial insanity in which only one faculty of the brain stopped working—an iconoclastic idea at a time when insanity was almost by definition a state of total, unrelieved derangement.

Phrenology began in late 18th-century Vienna, with research in craniology by its founder, Franz Joseph Gall (1758–1828). Gall's collaborator and most influential follower, the German physician Johann Gaspar Spurzheim, described how Gall arrived at his doctrine:

Dr. Gall, from his earliest youth, was attentive to the difference which existed between his brothers and sisters, and his school-fellows. He was particularly vexed, that while several of his school-fellows learned by heart even things which they did not understand, with great facility, he had the utmost difficulty in engraving in his memory a small number of words. On the other hand, however, he found that he excelled them in the powers of reflection and reasoning. He afterwards observed that in those individuals who had so great a verbal memory, the eyes were very prominent; and this observation was the commencement of all his future inquiries into psychology. . . .

It took years of study, however, for Gall to find the right track. For instance, he wasted time trying to correlate people's talents with "the whole form of their heads." . . . He had casts made of people's heads, collected skulls, and stopped people on the street if he noticed on their heads "any distinct protuberance." . . . In time, he wrote up his findings in a six-volume work, *On the Function of the Brain and Each of Its Parts*, first published in French in 1825. This work was eventually translated into English, but its late date of publication (1835) and unwieldy size meant that it was not much read in Britain or the United States. . . . The relative inaccessibility of Gall's work in Britain and the United States created a void filled by more timely and less cumbersome books on phrenology.

Spurzheim (1776–1832) compressed, systematized, and extended Gall's system in a single, English-language text, *The Physiognomical System of Drs. Gall and Spurzheim*, which, along with his other books, became the basis for the phrenological movement in Britain and the United States. Spurzheim identified 6 organs in addition to Gall's original 27 and, ingeniously, developed an easy-to-follow and easily reproduced head chart indicating the organs' locations. . . . Although Gall believed that climate, food, and drink can modify the faculties, and in fact used such changes to explain racial and ethnic differences in body build and character, he had only long-term modifications in mind. . . . Spurzheim, in contrast, taught that individuals' faculties can be modified in the course of a lifetime. "[B]ring men into favorable situations calculated to call forth their feelings, and these will be strengthened," Spurzheim wrote. "In order to cultivate benevolence, one should not frequent only the society of rich and opulent persons, and learn by heart descriptions of charity; he must experience misery himself." . . . Thus, Spurzheim gave the essentially deterministic doctrine an optimistic twist, adding the possibilities of self-help and treatment. In his view, the "inferior faculties"—those most responsible for crime—"stand in need of constant regulation." . . .

Although the social identities of phrenology's supporters differed over time and by country (sometimes by city), the first-stage advocates seem generally to have been middle-class reformers. Among the most enthusiastic were George Combe . . . and his brother Andrew Combe . . . , residents of the Scottish city of Edinburgh, where, for reasons that historians have explored extensively . . . , phrenology took its strongest and deepest hold. The substantial literature on the subject identifies phrenology's advocates as liberals, some with a radical and utopian bent, most of them antimetaphysical and, in France, also anticlerical. . . . They tended to be not members of social elites, but up-and-coming young Turks. The early 19th century was in any case a period of aspiration and widespread optimism. ("The most important way of preventing crime," wrote Spurzheim . . . , "is that of improving mankind.") In this context, phrenology provided a philosophical basis for those who hoped to rationalize governance and institute new means of maintaining order in the democratic state.

Phrenology's appeal lay partly in its implicit hierarchies. The doctrine naturalized the idea of social hierarchy through its division of labor between the head and lower parts of the body; it also taught the importance of harmony, balance, and cooperation among the parts and of obedience to natural law. Gall's system, as Cooter (1984) and others have noted, not only put the topmost part of the human form in charge, but also organized the faculties into a hierarchy. It located the lower propensities, which man was said to share with animals (Amativeness, Combativeness, and Destructiveness), on the lower section of the skull. Even more ignominiously, it relegated some of them to the back of the head. (Thus, Amativeness—sexuality—was to be found in the back and at the base of the skull.) Gall's intellectual faculties lay more toward the front and center of the skull, whereas at the top, crowning the whole, lay the moral faculties of Benevolence, Veneration, Firmness, Hope, and Conscientiousness. Here was a model of order and control for not only society, but also the individual, one in which goodness, rationality, and intelligence would control the impulsive, animalistic, and criminalistic. . . .

Spurzheim's *Physiognomical System of Drs. Gall and Spurzheim* (1815) remains an impressive book: clear, well organized, comprehensive, and closely argued. The first section, on the structure of the brain and nervous system, serves a credentialing function: Based on dissections and other direct observations of the brain, it shows itself to be the work of careful anatomists. Spurzheim enumerates past obstacles to scientific study of the brain and nervous system, including "the mania of forming systems upon a few solitary facts" and metaphysical assumptions. . . .

Spurzheim calls instead for close observation of "natural facts." We should "forsake hypothetical reasoning in order to follow the simple methods of experience . . . [We must adopt] a rational mode of judging from experiment and observation." . . . Later in the book, having explained the phrenological system in detail, Spurzheim proudly claims that "We never venture beyond experience [direct observation]. We neither deny nor affirm anything which cannot be verified by experiment." . . . Moreover, Spurzheim made a point of displaying his evidence for all to see. To some laymen and physicians thirsting for scientific understanding of human behavior, phrenology seemed to unlock the secrets of the human soul. . . .

This was the general scientific situation in which Gall and Spurzheim undertook their search for an explanation of human behavior. Their anatomical skills and empirical approach satisfied scientific requirements, but their doctrine's radical materialism—its reduction of free will and human nobility to bundles in the brain—meant that at first phrenology had few followers. Indeed, it might have sunk without a trace had Spurzheim not serendipitously . . . found a receptive social and cultural context in Edinburgh and the United States, had he not softened the doctrine's determinism to make phrenology palatable to reformers, and had the doctrine not attracted the superb publicist George Combe. Moreover, as the next sections show, phrenology provided middle-class reformers with exactly the science they needed to fight their jurisprudential and penological crusades. Similarly, specialists in mental disease and other fields discovered a scientific friend in phrenology. Through this fortuitous, stochastic process, then, phrenology found receptive constituencies—and thrived until changing circumstances made a successor science appear more persuasive.

EXPLANATIONS OF CRIME

Spurzheim's chapter on "The Organ of the Propensity to Destroy, or of Destructiveness" illustrates both his methods and phrenology's applicability to the study of crime. He begins by observing that animals vary in their propensity to kill, even within species and breeds. . . . In man, too, Spurzheim continues, the destructive propensity manifests itself with different degrees of intensity: Some people are merely indifferent to animals' pain, others enjoy seeing animals killed, and still others experience "the most irresistible desire to kill." . . . Spurzheim gives many examples, including that of the Dutch fiddler, and explores their implications. The examples seem to demonstrate that "the propensity to kill is a matter independent of education and training" . . . , a function of mental organization alone. Spurzheim also reports on the related research of Philippe Pinel, the French psychiatrist who at about the same time was observing in madmen a similarly "fierce impulsion to destroy," and he gives many of Pinel's examples. . . .

To Spurzheim, the conclusion seemed inescapable: There must be an organ of the brain that determines the propensity to kill, and it must function independently of other propensities, which continue to work normally even in extreme cases like that of the Dutch fiddler. Gall . . . had earlier identified an organ of Murder, having found a well-developed protuberance at the same spot in the skulls of two murderers. However, Spurzheim objects to naming an organ "according to its abuse" and therefore changes the name of Murder to Destructiveness, attributing to it the propensity, not only to kill, but also

to pinch, scratch, bite, cut, break, pierce, devastate . . . We are convinced, by a great number of observations, that the seat of this organ is on the side of the head immediately above the ears . . . It is commonly larger in men than in women; yet there are exceptions from this rule. . . .

In summary, on the basis of numerous examples, Spurzheim has identified the primary cause of homicide: overdevelopment of the organ of Destructiveness, which is the seat of both negative and useful forms of destruction.

The other faculties most relevant to criminology in Spurzheim's organology are Amativeness, Combativeness, Covetiveness, and Secretiveness. (He presents his commentary on Amativeness in Latin, a linguistic forerunner, perhaps, of TV's antipornography filters.) In these instances, too, Spurzheim insists that no organ is in and of itself evil; rather, the disproportionate enlargement of a faculty is the factor that leads to imbalance in a person's mental system and, hence, to criminal behavior. Covetiveness, for example, can be useful; we desire money and thus work for it. But when the organ of Covetiveness becomes overdeveloped, it leads to a propensity to steal. . . .

A deterministic doctrine, phrenology attributed criminal behavior not to free will, but abnormal brain organization. The fault might lie in poor heredity, poor environment, or a disease that had damaged the faculties—but not in individual choice. Yet phrenologists did not preach a gloomy, predestinarian message. Most people, they believed, are born with their faculties in harmonious balance; normality is the standard, and normal people, having been born responsible, do not commit crimes. "(T)he functions of a well formed and healthy brain," wrote the English phrenologist Marmaduke Sampson, "must always be consistent with virtue. From this you will see at once that all acts of an opposite nature must be attributed to a corresponding

unsoundness in [an] organ." . . . Moreover, because post-Gall phrenologists conceived of the brain as plastic, malleable, and capable of change, they were able to combine their determinism with an optimistic, rehabilitative approach to crime and other social problems without a sense of contradiction. Conceiving of character traits as heritable, but not fixed, they could simultaneously argue that criminals are not responsible for their crimes *and* that, with treatment, they can be cured of criminality. Sampson . . . , who tended to take extreme positions, viewed *all* criminals as "patients" who should be sent to moral hospitals.

In practice, most phrenologists dodged the full implications of their doctrine for free will by developing a typology of mankind according to degree of criminal responsibility. For example, the Edinburgh lawyer George Combe, the third most influential proponent of the doctrine after Gall and Spurzheim, delivered a lecture on "Human Responsibility" in Boston in the late 1830s, in which he explained that "Men may be divided into three great classes. The first comprehends those in whom the moral and intellectual organs are large, and the organs of the propensities [lower impulses] proportionately moderate in size." These men have free will and should be punished if they commit crimes. Members of the second class, whose organs are all large and about equal in size, have stronger criminal impulses, but are still responsible. In members of the third class, the propensities are large and the moral and intellectual faculties small. These are the "habitual criminals," the "incorrigibles"; "they are moral patients and should not be punished, but restrained, and employed in useful labour during life, with as much liberty as they can enjoy without abusing it." . . . In effect, Combe recommended totally indefinite sentencing for criminals in the third group, predicating release on their reformation. . . . His typology reflected ideas about social worth as well as degrees of criminal responsibility: Those in the first class were, by implication, most fit to govern, and those in the third class were most in need of governance.

Other phrenologists, too, created typologies based on the idea of biological variations in degree of criminal responsibility. Like Combe, James Simpson, an English lawyer, ranked humans into three classes according to their criminal propensities:

First, those whose criminal appetites or propensities are so powerful as to overbalance the restraining force of their moral and intellectual faculties . . . The *second class* of mankind are very numerous, those whose *animalism* is nearly as strong as in the first class, but whose moral and intellectual powers of restraint are . . . much greater . . . External circumstances in such persons turn the scales . . . The *third* class are the good ground . . . It is *physically* possible for such men to rob, or steal, or torture, or murder, but it is *morally* impossible. . . .

Although the major phrenological texts on issues of crime and justice were produced by professional men like Simpson and George Combe, anyone could add to the store of phrenological knowledge about crime. From Sydney to Stockholm, York to Heidelberg, and Rochester, New York, to Lexington, Kentucky, amateur phrenologists studied the heads of living and dead criminals, mailed their findings to phrenological journals, and reported them at meetings of phrenological societies. The 1834–1836 volume of the *Phrenological Journal and Miscellany*, for example, included a reader's article on a tame ram with unusually well-developed Destructiveness who violently butted adults and terrorized children. . . . Thus, phrenology enabled ordinary people to contribute to scientific knowledge, including knowledge about the causes of crime.

CRIMINAL JURISPRUDENCE

Phrenology took root in a period of remarkable upheaval in criminal jurisprudence, one in which revulsion against harsh punishments, especially of minor first offenders, property offenders, and the mentally ill, surged through Western Europe and North America. A transnational campaign against capital punishment took hold, and, as the first penitentiaries were built, citizens noisily debated the purposes of these new penal institutions. This rethinking of fundamentals of criminal jurisprudence occurred against a background of industrialization and urbanization that pushed legislators to find new methods of ensuring the survival and cooperation of the working class, including public health improvements, universal education, and measures to reform criminals. . . .

Engaging widely and deeply in this movement for criminal law reform, phrenologists rejected the principles of retribution and deterrence on which this body of law had traditionally rested. "Convicts are almost never reformed under the present system," Simpson . . . pointed out, voicing one common objection. George Combe found another argument in statistics on crime being published by the Belgian Adolphe Quetelet: The

stability over time in Quetelet's rates of crime and conviction seemed to prove that "crimes arose from causes in themselves permanent, and which punishment does not remove." . . . Because punishment makes no difference, Combe reasoned, reformation should become the goal of criminal law. Marmaduke Sampson, in turn, insisted that punishment is "irrational" and deterrence impossible because all criminals are sick and not responsible for their acts. Punishment actually increases crime, Sampson argued in an early version of amplification-of-deviance theory, by damaging offenders' constitutions and leading to the transmission of their enfeeblement to the next generation. . . .

Thus, phrenologists advocated a jurisprudential overhaul to reorient criminal law toward reformation and (in the case of those who proved incorrigible) social defense. . . . Phrenologists lobbied against debilitating punishments that might brutalize the faculties: the whip, the treadmill, and unrelieved solitary confinement. Some also lobbied for an end to transportation, a measure devoid of reformative value. Noting that "in dealing with criminals we are dealing with *mind*" . . . , George Combe and other phrenologists recommended individuation of punishment to recognize differences in capacity and predisposition toward crime. To C. J. A. Mittermaier, a law professor at the University of Heidelberg, one of the great advantages of phrenology was the way it encouraged law-makers to find ways to cultivate criminals' Benevolence and impede "the undue development of those organs which are liable, through abuse, to produce evil, such as Destructiveness." . . . Another advantage, in Mittermaier's view, lay in phrenology's guidance to judges trying to determine criminal responsibility; the doctrine made it clear that "Accountability . . . is influenced by the condition of the organs which we find in the offender." . . . *Do no harm* and *fit the punishment to the criminal*—these were the twin pillars on which phrenologists' programs for reformation rested.

The long-term thrust of these views was toward redefinition of the concept of dangerousness. Whereas 18th-century jurisprudence defined *dangerousness* in terms of crime seriousness, late 19th-century jurisprudence defined it in terms of the individual criminal's biological predisposition and capacity for crime. . . . Toward the century's end, the process of redefinition built up pressure for fully indefinite sentencing and eugenic approaches to crime control. Phrenology helped set this redefinitional process in motion. . . .

Curtailment of capital punishment in general was another legal reform that owed its success, in part, to phrenologists. Public sentiment against the death penalty was growing in any case, but phrenologists brought to the cause a united and vociferous insistence on abolition. Public executions brutalize onlookers, they argued, exciting destructive propensities and deadening moral sensibilities. . . . Moreover, they continued, it is folly to punish people who are not responsible (as, in the phrenological view, many criminals were by definition). Life imprisonment of murderers would satisfy the same end of social defense. Marmaduke Sampson, over the top as usual, not only argued that the death penalty stimulates crime; he offered to take members of a gallows mob and treat them for 1 month to "the wholesome influence of moral advice, coupled with *prison discipline*, and *medical treatment*," after which "it is probable that most of them would abstain from attending the execution at all." . . . Although Sampson was unusual among phrenologists in his optimism about the faculties' pliability, he was typical in his opposition to capital punishment.

Phrenologists' deterministic and materialistic analyses of criminal behavior, and their apparently sacrilegious recommendations for criminal law reform, scandalized traditionalists in the legal establishment. . . . However, it proved attractive to those searching for a new philosophical basis for discipline and social control—so much so that, by the end of the century, the reforms that phrenologists had advocated were by and large in place, although shorn of their organological language.

PENOLOGY

Phrenology, as its foremost historian observes, provided a "rational scientific umbrella" for "a vast range of ideas and beliefs which in themselves had little need of Gall's doctrine." . . . Nowhere is this truer than in the case of penology, an area in which phrenologists advocated a range of reforms that long outlived phrenology. To phrenologists, it seemed obvious that incarceration was the best possible punishment: Prisons isolated criminals from the rest of the population so they could not damage others' moral faculties while isolating criminals from enfeebling influences in the broader society. Phrenology's heyday coincided with the period in which American states began to build penitentiary-type prisons. Should these new institutions follow the Pennsylvania model of unbroken solitary confinement or should they adopt the practice of the prison at Auburn, New York, of solitary cells at night and group labor during the day? In deciding this and other penological issues, Gall's followers were guided mainly by George Combe and the American jurist Edward Livingston, the phrenologists who wrote most

extensively and authoritatively on prison policy. Both began with the idea that prisons should be designed to rehabilitate, and both endorsed measures to encourage convicts to improve themselves.

These ideas animated penology on both sides of the Atlantic for the next 150 years. They had been formulated originally by Gall, for whom the goal of criminal law should be "*to prevent crime, to reform malefactors and to protect society against the incorrigible*" . . . , and they became key to the international prison reform movement that started formally in Cincinnati, Ohio, in 1870. . . . Although phrenology was but one current flowing into this reform movement, it was a strong one. . . .

A well-ordered prison, in the phrenologists' view, was fundamental to the restoration of balance among criminals' faculties. Convicts should have fresh air and decent food. Corporal punishment, which only stimulates the lower faculties, must be prohibited, as must extended periods in solitary confinement. The prisoner's daily routine, George Combe explained in a letter to his German friend Mittermaier, must train him in "habits of sobriety, order, and industry, and at the same time, he must be furnished with intellectual, moral, and religious instruction." . . . Combe was serious about educating prisoners, estimating that there should be a teacher for every 8 to 10 convicts. . . . Mittermaier hoped that prison administrators would "study the individuality of the criminals, and direct their treatment in reference to it," diagnosing and treating offenders much as physicians diagnosed and treated patients. . . . Such recommendations, seconded by other phrenologists, laid the groundwork for later prison classification schemes. . . .

The phrenological recommendation that appealed most to prison administrators was the tiered system of rewards for good behavior. Edward Livingston proposed this system in his penal code . . . , a plan that, although never implemented by Louisiana, excited enthusiasm among phrenologists in the United States and Europe. Livingston outlined a graded system through which convicts would work their way up, enticed and reinforced by improved conditions along the way. They would start their sentences in the lower tier, characterized by solitary confinement, coarse food, and denial of opportunities to work. The inducements of promotion to the higher tier—books, better food, and opportunities for labor—would encourage them to exercise their higher faculties. Phrenologists with little direct involvement in prisons were impressed by the way that Livingston's system might encourage convicts to *choose* the path of improvement. . . . Prison administrators, in contrast, were probably more intrigued by the system's potential for increasing the control of convicts. At any rate, a graded system that could reward good behavior was soundly endorsed by the 1870 prison congress. Even earlier, it was implemented in famous experiments in prisoner reform by Alexander Maconochie at the Norfolk Island, Australia, penal colony . . . and by Sir Walter Crofton in Ireland. . . . Maconochie's work, in particular, may have been inspired by phrenological principles. . . .

During his 1838–1840 phrenological tour of the United States, George Combe visited prisons to collect evidence that might enable him to decide which system, the Pennsylvania or Auburn, was best. . . . Both approaches to convict discipline seemed to have virtues and drawbacks. Under the Pennsylvania system of perpetual solitary confinement, convicts grew weak, and their organs lost their vigor (the exception was the cerebellum or organ of Amativeness, which tended toward enlargement due to the many opportunities in the Pennsylvania system for self-abuse). Under the Auburn system, in contrast, prisoners were less susceptible to "deep moral and religious impressions." . . . Thus, Combe suggested combining the two approaches. Convicts should begin their sentences in solitary, with no opportunity for labor or other distractions while their lower organs softened and became vulnerable to moral influences. The next step should be "a very effective course of moral, intellectual, and religious instruction"; during this period of time, the convict would "be advanced to greater and greater degrees of liberty, of self-regulation, and of social enjoyment, in proportion as he showed himself to be capable of acting virtuously and wisely." . . . Next would come day release on "moral probation"—a presagement of the late 19th-century innovation of parole. . . .

"(N)o sound system of criminal legislation and prison discipline," wrote George Combe . . . "can be reached while the influence of the organism on the dispositions and capacities of men continues to be ignored." This idea lay at the heart of phrenology's program for penological reform. The specific influence of that program on subsequent theory and practice can be difficult to gauge partly because some reformers were reluctant to identify themselves with phrenology (de Guistino . . . puts Maconochie in this category) and partly because others had absorbed phrenological principles, but dropped the nomenclature. But it is undeniable that phrenologists' proposals to rationalize and medicalize prison management, put forth close to the inception of the prison system, and their vision of scientific rehabilitation, continued to drive Western penology right through until the 1970s onset of antirehabilitation.

The Achievements of Phrenology

Acceptance at first came slowly to phrenology. The Austrian emperor, alarmed by Gall's radical materialism and its implicit denial of free will, expelled Gall from the country; Paris, to which Gall and Spurzheim moved to carry on their research, proved only slightly less hostile. . . . Breaking with Gall and relocating to England, Spurzheim again encountered skepticism and ridicule. . . . Yet once he learned how to make Gall's doctrine accessible through his books and attractive through his teaching about the potential for human change, phrenology enjoyed greater success. . . .

Once the doctrine began to take root, its social context helped it to thrive. In a period when social reforms seemed both imperative and achievable, phrenology provided a sturdy platform on which to erect major programs of change. In a century when— to an extent difficult to comprehend today—ordinary people lived in fear of becoming insane, phrenology showed how insanity might be staved off through the cultivation of certain faculties. Equally important to psychologists and philosophers struggling to make sense of body–mind relationships, phrenology offered a way out of the mazes of Cartesian dualism by holding, simply, that the mind is not separate from the body, but rather a function of the brain. In an era of intense debate over the application of the insanity defense, the phrenological image of independent faculties in the brain offered a relatively clear way to conceptualize the new category of partial or moral insanity—a breakdown of a single organ while the rest continued to function normally.

Gall and Spurzheim had sketchily indicated their doctrine's implications for understanding and reforming criminal behavior. . . . Later phrenologists who built on this foundation worked mainly in the interstices between phrenology's two major stages after the basics had been established, but before disrepute set in among intellectuals. Catching phrenology at its peak of plausibility, they were able to achieve major reorientations in ways of thinking about social problems.

What, then, did phrenology accomplish in the area of crime and justice?

In criminology:

- Phrenology helped establish the idea that criminal behavior can and should be studied scientifically. It introduced scientific methods into the study of criminal behavior and inaugurated what became the positivist tradition in criminology.

- Phrenology produced the first systematic and comprehensive theory of criminal behavior, although it did not conceptualize its project in these terms.
- Breaking with the utilitarian model of Beccaria and Bentham, who were not much concerned with differences among criminals, phrenologists introduced the idea that people vary in their degree of criminal responsibility and in their propensity to commit crime.
- Phrenologists consolidated and advanced the medical model of criminal behavior, according to which criminals (or at least some criminals) are not bad, but sick. This concept of crime as a disease profoundly influenced later analyses of criminal behavior.
- By explaining criminality in terms of defective brain organization, phrenology established a biological foundation on which later criminologists built, including late 19th-century degenerationists and criminal anthropologists. It also laid the foundation for eugenic criminology.... The idea that the cause of crime may lie in brain defects (or genes that lead to brain defects) seems today to be making a comeback....

In criminal jurisprudence:

- Phrenology rationalized jurisprudence. At the dawn of the 19th century, on the threshold of the urban industrial world, it helped reorient criminal jurisprudence away from the principles of retribution and deterrence on which it had long rested and toward more systematic, proactive measures for reformation and social defense.
- The doctrine raised questions about criminal responsibility that in time led to new approaches to criminal insanity and new ways of conceptualizing dangerousness.
- Phrenologists proposed indefinite and indeterminate sentencing. In addition, they hinted at (without clearly articulating) the idea of sentencing according to biological fitness.

In penology:

- The first to propose a systematic program for reforming criminals, phrenologists advocated rehabilitative measures that shaped the course of "corrections" until the 1970s.

- Although rudimentary prisoner classification had been practiced in early lockups such as Philadelphia's Walnut Street Jail, phrenologists introduced the idea of *studying* convicts at the point of admission to prison and then dividing them into treatment groups according to intelligence and character. They also introduced the idea of classifying prisons and designating one for incorrigibles.
- More generally, phrenologists helped the next generation of prison administrators conceive of penology as a science that might professionalize prison management and medicalize work with convicts....

In summary, phrenology put into circulation powerful new concepts about crime and justice that eventually became part of the broader culture. The results lived on long after the husk of organology had fallen by the wayside.

***

By the 1830s, phrenology had begun to lose its plausibility among intellectuals and professionals. Some close students of the doctrine, like the English surgeon John Abernethy, had asked tough questions from the beginning. (How, Abernethy had demanded ..., were the organs coordinated? "By committees of the several organs, and a board of control?" Abernethy also worried about negative labeling: "[S]uppose a man to have large knobs on his head which are said to indicate him to be a knave and a thief, can he expect assistance and confidence from any one?") The social philosopher Auguste Comte, the psychiatrist Isaac Ray, and others who had begun as converts to phrenology gradually lost faith.... Still others, of course, had never seen anything in the doctrine but blasphemy and sympathy with criminals. Although phrenology remained popular through the mid-century and phrenologists continued to gather empirical proofs of their doctrine, to the scientifically inclined, it was increasingly clear that almost any evidence could be regarded as confirmation of such a multifaceted theory.... Nor did phrenologists conduct experiments to see whether their doctrine could be refuted. The aspect of phrenology that may have harmed it most, scientifically, was its redundancy: Even advocates eventually realized that one could reach the same conclusions about the nature of human behavior without recourse to organology....

Criminology and the Bad Science Issue

Phrenology is not the only disreputable ancestor in criminology's genealogy. Criminologists also have to come to terms with such forerunners as criminal anthropology, the feeblemindedness theory of crime, and Earnest A. Hooton's 1930's attempts to revivify eugenic criminology. To ignore a now discredited science like phrenology on the grounds that it was wrong is to miss an important opportunity to see how science is shaped by its social context and by the circumstances of those who generated it. . . .

Moreover, to proceed as if there were a bright line between good and bad science is to ignore the fact that social and historical factors shape the acceptance of *all* science—good, bad, anti-, pseudo-, pathological, partly right, Greek, Renaissance, and presumably authoritative 21st-century science. No scientific activity occurs in a vacuum, insulated from its social context, and thus it is futile to look for a pure, totally objective science. Even if science could be vacuum-packed, one could not easily distinguish between good science and pseudoscience. Finding ways to differentiate between sound and flawed science has been a major preoccupation of recent philosophers of science. Some have challenged the Enlightenment view of science as a rational, systematic, progressive activity. . . . They do not speak with one voice, of course, but individually or collectively they have argued that the scientific method is something of a myth because many scientific discoveries occur serendipitously, even anarchically, bypassing the step-by-step process enshrined in the just-so story of scientific methodology. The findings of even the physical and life sciences may be historically relative, in the view of some theorists, whereas others maintain that, although science can produce change, it does not produce progress. One need not swallow these critiques whole to recognize what they imply: To dismiss phrenology on the grounds that it was bad science is to take a naive, outmoded view of science. Perhaps only the passage of time can teach us which large-scale scientific research programs (and phrenology certainly fits this category) lead to truth or falsity. . . .

Sociologists and criminologists may continue to disregard phrenology on the grounds that it offered a *biological* theory of crime. Whereas in actuality it offered a biosocial theory, one that pictured a constant interaction between the faculties and environment, it did have a strong biological component. Thus, for the sake of argument, let us suppose for a moment that phrenology was an exclusively biological theory. Reflexive mistrust of biological theories per se, although it is historically and ethically understandable, is becoming increasingly suspect. As the phrenology example shows, biological theories are not necessary bigoted or conservative. Phrenology did biologize difference, but in its own context it was a progressive, even radical theory. One might well keep the liberalism and indeed progressivism of phrenology in mind today as biological theories make their comeback even while we also guard against their tendency to reach eugenic conclusions. Phrenology can help us remember that biological theories are no more inherently reactionary than sociological theories are inherently bias-free.

The history of criminology is generally an underdeveloped field, one to which Americans, in particular, have paid little attention. Thanks to David Garland . . . , Paul Rock . . . , and Neil Davie . . . , British criminologists have a relatively clear overview of their own disciplinary evolution, a solid scaffolding on which to construct more detailed studies. In contrast, U.S. criminologists have a shakier sense of their field's origins and development; in fact, the U.S.-based criminologist who has produced some of the best historical work—Piers Beirne . . .—was born and schooled in England. Americans' greater disinterest can be explained, at least in part, by conclusions reached by the historian Dorothy Ross in her *Origins of American Social Science* (1991). "American social science," Ross observes, "bears the distinctive mark of its national origins":

> Its liberal values, practical bent, shallow historical vision, and technocratic confidence are recognizable features. . . . To foreign and domestic critics, these characteristics make American social science ahistorical and scientist, lacking in appreciation of historical difference and complexity. . . . What is so marked about American social science is the degree to which it is modeled on the natural rather than the historical sciences. . . .

Ross ties the ahistorical nature of American social science to the experience of settling a new continent and untouched spaces. Americans "could relegate history to the past while they acted out their destiny in the realm of nature . . . they could develop in space rather than time." . . . Ross urges American social scientists to give more recognition to history to relativize their work and become more keenly aware that social science developed through human choices. Although Ross' analyses pertain specifically to U.S. social science, some of her conclusions are relevant to British as well as American criminologists.

Social science, as Ross recognizes, is constituted by activities as well as findings and results. It is not a constant, but rather an ongoing process. It is contingent on verification, of course, but it is also contingent on what is defined as scientifically interesting at any point in time and what methods of proof and disproof are available. Even our idea of what science is depends on the past. Our current understandings of the social roles of criminology, criminal jurisprudence, and "corrections" were shaped partly by phrenology. From today's perspective, phrenologists were wrong scientifically—the bumps of the skull do not reflect one's character, but they left a powerful legacy. If we try to ignore their work, we avoid part of ourselves as well.

Questions

1. Describe the role phrenology played in bringing about the eugenics approach to crime control.

2. Describe the contributions phrenology made in the area of penology.

CHAPTER 8

Nature *and* Nurture

Genetic and Environmental Influences on Behavior

Robert Plomin

Institute of Psychiatry, London

Kathryn Asbury

Social, Genetic, and Developmental Psychiatry Center

After 600 volumes of *The Annals of the American Academy of Political and Social Science* with hardly a mention of genetics, it is time to consider genetic as well as environmental influences on behavior. The theme of this chapter is that both genetics and environment, and the interplay between them, contribute importantly to the development of individual differences in behaviors, including mental health and cognition. Quantitative genetic research—exemplified by the twin design that compares identical twins (monozygotic [MZ]) and fraternal twins (dizygotic [DZ])—has gone beyond merely demonstrating the importance of genetic influence (heritability) to investigating more sophisticated issues, such as developmental change and continuity, heterogeneity and comorbidity, and the interplay between genes and environment.

Most exciting is the flood of molecular genetic research whose goal is to identify the specific DNA sequences responsible for genetic influence on common behavioral disorders such as mental illness and on complex behavioral dimensions such as personality. The latter are influenced by many DNA variants of small effect size, called quantitative trait loci (QTLs). . . . The most important implication of this research for social scientists is that, as multiple QTLs of small effect size for a particular trait are identified, they can be aggregated in a

"QTL set" that can then be used as a genetic risk index in the same way that environmental risk indices, such as socioeconomic status (SES) or education, are used. Unlike quantitative genetic research that requires unique samples such as twins, molecular genetic research only requires DNA, which can be obtained painlessly and inexpensively using cheek swabs. We look forward to exciting advances in understanding the interplay between genes and environment once DNA is incorporated into social science research. Our hope for this chapter is that it facilitates this integration.

In the first part of this chapter, we describe quantitative genetic research, emphasizing what it has taught us about the way the environment works to affect behavioral development. The second part considers the future of genetic research, which lies with DNA. . . .

The History of Nature and Nurture

The application of genetic research to human problems has experienced spectacular highs and lows over the decades since its inception in 1865. The study of nature and nurture in the development of behavioral traits began quietly with work from Francis Galton. . . . Pace and interest increased only gradually until, in 1924, the

Source: "Nature *and* nurture: Genetic and environmental influences on behavior," by Plomin, R., & Asbury, K., (2005), in *ANNALS of the American Academy of Political and Social Science, 600,* 86–98. Reprinted by permission of Sage Publications, Inc.

first twin and adoption studies in developmental psychology were published. . . . Events little more than a decade later complicated the course of progress. The slow but steady growth of genetic science was stopped abruptly by a world sickened by Nazi war crimes and all that was associated with them. The Nazi regime's abuse of genetics was high profile and terrifying to a world in mourning, a world whose way of life had been threatened. The emergence of behaviorism around the same time . . . proved a further roadblock in the development of genetic science, achieving a huge impact on the behavioral sciences with its ostensibly comforting theory of an environmental paradigm based on the assumption that we are what we learn.

Even from this poor midcentury soil, however, molecular genetic research managed to flourish, bursting onto the scientific stage in a Nobel Prize-winning blaze of glory with the discovery of the structure of DNA less than a decade after the end of World War II. . . . The genetic code was cracked in 1966, the four-letter alphabet (G, A, T, C) of DNA creating the three-letter words that code for the 20 amino acids that are the building blocks of proteins. The crowning glory of the century and the beginning of the new millennium was the Human Genome Project's working draft of the sequence of the 3 billion letters of DNA in the human genome, nucleotide bases that are the steps in the spiral staircase of DNA. . . .

During this time, genetic research on human behavior was slowly but steadily building a case for the importance of genetics as well as environment. The first textbook on behavioral genetics was only published in 1960, and it focused largely on research with nonhuman animals. . . . Since then, for nearly every area of behavior that has been studied, twin and adoption studies have shown strong genetic influence. . . . Genetic research has consistently shown heritable influence in many traditional areas of psychological research, such as mental illness, personality, cognitive disabilities and abilities, and drug use and abuse. Some areas showing strong genetic influence may be more surprising, such as self-esteem, interests, attitudes, and school achievement.

This research has led to growing acceptance of roles for both genes and the environment in the etiology of individual differences in behavior. This shift can be seen in the growing number of genetics papers in mainstream behavioral journals and in funded research grants. The public also accepts a major contribution of genetics. . . . Before the pendulum of fashion shifts too far from nurture to nature, it is important to emphasize that this same genetic research provides the best available evidence for the importance of the environment. . . .

Consider schizophrenia. Until the 1960s, schizophrenia was thought to be environmental in origin, with theories putting the blame on poor parenting to account for the fact that schizophrenia clearly runs in families. The idea that schizophrenia could run in families for genetic reasons was not seriously considered. Twin and adoption studies successfully changed this view. Twin studies showed that MZ twins are much more similar than DZ twins. This suggests genetic influence because MZ twins are genetically identical, like clones, whereas DZ twins, like non-twin siblings, are only 50% similar genetically. If one member of an MZ twin pair is schizophrenic, the chances are 45% that the other twin is also schizophrenic. For DZ twins, the chances are 17%. Adoption studies showed that the risk of schizophrenia is just as great when children are adopted away from their schizophrenic parents at birth as when children are reared by their schizophrenic parents, providing dramatic evidence for genetic transmission. There are now intense efforts to identify some of the specific genes responsible for genetic influence on schizophrenia. . . .

Back in the 1960s, when schizophrenia was thought to be caused environmentally, it was important to emphasize the evidence for genetic influence, such as the concordance of 45% for identical twins. Now that genetic influence is widely recognized, it is important to emphasize that identical twins are *only* 45% concordant for schizophrenia, which means that, in more than half of the cases, these pairs of genetic clones are discordant for schizophrenia. This discordance cannot be explained genetically—it must be due to environmental factors. Note that the word *environment* in genetic research really means *nongenetic*, a much broader definition of environment than is usually encountered in the behavioral sciences. That is, environment denotes all nonheritable factors, including possible biological events such as prenatal and postnatal illnesses, not just psychosocial factors. Nonetheless, the point is that genetics often explains half of the variance of behavioral traits, but this means that the environment explains the other half.

In addition to providing strong evidence for the importance of environmental influence, two of the most important findings from genetic research involve nurture rather than nature: nonshared environment and what has been called the nature of nurture.

Nonshared environment. Recent research shows that the environment works differently than we previously supposed. Theories of socialization have generally assumed that aspects of the environment such as SES or parental divorce will, for better or worse, make children growing up in the same family similar to each other.

Environmental research in genetically sensitive designs has consistently found a different pattern, namely, that the environments that affect behavioral development work by making children in the same family different.... We know this, for example, because genetically unrelated children growing up in the same adoptive family scarcely resemble each other for personality, psychopathology, and cognitive abilities after adolescence. Siblings are often similar, but their similarity is rooted in their genes, rather than in the environment they share. Environment is hugely important to human development, but genetic research has shown beyond a doubt that the most effective environmental influences are those that operate to make children in the same family different, not similar. These environmental influences are called *nonshared* because they are not shared by children growing up in the same family.

So why are children growing up in the same family so different? Research over almost two decades has attempted to identify specific sources of nonshared environment, exploring differential parenting, friendships, health, and chance experiences in relation to a wide range of behaviors. So far, progress has been modest, with many environments showing significant but small effects.... Although it is proving difficult to find specific nonshared environmental factors that account for large amounts of variance, it should be emphasized that nonshared environment is, in general, how the environment works to influence behavior. Although most research has focused on the family environment, it seems reasonable that experiences outside the family, with peers and individual life events, for example, might prove to be richer sources of nonshared environment.... It is also possible that chance contributes to nonshared environment in the sense of random noise, idiosyncratic experiences, or the subtle interplay of a concatenation of events. Compounded over time, small differences in experience might lead to large differences in outcome. Identifying the factors responsible for nonshared environment remains one of the big challenges for the future of this research.

The nature of nurture. Dozens of twin and adoption studies have shown that genetic factors substantially influence measures of behaviorally relevant environments, such as parenting, stress, or social support..., a phenomenon called *the nature of nurture*.... How can this be true given that environments have no DNA? The answer is that such environments can be considered as extended phenotypes, reflecting genetic differences between individuals as they select, modify, and construct their own experience of the world. In quantitative genetics, this phenomenon is known as genotype–environment

(GE) correlation because it involves correlations between genetic propensities and exposures to environment....

Given that environmental as well as behavioral measures show genetic influence, it is reasonable to ask whether associations between environmental and behavioral measures are mediated genetically. Multivariate genetic analysis (discussed later) can be used to analyze genetic and environmental contributions to the correlation between environmental and behavioral measures. Genetic factors can mediate the correlation to the extent that the environment represents a direct response to genetically influenced characteristics. For example, differences in parenting could be the genetic result of child psychopathology, rather than its cause. A general guideline from multivariate genetic research of this sort is that genetic factors tend to be responsible for about half of the phenotypic correlation between measures of the environment and measures of behavior. For this reason, environmental measures cannot be assumed to be truly environmental. A far-reaching implication of this research supports a shift from thinking about passive models of how the environment affects individuals toward models that recognize the active role we play in selecting, modifying, constructing—and reconstructing in memory—our own experiences....

In quantitative genetics, another type of GE interplay is known as GE interaction, which refers to differential sensitivity to experiences, in contrast to GE correlation, which denotes differential exposure to experiences. For example, in psychopathology, a particular type of GE interaction has been examined, called *diathesis-stress*, in which heritability is greater in high-risk environments.... GE interaction has been difficult to demonstrate in quantitative genetic analyses, in part, because of lack of statistical power to detect an overall effect of GE interaction on the variance of a trait.... However, several recent examples of GE interaction have been reported in analyses using measured genes as well as measured environments.... One example especially relevant to political and social science is that a functional polymorphism in the promoter region of the MAOA gene was shown to moderate the effect of child maltreatment on later antisocial behavior and violence....

In short, genetic research has made some of the most important discoveries about the environment in recent decades, especially about nonshared environment and the role of genes in experience. More discoveries about environmental mechanisms can be predicted as the environment continues to be investigated in the context of genetically sensitive designs. Nonshared environment and the role of genes in experience are two examples of ways in which quantitative genetic research strategies are being used to go beyond merely asking about the relative importance of nature and nurture. Two other examples of going beyond heritability estimates are developmental analyses of change and continuity and multivariate analyses of heterogeneity and comorbidity.

Developmental change and continuity. Change in genetic effects during one's development does not necessarily mean that genes are turned on and off during these stages, although this does happen. Genetic change simply means that genetic effects at one age differ from genetic effects at another age; that is, the same genes could have different effects in the brains of 8-year-olds and 18-year-olds. For example, developmental change in genetic effects is likely to be responsible for the fact that it is difficult to find behavioral markers in childhood for individuals who later become schizophrenic. Although it is possible that "schizophrenia genes" are not turned on until after adolescence, it is more likely that these genes operate the same way before and after adolescence, but that they only express their hallucinatory and paranoid effects after adolescent brain development enables such highly symbolic processing.

One of the more striking findings of genetic change involves general cognitive ability, often called intelligence and assessed by IQ tests. The magnitude of genetic influence increases steadily from infancy to childhood to adolescence to adulthood. . . . This is surprising because most people would think that environmental factors become increasingly important as experiences accumulate during the life course. It is not known why the heritability of general cognitive ability increases during development. It is possible that more genes come into play during development, but it is also possible that the same genes have greater effects. This latter hypothesis receives support from longitudinal genetic research on age-to-age change and continuity that suggests that the same genes are largely responsible for genetic influence throughout development. If the same genes are involved, how can genetic influence increase? One possibility involves GE correlation, which, as mentioned earlier, refers to correlations between genetic propensities and exposure to experiences. That is, increasing heritability may occur because small genetic differences may snowball as we progress through life, creating environments that are correlated with our genetic propensities.

Multivariate heterogeneity and comorbidity. Another important example in which genetic research is going beyond heritability is multivariate genetic analysis,

which, as mentioned earlier, focuses on the covariance (correlation) between traits, rather than the variance of each trait considered separately. It estimates the extent to which genetic factors that affect one trait also affect another trait. Multivariate genetic research in psychopathology suggests that genetic diagnoses of disorders often differ greatly from traditional diagnoses based on observable symptoms such as anxiety or depression. For example, several studies have shown that the same genes are largely responsible for anxiety and depression. . . .

Broad effects of genes have also been found in the cognitive domain. Despite the differences between cognitive abilities such as verbal, spatial, and memory abilities, the same genes largely affect all of these cognitive abilities. . . . Genetic overlap is also substantial across learning disabilities such as language, reading, and mathematics disability, leading to a "generalist genes" theory of learning disabilities. . . . Finding such substantial genetic overlap among cognitive abilities and disabilities has far-reaching implications for understanding the brain mechanisms that mediate these genetic effects. . . .

Sometimes multivariate genetic research suggests heterogeneity rather than comorbidity. An example of genetic heterogeneity that is especially relevant to the social sciences concerns psychopathic tendencies in childhood and antisocial behavior. Antisocial behavior in childhood and adolescence shows only modest genetic influence, and, unlike most traits, it shows some shared environmental influence. However, antisocial behavior in the presence of callous-unemotional personality traits is highly heritable and shows no shared environmental influence. . . . Another recent example concerns behaviors that are characteristic of autistic spectrum disorder (ASD). Diagnoses of ASD require deficits in both social and nonsocial behaviors, but multivariate genetic analysis reveals marked genetic heterogeneity between the social and nonsocial ASD related traits as assessed by teachers and by parents at 7 years. . . . In other words, different genes affect the social and nonsocial traits indicative of ASD.

The results of these multivariate genetic analyses have important implications not only for diagnosis, but also possibly for treatment and prevention. Their most immediate implication is that these quantitative genetic findings chart the course for molecular genetic research that attempts to identify specific DNA variation responsible for genetic influence. For example, the research showing that callous unemotional personality is the genetic core of psychopathic tendencies in childhood suggests that this should be the target for molecular genetic research, rather than the broader phenotype of antisocial behavior.

DNA

The future of genetic research on behavior lies in molecular genetic studies of DNA that will eventually identify specific DNA variants responsible for the widespread influence of genes in behavioral development. Identifying these DNA variants will make it possible to address questions such as those raised above—about GE, developmental, and multivariate mechanisms—with far greater precision and power. As compared with quantitative genetic studies of twins and adoptees, molecular genetics will have a far greater practical impact on behavioral research because molecular genetic research does not require special populations such as twins or adoptees. DNA can be easily and inexpensively obtained (from cheek swabs rather than blood for about $10 per individual), and genotyping of a DNA marker is also inexpensive (about 10¢ per individual). Moreover, devices called *gene chips* (microarrays) are available that can genotype hundreds of thousands of genes for an individual in 3 days. . . .

Finding genes associated with complex traits is difficult and expensive, but using genes already identified is easy and inexpensive and can add a powerful genetic dimension to behavioral research. . . . What has happened in the area of dementia in later life will be played out in many areas of behavioral research. The only known risk factor for common late-onset Alzheimer's disease (LOAD) is a gene, apolipoprotein E (APOE), involved in cholesterol transport. A form of the gene called allele 4 increases the risk fivefold for LOAD. Although the association between APOE allele 4 and LOAD was reported only a decade ago . . . , much research on dementia now genotypes participants for APOE to ascertain whether results differ for individuals with and without this genetic risk factor. . . . Genotyping APOE will also become routine in clinics if this genetic risk factor is found to predict differential response to interventions or treatments. Many large-scale behavioral studies are currently obtaining DNA on their samples in anticipation of the time when genes are identified that are relevant to their area of interest.

It should be noted that DNA variation has a unique causal status in explaining behavior. When behavior is correlated with anything else, the old adage applies that correlation does not imply causation. For example, parenting is correlated with children's behavioral outcomes, but this does not necessarily mean that the parenting causes the outcome. Genetic research has shown that parenting behavior in part reflects genetic influences on children's behavior. When it comes to interpreting correlations between biology and behavior, such correlations are often mistakenly interpreted as if biology causes behavior. For example, correlations between neurotransmitter physiology and behavior or between neuroimaging indices of brain activation and behavior are often interpreted as if brain differences cause behavioral differences. However, these correlations do not necessarily imply causation because behavioral differences can cause brain differences. In contrast, in the case of correlations between DNA variants and behavior, the behavior of individuals does not change their genome. The DNA sequence does not change. For this reason, correlations between DNA differences and behavioral differences can be interpreted causally: DNA differences cause the behavioral differences.

Behavioral science will be central to the new era of genetic research called the *postgenomic* era, in which the focus will shift from finding genes to understanding how these genes work. Such postgenomic research is usually considered in relation to the bottom–up strategy of molecular biology, in which a gene's product is identified by its DNA sequence, and the function of the gene product is traced through cells and then cell systems and eventually the brain. Behavioral research lies at the other end of the continuum in the sense that behavioral research represents an integrationist top–down level of analysis that begins with the behavior of the whole organism, rather than a reductionistic bottom–up level of analysis that begins with a single molecule in a single cell. For example, behavioral researchers can ask how the effects of specific genes unfold in development and how they interact and correlate with experience. . . .

This top–down behavioral level of analysis has been called *behavioral genomics* to distinguish it from the often-used phrase *functional genomics* because the latter phrase has become synonymous with bottom–up molecular biology. We suggest that behavioral genomic research is likely to pay off more quickly in prediction, diagnosis, and intervention, and eventually for behavioral preventions that use genes as early warning systems. Bottom–up and top–down levels of analysis of gene–behavior pathways will eventually meet in the brain. The grandest implication is that DNA will serve as an integrating force across all of the life sciences, including the behavioral sciences.

Nature *and* Nurture

As discussed earlier, the importance of genes as well as environment in the etiology of individual differences in behavior is increasingly accepted in science as well as in society. We predict that this trend will accelerate in the postgenomic era as specific genes are found that are responsible for the heritability of behavioral disorders and dimensions. However, as is the case with most advances in science, these new findings also raise new problems for medicine, parenting, education, employment, law, and insurance, as well as larger philosophical issues such as human dignity, free will, and moral responsibility. . . .

A general sense of unease about genetics comes from a feeling that genetic differences contradict equality: Are not all men (and women) created equal? Although this was a self-evident truth to the signers of the American Declaration of Independence, the founding fathers of the United States were not so naive as to think that all people are created identical. The essence of a democracy is that all people should have legal equality despite their individual differences, regardless of the environmental or genetic origins or those differences. Decisions, both good and bad, can be made with or without knowledge, but we believe firmly that better decisions can be made with knowledge than without. There is nothing to be gained by sticking our heads in the sand and pretending that genetic differences do not exist. The basic message of behavioral genetics is that each of us is an individual. Recognition of, and respect for, individual differences is essential to the ethic of individual worth. Proper attention to individual needs, including provision of the environmental circumstances that will optimize the development of each person, is a utopian ideal and no more attainable than other utopias. Nevertheless, we can approach this ideal more closely if we recognize, rather than ignore, individuality.

Questions

1. How have twin studies contributed to what we know about nature and nurture?

2. Describe the concept of *nonshared environment*.

CHAPTER 9

A Short History of Randomized Experiments in Criminology

A Meager Feast

David P. Farrington
Cambridge University

Advantages of Randomized Experiments

Randomized experiments are often regarded as the gold standard of evaluation evidence, even in criminology. . . . This is because they have the highest possible internal validity, or ability to demonstrate that a change in a treatment caused a change in an outcome. . . . The main advantage of a randomized experiment is that it equates persons in the intervention group with persons in the control group on all possible (measured and unmeasured) variables that influence key outcomes—providing that there are a sufficiently large number of people in each group.

This equating makes it possible to disentangle the effects of the intervention from the effects of other variables that influence key outcomes and from preexisting differences between the groups. A randomized experiment can establish the effect of an intervention more convincingly than alternative quasi-experimental evaluation methods that involve matched intervention and control groups, the comparison of predicted and actual outcomes in each group, or statistical adjustment for preexisting differences between groups. Basically, statistical control is not as good as experimental control. More worrying, results obtained in nonrandomized designs are usually different from those obtained in randomized experiments . . . , and effect sizes are usually larger in nonexperimental evaluations in criminology. . . .

In light of the advantages of randomized experiments, it might be expected that they would be used widely to investigate the causes of offending and the effectiveness of interventions designed to reduce offending. However, randomized experiments in criminology and criminal justice are relatively uncommon. . . . The history of the use of randomized experiments in criminology consists of feast-and-famine periods and a few oases (clusters of experiments) in a desert of nonrandomized research. The chapters in this volume describe some of these cases.

The California Youth Authority (CYA), 1960–1975

The Cambridge–Somerville Youth Study . . . is commonly believed to be the first large-scale randomized experiment ever conducted in criminology. . . . However, the first sustained program of experimental research on correctional effectiveness was carried out by the CYA from 1960 to 1975, and this is admirably described in the article by Ted Palmer and Anthony Petrosino. . . . Randomized experiments were also conducted elsewhere in California at the time. . . . The story of why these experiments flourished in the CYA and why they withered and died is fascinating and instructive.

Randomized experiments flourished because new types of policymakers were appointed who were knowledgeable about social science research and wanted sound empirical evidence to be the key basis for policy decisions.

Source: From "A Short History of Randomized Experiments in Criminology: A Meager Feast," by Farrington, D. P. (2003), *Evaluation Review, 27,* 218–227. Reprinted by permission of Sage Publications, Inc.

There was a belief in the effectiveness of rehabilitative programs and the value of empirical research. It was a time of hope and optimism. Key people (the director of the Research Division, the director of the CYA, and political appointees all the way up to the governor of California) supported scientific and experimental research. Key researchers . . . were trained as psychologists and, hence, believed in the importance of randomized experiments. The main funding agency was the National Institute of Mental Health (NIMH), which wanted high-quality, long-term experiments, not quick-and-dirty evaluations.

Randomized experiments withered and died because key personnel changed. CYA directors were increasingly appointed and replaced for political reasons, and this promoted a defensive and risk-averse mentality. Administrators increasingly wanted quick, policy-relevant answers. Researchers were increasingly trained in statistical rather than experimental control. There was increasing pessimism about the value of rehabilitation and increasingly get-tough policies as the just deserts model became popular with the political appointees. However, there were also more attempts to delay, modify, and suppress inconvenient research findings about the ineffectiveness of these get-tough policies and a decreasing belief in the value of research (because it did not produce the desired answers). Also, the main funding changed to justice agencies (Law Enforcement Assistance Administration and, later, National Institute of Law Enforcement and Criminal Justice), rather than the medical research agency NIMH. These justice agencies believed far less in randomized experiments and were far more concerned with political considerations and quick answers. . . .

The National Institute of Justice (NIJ), 1981–1988

. . . [T]he tenure of James K. "Chips" Stewart as the director of NIJ between 1981 and 1988 ushered in a new golden age of randomized experiments in American criminology. According to Weisburd and Petrosino . . . ,

> David Farrington, Lloyd Ohlin and James Q. Wilson . . . deserve credit for helping to put randomized experiments on the radar screen of criminologists in the mid-1980s. Their influential book entitled "Understanding and Controlling Crime" recommended the use of randomized experiments whenever possible to test justice innovations. This book had ramifications for the U.S. National Institute of Justice, which under the direction of

James "Chips" Stewart soon thereafter supported over two dozen such experiments.

. . . [T]his NIJ initiative in the 1980s . . . resulted from numerous influences. The most important factor was probably the Minneapolis Domestic Violence Experiment, which attracted enormous favorable publicity for NIJ when its results were announced in March 1983. . . . This randomized experiment showed that arrest caused fewer repeat incidents of spouse assault than separation or advice conditions. These results were welcomed by the U.S. Department of Justice and used to encourage police forces to arrest male perpetrators of domestic violence, rather than dealing with them in other ways. According to Sherman . . . , "The publicity helped to gain acceptance for the idea of randomized experiments." . . .

Another important factor was the critical review of NIJ by the National Academy of Sciences. . . . This said that NIJ had not been funding enough basic research work on deterrence and crime control theory and had not been using scientific peer review in selecting grant proposals for funding. It also recommended randomized experiments. In response, NIJ set up a Crime Control Theory program run by Dick Linster and Joel Garner and influenced by luminaries such as James Q. Wilson and Al Reiss, who supported randomized experiments.

Also in the 1980s, the National Academy of Sciences (NAS) Committee on Research on Law Enforcement and the Administration of Justice set up a Working Group on Field Experimentation in Criminal Justice, held a meeting in New Orleans, Louisiana, and produced a report on *Randomized Field Experiments in Criminal Justice Agencies*. . . .

Among the most important randomized experiments funded by NIJ were the Minneapolis Domestic Violence Experiment . . . and several replications in different locations, plus other Police Foundation experiments. . . . Also, the RAND Corporation carried out many path-breaking randomized experiments, including what was believed to be the largest randomized experiment on correctional effectiveness ever undertaken in the United States. . . . During this time period, Lawrence Sherman, David Weisburd, Peter Greenwood, and Joan Petersilia emerged as leaders of the new field of experimental criminology.

Joel Garner and Christy Visher were also (along with Dick Linster) important influences on the funding of randomized experiments in the 1980s from within NIJ. However, their article . . . focuses not on the golden age of American criminological experiments in the 1980s, but on the subsequent decline in NIJ funding of experiments in the 1990s. As more NIJ funds became available, fewer experimental designs were supported: from 6% of the budget in 1991 through 1995 to less than 1% in 1996 through 2000. This was partly because the average size of NIJ grants was dramatically reduced during the 1990s, making it difficult to mount randomized experiments. Once again, there is the familiar depressing story of exciting scientific progress in the feast years followed by progress backward in the famine years.

Yet this was not true of other developments. In particular, the 1980s were also a golden age for initiating prospective longitudinal studies in criminology and for criminal career research. . . . Again influenced by important bodies such as NAS . . . , American federal agencies . . . invested heavily in such studies. Perhaps because of their nature, these studies continued to be funded in the 1990s. So it was not generally true that NIJ, for example, abandoned fundamental long-term research.

The Home Office, 1964–1972

While the CYA experiments were being carried out, the Home Office in the United Kingdom was mounting a program of randomized experiments, and the history of four of these experiments is described by Chris Nuttall. . . . In many ways, developments paralleled those in California. As confidence in the effectiveness of treatment declined in the 1970s . . . , the Home Office abandoned all its research on correctional effectiveness, including randomized experiments. However, there were other important developments unique to the United Kingdom.

Before describing these developments, I should point out that there were other British randomized experiments sponsored or funded by the Home Office at that time, although not carried out by researchers in the Home Office Research Unit. . . . For example, the prison psychologist Mark Williams . . . randomly allocated 610 male borstal inmates to one of three open borstals differing in their regimes (traditional, group counseling, or casework). The experimental analysis did not begin until these borstals were full of randomly allocated inmates. It was found that the inmates treated in the case work borstal were significantly less likely to be reconvicted in a 2-year follow-up period (51% compared with 63% in the other two conditions, and a 63% probability for all borstal boys at that time). Contrary to the psychologists' predictions, the most disturbed boys did best and the least disturbed boys did worst in the traditional borstal.

Also, Rose and Hamilton . . . evaluated a police juvenile liaison scheme in Blackburn using a randomized experiment. Juveniles could be diverted into this scheme if they were first, minor offenders, if they admitted guilt, if their families were willing to cooperate and accept supervision from the police, and if the complainant was agreeable that the police should not prosecute. The police supervision lasted 6 months. All eligible arrested male juveniles (394) were randomly allocated to be either cautioned only or cautioned and supervised. A 30-month follow-up showed that the recidivism probabilities of these two groups were similar (26% to 27%), and hence it was concluded that police supervision was ineffective.

So why were few randomized experiments in criminology carried out in the United Kingdom after 1975? Chris Nuttall . . . correctly identifies the massive influence of Ron Clarke, who had originally been trained as a psychologist and who had originally advocated such experiments. However, Clarke's experience in an experiment at Kingswood training school . . . made him extremely doubtful about the value of randomized experiments. In the provocatively titled "The Controlled Trial in Institutional Research: Paradigm or Pitfall for Penal Evaluators?", Clarke and Cornish . . . concluded that "the additional certainty which experimental methods are supposed to be able to provide over correlational methods is either unattainable or not worth the extra costs involved."

Importantly, Ron Clarke became the intellectual leader of Home Office research and emphasized situational crime prevention as the main method of reducing crime. The idea was that situational factors could be changed more easily than individual or family factors. Because this method was targeted on crime in an area, rather than on an individual offender, it was difficult to evaluate using randomized experiments. Most evaluations used (at best) before and after measures of crime in experimental and control areas. . . . In introducing our nonrandomized experiment on the prevention of shoplifting . . . , Ron Clarke . . . stated that it "is especially noteworthy because it is one of the very first evaluations of situational measures to use an experimental design."

Another important influence on the Home Office was the Rothschild report of 1972, which specified that all Home Office research should henceforth have a specific customer such as the police, prisons, or courts. From then on, the amount of fundamental research carried out by the Home Office plummeted, especially fundamental research on the causes of offending, where there was no obvious customer in the criminal justice system. Also, Home Office research became more influenced by the views of policymakers and practitioners, who wanted quick results, had never heard of internal validity, and could not tell the difference between good and poor research.

In a previous article . . . , I detailed Ron Clarke's criticisms of randomized experiments and attempted to answer them. Also, David Weisburd ... provides a number of answers and counterarguments, most important that—to draw valid conclusions—it is unethical not to carry out randomized experiments. According to David Weisburd, the key question is why randomized experiments should not be used: "The burden here is on the researcher to explain why a less valid method should be the basis for coming to conclusions about treatment or practice." ... Other researchers have also attempted to outline and answer objections to randomized experiments ... arguing that scholarly societies, such as the American Society of Criminology, might play an important role in advocating such experiments.

Conclusions

Within the medical and psychological (as opposed to criminological) communities, randomized experiments have continued to be used; there have been no feast-or-famine periods. For example, most studies of family-based crime prevention reviewed by Farrington and Welsh ... used this method and were carried out by psychologists or child psychiatrists. Jon Shepherd ... suggests that randomized controlled trials dominate in medicine because most researchers are also practitioners and vice versa, whereas in criminology there is little overlap between researchers and practitioners such as police officers, judges, and prison officers. He advocates upgrading the quality of practitioners in criminology through university training.

The chapters in this volume show convincingly how feast-and-famine periods were influenced by key individuals. This is most undesirable. There should be a shared consensus among scholars, policymakers, practitioners, and funders that high-quality research is essential. Jon Shepherd is probably correct in suggesting that the answer lies in better education and training, especially of policymakers and practitioners, but also of the general public and the mass media. Surely, if the general public and the mass media could see the flaws in quick-and-dirty research, they would—as taxpayers—demand high-quality evaluations using the best possible methods, especially randomized experiments.

Questions

1. Describe the data collected in each of the three experiments by the California Youth Authority, the U.S. National Institute of Justice, and the British Home Office.

2. Why are randomized experiments the "gold standard"?

PART IV

PSYCHOLOGICAL THEORIES

Criminology, as explored in most introductory textbooks, is comprised of more sociological than psychological theories; the ways in which early psychological theories would explain criminality are often briefly presented. Contemporary forensic psychology is focused on psychopathology, or the study of mental illness as it relates to criminality. Here, two chapters presenting psychological approaches to criminality are included to acknowledge the perspective; both chapters were chosen for their unique and compelling topics. In *Psychopathology and Tattooing Among Prisoners*, Laura Manuel and Paul Retzlaff (chap. 10) examine the relationship between various personality types and having tattoos among prison inmates. In *The Terrorist Mind: Typologies, Psychopathologies, and Practical Guidelines for Investigation*, Laurence Miller (chap. 11) describes the main classifications of terrorists currently used by psychologists studying personality and the psychopathology of terrorism.

CHAPTER 10

Psychopathology and Tattooing Among Prisoners

Laura Manuel

Paul D. Retzlaff
University of Northern Colorado

Ever since Captain Cook returned from the South Pacific in 1769 with sailors bearing "tattaw" marks, people in the Western world have been obtaining tattoos. . . . Although tattoos enjoyed brief popularity in the mainstream culture in the 1920s . . . and possibly are enjoying a resurgence in the current culture . . . , tattoos are primarily associated with deviance . . . and criminality. . . . After their brief period of popularity in the 1920s, tattoos quickly returned to the domain of the socially marginal. . . . These "marks of disaffiliation" with society . . . become "voluntary stigma" indelibly marking their bearers as different from the mainstream culture.

Nationwide, the estimates of the number of people bearing tattoos range from a low of 7 million . . . to 12 million people . . . to a maximum of 20 million people. . . . It is generally agreed, however, that the practice of tattooing is more widespread among prison populations . . . , mental health institutions . . . , and the military . . . , especially among sailors. . . .

The association of tattoos with deviance and mental illness has been frequently investigated. Tattooing has been empirically associated with personality disorders . . . and psychopathic personality. . . . In Measey's . . . study of Royal Navy detainees, personality disorders increased as the number of tattoos increased. For those with no tattoos, 48% had a personality disorder. The percentage increased to 58% for those with 1 to 4 tattoos and up to 82% for those with more than 16 tattoos. Raspa and Cusack . . . found the association between personality disorders and tattoos so clear that they state

"finding a tattoo on physical examination should alert the physician to the possibility of an underlying psychiatric condition."

Among nonincarcerated groups, there is some evidence that the more extreme members of the population are more likely to obtain tattoos. In one study of 464 nonincarcerated adolescents, those with tattoos had higher problem behavior than those without tattoos. . . . In another study involving college students, male tattooed respondents reported smoking more cigarettes, having more sexual partners, and having been arrested more than nontattooed males. . . . In a study involving a cross-section of 18 universities, 24% of respondents with tattoos reported having 6 to 10 sexual partners and another 26% reported having more than 11 partners. . . .

In a recent study, Dhossche, Snell, and Larder . . . investigated the relationship between tattooing and suicide. They matched suicides and accidental deaths in a 3-year case-control study and found that 57% of the younger suicide victims were tattooed, compared with 29% of the accidental deaths. The authors concluded that tattoos may be possible markers for lethality from both suicide and accidental death due to the correlations with substance abuse and personality dysfunction.

People with tattoos have also been reported as more likely to engage in other forms of deviant behaviors. They have been reported to be more likely to engage in substance abuse . . . and risk taking. . . . Ceniceros . . . noted a strong correlation between playing Russian roulette and the number and types of tattoos. Buhrich . . .

Source: "Psychopathology and tattooing among prisoners," by Manuel, L., & Retzlaff, P. D., (2002), in *International Journal of Offender Therapy and Comparative Criminology*, 46, 522–531. Reprinted by permission of Sage Publications, Inc.

reported a strong association in males between tattoos and sadomasochism, bondage, and fetishism.

There is also a considerable body of research documenting the relationship between tattooed people and antisocial personalities . . . or actual criminal conduct. . . . More heavily tattooed Naval detainees were more likely to have a previous naval or civilian offense. . . . . Tattooed men in a mental hospital were also more likely to report having been arrested or court martialed. . . . Tattooed inmates were more likely to report liking criminals and admiring them. . . . In Fox's study . . . of women prison inmates, those with tattoos more frequently violated prison rules, were more likely to be charged with fighting, and were more likely to receive harsher punishments. In addition, Fox found that the female inmates with tattoos were more likely to have been in all four forms of institutions (e.g., juvenile facilities, reformatories, jails, and prisons). In a similar vein, Roc et al. . . . reported that, of 404 male inmates at the Utah State Prison, those with tattoos were more hostile, were more socially deviant, had more prison write-ups, and abused drugs more often.

The purpose of this study was to examine the relationship between specific psychopathologies and tattooing in a prison. By using a broad-based test of psychopathology, it is hoped that specific psychopathologies, and particularly personality disorders, may be mapped to tattooing behavior.

Method

RESPONDENTS

Respondents included 8,574 male inmates in the Colorado Department of Corrections. The men ranged in age from 18 to 90 and had an average age of 31.4 years (SD = 9.22). The respondents were 46.5% Caucasian, 30.3% Hispanic, 20.1% African American, and 2.0% American Indian. Respondents had a mean educational level of 11.3 years of schooling (SD = 1.91). Their median sentence was approximately 4 years, with a mean of approximately 10 years. Major categories of current incarceration charges included drug offenses (22.3%), burglary (9.9%), theft (9.3%), assault (7.7%), sex offenses (7.3%), escape (7.2%), robbery (4.7%), trespassing (4.0%), and homicide/murder (3.6%).

INSTRUMENTS

The MCMI–III corrections version . . . was used for this study and includes corrections-specific norming. It includes four validity and modifying indices, including an item-reading screen (Validity), Disclosure, Desirability, and Debasement. There are 11 Personality Disorder scales, including Schizoid, Avoidant, Depressive, Dependent, Histrionic, Narcissistic, Antisocial, Aggressive (Sadistic), Compulsive, Negativistic (Passive-Aggressive), and Self-Defeating. There are three scales of Severe Personality Disorders, including Schizotypal, Borderline, and Paranoid. The Basic Clinical Syndrome scales include Anxiety, Somatoform, Bipolar: Manic, Dysthymia, Alcohol Dependence, Drug Dependence, and Post-Traumatic Stress Disorder (PTSD). Finally, the three Severe Clinical Syndromes include Thought Disorder, Major Depression, and Delusional Disorder.

The test has only 175 items, and the true/false format is well tolerated by inmates. Using the validity and modifying indices, profiles that were invalid due to poor reading or motivation were eliminated. Of an initial sample, 894 (9.4%) were considered to be invalid, resulting in the current N of 8,574. Scores of 75 and above are seen as clinically significant and identify inmates with the particular pathology tapped by each scale.

PROCEDURE

The MCMI–III was administered to the inmates upon their admission to the system as standard procedure. This study is capitalizing on those available data. Approximately 2 years later, computerized records of Code of Penal Discipline (COPD) infractions were abstracted. Inmates' personality test results were compared to their tattooing infractions in this 2-year period.

RESULTS

Table 10.1 presents the MCMI–III descriptive data. As can be seen, there is a broad range of psychopathology among inmates. From a personality perspective, the usual inmate traits are seen, including 29% with Antisocial, 20% with Narcissism, and 17% with Sadistic personality traits. It is interesting that a number of "neurotic" personalities are quite prevalent, including Avoidant at 26% and Depressive at 19%. Clinical syndromes include Anxiety at 38% of this sample. This is probably somewhat situational given the stress induced by admission to prison. Other clinical syndromes include Alcohol Abuse at 29% and Drug Abuse at 16%.

Within the 2 years, 409 had committed a COPD for tattooing and 8,165 had not. Table 10.2 provides the means and standard deviations for the two groups. In addition, t statistics are provided. There were significant

Table 10.1 Means, Standard Deviations, and Percentage of Inmates Above 74 on Each Scale

Scale	Mean	SD	Percentage
1 Schizoid	47	26	11
2A Avoidant	40	32	26
2B Depressive	43	32	19
3 Dependent	41	26	15
4 Histrionic	53	16	10
5 Narcissistic	62	16	20
6A Antisocial	59	22	29
6B Sadistic	44	28	17
7 Compulsive	53	12	5
8A Negativistic	40	31	22
8B Self-Defeating	38	30	10
S Schizotypal	37	29	4
C Borderline	40	25	6
P Paranoid	41	28	6
A Anxiety	45	35	38
H Somatoform	28	29	1
N Mania	49	21	3
D Dysthymia	35	31	16
B Alcohol	57	24	29
T Drug	58	20	16
R PTSD	33	29	6
SS Thought Disorder	34	27	2
CC Major Depression	28	29	2
PP Delusional	37	28	2
N	8,574		

Note. PTSD, Post-Traumatic Stress Disorder.

differences at .001 between the two groups on the following personality scales: Depressive, Antisocial, Sadistic, Negativistic, Borderline, and Paranoid. Compulsive personality types engaged in significantly less tattooing. Clinical syndromes associated with more tattooing included Mania, Alcohol Abuse, Drug Abuse, PTSD, Thought Disorder, and Delusional Disorder.

Discussion

There appear to be quite a number of psychopathologies associated with inmate tattooing. They include classic criminal personality types, as well as more neurotic types. The traditional inmate personalities of Antisocial and Sadistic are more likely to be involved in tattooing. Negativistic personalities, along with the severe Borderline personality disorders, can also be seen. This is particularly interesting given the neurotic nature of these inmates.

There is also evidence that inmates are involved in tattooing for clinical reasons in addition to personality reasons. Just looking at the relative risk analysis, a wide range of clinical syndromes is associated with tattooing. The Mania scale points to energized inmates impulsively looking to "do something." The Drug scale may be a proxy for either personality disorder or gang involvement. The PTSD scale suggests that those who have been traumatized may be seeking relief in tattoos. Finally, the Thought Disorder scale points to a group of inmates who have little contact with reality and may be using tattooing as a means of fulfilling fantasy.

Going back to the personality scales, inmates probably tattoo for a number of different reasons associated with psychopathology. For antisocial personalities, these may include visual communication of gang membership, rank, or personal criminal accomplishments.... Lagramas (tear drop tattoos), for example, are well known as a symbol of time served or the number of people the inmate has killed. Inmates convicted of persons crimes (typically rape, robbery, and homicide) have been shown to wear more aggressive tattoos than those who were convicted of other types of crimes....

These kinds of tattooing would support the theory that tattoos are a form of exoskeletal defense, defined as an enhancement of the body suggesting that the bearer has attributes of strength and aggressiveness.... Hawkins and Popplestone proposed that tattoos are intended to signify physical strength and psychological aggressiveness and found evidence in their study that tattooed forearms were viewed in this manner. From ancient times, warriors tattooed themselves to appear fiercer and more aggressive. Tattoos remain symbolic of toughness and masculinity. Thus, clear-skinned men may be particularly eager to change their status in a prison situation regardless of institutional consequences.

Another popular tattoo in prisons is that of the Virgin Mary on the inmate's back. This has been proposed as a barrier to sexual assaults and could be viewed as another form of exoskeletal defense.

Tattoos are also frequently explained as marks of affiliation with a subculture that may be considered even more important in a prison system. Tattoos advertising a group membership important in prison may thus also be a form of defense.

Table 10.2   Means, Standard Deviations, and *t* Tests for Tattoo and Nontattoo Groups

Scale	Nontattoo		Tattoo		t *Test*
1 Schizoid	47	(26)	50	(25)	1.97*
2A Avoidant	40	(32)	41	(32)	.64
2B Depressive	43	(32)	49	(31)	3.51***
3 Dependent	41	(26)	49	(31)	1.14
4 Histrionic	52	(15)	54	(17)	1.88
5 Narcissistic	62	(16)	64	(18)	2.79**
6A Antisocial	58	(22)	66	(19)	7.18***
6B Sadistic	43	(28)	52	(28)	6.53***
7 Compulsive	54	(12)	49	(12)	7.05***
8A Negativistic	39	(31)	50	(31)	6.59***
8B Self-Defeating	38	(30)	42	(30)	2.68**
S Schizotypal	37	(29)	41	(29)	2.99**
C Borderline	39	(25)	48	(23)	7.42***
P Paranoid	41	(28)	47	(26)	4.65***
A Anxiety	45	(36)	49	(36)	2.10*
H Somatoform	28	(29)	32	(29)	2.36*
N Mania	49	(21)	56	(17)	6.47***
D Dysthymia	35	(32)	39	(32)	2.23*
B Alcohol	57	(24)	61	(22)	3.73***
T Drug	58	(20)	64	(19)	5.84***
R PTSD	33	(29)	37	(29)	3.28***
SS Thought Disorder	34	(27)	41	(27)	5.11***
Cc Major Depression	27	(29)	31	(29)	2.18*
PP Delusional	37	(28)	42	(27)	3.80***
N	8,165	409			

Note. PTSD, Post-Traumatic Stress Disorder.

*Significant at .05. **Significant at .01. ***Significant at .001.

Numerous authors have noted that a common characteristic of the tattooed person is low self-esteem.... This would appear to be common among incarcerated people as well, and self-esteem might be especially low early in their time served. This may explain the current finding of some neurotic type personality traits such as Borderline. Most of these authors have also noted that tattoos may be a mark of impulsiveness..., which should also be common among incarcerated criminals, particularly those with Antisocial Personality Disorder.

Tattooing has also been viewed as a way to express a negative attitude and violence toward oneself. Correlations between suicidal ideation or conduct and tattooing have been demonstrated.... Tattooing may be another indicator of an affective disorder. This is consistent with the negativistic traits found in this sample.

Tattoos may also simply indicate boredom and become something to do. Some research has noted that people with prison records favor tattoos that depict time references, such as clocks, calendars, spider webs, or years.... Whatever their reasons, tattooing in prisons has become so common that officials are considering allowing professional tattoo artists to work in prison so as to prevent the spread of hepatitis B and C, which are common in homemade tattooing....

This study has a number of limitations, including no data on how many tattoos the prisoners had upon entering the system. It is possible that some of the prisoners already had extensive tattooing on their bodies and thus did not add to their collection in the time period of this study. If considerable tattooing occurred prior to incarceration, it is possible that the inmate would not appear in this study of COPD infractions. The total number of tattoos and when they were obtained might have clarified some of the motivation concerning obtaining tattoos.

Further work examining the designs of the tattoos added in prison may clarify the motivations of the prisoners in obtaining the tattoos. Are the tattoos indeed exoskeletal defense mechanisms? Are prison-obtained tattoos symbols of affiliation, possibly suggestive of protectors within the system (e.g., gang tattoos)? Further study on the kinds of personalities and the actual tattoos obtained may clarify why the various personality types obtain tattoos.

Questions

1. Describe some of the traits and characteristics that researchers have found associated with tattooing.

2. What psychopathologies do Manuel and Retzlaff find associated with tattooing in the present sample?

CHAPTER 11

The Terrorist Mind

Typologies, Psychopathologies, and Practical Guidelines for Investigation

Laurence Miller

Independent Practice, Boca Raton, FL

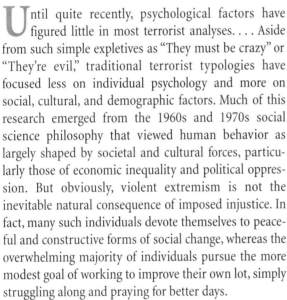

ntil quite recently, psychological factors have figured little in most terrorist analyses. . . . Aside from such simple expletives as "They must be crazy" or "They're evil," traditional terrorist typologies have focused less on individual psychology and more on social, cultural, and demographic factors. Much of this research emerged from the 1960s and 1970s social science philosophy that viewed human behavior as largely shaped by societal and cultural forces, particularly those of economic inequality and political oppression. But obviously, violent extremism is not the inevitable natural consequence of imposed injustice. In fact, many such individuals devote themselves to peaceful and constructive forms of social change, whereas the overwhelming majority of individuals pursue the more modest goal of working to improve their own lot, simply struggling along and praying for better days.

Something, then, beyond mere adversity turns a person into a terrorist. By examining the sociology and psychology of terrorism, we can identify the conditions that predispose some individuals to embrace violence as an ideological strategy. Furthermore, we can come to understand the kinds of people most prone to become the adherents and practitioners of terrorism. Of course, just as psychology influences the politics of people in small and large groups, the nature of a society's social and political forces correspondingly affects the psychological dynamics and the behavior of the people in it. This is especially true for societies in which there are

extreme imbalances in economic status and political influence. In science, the first step toward understanding is classification. Accordingly, the following sections summarize what we know about the kinds of people most likely to kill for a cause and how we can apply this knowledge to deterring and discouraging terrorist actions.

Terrorists and Psychopathology

A frequent comment heard among people following a suicide terrorist attack is something along the lines of, "Bad enough these suicide terrorists throw their own lives away, but don't they care that they're killing innocent people? That proves that only a crazy person would do such a thing." As a counterpoint to our reflexive revulsion at terrorists' seeming inhumanity, there are three basic forms of rationalization the terrorist mindset takes. . . . First, no target population is entirely innocent either because their own acts have targeted innocents as well or simply because they are evil by association with the enemy group by exemplifying or supporting the corrupt values and actions of the hated group. . . .

Second, the victims may, in fact, be innocent in the direct sense, but war is hell, and in all noble struggles, there is always collateral damage. As much was plainly spoken by Timothy McVeigh to justify the Oklahoma City bombing, and this is generally the attitude of military personnel who are tasked with pacifying hostile civilian

Source: "The terrorist mind II: Typologies, psychopathologies, and practical guidelines for investigation," by Miller, L., (2006), in *International Journal of Offender Therapy and Comparative Criminology, 50*, 255–268. Reprinted by permission of Sage Publications, Inc.

populations, whether in Northern Ireland, the Gaza Strip, Baghdad, or elsewhere. . . .

Third, and more grotesquely practical, if pure coercive terror is the goal, then the greater the number of innocents slain, the better. In fact, sophisticated terrorists know that responsibility for tragedy tends to affix itself to targets of proximity and opportunity, and populations will ultimately blame their own leaders for not protecting them if terrorist strikes continue to occur. Thus, in this latter mindset, targeting innocents is not a side effect or a regrettable necessity, but a deliberate strategic goal.

As for the issue of mental illness, it is tempting to view wicked behavior as crazy because doing so helps take some of the malevolent sting out of it. If someone commits a horrid, atrocious act out of pathology or insanity, the intentionality of it is diluted—on some level, they are "driven" to it. Such explanations are routinely proffered for the causes of street crime. . . . Reducing something to an anomalous scientific curiosity, no matter how perverse, gives us some intellectualized control over it. Detached clinical understanding inserts a psychological barrier between our knowledge of the act and the hideous feelings that knowledge provokes. It also gives us a motivational escape clause: If only we can determine the causes of these pathologies, we can potentially eliminate the danger.

Finally, pathologizing a violent act against us delegitimizes any traces of justification we may uncomfortably suspect underlies the act. If they are just crazy, then they would have attacked us no matter what, and nothing we could have done to assuage their alleged grievances would have dissuaded these delusional killers. But if it is not a sickness, if someone could coldly, rationally, and with full intention and self-justification commit such horrendous acts, then they are all the more frightening because maybe something we did, however remote, is partially responsible for our fate. Better to just regard them as a bunch of malevolent psychos.

Some authorities have pointedly disputed the idea that serious psychopathology underlies most terrorist activities. . . . For example, a few studies have explicitly compared politically motivated offenders with common street criminals . . . whose activities included various forms of violence, including murder. . . . In general, although the psychological profiles of the ordinary criminals tended to resemble that reported in the criminal psychology literature—low verbal IQ, impulsivity, poor planning and poor self-control, exploitive interpersonal relationships, and frequent alcohol and drug habits—the political criminals tended to be of at least normal intelligence and free of serious mental disorder or substance abuse.

These political terrorists lacked the early developmental antisocial pattern characterizing many chronic offenders, as well as any significant history of lawlessness prior to their involvement in violent political activity. They were better educated overall and capable of cooperative and collaborative decision making, organization, and action. They did not believe themselves to be mentally ill or to require psychiatric attention, yet they generally complied with the forensic examinations. When confronted with the human consequences of their acts, the political convicts showed steely reserve, but, unlike the cold-blooded remorselessness of the true psychopath, these political terrorists seemed to be able to rationalize and compartmentalize their violent activities, believing that these were necessary actions in fighting for their greater cause—the collateral damage concept. . . .

In this respect, then, psychological strength, not weakness, may underlie the characters of the most effective terrorists. A certain psychological resilience and philosophical resolve may be required for becoming a successful career political activist, whether this involves terror or nonviolent resistance. For example, nonviolent political activists who have been physically tortured by their regimes have been found to show milder posttraumatic psychological disturbance following their ordeals than ordinary civilians who were merely rounded up for questioning. . . . Indeed, because of their rebel status, the known activists typically underwent more prolonged and brutal torture than the civilians and yet showed less severe reactions. One reason is an obvious selection factor: Only those with a certain innate mental toughness and sense of loyalty are likely to opt for and stick with a style of life that offers few tangible rewards and many dangers. Yet it works the other way, too: An intense religious, philosophical, or political belief in what you are fighting for helps you fight all the more ferociously and resist interrogation more doggedly. . . .

Terrorist Typologies

Although what we can call the "modern" literature on terrorism is barely three decades old, the sheer number of attempts to ideologically, politically, and sociologically classify and categorize terrorist subtypes far exceeds the scope of this chapter. Accordingly, this section summarizes a few of the representative taxonomies of terror that have the greatest bearing on our attempts to get inside the terrorist mind. A later section presents a personality-based taxonomy of terrorism that can be practically applied to law enforcement and criminal justice.

"CRUSADERS, CRIMINALS, AND CRAZIES"

As in any complex organization, different roles are filled by different members of terrorist and other extremist groups, each with their own individual contributions to the goals and strategies of the organization. . . . One early classification system . . . divided terrorists into "crusaders, criminals, and crazies." The *crusaders* are the most ideologically driven of terrorists, motivated by their devotion to their cause, whether Islamic jihad or neo-Nazism. These individuals serve as the focal points of the group, rallying the group's commitment and planning strategic operations against the group's enemies, however those are defined.

The *criminals* are essentially violent individuals in search of an excuse to express their antisocial impulses through an ostensibly acceptable and noble cause. They are typically the least ideologically committed to the group and may easily change venues under the lure of new and better opportunities to practice their aggressive and sadistic craft. These are the odious, if necessary, thugs of the group who carry out the organization's dirty work largely because they are good at it and enjoy it.

The *crazies* are laboring under some mental disorder, which may either rivet their loyalty to the group or result in dangerous instability in terms of their commitment and behavior. Rootless, anomic, and disgruntled individuals of this type are commonly attracted to the anchoring philosophical certitude of many extremist groups. If their psychopathology can be channeled for the group's purposes, they may play useful roles within the terrorist organizational structure.

AMERICAN AND INTERNATIONAL TERRORISTS

Another prominent classification of terrorist group members grew out of Strentz's . . . study of the highly motivated and well-trained American and international terrorist organizations that emerged in the late 1960s and 1970s. For certain groups of modern terrorists, the substance of this analysis still applies today.

In this model, the *leaders* of terrorist groups usually exhibit an egocentric slant on reality, which may extend to the level of paranoia. They tend to see the world as a web of plots and conspiracies, especially by inferior cultures or religious infidels who are polluting and poisoning the purity of the self-defined chosen group. Rarely overtly psychotic, these leaders' characterological paranoia may be well hidden to the outside world, cloaked by the superficial persona of charismatic self-confidence and commanding presence—thus their emergence as messianic leaders.

Another subtype of terrorist organization member is the *activist-operator*, who typically has an antisocial or psychopathic personality structure. These types are frequently former or current mercenary soldiers or ex-convicts with long and varied rap sheets. They often have been recruited from a prison population by the terrorist leader, who then allows these opportunists to take the spotlight while the leader remains behind the scenes as the brains of the organization. For their part, the activist-operators exploit this opportunity to lead a thrillingly violent and hedonistic lifestyle with the tactical support and doctrinal blessing of the leader and the organization. However, activist-operators are rarely truly committed ideologically to the group's mission and may secretly harbor contempt for the abstract philosophies and lofty goals of the leader and his organization. Yet they stay in for the rush and the power trip they get from their role as organizational "muscle."

A third personality type in most terrorist organizations is the *idealist*, who may be genuinely dedicated to a better world, is willing to give his or her all, and is therefore eagerly coopted by the terrorist organization for its own ends. Ever the faithful servants, these idealists are often initially assigned routine maintenance and support duties until they prove themselves worthy of more sophisticated and dangerous operations. They are often desperate, dependent young people who are seeking truth and philosophical guidance and have fallen victim to the leader's rhetoric and the opportunist's deceit. . . .

TERRORIST SUBTYPES: COMMONALITIES

What all these typologies concur on is the identification of certain common subsets of terrorist group members, including:

- An ideologically driven charismatic leader
- A passel of acolytes who are drawn to the group's goals and ideals
- One or more "dirty work" operators who are likely to be in it for the thrill, the profit, or some combination of personal motives

Terrorist Personalities: Traits, Types, and Disorders

As noted earlier, most theorizing on terrorism has either ignored individual psychological factors or else has conceptualized the terrorist mind as mentally disordered by definition. But an analysis in terms of psychology need not automatically imply severe psychopathology. In this section, a terrorist typology is presented based on current psychological insight into personality theory.... Tactically, such a formulation can be useful for both profiling and identifying terrorist suspects as well as developing targeted interrogation strategies for gathering intelligence and other information. A psychological approach to terrorism or any other kind of violent behavior does not imply that such behavior is committed only by mentally disordered persons. Rather, psychological traits occur along a continuum, from normal variations on the theme of human diversity to extreme aberrations of thought, feeling, and action. Accordingly, an individual's personality may influence the course and direction of an otherwise perfectly rational and volitional choice to commit harmful acts in the name of either self-gratification or some higher purpose....

When features of character become more than minor variations, psychologists regard them not just as personality traits, but as personality disorders. The official definition of a *personality disorder* is "an enduring pattern of inner experience and behavior that deviates markedly from the expectations of the individual's culture, is pervasive and inflexible, has an onset in adolescence or early adulthood, is stable over time, and leads to distress or impairment." Thus, it is the extremes of their self-perception and conduct toward others that distinguish personality-disordered individuals from those with milder traits....

Again, it must be emphasized that conceptualizing terrorist mentalities within an established behavioral science context is not an attempt to clinically sterilize atrocious behavior by psychologizing or pathologizing it. Rather, the more we study deviant acts and life patterns with the lens of behavioral science, the better we may be able to understand how they affect us in the various venues of our daily lives, and—more important—how to manage them....

TERRORIST LEADERS: NARCISSISTIC AND PARANOID PERSONALITIES

Narcissistic personality is a pattern of grandiosity, sense of entitlement, arrogance, need for admiration, and lack of empathy for others' feelings or opinions. These are the classic cultic terrorist leaders convinced of their own authority and infallibility and regarding themselves as above the law because of their special powers of perception, insight, and judgment in matters of absolute truth and justice. They are often quite engagingly charismatic and able to ensnare impressionable devotees with their unshakable certitude, conviction of infallibility, and

infectious zeal for the cause. These are the leaders who give the orders and expect the followers to obey without question.

Paranoid personality is a pattern of pervasive distrust and suspiciousness so that others' actions and motives are almost invariably interpreted as deceptive, persecutory, or malevolent. Aside from the narcissistic personality style, these are the other main group of quintessential cult leaders, and, indeed, it is not uncommon for such leaders to combine various proportions of narcissistic and paranoid features in their personalities. The paranoid is less of an inviting charmer than the pure narcissist, who, as noted earlier, wants to be liked and admired above all. Instead, the paranoid leader's philosophy is more likely to have a racial or religious exclusionary focus, as well as a darkly conspiratorial tinge, in contrast to the expansive narcissist's universalist philosophy that is often broad enough to encompass the whole wide world. The paranoid leader is already convinced that it is him or her against everyone else; thus, he or she feels no compulsion to ingratiate him- or herself with the mass of inferior underlings except insofar as this will cement whatever allegiance among in-group members is necessary to accomplish the aims.

The paranoid person may be the most dangerous type of terrorist leader or group member because perceived external threats and the group's holy mission justify committing any kind of violent act to further his or her absolutist religious or political philosophy.... Thus, terrorist acts against religious infidels, political rivals, or racial inferiors are justified as perfectly legitimate defenses of the faith, social structure, or ethnic purity. As such, violent acts continue, and the world actually does come to hate the terrorist group and everyone connected with it, thus confirming the paranoid conspiracy theory in a vicious cycle.

The combined narcissistic-paranoid type seems to correspond to Strentz's ... definition of a leader and may be exemplified in religious terrorist or cult leaders who believe they are manifestly chosen to lead the masses to their own versions of salvation and spiritual perfection, which may well involve the annihilation of their enemies in the name of absolute religious and/or political truth. These are also the leaders who, when threatened, are most likely to lead their followers to mass suicide, believing that, without their own divine guidance, the underlings literally have no further reason to exist.

Paranoid terrorist leaders or group members are not likely to alter their fixed beliefs, which at extremes may attain a frankly delusional quality, and this renders them essentially impervious to logic or intimidation.

These are individuals who would rather go out in a blaze of glory than surrender their principles. Narcissistic underbosses or lieutenants may cooperate with law enforcement authorities if they can be persuaded that their own superior knowledge or talent has been squelched by less worthy leaders who have unfairly thwarted their rise to power in the group. . . . The key is for authorities to allow the narcissist to perceive a new and improved outlet for his or her own self-importance that involves cooperation with the authorities. Indeed, it remains unknown as to how many middle-level terrorist operatives have been "turned" in this manner. However, paranoid or combined paranoid-narcissistic leaders may well view their capture and interrogation as proof of their martyrdom, and this will only stiffen their resistance.

TRUE BELIEVERS AND UNSTABLE DECEIVERS: BORDERLINE AND ANTISOCIAL PERSONALITIES

Borderline personality is a pattern of erratic and intense relationships, alternating between overidealization and devaluation of others; self-damaging impulsiveness; emotional instability, including inappropriately intense anger and/or depressive mood swings and suicidality; persistent identity disturbance in self-image and interpersonal relationships; and a chronic feeling of emptiness that may lead to the quest for stimulation through provocation or escalation of conflict. Initially, borderlines may form ferociously powerful allegiances to group leaders and ideologies. Although the characteristic changeability of their attachments makes them unreliable long-term loyalists, their intervals of intense idealistic devotion and their willingness to take great risks in its service may make them useful—and expendable— functionaries for dangerous terrorist missions.

The mutability of the borderline's attachments may work to the advantage of law enforcement authorities should the borderline member become disillusioned with the terrorist group's ideals or feel slighted by the leader. Then, the fierce devotion may turn to rabid resentment, and the borderline will loathe the group with the same intensity as he or she once adored it. This is the place for authorities to step in and convince the borderline that his or her cooperation will right the wrong that has been done. If an interviewer can form a strong attachment bond with the respondent, this may encourage the borderline to reveal intimate details of the group's plans and activities. The only caution here is that the respondent may later "turn on" these same

authorities with equal intensity if he feels misused or rejected by them. . . . Also, borderlines' brittle and fragile emotional stability means that they are probably the terrorist subtype most at risk for impulsive suicide and so should be kept under careful observation while detained.

Antisocial personality is a pattern of consistent disregard for, and violation of, the rights of others. It is typically associated with impulsivity, criminal behavior, sexual promiscuity, substance abuse, and an exploitive, parasitic, and/or predatory lifestyle. Although possessed of similar qualities of entitlement and self-importance as the narcissist, antisocial personalities are distinguished by their complete lack of empathy and conscience, which allows them to treat other people simply as sources of their own gratification. They may join terrorist organizations for the sheer thrill of being able to wreak destruction on inferior, helpless citizens, and they are often the skilled assassins or bombers of the group. . . . They can also be quite shrewd in a cunning or conning type of way, and the more intelligent among these types may accumulate considerable fiefdoms of wealth and power or rise to positions of great authority within the terrorist organization. This personality type seems to most closely parallel Strentz's . . . cynical and hedonistic activist-operator terrorist subtype.

Unlike the narcissist or paranoid type, however, for the antisocial terrorist, there is no true loyalty—it is all a game. True identification with, or commitment to, any person or idea is entirely alien to his or her nature; when squeezed by authorities, the antisocial will qualmlessly betray compatriots to save his or her own skin. Tactically, authorities may exploit this self-serving character by offering a deal in exchange for intelligence. The only drawback is that antisocials tend to believe that they are more clever than everyone else and may try to outmanipulate the authorities by planting misleading information or trying to use law enforcement to strike back at their own enemies. This is further aggravated by the tendency of most antisocial personalities to be pathological liars in general. . . .

GOOD SOLDIERS AND WORKER BEES: AVOIDANT AND DEPENDENT PERSONALITIES

Avoidant personality is a pattern of social inhibition, feelings of inadequacy, and hypersensitivity to criticism. Even relatively neutral interpersonal interactions or confrontations are approached with trepidation. Although it is unlikely that many individuals with this personality pattern would choose a murderous vocation such as terrorism, some members may have initially been attracted to the helping and social justice aspects of some religious and political movements as a form of self-therapy or to garner good will and admiration from citizens and camaraderie from fellow group members. Indeed, the structure, order, predictability, and ideological certainty offered by many terrorist political and religious organizations are sublimely comforting to avoidant personalities, affording them respite from the moral ambiguities of the outside world while allowing them to perform an ostensibly useful function within a group of supportive comrades. Only later do they realize that these seductively benevolent organizations have a more violent side. . . .

Earning the investigatory cooperation of avoidant suspects usually occurs in proportion to the amount of security and safety that law enforcement authorities can provide for these individuals. Many disillusioned avoidant suspects will actually be relieved to free themselves of the terrorist group and will be happy to provide information in exchange for safety. A collaborative and supportive interview style, rather than a cold and confrontational interrogation, is the most productive approach with these individuals.

Dependent personality is a pattern of submissive and clinging behavior stemming from an excessive need for care and nurturance. Whereas avoidant suspects fear people and prefer to be away from them, dependent personalities desperately need people and fear only their rejection or insufficient support. Dependent personalities cling to others to provide guidance and direction, and a charismatic cult leader is the perfect object of this desire. Dependent members of terrorist groups may actually be good, dedicated soldiers so long as independent decision making is kept to a minimum. Interactions with colleagues or leaders are apt to be taken more personally than with other group members because dependents are always hungry for validation of their usefulness and worthiness. . . .

Facing questioning by authorities, dependent personalities may retain their loyalty to the terrorist group because of the sense of meaning, purpose, and validation that the group has given them. Presenting them with evidence that they have never really been regarded as respected group members, but rather have been duped and exploited by group leaders, may loosen their allegiance to the terrorist organization, or it may entrench it through denial to protect their own fragile self-image. A more effective strategy is to assume a supportive, collaborative approach to interview and interrogation, similar to

that with avoidant personalities. However, in this case, allowing the dependent individuals to gradually see themselves not as a criminal suspect in a hostile environment, but as a valued part of an important new team or family—the law enforcement agency and the accepting community it represents.

Borderline and dependent personalities probably define the ranks of many of the idealist terrorist subtypes in Strentz's . . . classification. The political or religious group provides them with meaning and validation, and they will be fiercely loyal to that group unless and until law enforcement authorities can provide a new focus for their dependent allegiance.

Limelight Seekers and Loose Cannons: Histrionic and Schizoid-Schizotypal Personalities

Histrionic personality is a pattern of excessive emotionality, attention seeking, need for excitement, flamboyant theatricality in speech and behavior, an impressionistic and impulsive cognitive style, and the use of exaggeration to maintain largely superficial relationships for the purpose of getting emotional needs met by being admired and cared for by others. . . . They are less strong on discipline and less willing to get their hands dirty than other types, but terrorist organizations may solicit these individuals as front men or women in the legitimate worlds of entertainment, the media, or politics to take their case to the larger world or to infiltrate mainstream organizations. The risk is that histrionics' hunger for recognition may eclipse their loyalty to the group, in which case they may draw too much attention to the group's activities and thus become an expendable liability.

This may prove an advantage to law enforcement authorities, who may be able to barter the promise of heroic media exposure for valuable information on the terrorist group ("I was a double-agent for al-Qaeda!"). Less theatrically, histrionic members may be the most likely type to drop out when "it's just not fun anymore." Then, similar to the narcissist, the promise of a positive public spotlight, combined with credible security against retaliation from the group, may render the histrionic individual a cooperative participant for law enforcement. Once again, information thus obtained should be independently validated given the histrionic personality's propensity for embellishment and self-aggrandizement.

The central characteristics of both schizoid and schizotypal personalities include avoidance of other people, severe deficits in social skills, generalized withdrawal from life, and sometimes impairment in perceptual and cognitive skills. *Schizoid personality* is a pattern of aloof detachment from social interaction with a restricted range of emotional expression. These are people who do not need people and are perfectly happy being left to themselves. The *schizotypal personality*, in addition, includes more serious disturbances of thinking and more bizarre behavior. It is thought that these two personality disorders really represent points on a continuum from schizoid to schizotypal to outright schizophrenia, with the latter characterized by severe distortions of thought, perception, and action, including delusions and hallucinations. In fact, schizoid and schizotypal personality disorders may episodically deteriorate into psychotic states, especially under conditions of stress.

Although such individuals are typically not joiners, the unstable identity structure of many schizoids and schizotypals may lead them on philosophical and spiritual quests that end up in social and religious movements with terrorist ties. They will be the "oddballs" of the group who mainly keep to themselves, but may show fierce commitment if the movement's philosophy appeals to their idiosyncratic worldview. However, they may have a tendency to decompensate and become delusional under prolonged, intense stress and are then more likely to become an expendable liability to the group.

If the goals and beliefs of the terrorist organization fit in with the schizoid or schizotypal's idiosyncratic worldview—especially if they contain fixed, delusional elements—these individuals may be as stubbornly resistant as the paranoid member to betraying the group. Even when they choose to cooperate, the sometimes bizarre and delusional nature of the information they provide may compromise its validity and usefulness. Overall, a firm and directive but not overtly hostile approach may be most effective in focusing the schizoid member's attention on simple, precise questions. These should be designed to yield specific, concrete bits of information that can then be fitted together to create a coherent narrative of useful information and intelligence.

Conclusions

Psychological principles will not, in themselves, solve all the problems of criminal and terrorist intelligence gathering, but inasmuch as interview and interrogation are uniquely human processes, their success will be informed by a mastery of the practical psychology of the criminal or terrorist mind. Indeed, practical psychology is a skill that is vital for all aspects of law enforcement and criminal justice.

Questions

1. What are the three forms of rationalization a terrorist might display?

2. Describe the personality disorders associated with the various terrorist types.

PART V

SOCIAL STRUCTURE PERSPECTIVE

Broadly, social structure theories study how various aspects of society, environmental factors, influence criminality. The approach's three main branches—strain, disorganization, and subculture—are presented here.

Strain

For Durkheim, *anomie* or *strain* referred to confusion about social norms and roles. Reconceived by Merton, strain is what results when a person's goals cannot be achieved through socially approved means. With his general strain theory, Robert Agnew attempted to account for why some individuals who experience stress and strain turn to crime, whereas others do not. In *Life Strain, Coping, and Delinquency in the People's Republic of China: An Empirical Test of General Strain Theory From a Matching Perspective in Social Support*, Wan-Ning Bao, Ain Haas, and Yijun Pi (chap. 12) examine the applicability of general strain theory (GST) to juvenile delinquency in modern-day China using a large sample of middle-school students. In *Marijuana Use as a Coping Response to Psychological Strain: Racial, Ethnic, and Gender Differences Among Young Adults*, Pamela Preston (chap. 13) applies GST, social learning, and self-control theories to examine an activity common among college students.

Disorganization

The ecological approach of social disorganization theory considers the role of a community's poverty and decline on crime. In *Neighborhood Context and Police Use of Force*, William Terrill and Michael Reisig (chap. 14) consider how the deviance or criminality of law enforcement officers who use excessive force is influenced by the environment in which it occurs. Combining social learning and social disorganization, Justin Patchin and colleagues (chap. 15) examine how youth adapt to the violence they witness in their communities in *Exposure to Community Violence and Childhood*

Delinquency. The authors consider why not all, indeed most, residents of disorganized neighborhoods engage in criminal activity.

Subculture

The group-specific social norms and values found in subcultures have been found to influence criminality. In *A Subcultural Study of Recreational Ecstasy Use*, Michelle Gourley (chap. 16) uses interviews and observations to investigate the influence of the drug-using subculture on the recreational use of the club drug ecstasy. In *Race, Victim-Precipitated Homicide, and the Subculture of Violence Thesis*, Lance Hannon (chap. 17) examines the subculture of violence theory that posits the existence of an African-American subculture that values violence and places great importance on a person's reputation among the group to explain their disproportionately high rates of involvement in homicide. The author analyzes a large sample (nearly 1,000) of homicides to determine whether incidents involving African Americans were more likely to involve victim precipitation, where the victim has a role in initiating the homicide.

CHAPTER 12

Life Strain, Coping, and Delinquency in the People's Republic of China

An Empirical Test of General Strain Theory From a Matching Perspective in Social Support

Wan-Ning Bao

Indiana University–Purdue University at Indianapolis

Ain Haas

Indiana University–Purdue University at Indianapolis

Yijun Pi

China University of Politics and Law

In the effort to clarify the causes of juvenile delinquency, theorists and researchers naturally focus on the patterns they have observed in their own society. How well their generalizations apply to other societies, especially ones with a different cultural heritage and social order, is rarely explored. In particular, the classic strain theories developed in mid-20th-century United States can be criticized for being so fixated on what was going on then and there that they neglected more general processes that might have more relevance elsewhere. This can be said of the theories pointing to the frustrations of lower class youth encountering barriers to educational and economic success in an increasingly meritocratic society . . . and of the theories emphasizing difficulties that middle-class youth may face in forming an identity . . . , living up to parents' high expectations . . . , and winning acceptance from peers . . . . The recent version of strain theory offered by Robert Agnew . . . seems less bound to a particular type of stressful experience or

to certain historical and geographic contexts. This is why we were inspired to investigate its utility for explaining juvenile delinquency in a non-Western country: the People's Republic of China.

In this chapter, we examine an important aspect of Agnew's general strain theory (GST): The availability of coping resources may mitigate the impact of strain on delinquency. With self-report data from a sample of 615 middle- and high school students in rural and urban areas, we investigate how Chinese adolescents' social and personal coping resources can condition their delinquent response to strain and can help explain why some youth turn to delinquent behavior, whereas others who experience similar strains in life do not do so.

We apply a "matching" perspective in social support to investigate whether social supports in a given domain (family, school, and peer group) buffer the effects of strain within that domain or spill over into other domains, and we also consider the category of

Source: "Life strain, coping, and delinquency in People's Republic of China: An empirical test of general strain theory from a matching perspective in social support," by Bao, W., Haas, A., and Pi, Y., (2007), in *International Journal of Offender Therapy and Comparative Criminology, 51,* 9–24. Reprinted by permission of Sage Publications, Inc.

coping resources that are not tied to any particular sphere. There is special attention to gender differences in the mobilization of social support and the formulation of personal coping strategies in the face of interpersonal strain.

GST

Agnew's GST represents a significant departure from the traditional strain theories in that it specifies conditioning factors that affect the likelihood of a delinquent response to strain. Therefore, it tries to answer a fundamental question of under what conditions strain leads to delinquency in a much more detailed way than earlier versions of strain theory did.

Defining *strain* as "relationships in which others are not treating the individual as he or she would like to be treated," Agnew . . . delineated three types of such negative relationships. The first type involves failure to achieve positively valued goals, including popularity among peers and achievement of good grades in school. The second type of strain involves removal of positively valued and familiar stimuli, as in rejection by a partner in romance or moving away from a comfortable environment. The third type of strain involves being subjected to negatively valued stimuli, such as beatings, scoldings, and ridiculings by parents, teachers, or peers.

GST recognizes that the likelihood of delinquent responses to strain is conditioned by social and personal factors. Drawing from other theories and studies, Agnew. . . suggested that delinquent adaptation to strain is more likely for those with weak conventional social bonds . . . , strong affiliation with delinquent peers. . . , and low self-esteem and low self-efficacy. . . . Conventional social bonds condition the impact of strain on delinquency by providing social support and constraining delinquent coping. For example, support from parents, teachers, and friends may facilitate nondelinquent approaches to coping with strain, and moral beliefs derived from these and other agents of socialization function as an internal control that inhibits delinquency. Affiliation with delinquent peers magnifies the effects of strain on delinquency because individuals exposed to such friends' deviant beliefs and behaviors receive support and reinforcement for delinquency. High self-esteem makes individuals more resilient in dealing with strain, whereas a strong sense of self-efficacy encourages them to feel responsible and capable of solving strain-producing problems.

PREVIOUS RESEARCH ON THE CONDITIONING MODEL IN GST

Agnew's GST has stimulated a number of investigations of the conditioning hypothesis. Researchers applied various analytical techniques, examined different conditioning factors, and found mixed results. Agnew and White. . . conducted the first study of this kind among middle-school students in New Jersey. They found that affiliation with delinquent peers and low self-efficacy interacted with strain to magnify the latter's impact on delinquency. Exposure to delinquent peers also interacted with strain to promote drug use. In a study of high school students in a large, metropolitan area in the midwestern United States, Mazerolle, Burton, Cullen, Evans, and Payne . . . found that affiliation with delinquent friends interacted with strain to increase the likelihood of violence and drug use. Lack of social bonds also magnified the impact of strain on drug use. Using longitudinal data from the National Youth Survey, Mazerolle and Maahs' . . . study revealed that a high level of moral beliefs, less exposure to delinquent peers, and low behavioral propensity toward delinquency buffered the impact of adolescents' life strain on delinquency. Agnew, Brezina, Wright, and Cullen . . . used data from the National Survey of Children and found that the personality trait of negative emotionality and/or low constraints made individuals more likely to experience intense emotional reactions to strain, less concerned about the consequences of delinquency, and more disposed to delinquency.

Other studies, however, failed to support the conditioning hypothesis derived from GST. In a longitudinal study of high school students, Paternoster and Mazerolle . . . examined the conditioning effects of moral beliefs, social support, delinquent peers, self-efficacy, and delinquent disposition on the strain–delinquency relationship. Their results revealed only one significant multiplicative interaction of strain and self-efficacy, but in an unpredicted direction. In a 3-year longitudinal study among adolescents, Hoffmann and Miller. . . found that the longitudinal effects of strain on delinquency were not conditioned by self-efficacy, self-esteem, or delinquent peers. When Aseltine, Gore, and Gordon. . . tested the conditioning effects of mastery, self-esteem, social support, and delinquent peers among high school youth, they found that interactions among these variables and strain had a significant impact on delinquency in only 6 of 96 models. In a study of college students, Mazerolle and Piquero. . . found that exposure to delinquent peers and moral constraints did not condition the impact of strain on delinquency.

The accumulating negative evidence on the conditioning hypothesis has raised questions about the conditioning assumptions of GST. One of the reasons for the inconsistency in the literature may be a lack of clear conceptualization of the buffering process on the part of researchers. Nearly all the previous studies used a global or aggregate measure of strain in testing conditioning effects. This common approach to measuring strain derives from the notion that various types of strain have a cumulative impact on delinquency. . . . This proposition, however, is questionable in examining strain-buffering processes because it precludes an investigation of how various specific social or personal coping strategies might be used to deal with particular types of strain. The conditioning of the strain–delinquency relationship may be harder to detect if strain is measured in a cumulative way that includes types of strain that have little to do with the posited conditioning variable.

Matching in Strain-Buffering Processes of Social Support

In the health literature, social support is widely viewed as having a "buffering effect" on stress. When individuals experience life stresses, social support functions to mitigate the potentially pathological consequences of the stress. . . . Two distinct conceptual elements in social support are support network resources and subjective appraisals of support. . . . With regard to the first element, the quality of important social relationships is crucial because it not only influences the likelihood of supportive behavior . . . , but also conditions the degree of attachment, social integration, reassurance of worth, and guidance. . . . Appraisals of supportive relationships are subjective assessments of the nature and quality of social network ties, taking forms such as satisfaction, a sense of belonging, and involvement . . . .

The integration of GST and social-support theory has been recognized and emphasized by scholars in an effort to build a more systematic GST of crime and delinquency. . . . Based on a multidimensional view of stressful events and social support, we suggest a matching model for examining strain-buffering processes, which focuses attention on "matches" between certain types of strain and certain types of coping resources. The concept of *matching* is central to theories of social support that hold that the source of support must correspond to the source of strain that individuals encounter to act as an effective buffer to life stress. . . .

This matching hypothesis has led to tests of "within-domain," "cross-domain," and "all-domain" buffering effects of social support. The concept of *within-domain buffering* implies that conflict and support from the same key relationships interact to affect outcomes for adolescents. To the extent that social support and conflict are relatively independent aspects of the same social relationship, parental support for adolescents may be as important as that from their friends, even in a conflicting relationship with their parents. . . . In addition, the large size and fluidity of the peer network allows adolescents to seek supporters from their peer group in dealing with negative peer experiences. . . .

In contrast, cross-domain buffering occurs when support from one social domain attenuates the adverse effects of stress from another social domain. For example, support from a peer group can help adolescents cope with family problems. Parents may be far less effective than friends in buffering the effect of family strains insofar as the former are a part of the problem. . . .

Finally, all-domain buffering occurs when something has a pervasive dampening effect, regardless of the source of the strain on the individual. For example, S. Cohen and Wills . . . argued that individuals in stressful circumstances may always benefit from relevant information and confidence in their own capabilities. Likewise, Gore and Aseltine . . . noted that personal resources, such as a sense of mastery and a sense of social integration, are likely to buffer the impact of stressors in all domains mainly because personality traits tend to be rather consistent through time and across a variety of situations. . . .

In the current study, we apply the "matching" perspective to test the conditioning model in GST. The current study focuses on interpersonal strain in three major life domains (family, school, and peer group) among Chinese adolescents. We predict that social supports from all of the previously mentioned domains have buffering effects on the relationship between interpersonal strain and delinquency, across and within these spheres. We also expect that moral belief, lack of delinquent peers, and personal coping resources have buffering effects in all domains.

Gender has been found to play a major role in the stress-buffering process among adolescents. For example, girls are more likely to seek and receive social support in times of stress . . . , whereas boys more often use "problem-focused" coping strategies. . . . So the current study also examines gender differences in Chinese adolescents' ability to mobilize effective coping resources in response to strain.

Method

SAMPLE

In the summer of 2002, data were collected from 615 students in the 8th to 11th grades in public schools in three locations in China. Roughly one third of the sample came from each of three locations: (a) the southern city of Guangzhou, (b) the northern city of Shijiazhuang, and (c) two rural schools near the latter. As the capital of Guangdong province, the coastal city of Guangzhou is undergoing rapid economic development, stimulated by proximity to Hong Kong, a major hub of international trade. Shijiazhuang, the capital of Hebei province and located about 300 kilometers south of Beijing, is typical of the inland cities in China in terms of its moderate rate of economic growth. In the rural district near Shijiazhuang City, the pace of change has been relatively slow; however, even here the same trends can be seen in incipient forms.

These locations were chosen to represent the wide range of trends of economic development and social change in different parts of China today. After the 1980s' economic reform that has given increasing free play to market forces, China has experienced rapid increases in urbanization and wealth inequality while traditional beliefs, norms, and social control have been undermined. . . . Crime rates are highest in the areas most affected by such trends because these trends are aggravating various strains in adolescents' lives, which contribute to the upsurge in juvenile delinquency. . . .

DATA COLLECTION

Drawing items from previous American tests of GST, a self-report survey form with 360 items was prepared in the Chinese language. To verify the equivalence of the Chinese and English versions, comparisons were made between the original English-language items and independently prepared back-to-English translations from the Chinese-language items. A pretest among 47 middle-school students in Beijing led to further adjustments in wording.

The parents of the selected participants were informed of the study by a letter that the students also saw before they filled out the questionnaire. Virtually all (98%) of the students who were invited actually participated. The survey was administered in an anonymous group setting, during regular class hours, with students marking their responses on computer-scan forms.

MEASURES

Apart from the single-item demographic control variables, we used multiple-item indicators to ensure more reliable measurement of the basic variables in Agnew's GST. These can be grouped into three categories: (a) exposure to negative stimuli (in the form of negative relationships with parents, teachers, and peers), (b) conditioning factors (social support from these same sources, and exposure to delinquent friends, moral beliefs, and personal coping resources), and (c) delinquent behavior (in the form of violence and property offenses). A scale was deemed suitable when it had loadings of .4 or more for each item on the rotated factor matrix and a reliability score (Cronbach's α) of .7 or more for each set of items.

Negative relations with parents were measured with a scale of 15 items designed to reveal perceived parental overbearingness, hostility, or dismissiveness. Using the response categories of 1 = *never*, 2 = *seldom*, 3 = *sometimes*, 4 = *often*, and 5 = *almost always*, youth reported how often their parents asked them and others what the youth did away from home, wanted to know who phoned and what was said, blew their tops when bothered by the youth, got angry about little things, acted as if the youth was in the way, made the youth feel unloved, told the youth how to spend free time and how to do his or her work exactly, insisted on obedience if the youth complained, acted strict and wanted to control whatever the youth did, forgot to help when needed, said no to anything asked for, and considered the youth's ideas silly.

Negative relations with teachers were measured using a scale of seven items designed to reveal whether respondents felt their teachers were mean. Youth were asked how often (1 = *never* to 5 = *almost always*) their teachers lost their temper, embarrassed the youth, talked down to the youth, made negative comments, criticized them in front of others, didn't forgive them, and isolated them.

Negative relations with peers were assessed with a scale of seven items. Using the response categories of 1 = *strongly disagree*, 2 = *disagree*, 3 = *neither agree nor disagree*, 4 = *agree*, and 5 = *strongly agree*, youth were asked whether they felt like they were lonely in school and among friends, they were put down by other students, nobody at school cared about or took an interest in them, their peers were demanding, and tensions or arguments with peers were common.

Family support was composed of seven items gauging attachment to parents. Youth indicated the extent to which they felt closeness to their parents; had feelings of respect, love, and confidence with regard to their parents; and wanted to be like their parents. The response categories were 1 = *not at all*, 2 = *not very much*, 3 = *not sure*, 4 = *somewhat*, and 5 = *very much*. Our justification for using indicators of attachment for this support scale (and the two that follow) is that previous research revealed that attachment to conventional others and institutions is a central ingredient in social support. . . .

School support included 12 items showing attachment to school using response categories of 1 = *strongly disagree* to 5 = *strongly agree*. Youth were asked whether school makes a difference in their lives, gives them chances to be with others of their own age and learn interesting things, gives them a feeling of accomplishment, and they felt satisfaction with school, perceived value of education, attraction of school, commitment to school, importance of learning, acquiring skills at school, and anticipated future benefits such as becoming a mature adult and a good citizen.

Peer support was gauged with two items. Youth were asked how easy (1 = *very hard*, 2 = *hard*, 3 = *not sure*, 4 = *easy*, and 5 = *very easy*) it was to find close friends and how often (1 = *never* to 5 = *always*) they were invited to parties and other activities by classmates.

Moral beliefs were composed of 16 items. Students were asked to indicate how wrong (1 = *not wrong at all*, 2 = *not sure*, 3 = *wrong*, and 4 = *very wrong*) it is to borrow money and not to repay it, cut classes and skip school, cheat on tests and copy another's homework, sass teachers, violate school rules, join gangs, steal things, destroy school property, drink alcohol, use drugs, bring a weapon to school, burglarize, and strike another without reason.

Delinquent friends included 13 items. Youth were asked how many close friends (1 = *none*, 2 = *very few*, 3 = *some*, 4 = *most*, and 5 = *all of them*) had smoked, drunk liquor, used drugs, sold drugs, stolen things, burglarized, shoplifted, used force to obtain something, taken part in gang fighting, damaged others' property, attacked someone, and carried a weapon.

Self-efficacy comprised five items indicating perceived personal control over the environment. Using response categories of 1 = *strongly agree* to 5 = *strongly disagree*, respondents indicated whether they felt like they faced problems they could not solve and were helpless, were being pushed around in life, had little control over the things that happen to them, and could do nothing to change many important things in life.

Self-esteem included eight items indicating judgments about one's self-worth. Respondents were asked to what degree (1 = *strongly disagree* to 5 = *strongly agree*) they feel like a person of worth, have a number of good qualities, can do things as well as others, take a positive attitude toward themselves, never think they are a failure, feel useless, not good at all, and are satisfied with themselves.

Delinquency was gauged with a scale of 16 items. About one half of the items referred to acts of violence: getting something by force, attacking someone, taking part in a group fight, getting into a serious fight and hurting someone badly, using a weapon in a fight, hitting a teacher or a parent, and having sex with someone against his or her will. The remaining items referred to property offenses: stealing things worth under or more than 50 Chinese yuan, shoplifting, burglary, stealing from school, making graffiti at public places, and damaging school property on purpose. Students indicated how often they had done each of these things in the past year using the following list of response categories: 1 = *never*, 2 = *once*, 3 = *twice*, 4 = *3 or 4 times*, and 5 = *5 or more times*. Forty-five percent of the participants committed at least 1 of the 16 offenses in the past year. Because the incidences of at least one violent offense and one property offense were quite similar (29% vs. 34%), it is clear that the single scale of delinquency truly picks up a variety of law-breaking forms.

There were four demographic control variables. For female sex, the coding was 1 = *male* and 2 = *female*. Each category comprised one half (50%) of the sample (307 males vs. 308 females). For age, the mean age was 15.6 years for males and 15.5 years for females, with a range of 13 to 18 years. For urban residence, the categories were 1 = *rural* and 2 = *urban*, with most (71%) of the sample in the latter group. Family living standard was based on the respondent's rating using the categories of 1 = *poor*, 2 = *nearly poor*, 3 = *just get along*, 4 = *relatively well off*, and 5 = *well off*. The mean was 3.1 for the sample.

We used one-tailed tests of statistical significance, deriving expected directions from predictions of GST or (in the case of the demographic controls) from patterns found in earlier studies. Because there is some overlap between various strain and conditioning variables in terms of the parties they refer to (parents, teachers, friends, or self), the possibility of multicollinearity has to be considered. Following the procedure recommended by Lewis-Beck . . . , we regressed in turn each of the strain and conditioning variables on the rest. We found that the resulting R^2 values (.36 or less) were far below the .80 threshold considered as a likely symptom of multicollinearity.

Results

Bivariate Correlations

The expected correlations for the key variables of GST are almost invariably significant in the posited direction. . . . [N]egative relationships with parents, teachers, and peers were all positively associated with delinquency. Six of the seven conditioning variables were linked to delinquency in the expected direction; only peer support had an insignificant correlation. As expected, males and students from poor families reported more delinquency; however, urban residence and age turned out to be unrelated to delinquency.

Interaction Effects of Interpersonal Strain and Conditioning Variables on Delinquency

Ordinary least-squares hierarchical multiple regression was used to test the first two hypotheses, which predict that support from family, school, and peers will have cross- and within-domain buffering effects on the relationship between delinquency and interpersonal strain in the settings of the home, school, and peer group, and that moral beliefs, delinquent peers, and personal coping will have all-domain conditioning effects. To test for buffering effects, multiplicative interaction terms were created by multiplying each of the interpersonal strain variables by each of the conditioning variables. All the variables used to construct the interaction terms were first centered by subtracting the mean from each variable score to reduce multicollinearity between the interaction term and its components in the analysis. . . . An examination of the variance inflation factors for the interaction and its components showed that all inflation factors were under 2, suggesting that multicollinearity is not a problem. . . .

We estimated a series of regression equations in which only one interaction term and its components were included along with all other strain, conditioning, and sociodemographic variables. . . . . Of 21 possible interactions, 9 were significant and in the predicted direction. This was a number far higher than would have been expected to occur by chance alone because only 1 of the 21 interactions would be likely to turn up significant just by accident at the conventional .05 level of significance. Students experiencing negative relations with teachers were less likely to respond to the strain with delinquency when they had school support, a finding indicating a within-domain buffering effect of social support. School support also buffered the effect of negative relations with parents on delinquency, and family support had a conditioning effect on negative relations with teachers. These findings revealed cross-domain buffering effects of social support. All-domain buffering is evident in the finding that moral beliefs condition the effects of interpersonal strain on delinquency in all three domains of family, school, and peer group. In addition, adolescents experiencing negative relationships with parents or teachers were more likely to turn to delinquency when they had more delinquent friends. Finally, self-efficacy was effective in buffering the impact of negative relations with parents.

Gender Differences in the Strain-Buffering Process

The third hypothesis predicts that females are more likely than males to use social support as coping resources in response to interpersonal strain. . . . Of 21 possible interactions, 8 are significant for girls and 7 for boys. Only two of these significant interaction terms involved within-domain buffering. Cross- and all-domain buffering was found for both sexes; however, both forms were generally more evident among girls.

For negative relations with parents, school support and self-efficacy had conditioning effects on the strain only among girls. Moral beliefs and delinquent peers buffered the strain for boys and girls. For girls, peer support had an unexpected magnifying effect on the strain–delinquency relationship. The concept of *differential social support* implies that social support is as important to generating nonconformity and crime as it is to producing conformity . . . , especially with regard to peers and cooffending. . . . A high level of peer support can magnify the impact of strain on delinquency because more close friends and more involvement in peer activities may increase the opportunities for delinquency. . . .

For negative relations with teachers, the only evidence of within-domain buffering came from the finding that school support had a conditioning effect on this type of strain among girls. Family support buffered the effect of the strain from negative relations with teachers among both sexes. Moral beliefs had a buffering effect on this type of strain for boys and girls, whereas delinquent peers conditioned the effect only for boys.

For negative relations with peers, there were two significant conditioning effects only for boys. On the one hand, peer support buffered the effect of the strain on delinquency, and, on the other hand, delinquent peers magnified the effect of interpersonal strain from peers.

Conclusions and Discussion

The purpose of the current study was to test whether delinquency-generating strains in the domains of family, school, and peer group are buffered by the conditioning factors identified in Agnew's GST. In particular, we examined whether sources of social support in these three domains have within- and cross-domain buffering effects on the relationship between interpersonal strain and delinquency. We also investigated the all-domain buffering effects of certain social learning variables and personal coping resources as these interact with interpersonal strain. We found evidence of all three types of buffering effects, although the magnitude of the standardized regression coefficients was modest (under .25) in all cases.

In the category of within-domain buffering, there was a significant dampening of delinquency from the interaction between school support and negative relations with teachers. Other studies have also found that school-related coping resources such as a sense of personal competence in academics can buffer the effects of stresses in the school domain, such as poor grades and academic failure. . . .

In the category of cross-domain buffering, we found that school support dampened the effect of negative relations with parents, whereas family support conditioned the effect of negative relations with teachers. These results indicate the importance of compensatory social support from two different social domains (viz., family and school) among Chinese adolescents. The relative independence of negative and positive aspects of social ties in different social domains suggests that individuals with social ties in a variety of social domains may be better prepared to cope with strain than individuals with limited social ties. . . .

All-domain buffering was also found. Indicating the important role of internal controls, moral belief conditioned the effects of interpersonal strains on delinquency in all three domains of family, school, and peer group. This pattern fits with Mazerolle and Maahs's . . . finding that moral beliefs against crime conditioned the cumulative effects of strain in various domains of American adolescents' lives. We also found that having delinquent friends magnified the effects of interpersonal strain in family and school on delinquency.

The analysis revealed differences between boys and girls in their patterns of using coping resources to respond to strain. Social support was more important for dampening strain's impact on delinquency among girls. Specifically, for girls, school support buffered the effects of negative relations with parents and teachers, and family support buffered the effect of negative relations with teachers. Girls also turned to friends for support when experiencing negative relations with parents, although such support amplified the effect of strain on delinquency. These findings are consistent with previous American studies that showed that, in the face of problems, adolescent girls are more likely than boys to seek help from family members and individuals outside the family . . . because such help seeking is deemed as a most suitable option for females in American culture. . . .

For boys, affiliation with delinquent peers was a key factor that magnified the effect of interpersonal strain on delinquency. Specifically, boys experiencing negative relations with parents, teachers, and peers were more likely to respond to the strain with delinquency when they had more delinquent friends. Unlike girls, boys often externalize conflict onto other persons or the environment and tend to take problem-focused rather than relationship-based coping strategies. . . . Boys experiencing strain are more likely to join or form delinquent peer groups, where they are exposed to delinquent beliefs, thus receiving reinforcement for their own propensity toward delinquency. . . .

The point of departure of the current study was our interest in applying the matching perspective for testing the strain-conditioning hypotheses of GST. Our findings suggest that some types of conditioning factors (e.g., social support) tend to operate in specific social domains, whereas others (especially moral beliefs) can function across all social domains. Therefore, future tests of the conditioning model in GST may depend on the development of the norms that define the appropriate match between source of strain and coping resources.

In terms of policy implications, our findings suggest that intervention programs to reduce delinquency could be made more effective if there was more attention to mobilizing those coping resources that are most linked with the specific types of strain in youths' lives. The revelation of substantial differences in sex suggests that it may not be a good idea to apply the same intervention approach to all types of youth. The salient role of the school in within- and cross-domain buffering suggests that strengthening school ties and increasing the supportiveness of school relationships may be especially fruitful in the search for ways to buffer the delinquency-generating impact of interpersonal strains in the main domains of Chinese adolescents' lives.

The relation between interpersonal strain and delinquency may be more reciprocal than implied by this analysis. Not only may interpersonal strain be antecedent to delinquency, but also being delinquent may increase strains with parents, teachers, and peers. Future research should use longitudinal data to further specify the relation between interpersonal strain and delinquency, which appears to be an important association in the People's Republic of China.

Questions

1. Describe the three sources of strain outlined in GST.

2. Describe the sources of strain which contemporary Chinese adolescents face.

CHAPTER 13

Marijuana Use as a Coping Response to Psychological Strain

Racial, Ethnic, and Gender Differences Among Young Adults

Pamela Preston

Penn State, Schuylkill, PA

Once limited to use by a small subculture, marijuana use has become common across age, social class, and ethnic groups. Young or traditional college-age adults use marijuana more often than other age groups. Data from the National Household Survey of Drug Abuse (2001) show that adults between the ages of 18 and 25 use marijuana an average of almost 28 days per year. This is almost 15 days per year more than juveniles (12–17 years old), 21 days more than 35- to 49-year-olds, and almost 27 days more than those ages 50 and older.

For many of these users, marijuana use is associated with a social event, something to do with friends on a weekend or special occasions. For others it is a more regular or even daily activity. This chronic marijuana user, as often as not, smokes alone. He or she no longer views marijuana use as a social activity; rather, it becomes a crutch needed to get through the day. It becomes a form of self-medication. The propensity to use marijuana on a regular (nonsocial) basis may have deleterious effects on the young adult's current situation and future. Chronic users enrolled in colleges and universities may miss classes, assignments, and exams, and all users may experience and/or exhibit depression or antisocial behavior. Although many campuses are concerned with drug use by both resident and commuter students, there may be a fundamental difference in causal factors between recreational and chronic marijuana users. Whereas the marijuana use may be problematic for the recreational user (leading him or her to miss important deadlines, etc.), marijuana use by the chronic user may be more a symptom of underlying problems or issues that affect his or her performance in school, on the job, and in life. Institutions and agencies devoted to addressing drug use and abuse by young adults need to be cognizant of possible differences of motives for drug use. This study compares the relative effects of strain, social learning, and low self-control on the level of marijuana use among young adults.

Past Research

Some of the factors associated with marijuana use addressed in past research include the role of (a) limited self-control, (b) social learning and the effect of the peer group, and (c) stress, strain, or anomie. Whereas some past research has focused specifically on a single theory, many have compared the relative effects of these three models on marijuana use.

SELF-CONTROL

Research focusing on the relationship between low self-control and marijuana use suggests limited association. Stylianou . . . found low self-control to be a mild

Source: "Marijuana use as a coping response to psychological strain: Racial, gender, and ethnic differences among young adults," by Preston, P., (2006), in *Deviant Behavior, 27*(4), 397–421. Reprinted by permission of Taylor & Francis.

predictor of marijuana use (among other behaviors). Bailey and Lott . . . found a mild negative relationship between self-control and a number of criminal offenses, including marijuana use.

SOCIAL LEARNING

Previous research shows more support for social learning theory. Akers . . . found social learning variables accounting for more than two thirds of the variance in marijuana use and more than one third of the variance in marijuana abuse. Hallstone . . . and Orcutt . . . also found significant social process/social learning factors associated with marijuana use.

STRESS/STRAIN

Research on the link between stress and substance use is not conclusive. O'Hare and Sherrer . . . , looking at the link between stress and substance abuse, found associations among stress, drinking, and marijuana use. Their study also addressed gender effects and indicated that women, rather than men, were more likely to respond to stress through substance use. Aseltine, Gore, and Gordon . . . , looking at the effect of anger in response to strain on subsequent delinquency, found no significant association with marijuana use. Hartnagel and Krahn . . . did find a relationship between unemployment/financial strain and marijuana use, as did a 1980 study by the Institute for the Study of Human Issues on chronic marijuana use in Costa Rica. Menard . . . also found that strain could explain from 14% to 34% of the variance in marijuana use and suggested that those studies finding no association may be a function of improper conceptualization of the strain variables, rather than inadequacies inherent in strain theory.

COMPARISON OF THE THREE THEORIES

Past research has also compared the relative effects of each of the three models on marijuana and other drug use. Akers and Cochran . . . found that social learning is most strongly associated with drug use, followed by social bonding, and little evidence to support anomie as a causal factor in drug use. Akers . . . found a limited relationship between anomie (defined as powerlessness) and marijuana use; however, Smith and Paternoster . . . , in a study of southeastern high school students, found that social bonding, differential association, strain, and deterrence are equally associated with frequency of marijuana use.

Some studies have suggested a link between parenting behaviors (which are integral in the development of self-control) and marijuana use, especially in tandem with social learning models. Svensson . . . found that there is a higher level of parental monitoring for females; conversely, this leads to greater contact with deviant peers for males. Combined with a lack of parental control, association with deviant peers contributes significantly to drug use. Andrews, Hops, and Duncan . . . found that a strong social bond with the parent will not necessarily protect an adolescent from drug use if the parent is also a substance user; rather, they would be more likely to model parental behavior when they were closely bonded; however, Dembo et al. . . . found that the effect decreases with the level of parental drug use. The effect of parental bonding does decrease with age as well; peer influence (as opposed to parental influence) was found to have a stronger influence on older adolescents. . . . Akers and Lee . . . found that there is an age-related curve in the effects of both social learning and social bonding. Past research shows that bonding and social learning interact and possibly intensify the effects of peer norms and values. They also address the differential effects of these factors on male and female adolescents; however, opinion is divided as to ethnic and gender differences.

Past research suggests that all three factors may contribute to marijuana use. Although there is evidence that males and females may respond to stress through substance use . . . , research addressing the differential effects of these factors on racial or ethnic minorities is lacking. This study contributes to the literature through an examination and comparison of the differential effects of peers (social learning theory), stress (general strain theory), and risk taking (social control theory) across both gender and racial/ethnic groups, thereby filling a gap in the current literature on the relationship between stress and deviant behavior (specifically chronic marijuana use).

Theory and hypotheses. Whereas past research has not shown a conclusive relationship between stress and marijuana use, this study suggests that stress does contribute to chronic, as opposed to recreational, marijuana use. It compares the effects of peers, stress, and risk-taking attitudes on chronic marijuana use across age and racial/ethnic groups of young adults. This study incorporates elements of general strain theory (GST) . . . , social learning theory . . . , and Hirschi and Gottfredson's concept of "low self-control."

In 1992, Agnew developed a revised GST that encompasses three dimensions: strain as the failure to achieve positively valued goals, strain as the removal of positively valued stimuli, and strain as the presentation of negative stimuli. Agnew's revised strain theory also attempts to address a major concern with Merton's original strain theory: Why do most people fail to engage in criminality as a form of goal attainment?

Criminality does not always ensue even in the face of overwhelming strain. Individuals have various coping mechanisms that allow them to adapt to both major and minor strain. Agnew . . . discusses major adaptations to strain and factors that may lead the individual to criminal or noncriminal adaptive techniques. There are cognitive, emotional, and behavioral adaptations to strain, one of which includes criminal behavior.

Cognitive adaptations allow the individual to minimize the importance or effect of a strain; for example, after being fired from one's job, he or she may minimize the importance by convincing him or herself that it was a terrible job and that he or she did not really want to keep the job anyway. There are three types of behavioral coping mechanisms. First, the individual may engage in behavior designed to achieve positively valued goals, guard or regain positively valued stimuli, or avoid negative stimuli. Finally, when adversity is believed to have been caused by others, the individual may engage in vengeful behavior. All types of behavioral coping mechanisms can involve criminal behavior. Finally, individuals faced with strain may cope through direct action on the negative emotions engendered by adversity. Emotional coping strategies act directly on the negative emotions engendered and include both legal and nonlegal methods, such as drug and alcohol use, physical exercise, meditation, and other activities designed to alleviate negative emotions, rather than addressing the strain or stress directly. Chronic marijuana use can, in this context, be considered an emotional coping strategy.

Akers' social learning theory . . . refines traditional differential association theory to include methods of learning. Akers also extends his theory to address crime and deviance that cuts across class boundaries and incorporates the effect of society on the learning process. Two of Akers' concepts are central to this study: differential association and definitions.

Differential association refers to the way one comes into contact with norms either favorable or unfavorable to deviant behavior—one's peer associations. Differential association can be dichotomized as interactional and normative. Interactional differential association includes direct contact with groups engaging in specific behavior (one's friends and family) and indirect contact with more abstract reference groups (the media). Normative differential association refers to the norms one comes into contact with due to his or her association with these groups. Naturally, the more drug-using friends that one has, the more one will be exposed to norms favorable to drug use.

One's definitions are derived from one's differential associations. Definitions are one's personal attitudes toward types of behavior. Akers further delineates between general and specific definitions. It is our specific definitions that govern our day-to-day behavior. The more one is exposed to norms favorable to drug use, the more likely one is to adopt these norms as his or her own (specific norms).

Another perspective suggests that the deviant has little control over his or her desires, and, in fact, he or she will often opt for the desires of the moment, which may include crime. . . . This person is a risk-taker, opting for the momentary pleasure at the possible expense of long-term goals and desires.

This study seeks to compare the differential effects of these three theories of deviance on disadvantaged groups, specifically racial/ethnic minorities and women. It sets out to test the following hypotheses based on previous research and the theories presented earlier.

H1. Strain (nervousness) is positively associated with chronic marijuana use.

H1A. The effect of strain is stronger for racial/ethnic minorities.

H1B. The effect of strain is stronger for females.

Past research has shown both gender and ethnic/racial differences in the effect of strain on criminal behavior. Mazerolle . . . and Hoffman and Su . . . , testing the effects of GST variables across genders, did not find significant variation. Agnew and Brezina . . . found a relationship between interpersonal strain, such as problems with interpersonal relationships, and both male and female delinquency, with the effect being more pronounced among males, with Hay . . . reporting that the effects of strain were more conducive to male delinquency. Conversely, Simpson and Elis . . . reported greater effects of school-related strain for women. Research has presented conflicting evidence of the relationship between race/ethnicity and strain. Whereas Eitle and Turner . . . state that Blacks tend to be exposed to more strain, Cernkovich, Giordano, and Rudolph . . . state that strain is only a factor in white delinquency and criminality. Although no studies have attempted to establish a link between strain and oppression among racial and ethnic minorities, Broidy and Agnew . . . did establish a link among GST, oppression, and female crime, whereas Katz . . . suggested that revised strain theory is a useful theory in understanding the effects of strain on criminality for women, particularly minority women, in a white male-dominated society.

GST indicates that deviant behavior is only one of many possible coping strategies. To this end, it is assumed that disadvantaged minorities and females (also operationalized as a disadvantaged group) will have fewer coping strategies available to them; therefore, they are more likely to become chronic marijuana users because other strategies may not be as readily available to them.

H2. Economic strain is positively associated with chronic marijuana use.

H2A. The effect of economic strain is stronger for racial/ethnic minorities.

H2B. The effect of economic strain is stronger for females.

Again, GST suggests deviant behavior as one strategy. Economic strain may be addressed through the emotional coping strategy of chronic marijuana use; disadvantaged groups may have fewer options available to them.

H3. Peer drug use is positively associated with chronic marijuana use.

H3A. The effect of peer drug use is stronger for racial/ethnic minorities.

H3B. The effect of peer drug use is stronger for females.

Although there is some evidence to suggest that the effects of social learning vary by ethnicity . . . , research is split on the differential effects of this theory on males and females. Whereas Smith and Paternoster . . . and Hartjen and Kethineni . . . found no across-gender differences, Heimer . . . also found that attitudes favorable to deviance affect both men and women similarly; however, she found differences between males and females in the effect of peer controls.

Disadvantaged groups may, by default, be more likely to depend on deviant peers for their social support networks. More traditional peer groups tend to consist of dominant or advantaged group members, and group boundaries may be less permeable, leading members of

disadvantaged groups to seek friendships within groups of deviant peers. Members of advantaged groups may also have deviant peers; however, they have more access to more traditional groups as well.

H4. Personal approval of drug use is positively associated with chronic marijuana use.

H4A. The effect of norms favorable to drug use is stronger for racial/ethnic minorities.

H4B. The effect of norms favorable to drug use is stronger for females.

Social learning and differential association suggest that exposure to a preponderance of deviant norms leads the individual to adopt deviant norms. Members of dominant or advantaged groups have more opportunity to be exposed to nondeviant norms, hence the effect of exposure to deviant norms is lessened.

H5. Willingness to participate in risky behavior is positively associated with chronic marijuana use.

H5A. The effect of participation in risky behavior is stronger for racial/ethnic minorities.

H5B. The effect of participation in risky behavior is stronger for females.

Past research has shown both gender and ethnic/racial differences in the effect of self-control on crime and deviant behavior. Although Higgins . . . found that self-control theory was a usable theory in explaining deviance by both genders, other researchers such as Keane, Maxim, and Teevan . . . ; Vazsonyi and Croswhite . . . ; Blackwell and Piquero. . . . ; and Burton, Cullen, and Evans . . . found that, although self-control is applicable to males and females, the effects generally differ between genders or, in some cases, fails to apply to all groups. . . . La Grange and Silverman . . . found differences between males and females in preference for risk-taking, with males much more likely to take risks. Findings conflict on the relationship between minority group status and self-control. Lynskey, Winfree, et al. . . . found that self-control was lowest among white gang members (compared with African Americans and Asians); however, Heilbrun and Heilbrun . . . found lower self-control among black violent offenders.

There are legitimate and extralegal means of engaging in risky behavior. Individuals from advantaged groups who enjoy participating in dangerous or risky activities may opt for legitimate thrill-seeking activities, such as extreme sports. Members of disadvantaged groups do not have access to these activities; therefore, they are more likely to engage in the relatively accessible and inexpensive activity of drug use.

Methodology

DATA

Data for this study represent a subset of 18- to 25-year-old subjects taken from the 2001 National Household Survey of Drug Abuse. This is a multistage area probability sample and includes data from all 50 states and the District of Columbia. The sample was stratified on three levels: state, field interviewer regions, and area segments of adjacent census blocks. The universe represented by the study includes the noninstitutionalized civilian population of the United States ages 12 and older.

The dataset was then modified to include only those subjects who reported having used marijuana within the past year. Subjects not having used it within the past year are assumed to be nonusers, whereas subjects who have used it at least once within the past year are assumed to be users. This resulted in a total sample of 4,601 subjects. This subsample will not reflect the general population because it has been modified to include only those subjects who report having used marijuana within the past year.

OPERATIONALIZATION

The dependent variable in this study is marijuana frequency. This variable is dichotomized to reflect either recreational or chronic marijuana use. *Recreational marijuana use* is defined as using less than 12 times a month. Chronic marijuana use is defined as using 12 times a month or more. The rationale behind this is that persons using 12 times a month (an average of 3 days a week) are not limiting their use to weekends and special occasions. Those who use less than 3 days a week or have not used in the past month, but have used in the past year, are assumed to be using marijuana in a social context—in the course of partying or other social activity.

Independent variables include strain, economic strain, norms favorable to drug use, number of friends who use drugs, and favorable attitudes toward risky behavior.

Strain is measured by a four-item index. Survey questions include: Are you more nervous than most people about crowds? Are you more nervous than most people about public places? Are you more nervous than most people about traveling? Are you more nervous than most people about being away from home? The alpha for this index is .718. The range is 0 to 4, with 0 indicating no strain and 4 indicating a maximum level of strain.

Economic strain, measured by how much public assistance the respondent's family received, was measured by a series of questions with binomial (yes/no) response categories asking whether their family received specific types of public assistance. . . .

Norms favorable to drug use was measured by a four-item index that included the following questions: How does respondent feel about adults smoking one or more packs of cigarettes a day? How does respondent feel about adults trying marijuana or hashish? How does respondent feel about adults drinking alcohol daily? How does respondent feel about adults driving after one or two drinks? The alpha for this index is .924, with a range of 4 to 12.

Number of friends who use drugs was measured by a four-item index that included the following questions: How many of the respondent's friends smoke cigarettes? How many of the respondent's friends use marijuana or hashish? How many of respondent's friends drink alcohol? How many of respondent's friends get drunk weekly? The alpha for this index is .8693, with a range of 4 to 16.

Liking risky behavior was measured by a four-item index that included the following questions: Does respondent get a real kick out of doing dangerous things? Does respondent like to test him or herself by doing risky things? Does respondent wear a seatbelt when riding in the front passenger seat of a car? Does respondent wear a seatbelt when driving a car? The alpha for this index is .777, with a range of 4 to 16.

There are three control variables in the study: marital status, employment status, and education. In each case, the variable was dichotomized to reflect the following risk categories: not married, not in labor force, and did not finish high school. Although it could be argued that unemployed persons, unmarried persons, and persons who did not finish high school also represent a disadvantaged status, the relatively young age of this sample (18- to 25-year-olds) makes it likely that most are not married, many may not be employed because they are in college, and some may still be in high school. Therefore, although the sample is stratified by race/ethnicity and gender, these three items are treated as demographic variables. . . .

Results

BIVARIATE RESULTS

. . . [M]ales are more likely to be chronic marijuana users than females. This runs counter to the original hypothesis, and gender was recoded to reflect male as the risk category. Native American/Pacific Islanders are most likely, followed by mixed-race respondents, then African Americans. Asians are least likely. Although few subjects in the sample were married, they were less likely to use chronically. Those not in the labor force and those who did not finish high school were also more likely to be chronic users. . . .

[C]hronic users experience significantly more strain, have a higher level of approval of drug use, have more friends who use drugs, and are more likely to like engaging in risky behavior. There is no significant difference between groups in level of economic strain. Therefore, this variable will not be included in the multivariate model.

MULTIVARIATE RESULTS

. . . Gender, minority group status, and education are all significantly associated with chronic marijuana use. Males are 1.05 times as likely as females, minority group members 1.24 times as likely as nonminority group members, and persons not having finished high school are 1.44 times as likely to be chronic marijuana users. Strain, approval of drug use, the number of friends who use drugs, and a liking for risky behavior are all positively associated with the likelihood of chronic marijuana use, as predicted by the hypotheses.

. . . Analyses of nonminority and minority groups included gender in the model (female being the risk factor), and analyses of male and female groups included minority group status in the model. . . .

Gender and education are risk factors only for nonminority group members, whereas marital status is a risk factor only for minority group members. Hypotheses 1 through 5 state that all independent variables affect minority group members more than they do nonminority group members. Economic strain (hypotheses 2, 2A, and 2B) did not have a significant effect on the dependent variables, therefore it was excluded from the analysis. Hypothesis 1A appears to be supported because strain has a stronger effect on chronic marijuana use by minorities. However, approval of drug use and the number of friends who use drugs are more strongly associated with the dependent variable for nonminority group members. Hypotheses 3A and 4A do not appear to be supported. Liking to engage in risky behavior is significantly associated with the dependent variable for minority group members only; therefore, hypothesis 5A also appears to be supported.

Minority group status is significantly associated with chronic marijuana use for females only; however, education is significant for both males and females and, in fact, has a stronger effect of chronic marijuana use by males than females. Hypotheses 1B, 3B, 4B, and 5B are all supported because the effect of strain, approval of drug use, number of friends who use drugs, and liking to engage in risky behavior are all more strongly associated with chronic marijuana use by females.

Discussion

This study only looks at levels of use within the marijuana-using population. Within this population, males, minority group members, high school dropouts, persons experiencing strain (defined as social anxiety), those who personally approve of drug use, those who have friends who use drugs, and those who like to engage in risky behavior are more likely to be chronic, as opposed to recreational, drug users. However, this study attempted to ascertain whether there were differences between advantaged and disadvantaged groups, as defined as racial/ethnic minorities and females. For the most part, the hypotheses were supported.

Among nonminority group members (whites), males were slightly more likely (1.03 times) than females to be chronic users. Those who did not finish high school were 1.6 times as likely as those who did. Strain, approval of drug use, and the number of friends who use drugs were also associated with chronic use; however, risky behavior was not. Nonmarried minority group members were 2.2 times as likely as married ones to be chronic users, and strain, approval of drug use, number of friends who use drugs, and risky behavior were associated with chronic use. Notable differences between nonminority and minority groups include gender and education affecting only nonminorities and marital status and risky behavior affecting only minorities. Strain significantly affects both groups' level of marijuana use, indicating support for GST; however, the fact that it has a stronger effect on minority group members suggests the possibility that minorities, lacking resources, may have fewer alternative strategies for dealing with strain and, hence, may be more likely to become chronic users. Social learning appears to have a stronger effect on non-minorities, whereas self-control is only significantly associated with level of use for minorities.

Females were also defined as disadvantaged minorities. The data suggest that minority group status does have a significant effect on female level of marijuana use; in fact, minority females are almost $1^1/_2$ times as likely as nonminority females to be chronic users. This may tie into strain theory because the experience of being a double minority could create a form of strain. Education affected both male and female levels of use, although it had a stronger effect on males. This also may reflect a form of strain; the male who did not finish high school will most likely experience a higher level of strain than the female because the employment expectations for males have been traditionally higher, and this group of males may feel shut out of the economic structure and cope with the strain through higher levels of use. The data show that, although social learning and self-control affect both males and females, they have a stronger effect on females, and strain is associated with female chronic use. Females, like minority group members, may have fewer alternative coping strategies (as addressed by GST). Peer effects (social learning) also have a stronger effect; this may reflect the greater importance women traditionally place on personal relations, which then intensifies peer group effects. Finally, low self-control, at least with regards to marijuana use, has a stronger effect on women.

. . . The net effects of each theoretical construct presented . . . clearly show that, regardless of gender or minority group status, social learning variables have the strongest effect on chronic marijuana use. Most important is association with deviant peers, operationalized as the number of friends who use drugs, followed by a personal approval of drug use. Strain, operationalized as nervousness in social situations, has the third strongest net effect. Self-control, although significantly associated with chronic marijuana use, has the weakest effect. Overall, social learning appears to have the greatest explanatory power for this type of behavior.

However, the relevance and power of each theoretical construct varies between groups. Among nonminority group members, social learning explanations are most significant (again, the number of drug-using friends is the strongest effect, followed by personal approval of drug use), followed by strain. Self-control (as measured by a liking for risky behavior) is not associated with chronic marijuana use in this population. However,

when looking at the relative effects of the three theories on minority group marijuana use, strain becomes the most significant factor. Although Cernkovich, Giordano, and Rudolph . . . state that strain is only a factor in white delinquency and criminality, these data suggest that it is a major factor in chronic drug use by racial/ethnic minority group members.

The relative effects of social learning and strain among males closely reflects the patterns found in the nonminority group subsample. Social learning variables clearly had the most explanatory power, with the number of drug-using friends having the strongest effect. Among males, the self-control variable is significantly associated; however, this may be a reflection of the fact that nonminority and minority males (among whom self-control was a significant factor) are included in this subsample.

Social learning and strain appear to have near-identical effects on chronic marijuana use by females, with the number of drug-using friends most strongly associated, followed by strain. Furthermore, a comparison of the betas for minority group members and for females on the strain variable (.201 and .218, respectively) suggest a similar effect. Additionally, the significant effect of minority group status on marijuana use by females only suggests that, reflective of Katz's . . . study, strain theory is a useful tool in the study of crime and deviance among women, and particularly minority women. Thus, perhaps, double minorities, such as racial/ethnic minority women, are most susceptible to the effects of strain and subsequent deviant behavior.

Implications of the Present Study

As stated earlier, young adults are more likely than any other age group to use marijuana. Because this age group also encompasses the traditional college age population, the results of this study may point professionals both on and off campus toward more effective means of addressing drug (especially marijuana) use by this population. It also distinguishes between chronic and recreational users. This is important because it is the life of the chronic user that is more likely to be negatively impacted by his or her drug use. In targeting the chronic user, universities and other agencies dealing with this population may be able to conserve resources and target their programs to individuals who are using the drug more than recreationally.

Based on these data, agencies may want to tailor their programs to address the needs of unique populations. For example, strain appears to have a stronger effect on minorities and females. Therefore, counselors and programs may want to emphasize coping strategies for these populations and, when dealing with male clients, focus their efforts on educational attainment. For many years, Alcoholics Anonymous has tailored programs to meet the needs of diverse populations (e.g., there are meetings for Latinos, Gays, women only, etc.). Although Narcotics Anonymous has adopted similar programming, by focusing only on those groups that use drugs more than recreationally and targeting programming to specific populations, agencies working with drug users may find their programs more effective and less costly.

Questions

1. How do recreational users of marijuana differ from chronic users?

2. How do the authors define and measure strain in this study?

CHAPTER 14

Neighborhood Context and Police Use of Force

William Terrill

Northeastern University

Michael D. Reisig

Michigan State University

orce lies at the core of the police function . . . . It is no surprise, then, that this form of police behavior has long been a primary focus among those who study the police. . . . A considerable portion of this research centers on why officers resort to force. Much of this work focuses on situationally based determinants and officer attributes inherent in police–citizen encounters. To a lesser extent, researchers have also sought to investigate the influence of organizational factors on police use of force. With but a few notable exceptions . . . , multivariate examinations of the role of neighborhood context on police use of force practices are noticeably absent.

Using data collected as part of a systematic social observation study of the police in Indianapolis, Indiana, and St. Petersburg, Florida, the research reported here examines the degree to which forceful authority toward suspects is influenced by the type of neighborhood in which police–suspect encounters occur. Our objective is to determine the effect of neighborhood context on the day-to-day exercise of force by patrol officers. Do officers exercise force differently in some neighborhoods as opposed to others? . . .

Explanations of Police Use of Force

For more than three decades, researchers have expended considerable effort to explain the causes of police use of

force. These efforts generally have been framed within three broad perspectives. Two in particular—sociological and psychological—have guided a majority of prior systematic inquires. Within the sociological (or situational) domain, researchers have assessed the influence of social status on punitive police behavior. . . . For example, Black . . . posited that the application of punishment by legal agents can be explained in terms of various types of social space in which the subjects of control are located. Black . . . hypothesized that the police will be more punitive (e.g., forceful) toward suspects with lower economic or marginal cultural status, such as the poor, minorities, and the young. Furthermore, those who are under the influence of drugs and/or alcohol, mentally deranged, disrespectful, resistant, or filled with anger are placed in a negative normative space. These suspects are said to offend society's—and the police officer's—standards of appropriate behavior, or they appear to lack self-control. In either case, these suspects are viewed by the police as more deserving of control and punishment. . . .

A second perspective is framed within a psychological (or individual) orientation. According to this approach, officer characteristics, experiences, views, and outlooks are posited to affect police behavior. . . . Simply stated, is there something about particular officers that help explain why they use force? This explanation rests on the assumption that officers with certain traits, experiences, or attitudes will respond differently in similar

Source: "Neighborhood context and police use of force," by Terrill, W., & Reisig, M. D., (2003), in *Journal of Research in Crime and Delinquency, 40,* 291–321. Reprinted by permission of Sage Publications.

situations. Muir's . . . theoretical orientation may best illustrate the role of the individual. Muir . . . was primarily interested in characterizing "good" versus "bad" police officers. He constructed a fourfold typology into which officers could be grouped depending on the following two dimensions: their view of human nature and their attitude toward the use of coercive authority.

A third approach involves examining the role of the organization in use-of-force practices. Different variants of organization theory have been proposed that emphasize formal and informal features of the organization. . . . For example, Wilson . . . posited that the formal structure of an organization and the political environment within which it operates create predictable patterns of police behavior. More specifically, Wilson presumed that styles of policing reflect organizational rules, regulations, standard operating procedures, incentives and disincentives, and administrative direction. In other words, a common vision becomes part of each officer's mindset of how to handle the everyday aspects of police work. Accordingly, individual officers will handle similar incidents that occur at the street level in a consistent manner. A different perspective looks to the effect of the informal structure (e.g., police culture), rather than the formal structure. . . . According to this framework, the police culture serves to protect and isolate officers from internal and external scrutiny more than it does to forge a particular style of policing. Instead, operating through the protection of one another, officers are able to develop their own unique styles.

Although these conceptual frameworks have contributed to our understanding of police use of force, several limitations are apparent. Perhaps most important, each of these perspectives fails to take into account the possibility that police use of force varies according to the broader context concerning where the encounter takes place. Given the likelihood that aggressive police tactics are not evenly distributed across urban neighborhoods . . . , the potential for spurious findings at the encounter level is a real possibility. To better understand the dynamics of police use of force, a rigorous empirical assessment, which entails the estimation of a well-specified multilevel model, is needed.

The Ecology of Police Force

In the Chicago School's tradition of neighborhood ecology . . . , police researchers have begun to focus on the effects of neighborhood context on police behavior. . . . Nevertheless, research in this area remains sparse.

Concerning the link between police behavior and neighborhood context, Slovak . . . noted,

> there is no solid lead to follow from the research of others in this regard, for almost no serious efforts to tie ecological variations within a city to police patterns in particular or to social control efforts in general have yet appeared. . . .

Ten years later, Klinger . . . echoed Slovak's observation, stating, "A few studies have considered the possibility that police action might vary across urban neighborhoods . . . but none contains any systematic theory linking police activity to the ecological contexts in which it occurs." . . . Clouding matters further, the literature dealing specifically with police use of force in this regard is even more remote. However, despite the lack of a logically ordered set of propositions that explain and predict use of force across neighborhoods, the literature does provide some guidance.

Although a few scholars previously speculated on the relationship between neighborhood context and police behavior . . . , it was not until the 1960s that researchers began to seriously consider the issue. One of the most illuminating studies was conducted by Werthman and Piliavin . . . , who observed and interviewed Oakland and San Francisco, California, patrol officers. The authors concluded that officers tend to associate neighborhoods with the degree to which they encountered suspicious persons. Officers not only rely on various cues to define a so-called suspicious person (e.g., running from police, appearing to conceal a weapon or contraband, and previous arrests), but also define geographic areas as suspicious places. . . .

Werthman and Piliavin . . . referred to this process as "ecological contamination," whereby *everyone* encountered in designated "bad" neighborhoods assumes moral liability. In effect, the socioeconomic character of the area in which the police encounter the suspect may attach to the individual suspect independent of the suspect's personal characteristics or behavioral manifestations.

Bayley and Mendelsohn . . . also picked up on the neighborhood–police behavior nexus, arguing that police are more aggressive (e.g., stopping citizens and using force) and punitive (e.g., making arrests) when operating in lower class and high-crime neighborhoods. In these neighborhoods, the authors argued, greater social distance exists between police officers and citizens. Consistent with Werthman and Piliavin's . . . ecological contamination hypothesis, Bayley and

Mendelsohn . . . posited that a suspect's mere presence in a bad neighborhood increases the likelihood that the suspect will be the recipient of police aggression.

Perhaps the most rigorous study exploring the effect of neighborhood context on police behavior was conducted by Smith . . . , using data from the Police Services Study. Smith examined the effect of a number of different community characteristics (e.g., crime rate and socioeconomic factors) on different forms of police behavior (e.g., arrest, coercive authority, and filing official reports). One of his primary conclusions was strikingly similar to Werthman and Piliavin's . . . ecological contamination hypothesis. At the encounter level, officers were significantly more likely to use force on Black suspects, but this effect was mediated when neighborhood context was considered. Smith . . . concluded that the "propensity of police to exercise coercive authority is not influenced by the race of the individual suspect per se but rather the racial composition of the area in which the encounter occurs." . . . Furthermore, he found that citizens encountered in low-status areas ran three times the risk of arrest. To date, however, empirical support for Smith's . . . findings remain elusive. For example, Slovak's . . . examination of organizational and environmental characteristics in three medium-sized cities led to his conclusion that police aggressiveness is "generally similar across the neighborhoods of a given city." . . .

More recently, an ecological theory has been articulated to account specifically for variations in the vigor with which formal police authority is applied. Klinger . . . referred to vigor as a form of "legal authority in encounters with citizens by making arrests, taking reports, conducting investigations, and so on." . . . Drawing on Durkheim and other social theorists, Klinger . . . postulated that formal police efforts are less vigorous in districts in which deviance levels are high. Levels of deviance affect workload and resource constraints for dealing with crime and disorder, as well as officers' understanding of what constitutes so-called normal crime, how to define deserving victims, and cynicism about the effectiveness of the department's and the justice system's efforts to control deviance. Like other community-level explanations, Klinger's . . . perspective might be adapted to explain police force according to the socioeconomic character of the neighborhood where police encounter criminal suspects.

One of the difficulties with using Klinger's . . . theory as a conceptual guide to model police use of force is determining the direction of the influence of neighborhood context. For example, a loose definition of police force would include all forms of legal authority

(e.g., not just arrest), and we might hypothesize that police use less force in disadvantaged, high-crime neighborhoods. Klinger . . . noted that, unlike arrests, police use of force does not always entail a high level of vigor. For example, physically restraining a suspect or using chemical mace without making an arrest may actually constitute less vigor. Complicating matters more with respect to the study at hand, Klinger's . . . theory is directed at a unit of analysis (e.g., police district) much larger than the individual neighborhood. Whether Klinger's . . . theory predicts less or more coercive policing in disadvantaged and high-crime neighborhoods remains open to debate.

Other police scholars have also communicated a certain reluctance to support the notion that police officers are more aggressive in poor, crime-ridden neighborhoods. For example, after examining police practices in one depressed neighborhood, Goldstein . . . reported that police rarely took an official report or made an arrest in serious assault cases. Similarly, Reiss and Bordua . . . noted that, although officers act more aggressively in depressed neighborhoods in certain situations, officers were reluctant to intervene in others . . . . In combination, these studies suggest that as levels of deviance and socioeconomic distress increase in a given area, a number of factors, such as those mentioned by Klinger . . . (e.g., workload, regularity of crime, cynicism, attached worth given to the victim, etc.), will also influence officers' use of coercive authority unless the incident in question is of a serious nature (e.g., homicide incident).

Where does this leave us? There are clearly similarities and differences found in the literature with respect to the role of neighborhood context. One of the difficulties with comparing extant research concerns the variation in methodological approaches (e.g., ethnography and official records), as well as the ambiguity of conceptual definitions, such as police aggressiveness and vigor. Nevertheless, with the exception of Slovak's . . . study, a consistent theme has emerged: Police behavior is patterned territorially. Police officers come to readily compartmentalize various geographic areas, within which the potential exists to behave in accordance with the environment, as opposed to the suspect's characteristics. This may result in suspects encountered in disadvantaged and high-crime neighborhoods being subjected to higher levels of force. However, it may also result in less forceful behavior. Moreover, we must also consider that suspect behavior also varies across neighborhoods. For example, McCluskey and colleagues . . . found that criminal suspects encountered by police in neighborhoods characterized by comparatively higher levels of concentrated disadvantage were significantly more likely to display disrespect toward the police. Most studies have found that suspect behavior is a significant determinant of police use of force. . . . Accordingly, we might expect to observe higher levels of police use of force in disadvantaged neighborhoods.

We seek to inform this line of inquiry using recently collected data and statistical modeling techniques designed specifically for nested data. We examine the role of neighborhood context after adjusting our models for a host of encounter-level and officer-based determinants of police use of force. Uncovering patterns of police use of force is challenging because of the degree of sensitivity that such a topic presents. Systematic observational inquiry provides a rare opportunity to experience firsthand forceful police practices as they occur on the street, a picture difficult to obtain using other methodologies. Official records, police surveys, and citizen complaints are common data sources used to study police use of force, but in each instance the party responsible for detailing the circumstances has a stake in the reporting. In contrast, systematic field observations rely on disinterested third parties trained to remove themselves from the target of observation. In summary, we seek to advance the police use-of-force literature by using systematic social observational data, which is well suited for the task at hand.

We also seek to contribute to the research literature by addressing various technical shortcomings that may have been present in previous attempts to better understand the role of neighborhood context. For example, previous endeavors have relied on multivariate statistical techniques not specifically designed to model data with a nested structure (e.g., police–suspect encounters nested within neighborhoods). Relying on such techniques (e.g., ordinary least squares regression) raises several important issues. . . .

Methods

Data

This study uses the following four sources of data originally collected by the Project on Policing Neighborhoods: systematic social observations, census data, police crime records, and in-person interviews with police officers. Twelve beats in each city (Indianapolis and St. Petersburg) were selected as study beats, and observers were assigned to ride with the officers assigned to these beats. The study beats from each site were

selected to closely match the degree of socioeconomic distress (i.e., the sum of percentage of poverty, percentage of female-headed families, and percentage unemployed). Omitted in the sampling design were police beats with the lowest levels of socioeconomic distress (i.e., the most affluent districts). In other words, observers were assigned to officers patrolling areas in which police–citizens encounters were expected to be more frequent. Nonetheless, because of the nature of workload requirements (e.g., calls for service), officers often interacted with citizens in nonstudy beats as well. Hence, systematic observations were recorded in 97 of the 98 total beats (50 in Indianapolis and 48 in St. Petersburg). Each site drew beat boundaries to reflect as closely as possible existing neighborhood boundaries; hereafter, these aggregates are referred to as neighborhoods.

In the summer months of 1996 and 1997, trained graduate and honor undergraduate students served as field observers. Field observers accompanied officers assigned to selected neighborhoods throughout a matched sample of work shifts. Observation sessions oversampled busier days and shifts. During their time with officers, observers took notes and spent the following day transcribing their notes into detailed accounts and coding them according to a predefined protocol. Approximately 240 hours of observation were carried out for officers assigned to each neighborhood. . . . A police–citizen encounter was defined as a face-to-face communication between officers and citizens that was more than a passing greeting. In all, 6,500 citizen encounters were observed in Indianapolis and 5,500 in St. Petersburg. The length of police–citizen encounters ranged from less than a minute to several hours. The citizens included crime victims, witnesses, a variety of service recipients, and criminal suspects. The analysis presented here focuses on police–suspect encounters.

Suspects were defined as wrongdoers, peace disturbers, or persons for whom a complaint was received. More specifically, individuals were considered suspects by observers if any of the following criteria were met: police identified the citizen as a suspect, interrogated, searched, issued threats or warning, used force to prevent or stop wrongdoing, arrested, or cited the citizen, or if the citizen admitted wrongdoing. This presents a somewhat difficult problem, in that part of the inclusion criteria for becoming a suspect involves the dependent measure (i.e., force), which is akin to partially sampling on the dependent variable. In the present case, however, this is unavoidable. The alternative would have been to exclude such cases, which clearly would present a much greater problem—the fact that there would be no way to analyze any of the force cases because there would be none. Furthermore, there were several cases in which the officer used force on citizens not labeled as suspects (e.g., victims requiring restraint after being told their partner was killed in an automobile accident). Observers were instructed not to regard the inclusion criteria in such strict terms so as to skew or alter the overall meaning of the word *suspect*. Overall, 3,544 police–suspect encounters involving 305 officers were observed. . . .

Dependent Variable

Extant research demonstrates that, in any given police–citizen encounter, officers can and do apply numerous forms of both physical and nonphysical force (e.g., verbal threats). To capture this variation, we define police force as acts that threaten or inflict physical harm on suspects. This definition is based on the National Academy of Science's (NAS) definition of violence and has been applied in previous studies of police use of force. . . . Traditionally, researchers have focused on physical forms of force, especially actions that are above and beyond simple restraint techniques (i.e., excluding pat downs and handcuffing). Doing so seems fairly reasonable given that researchers have often been interested in excessive force, which usually entails more extreme forms of physical force. Nonetheless, such a conventional or traditional definition of force has often carried over to additional studies that have not focused on excessive force. This is somewhat puzzling given that the mere definition of physical force involves exactly that—physical force, which indeed involves pat downs and handcuffs. Failure to include such forceful acts within a measure of force would be misleading at best and wholly inappropriate at worst. Clearly, the act of physically restraining a suspect, either through a pat down search or the use of handcuffs, constitutes a degree of harm consistent with how the NAS defines violence and how previous researchers have conceptualized forceful police behavior. . . .

In addition, researchers have generally not considered verbal forms of force (commands and threats) in their definition of force. In recent years, however, researchers have come to recognize the importance of adopting a broader definition of force. For instance, several scholars . . . have called on researchers to consider commands and threats in the universe of behaviors considered force because of the coercive nature of these acts. In the case of commands, the threat to do harm is implicit, whereas a threat is explicit. Garner et al. . . . , Klinger . . . , and Alpert and Dunham . . . all recognized that verbal force does not have to include an explicit

threat outright. For example, Garner and colleagues . . . considered verbal force to include instances when "officers shouted or used a command voice." . . . Klinger . . . defined verbal force as "verbal orders that officers issue to citizens." . . . Alpert and Dunham . . . placed verbal force in their minimal force classification, which includes "strong directive language." . . .

Within this context, our dependent variable includes forceful police behavior that captures a variety of behaviors located throughout the force continuum—both physical and verbal manifestations. More specifically, the highest level of force reflects the severity of force imposed on suspects and placed along a continuum ranging from least to most severe harm . . . . Force was ranked in the following manner: none, verbal (commands and threats), physical restraint (pat downs, firm grip, and handcuffing), and impact methods (pain compliance techniques, takedown maneuvers, strikes with the body, and strikes with external mechanisms). Coded observations ranged along a four-point scale, from 1 (*no force*) to 2 (*verbal force*), 3 (*restraint techniques*), and 4 (*impact methods*) at the encounter level (mean = 1.81, $SD = .81$). The percentage of encounters in which each form of force represented the highest level of force used by officers is as follows: verbal (37%), restraint techniques (19%), and impact methods (2%). In 42% of police–suspect encounters, no force was used. Because the distribution of our dependent variable, level of force, was positively skewed (i.e., toward the right of the mode frequencies taper off), we used a natural log transformation so as to better approximate a normal distribution (mean = .49, $SD = .45$).

It is important to note that police sometimes use more than one level of force on a given suspect. However, for this analysis, interest lies only in the highest level used. The dependent measure does not reflect attempts by officers to use lower levels, either before or after the highest level was applied. Accordingly, we do not attempt to distinguish officers who began with low levels of force, such as commands or threats, escalating only to higher levels of physical force when lower levels failed to achieve their objectives. Although the dynamics of force within an encounter are worthy of inquiry for exploring the evolution of police tactics during encounters, such an analysis is beyond the scope of the present research. The focus here is on how much force was ultimately applied so as to judge the effect of the various determinants on force generally and neighborhood factors specifically. In addition, only the force used by the officer selected for observation was coded. Force applied by other officers who were present was not attributed to the observed officer, which would introduce error when attempting to associate characteristics of the officer with the decisions he or she made.

Finally, we do not attempt to distinguish whether the application of force satisfied a particular standard (e.g., excessive vs. not excessive). Although certainly worthwhile, that is an entirely different enterprise. By limiting our analysis in this way, we cannot judge whether police over- or underused force in any instance. We can, however, characterize patterns in the distribution of force and speak to questions about economy in the use of force, which Bittner . . . noted as the defining value of contemporary Western society for good policing.

Independent Variables

Neighborhood-level variables. We operationalized neighborhood structure using 1990 census data. Concentrated disadvantage is a weighted factor score that includes the following census items: percentage poverty, percentage unemployed, percentage female-headed families, and percentage African American (eigenvalue $= 3.07$, factor loadings $> .80$). Extant theory and research suggests that this measure represents racially segregated, economic disadvantage. . . . Descriptive statistics revealed that the distribution of concentrated disadvantage was skewed. To correct for this, we added a constant (1.5) to the term, thus eliminating negative values, and we adjusted the distribution using a natural log transformation. . . .

To capture variations in crime, a second neighborhood-level variable, homicide rate, was included in the analysis. We selected homicide because it is widely considered by criminologists to be the most reliable measure of crime that is least sensitive to underreporting. . . . Homicide rate was the rate of police-recorded homicides per 1,000 neighborhood residents. Data from the calendar year 1995 were used for Indianapolis neighborhoods (number of homicides $= 93$), and 1996 data were used for neighborhoods located in St. Petersburg (number of homicides $= 23$). Because the distribution was skewed, we analyzed the natural log.

Encounter-level variables. We included an array of variables at the encounter level. Among these factors are suspect sociodemographic characteristics, such as male, minority, age, and wealth. . . . We also included a number of additional variable clusters at the encounter level, consistent with previous theory as noted earlier (e.g., sociological and psychological), including suspect presentation (e.g., suspect resistance, alcohol use, and mental impairment), officer characteristics (e.g., sex, race,

education, and training), officer attitudes (e.g., crime-fighting orientation), and additional measures used as statistical controls (e.g., citizen audience) in some of the multivariate models. Variable descriptions and coding schemes, as well as bivariate associations for the encounter-level variables used in the analysis, are presented in the appendixes.

Finally, citizen behaviors must have occurred prior to the highest level of force. Studies that seek to explain or predict use of force decisions often look at the police–citizen encounter as if it were a single discrete event without noting the developmental nature over time within that event. Nonobservational studies in particular are often lacking in this regard because reconstruction of when during the encounter various citizen actions occur cannot usually be determined. Researchers are left to speculate or assume that certain actions occurred prior to the use of police force. Nonetheless, even studies based on observational data can be limited to some extent. For instance, Worden . . . in his analysis found that antagonistic citizens were significantly more likely to be on the receiving end of some type of physical force. However, we do not know whether the citizen's antagonistic behavior preceded or followed an officer's forceful behavior. Unless careful attention is given to when various behaviors occur, one cannot establish a causal relationship. As a result, five of the predictor variables (e.g., suspect disrespect, suspect resistance, arrest, weapon, and citizen conflict) used in the present inquiry are referred to as timing variables, meaning that they needed to be coded according to when they occurred during the encounter. Unlike a static variable (e.g., citizen gender), which cannot change during the course of the encounter, timing variables can. Hence, these five timing variables are coded to ensure a causal relationship (e.g., occurred prior to the highest level of force).

Results

We now turn our attention to the multivariate analyses. Our primary interest concerns the effects of neighborhood context on the level of force police use during encounters with criminal suspects. Table 14.1 presents three different multivariate models for level of force. Model 1 reports estimates derived from a weighted least squares (WLS) regression model. Here, the outcome measure is the neighborhood mean for level of police force ($N = 80$). Descriptive statistics revealed that a few high-end outliers existed. To reduce the skewing effect, we analyze a square-root transformation of level of force . . . . Unlike traditional ordinary least squares regression, WLS allowed us to give more weight to neighborhoods where more observations of police–suspect encounters were recorded. Each case was weighted by the square root of the number of police–suspect encounters per neighborhood. The results suggest that concentrated disadvantage and homicide rate are both linked to level of force. In terms of relative importance, the magnitude of the coefficients appear similar (β = .23 and .27, respectively). Overall, model 1 shows that higher levels of force were significantly more likely to be used against suspects encountered in crime-ridden and disadvantaged neighborhoods. Because these effects were observed in the absence of encounter-level statistical control variables, this represents a relatively lenient test of the effects of neighborhood context on level of police force.

Model 2 in Table 14.1 is an encounter-level ordinary least squares regression equation (N = 3,330). In this model, we seek to determine whether the suspects' sociodemographic characteristics influence the level of force used by police. The results show that male, minority, youthful, and lower income suspects were more likely to be on the receiving end of higher levels of police force, net of encounter-level statistical controls. These results support our contention that a true test concerning the effects of neighborhood context on level of force should include a host of encounter-level variables, such as suspect sociodemographic characteristics, to control for within-neighborhood variance in observed instances of police use of force.

To stage a more rigorous test of the effects of neighborhood context, which would adjust for encounter-level covariates, we proceeded to simultaneously regress level of force on both neighborhood- and encounter-level variables using hierarchical linear modeling techniques. We

Table 14.1 Multivariate Models for Level of Force

Item	Model 1			Model 2[a]			Model 3[a]		
	b	β	t Ratio	b	β	t Ratio	b	β	t Ratio
Constant	1.35 (.01)	—	124.51***	.31 (.08)	—	4.08***	.48 (.01)	—	39.06***
Male	—	—	—	.09 (.02)	.09	6.03***	.09 (.02)	.09	5.48***
Age	—	—	—	−.03 (.01)	−.10	−6.17***	−.03 (.00)	−.10	−6.13***
Wealth	—	—	—	−.05 (.01)	−.06	−4.07***	−.03 (.01)	−.04	−2.55*
Concentrated disadvantage	.02 (.01)	.23	2.14*	—	—	—	.03 (.01)	.21	2.01*
Homicide rate	.03[b] (.00)	.27	2.53*	—	—	—	.04[b]	.26	2.65*
F ratio		7.38***		38.60***				—	
Within-neighborhood explained variance		—			.23			.22	
Between-neighborhood explained variance		.14[c]			—			.08	
Chi-squared		—			—			217.08***	

Note. Standard error in parentheses.

[a]Estimates control for encounter-level variables reported in Appendix B.

[b]Multiplied by 10.

[c]Coefficient of determination (adjusted).

*P < .05. **P < .01. ***P < .001 (two-tailed test).

began by first estimating a one-way ANOVA model for level of force at the encounter level. . . . Doing so provided us with several descriptive statistics to determine whether hierarchical modeling is appropriate for these data. First, we assessed the neighborhood reliability of the outcome measure at the neighborhood level. We calculated the reliability (λ) of the sample mean, β_{0j}, as the average of neighborhood-specific reliabilities across the set of neighborhoods, j, using the following formula: $\lambda_j = \Sigma \; (\tau_{00}/[\tau_{00} + \sigma^2/N_j])/_j$, where τ_{00} is the between-neighborhood variance, σ^2 is the within-neighborhood variance, and N equals the sample size in each of j neighborhoods. The reliability estimate for level of force ($\lambda = .58$) indicated that the sample mean was a reliable indicator of the true neighborhood mean. In other words, we concluded that we would be able to model neighborhood-level effects with an acceptable degree of precision.

Next, we calculated an intraclass correlation coefficient (ρ) for the outcome measure: $\rho = \tau_{00}/(\tau_{00} + \sigma^2)$. The intraclass correlation (ICC) reveals the proportion of variance between neighborhoods in the outcome variable. The ICC for level of force was .04, which indicates that approximately 4% of the variance in level of force was between neighborhoods. Stated differently, the amount of variation within neighborhoods plus variation attributable to measurement error for level of force was approximately 96%. Prior researchers using multilevel models have reported similar results . . . . The question remains, however, whether enough variation in level of force exists between neighborhoods to model as a function of contextual factors. To address this question, we turn to the chi-square value for between-neighborhood variance. The chi-square statistic is statistically significant ($\chi^2 = 203.70, P < .001$). We can therefore reject the null hypothesis that no differences in level of force exist across neighborhoods. Overall, the neighborhood reliability, ICC, and chi-square indicate that the data were suitable for estimating hierarchical linear models.

Model 3 in Table 14.1 is a fixed-effects hierarchical regression model. Using the fixed-effects model allows us to constrain the encounter-level slopes, thus not allowing them to vary as a function of neighborhood-level conditions. This adjustment is consistent with the objective of the analysis—to test the effects of neighborhood-level predictors, not to investigate the potential for multilevel interactions. The constant, β_{0j}, was allowed to vary across neighborhoods and is modeled as a function of neighborhood-level conditions (e.g., concentrated disadvantage). The neighborhood-level model took the following form:

$$\beta_{0j} = \gamma_{00} + \gamma_{01} \; (\text{concentrated disadvantage}) + \gamma_{02} \; (\text{homicide rate}) + u_{0j}.$$

In the neighborhood-level model, b_{0j} is the neighborhood mean for level of force. The model is also specified with a random error term (u_{0j}), which represents the variability remaining once the neighborhood-level predictors are controlled. The neighborhood-level variables were centered on the grand mean, and encounter-level variables were centered around the group mean. . . .

The neighborhood effects observed in model 1 persist in model 3. In other words, both concentrated disadvantage and homicide rate are related to level of force in the expected direction, net of 26 encounter-level variables. Simply put, police are significantly more likely to use higher levels of force when encountering criminal suspects in high-crime areas and neighborhoods with high levels of concentrated disadvantage independent of suspect behavior, officer characteristics, and other statistical controls. When comparing model 1 to model 3 in Table 14.1, an interesting finding emerges. The effect of minority diminished below statistical significance in the hierarchical model ($P = .17$). More specifically, the standardized coefficient (β) for minority was reduced by 50% (from .04 to .02). In summary, it appears that race is confounded by neighborhood context: Minority suspects are more likely to be recipients of higher levels of police force because they are disproportionately encountered in disadvantaged and high-crime neighborhoods. It is also worth noting that the effects of male, age, and wealth persist once neighborhood contextual variables are entered into the equation. The standardized regression coefficients indicate that age and male are stronger predictors ($-.10$ and $.09$, respectively) when compared with wealth. The magnitude of these effects, however, is relatively modest when compared to homicide rate ($\beta = .26$) and concentrated disadvantage ($\beta = .21$).

Further Tests

In a recent review of contemporary urban poverty research, Small and Newman . . . noted that the use of poverty-related indexes, such as concentrated disadvantage "do not help us discern which neighborhood characteristics affect people and which do not." . . . We adopted the use of concentrated disadvantage for the following three reasons: (a) the use of a composite poverty index is parsimonious, (b) the census items used to construct concentrated disadvantage are highly correlated with one another, and (c) we were interested in the level of force police used during encounters with criminal suspects in neighborhoods characterized by the conditions described by Wilson. . . . Nevertheless, we do find merit in Small and Newman's observation, and the bivariate relationships between the four census items used to construct concentrated disadvantage and the outcome variable of interest (i.e., level of force aggregated to the neighborhood level) are provided in Table 14.2. The economic variables (i.e., poverty and unemployment) were, in relative terms, more strongly correlated with level of force. Family structure and race were more modestly associated with neighborhood levels of police force. It should be noted that these four bivariate relationships were weaker when compared with the association between neighborhood level of force and concentrated disadvantage ($r = .27$). The high intercorrelations between the items used to construct concentrated disadvantage (from .58 to .81) precludes the estimation of a multivariate model. Although the results reported in Table 14.2 are informative, it appears that grouping these measures into a weighted index, which reflects racially segregated economic disadvantage, provides a more parsimonious and powerful indicator of neighborhood context that can also be used when estimating multivariate models.

Discussion

The findings presented here support Werthman and Piliavin's . . . "ecological contamination" hypothesis. We find that officers are significantly more likely to use higher levels of force when encountering criminal suspects in high-crime areas and neighborhoods with high levels of concentrated disadvantage independent of suspect behavior and other statistical controls. There are a number of plausible interpretations that might explain such behavior. First, based on previous experience, officers may come to know or identify certain places as problem places just as they may come to know certain persons as problem persons. Within the framework of police work, this often involves a certain degree of perceived danger. . . . Problem places correspond to dangerous places and dangerous places correspond to officer safety. As noted by Herbert . . . , "incidents are considered especially dangerous depending upon their geographic location . . . considerations of safety, in other words, lead officers to define particular areas as laden with danger, and they respond accordingly." . . . Hence, when officers operate in areas of heightened danger (characterized by high levels of distress and crime), they may be more likely to apply higher levels of force.

A second explanation may result from the perception that force is seen as an acceptable mechanism of conflict management in an environment in which force by forceful means is more the norm . . . . Officers may simply be more likely to resort to force because this is the manner in which conflict is resolved in these types of neighborhoods. As noted by Fyfe . . . , one might readily expect more police violence where there is more crime and violence in the community. More specifically, the use

Table 14.2   Additional Bivariate Statistics at the Neighborhood Level

Item	1	2	3	4	5
1 Level of force	1.0				
2 Percentage poverty	.23*	1.0			
3 Percentage unemployed	.18	.77**	1.0		
4 Percentage female-headed families	.11	.81***	.65**	1.0	
5 Percentage African American	.13	.61**	.58**	.71**	1.0
Mean	.48	22.92	9.13	18.42	42.63
SD	.13	13.60	5.12	10.87	37.66
Minimum	.15	4.47	1.15	2.68	.00
Maximum	.90	66.25	23.75	60.24	100.00

*$P < .05$. **$P < .01$ (two-tailed test).

of force may be seen as a more acceptable way of doing business. In addition, officers may feel isolated from external consequences in such neighborhoods. . . .

So-called getting away with using force in distressed and high-crime neighborhoods might be seen as easier than if applied in other types of neighborhoods. In essence, the resulting consequences are not great. Relatedly, it may also help explain why residents of such areas generally view the police less favorably. . . .

Yet another explanation might be characterized as the so-called *dirtbag syndrome*. Reiss and Bordua . . . observed that police officers tend to place people into one of two categories—those who deserve to be punished and those who do not. Those falling in the latter category are often informally (and derogatorily) referred to by police as *dirtbags*. This type of dichotomy may spill over and attach to locations just as it does to people. Numerous scholars have noted the cynical nature of police officers . . . . Such cynicism may translate into the perception that those occupying certain neighborhoods must be up to something, which translates into more coercive patterns of behavior. If the suspect is from the area, the officer may believe this person is involved in some deviant behavior by the very fact that he or she lives in this environment. If the suspect is not from the area, the degree of suspicion may be enhanced even further. Why else would this person come to this part of town? Officers may reason that this person must be here to score his or her next high or to meet with someone in the area engaged in some form of illegal behavior.

Embedded within each of these potential explanations is the influence of key sociodemographic variables such as race, class, gender, and age. As the results show, when these factors are considered at the encounter level, they are significant. However, the race (i.e., minority) effect is mediated by neighborhood context. Perhaps officers do not simply label minority suspects according to what Skolnick . . . termed "symbolic assailants" as much as they label distressed socioeconomic neighborhoods as potential sources of conflict. If, as noted by Skolnick . . . , officers tend to view minorities as individuals associated with an increased likelihood of violence, it may also be that officers apply a similar, and even more powerful, perceptual framework around geographic space. Within this context, the influence of so-called symbolic neighborhoods outweighs the perception of individual symbolic assailants with respect to how the police go about applying coercive forms of control. Interestingly, however, the other key sociodemographic variables are not mediated

by neighborhood context. That is, officers are more likely to use higher levels of police force on male, young, and lower class suspects irrespective of neighborhood context, countering a symbolic neighborhood explanation with respect to these characteristics.

The fact that officers are more forceful in areas characterized by high levels of disadvantage and crime—irrespective of suspect behavior at the police–suspect encounter level—suggests the need for emphasizing departmental values and initiating open discussions on the importance of accountability to the law. When the police act as a mechanism to distribute force disproportionately to those located in so-called bad neighborhoods, legitimacy is undermined. Ultimately, progress is difficult to achieve unless force is rooted within legal justifications for its use.

Future research should continue to examine the role of neighborhood context on police use of force. Such an effort might begin with a better understanding of officers' views toward neighborhoods and how such views may prompt their decision-making behavior. We have laid out three potential interpretations for why officers were more likely to use force in areas characterized by concentrated disadvantage. At this stage, they are nothing more than post hoc interpretations. Future work that incorporates officers' views of neighborhood context may enable researchers to draw a more explicit theoretical framework, which will then permit additional empirical testing.

Researchers might also consider the level of activity emanating from community groups in each neighborhood. One might posit that where community groups are active, the use of police force will be substantially higher (or lower) than where they are not. A more sophisticated approach might look at what community groups in each neighborhood are mobilized to do or what they request of the police. Perhaps officers are more forceful in certain areas simply because the citizens in such areas are asking for stepped-up enforcement. Finally, research identifying additional neighborhood factors, beyond concentrated disadvantage, will help to better understand forceful police behavior.

Questions

1. What are the characteristics of a disorganized neighborhood?

2. Outline each of the three explanations Terrill and Reisig offer for their results.

CHAPTER 15

Exposure to Community Violence and Childhood Delinquency

Justin W. Patchin
University of Wisconsin-Eau Claire

Beth M. Huebner
University of Missouri-St. Louis

John D. McCluskey
University of Texas at San Antonio

Sean P. Varano
Northeastern University

Timothy S. Bynum
Michigan State University

The effect of neighborhood environment on child development has received significant scholarly attention in recent years. . . . Research has suggested that children reared in disadvantaged neighborhoods are at an elevated risk to engage in deviant behaviors. . . . Other research, however, has shown that the vast majority of children who grow up in disorganized environments fail to initiate serious offending. . . . The goal of this research is to examine why some children, raised in neighborhoods with similar structural and economic disadvantages, engage in delinquent behaviors, whereas others abstain from crime.

Traditionally, researchers have explored the effects of community context on delinquency using social disorganization theory. . . . Specifically, it has been argued that disadvantaged, disorderly, and decaying neighborhoods foster an environment in which deviance becomes widespread. . . . In addition, these characteristics preclude the development of social networks within the neighborhood that could potentially redress the maladies associated with crime and deviance. . . .

The social disorganization literature has shed considerable light on the between-neighborhood processes associated with delinquency. However, less is known about the within-neighborhood mechanisms associated with delinquency. Specifically, little research has been conducted on the role of witnessing community violence on delinquency. This dearth in the literature is surprising given that researchers have found that exposure to violence is commonly reported among youth living in disorganized neighborhoods. . . .

The purpose of this study is to extend previous research by examining the effect of exposure to community violence on delinquency among a sample of

Source: "Exposure to community violence and childhood delinquency," by Patchin, J. W., Huebner, B. M., McCluskey, J. D., Varano, S. P., & Bynum, T. S., (2006), *Crime and Delinquency, 52,* 307–332. Reprinted by permission of Sage Publications, Inc.

9- to 15-year-old youth who reside in disorganized neighborhoods. Although numerous studies have examined the relationship between neighborhood context and delinquency, as noted earlier, few researchers have considered the effect of exposure to violence on delinquency or the effects of exposure to community violence net of delinquency correlates and neighborhood disadvantage. Inclusion of multiple controls for neighborhood disadvantage and delinquency correlates (e.g., attachment to school) helps isolate the effects of exposure to community violence. The sample selected for examination is unique in that efforts were made to include active offenders and youth who are most at risk to engage in delinquent activities. The examination of early, serious delinquency is also of particular importance because research has shown youth who engage in delinquent behaviors prior to the age of 14 are at high risk to continue participation in crime and deviance throughout the life course. . . . Data for the study were obtained from youth interviews and the *U.S. Decennial Census* (U.S. Census Bureau, 2000). Ordinary least squares and logistic regression models are estimated to test the hypothesis that youth who witness more violence in their neighborhoods are more likely to report assault and weapon carrying.

Literature Review

Scholars in the Chicago School of Sociology . . . and elsewhere have argued that "characteristics of the urban environment are critical to explaining the emergence of crime in specific communities." . . . Specific theoretical and empirical attention has been devoted to structural characteristics such as residential mobility, concentrated disadvantage, and population heterogeneity. . . . Each of these elements is thought to have direct and indirect effects—through decreased informal social control capabilities—on crime. . . . In addition, researchers have also argued that the deviance that occurs within disorganized neighborhoods may negatively affect the residents by making them feel compelled to use violence as a response to a threatening urban environment. . . .

Ecological research has consistently linked community disadvantage to between-neighborhood differences in violence and crime. More recently, researchers have begun to examine the factors within neighborhoods that are associated with delinquency, specifically exposure to community violence. The results from this research have been mixed. For example, Stewart and colleagues . . . found that neighborhood affluence was significantly

related to preadolescent violence, whereas neighborhood violence was not. They reason that neighborhood-level factors may be less important for younger children than for older adolescents, who may be more embedded in the neighborhood culture. . . . Similarly, Wilson and Herrnstein . . . argued that serious and persistent offenders begin offending early in life—before contextual factors such as antisocial peers or neighborhood disorganization can negatively affect their development. Other research has indicated that youth who are consistently subjected to violence in their neighborhoods become desensitized to it and are therefore not negatively affected by it. . . .

Aggressive reaction to noxious stimuli such as exposure to community violence is also consistent with broader criminological theories such as Agnew's . . . general strain theory (GST) and Bernard's . . . theory of angry aggression. Consistent with GST, delinquent coping behaviors may result when vicarious strain (in the form of neighborhood violence) leads to anger or frustration. According to Agnew . . . , strains that occur "in settings that are frequented by the individual" . . . , such as his or her immediate neighborhood, are particularly salient. Thus, one avenue through which exposure to community violence has been found to influence youth is through psychological functioning, in the sense that there is increased anxiety and promotion of anger in those who witness violence. . . . Rosenthal's . . . work on exposure and victimization indicated that there was modest support for a link between those experiences and anger and anxiety. Similarly, Aneshensel and Succoff . . . also found direct and positive associations between "ambient hazard" and both anxiety and depression. Aggressive behaviors could be coping mechanisms to deal with the psychological effects that exposure to violence exacted on youth.

Exposure to community violence may also contribute to the generation of learned aggressive behaviors. The use of aggressive situational responses or adoption of weapons for self-defense could be viewed as "learned" responses, consistent with social learning theory . . . and cultural perspectives. As Anderson . . . noted, children quickly "learn to deal with their social environment." . . . In a violent environment, willingness to express toughness is often revered. Youth who understand this "code" may be more inclined to engage in assaultive behaviors or to carry a weapon such that they gain respect from their peers.

Studies in other fields (notably public health) have also linked exposure to community violence with negative behavioral outcomes in children and adolescents, most notably aggressive behavior.... For example, Colder and colleagues ... found that perceived neighborhood danger was associated with positive beliefs about aggression. In addition to promoting aggressiveness, exposure to violence promotes dysfunctional defensive responses such as weapon carrying and fighting behaviors. Durant and colleagues ... analyzed data on a sample of African-American adolescents and also found a strong positive association between exposure to violence and the use of violence by adolescents. Similarly, Sheley and Wright ... found that youth's gun possession was strongly related to a self-reported need for protection. In short, exposure to violence may directly influence aggressive behavior through the changing of the mental calculus of those most often exposed.

Recently, scholars have attempted to better understand the complex relationship between individual- and community-level factors and adolescent development.... For example, Wikström and Loeber ... found that "there is a significant direct effect of neighborhood disadvantage on well-adjusted children influencing them to become involved in serious offending as they reach adolescence." ... They concluded that "community context may have an important indirect influence on early onsets through its potential impact on the development of individual dispositions and, particularly, aspects of the individual social situation (family, school, peers) related to serious offending." ... In short, individual and environmental attributes interact to influence the behavior of adolescents. This study serves to expand on this line of research by isolating the effect of exposure to community violence on delinquency from that of neighborhood disadvantage and individual social situation.

Method

DATA

Data for the study were drawn from a larger research project designed to examine the efficacy of police-centered intervention programs in reducing serious, violent behavior among preadolescent and adolescent youth. Individual-level data were obtained through comprehensive interviews of youth, and community-level data were acquired from the U.S. Census Bureau.... Personal interviews conducted with 187 youth between the ages of 9 and 15 living in a moderately sized midwestern city served as the foundation of the research. Youth who resided in neighborhoods within the northwest quadrant of the city were targeted for the study because the area had been identified by city officials as disproportionately disadvantaged. In addition, the target area had been designated in 1993 as a Weed and Seed community where proactive citywide response was necessary to address many prevailing community concerns.

Specifically, youth were selected to be included in the study in one of three ways. First, youth were recruited to be interviewed from the middle school in the target area. Teachers informed youth in their classes about the project, and interested students were required to have their parent or guardian sign and return a permission slip to participate. Because of this active consent procedure, the participation rate was relatively low (about 25%). Second, youth were recruited from two recreation centers in the neighborhood. Flyers were distributed, and the supervisors at each center agreed to solicit participants. Active consent was also secured from the parents of these youth. Finally, youth who lived in the target neighborhoods who were arrested during a 3-year period were also included in the sample. Arrested youth were generally interviewed within a few weeks of coming into contact with the criminal justice system. All youth were given $20 for a 30- to 40-minute interview. In total, 34% of the youth were interviewed at the school, 29% were recruited from the recreation centers, and 37% were included because they were arrested.

Although the sample does not consist of youth who were randomly selected from a larger population, it builds on traditional school-only samples, which may fail to capture the most active offenders who may be missing due to absence. By recruiting youth from recreational centers and including those who have been arrested, the sample attempts to include the most active and at-risk youth in the target neighborhoods. Indeed, many nationally representative samples of youth may fail to include sufficient numbers of active offenders to allow for accurate analysis....

Data on neighborhood disadvantage were obtained from the 2000 U.S. Decennial Census. Census data included in this analysis were aggregated to the block group area—the smallest unit commonly available to the general public. Census data were linked to the individual based on the block group area in which the youth reported living at the time of the interview. Sample members lived in 40 different block group areas within the same general area of the city. In the city examined here, there are 148 block group areas, with an average of 1,500 residents and 600 housing units within each area.... As described earlier, the target area is generally more disadvantaged than the city as a whole. For example, there is a higher proportion of families below the poverty level, households receiving public assistance, and unemployed residents who live in the target area than in the city. Moreover, there is a higher proportion of abandoned buildings and more concentrated disadvantage in the target area.

Measures

DEPENDENT MEASURES

The goal of this research is to examine the effect of exposure to community violence on child participation in serious personal delinquency, controlling for individual-level demographic factors and delinquency correlates. The main research question, then, is as follows: Are youth who live in disorganized neighborhoods, or who perceive their immediate environment to be violent, more likely to carry a weapon or engage in assaultive behavior? Because juvenile weapon involvement and violence continue to be national public health concerns . . . , identifying the community-level factors associated with the early initiation of such behaviors aid in our overall understanding of those activities.

Self-reported weapon possession and assaultive behavior serve as dependent variables. The personal assault measure is dichotomous (1 = individual reported that he or she had assaulted an adult, assaulted a peer, or thrown rocks or bottles at others during the previous 12 months; 0 = respondent did not report assaultive behavior during the past 12 months). The weapon possession measure includes individuals who reported that they had carried a weapon for any reason during the previous 12 months (1 = youth reported possessing a weapon on one or more occasions during the last 12 months; 0 = youth did not report weapon possession). . . .

Although the average age of the sample was quite young (mean = 12.0), the participants reported substantial involvement in serious delinquency during the prior year. More than half (58%) of the sample members reported that they had committed assaultive behavior during the past year, and 18% of youth indicated that they were in possession of a weapon during the past 12 months. Specifically, of those youth who were in possession of a weapon, 54% reported carrying a knife and 41% reported carrying a gun. The type of weapon was unspecified for the remaining respondents.

Neighborhood Influences

Two measures of neighborhood influence are included in the models. The first variable, exposure to community violence, measured at the individual level, was designed to reflect personal experience with neighborhood violence and is operationalized using a seven-item additive scale (Cronbach's α = .857). Respondents were asked how often in the previous 12 months they heard gun shots, saw somebody arrested, saw drug deals, saw someone being beaten up, saw someone get stabbed or shot, saw gangs in their neighborhood, and saw somebody pull a gun on another person. Response items ranged from 1 to 4 (1 = *none*, 2 = *once or twice*, 3 = *a few times*, and 4 = *many times*).

The neighborhood disadvantage construct is an adaptation of the Sampson et al. . . . indicator of concentrated disadvantage. A six-item factor score was calculated using 2000 U.S. Census data and included the percentage of residents below the poverty line, households receiving public assistance, female-headed households, residents older than 16 who are unemployed, population younger than 18 years old, and population that is African American (eigenvalue = 3.83, factor loadings > 0.63, Cronbach's α = .812).

Individual Characteristics and Delinquency Correlates

Consistent with previous delinquency research, a number of individual-level variables are included in the model as controls. Two dichotomous variables are included in the models as measures of gender and race. Gender was dichotomized into male respondents and female respondents (1 = male, 0 = female). Race was dichotomized into non-White and White (1 = African American, Asian, Hispanic, or other race; 0 = White). The age variable represents the youth's age in years. A final dichotomous, individual-level measure is included in the models to control for previous arrests (1 = individual had one or more arrests during the past year; 0 = youth was not arrested during the past year). The previous arrest measure was included to control for the fact that those who were arrested have a greater likelihood of self-reporting deviant behaviors irrespective of the community-level variables of primary interest in the current study. [Sixty-four percent] of youth in the sample were male, 58% were non-White, and 37% had a previous arrest.

In addition, research has also suggested that factors such as parenting . . . , peer relationships . . . , and school relationships . . . may influence the relationship between community context and delinquent outcomes. . . . For example, youth who are strictly supervised by a parent may be less likely to witness or be negatively affected by violence that occurs in their neighborhood. Stern and Smith . . . found that neighborhood disadvantage was related to delinquency both directly and indirectly through decreased involvement and supervision by parents. Similarly, recent research has found that peer networks moderate the relationship between social disorganization (socioeconomic status, ethnic heterogeneity, residential stability, family disruption, and level of urbanization) and delinquency. . . . Finally, features of school environments (e.g., school climate) are important considerations and can reduce the negative effects of neighborhood environments. Youth who are strongly attached to school may spend more time with prosocial adults in that context, thereby limiting their exposure to community violence.

Informed by these previous studies, four variables are included in the models as delinquency correlates, both to control for their individual effects and to determine their potential relationship to neighborhood-level factors in terms of serious childhood violence. Family context is measured in relationship to family structure and parental supervision. The single-parent family construct reflects whether the child lived with only one primary caregiver or otherwise (1 = child currently resides with only one parent/guardian; 0 = child resides in a two-parent/guardian household). Family supervision is measured using a five-item additive scale (Cronbach's α = .724). Respondents were asked, "How much does your primary caregiver know about: who your close friends are; what you do with your friends; who your close friends' parents are; who you are with when you are not at home; and, what you are doing in school?" Response items were 1 (*knows nothing*), 2 (*knows very little*), 3 (*knows something*), and 4 (*knows everything*).

In addition, a four-item additive scale was designed to measure the respondent's attachment to school (Cronbach's α = .675). Individuals were asked to report their agreement with the following statements: "I try hard in school," "Education is so important that it is worth it to put up with things I don't like," and "In general, I like school." Response items ranged from 1 to 4 and included the following: 1 = *strongly disagree*, 2 = *disagree*, 3 = *agree*, and 4 = *strongly agree*. Students were also asked to respond to the item "Homework is a waste of time" using the following response options: *strongly agree, agree, disagree*, and *strongly disagree*.

Finally, an eight-item additive scale is included representing peer delinquency (Cronbach's α = .823). Respondents were asked in the past year how many of their friends drank beer, wine, or liquor; used a weapon or force to get money or things from people; attacked someone

with a weapon or with the idea of seriously hurting him or her; hit someone with the idea of hurting him or her (e.g., fist-fighting); stole something worth more than $100; stole something worth more than $5 but less than $50; damaged or destroyed someone else's property on purpose; or took a car for a ride without the owner's permission. Response items ranged from 1 to 4 and included *none of them, a few of them, some of them*, and *all of them*.

Analyses

The goals of the research are twofold. The primary goal is to estimate the effect of exposure to community violence on weapons possession and assaultive behavior. In response to research that suggests that factors such as parenting, peer relationships, and school attachment affect the relationship between community context and delinquency outcomes . . . , the second goal of the research is to assess the effects of exposure to community violence on personal assault and weapon possession through a series of delinquency correlates.

The statistical analyses are conducted in two phases. First, ordinary least squares regression is used to estimate the effect of neighborhood influences (neighborhood disadvantage and exposure to community violence) on each of the delinquency correlate predictors—parental supervision, school attachment, and negative peers—controlling for individual demographic characteristics. The purpose of this stage of the analysis is to explore the relationship between neighborhood context and delinquency correlates. For example, is exposure to community violence related to a decrease in family supervision or school attachment? Results from this initial stage will help to clarify the relationship between community-level attributes and delinquency and inform policy recommendations.

The second phase of the analysis involves estimating the impact of neighborhood influences on delinquency, net of individual controls, and delinquency correlates. Logistic regression is used as the analytic technique in these models. . . .

Findings

Neighborhood Influences and Correlates of Delinquency

. . . [E]xposure to violence had a moderately strong and significant effect on each of the delinquency correlates, net of individual controls. Youth who indicated personal exposure to neighborhood violence reported lower levels of parental supervision and school attachment and were more likely to associate with delinquent peers. As expected, community disadvantage had little effect in the models. Because youth resided in the same general neighborhoods, there was little variation in the level of disorganization. Nevertheless, it appears that youth's perceptions of neighborhood violence are more indicative of delinquency correlates than the global indicator of neighborhood disadvantage.

The effect of individual characteristics on delinquency correlates also deserves mention. Gender was the only significant predictor in the school attachment model, with males more likely to report reduced school attachment. Age, gender, and previous arrest were all significantly and positively related to peer involvement in delinquency. None of the individual demographic measures was significantly related to parental supervision.

Overall, the amount of variance explained by the neighborhood influences and individual characteristics varied by outcome. The explanatory power for the parental supervision and school attachment model was quite small, as evidenced by the R^2 of .110 and .107. In contrast, the R^2 was .483 for the peer delinquency model, which is greater than four times that of the parental supervision and school attachment equations.

PERSONAL ASSAULT

Three separate logistic regression models are estimated to ascertain the unique effects of individual characteristics, neighborhood influences, and delinquency correlates on personal assault. . . . In Model 1, males and youth with a previous arrest were more likely to report committing an act of personal assault in the previous 12 months. The strength of the relationship among arrest history, gender, and personal assault was quite strong. Both males and individuals with a previous arrest were greater than three times as likely to report a personal assault when compared with females and individuals without previous exposure to the criminal justice system. Overall, this preliminary model had relatively weak explanatory power as evidenced by the Nagelkerke R_L^2 of .209.

The inclusion of neighborhood influences in Model 2 improved the explanatory power of the model, although the exposure to violence construct was the only measure found to be statistically significant. The Nagelkerke R_L^2 for Model 2 was .318. The results of this

model also support the study hypotheses. Individuals who reported higher levels of exposure to violence in their community were significantly more likely to report participation in personal assault behaviors over the previous year. However, the strength of association for community violence exposure was small; for every 1 unit increase in the exposure to violence construct, youth were 1.16 times more likely to report personal assault.

None of the delinquency correlates was found to be statistically significant in the final model (Model 3). Moreover, the inclusion of the delinquency correlates did little to change the effect of exposure to violence on personal assault. Net of individual controls and ecological domains, individuals who reported higher exposure to violence in their neighborhoods were more likely to indicate participation in personal assault. The delinquency correlates increased the explanatory power of the model (Nagelkerke R_L^2 of .367), suggesting they may play a role in the explanation of childhood delinquency, although the constructs derived for this analysis did not achieve statistical significance.

WEAPON POSSESSION

. . . In Model 1, the inclusion of individual characteristics generated only one significant predictor. Namely, individuals with previous arrest histories were significantly more likely to report possessing a weapon during the past year. In fact, youth with previous arrest histories were nearly 14 times more likely to report possessing a weapon. Overall, the individual characteristics model had moderate explanatory power, with a Nagelkerke R_L^2 of .337.

The importance of considering exposure to community violence when estimating youth involvement in serious, personal delinquency was further confirmed in Model 2. The exposure to community violence measure was significantly related to weapon possession; for each unit increase in the exposure to violence measure, youth were 1.22 times more likely to report the possession of a weapon during the past year. Consistent with the results from the personal assault model, neighborhood disadvantage was not significantly associated with weapons possession. Including neighborhood influences in the equation did increase the explanatory power of the model, with an overall Nagelkerke R_L^2 of .464.

Contrary to the assault model, peer influence was significantly related to weapon possession. The explanatory power of the delinquency correlates as a whole were also moderately strong; including the delinquency correlates in the model increased the Nagelkerke R^2_L from 0.464 to 0.533. The effect of peer delinquency was particularly strong, with a 1-unit increase in the measure of peer delinquency associated with a 23% increase in the likelihood of weapons possession. This finding highlights the importance of peer influences in understanding certain forms of serious personal delinquency, specifically weapons possession.

Discussion

Before discussing the implications of the study, a few limitations merit acknowledgment. First, the sample size is small and was not randomly collected from a discrete population. As noted, the sample is disproportionately composed of young youth with prior experience with the criminal justice system. Although this attribute is a strength, in the sense that it allowed us to look at the serious violence of a young cohort, the vast majority of youth at this age are not carrying weapons or engaging in serious assaultive behavior. There may be differences between youth in the current sample and youth who do not come into contact with the criminal justice system that were not accounted for in the analysis. Because this is a unique sample, the generalizability of the findings to a larger population is difficult. Nevertheless, the results are informative and build on previous research in this area.

Another limitation is that the individual-level data are self-reported perceptual measures. That is, the actual violence that occurs in one's neighborhood may be different from that which is perceived. Future studies should seek to supplement resident perceptions with actual measures of violence in the neighborhood (i.e., official crime or observational data . . .). Finally, due to the cross-sectional nature of the data, causality cannot necessarily be inferred. Although it appears that youth who witness violence are impelled to carry a weapon or engage in assaultive behaviors, it could also be that youth who get into fights or carry a weapon are more likely to witness community violence (perhaps because they are a party involved in the violence). Future analyses should measure community-level variables at one time period and delinquency at a future time point to ensure proper temporal ordering.

Despite these limitations, the study was able to build on previous research by more fully exploring the neighborhood-level variables associated with childhood violence. The specific research question posed was as follows: What community-level factors differentiate offenders from nonoffenders who live in the same communities? Results from the analyses supported the hypothesis that individuals who are exposed to more community violence are more likely to engage in serious personal violence. Youth who reported higher levels of exposure to community violence were significantly more likely to report possessing a weapon and engaging in personal assault. As noted, previous research has primarily focused on the relationship between community violence and psychological outcomes; this study finds similarly negative effects on violent behavior in a sample of youth.

In contrast, larger social indicators of neighborhood disadvantage did not have a significant effect on delinquency. This is not to suggest that disadvantage, per se, is unimportant. Indeed, several of the studies reviewed above testify to its salience. It could be that the level of disadvantage in the target area is not comparable to that of communities from other studies. For example, having 13% of families living in poverty is much less than the cutoff Wilson . . . designated as a neighborhood truly disadvantaged (40%). A more plausible explanation relates to the nature of the target neighborhoods considered in this analysis. The target area as a whole was more disadvantaged than the city; however, there may not have been enough variation in level of disadvantage within the targeted area to reveal a significant relationship. Nevertheless, research that simply tests the relationship between structural or physical attributes of the community may miss another important variable, namely, the exposure to community violence that often occurs in these contexts.

The research also highlights the importance of considering the potential effect of delinquency correlates in understanding involvement in serious, personal delinquency. Exposure to violence was significantly related to parental supervision, school attachment, and peer delinquency. The effect was particularly strong for the peer delinquency model as evidenced by a standardized β of 0.56 for the exposure indicator. It is noteworthy that the exposure to violence measure remained significantly associated with childhood violence, even after controlling for other common correlates of delinquency. Although associating with delinquent peers does appear to influence the relationship between exposure to violence and weapon possession, exposure to violence did have a significant effect on weapon possession and personal assault, net of controls for individual demographic characteristics and delinquency correlates.

These findings offer important implications for policy. First, the study suggests a need for a more comprehensive notion of victimization, that is, a vision that extends beyond the immediate victim to others in the community who witness the incidents. As victim advocates and other concerned groups call for a more victim-centered approach to criminal justice, consideration must also be given to the potentially harmful effects to others not directly related to the incident.

The current research also speaks to the importance of developing broader community intervention models. Efforts that build a sustained community capacity to intervene with those directly and indirectly involved in violence hold the potential to prevent violence in the future. Furstenberg, Cook, Eccles, Elder, and Sameroff . . . argued that these sorts of neighborhood resources have both direct and indirect effects on child development and increase the chances that children will successfully navigate the most deleterious, dangerous, and disorganized environments.

Finally, results of this study support the development of social networks within one's community as a way to control both unruly adolescents . . . and crime more generally. Findings suggest that a proximal approach to delinquency prevention may be to protect youth from the deviance and social disorder that occurs within their neighborhoods. This protection could come in the form of more supervised after-school activities for youth or more positive mentoring by parents or other prosocial adults. This suggestion warrants further exploration because the current study found evidence that exposure to violence was inversely related to parental supervision, but that parental supervision was not directly related to participation in delinquent behaviors. Organized activities may limit exposure to violence, and parents, teachers, or other overseers could immediately step in to comfort children if they witness violence. Moreover, parents and teachers can be proactive by discussing community violence in schools and at home. This may help youth cope with what they see in the streets. Although results stress the virulent effects of witnessing community violence as opposed to disorder or disadvantage per se, community mobilization that enables citizens to proactively protect adolescents, particularly those most at risk for delinquency, appears to be a viable crime-reduction strategy.

Questions

1. Identify the dependent variables measured by Patchin, Huebner, McCluskey, Varano, and Bynum.

2. Describe the implications of the authors' findings.

CHAPTER 16

A Subcultural Study of Recreational Ecstasy Use

Michelle Gourley

Australian National University

Early research on youth drug use suggested that it occurred predominantly in deviant subcultures. Subcultural theories of deviance have therefore been the dominant theoretical framework within which youth drug use has been examined and understood since the 1950s. Subcultural theories focus on the importance of deviant subcultures to the initiation and maintenance of deviant acts. They argue that deviance is the result of a learned acquisition of deviant values and norms within the context of a subculture. . . .

Past research has shown that the social controls and learning processes that operate in drug subcultures are the framework within which people decide how a certain drug should be used and how it will be experienced. . . . A pioneering work on subcultural drug use was Howard Becker's study of marijuana use published in his book *Outsiders* in 1963. Becker focused on the conditions necessary for becoming a marijuana user and emphasized the importance of learning within a subculture of drug users in the initiation and maintenance of marijuana use. He found that learning to perceive and enjoy the effects of marijuana is mediated by a subculture of experienced users. He argued that individuals were able to use a drug for pleasure only when they had learned to conceive of it as a substance that could be used for pleasure. This process was found to take place when three conditions were met: the user had learned the correct technique, the effects of the drug, and how to enjoy the effects of the drug. For Becker, these three conditions take place through an individual's interaction with a group of other users who equip the beginner with the necessary concepts with which to organize the drug experience. . . .

Today the nature of drug use in society has changed somewhat from the time when subcultural theories of deviance were first developed and most widely applied. We are now seeing the emergence of widespread recreational drug use among relatively large numbers of ordinary youth. Recent drug research indicates that there has been a reduction in ethnic, gender, and social class differences in drug use, which suggests that drug-related behavior is becoming accommodated into a larger grouping of society. . . . Many young people no longer think of recreational drug use as deviant, but see it as rational and informed. . . . The majority of young recreational drug users today are not cut off from conventional society nor are they associated with problems of addiction, delinquency, or crime, which are traditionally linked to drug use. . . . Such recent trends in the use of illicit drugs have raised doubts as to whether recreational drug use still takes place within a subcultural context.

A position held by a number of postmodern writers is that the subcultural context of drug use has diminished and, thus, subcultural theories are outdated. . . . They argue that subcultural theories were developed when drug use was seen as atypical and the act of delinquents, and therefore they do not represent the widespread recreational drug scene of today. . . . They also argue that, as a result of postmodernism, there are no longer any clearly differentiated subcultures or specific

Source: "A subcultural study of recreational ecstasy use," by Gourley, M., (2004), in *Journal of Sociology*, *40*, 59–73. Reprinted by permission of Sage Publications, Ltd.

youth cultural styles due to the individualization and diversification of the music and fashion industries. . . . From this perspective, the concept of subculture is deemed unworkable as an analytical tool in the sociology of youth, music, and style in postmodern society. . . .

The relevance of subcultural theories to modern-day drug use has been challenged by a normalization perspective on youth drug use that has recently emerged in sociological literature. The work of Howard Parker and colleagues has been most influential in this area. They argue that drug use is a common form of behavior among youth who see it as a normal aspect of their lives. They characterized the period of the 1950s to the 1980s as one in which subcultural drug use prevailed, but saw a normalization of drug use emerge from the 1990s onward. The proposal that drugs are so widely spread to be accepted as normal would appear to have little empirical support, however. . . . The normalization thesis seems to be an oversimplification of the way in which drug use can be understood today, which raises doubts over whether the criticisms of subcultural theories in relation to drug use are well founded.

The Study

The purpose of this chapter is to question the argument that in contemporary society the relationship between subcultures and drug use has diminished and to show that subcultural theories of deviance are still relevant to understanding recreational drug use. Specifically, Howard Becker's subcultural theory of deviance, developed from his study of marijuana users in the 1960s, was examined and applied to ecstasy use among youth.

Ecstasy was chosen as the drug of interest in this study for two main reasons. First, because of the relative newness of the drug, few studies have looked at ecstasy use in any qualitative way. . . . Second, ecstasy has become a common recreational drug for middle-class youth. Australian statistics from 2001 show that the lifetime use of the drug ecstasy is 19.7% for people ages 20 to 29 years old, which makes it the third most popular drug for young people after marijuana and amphetamines. . . . The growing popularity of ecstasy is strongly associated with the development of the rave/dance culture in the late 1980s. It is important to note that the ecstasy and dance cultures are not one and the same phenomenon, although they are strongly linked. . . .

Observation and semistructured interviewing were used to investigate ecstasy use in the young population. The observations were drawn from approximately six venues in Canberra and Sydney at which recreational drugs were commonly used, such as dance events, nightclubs, and music concerts. These direct observations were accumulated over approximately 3 years. In addition, semistructured interviews were conducted with 12 recreational ecstasy users (6 female and 6 male) between the ages of 20 and 22. They were all of middle-class background and were either university students or in full-time work. The interviewing sessions aimed to uncover subcultural characteristics such as norms of behavior, values and shared understandings surrounding ecstasy use, and the subcultural learning and socialization processes involved in ecstasy use.

Initiation Into Ecstasy Use

Subcultural theories argue that drug users acquire motivations to use a drug in interaction with other users. Howard Becker argued that people's initiation, maintenance, and discontinuance of drug use are the consequences of changes in their conception of the drug and that membership in a drug subculture can vary over time as interactions with other users and acceptance of drug lore change. . . . Individuals' socialization into ecstasy use can thus be looked at as a function of their degree of interaction with users and their attitude change over time toward the use of illicit drugs.

Interviewees reported that, at some stage in the past, their attitudes toward drugs were fairly negative and that they considered all drugs to be destructive. . . . However, they stated that, as they grew older, they became increasingly exposed to certain drugs such as ecstasy and discovered that these drugs were being used by normal, conventional youth. This led to a change in their attitude toward drug use. They were now of the view that maybe all drugs were not such a bad thing and could in fact be used to have fun. Such an attitude change had not taken place for other drugs, such as heroin. As one interviewee said: "Smackees [heroin users] give drug users a bad name as they go past the point of recreation."

Ecstasy seems to be a substance used intensely for a short period of time, before there is a move to light recreational use. Users come to have a more cautious view of the drug as they discover that every ecstasy experience is not necessarily as good as the last one. As one interviewee remarked, when someone has experienced a good ecstasy pill, they go through a period where they want to take the drug all the time, but this does not last.

Interviewees attributed their declining ecstasy use to the fact that they were going to raves and other social events less often and were therefore growing out of the ecstasy scene. This is evident from the following quotes from male and female interviewees, respectively: "I am now disenchanted with the whole scene" and "I am coming to see that using ecstasy every weekend is pointless as we do the same things." It would seem that as users grow older, they tend to move out of the drug scene and out of the subcultures that embrace recreational drug use and look for other leisure activities.

Peer involvement with ecstasy was a key factor in an individual beginning and maintaining ecstasy use. The interviewees in this study shared similar experiences in terms of entry into drug networks and patterns of consumption through involvement in friendship networks that provided them with access to ecstasy and to a social setting for its consumption. The majority of the interviewees' first experiences with ecstasy occurred with friends from their immediate social networks who had used ecstasy before and who played a major role in their decision to try the drug. The importance of being with friends who were accepting of ecstasy use and being in a setting that was conducive to ecstasy use was stressed by the interviewees for all occasions of use. The need for these conditions to be met when using ecstasy highlights the subcultural underpinnings of ecstasy use.

None of the participants had used ecstasy when they were on their own and did not know of anyone else who did so. They believed that ecstasy was only beneficial when it was used in groups—that it was considered abnormal for someone to use ecstasy alone and that he or she would be frowned on for doing so. For example, one of the interviewees said that anyone using ecstasy alone would be regarded as "some kind of druggo [drug addict]." These findings strongly suggest that ecstasy use is a group-orientated activity and that there is a norm in the ecstasy culture that one does not use the drug alone.

Initial fears of dangerous experiences from taking ecstasy were challenged by the reassurances of other users who had engaged in ecstasy use with little trouble. It was stressed that friends who were experienced users gave advice and information on safety issues and on the effects of ecstasy before the interviewees made the decision to take ecstasy for the first time. Interactions with friends who use drugs and, in turn, participation in a drug using subculture persuade the beginner that drug use can be safe. This finding supports Zinberg's work, which suggests that the drug-using group reinforces an individual's discovery that use of a particular drug is not a bad activity and is worthwhile engaging in. . . .

The importance of having friends within the drug subculture to one's maintenance of ecstasy use is supported by the finding that many of the ecstasy users interviewed said that there were social occasions when they did not plan to take ecstasy, but had ended up doing so because they were with friends who were using the drug. The participants also explained that when they take ecstasy, they want their friends to have as good a time as them and therefore may try to persuade other users to take ecstasy on a particular occasion. As one respondent said: "When I use drugs I like to have others with me taking a pill so we can all have a shared [drug] experience." If interaction with a drug subculture is maintained, a user can be both influenced by and have an influence on other users to take ecstasy regularly.

Learning to Perceive the Effects of Ecstasy

According to Becker's subcultural theory of deviance, users learn to perceive a drug's effects through participation in a drug-using subculture. Becker stressed that the novice drug user acquires the concepts that make an awareness of being high possible through direct communication with other users or via picking up cues from other users within a subcultural context. . . .

Being high not only involves the presence of symptoms, but the recognition and perception of those symptoms and their connection with use of the drug by the user. . . . In the present study, ecstasy users were asked about their own experiences of being high from ecstasy use and their observations of others. All those interviewed said that they had seen people who were high on ecstasy, but did not believe they were high themselves. This was especially the case with first-timers, whom the respondents believed were in denial about the drug's effectiveness and needed to be coached through the experience to be able to recognize the effects of ecstasy. A respondent explained that sometimes people need someone to point out their abnormal behaviors to alert them to the fact that they are high because they are not always conscious of their behavior. . . .

A further example of how interaction with other users can lead to an awareness of being high is this description by a female interviewee of her first experience: "I ended up taking five ecstasy tablet halves because I couldn't feel anything [drug effects] for ages." She recalled that her friends (who were experienced users) kept asking her, "Can you feel anything yet?", to which she would reply, "What am I supposed to feel?" This prompted her friends to inform her of the kind of drug effects she should be looking for so she would know when the drug was working. Such conversations with other users made her become more aware of certain parts of her drug experience and led her to perceive what she described as "a sudden rush" and connect such a feeling with the notion of being high.

Observations of groups of ecstasy users also brought to light the fact that failure to feel high worries users and leads them to ask more experienced users for advice and reassurance. Some examples of the types of advice and reassurances given by other users within the ecstasy subculture are that smoking a cigarette can help to kick-start the effects and that the drug will work if you are relaxed, clear-headed, and not concentrating on the absence of effects.

Previous subcultural research has found that first-time experiences with a drug are associated with the presence of an experienced user to act as a guide. . . . In the present study, the role of an experienced user assumed some importance to how first-timers came to interpret the effects of ecstasy and made sense of the drug experience that would otherwise be vague and ambiguous. This is evident from the response of a female interviewee when asked about the effects of ecstasy: "You only really know the meaning of what you are feeling when someone diagnoses it for you, otherwise it is hard to let go and you end up pushing the effects away." This is further supported by a respondent who stated that he used ecstasy for the first time without other experienced users being present. He recognized when the ecstasy pill was starting to take effect by the fact that he felt "different," but he did not know how to interpret what he was feeling.

Conversations focused around describing one's elevated mood (being high) are typical among ecstasy users. Users often indicate to others who have taken an ecstasy pill when they are starting to feel the effects. To begin with, users may go into detail about what they are feeling. As one interviewee said: "You get excited about being smashed and want to broadcast it to everyone." However, with time and experience, everyone in the group comes to know the meaning of what it feels like to be high on ecstasy and therefore individuals do not need to describe it in such detail anymore. A shared language develops among users, in which a simple word or gesture communicates to others that one is high. . . .

Learning to Define the Effects of Ecstasy as Pleasurable

Becker argued that drug users learn the pleasures to be derived from an act in the course of interaction with more experienced deviants. . . . He stated that, before engaging in the activity of drug use, people have little notion of the pleasures to be derived from it. It is only through experience with the drug, coupled with subcultural support, that an individual can conceive of the drug experience as pleasurable. . . .

Experienced users are important to those having doubts about first using ecstasy and to those deciding whether to continue use after a bad experience with the drug. Becker outlined in his work on marijuana use that it is common for users to have an unpleasant experience with a drug, which they cannot define as pleasurable. He argued that the likelihood of a redefinition of the drug as again capable of producing pleasure depends on the degree to which the individual interacts with other users. . . . In the present study, all but one interviewee had at least one unpleasant experience with the drug ecstasy, but it did not lead them to cease use. One of the reasons for this was that by the end of the week users had forgotten about their bad experiences, and the excitement of the weekend, going out, and socializing had taken over. Their wish to continue interacting with an ecstasy using group of peers was a major influencing factor in users' definitions and perceptions of ecstasy use and thus their ecstasy-using behavior.

Becker's work on marijuana demonstrated how subcultural support in the form of help and advice from experienced users is important to how a user will overcome an unpleasant drug experience. . . . When asked about their not-so-pleasant experiences with ecstasy, most respondents reported that other users had helped them through such events by attempting to talk them out of feeling scared or paranoid and by reassuring them that any negative drug effects would pass. Observations also brought to light the commonality of experienced users giving water to users feeling ill and teaching inexperienced users to regulate their use so as to avoid unpleasant comedowns in the future.

Paul Willis argued that drug experiences are socially constructed, culturally learned, and defined in the context of subcultural use, rather than being based on the properties of different types of drugs. . . . Most of the respondents in this study attributed their best experiences with ecstasy to the atmosphere, their frame of mind, and the presence of close friends. The purity of the pill was considered only a secondary influence. For example, one respondent said that her best experiences with ecstasy were not the result of a good pill, but had been when she was around a group of people who were all in a good mood and in a setting conducive to ecstasy use. . . .

It is through involvement in a subculture in which drug use is normalized that a user can get the most out of the drug experience by having access to a drug-conducive environment and interaction with other like-minded users.

Transmission of Knowledge Within the Ecstasy Subculture

Becker's studies of marijuana use along with more recent drug research have emphasized that communication and transmission of knowledge about drugs through stories and folklore represent important aspects of user subcultures. . . . Cultural information and options for behavior are spread through interacting social networks, which leads to a common world of discourse for the members of a subculture. . . .

The importance of expert knowledge, which is accumulated within subcultures, is emphasized in Grebenc's study of drug subcultures, in which prohibited knowledge was shown to circulate among drug users through storytelling. . . . A picture emerged from observations and interviews that much expert knowledge is accumulated inside the ecstasy culture. For example, it is common knowledge among ecstasy users that if you chew rather than swallow an ecstasy pill it will work faster, that smoking marijuana during the come-down phase helps to alleviate the negative effects of ecstasy, and that sucking a lolly-pop prevents the jaw grinding associated with ecstasy use.

Becker illustrated the importance of an informed user subculture as a way to create a safe context for drug use. He found that a continually evolving folklore educates users which results in individuals being able to gain experience with the drug and communicate their experiences to other users. . . . Within the ecstasy culture stories are transmitted from user to user about how to use the drug safely. For example, stories involving instances of people getting caught with ecstasy or having an unpleasant experience with the drug provide users with the appropriate information and knowledge to guide their own drug-related behavior.

Drug stories are also used to affirm the decision to take particular drugs. . . . Most of those interviewed said that they had heard about the drug ecstasy through other users and through stories in the media and came to associate its use with an image of high-energy dancing and partying. This had an influence on their perception of ecstasy as a soft party drug and on their decision to use it. Two interviewees said that they wanted to try ecstasy because of all the hype surrounding it in the media and in the young population. Thus, information with regard

to drug use is not only transmitted though face-to-face interaction, but also circulated through a wider interlocking social network.

Deviant activities tend to generate a specialized language to describe the events, people, and objects involved, which is learned through participation in the deviant subculture and through interaction with other members. . . . Within the culture surrounding ecstasy use, drug lingo is common among users. There is a vast array of specialized terms used for taking ecstasy, being high, coming down, and names for both the drug and ecstasy users themselves. For example, *dropping, racking up, pilling, peaking, scattered, lollies, disco biscuits,* and *eccy-heads* are all terms that have little meaning to those outside the ecstasy subculture.

SHARED UNDERSTANDINGS/VALUES

Subcultural theories maintain that membership in a drug subculture requires evidence that drug users share similar cultural ideas about drugs. . . . Part of the underlying symbolism of drug use is the shared understandings that organize and make sense out of the reality of drug use. . . . The information obtained from interviews with, and observations of, ecstasy users reveals that there are shared ideas, values, and beliefs that govern the use of ecstasy among groups of users, which suggests the presence of a drug subculture.

When the effects of ecstasy were discussed with those interviewed, it became clear that users share similar cultural ideas about the positive effects of ecstasy. All those interviewed believed that the drug reduces people's inhibitions by making them more honest and open and enhances communication and closeness with others.

Interviewees gave similar reasons for why they use the drug ecstasy. One of the most common reasons was that interviewees wished "to be on the same level" as their friends when out as a group, and thus they were much more inclined to use ecstasy on a particular occasion if their friends were using the drug. One respondent was adamant that "certain circumstances call for ecstasy use," such as being at a major dance event (rave). Another common response was that ecstasy was used to enable people to party all night and to make the fun and excitement of the night last longer. . . . Most interviewees used ecstasy to enhance their mood and to relax or unwind after a week of work or university. The data show some support for the view that recreational drug use fits into young people's idea of time out from the stresses and strains of everyday life. . . .

Becker stressed that most deviant subcultures have a self-justifying rationale to neutralize conventional attitudes and legitimize the continuance of the deviant act.... Justifications for ecstasy use were similar among respondents and can be placed into three main categories. The first type of justification has to do with the perceived safety of the drug. All interviewees were aware that there may be long-term dangers associated with ecstasy use, such as brain damage. They showed little concern, however, and focused on the fact that they hadn't personally seen or heard of many bad experiences with the drug and believed that they did not find it addictive.... Ecstasy's reputation as easily controllable and user-friendly relieves the fears of many people....

The second self-justifying rationale that came to light when interviewing ecstasy users was that ecstasy use is thought to be so commonplace among young people that the respondents had difficulty in perceiving ecstasy users as committing a criminal act. One respondent said that people see other people using ecstasy who aren't risk takers or the type of people typically associated with drug use and therefore come to see ecstasy use as legitimate behavior. None of the users interviewed regarded ecstasy use as deviant or as a rejection of social convention. It would seem that the drug ecstasy has had a huge impact on young people's perceptions of drug-taking, in that it has given ordinary youth a positive experience of illegal drug use.

The third main justification that users gave for their drug use was that ecstasy, like alcohol and tobacco, is used as part of people's leisure. Many interviewees considered ecstasy use to be a good alternative to drinking alcohol. This is because a night out can be cheaper when using ecstasy than drinking alcohol and enables users to drive home without the fear of being caught for drunk driving.... Some respondents even saw ecstasy as less of a danger than alcohol, believing it allowed people to stay more in control of their bodies.

Norms of Behavior/Sanctions

Subcultures, like cultures in general, prescribe norms that regulate conduct and are ordered socially.... This study identified norms of conduct and social sanctions surrounding the use of ecstasy that define moderate and acceptable use, condemn compulsive use, limit use to settings conducive to the drug experience, and routinize use.

A picture emerged from interviews and observations that characteristic occasions when ecstasy was used were planned activities, and that a cycle of socializing, dancing, and drinking is the norm when the drug is used. Ecstasy can be both a social and an antisocial drug. There are times when users can't stop talking and want to be with others, and there are times when they just want to dance for hours by themselves, get immersed in the music, and block out those around them. Part of learning the effects of ecstasy and the norms that go with it is that there are times to be sociable, times to dance, and times for self-contemplation, especially when the comedown is experienced.

When asked about where ecstasy is taken, interviewees reported that they had used ecstasy most often at raves or dance events because of the drug-conducive atmosphere of such settings. They said that they had only used ecstasy at specific clubs, bars, and house parties where their drug-using behaviors were accepted by those around them. It was clear from observations that social sanctions limit ecstasy use to settings conducive to the drug experience....

There are also social sanctions that condemn compulsive use in the ecstasy culture. People who use ecstasy compulsively often find themselves excluded from their drug-using peer group. For example, many of the interviewees said that they no longer socialized with friends who they believed had taken ecstasy use to an extreme. Therefore, mechanisms such as social exclusion help to ensure that individuals will conform to convention. Unspoken rules of the drug subculture exert a powerful influence in regulating individual drug-taking behavior and conduct.

Conclusion

The purpose of this research was to question the recent arguments that the relationship of subcultures to drug use has weakened and that subcultural theories of deviance are outdated. The findings from this study suggest that subcultural theories of deviance are still relevant to understanding recreational drug use in contemporary society.

First, the findings indicate that ecstasy use occurs in an ecstasy-using subculture. Specific norms of behavior, social sanctions, and shared understandings and values can be identified that are particular to ecstasy users, as well as clear rules concerning why, where, and how much it is considered legitimate to use ecstasy by groups of users. The research suggests that there is a great deal of normality in user perceptions of their drug use and in the way ecstasy is used by groups in specific social contexts. This supports an underlying assumption of subcultural theories that deviance needs to be understood as normal behavior in specific social circumstances. It is evident that knowledge and behavior concerning ecstasy use are transmitted through an interlocking social network, which further suggests the presence of an ecstasy subculture.

Second, the findings highlight the importance of learning within a drug subculture to the initiation, maintenance, and experience of ecstasy use. It is through the course of experience in drug-using groups that users acquire the norms, values, and shared understandings surrounding the use of a drug. The findings indicate that the experience of ecstasy use is a social one, involving a process of initiation into use of the drug through exposure to the drug subculture. Ecstasy users learn to perceive and enjoy the effects of the drug through interaction with experienced users within a subculture who pass on the customs for doing so. . . . This research therefore confirms subcultural drug research, and in particular Howard Becker's theory of deviance, and extends it to ecstasy use. The findings of this study suggest that Becker's research on what was considered a deviant subculture approximately 40 years ago still has relevance to what is considered more of a mainstream recreational subculture in today's society. They also suggest that no better conceptual framework for understanding youth

drug use has appeared since subcultural theories of deviance were first developed and applied.

No matter how subcultural theories are challenged, whether by a normalization perspective of drug use or by postmodern discourse that envisions a fracturing and fragmenting of youth culture, the subcultural perspective helps us to understand ecstasy use in contemporary society. The subcultural perspective may not provide a complete understanding of illicit drug use in modern times, but it does present useful guidelines for research and investigation. One conclusion to be drawn from this research is that the meaning of drug use has to be looked at in the context of the norms of behavior and shared understandings of the drug-using group in which they are learned. There is little doubt that subcultural theories still have a lot to offer to the sociological understanding of deviance, drug use, youth culture, and social interaction in contemporary society.

Questions

1. Describe the normalization perspective of youth drug use.

2. How is peer involvement with ecstasy a key factor in an individual beginning and maintaining ecstasy use?

CHAPTER 17

Race, Victim-Precipitated Homicide, and the Subculture of Violence Thesis

Lance Hannon
Villanova University

Introduction

Despite recent declines in homicide, African Americans continue to have a homicide victimization rate over six times that of Whites. Although African Americans make up approximately 13% of the total population, they constitute 49% of all those arrested for homicide.... Undoubtedly, homicide disproportionately plagues African-American communities. What remains uncertain, however, is the exact cause of the overrepresentation of African Americans in homicide statistics. Some criminologists claim that African Americans have a higher homicide rate than Whites solely because African Americans face greater economic hardship and other structural obstacles. Other criminologists suggest that structural factors explain only part of the discrepancy; cultural differences between Whites and African Americans are also at work.

The cluster of theories emphasizing the importance of culture in the explanation of African Americans' disproportionately high homicide rate is known as the subculture of violence perspective. This viewpoint is based on two related arguments, both of which stress the relatively unique socialization experiences of African Americans stemming from their distinctive history in the United States and their present position in a highly segregated society. The first argument suggests that the legacy of slavery has created a type of normative defensiveness where African Americans are more likely to perceive relatively minor affronts as symbolic of an attempt to label them as inferior. The second argument implies that learned distrust of mainstream social institutions, particularly the criminal justice system, has led to the creation of social norms emphasizing nonlegal and frequently violent means of dispute resolution.

The primary scholarly source for the African-American subculture of violence perspective is Wolfgang and Ferracuti's . . . often-cited classic, *The Subculture of Violence*. In this book, the authors discuss a variety of deviant subcultures beyond those that are race-based, including, most notably, a subculture of violence in the Southern region of the United States. Wolfgang and Ferracuti focus their analysis on the crime of homicide and take an inductive approach in formulating their empirically driven theory:

> We suggest that, by identifying the groups with the highest rates of homicide, we should find in the most intense degree a subculture of violence, and, having focused on these groups, we should subsequently examine the value system of their subculture, the importance of human life in the scale of values, the kinds of expected reaction to certain types of stimulus, perceptual differences in the evaluation of stimuli, and the general personality structure of the subcultural actors....

Source: "Race, victim-precipitated homicide, and the subculture of violence thesis." By Hannon, L., (2004), in *Social Science Journal, 41*, 115–121. Reprinted by permission of Elsevier via Copyright Clearance Center.

Wolfgang and Ferracuti first ask the question "In what populations is homicide most frequent?" They then attempt to explain why homicide is so frequent in these populations by examining the cultural characteristics of offenders and victims.

In terms of a racial subculture of violence, Wolfgang and Ferracuti . . . point to culturally supported defensiveness among African Americans:

> The significance of a jostle, a slightly derogatory remark, or the appearance of a weapon in the hands of an adversary are stimuli differentially perceived and interpreted by Negroes and Whites . . . Social expectations of response in particular types of social interaction result in differential "definitions of the situation."

It should be noted that Wolfgang and Ferracuti do not argue that all African Americans are equally socialized into this subculture of violence. Nor do they argue that those fully socialized into this subculture inherently value violence for the sake of violence. Rather, they propose that, among African Americans, violence is simply more likely to be considered an appropriate response to what would appear to an outsider as a minor act of disrespect or provocation.

Lynn Curtis . . . , a student of Wolfgang, expanded on Wolfgang and Ferracuti's pioneering research with *Violence, Race, and Culture*, a book focusing exclusively on the racial aspects of the subculture of violence thesis. Like Wolfgang, Curtis argues for the existence of culturally supported defensiveness among African Americans, particularly those from poverty backgrounds. He notes:

> The first probability reflects a brittle defensiveness and a reiteration of expressive, physical manliness in word and action that can generate heated standoffs in situations that persons not accepting contraculture might find trivial. Once an altercation or other conflict has been initiated, the second probability is raised by the precedent of violent conflict resolution learned through past socialization experience. . . .

In addition, Curtis suggests that the history of African Americans in the United States has created an intense distrust of the conventional institutions utilized by the majority for dispute resolution. Thus, according to Curtis, many African Americans have been socialized to believe that taking matters into their own hands, using violence, is an appropriate way to handle conflict.

In summary, Wolfgang and Ferracuti . . . and Curtis . . . argue that African Americans are more likely to respond to minor transgressions with lethal force because of a culturally defined need to protect one's reputation and a normative aversion to conventional forms of dispute resolution. Using data on more than 950 nonjustifiable homicides from police files, the present study tests this hypothesis by examining race-specific patterns of the victim's role in initiating homicides. If, as the theory suggests, African Americans are more likely than Whites to respond to minor affronts with lethal violence, then African-American homicide incidents should be characterized by more minor acts of provocation.

Previous Studies

As Cao et al. . . . have noted, the subculture of violence thesis is one of the most cited, but least tested explanations for the disproportionately high homicide rate among African Americans. The most prominent method for testing the subculture of violence thesis utilizes survey methodology. The major strength of the survey method is that it tests for cultural differences directly, rather than inferring cultural differences from unexplained variation after controlling for structural factors. . . . The central question for researchers using the survey approach is, "Do African Americans have significantly different attitudes regarding the appropriate use of violence?" Overwhelmingly, these studies find that African Americans are not more likely than Whites to endorse the use of violence in a variety of hypothetical circumstances. . . . Thus, studies using survey methodology have generally failed to support the subculture of violence thesis as a legitimate explanation for disproportionately high African-American homicide rates.

Still, the attitudinal survey design is not entirely true to the methodology advocated by Wolfgang and Ferracuti, the forefathers of the subculture of violence perspective. Wolfgang and Ferracuti propose an inductive approach to studying violence. From their viewpoint, rather than sampling from the general population as most survey studies do, it is better to work backward from the crime scene because the subculture of violence theory does not claim that all African Americans are equally socialized into the subculture. The subculture of violence thesis is meant to explain why African Americans are disproportionately involved in violent crime, particularly homicide. It does not argue that most or even a sizable minority of African Americans will involve themselves in such violence or endorse such acts. In other words, the subculture of violence thesis is meant to explain behavior that is, although far too frequent for a supposedly progressive society like the United States, statistically rare even among African Americans. Thus, the use of general population surveys and a general-to-specific investigative framework biases the results in favor of finding no difference among racial groups simply because of the relative rarity of a phenomenon like homicide.

Of course, the inductive approach to studying violence advocated by Wolfgang and Ferracuti is not without its own methodological problems. In particular, examining the characteristics of homicide offenders and victims to explain variation in homicidal behavior greatly increases the risk of tautological argument (i.e., people with the characteristics of killers tend to be more likely to kill). But when used cautiously, the inductive approach to studying violence is as useful as the deductive approach; what it loses in terms of generalizability it gains in terms of specificity and avoidance of aggregation bias. The current analysis goes beyond the existing survey-based literature by utilizing the inductive approach to provide a test of the African-American subculture of violence thesis that is consistent with the methodological stance taken by its creators.

Data and Sample

The data for the current analysis were originally collected by Zahn and Riedel . . . for the National Institute of Justice. The original purpose of the dataset was to examine an array of issues related to the "nature and patterns" of homicide in U.S. cities. Detailed information on homicide incidents was gathered from police files for eight American cities in 1978: Philadelphia, Newark, Chicago, St. Louis, Memphis, Dallas, Ashton, and Oakland. These cities were selected based on population size and the researchers' desire to represent multiple regions in the sample.

This dataset is ideal for the current analysis because, in addition to demographic variables for both victims and offenders, it contains detailed information on the victim's role in initiating the homicide event (their behavior immediately before the homicide took place), what Wolfgang . . . termed "victim precipitation." Not only do Zahn and Riedel code the homicide reports in terms of whether the victim flashed a

weapon before the offender resorted to lethal force, the most common operationalization of victim precipitation, but they also code more subtle forms of provocation such as verbal threats. Thus, the data allow for a test of the subculture of violence hypothesis that African Americans are more likely to respond to minor acts of provocation with extreme violence. Although the data are more than 20 years old and are only from urban areas, there are no provisions in the African-American subculture of violence theory that would limit the generalizability of the perspective to a specific time or place.

The current analyses utilize a subsample of Zahn and Riedel's dataset that excludes homicides classified as justifiable because legitimately killing in self-defense is, by definition, not an overreaction to a victim's provocation. Missing data related to the offender's race and whether and how the victim initiated the homicide event further reduced the sample by about 30%. Following convention at the time, Zahn and Riedel did not code "Hispanic" as an ethnic background (i.e., their coding scheme does not allow for the possibility that an individual could be African American or White and also of Hispanic origin). Thus, the current analyses are built around a comparison of non-Hispanic African Americans and non-Hispanic Whites. Seven homicide offenders classified as "other race" were removed from the sample because their small sample size precludes reliable statistical analysis. After excluding these cases and other cases with missing data, the final sample consisted of 967 homicides.

Results

Table 17.1 displays the results of a logistic regression analysis of the probability that the victim initiated the homicide event, usually by verbally taunting the offender, physically assaulting the offender, or displaying a weapon to scare the offender. The equation included a dummy variable for whether the offender's race was classified as African American and a dummy variable for whether the offense took place in one of the Southern cities (Dallas, St. Louis, or Memphis). The coefficients for the race variable failed to achieve statistical significance at the .05 level, indicating that cases with African-American offenders were not significantly different from cases with White offenders in terms of victim precipitation. Interestingly, consistent with the Southern subculture of violence thesis, homicides in the

Table 17.1   Logistic Regression Estimates for Victim Precipitation in Homicide Cases

Variables	b	S.E.
Southern city	.425*	0.197
African American offender[a]	−.152	0.182
Intercept	−.592*	0.167
Model χ^2	5.29	

Note. This sample was limited to cases with offenders not of Hispanic origin.

d.f. = 2.

$N = 967$.

[a]White offender is the reference group.

*P < .05.

three Southern cities were significantly (at the .05 level) more likely to be characterized by victim precipitation. It should be kept in mind, of course, that this sample is far from representative of the entire Southern region.

Table 17.2 displays the results of an analysis of whether and how the victim initiated the homicidal drama by race of the offender. As expected from the coefficients for the logistic regression analysis, the percentage of homicide events that were not victim precipitated was roughly equal for both racial groups (63.3% for Whites and 66.5% for African Americans). Furthermore, among those cases that were victim initiated, African Americans and Whites had similar levels of minor acts of provocation. Most notably, African Americans did not have higher levels of victim precipitation by verbal taunting or challenges. Thus, contrary to Wolfgang and Ferracuti's . . . perspective, "the significance of a jostle, a slightly derogatory remark, or the appearance of a weapon in the hands of an adversary" does not seem to vary substantially between racial groups, at least in terms of homicide.

In alternate analyses, the sample was limited to nonfelony-related homicides (e.g., not in the course of a robbery or drug deal) to examine possible differences between racial groups for killings that were more likely to be "heat of passion" crimes. Excluding felony homicides from the sample did not reveal any racial differences in victim precipitation and in fact seemed to slightly increase the similarities between African Americans and Whites. In another supplemental analysis, a logistic regression model focusing on interracial homicides (only 15% of the total sample) produced nearly identical results. That is, cases with an African-American offender and a White victim had similar levels of victim precipitation as cases with a White offender and an African-American victim. Other alternate analyses demonstrated that cases with offenders of Hispanic origin did not have significantly different levels of victim precipitation than those with offenders not of Hispanic origin.

Summary and Conclusion

The present analysis tested the African-American subculture of violence thesis that proposes that African Americans have a high homicide rate because they have been uniquely socialized to be hypersensitive to minor affronts and to believe that violence is an acceptable way to deal with conflict. . . . Thus, the theory suggests that African-American homicides should be more likely to be characterized by what would appear to an outsider as a trivial conflict or minor dispute. Unlike previous studies, the current analysis adopted a "work-backward-from-the-crime-scene" approach that is consistent with the research strategy advocated by the primary subculture of violence theorists. Still, like previous studies, the results failed to provide support for the notion of a unique subculture of violence among African Americans. Homicides appear similar across racial groups in terms of whether and how the victim initiated the violent event.

Table 17.2   Offender's Race by Type of Victim Precipitation

Offender's Race	Verbal Taunting (%)	Simple Assault (%)	Display Weapon (%)	Other Precipitation (%)	Not Victim Precipitated (%)
White ($N = 158$)	6.3	9.5	10.1	10.8	63.3
African American ($N = 809$)	4.9	10.6	10.5	7.4	66.5

Note. Percentages may not add to 100 because of rounding error.

Therefore, these findings cast doubt on Wolfgang and Ferracuti's . . . assertion that, "the significance of a jostle, a slightly derogatory remark, or the appearance of a weapon in the hands of an adversary are stimuli differentially perceived and interpreted" by African Americans and Whites. In regard to what triggers a homicide, African-American offenders and White offenders seem to be similarly affected by minor affronts.

Questions

1. Explain the arguments underlying the subculture of violence theory.

2. How does provocation play a role in violence according to this theory?

PART VI

SOCIAL PROCESS PERSPECTIVE

Because not all people exposed to negative societal conditions (such as strain or disorganization) engage in crime, social process theorists examine the influence of social interactions that take place among all segments of society. The approach's four main branches—social learning, labeling, social bond, and self-control—are presented here.

Social Learning

According to social learning theories, people acquire the techniques and thinking associated with crime from relations with others who are engaged in the behaviors. When criminality is rewarded more than punished, or its benefits outweigh its risks, it is reinforced and more likely to reoccur. Tammy Castle and Christopher Mensley (chap. 18) explore the link between military experience and serial killers in *Serial Killers With Military Experience: Applying Learning Theory to Serial Murder*. Although not the only cause of serial killing, the authors describe the role of the military in teaching and reinforcing violence, aggression, and killing. Allison Chappell and Alex Piquero (chap. 19) test Ronald Akers' theory in *Applying Social Learning Theory to Police Misconduct*. For Akers, learning occurs when there is association with those engaged in the behavior, reinforcement and favorable definitions of the behavior, and available role models. Since one of the main underlying principles of social learning theory is that it takes place in all of us, this chapter examines how the police may learn to engage in criminal behaviors.

Labeling and Reintegrative Shaming

Society's reaction to crime, whether through negative labeling and stigmatizing or the more progressive stance of reintegrative shaming, plays a role in a person's criminality. Although some people may be more likely to engage in crime due, in part, to the influence of a negative label, there are also people who are less likely to engage in crime in order to avoid that label. The duality of stigma is explored in the cross-cultural chapter by Patricia Funk (chap. 20) in *On the Effective Use of Stigma as a Crime Deterrent*, where the author considers stigma policies in the United States, Spain, and Switzerland. Another comparative study of labeling is presented in *Social Control in China:*

Applications of the Labeling Theory and Reintegrative Shaming Theory, by Xiaoming Chen (chap. 21). The author notes the limits of labeling theory in non-Western cultures and outlines how Chinese society uses stigma and labeling to achieve the goals of reintegrative shaming.

Social Control/Bond

In social control theory, Travis Hirschi maintains that criminality occurs when a person is only weakly connected to conventional others. The bond, according to his theory, is comprised of attachment, involvement, commitment, and belief. In *The Effect of Social Bonds on Successful Adjustment to Probation: An Event History Analysis* John Hepburn and Marie Griffin (chap. 22) examine how social bonds with others influence the probation experiences of people convicted of child molestation. The authors use what is arguably the most stigmatized and estranged group of offenders to be released from prison to test the hypothesis that bonds to others will affect successful adjustment to probation. In contrast to social bond theory is Michael Gottfredson and Travis Hirschi's general theory of crime, in which they maintain that criminality is the result of individual differences in levels of self-control. In *Self-Control and Social Bonds: A Combined Control Perspective on Deviance,* Douglas Longshore, Eunice Chang, Shih-chao Hsieh, and Nena Messina (chap. 23) consider how social bonds and self-control are related in a sample of adult male drug offenders.

Self-Control

Gottfredson and Hirschi's general theory of crime argues that criminal propensity is fixed within an individual early in life (by age 10). L. Thomas Winfree, Terrance Taylor, Ni He, and Finn-Aage Esbensen (chap. 24) test that premise using longitudinal data in *Self-Control and Variability Over Time: Multivariate Results Using a 5-Year, Multisite Panel of Youths.* The authors examine levels of self-control, self-reported engagement in criminal activity, and attitudes exhibited in a large sample (more than 950) of youth in six cities at five points in time.

CHAPTER 18

Serial Killers With Military Experience

Applying Learning Theory to Serial Murder

Tammy Castle
James Madison University

Christopher Mensley
Institute for Correctional Research and Training

The term *serial murder* was first introduced to differentiate between individuals who killed over a prolonged period of time and mass murderers who killed several victims in one episode. Although the term was not popularized until the 1980s, serial murder has existed for hundreds of years. The first documented case of serial murder occurred in the 15th century. Gille de Rais, a French nobleman and friend of Joan of Arc, was executed for torturing and murdering approximately 100 children. . . .

Although serial murder remains a relatively rare phenomenon, the number of serial murders has risen in the United States in the past 20 years. Hickey . . . profiled 337 cases of serial murder that occurred in the United States from 1800 to 1995. The majority of these cases (302) occurred between 1980 and 1995. Although serial killings appear more frequently, a portion of this increase may be due to enhanced technology that allows law enforcement officials the necessary information to link possible serial homicides. In addition, media attention has played a large part in increasing public awareness of serial murder. However, media attention alone cannot account for the increase in serial murder during the past couple of decades. Regardless, serial murder remains a rare occurrence. . . .

The study of serial homicide remains in its infancy. Studies have focused on the motivation and causation, which has encompassed biological, sociological, and psychological factors. Scholars have examined whether the propensity for serial murder is the result of heredity, head trauma, environmental factors, parental influences, or mental illness. There are no variables that can account for all cases of serial murder. Therefore, research must continue in this area to determine what other factors contribute to the making of a serial killer. One link observed in the case studies of serial killers is that some of them have served time in the military. This link has not been addressed in previous literature on serial murder, although the military is a social context that promotes violence and aggression. Therefore, the focus of this chapter is to explore the military as a social context where future serial murderers may learn the necessary skills to kill.

Definitions of Serial Murder

Serial murder is a term generally used to describe murders that are committed sequentially or in repetition. In the early 1980s, FBI officials first used the term serial

Source: "Serial killers with military experience: Applying learning theory to serial murder," by Castle, T., & Hensley, C., (2002), *International Journal of Offender Therapy and Comparative Criminology, 46,* 453–465. Reprinted by permission of Sage Publications, Inc.

murder to define this phenomenon and distinguish this type of murder from *mass murder*. Serial murder was defined by law enforcement officials as sexual attacks and resulting deaths of young women, men, or children committed by male killers who tend to follow physical or psychological patterns. . . .

In 1988, the FBI revised its definition, describing serial killings as three or more murders committed separately, with an emotional cooling-off period between the homicides. . . . Also in 1988, Brooks, Devine, Green, Hart, and Moore published a report offering a more detailed definition of serial murder. The report defined *serial murder* as

> a series of two or more murders, committed as separate events, usually, but not always by an offender acting alone. The crimes may occur over a period of time ranging from hours to years. Quite often the motive is psychological, and the offender's behavior and the physical evidence observed at the crime scenes will reflect sadistic, sexual overtones. . . .

Holmes and DeBurger . . . described five elements that further distinguished serial murder from other types of multiple homicides. The first element contained repetitive homicides. The serial killer continued to kill during a period of months or years. The second element explained that these murders were typically one on one, although some "team killers" did exist. The third element suggested that serial murder rarely occurred between people who were intimates. Typically, no prior relationship existed between victim and killer. The fourth element implied that the serial killer felt a compulsion to kill; thus, the murders were not crimes of passion and did not stem from victim precipitation. The fifth element suggested that economic motives may have been missing in most cases of serial murder.

In 1990, Egger limited the definition of serial murder to include seven major components. The first component of serial murder is when one or more individuals commit a second and/or subsequent murder. The second component asserts that there is generally no prior relationship between victims and their attacker. Third, the subsequent murders take place at different times and have no apparent connection to the prior murder. The fourth characteristic is that the murders are usually committed in different geographical locations. Fifth, the motive is not for material gain. Rather, the motive is the murderer's desire to have power or dominance over victims. Sixth, victims may have symbolic value for the

murderer. The murderer may also perceive victims as powerless given their situation in time, place, or status within their immediate surroundings. For this reason, the seventh component is that victims tend to be those who are most vulnerable, least valued, or marginalized by our society. These people include the homeless, prostitutes, homosexuals, vagrants, missing children, individual women out alone and moving in isolated areas, college students, older women, and migrant workers. . . .

Some researchers suggest that Egger's . . . definition is too specific and that a broader definition of serial murder should be used. Hickey . . . argued that the definition of serial killers should include anyone who commits multiple murders during an extended period of time. Many women who commit multiple murders often kill acquaintances or are motivated by profit. Hickey's definition of serial murder would encompass more women in this otherwise predominantly male phenomenon.

Although scholars disagree on the precise definition of serial murder, psychological factors are often examined in research on serial homicide. The heinous nature of serial murder propels many to question the sanity of those who commit such crimes. The next section discusses the issue of mental illness in the case of serial murder.

Mental Illness

Many people in society prefer to explain serial murder by labeling killers as insane. However, most serial killers are not insane. Using the legal definition of *insanity*, the vast majority of serial killers know the difference between right and wrong at the time of commission of the crime. Fewer than 4% of serial killers have attempted to use insanity as a defense. Only 1% of those who used this defense were found not guilty by reason of insanity. . . . In other cases of homicide, less than 1% of these used insanity as a defense. Only 25% of these cases were successful. . . . Although it is not insanity, most scholars agree there is some pathological process associated with the commission of such crimes. . . .

Norris . . . took a biological approach to serial murder. In his book *Serial Killers*, he suggested that some serial killers may be suffering from a neurological disorder. This is often due to head trauma they experienced in childhood. The head trauma may damage certain areas of the brain, causing episodic aggressive behavior.

Although Norris . . . focused on structural brain abnormalities, he acknowledged the contributions of environmental and psychological factors. Norris noted 21 patterns indicative of episodic aggressive behavior, including

> ritualistic behavior, masks of sanity, compulsivity, search for help, severe memory disorders, chronic inability to tell the truth, suicidal tendencies, history of sexual assault, deviant sexual behavior and hypersexuality, head injuries or injuries that occurred at birth, history of chronic drug or alcohol abuse, alcohol or drug-abusing parents, victim of physical or emotional abuse, cruel parenting, result of unwanted pregnancy, product of a difficult gestation period for the mother, interrupted bliss or no bliss in childhood, extraordinary cruelty to animals, arsenal tendencies without obvious homicidal interests, symptoms of neurological impairment, evidence of genetic disorders, or feelings of powerlessness or inadequacy. . . .

Some serial killers have suffered episodes of psychosis, neurosis, and paranoia. Episodes of psychosis involve the individual having some form of break with reality during which they may exhibit dangerous or violent behavior. Neuroses, in contrast, are less severe and include many of the behaviors associated with personality disorders. . . . Paranoia is the sense that an individual is being endangered, threatened, or plotted against. Paranoia is symptomatic of many neuropsychiatric disorders, including senility, seizures, brain damage, and schizophrenia. . . .

Schizophrenia is often first diagnosed in the teenage years or the early 20s. Symptoms include disorganized thought processes, psychosis, hallucinations, delusions, and feelings of being controlled from the outside. There are different subtypes of schizophrenia; however, most fall within the categories of paranoid or nonparanoid. . . .

Paranoid schizophrenics are often associated with unprovoked bouts of violence. In most cases, the violence is due to hallucinations or delusions. . . . Some report hearing voices that command them to kill. David Berkowitz, also known as "Son of Sam," tried to use schizophrenia as a defense at his trial. Berkowitz claimed that the next door neighbor's dog commanded him to kill, but later recanted. . . .

Violence in schizophrenics is often committed during a psychotic episode. However, few believe that this explanation holds true for serial murderers. Some single episodes of homicide can be accounted for by temporary insanity due to schizophrenia, but there has never been an authenticated case of a schizophrenic committing serial murder. . . .

Other types of mental illness that have been used as an explanation for serial murder fall into the category of dissociative disorders. One of these illnesses, dissociative identity disorder (DID), is also known as multiple personality disorder. DID is characterized by the existence of two or more different personalities or personality states. . . . Psychologists believe that DID develops in response to some traumatic experience in childhood. The personalities develop as a way to dissociate from the pain of the experience. . . . DID has been used successfully as a defense in one instance of a single homicide. However, it too has never been authenticated in any serial killer. . . . .

Biological abnormalities and severe mental illness are rare in serial killers. However, some pathological process is often present. The most common psychological factor experienced by serial killers is a personality disorder. The next section discusses the types of personality disorders that are most commonly associated with serial killers.

Personality Disorders

Personality disorders, unlike severe mental illness, are often difficult to detect. Individuals with personality disorders do not show any overt symptoms such as those associated with psychoses or schizophrenia. Personality disorders are insidious and often present as simply aspects of an individual's character. . . .

The *Diagnostic and Statistical Manual of Mental Disorders–IV* (*DSM–IV*); . . . is the guidebook used by psychiatrists, psychologists, and social workers to assess and diagnose mental disorders. The *DSM–IV* describes personality disorders as "enduring patterns of inner experience and behavior that deviate markedly from the individual's culture." . . . For a personality disorder to be diagnosed, the *DSM–IV* states that two of the following four areas must be affected: cognition (perception and interpretation of self, others, and events), affectivity (intensity, range, and appropriateness of emotional response), interpersonal functioning, and impulse control. . . . The most common personality disorder linked with serial killers is antisocial personality disorder. . . .

Historically, the term *psychopath* was used to describe someone that today would be diagnosed with antisocial personality disorder. In the 1960s, a psychopath was characterized by lacking feeling toward other humans, being emotionless, showing no remorse, acting on impulse without thought, and lacking drive or motivation. Psychologists also acknowledged the lack of any psychoses or mental deficits. . . .

In 1976, Hervey Cleckley released a publication called *The Mask of Sanity*. In this publication, Cleckley devised a checklist of symptoms of the individual suffering from a psychopathic disorder. These symptoms included superficial charm, intelligence, unreliability, malingering, lack of remorse and shame, lack of motivation, lack of delusions, narcissism, trivial sex life, and lack of long-term goals. Many scholars agree that not all serial killers exhibit all of these qualities. To the contrary, some serial killers actually do experience remorse. To extinguish the guilt, they negate their feelings or rationalize their behavior.

Based on Cleckley's observations, Hare . . . revised the psychopathy checklist. He argued that psychopaths exhibit superficial charm, narcissism, pathological lying, manipulation, lack of remorse and guilt, shallow affect, lack of empathy, and failure to accept responsibility for their actions. The psychopath's lifestyle is described as parasitic and prone to boredom, with poor behavioral controls, lack of long-term goals, impulsivity, irresponsibility, juvenile delinquency, promiscuous sexual behavior, short-term marriages, and criminal versatility.

Current scholars contend that serial killers may exhibit some of these traits, but not all of them. Psychopathy is a broad category that should not be used to describe serial killers due to the variety of types of offenders. Today, psychologists have replaced the term *psychopathy* with *antisocial personality disorder*. The common pathology among serial killers tends to reflect a high degree of anger, hostility, frustration, low self-esteem, and feelings of inadequacy. . . .

Fox and Levin. . . . suggested that, rather than suffer from psychopathy, many serial killers possess psychological facilitators for neutralizing guilt and remorse.

They are able to compartmentalize their attitudes by conceiving of at least two categories of human beings—those whom they care about and treat with decency, and those with whom they have no relationship and therefore can victimize with total disregard for their feelings. . . .

Fox and Levin . . . . also asserted that compartmentalization is a method used by serial killers to separate themselves from their crimes. However, compartmentalization is learned and used by individuals in their everyday roles. Individuals separate the positive and negative aspects of their personalities and create two separate selves: one may be a cutthroat businessman at work, whereas the other is a loving husband and father. . . .

Fox and Levin . . . . contended that, along with compartmentalization, dehumanization is another neutralization method learned by serial killers. Dehumanization is another psychological process that effectively permits killing without guilt. . . .

In the case of serial killers, dehumanization is often used when selecting the victims. Prostitutes, homosexuals, and the homeless are viewed by serial killers as subhuman elements of society. However, in some cases, dehumanization does not occur until after victims have been captured. Victims then become objects that serial killers can rape, torture, mutilate, and eventually murder. . . .

Serial killers may suffer from personality disorders. However, some scholars believe the behavior they exhibit can also be learned in different environments. The next section explores the military as an environment that promotes violence and teaches individuals to kill.

Teaching Servicemen to Kill

Some scholars propose that the military provides the social context where servicemen learn aggression, violence, and murder. Grossman . . . ., a military expert on the psychology of killing, discusses these methods in *On Killing: The Psychological Cost of Learning to Kill in War and Society*. Grossman coined the term *killology* to describe a new interdisciplinary field: the study of the methods and psychological effects of training military recruits to circumvent their inhibitions to killing fellow human beings.

Grossman . . . .noted that previous military research showed that servicemen were not inclined to kill. During the Civil War, only a tiny percentage of servicemen fired to hit, whereas the vast majority fired over the enemy's head. A team of researchers, studying what servicemen did in battle during World War II, discovered that only 15% to 20% of individual servicemen were able to fire at an exposed enemy. Considering this unwillingness to kill in battle a problem, the military adopted different techniques in an attempt to increase this percentage. By the time of the Korean War, the rate of servicemen willing to fire to kill increased to 55%. During the Vietnam War, the rate had risen to more than 90%. . . .

Grossman . . . stated that today the military uses various training methods to increase the killing rates of servicemen, including brutalization, classical conditioning, operant conditioning, and role modeling. Brutalization and desensitization to violence are first encountered at boot camp. Cadets are verbally and physically abused by superiors for the entire duration of boot camp. Cadets also lose all individuality by being forced to act and dress alike. The author reports that this brutalization is designed to break down existing mores and norms and to accept a new set of values that embrace violence and death as a way of life. Cadets eventually become desensitized to violence and accept it as a normal and essential survival skill. . . .

Operant conditioning, the procedure of repetitive stimulus–response reinforcement chaining, is also used by the military to condition servicemen to react a certain way. An appropriate example of operant conditioning by the military is the use of flight simulators to train pilots. When pilots are flying and experience a problem, they will react reflexively due to the hours of training on the flight simulator. . . .

Grossman . . . also suggested that conditioned responses are beneficial in various ways. Servicemen and police officers, for example, are trained to shoot at man-shaped targets. This is the stimulus. The conditioned response is to shoot the target. The trainees repeat these procedures many times. Later, servicemen and police officers will reflexively shoot to kill when faced with the same situation.

According to Grossman . . . , role models are also used by the military. Servicemen are provided immediate role models, their drill sergeants. Drill sergeants personify violence and aggression, and servicemen strive to be like their role models. Dehumanization also contributes to servicemen learning to kill. Enemies are viewed as subhuman and become objects. The learned, conditioned responses take over, and servicemen then become killers. . . .

Unfortunately, only one empirical study has examined the possible link between serial murder and military experience. Using data collected from 354 previously identified case studies, Castle . . . identified 25 American serial killers with previous military experience. Thus, approximately 7% of all the serial killers identified in her study had a military background. In the next section, we apply learning theory to serial murder with a special emphasis on military experience.

Applying Learning Theory to Serial Murder

Learning theorists contend that deviant and criminal behavior that can be learned can also be unlearned.

Although there are many criticisms of learning theory, it is still used today by researchers. Serial murder is one area to which scholars have attempted to apply learning theory. Hale . . . suggested that serial murder is a crime that can also be learned.

Hale . . . noted that the internal drives of a serial killer are often overlooked as motivation. Previous case studies of serial killers suggested that killers' victims often resemble persons who caused the killers humiliation. Hale proposed that early humiliation in the lives of serial murderers can eventually translate into criminal behavior. This happens, however, only if killers recognize and internalize the humiliation as a motive.

Hale . . . used Amsel's . . . frustration theory to explain how killers internalize the perceived wrong and use it as a justification for murder. Based on this theory, killers associate certain cues from the situation in which the humiliation initially occurred with the later humiliation. The later or current humiliation is referred to as a *nonreward situation*. Nonreward presented in a situation in which reward previously occurred produces an unconditioned frustration response. The cues that are present during the humiliation become conditioned to produce an anticipatory frustration response. This response also produces distinctive internal stimuli, which motivates the individual to avoid potentially humiliating situations in the future.

The Hull . . . and Spence . . . theories of discrimination learning explain why killers are not able to discriminate one instance of humiliation from another. Situations in which killers have experienced a reward (reinforcement) allow them to discriminate between stimuli and choose the behavior that produces the reward. However, killers have experienced few, if any, situations that produce a reward. Therefore, in all situations in which the cues indicate a potential humiliation to the killers, the killers associate them with a nonreinforcement situation. The abundance of these nonreinforcement situations does not allow killers to discriminate one situation from another.

Hale . . . also uses Dollard and Miller's . . . theory of learning to explain why killers "instigate" a certain behavior. An instigated behavior is a behavior where the predicted response is the consequence. This consequence has been observed or inferred by the individuals. The behavior may be instigated to seek approval or some other desired goal. Frustration occurs when a barrier prevents the individuals from reaching the desired goal.

This frustration is the result of a basic impulse or drive being blocked. The aggressiveness is blocked, but must eventually be released. The aggressive impulses may be released indirectly through displacement to less threatening objects. Using Freud's idea of transference, Dollard and Miller . . . suggested that responses may be transferred from one object to another through generalization.

In the application to serial murder, killers are under the control of individuals who originally caused the humiliation. Killers may release the frustration and aggression on the original individuals. However, the control and humiliation often prevent killers from doing this. Therefore, the humiliation becomes internalized and is not corrected. Through generalization, killers transfer this internalized humiliation to their victims in an attempt to rectify the past humiliation. . . .

Hale . . . focused on the internal drives of killers in applying learning theory to serial murder. Based on previous case studies that report killers' victims often resemble someone who caused them humiliation, Hale suggested that the early humiliation can eventually translate into criminal behavior. Killers internalize a perceived wrong and use it as justification for murder. The abundance of nonreinforcement situations makes it impossible for killers to discriminate one situation from another. Eventually, killers, using generalization, transfer internalized humiliation to their victims. The killers are unable to discriminate between different stimuli. Hale asserted that this transference occurs only if killers recognize and internalize the humiliation as a motive for the murders. However, although most victims have some symbolic value for the killers, not all of the victims resemble someone from their past.

Hale . . . , like other learning theorists, contended that serial murder can be unlearned. Killers are unable to discriminate or specify the differences and similarities between comparable stimuli. Serial killers are confusing cues from the past with ones in the present. Therapy may be able to help serial killers identify these faulty generalizations and expand their learning processes. . . .

Burgess and Akers' . . . theory of differential association reinforcement follows the logic of operant principles while acknowledging the cognitive processes that contribute to such associations. The principles of their learning theory as well as contributions by Grossman . . . can be applied to serial killers who have served in the military. Although branches, ranks, and types of military service may differ among the cases, military boot camp provides a common social context in which servicemen can transfer violence and aggression into learning how to kill. War and combat experience may help to strengthen or reinforce the behavior; however, the learning experiences provided in boot camp are sufficient.

The first principle of Burgess and Akers's . . . theory asserted that deviant behavior is learned according to the principles of operant conditioning. This repetitive procedure of stimulus–response conditions servicemen to react in a certain way. . . .

The behavior can be learned in nonsocial situations, where the behavior is either reinforcing or discriminating, and through social interactions of other persons, where their behavior is observed to be reinforcing or discriminating. The likelihood that the behavior will be repeated in the future is governed by positive and negative reinforcement. Killing in the military or eliminating the enemy threat is deemed an essential survival tool. Servicemen are positively reinforced for this behavior. Servicemen also are exposed to the interactions of other servicemen being reinforced for their behavior. Grossman . . . discussed this in his study, contending that the military uses positive role modeling and that the role models usually represent people who personify violence and aggression.

The principal part of learning deviant behavior occurs in the groups that control individuals' major source of reinforcements. When individuals enter the military, that group becomes the individuals' major source of reinforcements. As Grossman . . . reported, brutalization is a technique used by the military to break down individuals' existing mores and norms and to embrace violence and aggression as a new way of life. The military then becomes the individuals' primary social group.

The specific techniques, attitudes, and avoidance procedures of deviant behavior are learned in reinforcing situations. Servicemen not only learn to accept death and killing as a way of life, but also the techniques of killing and the attitudes that reinforce this type of behavior. Dehumanization and compartmentalization are also learned as methods to neutralize remorse and guilt. Servicemen are taught that there are two groups of people: fellow servicemen and enemies. Enemies are viewed as subhuman, which neutralizes the guilt of killing them. . . .

The potential for persons to commit deviant behavior is increased in situations where the presence of normative definitions and verbalizations over conforming behavior has acquired discriminatory value. In the military, servicemen learn that killing is a normal and accepted way of life. Serial killers learn that conforming to behavior in the military is to embrace a way of life that encourages violence and aggression. This way of life is not considered conforming behavior in civilian life, although killing is defined as normal in the military. This behavior has been reinforced in the military, and serial killers apply these learned skills in civilian life.

Finally, the strength of deviant behavior is a direct function of the amount, frequency, and probability of its reinforcement. Violence and aggression are continuously and consistently reinforced in the military. Servicemen learn that these values will be positively reinforced. Although the specific reward changes, serial killers murder because it provides them with some kind of reinforcement. However, as Holmes and Holmes . . . pointed out when describing the cyclic nature of serial murder, the ritual often leaves serial killers depressed and unsatisfied. Serial killers begin the cycle again, believing that this will cure the depression. As serial killers continue to cycle, rarely do the murders leave the killers feeling satisfied or rewarded. Yet the behavior has been frequently reinforced; therefore, it is more likely to be repeated in the future.

Conclusion

Although serial murder has existed for hundreds of years, the study of serial murder remains in its infancy. Scholars have endeavored to study serial murder by focusing on biological, psychological, and sociological factors. Some of these studies have provided support in hindsight for these various factors by noting their evidence in the case histories of serial killers. However, none of these factors exist in all cases of serial murder.

The general theory of social learning, as formulated by Burgess and Akers . . . , was applied to show how the military provided a social group through which potential or future serial killers learn the skills and neutralization techniques of killing. Grossman's . . . research in the military on the psychology of killing supports the idea that murder, like other forms of crime and deviant behavior, can be learned. Although researchers have used social learning theory to support crime and deviant behavior, Hale . . . was the first scholar who attempted to apply learning theory to serial murder.

Like other variables previously considered in the study of serial murder, military experience is not present in all cases. Therefore, the military may be just one social group that provides the serial killer with the associations and reinforcements necessary to learn how to kill. However, future serial killers may be attracted to military service for this reason. Because the study of serial murder remains a new area of research, future studies might examine this relationship further.

Questions

1. Describe the training methods used by the military today to increase the killing rates of service people.

2. How does military training influence serial killing according to the general theory of social learning?

CHAPTER 19

Applying Social Learning Theory to Police Misconduct

Allison T. Chappell
University of Florida, Gainesville

Alex R. Piquero
City University of New York, John Jay College

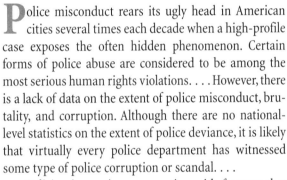olice misconduct rears its ugly head in American cities several times each decade when a high-profile case exposes the often hidden phenomenon. Certain forms of police abuse are considered to be among the most serious human rights violations. . . . However, there is a lack of data on the extent of police misconduct, brutality, and corruption. Although there are no national-level statistics on the extent of police deviance, it is likely that virtually every police department has witnessed some type of police corruption or scandal. . . .

Policing is a unique occupation with features that contribute to the opportunity for deviant behavior. . . . Police officers enjoy many freedoms that are not accorded to regular citizens, such as speeding, using deadly force, and seizing property. Not only does the occupation provide many opportunities for deviance, but it also provides justifications if the behavior is questioned. Moreover, deviant officers are unlikely to be detected because of loose supervision and the fact that officers often work in isolation from public observation.

Police misconduct has been defined in many ways, and the term has been used to describe many different actions, including drug using and selling, brutality, protection of illegal activity, insubordination, and neglect of duty. In this chapter, we focus on accepting gifts and meals from the public, opportunistic theft, and the use of excessive force.

According to Alpert and Dunham . . . , acceptance of meals and gifts is the most common and extensive form of police corruption. . . . Many cities actually allow officers to accept free or discount meals. It is often accepted behavior when it is an act of gratitude toward the police, but sometimes the motive is to buy protection from the police. In other words, some businesses offer free items or services in expectation for quicker response times and extra protection from the police. . . .

Alpert and Dunham . . . describe "opportunistic theft" as a result of situations that provide unusual opportunities for theft. For example, the police are likely the first respondents to a burglary call. When belongings or merchandise have already been taken illegally, the opportunity presents itself to steal something and blame it on the burglary. Another example is taking money or drugs from drug dealers and failing to report it to the police department.

The term *excessive force* is used to describe "force that exceeds what is objectively reasonable and necessary in the circumstances confronting the officer to subdue a person." . . . Police officers are to use force only when necessary and only to the extent required for the performance of their duty. It includes, but is not limited to, unjustified shootings, severe beatings, fatal chokings, and rough treatment. . . .

Source: "Applying social learning theory to police misconduct," by Chappell, A. T., & Piquero, A. R., (2004), in *Deviant Behavior, 25*(2), 89–108. Reprinted by permission of Taylor & Francis.

Although useful documentation of police deviance has occurred, researchers and practitioners continue to struggle in developing a comprehensive theoretical picture of police misconduct. Previous attempts have viewed police misconduct as a product of the authoritarian personality . . . , individual deviance (i.e., the "bad apple approach") . . . , organizational or group deviance . . . , a social ecological phenomenon . . . , the breakdown of deterrence and rise of impulsivity . . . , and the larger police subculture and occupational socialization. . . .

This chapter analyzes police misconduct from a unique theoretical base. We believe that the social-psychological behaviorist approach of Akers' social learning theory provides a unique theoretical lens through which to view police misconduct. Herein, we examine how officer attitudes and perceptions of peer attitudes and ideas about the likelihood of punishment influence officially documented citizen complaints.

Prior Research on Citizen Complaints

Little is known about the extent of police misconduct. This lack of information is largely due to a lack of accurate reporting of police misconduct incidents, and to the fact that misconduct, in general, is a relatively rare event. One of the ways it has been measured is with citizen complaints. . . . This approach is not without limitations. There are under- and overreporting problems; only one third of people who believe they have been mistreated by the police actually file a complaint. . . .

In general, there are at least three issues associated with citizen complaints that must be recognized. First, citizen complaints have been used to measure multiple concepts, including police misconduct, police–citizen relations, and police productivity. It has been observed that police officers who are most active are more likely to receive complaints, regardless of whether they are participating in misconduct. . . . A second problem lies in the validity of citizen complaints to measure police misconduct. Lersch and Mieczkowski . . . examined this issue by comparing the occurrence of externally (citizen) generated complaints to internally generated complaints filed with the internal affairs office of a large police agency in the southeast. They found that officers identified by citizens as having engaged in misconduct were significantly more likely to be accused of misconduct by their peers. A third issue is that complaints are filed from the perspective of the citizen. Previous research suggests that police officers tend to define misconduct narrowly, whereas citizens define it more broadly. . . . There also is

concern about the method by which complaints are handled in an agency. If citizens are aware that their department takes complaints seriously, this may affect their decision to file a complaint. Thus, departments with excellent community relations may actually have higher rates of citizen complaints because people feel more comfortable reporting misconduct to the agency. . . . Alternatively, complaint processes and procedures that are intimidating or complicated can affect the decision to file a complaint. If the victim has a criminal record, he or she may not want to draw attention to him or herself. . . . Finally, if officers perceive that their department does not investigate complaints thoroughly, then they may be less likely to modify their behavior in response to complaints, thus affecting the number of future complaints filed.

Unfortunately, although researchers have been successful in documenting police misconduct, extant research has been slow to provide a theoretical lens through which to view police misconduct. In the next section, we highlight one criminological theory that we believe offers unique insight into the causes of police misconduct.

Social Learning Theory

Akers developed social learning theory as an extension of Sutherland's differential association theory to explain acts that violate social norms. . . . The basic assumption behind social learning theory is that the same learning process can produce both conforming and deviant or delinquent behavior. Akers posits that four variables function to instigate and strengthen attitudes toward social behavior: differential association, definitions, reinforcement, and modeling. The balance of these influences determines whether one will be prone to engage in conforming or deviant behavior. The central variable in social learning theory is differential association, or the influence of those with whom one associates frequently. Akers argues that individuals develop favorable or unfavorable definitions to deviance in interactions with their peers. These definitions are then reinforced, positively or negatively, by the rewards or punishments (either real or perceived) that follow their behavior. Additionally, peers provide models of behavior to follow.

Social learning theory has received considerable scholarly attention and empirical support; however, its focus has tended to be on explaining crime and delinquency more generally, and not police misconduct in particular. Next, we provide a brief review of how social learning has been dealt with in the policing literature.

DIFFERENTIAL ASSOCIATION

As it applies to the police, the subculture is the primary peer group in which officers learn definitions. According to Alpert and Dunham . . . , one of the most profound pressures operating in police agencies is peer influence. In this vein, most researchers and police officers acknowledge the existence of a police subculture. . . . The subculture may facilitate deviant behavior by transmitting the beliefs, values, definitions, and "manners of expression" that depart from acceptable behavior. This happens because the subculture's shared value system allows them the opportunity to rationalize, excuse, and justify deviance. . . . Alpert and Dunham . . . maintain that because social isolation is a feature of the police subculture, officers are likely to withdraw into the subculture for support and approval. The result is that the police officer is "subjected to intense peer influence and control," and this can involve the acceptance of deviance. . . .

Due to the isolation that police officers often feel, they tend to spend more time with other officers, especially for social purposes. Therefore, it becomes more important for the officer to feel accepted by the peer group for the development of a satisfactory self-concept. . . . Accordingly, Skolnick . . . reported that the strength of the organizational culture in a police department was so salient that, regardless of personal differences, individuals adopted the beliefs and definitions of the department.

The police subculture provides an opportunity to learn deviant activity because attitudes, values, and beliefs are transmitted from one generation to another in a learning process. . . . Skolnick . . . asserts that the police develop "cognitive lenses" through which to view the world. Sherman . . . further contends that police corruption may be explained as the transmission of cultural values via the influence of reference groups.

Savitz . . . looked at police recruits' attitudes toward police deviance at three different time periods. He found that as recruits advanced from the police academy to the streets, exposure to the police subculture increased, and their attitudes became more permissive regarding deviance. The officers began to favor less severe punishments for various forms of misconduct, such as accepting bribes and theft. . . .

DIFFERENTIAL REINFORCEMENT

Police scholars often comment on the importance of peer acceptance and approval regarding their own behavior and beliefs. According to Herbert . . . , officers engage in certain behaviors to maintain good standing in a desirable occupational environment. It is suggested that officers learn corrupt behavior through the reinforcements obtained from the subcultural group. . . . According to Conser . . . , the subculture is a powerful reference group that has a great capacity for the reinforcement of corrupt behavior. He suggests that corruption arises through a process of interaction, during which the individual officer learns such behavior in accordance with the responses of others. Akers . . . notes that the selection and continuation of associations are functions of differential reinforcement. However, in the special circumstance of the police subculture, it would be more difficult to separate whether peers are deviant. One study found that receiving free meals, services, or discounts was viewed by many police officers as a fringe benefit of the job and anticipated little risk of punishment for these behaviors. In summary, it is likely that the police subculture reinforces and encourages certain types of police misconduct. . . .

Current Study

In this chapter, we present what we believe is the first application of Akers' social learning theory . . . to account for police misconduct. As it applies to the deviant subculture of the police, social learning theory suggests that officers develop peer groups within the department. These peer groups either hold conventional or nonconventional, prodeviance beliefs. Assuming that the subculture is already formed, the theory would argue that as a new officer enters the peer group, he or she will be exposed to models of behavior that will influence his or her own attitudes and behavior. Because police officers are exposed to their coworkers much more often than others, it is likely that the officer will learn to accept and internalize the definitions shared by other officers.

We employ data from a random sample of police officers from Philadelphia who were queried on a number of issues related to police misconduct. Three hypotheses are examined. First, officers who associate with deviant peers are more likely to have citizen complaints. Second, officers who consider misconduct to be less serious will have a higher likelihood of citizen complaints. Third, officers who anticipate less punishment for misconduct are more likely to have citizen complaints.

Data and Methods

The data are drawn from a survey administered to a sample of police officers from the Philadelphia Police

Department (PPD). The population of study includes all Philadelphia police officers assigned to patrol, including the ranks of Police Officers, Sergeants, and Lieutenants, as of January 2000. This amounts to 3,810 officers from the 23 Philadelphia patrol districts. A simple random sample of 504 officers was drawn from this population, the majority (91%) of whom were patrol officers. Out of the possible 504 officers, only 5 officers refused to participate, leaving a sample of 499 available for analysis. Males comprised 68% of the sample; 53.5% of the sample was non-White (45.7% were Black). Respondents ranged in age from 20–61, with a mean of 35 years. On average, respondents had 7.5 years of police experience. Finally, 46% of the sample was married. There were no substantive differences in the demographic characteristics for the sample used in this study and the larger population of officers.

Researchers attended roll-calls in all 23 Philadelphia police districts. . . . The survey was administered to officers immediately following their roll-call, prior to going out on the street. On average, it took about 15 minutes for an officer to complete the survey. . . .

Dependent Variable

Police misconduct was measured by the presence of citizen complaints. Officers were asked whether they had ever been the subject of a formal citizen complaint. About half of the sample had received at least one complaint. In this study, we compared officers who had no complaints to officers who had one or more complaints. Because of the categorical nature of the dependent variable, logistic regression was employed.

Independent Variables

Several independent variables were obtained via officers' responses to several hypothetical vignettes (i.e., scenarios). The vignettes, or third-person scenarios, were designed to present respondents with realistic examples of a variety of deviant and conforming behavior. This methodology has previously been applied to the study of police behavior and deviance . . . and is a common technique in the social sciences. . . . In the Klockars et al. . . . scenario study of police integrity, officers were asked to respond to several hypothetical scenarios, such as theft, bribery, and accepting gifts. Officers were asked to rate the seriousness of each act from their own perspective, as well as from the perspective of their peer officers on 5-point Likert scales. They also were

asked to rate the amount of discipline they thought would follow the act.

In this study, we employed five of the hypothetical scenarios used by Klockars et al., and the questions following the scenarios were used to measure social learning concepts. The first two scenarios involved (a) accepting meals and objects of small value, and (b) accepting gifts from merchants on holidays. The second two scenarios involved theft from a crime scene: (a) stealing a watch after a jewelry store burglary, and (b) stealing money out of a lost wallet. The fifth scenario involved using excessive force. As is seen in the next section, scales of the social learning indicators were created by summing responses for items that loaded .50 or above on the factor in a factor analysis.

Peer Associations

Akers . . . argues that the perception of peer behavior may be just as important as the actual behavior. Even if deviant peer behavior is misperceived as more or less than it actually is, the peer influence will still operate through that perception. . . . Three variables measured the perception of peer behavior, and for each item respondents were asked, "How serious do most police officers in the PPD consider this behavior to be?" The first measure indicated whether officers perceived their peers to consider behaviors, such as accepting gifts and meals, to be serious (α = .75, M = 7.53). Response options ranged from 1 (*very serious*) to 5 (*not at all serious*) for each behavior. The second measure indicated peer attitudes about two types of theft (α = .71, M = 2.86). Response options ranged from 1 to 5. The third measured peer attitudes about excessive force (M = 2.57). Response options ranged from 1 to 5. Because higher values correspond with the perception of decreased seriousness, we expected that peer associations will be positively related to misconduct and, thus, citizen complaints.

Definitions

Definitions refer to one's attitudes and beliefs that define the commission of an act as right or wrong. . . . According to the theory, the stronger one's feelings are against certain acts, the less likely one is to engage in them. Officers were asked to respond to several acts committed in each of the three scenarios (accepting gifts and meals, theft from a crime scene, and using excessive force). Specifically, officers were asked: "How serious do you consider this behavior to be?" Response options ranged from 1 (*very serious*) to 5 (*not at all serious*) for accepting gifts and meals ($\alpha = .72$, $M = 6.84$), for two types of theft ($\alpha = .72$, $M = 2.32$), and for excessive force ($M = 2.10$). Because higher values correspond to a more accepting attitude toward criminal behavior (i.e., decreasing levels of seriousness), these variables are expected to be positively related to citizen complaints.

REINFORCEMENT

Reinforcement refers to anticipated rewards or punishments associated with certain behaviors that serve to determine whether someone will repeat the behavior. In an effort to measure this concept, the following question was used: "If another officer engaged in this behavior and was discovered doing so, what if any discipline do *you* think *would* follow?" Choices ranged from none (0), to verbal and written reprimands, suspension without pay, demotion in rank, and dismissal (6) and were reverse-coded so that higher values correspond to lower expected punishment. The question was asked in accordance with the three domains of misconduct noted earlier. Response options ranged from 1 to 6 for each item (two for accepting gifts and meals [$\alpha = .89$, $M = 8.14$], two for theft [$\alpha = .83$, $M = 3.10$], and one for excessive force [$M = 3.39$]).

Analytic Plan

Our analysis follows three steps. First, we predict citizen complaints with a series of controls to capture baseline estimates. Then, we examine the effects of peer, definition, and reinforcement variables, as well as all of the aforementioned variables combined in an effort to predict citizen complaints.

Results

In general, officers consider stealing and using excessive force to be serious violations, whereas they consider accepting free gifts and meals from the public as not so serious violations. They perceive their peers' attitudes to be similar to their own. When asked what kind of discipline they thought would follow, they perceived verbal or written reprimands for accepting gifts and meals, but they perceived much more serious punishment for theft and excessive force. Most officers believed if they were

caught stealing, they would be dismissed, whereas if they were caught using excessive force, they would be "suspended without pay." It is interesting to note that they perceive theft to be most serious, as evidenced by their anticipation of the harshest punishment for it.

. . . [A] baseline analysis of the influence of control variables on citizen complaints . . . shows that both length of tenure and gender have a significant influence on citizen complaints. Males and those officers with more tenure are more likely to have citizen complaints.

. . . [W]e add[ed] the peer association variables to the baseline model and examin[ed] their relation to citizen complaints. Measures representing male and tenure remain significant in this model. Additionally, two of the peer variables are significant. Consistent with Akers . . . , respondents who think their peers consider using excessive force to be less serious are more likely to have citizen complaints. However, and inconsistent with Akers, respondents who think their peers consider theft to be less serious are less likely to have citizen complaints.

[A further] regression . . . adds the social learning effect of definitions to predict citizen complaints. Again, measures of tenure and being male continue to be significant and positively associated with citizen complaints. Definitions about gifts and theft are not significantly associated with citizen complaints, but definitions about using excessive force are significant predictors of citizen complaints. The results show that, to the extent that officers do not consider using excessive force to be serious, they are more likely to have citizen complaints, a finding consistent with social learning theory.

The next analysis . . . show[ed] the effects of reinforcement variables on citizen complaints. As in the previous model estimations, measures of gender and tenure remain significant and positive. The only significant reinforcement variable concerns the use of excessive force. To the extent that respondents anticipate less punishment for using excessive force, they are more likely to have citizen complaints.

. . . Table 19.1 presents the results for the complete model. Consistent with the previous models, measures of tenure and gender were significantly and positively related to citizen complaints. One's perception of peer attitudes about theft was significantly related to complaints, but in the opposite direction. Also, the less serious an officer considered the use of excessive force, the more likely he or she was to have citizen complaints. Finally, if officers anticipated lesser punishment for theft, they were more likely to have citizen complaints (consistent with a learning approach).

Table 19.1   Logistic Regression Model Predicting Citizen Complaints With Social Learning Variables: Full Model

Control Variables	B	S.E.	Odds Ratio
Tenure	.097	.019	1.102*
Race (1 = non-White)	.121	.222	1.129
Marital status (1 = married)	.111	.223	1.118
Gender (1 = male)	.588	.239	1.800*
Peer associations			
Gifts	.073	.074	1.075
Theft	−.187	.102	.830*
Force	.012	.121	1.012
Definitions			
Gifts	−.070	.070	.933
Theft	.067	.148	1.069
Force	.178	.128	1.195*
Reinforcement			
Gifts	−.043	.056	.958
Theft	.105	.069	1.111*
Force	.111	.109	.118
Intercept	−1.733	.626	.177*
Pseudo R-square	.185		

*$P < .05$. P values computed for one-tailed significance tests.

Discussion and Conclusion

. . . Three key findings emerged from our effort. First, accepting gifts from the public or from businesses is considered by this sample of officers to be normative and not indicative of other more serious forms of misconduct. Second, officer attitudes about the use of excessive force were related to citizen complaints more so than attitudes about theft or accepting gifts. Third, officers anticipated more punishment for theft than for using force, but variables related to force were the most consistent predictors of citizen complaints. In summary, the results of this study indicate that Akers' theoretical framework may provide a useful theoretical lens through which to view the problem of police misconduct. . . .

As with most research, several limitations of the current study should be recognized. Most notably, our measures were indirect and only tapped into a few pieces of Akers' theoretical framework. Additionally, because the concept of peer involvement takes a unique form in the policing context, our measures focused on the perceived deviance of peers, instead of the frequency and intensity of interaction with deviant peers. Third, only one measure of behavior, citizen complaints, was examined in this study, and we did not partial the complaints indicator into "type" of complaint. Thus, whether these attitudes relate to other behaviors remains unknown. Fourth, our data came from one large police department. The extent to which the results hold in smaller jurisdictions is an empirical question. Finally, our data were cross-sectional in nature. To be sure, a more complete test of Akers' theory would employ longitudinal data to sort out the bidirectional relationships between attitudes and behavior.

With these limitations in hand, we hope that interested researchers will continue to examine officers' attitudes about different types and levels of misconduct to fully gauge where attitudes begin to affect complaints on the continuum of police misconduct. Much theoretical and policy knowledge is to be gained from such a concerted approach. Our analysis is but one step in this direction.

Questions

1. Describe the four factors that predict delinquency and crime according to Akers' social learning theory.

2. Identify three possible limitations of using citizen complaints to measure police misconduct.

CHAPTER 20

On the Effective Use of Stigma as a Crime-Deterrent

Patricia Funk

Universitat Pompeu Fabra

Introduction

Economic models of crime elaborate on the role of governmental punishment in achieving deterrence. Yet, theoretical arguments as well as empirical evidence suggest that the formal (governmental) punishment that a convicted criminal is confronted with constitutes only part of the whole penalty. If the act of committing a crime lowers productivity or if criminal and unproductive characteristics of workers are positively correlated in a world of asymmetric information, then a rational employer stigmatizes a convicted criminal by reducing his wage. . . . Empirical evidence confirms that wage reductions after conviction are substantial. Depending on the crime committed, these stigmatization costs (in terms of wage reductions) may far exceed the governmental penalty.

Occurrence of "punishment" in the labor market (hereafter abbreviated by stigmatization or informal punishment) can partly be controlled by the government. By handing out criminal records to the employers or not, the degree of stigmatization is varied. Although in the United States there seems to be a tendency toward facilitating the access to criminal records (e.g., "Megan's Law" encourages the stigmatization of sexual offenders), the opposite holds true for Switzerland: Legal changes are planned after which an employer asking for a criminal record will only be informed about serious offenses. Less serious offenses that are punished by no more than 3 years of prison will no longer be listed in the criminal

record. Therefore, "mild offenders" cannot be stigmatized anymore. . . .

In view of these internationally contrasting policies, a complete understanding of how stigma shall be used seems indispensable.

The seminal article on informal sanctioning in *the labor market* is Rasmusen. . . . In two models (differing with respect to the employer's motivation to reduce a criminal's wage), he explains the amount of stigmatization and shows that greater stigma reduces crime. Therefore, Rasmusen concludes that "stigma shares with fines the advantage of deterring the criminal without creating real costs. . . ." As such, complete publication of criminal records is called for to exploit informal punishment to the largest extent.

In contrast to Rasmusen's . . . model, which only considers unconvicted offenders, Furuya . . . restricts his attention to formerly convicted offenders. Because non-employment of stigmatized ex-convicts is assumed to impose *exogenous* costs on society (social welfare payments and recidivism), Furuya . . . derives conditions under which public employment of ex-convicts is socially beneficial.

The goal of this chapter is to reevaluate stigma's role as a crime-deterrent in a more comprehensive model accounting for unconvicted as well as convicted offenders.

By considering the reactions of convicted as well as unconvicted offenders, stigma's benefits (Rasmusen's . . . deterrence idea) as well as stigma's costs (Furuya's . . . recidivism idea) can be compared. In contrast to Furuya . . . , who

Source: "On the effective use of stigma as a crime-deterrent," by Funk, P., (2004), in *European Economic Review, 48*, 715–728. Reprinted by permission of Elsevier via Copyright Clearance Center.

assumes *exogenous* costs of stigmatization, I make the link between stigma and a convicted offender's incentive to commit a crime explicit. Therefore, in addition to deriving the different effects of stigma on crime, I am able to analyze through which measures government can mitigate potential negative side effects of stronger stigmatization.

My model clearly builds on Rasmusen's . . . work, but differs from it in two respects. First, in Rasmusen's . . . analysis, neither crime nor legal activities requires employment of any resources. However, as pointed out by Ehrlich . . . , a realistic model would assume legal and illegal activities being time-consuming and being used in a substitutive manner. Therefore, the criminal decision is formulated as a time-allocation problem between legal and illegal activities, where stigma hits a convicted criminal in the period after conviction. Second, in contrast to Rasmusen . . . , the effect of stigma on criminal behavior is not only analyzed for an unconvicted, but also for a convicted individual.

The main results are the following:

1. In the basic model where illegal earning opportunities are prevalent outside the workplace (separate legal and illegal markets), stronger stigma induces opposite effects. Whereas strong stigma deters an unconvicted individual from committing crimes (*deterrence effect*), it simultaneously enhances recidivism of a convicted and stigmatized offender (*recidivism effect*). The cause of this undesirable side effect is the reduction of legal wages for stigmatized criminals, which favors the relative attractiveness of crime.

   Therefore, in contrast to Rasmusen's . . . research, which considers stigma as an effective deterrent without social costs, I show that increasing stigma may even be countereffective. Conditions under which stigma proves to be effective (or not) are derived.

2. As a second important result, it is demonstrated that stigma's effectiveness can be ensured by complementing it with adequate formal punishment: Notably, a strong punishment for repeat offenders helps counterbalance the negative incentive effects of stronger stigmatization (which occur after conviction).

   As such, the "recidivism costs" from stigmatization can be reduced by increasing the punishment of repeat offenders, which can be costly depending on the type of formal punishment used.

3. Finally, if illegal earning opportunities are present at work (extended model: overlapping legal and illegal markets), I show that the negative-incentive effects of stronger stigmatization get weaker. Because a criminal record may prevent a criminal from being hired at places with high illegal gains (e.g., a child molester from being employed at a kindergarten), stigma may actually *decrease recidivism*. Hence, the negative-incentive effects of stigma get smaller, and the more illegal earning opportunities are tied to the legal workplace.

   As for the degree of stigmatization, it turns out to depend on formal punishment as follows: The higher the formal punishment for repeat offenders, the smaller is the risk of crime at work and also the amount of wage reduction. Therefore, informal punishment is used as a *strategic substitute* to formal punishment.

Relating my chapter to the literature on nonlegal sanctions in general . . . , there is one important distinction. This chapter focuses on stigmatization *in the labor market* and challenges the view that stigma is a cost-effective deterrent by providing arguments that are specific to the labor market. Even more different from my analysis is the research on reputational penalties of firms. Although Karpoff and Lott . . . analyze the interaction between fines (governmental) and reputational penalties for firms engaging in criminal fraud, the firms' incentives to cheat on product quality are so different from the individuals' incentive to commit a crime that their results are not applicable to my analysis.

The rest of this chapter is structured as follows: In the next section, the basic model is presented, together with some results from comparative statics. An extension of the model, which allows for illegal earning opportunities at work, is given in the following section. Implications for public policy are discussed in the final section.

The Basic Model

I focus on risk-neutral individuals seeking to maximize total earnings. Assume that two independent markets of employment exist: one for legal activities and one for illegal activities. The problem facing a potential criminal is how to allocate a fixed amount of working time $\bar{t} \geq 0$ to these different sources of income. Returns in either market are assumed to be linearly dependent on working time as well as wages. $L = w \cdot (t - t), w \geq 0$ describes the legal return function and $G = g \cdot t, g \geq 0$ the corresponding illegal one. t, with $0 \leq t \leq$ t represents time allocated to illegal activities.

If a positive amount of t is chosen, the offender gets convicted with probability $p = \theta \cdot t, p \in [0, 1]$ and incurs a public penalty of the amount $F = f \cdot t, f \geq 0$. Additionally, stigmatization affects him a period later. $L = s \cdot w \cdot (t - t)$ represents the legal earning function of a stigmatized individual. $s \in [0, 1]$ captures the stigma effect and assumes a value of 0 in the case of complete stigmatization and a value of 1 if there is no stigmatization.

The extent of stigmatization s depends on (a) whether the employer obtains information about past crimes, and (b) given that he obtains the information, the perceived productivity discount of a criminal compared with a noncriminal person. For instance, convicted criminals might have experienced a depreciation of human capital during their prison stay, or even during their criminal careers they might have had less time to invest in (noncriminal) human capital. As such, if the employer expects an output q from an unconvicted person, but only $\alpha \cdot q$ ($\alpha < 1$) from a convicted person, he might discount a convicted criminal's wage by $s = \alpha$.

Figure 20.1 represents the individual's decision tree. The probabilities of getting in the state conviction/no conviction are indicated on the branches, the payoffs in these states at the end of the branches. As for the notations on illegal time t, numbered subscripts always indicate the period. The time allocations in the second period depend on the conviction state $S_1 \in (c, n)$ at the end of period one, which can be either conviction (c) or nonconviction (n). To save on space, I introduce the following abbreviations: $t_{2|n} \equiv t_2 \mid S_1 = n, t_{2|c} \equiv t_2 \mid S_1 = c$.

Stigma and Criminal Behavior

Let us calculate how the individual's optimal illegal time depends on the level of stigma. Applying backward induction, I first solve for the second-period time allocations.

An individual who was not convicted in the first period maximizes his expected payoff:

$$E\pi(t_{2|n}; w, g, f, \theta, \bar{t}) = \theta \cdot t_{2|n} \cdot (w \cdot (\bar{t} - t_{2|n})$$
$$+ g \cdot t_{2|n} - f \cdot t_{2|n}) + (1 - \theta \cdot t_{2|n})$$
$$\cdot (w \cdot (t - t_{2|n}) + g \cdot t_{2|n}) \tag{1}$$

under the constraint that $0 \leq t_{2|n} \leq \bar{t}$.

Assuming interiority, maximization of (1) yields

$$t_{2|n}^* = \frac{g - w}{2 \cdot \theta \cdot f}. \tag{2}$$

For an individual convicted in period 1, the expected payoff in period 2 is represented by

$$E\pi(t_{2|c}; w, g, f, \theta, s, \bar{t}) = \theta \cdot t_{2|c} \cdot (s \cdot w \cdot (t - t_{2|c})$$
$$+ g \cdot t_{2|c} - f \cdot t_{2|c}) + (1 - \theta \cdot t_{2|c})$$
$$\cdot (s \cdot w \cdot (t - t_{2|c}) + g \cdot t_{2|c}). \tag{3}$$

The interior solution to the maximization of (3) is

$$t_{2|c}^* = \left. \frac{g - s \cdot w}{2 \cdot \theta \cdot f} \right| \tag{4}$$

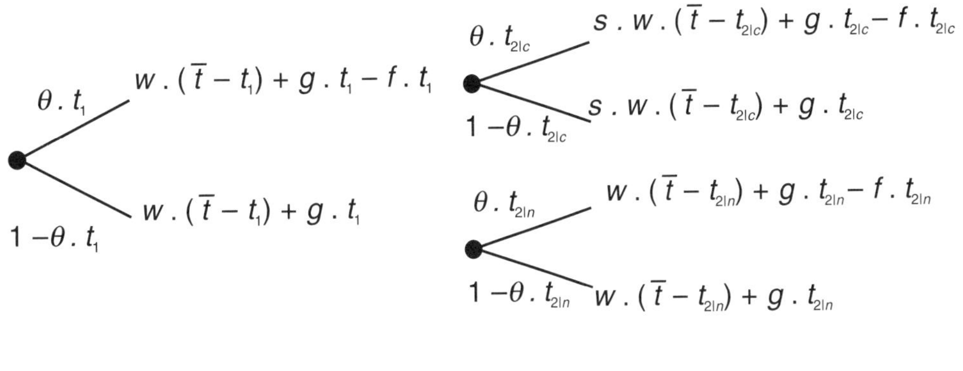

$$\theta \cdot t_{2|c} \diagup s \cdot w \cdot (\bar{t} - t_{2|c}) + g \cdot t_{2|c} - f \cdot t_{2|c}$$
$$1 - \theta \cdot t_{2|c} \diagdown s \cdot w \cdot (\bar{t} - t_{2|c}) + g \cdot t_{2|c}$$

$$\theta \cdot t_1 \diagup w \cdot (\bar{t} - t_1) + g \cdot t_1 - f \cdot t_1$$
$$1 - \theta \cdot t_1 \diagdown w \cdot (\bar{t} - t_1) + g \cdot t_1$$

$$\theta \cdot t_{2|n} \diagup w \cdot (\bar{t} - t_{2|n}) + g \cdot t_{2|n} - f \cdot t_{2|n}$$
$$1 - \theta \cdot t_{2|n} \diagdown w \cdot (\bar{t} - t_{2|n}) + g \cdot t_{2|n}$$

Figure 20.1   The decision tree

The expected payoff of an individual in period one is given by

$$E\pi(t_1; w, g, f, \theta, s, \overline{t}) = \theta \cdot t_1 \cdot (w \cdot (t - t_1)$$
$$+ g \cdot t_1 - f \cdot t_1) + (1 - \theta \cdot t_1) \cdot (w \cdot (t - t_1) + g \cdot t_1)$$
$$+ \theta \cdot t_1 \cdot E[\pi_{2|c}] + (1 - \theta \cdot t_1) \cdot E[\pi_{2|n}]. \tag{5}$$

$E[\pi_{2|c}]$ denotes the expected second period payoff in the state of conviction (given optimal time allocations in this state) and comes to

$$\frac{(g - s \cdot w)^2}{4 \cdot \theta \cdot f} + s \cdot w \cdot \overline{t}.$$

$E[\pi_{2|n}]$ represents the respective expected payoff in the state of nonconviction (given optimal time allocations) and is given by

$$\frac{(g - w)^2}{4 \cdot \theta \cdot f} + w \cdot \overline{t}.$$

Clearly, for $s < 1$ and $t^*_{2|c} < \overline{t}$, the expected payoff in the state of conviction is lower than the expected one in the state of nonconviction as legal wages are reduced.

The interior solution to the maximization of (5) is given by

$$t^*_1 = \frac{g - w}{2 \cdot \theta \cdot f} + \frac{\theta}{2 \cdot \theta \cdot f} \cdot E[\pi_{2|c}] - \frac{\theta}{2 \cdot \theta \cdot f} \cdot E[\pi_{2|n}]. \tag{6}$$

The first main result of the chapter can now be established.

PROPOSITION 1:

If stigmatization exists, there are two opposite effects resulting from stronger stigmatization:

1. On the one hand, an unconvicted individual's illegal time is reduced (deterrence effect).

2. On the other hand, a convicted individual's illegal time is raised (recidivism effect).

PROOF

Part 1:
$$\frac{\partial}{\partial s}(t^*_1) = -\frac{w}{2 \cdot f} \cdot \left[\overline{t} - \frac{g - s \cdot w}{2 \cdot \theta \cdot f}\right]$$

which is larger than zero for $t^*_{2|c} < \overline{t}$ and zero otherwise (recall that increasing s means *less* stigmatization).

Part 2:
$$\frac{\partial}{\partial s}(t^*_{2|c}) = -\frac{w}{2 \cdot \theta \cdot f}.\Big|$$

The intuition behind Proposition 1 is straightforward: For an unconvicted individual, the threat of stronger stigmatization presents a greater potential loss of legal earning opportunities. Therefore, there is a strong incentive to reduce the risk of becoming stigmatized by spending less time on illegal activities in period 1. In contrast, stronger stigmatization reduces legal wages of an already convicted offender. Therefore, illegal activities become relatively more attractive, and the substitution of legal through illegal time is the rational consequence.

In view of these opposed effects, it is unclear whether stronger stigma raises or lowers total expected illegal time. The conditions, under which the former or latter holds true, are established in Proposition 2.

PROPOSITION 2:

1. Ceteris paribus, stronger stigma reduces the expected sum of illegal time if

$$(t - t^*_{2|c}) + \theta \cdot (t - t^*_{2|c}) \cdot (t^*_{2|c} - t^*_{2|n}) - t^*_1 > 0.$$

2. The expected illegal time increases due to stronger stigmatization if

$$(t - t^*_{2|c}) + \theta \cdot (t - t^*_{2|c}) \cdot (t^*_{2|c} - t^*_{2|n}) - t^*_1 < 0.$$

3. The derivative of the left-hand term with respect to w is positive and with respect to g negative. Therefore, high legal and low illegal wages foster the effectiveness of stigma in reducing crime.

<u>PROOF</u>

Proposition 2 follows directly from differentiating an individual's expected illegal lifetime ($E[t^*] = t^*_1 + (\theta \cdot t^*_1 \cdot t^*_{2|c} + (1 - \theta \cdot t^*_1) \cdot t^*_{2|n})$) with respect to s.

Therefore, findings of current research, which propose stigma as an effective crime-deterrent, must be taxed as premature. However, can different punishment of first and repeat offenders be used to eliminate the undesirable recidivism effect of stronger stigma?

Extension: Different Punishment for First and Repeat Offenders

Let us enrich the analysis undertaken thus far by allowing for different punishment for first and repeat offenders. f_1 denotes the marginal penalty of a first-time convicted offender, f_2 the one of an offender convicted for the second time.

<u>PROPOSITION 3</u>:

$$\exists \tilde{f}_2 \text{ with } - \frac{\partial}{\partial s}(E[t^*]) < 0 \text{ for } f_2 > \tilde{f}_2.$$

Proposition 3 states that with harsh enough punishment for repeat offenders, stigma proves to be effective. Proposition 3 holds because deterrence of unconvicted individuals is stronger with higher

$f_2\left(\frac{\partial}{\partial s}(t^*_1) = \frac{w}{2 \cdot f_1} \cdot \left[\bar{t} - \frac{g - s \cdot w}{2 \cdot \theta \cdot f_2}\right]\right)$, but also because

the recidivism effect is smaller with increased

$f_2\left(\frac{\partial}{\partial s}(t^*_{2|c}) = - \frac{w}{2 \cdot \theta \cdot f_2}\right)$. Therefore, the threat of harsh

enough punishment for repeat offenders mitigates the negative-incentive effect of stigma, which stems from the ex-convict's drive toward recidivism.

By analyzing punishment of first and repeat offenders in a context of stigma being present, I also provide a powerful justification as to why the practice of punishing repeat offenders more severely than first offenders may be efficient: It reduces the higher propensity toward crime after conviction.

So far, economists have encountered difficulties finding an explanation as to why, in practice, repeat offenders are punished harsher than first offenders.

However, all the studies assume that legal and illegal earning opportunities are the same before and after conviction, which is unlikely due to stigmatization.

The General Case: Illegal Earning Opportunities Inside and Outside the Legal Workplace

In this section, I extend the basic model by allowing illegal earning opportunities to be present on and off the workplace. Therefore, an individual can allocate a fixed amount of working time $\bar{t}$ to illegal activities at work (t_w), to illegal activities outside the workplace (t), or to legal activities ($t - t_w - t$). In analogy to the previous section, the probability of conviction is now given by $p = \theta \cdot (t + t_w)$, the penalty by $F = f \cdot (t + t_w)$, the legal earning function by $L = w \cdot (t - t)$ and total illegal earnings by $G = g \cdot t + g_w \cdot t_w$. For a convicted criminal, the legal return function is reduced to $L = s \cdot w \cdot (t - t), s \in [0, 1]$ and illegal earnings are newly given by $G = g \cdot t + g_w(s) \cdot t_w$. Because illegal earning opportunities at work might be affected by the presence of a (nonempty) criminal record, $g_w = g_w(s)$.

Although the prior section represented the special case with $g_w = 0$, I start with the polar case, where illegal earning opportunities are exclusively present at work ($g = 0$).

Illegal Earning Opportunities Only at the Workplace

Again, the potential criminal maximizes his expected utility in each period and therefore spends

$$t^*_{w1} = \frac{g_w}{2 \cdot \theta \cdot f_1} - \frac{\theta}{2 \cdot \theta \cdot f_1} \cdot \left(E[\pi_{2|n}] - E[\pi_{2|c}]\right), t^*_{w2|n} = \frac{g_w}{2 \cdot \theta \cdot f_1}$$

and $t^*_{w2|c} = \frac{g_w(s)}{2 \cdot \theta \cdot f_2}$ on illegal activities at work (given interior solutions). To evaluate the effect of stigma on crime, it has to be determined to what extent illegal earning opportunities are affected by the presence of a criminal record ($g_w(s)$ in $t^*_{w2|c}$).

First of all, we know that, due to heterogeneity in illegal gains, conviction is a signal of high illegal gains at work. Therefore, an employer pays an ex-convict a wage $s \cdot w$, which equals the expected output $\alpha \cdot q \cdot \left(\frac{\bar{t} - t_{w2|c}}{\bar{t}}\right)$

minus the expected harm from crimes being committed at work $\hat{g}_{w|c} \cdot \frac{\hat{t}_{w2|c}}{\bar{t}}$ (a hat denotes estimated values because g_w is unknown to the employer).

Because a criminal record reveals information about past offenses committed, it helps an employer estimate the illegal gains a potential employee has at work. Ideally, a criminal record is "fully informative" (i.e., it allows to correctly estimate the illegal gains $\hat{g}w = gw$). In this case, it is a straightforward point that with illegal gains exceeding a certain threshold level $\bar{g}w$, the employer is no more willing to employ the ex-convict ($s = 0$). Thus, illegal gains depend on the degree of stigmatization as follows:

$$g_w(s) = \begin{cases} 0 & \text{if } s = 0 \iff g_w \geq \bar{g}_w \\ g_w & \text{if } s > 0 \iff g_w < \bar{g}_w \end{cases}$$

Therefore, stigma exerts a *precaution function* by excluding the ex-convict from workplaces with high illegal earning opportunities. Proposition 4 summarizes the most important implications of this model.

PROPOSITION 4:

If illegal earning opportunities are only present at work and a criminal record is fully informative, stigma affects behavior as follows:

1. Stigma deters unconvicted offenders (*deterrence effect*).

2. Stigma reduces recidivism (*precaution effect*).

PROOF

Part A. Because stigma decreases legal and illegal earning opportunities after conviction, higher stigma increases ($E[\pi_{2|n}] - E[[\pi_{2|c}]]$) and, hence, decreases the incentive to allocate time to illegal activities in period 1.

Part B. Because $t^*_{w2|c} = \frac{g_w(s)}{2 \cdot \theta \cdot f_2}$ and $\frac{\partial}{\partial s}(g_w) \geq 0, \frac{\partial}{\partial s}(t^*_{w2|c}) \geq 0$

(recall that increasing s means less stigmatization).

Therefore, although stigma increases recidivism if illegal earnings are unrelated to the legal workplace, the opposite might occur if illegal earning opportunities are only present at work.

Note also that for $gw < \bar{g}w$, the employer is willing to employ the ex-convict at a wage

$$s \cdot w = \alpha \cdot q - \alpha \cdot q \cdot \frac{gw}{2 \cdot \theta \cdot f_2 \cdot \bar{t}} - \frac{g_w^2}{2 \cdot \theta \cdot f_2 \cdot \bar{t}}.$$ As can be

seen from the wage function, the degree of stigmatization (compared with an unconvicted criminal's wage q) is the lower, the higher the formal punishment of repeat offenders. Because the employer anticipates that a higher punishment in the case of recidivism decreases the likelihood of crimes being committed at work, the wage reduction gets smaller. In this case, informal punishment turns out to be a *strategic substitute* to formal punishment.

Illegal Earning Opportunities Inside and Outside the Workplace

Although in this general model illegal earning opportunities are available in two different markets (inside and outside the workplace), it is generally not optimal for a criminal to operate in both illegal markets in one single period. Because both types of illegal activities have the same marginal cost functions, the individual selects the illegal activity with the higher marginal return. For instance, if $g - w > g_w$, a criminal only spends time on illegal activities outside the workplace, before and after conviction. However, if $g - w < g_w$, an unconvicted offender focuses on illegal activities at work, but may switch to illegal activities outside the firm after conviction (e.g., if $g(s) = 0$ and $g - s \cdot w > 0$).

As for the effect of stigma on crime, it clearly serves as a deterrent for unconvicted individuals. Again, stigmatization reduces legal as well as possibly illegal earnings. Therefore, an unconvicted individual has an incentive to reduce the risk of becoming convicted and stigmatized by spending less time on illegal activities. For an already convicted offender, the effect of stigma depends on the market in which the criminal is operating. If before conviction crimes were committed outside the workplace, stigma enhances recidivism. In contrast, if the unconvicted offender had higher illegal returns at work, stigma reduces recidivism as long as the criminal does not change the market (precaution effect). However, if stigmatization induces the offender to abandon crimes at work in favor of illegal activities outside the workplace, the impact on illegal time is a priori not clear. Therefore, the strength of stigma's precaution effect depends on how easily illegal earnings at work may be substituted by illegal earnings outside the workplace.

Discussion

The fact that ex-convicts face different conditions on the labor market than employees with a blank criminal record has been widely recognized. Yet, the implications drawn for stigmatization policy differ sharply between countries. Whereas the United States facilitates access to criminal information, Switzerland pursues a policy of restricting criminal information. Next to these polar cases of "full stigmatization" (for certain offenses) and "no stigmatization" (for certain offenses), there are countries that are located somewhere in between. Spain, for example, gives criminal records to the labor market, but wage subsidies for ex-convicts are granted in certain situations.

The model outlined in this chapter provides a theoretical framework for analyzing and understanding the complex relationship between stigma and crime. By showing that stigma exerts different effects on unconvicted (*deterrence*) and convicted (*recidivism, precaution*) offenders, the model captures the different rationales behind differing stigmatization policies.

According to my model, the American stigmatization policy has a strong deterrence effect on unconvicted offenders. At the same time, it might have a high degree of recidivism for stigmatized ex-convicts. The Spanish solution contributes to reduce the recidivism effect because it de-facto weakens the amount of stigmatization. Unfortunately, it also reduces deterrence because unconvicted offenders anticipate the less devastating consequences on the labor market after conviction. The Swiss model, finally, suppresses stigma's deterrence function for the offenses excluded from the criminal record. Simultaneously, it increases the ex-convicts' incentive to apply for legitimate work.

As such, it remains unclear at the theoretical level which policy is most beneficial in terms of crime deterrence. In fact, I showed that the only way to guarantee the effectiveness of stigma is to supplement it with harsh enough punishment for repeat offenders. Therefore, the harsher a country's punishment for recidivists, the more likely is stigma going to be effective.

Although stigma may deter crime, its employment must not be *optimal*. Because stigma's effectiveness has to be bought at potentially costly higher punishment of repeat offenders, stigma (as opposed to fines) is not necessarily a cost-free deterrent. However, stigma may have a beneficial impact on the efficiency of the labor market next to its function as a crime-deterrent....

It seems that the benefits from stigmatization in terms of (inexpensive) crime reduction and allocative efficiency improvements are the highest if high illegal earning opportunities prevail at the workplace. Because stigma may exclude the ex-convict from jobs with high illegal earnings, there might be even less recidivism in addition to stigma's deterrent effect. Additionally, the allocative distortions from having employed a criminal rather than a noncriminal worker would be the greatest if a lot of harm could be done at work. Therefore, it seems important to pass on criminal information to those employers, where a connection between an ex-convict's past and future offenses at work is probable and dangerous (an illustrative example is to hand out the information about a former child molester to the owner of a kindergarten).

For the offenses, which are unrelated to (a certain type of) work, the benefits of stigma are less clear. From an enforcement perspective, the use of stigma is dominated by the use of fines. Not only do fines deter crime without social costs, but they also enable one to relate the penalty to the damage.... Because fines are usually used for punishing mild offenses, replacement of stigma through fines most likely makes sense for these kinds of offenses (as is done in Switzerland). However, there is still a trade-off between optimal enforcement and allocative efficiency. In the case where the wage reduction (stigmatization) reflects the employer's distaste against hiring criminals (instead of a productivity discount), the consequences in the labor market may be distributional rather than allocative and the "harm" from suppressing stigma smaller.

For future research, I think a survey that explored in more detail the employers' reasons for not hiring ex-criminals or reducing their wage (such as precaution, productivity concerns, distaste against criminals, etc.) would be helpful for further assessing stigma's costs and benefits.

Questions

1. Describe the role of rational choice in criminal behavior.

2. Describe how stigma and deterrence are related.

CHAPTER 21

Social Control in China

Applications of the Labeling Theory and the Reintegrative Shaming Theory

Xiaoming Chen

Law School of Xiamen University

Social Control: Chinese Philosophy and Perspectives

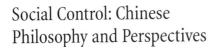

In every society, a normative order must be accompanied by a formal and informal structure for maintaining this normative order. Although crime and social control are universal facets of social life, every society exercises a cultural option when it develops a specific way of looking at crime and delinquency and a characteristic mechanism for controlling them. . . . China offers a valuable context for extending previous—mainly American and European—research because of the profound sociocultural differences between Chinese and Western societies.

Something called *social control* takes place in all societies because every society has a set of social norms. Social control is found wherever and whenever people hold each other to certain standards. The concept of social control has appeared in various radical, critical, or revisionist writings about crime, delinquency, and law over the past three decades. However, there are big differences within this literature—among labeling theory, reintegrative shaming theory, Marxist critical criminology, abolitionist theory, and left realism. Social control and crime cannot be studied in the abstract, but certain abstract concepts do have general applicability. Although social control takes many forms and appears in many places, it always is a manifestation of the same essence. *Social control* should be considered as a generic term for response

to nonconformity, including both perception of and reaction to rule breaking. . . . In other words, it includes the formal and informal ways that society has developed to help ensure conformity to social norms. Social control takes place when a person is induced or forced to act according to the values of the given society, regardless of whether it is in accordance with his or her own interests. The aims of social control are "to bring about conformity, solidarity, and continuity of a particular group or society." . . . Due to different cultures and traditions, different models of social control exist in different societies. Compared with the West, Chinese society has developed a different model of social control. . . .

China's traditional value system is a complex amalgam of ideas that evolved over thousands of years and was shaped by Confucianism, Daoism, Buddhism, and other influences. Traditional thought accepted social stratification as natural and considered social groups to be organized on hierarchical principles. Much concern centered on the need for properly ordered social relationships. Confucius stressed that for a society to have order, there must be social stratification, and obligations of each level must be made clear. He believed that without a distinction between the nobility and the common people, there could be no imperial country. . . . Therefore, traditional Chinese philosophical texts are full of descriptions of what it means to be a dutiful son, a loyal official, and even a benevolent ruler. Social status in traditional China was based on respectability, which is

Source: "Social control in China: Applications of the labeling theory and the reintegrative shaming theory," (2002), by Chen, X., in *International Journal of Offender Therapy and Comparative Criminology, 46,* 45–63. Reprinted by permission of Sage Publications, Inc.

rooted in Confucianism's ideal type of social relationship. Ancestor worship was an important act by which an individual became a member of a group and his or her position within this group was clearly defined. . . . It is generally assumed that the secular function of ancestor worship interacted with the spiritual practice of honoring and protecting the soul of an ancestor and stabilized social-political order. The ceremony was designed to express the government's veneration for old age and to encourage others to show respect for their elders, thus guaranteeing a stable cultural value system. . . .

With a preeminent emphasis on societal order and value consensus, it is perhaps not surprising that notions of individualism never flourished on Chinese soil. Individuals were seen as finding their meaning as members of ordered collectivities. Individual success was usually seen as the result of the support of one's family or other collectivity and not solely an individual matter. Similarly, individuals who committed crimes were regarded as products of bad family and other social influences. Credit or blame for an individual's acts was spread outward to affect these wider social groups. Thus, it is clear that China's traditional value system evolved over many centuries in directions that are quite distinct from the West. For example, the Western emphasis on individualism, human rights, and equality never assumed primary importance in traditional China.

Contemporary social control is rooted in the Confucian past. The Confucianism that remains the dominant Chinese philosophy has influenced Chinese society and provided the basis for the social order throughout Chinese history. Although another ancient school of thought, Legalism—which maintained that man was by nature evil and had to be controlled by strict rules of law—was opposed to Confucianism, it lacked the enduring impact of the latter and prevailed over Confucianism only during the Qin dynasty (221–207 BC). Since the Han dynasty (206 BC–221 AD), Chinese social and political institutions have been based on Confucian ideology, and social control has been founded on ethical and moral persuasion backed by a state penal code as a last resort. . . .

Therefore, for a long time, social order in Chinese society has mainly been based on moral socialization, not on the deterrence of law. In other words, conformity to proper modes of conduct is not obtained through fear of formal sanctions, but from an understanding and acceptance of the rules based on an early and ongoing educational process. This is consistent with the traditional Chinese concept that persuasion and education are more powerful than force. The Chinese have a strong belief in internalizing rules of conduct to the point at which the individual will conform to accepted behavior due to moral persuasion, rather than due to the fear of punishment.

The influence of the West came particularly in the late 19th and early 20th centuries. When Western values were introduced to Chinese education, Marxism, a Western doctrine, eventually was proclaimed the basis for the official values of the Chinese socialist society. Marxism provided a critical basis for a reexamination of Chinese values and customs. When the Chinese communists came to power in 1949, they set about to produce major changes in the way Chinese society was organized. Their goal was a radical social revolution and not simply a political revolution. Many aspects of traditional social life—class relations, family organization, women's roles, personal values, and so on—did not meet the requirements of the socialist revolution and construction and were slated for fundamental change. . . . New organizational structures ranging from "macrosocial and political networks to the smallest human groups" replaced the traditional Chinese pattern. . . . However, many of the social forms in China had evolved slowly over the centuries and were imbued with deep meaning for the general population. All could not simply be swept aside overnight. Moreover, the Chinese communist leaders had also been schooled within the Chinese traditions before they became exposed to Western and Soviet influences. As a result, they developed deeply ambivalent feelings about traditional values. At the same time, to mobilize the population in support of the goals of the Chinese Communist Party, the Chinese government had to selectively build on and reinforce some elements of traditional social life to try to change other elements. Based on this consideration, the bundle of traditional ideals and values was not rejected completely by the Chinese government. Rather, some traditional values continued to be accepted as natural and proper, whereas others were expected to be eradicated or changed. The result of this complex change process has been a fundamental transformation of Chinese society. However, the contemporary social system and social values are in many clearly identifiable ways still Chinese. The main form of social control is still before-the-fact socialization, not after-the-fact arrest. . . . A unitary set of values required by society remains a basic way of thinking in contemporary China. Likewise, accepted as a matter of course is the notion that individuals are malleable and can be socialized and influenced to behave in proper ways. Given these continuities, persuasion is still seen as preferable to coercion as a means of social control. . . .

In the social and legal control mechanisms of contemporary China, mass participation, based on the Confucian tradition of stressing the value of the group and the destructiveness of selfishness . . . , is still regarded as a key tenet. The social order in China is supposed to be maintained by "the capacity of society's members to understand one another and to act in concert in achieving common goals through common rules of behavior." . . . The heavy emphasis is clearly on informal rather than formal methods of social control. The Chinese experience indicates that collective citizen action is an effective strategy for controlling crime, reducing fear of crime, and building a peaceful society. Indeed, social control in Chinese society is so strong that dropping out, becoming invisible, or carving out an area of one's life and declaring it out of bounds to anyone but oneself or one's family seem to be impossible. . . . Dorothy Bracey . . . aptly described how and why the Chinese social and legal control systems work in practice. . . .

When the Chinese say that crime is a social problem, they are not simply saying that an individual is a product of the social environment and therefore is not totally responsible for his behavior. They are saying that the social group—not an abstract "society" but a village, neighborhood, or work group—is both responsible for and a victim of crime. The conclusion they reach is that the social group has the right and duty to intervene in behavior that might lead to crime. . . .

Clearly, although Chinese society today has changed greatly and is not the same as it was in the past, informal social control has adapted to significant political and ideological shifts over the centuries. Although China is undergoing major changes in the direction of a free-market economy, the traditional focus on matters pertaining to social and legal control and mass group involvement do not seem to have diminished. The basic social unit in the present Chinese society continues to be the group rather than the individual. People first learn to behave in response to the family's needs; this helps set the stage for behaving in terms of the school's needs, the work unit's needs, and the neighborhood's needs. Thus, social control rests with these same groups—the family, the school, the work unit, the neighborhood group, and, only as a last resort, the state. Ultimately, however, the state, as a definer and protector of the nation's needs, is the apex of this structure. All crimes, as a consequence, are regarded as crimes against the state.

Today's China is different from China of the past. Chinese approaches to social control have been undergoing changes, in some areas slowly and in others with breathtaking speed. The Chinese have realized the limitations of control by the masses and informal procedures. As a part of the legalization drive, the Chinese government is promoting and strengthening legal control in Chinese society. The trend in the Chinese social control model is toward being more formal and professional to provide equality and protect individual rights. Nowadays, China has developed an extensive array of coded laws and made a massive effort to train and professionalize lawyers, police, prosecutors, and judges. Law is now officially recognized as a principal tool for the achievement of socialist justice, social stability, and economic development. Nevertheless, this trend cannot be viewed as a phenomenon related to the transition to Western practices. Rather, it represents the adjustment of an old model to a new social environment. This adjustment is characterized by an attempt at a parallel development of social and legal control systems, which are part of what the Chinese government called "socialism with Chinese characteristics," intended to meet the new situations of a market economy. There are still many fundamental differences in the social and legal control of crime and delinquency between Western and Chinese societies. They mainly reflect differences in philosophical and ideological value judgments. Although the West does not deny the existence and importance of groups, its primary concern is with the individual—whether in terms of legal status, religious salvation, or personal fulfillment.

Consequently, the Western system stresses individuality, privacy, and diversity. Chinese society places less importance on the individual and greater emphasis on how he or she functions within the context of a larger group. Thus, although China is engaged in the construction of socialist legalism, it is still emphasizing mass participation and a parallel development of formal and informal social control. The stress on informal models and mass participation may be seen as contributing to the preservation of traditional values as it places responsibility on a range of social groups. Social groups, such as neighborhood committees, are becoming less militant and conspicuous, but they are still counted on for preventing and controlling crime and delinquency and providing support to the formal criminal justice system. Perhaps due to the sheer size of China and its population, this appears to be the only practical approach to controlling crime. In China, a primary reliance on the formal criminal justice system in maintaining the public order would not only be socially impractical, but also financially unviable.

However, the theory and practice of Chinese social control indicate that it is not a completely informal system; rather, it is formally invested in less formal structures—in mass groups more than in traditional social institutions. For example, some local neighborhood groups, such as public security committees and mediation committees, are legitimized and often trained by local justice organs or police agencies. Formal agencies make informal groups the locus of social control. Therefore, the term *informal*, as it is used here, has a different meaning from that common in the West. From a strict point of view, it should be considered to be a specific form between *formal* and *informal*, which may be more properly called *quasi-formal*. Because informal institutions do not form a part of the formal criminal justice system, they are established based on certain legal regulations. As Ronald Troyer . . . stated, "While these residents' committees and residents' small groups are often referred to as 'mass organizations,' they are not volunteer associations in the U.S. sense; they are government organized and controlled entities." . . .

In emphasizing the differences between Chinese and Western systems of social control, we should not lose sight of the fact that there are also some similarities. For example, in theory, the system of Chinese social control appears to reflect the basic principles of two influential Western approaches to crime control—namely, informal social control and opportunity reduction. . . .

In practice, many Western countries seem to have grappled with the idea of informal control of delinquency. For example, some studies in the United States suggest that community-based treatment of delinquency may provide a promising alternative for improving results in reducing delinquent recidivism. . . . In fact, appeals to community for crime and delinquency prevention become more and more conspicuous all over the world. They emanate from both the political left and right. For the right, the notion of community has largely been associated with top–down intervention that seeks community support for the existing formal criminal justice system. For the radical left, community has come to be associated with strategies of local "empowerment" through grassroots or bottom–up activities that, as a consequence, may result in more oppositional relationships with formal state agencies. . . .

In conclusion, although social control in China has changed considerably as a result of social development, often these changes should be seen more as responses to changing political situations or to modern technology than to shifts in attitudes among the general public. Law has traditionally been regarded as, at best, irrelevant and,

at worst, disruptive of harmony. Neither written codes nor legal institutions and practices have traditionally been seen as important by the Chinese. . . . The function of legal control was minimized by the effectiveness of strong social control within Chinese society. The concept of Confucian morality, the family ties, and other mechanisms of social control have been important factors in maintaining social order.

Brief Reviews of the Labeling Theory and Reintegrative Shaming Theory

Labeling theory holds the view that formal and informal societal reactions to delinquency can influence delinquents' subsequent attitudes and behavior. This was recognized early in the 1900s. According to Donald Shoemaker . . . , Frederick Thrasher's work on juvenile gangs in Chicago . . . was one of the first instances in which the consequences of official labels of delinquency were recognized as potentially negative. . . . Thereafter, Frank Tannenbaum . . . introduced the term *dramatization of evil*, in which he argued that officially labeling someone as a delinquent can result in the person becoming the very thing he is described as being. Edwin Lemert . . . developed the concepts of primary and secondary deviance, which became the central elements of the first systematic development of what has come to be known as labeling theory. These concepts all stress the importance of social interactions in the development of self-images and social identities.

The central tenet of labeling theory is quite straightforward: Deviance and social control always involve processes of social definition . . . Howard Becker . . . made the following succinct comments:

> Social groups create deviance by making the rules whose infraction constitutes deviance, and by applying these rules to particular people and labeling them as outsiders. From this point of view, deviance is not a quality of the act the person commits, but rather a consequence of the application by others of rules and sanctions to an "offender." The deviant is one to whom that label has successfully been applied; deviant behavior is behavior that people so label. . . .

Labeling theory attempts to account for the mutual effects of the actor and his audience. The theory is concerned not only with what the actor and reactor do, but also with how each one's actions affect the behavior of the other. . . . It is thus clear that one of the most central issues with labeling theory is the connection between behavior and the societal reaction to it. . . .

Another issue with labeling theory is the matter of how the label is handled by the labelee. The importance of groups and associations in the actor's reception of societal reactions to his behavior is emphasized. For example, Howard Becker . . . thought that a final step in the career of a deviant is the identification with an "organized deviant group." . . . It suggests that group support of a labeled deviant may either push him further into an identity as a deviant or serve as a catalyst for a transformation from a socially shunned role to a more positive social status.

The origins of the reintegrative shaming theory may be traced to John Braithwaite's . . . publication of *Crime, Shame and Reintegration*. Here, he wrote,

> The first step to productive theorizing about crime is to think about the contention that labeling offenders makes things worse. The contention is both right and wrong. The theory of reintegrative shaming is an attempt to specify when it is right and when wrong. The distinction is between shaming that leads to stigmatization—to outcasting, to confirmation of a deviant master status—versus shaming that is reintegrative, that shames while maintaining bonds of respect or love, that sharply terminates disapproval with forgiveness, instead of amplifying deviance by progressively casting the deviant out. Reintegrative shaming controls crime; stigmatization pushes offenders toward criminal subcultures. . . .

Braithwaite's . . . statement reflects that the core of the reintegrative shaming theory is about the positive effectiveness of reintegrative shaming and the counterproductiveness of stigmatization in controlling crime. He argues that "shaming is counterproductive when it pushes offenders into the clutches of criminal subcultures; shaming controls crime when it is at the same time powerful and bounded by ceremonies to reintegrate the offender back into the community of responsible citizens." . . . Therefore, individuals should be confronted in the communities to which they belong and reintegrated back into them, rather than cast out of the community. Otherwise, they may be driven into one of the variety of criminal subcultures that are available. According to Braithwaite . . . , informal shaming by those around us is

far more effective in preventing criminal behavior than the threat of punishment. Thus, the key to crime control lies in cultural commitment to shaming in ways that are more "reintegrative" than stigmatizing. . . .

The reintegrative shaming perspective is not just an abstract theory. Two major movements, in both formal and informal justice systems, have endeavored to promote and apply shame-based strategies in practice. One movement advocates the use of judicial shame penalties, such as public exposure and apology. According to David Karp . . . , the shame penalty is meant to reaffirm normative standards and deter future transgressions by creating an opportunity for the offender to experience shame. The threat to the social status of the offender is the primary sanction in the shame penalties.

The other movement promotes a model developed through the well-known Family Group Conferencing Project initiated in Australia and New Zealand. . . . The project aimed to involve a wide-ranging group of people connected to the victim(s) and offender(s) in responding to offenses by juveniles, thereby returning conflicts to the community. The offender is urged to take responsibility by caring about what he or she has done. This model provides a public arena and a ceremony in which the offender and the victim consider the offense and what should be done about it. Rather than a formal ceremony dominated by the arcane language of the law, these are informal sessions in which support systems of the victim and the offender and interested local residents meet to discuss the impact of the crime and how the offender might deal with that impact. Under this model, Braithwaite and Mugford . . . outlined the conditions for successful reintegration.

1. In contrast to identifying both the act and the offender as counternormative, only the act is identified as such.

2. The offender is not defined by the act, but neither is the act condoned ("hate the sin, love the sinner").

3. The denouncer is viewed as a part of a community of relations, of which offender, victims, and others are a part. Denunciation is in the name of victims and the interest of the community.

4. Through a process of reconciliation in which the offender expresses remorse and commits to reparation, the community responds with forgiveness and decertification of the deviant label, closing the distance between the offender and the community. . . .

Generally, the reintegrative shaming theory and practice aim at maximizing shame while maintaining community links and providing opportunities for the offender to make amends to those injured. According to John Braithwaite . . . , crime is best controlled when members of the community are the primary controllers through active participation in both shaming offenders and concerted efforts to reintegrate them back into the community of law-abiding citizens. . . .

Social Control in China and the Postulates of the Labeling Theory and the Reintegrative Shaming Theory

Labeling theory (LT) is picked because it has received certain empirical support from many Western criminological studies, but cross-cultural verification seems to be lacking. Interestingly, the Chinese system seems to rely greatly on benefits of labeling in preventing and controlling juvenile delinquency. I have considered the reintegrative shaming (RS) theory because John Braithwaite . . . , in his original exposition of RS, argued that Japan represented an interdependent and communitarian society that practices RS writ large. . . . Due to the influence of Confucianism, there are many similarities between Japanese and Chinese societies. Probably, it is more meaningful if this theory can be tested in the light of Chinese experience because China is a more typical interdependent and communitarian society.

Evidence available from the Chinese society will be used to assess the main tenets of these theories and to probe both their cultural specificity and possible universality. A closer, cross-cultural look at these theories may prove illuminating for both Western and Chinese scholars. Given, however, the cultural disparity between the Western and Chinese ways of thinking, theoretical concepts have to be contextualized and explored differently in each culture. Therefore, many of my ideas may have to be reconceptualized in the process of my analysis.

LT: The primary factor in the repetition of delinquency is the fact of having been formally labeled as a delinquent.

RS: Shaming carries a risk of alienating the first-time offender if it is not combined with positive reintegrative efforts. These efforts are more likely to succeed in a society tied by strong informal bonds.

The Chinese approach to delinquency assumes that labeling a delinquent does not necessarily produce his or her secondary deviance despite the existence of an effect of official labels on delinquent identities and behavior. In Chinese society, it is recognized that the social reaction to delinquency (labeling) may have both positive and negative effects, but a greater emphasis is placed on its potential for positive effects. In China, stigma is regarded as a great deterrent; it is shameful and therefore people try to avoid it. It is also believed that labeling contributes to rehabilitation. In Chinese society, on being labeled deviant, a person is subject to negative reactions and moral condemnation from society and is initially removed from his or her normal position in society and assigned a special role—a distinctive deviant role. This strategy is expected to force the individual to feel "pain" and recognize that he or she indeed has some problems and therefore become motivated to rehabilitate him or herself.

However, this process of labeling takes place in a distinct cultural context. Chinese society is a highly interdependent and relatively communitarian society in which individual survival depends on the survival of groups, and the functioning of groups depends on the capacity of their members to cooperate. . . . In such a society, social comparison becomes a major concern of members of society. Individuals care profoundly about what others think of them and their positions in the social world. . . .

Because individuals strongly depend on others for fulfillment of basic needs, pride and shame serve as indicators of the strength of the individual's social connection to others in Chinese society. Because of this sense of interdependence, the Chinese have the greatest esteem for those who make progress in accepting conventional norms. The role of a (positively labeled) model is always emphasized. To the Chinese people, to be praised as a model citizen—as the chaste widow or the dutiful son were praised by Confucians—is regarded as the most legitimate and desirable form of reward because it moves others to imitate and respect them. . . . This thought continues to exert a strong influence in the present China. Many officials of correctional institutions are convinced that the use of models provides the most desirable mode of learning and is especially effective because peer respect is a powerful human need. . . . Therefore, the inmates are urged to learn from good examples. Emulated models may be living or dead, national or local. For example, Lei Feng, a late soldier of the People's Liberation Army, is renowned throughout the whole country for his hard work, selflessness, and patriotism.

A model may exhibit general virtues, such as "selflessly serving the people," or particular ones, such as "working or studying hard." The other side of this emphasis on the model is to encourage people to become models themselves. Thus, inmates are exhorted to act as models for other inmates. Those chosen as models of neatness, productivity, helpfulness, or some other virtue are often lauded at many different occasions, and others are encouraged to follow their example. For example, there are blackboards in almost every correctional institution that display inmates' good deeds. Many officials believe that the model's example helps to develop an entrenched attitude, which is far more stable than a fear of punishment. Coercive methods are regarded as being a second choice.

For social control to be effective, however, the effect of negative labeling and shame is also emphasized. The effect of shaming lies not only in deterrence, but also reintegration. Although at first shaming can stigmatize and alienate the juvenile offender when the community expresses disapproval not only of the act but also of the person . . . , the need to regain or protect one's social status is a strong motivation for conforming behavior. This is facilitated by the subsequent reintegrative efforts of the collective.

Shaming is particularly meaningful in societies with strong social bonds. In China, people, especially juveniles, are closely attached to their family, school, and neighborhood. Strong social bonds make shame have a greater effect on offenders because shame is the emotional cognate to the social bond, and shame is felt when the bond is threatened. . . . Once a person is shamed, the shame is often also borne by his or her family and, although to a lesser degree, by neighborhood and school. Under these circumstances, juvenile offenders as well as their families, schools, and neighborhoods endure painful humiliation. This situation can force shamed persons to regret their behavior because they accrue greater interpersonal costs from shame. . . .

Shaming is powerful, and where there is power there is also a risk. John Braithwaite and Stephen Mugford . . . argued that stigmatization and exclusion are the most significant risks of shaming. Braithwaite . . . pointed out that shame can take dramatically different forms. They range from stigmatizing or disintegrative shaming, which brings a degradation in social status, to RS. . . .

Indeed, a shame-induced negative or delinquent self-image has a detrimental effect on some juveniles. In China, some informal or formal control measures, such as early social-educational intervention and confinement in a work-study school or juvenile reformatory,

result in considerable stigma. This may persist although these measures do not attempt to demean and humiliate offenders and emphasize reintegration into the community following treatment at an institution. For example, according to Article 152, the Law on Criminal Procedure, trials of those who are 18 years of age and younger are not open to the public. Clearly, this provision of the Law on Criminal Procedure is intended to protect juveniles from stigmatization and increase the possibility that a rehabilitated offender becomes again part of the community. In addition, social-educational teams, which are composed of not only their parents, relatives, teachers, colleagues, and neighbors, but also the police, may be assigned to monitor and help reintegrate the returning delinquent. Concrete measures are supposed to be selected according to the nature of the offender and the offense to "suit the remedy to the case" (a Chinese proverb). For different cases, there are different educators and methods, ranging from heart-to-heart talks to group study of the Party and governmental documents, laws and regulations; to public discussion of the deviant's problems and offering of suggestions and criticisms; to visiting factories, farms, and historical and cultural sites and solving young people's practical problems, such as housing, schooling, employment, and so on.

Although many measures have been taken, it is impossible to erase stigma completely. Once stigmatized with a deviant label, some juveniles, especially those from broken families, may lose love, dignity, and respect. In some areas, many schools, factories, and other institutions are reluctant to accept youngsters with a criminal or delinquent past. These young people usually have fewer opportunities to enter school, to find jobs, to join the army, or even to establish a family. Thus, they may experience a sense of injustice at the way they are victimized by agents of social control. This situation may indeed influence some juvenile offenders to have more negative attitudes toward society, become more involved with delinquent peers, and regard themselves as more delinquent. Under these circumstances, deviance becomes and is rationalized as a defensible lifestyle, which is difficult to change. This partly explains the phenomenon of recidivism in China.

> LT: Formal labels eventually alter a person's self-image to the point at which the person begins to identify him or herself as a delinquent and acts accordingly.

> RS: Shaming may damage a person's self-esteem if it is directed at the individual identity not the act and is not followed by positive reintegrative ceremonies.

According to the Chinese experience, whether one resists the negative effects of labeling and becomes positively influenced by the label depends not only on the labelees, but also on the efforts of the whole society. On one hand, stigmatization by certain agents of social control can indeed increase the attraction of outcasts to subcultural groups that provide social support for crime. On the other hand, concerted efforts of the community can change this situation. . . .

Families, friends, neighbors, schools, work unit, and the police intervene at the first sign of possible trouble. Chinese people do not mind only their own business; they prefer to handle crime and juvenile problems in their neighborhood, rather than hand them over to professionals. As a result, almost all members of the society seem to have become active controllers of crime and delinquency. Families, neighborhood communities, work units, and schools act as positive solvers of problems instead of silent observers. Their active participation is believed to have great effect on improving the offenders' legal and moral conscience, heightening their immunity to delinquent influences, decreasing attractive opportunities for participation in subcultures, and reintegrating them back into the community of law-abiding citizens.

As the first line of defense against criminal activity, the family and the grassroots community organizations play the most important role. In the vast majority of cases, delinquents are put under the supervision of their families and the relevant local authority—neighborhood committee, school, or work unit (depending on the delinquent's status). . . . According to Article 17 of the Criminal Code of China, parents or guardians of offenders under the age of 16 have the obligation to discipline their children. Under the watchful eyes of those with whom the delinquents have the most frequent daily contact, they are encouraged to reform and develop a sense of social responsibility, which will lead to their reintegration into the society.

Various specialized organizations, through their local branches, also take a hand in urging delinquents to rehabilitate themselves. Many state or regional leaders and other high-ranking officials often visit the institutions and show interest in inmates' study, labor, and life. Different levels of the People's Congress, government, and other organizations, such as labor unions, the Young League, women's associations, and even military organs, all are assisting reformatories with reforming delinquents. . . . Perhaps, mass involvement in reforming delinquents is one of the most striking aspects of the Chinese justice system that differentiates it from Western models.

Unlike in the RS approach, however, the deliberate focus of labeling in China seems to be both on the offense and the offender. Offenders are first labeled deviants and educated to understand that what they have done has detrimental psychological, social, and economic consequences for victims and also for themselves and other parties and to assume responsibility for what they have done. Then they are shown concern and love, accompanied by attempts to solve their practical problems, such as housing, schooling, and employment. This two-stage approach both expresses community disapproval and symbolizes reacceptance of offenders while offering a practical basis for reintegrating offenders. Thus, community not only reaffirms the normative order by shaming offenders but also provides them with opportunities for conventional reintegration. . . .

It is worthy of note that police and judicial organizations are also expected to play active roles in reintegrating offenders. In China, educating and helping offenders, especially juvenile delinquents, has become one of the main tasks of the police who are working in neighborhood police stations. They always work closely with local government, factories, enterprises, schools, neighborhoods, and other institutions to maintain public order, "prevent, reduce and forestall crimes through ideological, political, economic, educational, administrative and legal work," and create a better social environment. . . . They not only provide community surveillance, but also conduct many education programs at the neighborhood level, such as distributing legal materials and educating the residents in the neighborhood about laws and rights; holding community meetings to discuss justice and social problems; preparing messages involving legal and crime prevention matters and persuading residents of the necessity of rules for public security and individual protection; and visiting offenders and their families, friends, and relatives to determine what the problem is, seek solutions outside of the criminal justice system, and help them solve such problems as unemployment. In some cases, for example, according to Leng . . . , the police station in a neighborhood community may draw up a contract between the juvenile and his or her parents, the neighborhood, and the school. If the juvenile meets the terms of the contract within a specified time, then a certificate of good behavior is issued to the youngster, and the case is considered closed. If the adolescent does not meet the terms of the contract or commits a new violation, then the contract is extended or revised. Although the emphasis is on the collective nature of the treatment program—it is more than just an agreement between the juvenile and the police—direct involvement by the police is also intended as a reminder that an arrest can still be effected if the juvenile offender strays farther from the beaten path. The aim is to put greater pressure on delinquents. In reality, although the police participate directly in the early intervention, they are not concerned with law and punishment as such, but rather with helping offenders become law-abiding and useful citizens. The mere presence of the police is considered to be able to strengthen intervention and has in fact become an integral part of it. The extent and diversity of activity performed by the Chinese police indicate that policing not only is a prime force in enforcing the criminal law, but also plays an important role in the elaborate system of informal social control.

Although the judicial shame penalties, such as public exposure and debasement penalties (generally achieved by associating the offender with a noxious activity), that exist in the United States do not exist currently in China, China does have some judicial options, such as mass trials and sentence-pronouncing rallies, that can reach the same effect as shame penalties. They are designed to convey moral condemnation and inform the public about the offense and the offender to elicit public shaming of the offender. In the Chinese social environment, these legal measures can work as both a specific and general deterrent of possible future transgressions. With respect to young people, the educational sessions conducted by juvenile courts before disposition of cases may have a similar effect.

The Chinese experience suggests that informal and quasi-informal social education, including various education and training programs operated by parents, relatives, friends, or a relevant collectivity, has a greater effect on the juvenile's future behavior and self-identification than sanctions imposed by a remote legal authority. Social education can induce juveniles to recognize the harmfulness of their conduct and eventually to rehabilitate themselves. This is especially true in Chinese society because of its collectivist nature. . . .

In fact, through many kinds of education and help, operated by the society at large, and through positive inducement, rather than merely criticism or negative incentives, the vast majority of the young people initially labeled as criminals or delinquents eventually leave these deviant statuses well and truly behind them. This is indicated by the low rate of recidivism in China. A number of different sources suggest that recidivism rates among those released from reformatories are between 8% and 15%. . . . Despite different estimates, it is clear that the recidivism rate is quite low. From the limited data available, it is difficult to judge what causes low recidivism rates for the released inmates; however, community involvement, tight social control, or postrelease surveillance and rehabilitation all should be regarded as contributing factors.

Conclusion

The limitations of LT are quite clear in the light of the Chinese experience. This may explain why LT obtains only a limited empirical support for its key predictions even in Western countries. Furthermore, the LT ignores the cultural characteristics of different countries. For example, the concept of shaming is consistent with the cultural ethos of Chinese collectivism, rather than Western individualism. Therefore, LT assertions regarding the relationship of a formal delinquency label and secondary deviance do not seem particularly relevant to the Chinese experience. Rather, the Chinese experience tends to support the RS theory developed by John Braithwaite—the collectivist nature, strong social bonds, effective informal social control, and an emphasis on social education all make shaming a positive rather than negative tool of social control in Chinese society.

Questions

1. Define social control and identify its goals.

2. Describe social relations according to the ideals of traditional Chinese culture.

CHAPTER 22

The Effect of Social Bonds on Successful Adjustment to Probation

An Event History Analysis

John R. Hepburn

Arizona State University

Marie L. Griffin

Arizona State University

Although social bonds are widely thought to be a significant predictor of successful probation outcomes, recent research provides inconsistent findings on this issue. MacKenzie, Browning, Skroban, and Smith . . . and MacKenzie and Li . . . , for example, concluded that the observed decrease in criminal behavior among probationers while on probation was due to the deterrent effect of probation supervision, rather than to positive social bonds. In contrast, Kruttschnitt, Uggen, and Shelton . . . and MacKenzie and Brame . . . found that, respectively, social bonds and prosocial activities were significant predictors of probation success.

The objective of the present chapter was to examine the effect of social bonds on offenders' successful adjustment to probation. In doing so, this chapter contributes to the ongoing investigation in four ways. First, unlike most previous research, this chapter's focus is on the quality of the social relationships with family and friends. Second, measures of social bonds were obtained after entry to probation, rather than at the time of arrest or conviction, thus making them proximate to the observation period. Third, the use of a highly stigmatized offender population creates a more rigorous "test" of the effect of social bonds on probation adjustment. Finally, the use of an event history analysis permits an examination of the effects of social bonds on the time to failure—in this case, measured as an unsuccessful adjustment to probation.

Social Bonds as Informal Controls

Laub and Sampson . . . outlined a "life-course theory of age-graded informal social control" to explain desistance from crime. Focusing attention largely on young adult offenders, this model suggests that criminal behaviors decrease as aging adolescents form attachments and investments in conventional social groups and activities. For adolescents, social bonds are formed to parents, peers, and school; in adulthood, these bonds are extended to include work and marriage. Social bonds increase the individual's social investment and create a web of reciprocal relationships, both of which exercise constraints over criminal behavior. The formation of social bonds, then, is a "turning point" in the criminal trajectory of the offender that leads to desistance.

Because the formation of social bonds is a slow and incremental process, desistance is a gradual process that reflects the cumulative effects of these social bonds. . . . The social costs of crime increase with an increased

Source: "Effect of social bonds on successful adjustment to probation: An event history analysis," Hepburn, J. R., & Griffin, M. L., (2004), in *Criminal Justice Review, 29,* 46–75. Reprinted by permission of Sage Publications.

investment in conventional social relationships and social activities, and criminal behavior is voluntarily suspended. Laub and Sampson . . . , for instance, noted that "the key elements seem to be aging; a good marriage; securing legal, stable work; and deciding to 'go straight,' including a reorientation of the costs and benefits of crime."

To date, employment and family have received the most attention. Laub and Sampson . . . unreservedly asserted that "ties to work and family . . . reduce the probability that criminal propensities will be translated into action." . . . Horney, Osgood, and Marshall . . . and Shover . . . noted that employment was a major factor leading to desistance among long-term, frequently offending males. Simons, Stewart, Gordon, Conger, and Elder . . . also found that criminal behavior was affected by job attachment among young adults, but Uggen's findings . . . suggest that employment is more likely to be a turning point for older offenders (beyond age 26) than for younger offenders. Ties to the family have been linked to the prevalence of delinquency for quite some time . . . current studies among adults have focused on family relationships in adulthood, especially romantic relationships and marriage. . . . Moreover, recent evidence has called attention to the quality of these romantic relationships. . . . Criminal acts are less likely when these partnerships develop . . . , and they appear to resume when these partnerships are weak or are terminated. . . .

The Effect of Social Bonds While on Probation Supervision

If rule-breaking behavior is associated with the strength of the offender's ties to stable, conventional social relationships, there is a clear prescription for probation supervision: increase and stabilize the probationer's social bonds to society, especially those that arise from employment and social relationships. Indeed, probation supervision is designed to encourage or coerce participation in conventional social activities (e.g., school and employment) and relationships with conventional others (family and peers) while discouraging or banning participation in unconventional activities (e.g., drug use and homelessness) and association with unconventional others (e.g., known felons). Although probation supervision cannot compel strong social bonds, these efforts to increase the likelihood that such bonds may form are consistent with the widely held view that success on probation is associated with social bonds.

However, recent research with probationers has provided mixed results. MacKenzie et al. . . . studied the

effects of probation supervision on reoffending. That study of the self-reported behaviors of 107 adult probationers observed that both the number of probationers who reoffended and the rate of reoffending decreased during the first 6 months of probation supervision. Monthly measures of work, school attendance, and living with a significant other were included in the analyses, yet these measures of social bonds were found to be poor predictors of criminal reoffending. Nonetheless, the rate of reoffending was reduced during probation, leading MacKenzie et al. to conclude that "this study indicates that probation can be a viable method of short-term crime control. Probation reduces the number of offenders who commit crimes and the rate of offending for those who continue to offend." . . . MacKenzie et al. also noted, however, that, although some persons continued to commit crimes while on probation, the reoffending was unrelated to measures of social bonds.

This conclusion was reinforced in the reanalysis of these data by MacKenzie and Li . . . , who hypothesized that arrest and probation may serve to increase conventional bonds and, as a result, reduce criminal behavior. Using a time series analysis to make comparisons in the likelihood of attending school, having a job, and living with a spouse at three points in time—the year prior to arrest, the time of arrest, and the time on probation—MacKenzie and Li reported the following finding:

> Social bonds did not increase after arrest and probation. In fact, those who remained in the community during the period between arrest and probation were less apt to live with spouses, attend school, or have jobs, possibly indicating the negative impact of arrest on social bonds. There were no differences in social bonds between the prearrest period and probation. Thus, although arrest and probation are associated with a decline in criminal activities and risk behaviors, there is no evidence that social bonds increased as a result of arrest or probation. . . .

Absent any increase in social bonds among probationers, MacKenzie and Li concluded that the observed reduction in criminal reoffending during the first year of supervision could not be attributed to any increase in social bonds.

Nevertheless, support for the effects of social bonds was provided in two other studies. In the first, MacKenzie and Brame . . . examined the success of community supervision among nonequivalent groups of male offenders who had been sentenced to boot camp, to prison, and to probation in four southern states. The authors found that supervision intensity was strongly associated with the level of prosocial activities while on probation, indicating that supervision requirements and the intensity of supervision increased the probationer's social bonds to conventional activities. Further, the level of involvement in prosocial activities was related inversely to supervision failure, which was defined as a revocation prompted by an arrest for a new offense during the first year of supervision. These findings suggest that community supervision has the potential to improve the social bonds of probationers to the community and that those strengthened social bonds will be significant in the probationers' criminal desistance.

Kruttschnitt et al. . . . also found limited support for the effect of social bonds among probationers. This study of 556 sex offenders examined the effects of job stability and marital stability on probation success, which was operationalized as the absence of any new crime or probation violation during the first 5 years of probation supervision following conviction. "Job stability" was considered to have occurred if the probationer had been working for at least 6 months with the same employer prior to conviction, and "marital stability" reflected any change in marital status between the time of the offense and the time of sentencing. Kruttschnitt et al. observed a small decrease in the percentage of probationers who were married or cohabiting between the time of the offense and the time of conviction and noted that "this finding suggests that formal processing for the instant offense may have disrupted family stability for some offenders." . . . The authors also reported that neither marital status at sentencing nor marital stability predicted the occurrence of a reoffense during probation. In comparison, job stability was found to be a significant predictor of reoffending.

Sex Offenders on Probation: Establishing Social Bonds

The importance of social bonds to successful probation outcomes is underscored in the case of child molesters. Child molesters tend to have an existing relationship with the victim and with the victim's family, in which case the crime represents a violation of trust that threatens to rupture the existing social bond. Child molesters are among only a few types of offenders whose behavior is attributed largely to psychological or emotional characteristics that create propensities to crime, most notably impulsivity . . . and intimacy deficits . . . , and these criminal propensities are believed to be rather stable over the life course. . . . Lengthy incarceration appears to have little deterrent effect following release . . . , and

evaluations of treatment programs have yielded mixed results. . . .

Child molesters represent high-profile offenders who have been convicted of one of the most serious and offensive transgressions of social life. Their behavior is so morally offensive and socially threatening to the community that, following conviction, most jurisdictions require these offenders to register with local law enforcement as a "sex offender" and, furthermore, require local law enforcement to notify residents of an offender's presence in their neighborhood. In addition, by the conditions of their probation, child molesters are often restrained from living with their spouse or visiting with their children. Where they work and where they live are also closely regulated by probation supervision to restrict their access to potential victims. These formal responses to the offender undermine the offender's attempt to normalize social relationships and often weaken existing bonds to family and friends.

Research Problem

The objective of this chapter was to examine the effect of social bonds on offenders' successful adjustment to probation. By limiting the analysis to child molesters, the focus is placed on an offender population that is thought to have durable criminal propensities and an offense that maximizes the physical and social estrangement from society: Existing social bonds may be weakened or destroyed, and new social bonds are likely to be slow in forming. These factors undermine the likelihood that social bonds will be a significant predictor of probation outcomes, so any observed relationship between social bonds and adjustment to probation will be a strong statement of support for the hypothesis that a successful adjustment to probation is significantly predicted by a probationer's social bonds to conventional society.

Data and Methods

Serving the greater Phoenix, Arizona, metropolitan region, the Maricopa County Adult Probation Department created a specialized unit to supervise adult sex offenders. The probationer caseload was lowered somewhat for probation officers in this unit, and their work is supported by surveillance officers who monitor the weekend and evening activities of offenders. Arizona law authorizes lifetime probation for certain sex offenders, resulting in an increasingly large proportion of sex offenders who will remain on probation indefinitely. All child molesters are required to register with the Sheriff's Office as sex offenders and to adhere to a list of 16 other specialized probation terms for sex offenders (in addition to the standard terms of probation), most of which were designed to (a) reduce the probationers' opportunity to have contact with children; (b) reduce the probationers' access to places, electronic and print materials, and activities that might provide a situational inducement to another sexual offense; and (c) compel participation in treatment.

SAMPLE SELECTION AND DATA COLLECTION

The sample consisted of the 258 adult males who entered probation during the 30-month period between January 1, 1997, and June 30, 1999, following conviction for child molestation. The progress of each probationer was followed from the date of entry to probation to either the probationer's termination from probation supervision or the end of data collection, March 30, 2001. This created a follow-up period that ranged from 21 to 51 months; the mean length of observation was 35.3 months ($SD = 8.0$ months), and the median period was 35 months.

All data were collected from official records of the presentence investigation as well as from the court, the probation department, and local law enforcement agencies. At entry, data were obtained on a number of static factors, including the sociodemographic characteristics of each probationer, his criminal justice and substance abuse history, and select information about the offense of conviction. Dynamic postconviction measures of social bonding at the time the offender was reentering the community were obtained from the first progress report completed by the probation officer after the offender's first 6 months on probation. These interim reports included information regarding the probationer's employment status and relationships with family and friends. Finally, data regarding any technical violations or new crimes were recorded as the occasion arose, and final disposition information was recorded for all cases that were terminated during the observation period.

MEASUREMENT OF THE CONTROL VARIABLES

A profile of the sample is presented in Table 22.1, which summarizes information about each of the sociodemographic and criminal history factors used in the analysis. The average age at entry to probation, for example, was 33.7 years ($SD = 14.8$), with a median age

of 30.5 years. As is evident in Table 22.1, the majority of probationers were White, non-Hispanic, with 23.6% Hispanic and 9.3% African American. The mean number of years of formal education was 11.3 ($SD = 2.3$), and 57.2% of the probationers had a high school degree or its equivalent.

Prior treatment is a potentially important control variable, and records indicate that 18.7% of the sample had received prior treatment for emotional or mental health problems, 19.6% had received prior treatment for substance abuse, and 21.1% had received prior treatment for sexual aberrant behavior. Prior criminal history is also an important control variable, and official records revealed that fewer than half of the sample had had a prior arrest as a juvenile (21.7%) or as an adult (48.1%), and 42.6% had had a prior arrest (as either an adult or a juvenile) for a sex offense against a child. Finally, a measure of the legal severity of the instant offense was observed by noting that 14.6% of the sample entered probation directly after sentencing, 15.4% entered probation after serving time in the state prison (mean = 5.9 years, $SD = 3.2$ years), 64.6% entered probation following a jail sentence (mean = 9.4 months, $SD = 3.8$ months), and another 5.4% first served a period of jail confinement with work furlough (mean = 7.4 months, $SD = 4.5$ months).

For analysis purposes, each control variable except age at entry to probation and education was dichotomized, with values of "0" assigned to the reference category and "1" assigned to the attribute identified. Accordingly, ethnicity was dichotomized into non-White (35.3% = 0) and White (64.7% = 1). Similarly, prior treatment was transformed into those probationers with no history of prior treatment (40.3% = 0) and those probationers who had had mental health, substance abuse, or sexual behavior treatment (59.7% = 1). Prior arrest was dichotomized to represent those with no prior arrests (41.5% = 0) and those with one or more prior arrests (58.5% = 1). Finally, point of entry to probation was dichotomized to reflect those who entered probation with no time in state prison (84.6% = 0) and those who entered probation following a period of incarceration in state prison (15.4% = 1).

MEASUREMENT OF THE INDEPENDENT VARIABLES: SOCIAL BONDS

Laub and Sampson's attention to the web of reciprocal relationships that create the social bonds to constrain inherent criminal tendencies . . . has focused principally on lawful employment and conventional

Table 22.1   Characteristics of the Sample

Control Variables	Number of Cases	Percentage of Total	Mean	SD
Age at entry	258		33.68	1.48
Ethnicity				
White	167	64.7		
Hispanic	61	23.6		
African American	24	9.3		
Other	6	2.3		
Education			11.32	2.3
Less than high school graduate	107	42.8		
High school graduate/GED	104	41.6		
Some college	29	11.6		
College graduate	10	4.0		
Prior treatment experience				
Alcohol and drug use	48	19.6		
Sexual dysfunction	52	21.1		
Mental health	45	18.7		
Any one of the above	154	59.7		
Prior arrests (one or more)				
As a juvenile	56	21.7		
As an adult	124	48.1		
For sex offense against a child	110	42.6		
Any arrest (as juvenile or adult)	151	58.5		
Entry to probation				
From court	38	14.6		
Postincarceration, jail	182	70.0		
Postincarceration, prison	40	15.4		
Independent variables				
Employed full time	139	57.0		
Social support from family	171	66.3		
Social support from friends	120	53.5		
Total social support				
Neither family nor friends	52	20.2		
Either family or friends	103	39.9		
Both family and friends	103	39.9		
Dependent variables				
Revocation petition filed	116	45.0		
Unsuccessful termination	53	20.5		

social relationships. Following this emphasis, social bonds were defined in terms of full-time employment and positive social supports from family and friends. Full-time employment is not merely a source of income or an activity that consumes time; it represents a system of obligations and restraints that links the probationer to conventional society. Accordingly, employment while on probation was a dichotomized independent variable; 43% were not employed full time (0) and 57% were employed full time (1).

The attention to positive social supports highlights the theoretical importance of the quality of the social relationship. It is not simply a matter of whether the offender is married or has friends; it is the nature of the offender's relationships with a partner, with family members, and with conventional friends that is important. . . . With a measure of the quality of the relationships, this chapter is able to provide a better understanding of the role of the social bond in desistance.

The social support of family and friends was measured on the basis of probationer responses to several items that were asked during the 6-month progress report. First, probationers were asked to report the nature of their relationships with four possible groupings of family members: "wife or significant other," "mother," "father," and "other relatives." At the conclusion of this discussion, the probation officer categorized each relationship into one of four categories: "positive influence," "negative influence," "mixed influence," and "neutral or absent." Probationers who reported a positive influence from any one of the four possible groupings (i.e., wife, mother, father, and other relatives) were defined as having the social support of family (66.3% = 1).

Second, probationers were asked to report the nature of their relationship with "close friends," and their response was again categorized by the probation officer into one of the four categories: "positive influence," "negative influence," "mixed influence," and "neutral or absent." This was followed by the probationer being asked, "Do you have at least one significant person in your life, other than a relative, who is aware of the offense and who can be counted on for support?" Those probationers who reported a positive influence from close friends or who reported that they had at least one friend who could be counted on for support were defined as having the social support of friends (53.5% = 1).

Finally, the support of both family and friends was combined into a single indicator to represent the total social support available to the probationer. As indicated in Table 22.1, 39.9% of the probationers reported the support of both family and friends; another 39.9% of the probationers reported the support of either family or friends, but not both family and friends; 20.2% of the probationers reported that they received social support from neither family nor friends. For analysis purposes, this measure of total social support was treated as a dummy variable: Support of either family or friends (1) and support of both family and friends (1) were examined against the reference category of support of neither family nor friends (0).

MEASUREMENT OF THE DEPENDENT VARIABLE: UNSUCCESSFUL PROBATION ADJUSTMENT

Unsuccessful adjustment to supervision has been noted to be a significant predictor of subsequent recidivism among sex offenders. . . . The present analysis utilized two measures of unsuccessful adjustment to probation. The more liberal measure of an unsuccessful adjustment to probation was the issuance by the probation officer of a petition to revoke probation. A probation revocation petition, which may be occasioned by the commission of one or more technical violations or by the commission of a new crime, is a strong statement to the court that the probationer is not abiding by the conditions of supervision. This dichotomous outcome measure was coded 0 (55.0% received no petition to revoke probation) or 1 (45.0% received one or more petitions to revoke probation).

The second and more conservative outcome measure was defined by the termination status of each probationer. A probation revocation petition filed after the commission of any new criminal offense or technical violation could lead to one of two general outcomes: Either the probationer is continued on probation supervision, with or without some changes in the conditions of probation (e.g., assignment to intensive probation supervision), or the probationer is terminated from probation and transferred to the county jail or state prison. Those who are terminated and incarcerated have "failed" probation, whereas those who are returned to probation and continue to satisfy the conditions of their probation are viewed by the Adult Probation Department and others as a "successful" outcome. Unsuccessful probation termination, then, was analyzed as a dichotomous measure of probation failure, with a value of "0" assigned to those 79.5% of the probationers who remained on probation throughout the observation period and a value of "1" assigned to those 20.5% of the probationers who were terminated unsuccessfully.

The two measures of probation failure are not conceptually distinct, but both measures were used because they reflect an important difference in the severity of the probation violation. Fewer than half of all the revocation petitions resulted in a revocation of probation, but the remaining petitions often produced more intensified conditions of probation supervision. Therefore, either measure represents an unsuccessful probation adjustment, and social bonds were expected to be a significant predictor of both measures.

STATISTICAL ANALYSES

Event history analysis was used to model the time to an unsuccessful probation adjustment, which was operationalized by two dimensions: a probation revocation petition and an unsuccessful probation termination. Because the data included censored cases (cases for which probation failure had not yet occurred), more traditional regression models were inappropriate. Instead, event history allowed for the inclusion of predictor variables in models of the probability of failure at different points in time. The emphasis on time to failure permitted an examination of the question of whether social bonds had any effect in extending the probationer's life on probation.

The analysis began by estimating life tables of the survival rates of probation adjustment during the observation period. The life tables procedure allowed the sample to be grouped by an independent variable of interest, and then each group was treated as if it were a sample from some larger population to test the null hypothesis that the survival distributions would be the same for each group. The life table analysis was extended to include tests of equality across (a) the offender group members who were employed full-time versus the offender group members who were not employed full-time, (b) the offender group members who had positive social support from family versus the offender group members who lacked family support, (c) the offender group members who had positive social support from friends versus the offender group members who did not have the support of friends, and (d) the three offender groups represented by total social support: no support of family or friends, support of either family or friends, and support of both family and friends.

The effect of social bonds on probation adjustment was further analyzed by regression equations that were estimated using survival analysis procedures that allowed an estimation of the net effects of variables included in the model on the dependent variable with right censoring. . . . Because the model included multiple covariates as predictors, the Cox regression model, which includes time at risk in the analysis, is an appropriate technique for data that contained censored observations. . . .

Findings

SURVIVAL DISTRIBUTION CURVES

Figure 22.1 provides the survival distribution functions, grouped into 30-day intervals, among the pooled probationers for both measures of probation failure: time to a probation revocation petition and time to an unsuccessful termination from probation. There was an early and somewhat abrupt decline in the revocation petition survival rate throughout the period of observation. Nearly 40% of all those who would receive a revocation petition did so within the first year, and about 80% of those who would receive a revocation petition did so within the first 2 years. The survival distribution function of unsuccessful termination for the pooled probationers, which is also presented in Figure 22.1, reveals a slower rate of failure during the first 12 months, after which the decline becomes more precipitous.

TESTS OF EQUALITY OF SURVIVAL CURVES: THE EFFECTS OF SOCIAL BONDS

Our focus is on whether the survival curve significantly differed for probationer group members who differed in social bonds. Turning first to the survival curve for time to a revocation petition, it is evident in Figures 22.2a through 22.2d that probationers who had social bonds experienced a longer time to failure than probationers who did not have these bonds. From Figure 22.2a, we see that probationers who worked full time experienced a significantly longer time to a revocation petition than probationers who were not employed full time. Figure 22.2b illustrates the magnitude of the difference in survival time between those who had the support of family and those who did not, and Figure 22.2c depicts the significant difference in survival time observed between those who had the support of friends and those who did not. In each case, social support was associated with significantly longer rates of survival on probation.

Finally, the equality of survival curves among the three groups that were formed by combining support of family and support of friends is presented in Figure 22.2d. The overall difference in the three curves is statistically significant: Those probationers who had the support of neither family nor friends had the shortest survival time on probation, and their survival curve is significantly different from that of both probationers who had the support of either family or friends (Wilcoxon statistic = 19.954, $df = 1$, $P < .001$) and probationers who had the support of both family and friends. . . . The survival curve of those probationers who had the support of only family or friends is observed in Figure 22.2d to differ from the survival curve of probationers who had the support of both family and friends, but this difference is not statistically significant. . . .

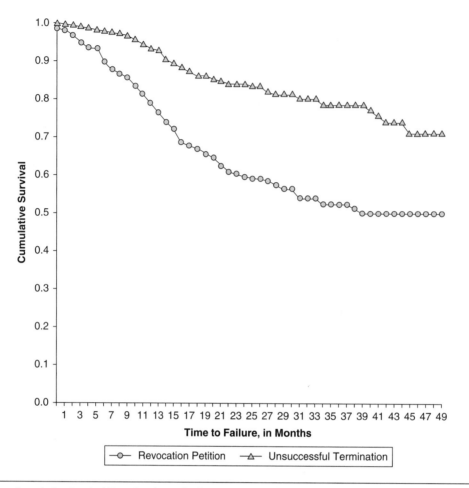

Figure 22.1   Cumulative Survival Function for Each of Two Measures of Failure on Supervision

Similar analyses of the survival distribution of unsuccessful probation termination by social bond strata are presented in Figures 22.3a through 22.3d. The test for equality among those who were employed full time and those who were not employed full time is represented in Figure 22.3a, and it is apparent that those who were not employed full time had a significantly shorter time to unsuccessful termination from probation. The effect of family support on the time to termination is evident in Figure 22.3b: The rate of failure among those without positive family support was significantly greater than the rate of failure among those who had positive family support. Figure 22.3c shows that the rate of unsuccessful termination also differed significantly by the presence of support from friends: Those probationers who lacked the positive support of friends were terminated much more quickly than those who received the support of friends.

Figure 22.3d examines the equality of survival curves among the three groups representing different levels of social support. The overall comparison is statistically significant, largely as a result of the finding that probationers who did not have the support of either family or friends were significantly less likely to survive on probation than those probationers who had the support of either family or friends . . . and those probationers who had the support of both family and friends. . . . Although probationers who had the support of only family or friends appeared to fail more quickly than probationers who had the support of both family and friends, this difference is not statistically significant. . . .

In summary, the data presented in Figures 22.2a–22.2d and Figures 22.3a–22.3d graphically illustrate the significant effects of the social bonding measures on the probationers' survival time to either a revocation petition or an unsuccessful termination. The length of time on probation before either the receipt of a revocation petition or an unsuccessful termination was significantly longer among those probationers who were employed full time (compared with those who were not), those

(text continues on p. 195)

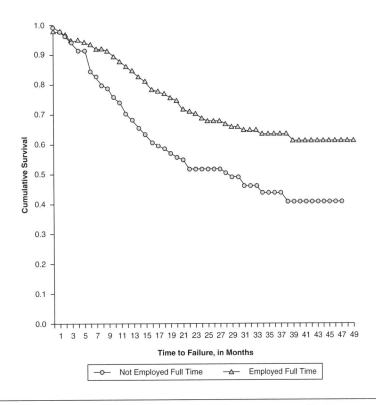

Figure 22.2a   Survival Curves for Time to Revocation Petition for Probationers Grouped by Measures of Social Bonds—Employment Status

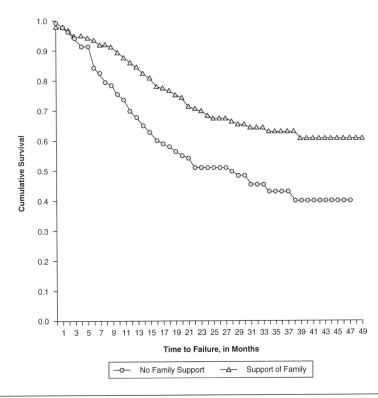

Figure 22.2b   Survival Curves for Time to Revocation Petition for Probationers Grouped by Measures of Social Bonds—Positive Support from Family

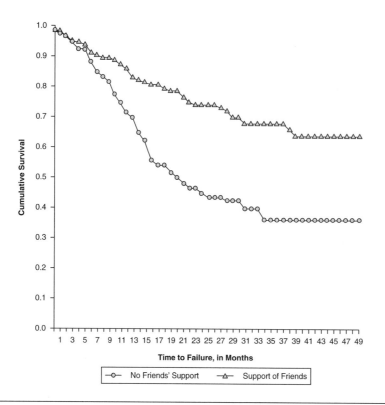

Figure 22.2c   Survival Curves for Time Revocation Petition for Probationers Grouped by Measures of Social Bonds—Positive Support from Friends

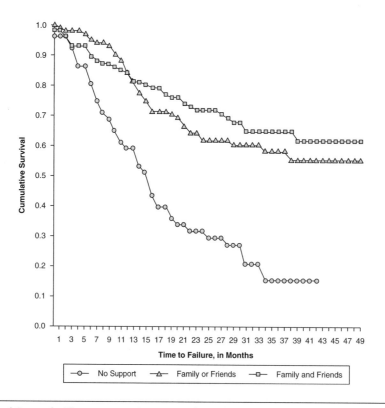

Figure 22.2d   Survival Curves for Time to Revocation Petition for Probationers Grouped by Measures of Social Bonds—Total Social Support

probationers who had the support of family (compared with those who were without family support), those probationers who had the support of friends (compared with those who were without the social support of friends), and those probationers who had the support of family and/or friends (compared with those who had the support of neither family nor friends). These findings offer rather uniform support for the hypothesis that positive social bonds enhance offenders' positive adjustment to supervision.

Multivariate Analysis

A more rigorous examination of the degree of support for the hypothesis was provided by the use of Cox regression models to analyze the independent and additive effects of each social bonding measure on the survival time to revocation petition when the effects of the salient sociodemographic and criminal history factors were simultaneously controlled. In the first model, time to receipt of a petition to revoke probation was regressed on just the sociodemographic and criminal history factors of the probationers. Age had a significant direct effect on the time to receipt of a revocation petition; a 1-year increase in age decreased the likelihood of a revocation petition by 3.9%, so the revocation petition was more likely for younger offenders. Prior arrests significantly increased the risk of failure ($B = .672$), such that those with one or more previous arrests were 1.96 times as likely to receive a revocation petition as those who had no prior arrests. Education, prior treatment, and entry from prison did not significantly affect the likelihood of a petition to revoke supervision.

The second model . . . introduces each of three measures of social bonding, permitting an analysis of the direct effect of each measure of conventional social ties on the time to a revocation petition while controlling for the effect of the sociodemographic and criminal history factors. The effects of age and prior arrest on the time to revocation petition continued to be significant when these three measures of social bonds were introduced to the model. Full-time employment did not have a significant effect on the time to a revocation petition, but probationers who had the positive support of family and probationers who had the positive support of close friends survived on probation significantly longer than probationers who did not have these bases of support. The relative risk of failure among those with positive family support was 59.8% of the risk of failure among those without positive family support, and the relative risk of failure among those with positive friends' support

was only 42.5% of the risk of failure among those without the positive support of friends.

The third model . . . replaced the separate measures of support of family and support of friends with the composite measure, total social support. In this case, the emphasis was on the degree to which probationers received positive social support from both family and friends or from family or friends, in contrast to probationers who received support from neither family nor friends. Again, there was a statistically significant negative effect of age on time to a revocation petition and a strong positive effect of prior arrests on the time to a revocation petition. Full-time employment continued to be a nonsignificant predictor of time to a revocation petition.

The findings presented . . . support the hypothesis. Compared with the reference category of probationers who were without the positive social support of family or friends, those who had the support of either family or friends survived on probation significantly longer; indeed, they had a relative risk of failure that was only 27.2% that of probationers with no positive social support. Similarly, those probationers who had the positive social support of both family and friends survived on probation significantly longer than those probationers who lacked the positive support of either group; their relative risk of failure was only 24.3% that of the latter group. These findings indicate that positive social support by family or friends, or by both groups, during the early phase of community supervision significantly improved the probationers' adjustment to community supervision as measured by the filing of a revocation petition.

. . . It is noteworthy that ethnicity, education, and, especially, age did not significantly affect time to probation failure. Further, neither measure of criminal history—prior arrests and entry to probation from prison—had a significant effect on time to probation failure. Prior treatment, however, did have a significant independent effect on time to unsuccessful probation termination. The observed B ($-.672$) indicates that prior treatment reduced the risk of an unsuccessful probation termination.

The effect of prior treatment on unsuccessful probation termination remained significant when the three measures of social bonding were included in the equation. . . . Moreover, each of the measures of social bonding had a significant effect on time to probation failure. First, full-time employment was a significant predictor of the time to probation failure: Those with full-time jobs were about half as likely as those without full-time employment to be terminated unsuccessfully from probation. Second, time to probation failure was significantly greater among probationers who had the positive support of family (compared with probationers who were without the positive support of family) and among probationers who had the positive support of friends (compared with probationers who were without the positive support of friends). The log-odds ratio indicates that those who had positive family support were only 45% as likely as those without family support to be terminated unsuccessfully from probation, and probationers who had the positive support of friends were only about 32% as likely as those without supportive friends to be terminated from probation.

. . . Prior treatment continued to be a significant predictor of time to probation failure, and again it was the only control variable observed to have a significant effect on the likelihood of probation failure. Full-time employment, however, ceased to be a significant predictor of time to probation failure.

. . . [T]he positive support of family or friends, compared with the support of neither family nor friends, continued to be a significant predictor of probation survival: Those who had the positive support of family or friends were only 24.7% as likely as those who were without the support of either family or friends to be unsuccessfully terminated from probation. In light of the predictive effect of the positive support of either family or friends, it is not surprising to observe . . . that those who had the positive support of both family and friends were only 16.7% as likely as those who were without the support of either to be unsuccessfully terminated from probation. The observed effects . . . indicate that the length of time to unsuccessful termination from probation was significantly affected by measures of conventional social ties, independent of criminal history, prior treatment, or salient sociodemographic characteristics of probationers. Whether individually (family support or friends' support) or together (support of both family and friends), these measures of positive social support are significant predictors of the sex offender's survival on probation.

Discussion

What factors explain why some offenders make a successful adjustment to community supervision and other offenders do not? A number of current developmental and life-course theorists . . . have suggested that strong social bonds to conventional activities and social groups constrain criminal behavior, but recent research with probationers has provided inconsistent support for the effect of social bonds on adjustment to probation. On the

one hand, studies of the self-reported behaviors of a small number of adult probationers in Virginia who had been convicted of an assortment of offenses uniformly concluded that social bonds and prosocial activities had no effect on the likelihood of new offenses while on probation. . . . In contrast, prosocial activities were found to be a significant predictor of probation success among adult sex offenders in Minnesota . . . and among adult probationers convicted of an assortment of offenses in four states. . . .

The present analysis of child molesters provides strong and consistent support for the hypothesis that social bonds affect the offender's adjustment to probation during the first 3 years of supervision. First, bivariate tests of equality of survival curves indicated that the social bond had a significant effect on sustaining probation success over time. Probationers who were employed full time experienced a longer time to a revocation petition and a longer time to an unsuccessful termination from probation than those probationers who did not have full-time employment. Also, a significantly longer time to a revocation petition and to an unsuccessful termination was observed among probationers who had the positive support of family (compared with those who were without family support), among probationers who had the positive support of friends (compared with those who were without friends' support), and among those who had the support of either family or friends (compared with those who had the support of neither family nor friends). Second, these effects of social bonds were confirmed in multivariate regression models. Full-time employment was found to have a significant effect only on the time to unsuccessful termination, but support of family and support of friends were found to affect the time to a revocation petition and the time to an unsuccessful termination.

Limitations

It appears that the observed differences in adjustment to supervision are due, at least in part, to differences in social interdependence among the probationers. Although this finding suggests that social bonds are an important factor in the probationer's successful adjustment to community supervision, that conclusion must be viewed within the limitations of this analysis. One limitation is that the probationers were under supervision throughout the observation period. A stronger test of the hypothesis would examine outcomes after supervision is terminated (and, presumably, the opportunities for unsanctioned crime are increased). However, fully

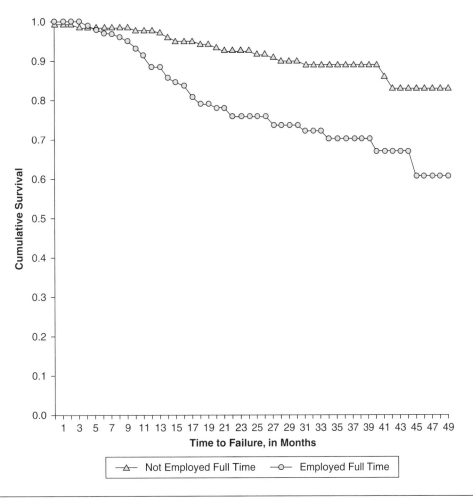

Figure 22.3a   Survival Curves for Time to Unsuccessful Termination for Probationers Grouped by Measures of Social Bonds—Employment Status

91% of the child molesters in this study were serving lifetime probation and will always be supervised while in the community. Because of the invariability of supervision, we framed our analysis in terms of the probationers' successful entry and adjustment to probation. As noted earlier, adjustment to supervision has been found to be a significant predictor of subsequent recidivism among sex offenders....

Another limitation is that probationers were observed for an average of only 3 years following entry to supervision. Studies of probation outcomes and recidivism often examine a period of 3 years or less ..., but longer follow-up periods are desirable. Recent studies of recidivism among sex offenders have argued the need for a period of 5 years ... or even longer.... A longer follow-up period may yield the same findings, but it

would provide increased confidence in the stability of those findings. At a minimum, we hope to have made the case that a 3-year follow-up period is long enough to determine whether probationers make a successful adjustment to supervision.

Also, the two measures of unsuccessful probation adjustment used in the present analysis—revocation petition and probation failure—are activities or outcomes that are produced by probation officers and other officials and are not direct measures of the probationers' behavior. As in the case of arrest or conviction data, we are assuming that these outcomes are produced by unbiased and uniform responses of officials to the objective behaviors of the probationers. Although self-reported measures of probationer adjustment are not without their own limitations, such measures

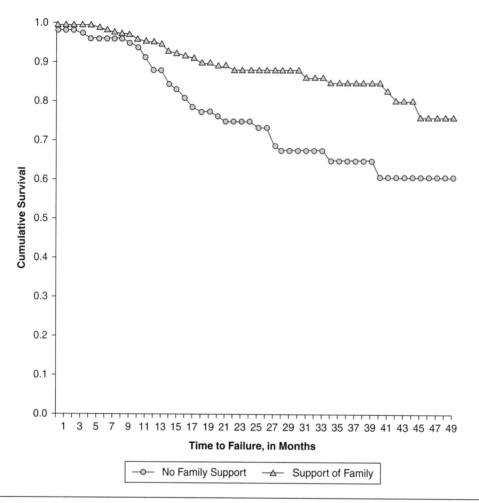

Figure 22.3b   Survival Curves for Time to Unsuccessful Termination for Probationers Grouped by Measures of Social Bonds—Positive Support from Family

would be a useful complement to the official measures utilized in this analysis.

Moreover, the use of probation officers to determine the level of social bonds raises the issue of the independence of the measures of the independent and dependent variables. Although this question is often raised in connection with the use of data from probation files, it is nonetheless important to ask: To what extent are the observed effects of social bonds on successful adjustment an artifact of the probation officers' actions to petition for revocation on the basis of their biases pertaining to the measures of social support of family and friends? For that matter, to what extent does the probationer's social bond to the probation officer affect the probationer's success on probation? Although this represents a potential confounding effect between the independent and dependent variables, the conclusions are strengthened by the fact that they are consistent

with those reported in analyses that did not face this limitation. . . .

Finally, we must be cautious in asserting a causal relationship between social bonds and rule-breaking behavior until the relationship among criminal propensity, social bonds, and criminal behavior is resolved. Impulsivity, low empathy, and antisocial tendencies—generally regarded as measures of criminal propensity . . .—may be the cause of both the failure to form social bonds and the unsuccessful adjustment to probation supervision. If this is the case, the observed relationship between social bonds and successful adjustment is spurious. Nevertheless, other life-course theorists either deny the presence of a stable criminal propensity . . . or argue that social bonds inhibit the criminogenic effects of criminal propensities. . . . As is true of the previously cited studies of the effect of social bonds on probation outcomes, this chapter used prior arrest record, an admittedly weak

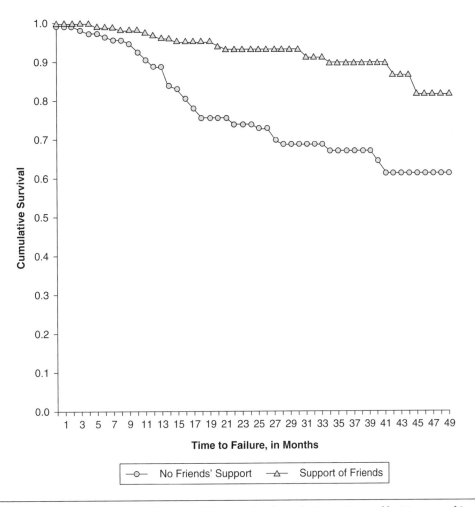

Figure 22.3c   Survival Curves for Time to Unsuccessful Termination for Probationers Grouped by Measures of Social
Bonds—Positive Support from friends

measure of criminal propensity, as a control variable. In the absence of stronger controls for criminal propensities among probationers, it is possible that a selectivity effect has occurred in these earlier studies and in the study reported in the present chapter.

These and other limitations notwithstanding, the study reported in this chapter makes an important contribution to the research literature in support of desistance theory. First, it is among only a few studies that use proximate and qualitative measures of social bonds. Typically, social bonds such as employment and marital status are static measures based on observations made at the time of arrest or conviction. In contrast, this study observed social bonds during the early months of supervision, when the offender was at risk of failure. Furthermore, recent efforts have moved beyond the simple

distinction between married and unmarried offenders used by Kruttschnitt et al. . . , MacKenzie and Brame . . . , and MacKenzie et al. . . . and have examined the strength of the marital bonds . . . or the quality of ties to family and friends. . . . Following a felony conviction, especially a conviction for child molestation, the nature of the social bond to family and friends is better captured by a measure of the quality of the relationship or the nature of the social support within the relationship than by a simple dichotomy between married and unmarried. In addition, the married/unmarried dichotomy fails to examine the impact of parents, siblings, and other family members. The importance of social support is evident in our finding that probationers who had the support of family or the support of friends during the early months of probation supervision

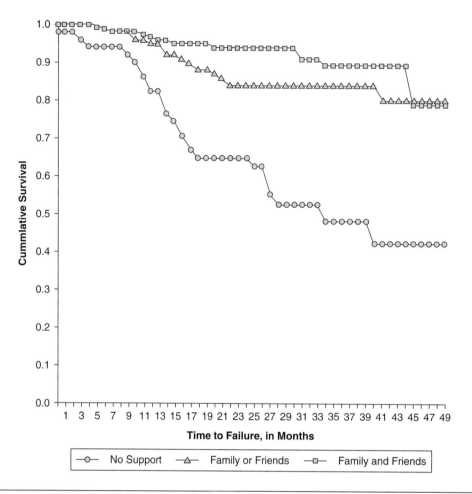

Figure 22.3d   Survival Curves for Time to Unsuccessful Termination for Probationers Grouped by Measures of Social
Bonds—Total Social Support

survived on probation significantly longer than probationers who did not have the positive support of either family or friends at this critical time.

Second, this study was a prospective analysis that examined the time to failure rather than, as is more typical, the presence or absence of failure. Consistent with the concept of desistance as a process rather than an outcome, an event history analysis is advantageous because it estimates the overall probability of a negative outcome occurring at different points in time. This chapter asks the question: "Do social bonds have any effect in extending the probationer's life on probation?" A comparison of the survival rates on probation permitted us to determine that social bonds, particularly the positive social support of family or friends, improved the survival rate of probationers relative to those probationers who were without these social bonds.

Finally, the analysis tested the effects of social bonds with a group of probationers who had been convicted of child molestation. The desistance process may be unique to distinct offender categories . . . , and "child molesters" are a more homogeneous grouping than "sex offenders." . . . Certainly, child molesters represent a distinct category of offenders in terms of the enduring criminal propensities attributed to them . . . and the social isolation that they experience. . . . The social stigma of child molestation is so strong that these offenders have difficulty maintaining conventional employment as well as the support of family and friends. Perhaps it is precisely because the offense so seriously threatens conventional social bonds that we found the presence of social bonds to be significant predictors of these offenders' ability to survive on probation.

IMPLICATIONS

Desistance theory informs the debate on strategies of intervention with offenders.... It is apparent that employment and relationships with family and friends are social ties that enhance the offender's ability to successfully adjust to the problems of community reentry.... Social ties appear to be even more important among offenders who have the greatest propensities to crime.... Nevertheless, efforts to build and maintain strong social bonds are often inconsistent with the broader societal effort to publicly stigmatize and socially isolate the offender, especially the sex offender. Community notification procedures rely on stigma to create a public identity of the offender as a deviant.... The offender is ascribed a master status ... as a "child molester" or a "sex offender," and the social reaction of the community creates problems of adjustment for the offender.... Reentry to the community is restrained by probation restrictions that govern living arrangements, employment opportunities, and even visits with family members. When the offender faces a lifetime on probation, there is no end in sight for these official restraints. These and other formal responses rely on incapacitation and the threat of punishment to reduce future rule-breaking and criminal behavior. To the extent that cessation occurs, it is involuntary and temporary.

Formal authorities are in a position to assist the offender in developing and strengthening social bonds to conventional activities and to the offender's family and friends. In fact, MacKenzie and Brame ... argued that probation officers should employ strategies of "coerced reintegration" to take advantage of this opportunity to establish positive social bonds that will persist long after any possible deterrent effects of supervision. However they are formed, there is strong evidence that social bonds are an important factor in an offender's successful adjustment to community supervision.

Employment and relationships with family and friends are not static variables, however, and continued success on probation will depend on the persistence of strong social ties to these conventional activities and groups. The strength of social bonds is a dynamic variable that can vacillate over time while offenders are under probation supervision. Future research must examine this hypothesized linkage between social bonds and successful adjustment to probation by obtaining repeated observations of both social bonds and probation outcomes at several points over an extended time. With added controls for the possible selectivity effect of criminal propensities, the link between dynamic social bonds and probation adjustment over a longer time frame can be investigated.

Questions

1. How do social bonds act as informal controls on criminality, according to this article?

2. Explain the policy implications of the authors' findings for future strategies of interventions with offenders.

CHAPTER 23

Self-Control and Social Bonds

A Combined Control Perspective on Deviance

Douglas Longshore

Eunice Chang

Shih-chao Hsieh

Nena Messina

University of California, Los Angeles, Integrated Substance Abuse Programs

According to the general theory of crime . . . , variation in the propensity to engage in crime and other deviance is mainly a function of individual differences in self-control. The general theory of crime, featuring self-control as the central explanatory factor, contrasts with Hirschi's . . . social bonding theory, in which deviance is a result of weak social bonds such as poor attachment to others and low involvement in conventional activities. It is not clear whether or how these two perspectives in control theory can be reconciled. One possibility, explored in the current study, is that social bonds mediate the relationship between self-control and deviance. It has also been suggested that association with deviant peers may mediate the influence of social bonds on deviance . . . ; that is, people whose peers expose them to and reinforce deviance are more likely to engage in deviance and to have weak bonds to conventional peers. . . . In addition, association with deviant peers may be characteristic of people with low self-control and may mediate the effect of low self-control on deviance. Prior research has not tested these possibilities.

Theory integration can help to resolve disparate conceptual approaches in the field of criminology. . . . Through identification of dominant themes, premises, hypotheses, and findings common across different disciplines or causal propositions, theory integration may lead to an "intellectual account" . . . that offers more conceptual richness and greater predictive power than any one theory individually. For reasons explained next, we believe that the self-control and social bonding perspectives might be combined into one explanatory model in which social bonds and deviant peer association are treated as processes through which low self-control exerts some of its influence on deviance. Using longitudinal data from a sample of 1,036 adult male drug offenders, we examined relationships among self-control, social bonds, deviant peer association, and drug use. We also tested the degree to which social bonds and peer association mediate the relationship between self-control and drug use.

Theoretical Background and Literature Review

Gottfredson and Hirschi . . . defined *self-control* as the degree to which a person is "vulnerable to the temptations of the moment." . . . They viewed low self-control as a

Source: "Self-control and social bonds: A combined control perspective on deviance," by Longshore, D., Chang, E., Hsieh, S., & Messina, N., (2004), *Crime and Delinquency, 50,* 542–564. Reprinted by permission of Sage Publications, Inc.

behavior pattern arising from ineffective socialization early in life. This pattern was said to be quite stable, when established, and was cited as the primary individual-level factor explaining crime, drug use, and other forms of deviance. Many studies have found the expected relationship between low self-control and adult crime . . . , juvenile delinquency . . . , drunk driving . . . , and other imprudent behavior by adults and youth. . . .

The general theory of crime, featuring self-control as the central explanatory factor for individual differences in deviant conduct, departs from Hirschi's . . . social bonding theory, perhaps the preeminent control perspective in criminology. . . . In social bonding theory, the primary explanatory factors for deviant conduct are weak social bonds—specifically, poor attachment to others, low involvement in conventional activities, lack of commitment to a conventional lifestyle, and low endorsement of conventional moral belief. . . . Empirical research has confirmed the hypothesized relationships between social bonds and crime, delinquency, drug/ alcohol use, and smoking. . . . However, most of this research has focused on juveniles, not adults. . . . In addition, studies are inconsistent regarding the strength of the bonds/deviance link in relation to the seriousness of deviance. In some research, this link is stronger for minor deviant acts such as petty larceny and adolescent smoking than for serious misconduct such as theft, assault, and robbery. . . . Other research has suggested the opposite . . . or found no such differences. . . .

Hirschi's . . . original formulation of social bonding theory did not fully explore possible complexities in attachment and peer influence. His hypothesis was that attachment per se promotes conformity. As summarized by Akers . . . , "It is the fact of attachment to other people, not the character of the people to whom one is attached, that determines adherence to or violation of conventional rules." . . . That hypothesis has been called into question by research indicating that attachment to peers is conducive to conformity only when peers are law-abiding. . . . Additional research has distinguished between bonds to conventional others and bonds to deviant others. Findings indicate that deviance is less common among persons with close ties to law-abiding others and more common when close ties exist to deviant others. . . . Finally, some studies have tested peer influence as a variable mediating the relationship between social bonds and deviance. Marcos et al. . . . and Krohn et al. . . . found that deviant peer association partially explained the effects of social bonds on adolescent smoking and drug use. . . . In Agnew . . . , the relationship between social bonds and delinquency was

mediated by deviant peer association. In short, an adequate test of social bonds as correlates of deviance requires a careful definition of the attachment bond and recognition of the possibility that association with deviant others may be causally relevant as a mediator of the relationship between social bonds and deviance.

In their 1990 book introducing the general theory of crime, Gottfredson and Hirschi advanced the argument that the link between weak social bonding and deviance may be spurious inasmuch as both are products of the same causal factor, namely low self-control. Their argument implies that nothing of theoretical importance is likely to be gained in research testing an integrated model of self-control and social bonding. However, Akers . . . emphasized the need to explicate the conceptual links between self-control and social bonding. Other criminologists have made the same point. . . . In addition, bonding theory does not address "how people become bonded in the first place." . . . Given the general theory's proposition that social bonds are a product of low self-control, it seems germane to put that proposition to the test, and doing so requires an integrated perspective linking self-control and social bonding. Finally, the authors of the general theory stated that weak social bonds are "to some large degree products of low self-control." . . . Traits representing propensity to engage in deviance may "affect the settings in which the individuals possessing them are located, e.g., the amount of education they obtain, the kind of job or marriage they achieve, the area of the city in which they live." . . . These statements suggest relationships that are causal, not merely artifactual; that is, low self-control, as a propensity established early in life, may have negative effects on the development of social bonds later in life. The person with low self-control may be less likely to form and maintain stable friendships, more likely to associate with others who lack self-control and who are similarly deviant, less able to adjust to the demands of school and workplace, and less likely to place high value on conventional ties. . . . The importance of exploring the causal link between self-control and social bonds is underscored by the fact that self-control, as a trait established early in life, exerts any influence on serious deviance quite distally, that is, over a span of years. Some of that influence may be direct, reflecting an enduring propensity for deviant conduct. However, it remains important to see whether any part of its influence might be exerted through causal processes involving more proximal factors.

The foregoing implies an integration of self-control and social bonding perspectives in which the relationship between low self-control and deviance is mediated at least partially by one or more social bonds. Tests of that possibility may add depth to our conceptual understanding of deviance and would help to specify the causal chain linking self-control and deviance. There is little empirical work on this possibility, however. Wright, Caspi, Moffitt, and Silva . . . , using cohort data from the Dunedin Multidisciplinary Health and Development Study . . . , found that low self-control in childhood predicted weak social bonds and greater criminal behavior later in life. The authors also found that social bonding and adolescent delinquency predicted adult crime, and the effect of self-control on crime was largely mediated by social bonds. . . .

The analysis reported here is based on longitudinal data from a sample of adult men with serious criminal histories, a population often overlooked in studies on self-control and social bonds. We examined low self-control, social bonds, and deviant peer association as predictors of drug use across a 6-month follow-up period. We also tested social bonds and deviant peer association as mediators of the relationship between low self-control and drug use. Deviant peer association was among our set of possible mediators because the effect of low self-control and social bonds on deviance may be mediated partly by peer influences. . . . Peer association may therefore play a role in a combined control perspective on deviance; it may help to explain the effect of low self-control, social bonds, or both.

Method

SAMPLE

This chapter is based on data collected between 1991 and 1995 for an evaluation of Treatment Alternatives to Street Crime (TASC) programs in five U.S. cities. TASC programs assess the drug treatment needs of offenders in local criminal justice systems, refer drug-involved offenders to treatment and other services, and monitor their status. Treatment may be in lieu of, or an adjunct to, routine criminal justice processing. Evaluation results are reported in Anglin, Longshore, and Turner . . . and Turner and Longshore. . . .

Data required for this analysis were completed for a sample of 1,036 adult male offenders. The ethnic breakdown of this sample was 59% African Americans; 35% non-Hispanic Whites; and 5% others, mostly Hispanics. Ages ranged from 18 to 64 years ($M = 30.8$), and offenders had completed 10.3 years of school on average. Of the sample, 25% said they were currently married or living

with someone, and 66% were not employed at the time of the baseline interview. Most offenders had extensive criminal histories, two thirds (66%) had at least two prior felony convictions, and just more than one third (36%) had been younger than 15 years when first arrested. Most (77%) had been incarcerated at least once, and all offenders were on probation at the time of the baseline interview. Involvement in drug use was extensive, as would be expected in a sample of adult drug offenders referred to treatment by criminal justice. Lifetime use of marijuana was reported by 91% of the sample, crack cocaine by 47%, powder cocaine by 54%, and heroin by 28%.

The original sample included female as well as male offenders. However, psychometric properties of the self-control measure may not be adequate for women . . . perhaps because the etiology and consequences of low self-control differ by gender. . . . We therefore excluded female offenders from this analysis.

MEASURES

Items intended to capture the constructs of interest were factor analyzed in SAS by means of maximum likelihood estimation and direct quartimin rotation. Items that formed reliable and distinct factors corresponding to the intended constructs were retained in confirmatory factor analyses and employed as factor indicators in subsequent analyses. Where appropriate, items were scored in reverse. Factor loadings from the confirmatory factor analysis are shown in Table 23.1. Low self-control, social bonds, deviant peer association, and baseline drug use were measured in an initial interview. Subsequent drug use was measured in a follow-up interview 6 months later. More than 80% of the sample were located and completed the follow-up interview.

Low self-control. Low self-control was measured with three multi-item indicators: impulsivity, based on four self-report items (e.g., "you act on the spur of the moment without stopping to think"); self-centeredness, based on four self-report items (e.g., "you look out for yourself first, even if it makes things hard on other people"); and volatile temper, based on four self-report items (e.g., "you lose your temper pretty easily"). Response options were *never, rarely, sometimes, often,* and *almost always.* When necessary, item scores were reversed so that higher values represent lower self-control.

Distinctive relationships between deviant conduct and some of self-control's constituent elements have been found. . . . However, self-control can defensibly be

Table 23.1   Confirmatory Factor Analysis

Factor	Standardized Factor Loadings
Low self-control	
Impulsivity	0.55
Self-centeredness	0.61
Volatile temper	0.64
Attachment	
Cooperation	0.81
Enjoyment	0.83
Listening/helping	0.78
Involvement	
Currently married/living with	0.64
Ever married/lived with	0.70
Duration of current/last employment	0.37
Beliefs	
Children should obey	0.27
Things called crime don't hurt	0.42
Okay to sneak into game/movie	0.59
Okay to sell alcohol to minors	0.52
Religious commitment	
Religion important	0.70
Religious preference	0.66
Born again	0.52
Drug/alcohol peers	
Friends like to drink	0.62
Friends use drugs	0.97
Previous drug use	
Number of drugs used	0.71
Frequency of use (logged)	0.99
Days of use (logged	0.98
Follow-up drug use	
Number of drugs used	0.72
Frequency of use (logged)	0.99
Days of use (logged)	0.98

analyzed as a unidimensional construct . . ., at least among men . . . , and a unitary measure of self-control is appropriate in an analysis testing hypotheses derived from a theory in which self-control is viewed as a unitary construct. . . .

Attachment. Attachment was measured by three indicators of affective ties among family members "when you are around other members of your family." Questions asked how often there is (a) "a feeling of cooperation," (b) "enjoyment in being together," and (c) "an interest in

listening and helping each other." The recall period for these questions was the past 6 months. Response options were *never, sometimes, about half the time, usually,* and *always.* Higher values indicate stronger attachment.

These questions, derived from Marcos et al. . . . and Krohn et al. . . . , are typical of attachment indicators employed in tests of social bonding theory. . . . Because our focus was on bonds constraining adult behavior, questions pertained to the current family, not the family of origin. All men in the sample reported interaction with their families during the baseline recall period (past 6 months); thus, coding and interpretation of responses was not complicated by lack of recent interaction with family members.

Involvement. Involvement in a conventional lifestyle is the temporal aspect of social bonding. Involvement indicators in our dataset pertained to the person's history and stability of intimate relationships; specifically, (a) whether the person is currently married or living with someone, (b) whether he has ever been married or lived with someone, and (c) the duration of current or most recent employment. Higher values indicate greater involvement. . . .

Moral belief. This bond represents adherence to a general belief that the rules of conventional society are binding. Our belief factor was based on endorsement of four items: (a) "many things called crime do not really hurt anyone"; (b) "when parents set down a rule, children should obey"; (c) "it is okay to sneak into a ballgame or movie without paying"; and (d) "even though it is against the law, it is okay to sell alcohol to minors." Response options were *strongly disagree, disagree, undecided, agree,* and *strongly agree.* Scoring on items 1, 3, and 4 was reversed so that higher values represent stronger endorsement of conventional moral belief. . . .

Religious commitment. The fourth bonding factor is stake in conformity, or devotion to conventional lines of action. . . . Commitment is typically measured as educational or job aspirations, time spent on homework or other conventional activities, and/or religiosity. . . . However, a key problem in bonding studies is that commitment, so measured, is difficult to distinguish from involvement, especially when the commitment indicators implicitly or explicitly ask about time spent in conventional activities or time invested in conventional goals. . . .

In accord with other research . . . , we used indicators of religiosity to capture the constraining effect of commitment. The three indicators were (a) "how important is religion in your life" (*not important, a little important, important,* or *very important*); (b) "how would you describe your current religious preference" (*none* vs. *Catholic, Protestant, Jewish,* or *other*); and (c) "do you consider yourself a born-again Christian" (*no* or *yes*). Higher values indicate stronger religious commitment.

Association with substance-using peers. For a deviant peer association measure specific to the deviant conduct at issue (drug use), we used two indicators: (a) "how many of your friends like to drink" and (b) "how many of your friends use illegal drugs" (a third possible indicator, "how many of your friends are involved in crime," did not load on this factor). Response options were *none, some, about half, most,* or *all.* Higher values indicate greater association with substance-using peers.

Notably, this measure is not based on a simple count of peers who used drugs or alcohol. By measuring substance-using peers as a (non-numerical) proportion of total peers, we accounted for the fact that social networks can include conventional as well as deviant others in varying proportions and that ties to deviant others may not contribute to misconduct if such ties are outweighed by conventional ones....

Drug use. At baseline and follow-up, offenders were asked to report their drug-use patterns over the prior 6 months. Respondents reported drug use for the 6-month period on a month-by-month basis moving backward. This procedure followed previous interview techniques shown to produce good recall data on alcohol and drug use.... Indicators for this factor were number of drugs used, frequency of drug use (log transformed), and number of days of drug use (log transformed) in the prior 6 months.

ANALYSIS OF DATA

As a first step in the analysis, we adjusted for possible effects of assignment to TASC and demographic variables (race and age). Following the procedure employed by Newcomb and Bentler..., we partialed all three variables out of each relationship in the correlation matrix, thus removing their influence from the entire system of theory-relevant factors. In subsequent causal modeling, we were therefore able to maintain focus on predictors drawn from the two control perspectives. This procedure reduced the possibility of misspecification of the relationships of theoretical interest and, at the same time, avoided adding unduly to the complexity of the analytic model. Race and age indicators were based on self-report.

TASC assignment was measured as a dummy variable (TASC group = 1, comparison group = 0)....

Using the two-step approach recommended by Anderson and Gerbing... and the Mplus statistical modeling program..., we used confirmatory factor analysis to test the adequacy of the proposed measurement model and relationships among the latent factors. Each hypothesized factor predicted its proposed indicators, and factors were allowed to intercorrelate. Next we tested a structural equation model in which (a) low self-control predicted all four social bonds, (b) these five factors predicted substance-using peer association, and (c) all six factors predicted drug use at follow-up. Baseline drug use was employed as an additional predictor so that scores on the follow-up measure would reflect greater involvement in drug use after adjustment for baseline use. We did not allow correlated errors between latent factors because we had no theoretical basis for doing so.... Paths were dropped from the initial model if they were not significant. The significance of possible indirect effects of low self-control on drug use was also examined....

Our measures of low self-control, social bonds, peer association, and baseline drug use were coterminous. The outcome measure was drug use during the 6-month follow-up period; after adjustment for baseline use, this measure reflected change in degree of drug-use involvement over that period. Thus, the temporal order is clear from predictors to outcome measure, but not among the predictors. We do not see the latter as a major problem. In the general theory of crime, self-control is said to be established early in life and to remain stable thereafter.... In his analysis of data from the Cambridge delinquent development study, Polakowski... found that self-control had indeed remained "moderately stable" across a 4-year span.... Thus, it is logical to use a coterminous self-control measure as an exogenous factor in an analysis in which the endogenous factors (e.g., social bonds and deviant peer association) are based on data also collected at baseline.

Results

We examined bivariate relationships between low self-control and other factors to be included in the model.... Low self-control was strongly and inversely related to all four factors, indicating strength of conventional social bonds. Offenders with low self-control also reported that a greater proportion of their peers were involved in substance use. Finally, measures of drug use were higher among persons with low self-control.

The four bonding factors were related consistently, although not always significantly, to drug use. The direction of these relationships was as hypothesized. Persons reporting more drug use at follow-up appeared to have weaker conventional bonds. Moral belief was the bond most strongly linked to subsequent drug use. The other bonding factors were modestly related to subsequent drug use. The substance-using peer factor was associated positively with subsequent drug use.

Discussion

In the general theory of crime . . . , the propensity to engage in crime and other deviance is determined mainly by individual differences in self-control. This proposition contrasts with Hirschi's . . . own earlier view that deviance is mainly a result of weak social bonds. We tested the possibility that these two control perspectives might be integrated by positing social bonds, along with deviant peer association, as outcomes of low self-control and as mediators of the relationship between low self-control and drug use. Moreover, this test was based on a dataset that addressed important issues in prior research: Data were longitudinal rather than cross-sectional; the sample was composed of adult men rather than juveniles; and deviant involvement, specifically illegal drug use, was substantial among these men.

All four bonding factors and the peer association factor were related strongly, in the expected direction, with low self-control. These results are consistent with the proposition that people with low self-control will also lack close emotional ties to conventional others, spend less time in conventional activities, evince a weaker commitment to conventional lifestyles, reject the view that prevailing moral values are binding on the individual, and associate with others involved in deviant conduct. . . . Bonding factors were also related as expected to drug use, although the relationship for three of the factors was weak. These results are consistent with social-bonds research using samples drawn from nonoffender or juvenile populations. That research has confirmed hypotheses in social bonding theory, but has typically found that bonding measures explain only a modest portion of the variance in deviant outcomes. . . .

Conventional moral belief was the only social bond that mediated the relationship between low self-control and drug use. This result too is consistent with research using nonoffender and juvenile samples—research in

which moral belief has emerged as the social bond most consistently correlated with deviance. . . . For example, in Elliott and Menard . . . , moral belief was the sole bonding factor associated with juvenile delinquency in general and with drug use in particular. Burkett and Warren . . . found an association between moral belief and adolescent marijuana use. . . . In Williams . . . and Williams and Hawkins . . . , crime and marijuana use by adults were associated with moral belief. . . . Finally, in the study by Evans et al. . . . reported earlier, moral belief ("internal criminal values") appeared to mediate partially the relationship between low self-control and adult crime.

Gottfredson and Hirschi . . . argued that the apparent influence of weak social bonding and deviant peer association on deviance is spurious because all these characteristics can be traced to low self-control, a trait emerging early in life and remaining stable. Our findings argue against viewing social bonds and deviant peer association as causally trivial or irrelevant. Instead, an integrated explanatory model served to identify the more proximal processes through which low self-control may exert at least some of its influence on deviance. More specifically, and in accord with the implications of findings in Evans et al. . . . , we were able to identify moral belief and deviant peer association as the mediating processes at work.

Although results support an integrated theoretical control perspective, only about 19% of the variance in drug use was explained by our model. The measures available to us may not have captured the underlying constructs adequately. However, other longitudinal research on low self-control has explained, at best, about the same portion of the variance in crime and other outcomes. . . . Similarly, longitudinal research on social bonds has explained only a limited portion of the variance in the outcomes tested. . . . For example, bonding factors explained about 15% of the variance in adolescent smoking and about 2% of the variance in delinquency in longitudinal analyses reported by Krohn et al. . . . and Agnew. . . , respectively. One possible reason is that samples used in many prior studies were not involved in serious deviance; variability in the outcome measures may accordingly have been low. Unlike those samples, ours was composed of adult male offenders with extensive criminal histories, and the dependent variable in our analysis captured serious deviant involvement (frequent use of illegal drugs, chiefly marijuana and cocaine). Still, most of the variance in that outcome was left unexplained. . . .

Limitations and Conclusions

At least three limitations of the analysis are notable. First, because our sample was composed of adult male offenders, findings may not represent causal processes among adult female offenders or juveniles, and variability in any of the predictors may have been more restricted than is likely in samples providing greater diversity. Range restrictions may explain why these predictors in combination were able to explain only a modest proportion of variance in subsequent drug use. However, despite the possible range restrictions, findings were in some important respects consistent with a combined control perspective. All four measures of social bonds were strongly related to low self-control; and one of the bonding factors, moral belief, mediated the path from low self-control to drug use.

A second limitation has to do with bonding measures available in the dataset. The attachment measure, for example, was based on emotional ties to family members; and the involvement measure was based on stability of one's employment and intimate relationship, if any. Measures using other indicators, such as quality of one's intimate relationship, job satisfaction, and participation in adult education or social/recreational activities, might have led to different results. . . . In addition, our measure of commitment, or investment in conventional life, focused on religiosity. Other studies have operationalized commitment as educational or job aspirations, time spent on homework, or other conventional activities. Some of these operationalizations, notably aspirations and time spent on homework, may conflate commitment with other types of bonds . . . and/or seem more applicable to adolescents than to adults. Thus, they were not optimal for the current study. Moreover, research on religiosity and deviance can easily be read as support for the protective function served by commitment. . . . Finally, Burkett and Warren . . . , Krohn et al. . . . , and LeBlanc and Caplan . . . have used religiosity as an indicator of the commitment bond. A religion-based measure of this bond, therefore, seemed defensible. However, religious commitment may not be a strong deterrent of drug use among criminal offenders. There is a need for further work in which the bonding measures tested as mediators of self-control are based on diverse and conceptually distinguishable indicators. However, we do not think measurement problems are likely to have undermined the self-control factor. Psychometric evidence on the self-control indicators is quite favorable. . . .

Third, a unidirectional model does not account for the possibility of feedback effects; for example, deviant involvement may affect the strength of social bonds measured later. . . . Bidirectional modeling may be essential in studies that postulate a dynamic relationship between variables in a long-term developmental course spanning childhood into adulthood. However, unidirectional modeling seemed defensible for a sample composed entirely of adults and a time frame as short as 6 months. In addition, Hirschi's formulation of control theory is unidirectional (bonding influences deviance), as is the general theory proposed by Gottfredson and Hirschi (low self-control influences deviance). Thus, a unidirectional model seemed appropriate for an initial exploration of a combined control perspective.

The only bonding factor mediating the relationship between low self-control and drug use was conventional moral belief. This finding suggests that the mediating role of social bonding occurs mainly in the realm of internal constraint (moral belief), rather than the realm of affective ties (attachment), investment in a conventional lifestyle (religious commitment), or time spent in conventional activity (involvement); that is, if low self-control influences deviance via social bonding, its effect may operate through internalization of deviant values and/or neutralization of conventional values. . . . In addition, conventional moral belief has been found to predict help seeking for drug problems and unfavorable attitudes toward drug use . . . , and the desire to regain moral standing as a member of conventional society seems central to the recovery process. . . . The mediating role of moral belief suggests that low self-control influences drug use partly by weakening the person's stake in conformity or, conversely, by elevating the person's feelings of social exclusion or stigma.

The predictive strength of substance-using peers may reflect differential association or social learning; that is, deviant conduct may be determined, in part, by normative and interpersonal influences, differential reinforcement of deviance, and modeling effects of substance-using peers. . . . Such effects are not anticipated in theories of self-control or social bonding. However, the path from substance-using peers to deviant conduct can be read as consistent with control perspectives. It may, first, represent a sorting effect; persons with low self-control tend to flock together and share a taste for risk. . . . Substance-using peers may, second, represent exposure to greater opportunity for drug use. . . .

We suggest three avenues for control-theory research attempting to increase the amount of variance explained in deviant conduct. First, the causal link from low self-control to bonds has been conceptualized in a simple one-way model, in which low self-control is established early in life, remains stable, and later has adverse effects on social bonds. The causal processes may be more dynamic, however. Weak social ties early in life may undermine the development of adequate self-control and sensitivity to others, thus setting in motion a vicious cycle in which weak social bonds and low self-control reinforce each other. . . . Greater variance might be explained in datasets designed to model these more complex causal processes.

Second, control theorists may gain insight by examining the role of low self-control and social bonds within more comprehensive integrated models, such as modified strain . . . , problem behavior . . . , or control balance. . . . Causal factors in the problem behavior model, for example, are deviant as well as conventional bonds, early socialization, strain, and social disorganization. Low self-control might be folded into that model as an outcome of early socialization with effects on subsequent strain and on both types of bonding. In control balance theory, self-control might be handled as a constituent element of constraint . . . or as a factor influencing one's ability to balance control effectively and thus reduce the likelihood that the person will use deviance to try to resolve a control imbalance. . . . Integrated theories can explain a healthy proportion of variance (50% or better) in crime and delinquency . . . and may be especially applicable to more serious and persistent deviance. . . . In short, research using an integrated theory approach might illuminate the conditions under which control factors exert strong effects on deviant behavior and might serve to locate these factors within an overall causal nexus.

A third approach to improving the variance explained by control factors is to identify moderators, that is, contingencies under which self-control and/or social bonds exert more influence on deviance. Among the set of potential moderating factors are aptitudes and skills for crime, motivations to commit crime, competing motivations that might divert people from crime

despite low self-control or weak bonds, and rational choice variables. . . . Another possibility is that self-control is most closely linked to crime in early onset than in late onset offenders. Among early onset offenders, behavioral problems indicative of low self-control manifest themselves early in childhood and result in weakened bonds to parents and others. Crime and other deviance are more serious and persistent among early onset cases. . . . Thus, the causal processes in which control factors are pivotal in the production of later deviance may be stronger and easier to model among early onset cases.

Finally, apart from social bonds, what other mediators might help to explain the effects of low self-control on deviance? As noted, people with low self-control may experience greater strain, which may, in turn, lead to more deviant involvement. . . . Deterrence or rational-choice factors such as perceived pleasure of offending and perceived consequences of offending may play a mediating role as well . . . if people with lower self-control derive more pleasure from offending, fail to foresee negative consequences, and discount such consequences more heavily.

In summary, the combination of self-control and social control perspectives shed some light on the causal processes by which low self-control may influence later deviance. However, more conceptual clarity may be gained by testing low self-control within broader integrated theories that account for factors outside the control tradition; identifying personal traits or social circumstances under which low self-control has more predictive value; and exploring the processes or mediating factors, including but not limited to social bonds, that explain the effects of low self-control on deviance.

Questions

1. Why do the authors argue it can be advantageous to combine or integrate theories of criminality?

2. Describe how the authors measure low self-control.

CHAPTER 24

Self-Control and Variability Over Time

Multivariate Results Using a 5-Year, Multisite Panel of Youths

L. Thomas Winfree, Jr.
New Mexico State University in Las Cruces

Terrance J. Taylor
Georgia State University

Ni He
Northeastern University

Finn-Aage Esbensen
University of Missouri-St. Louis

At the core of Gottfredson and Hirschi's . . . general theory of crime—what is also known as event-propensity theory . . . and self-control theory . . . —is the stability across the life course of certain propensities that predict short-term, circumscribed events, specifically crimes and theoretically related acts. Once established, these propensities do not change. In describing crime-prone persons as lacking sufficient restraint, Gottfredson and Hirschi . . . advanced the idea that such propensities are more similar to the notion of the conscience than criminality, but they use the term self-control as an all-inclusive construct. That is, persons with lower levels of self-control are less restrained from committing crimes than are persons with higher levels of self-control: "Lack of restraint or low self-control allows almost any deviant, criminal, exciting, or dangerous act." . . .

Gottfredson and Hirschi . . . earlier described low self-control persons as impulsive, aggressive, and self-centered, but in a general theory of crime (1990), they identified a series of specific self-control elements. Importantly for those who would later test self-control theory, Grasmick and associates . . . provide operational restatements of these elements. For example, Gottfredson and Hirschi wrote that low self-control persons seek immediate gratification because they have a here-and-now orientation; in a related vein, crimes provide few or meager long-term benefits. Grasmick and associates . . . viewed these twin elements as evidencing the single trait of impulsivity. Second, criminal acts "provide easy or simple gratification of desires" . . . , suggesting to Grasmick and associates a preference for simple tasks. Third, Gottfredson and Hirschi . . . noted that criminal acts are often exciting, risky, or thrilling; hence, people with low self-control tend to be "adventuresome, active, and physical." For Grasmick and associates . . . , these traits added a risk-seeking component to self-control. Fourth, Gottfredson and Hirschi saw crimes as generally requiring little skill or training, and those lacking in

Source: "Self-control and variability over time: Multivariate results using a 5-year, multisite panel of youths," by Winfree, Jr., L. T., Taylor, T. J., He, N., & Esbensen, F., (2006), in *Crime and Delinquency, 52*, 253–286. Reprinted by permission of Sage Publications.

self-control tended to avoid or devalue cognitive and academic skills generally, elements that Grasmick and associates . . . viewed as collectively supporting a physical activity's component. Fifth, low self-controls exhibited little concern for the care, discomfort, and welfare of those they harm, characteristics Grasmick and associates circumscribed within the trait of self-centeredness. Finally, according to Gottfredson and Hirschi . . . , crime allows low self-control persons a means to vent their intolerance for frustrations, especially given their proclivity for responding to conflict physically rather than verbally. Grasmick and associates . . . saw a temper component in this part of self-control.

Gottfredson and Hirschi . . . noted that early child-rearing practices are the source of these essential traits. Poor or inadequate childrearing practices in the first decade of life set in motion forces, traits, or propensities that do not, in themselves, lead inevitably to crime, but "in the absence of socialization the child will tend to be high on crime potential." . . . This notion—that children as young as 10 may possess the necessary propensities toward crime—suggests that other criminological theories that locate the crime-causing forces closer to the law-violating event are wrong. Other things happen to the low self-control children, claimed Gottfredson and Hirschi, such as poor school performance or chronic difficulties with other adults and authority figures such as police and employers, but these are consequences, not causes. As a result, low self-control children—and later the young adults—enter school, the workplace, and the social world with traits that are often in contradiction to their immediate social environment.

Gottfredson and Hirschi . . . also saw sex and race as uniquely tied to the extant patterns of self-control in a given youth. However, consistent with the core assumptions of their theory, they observe that "low self-control is not produced by training, tutelage, or socialization. . . . [T]he causes of low self-control are negative rather than positive; self-control is unlikely in the absence of effort, intended or unintended, to create it." . . . What happens is largely a result of the variable patterns of early childhood supervision experienced by boys versus girls and Whites versus ethnic and racial minorities. Parents and guardians supervise girls more closely than boys, but socialize them the same, claimed Gottfredson and Hirschi . . . : "Parents may foster the same antidelinquent attitudes and behaviors in their children even as they supervise them differently." . . . As a result, females have higher levels of self-control than boys and less subsequent delinquency or analogous behavior. Similarly, parents of White children—even boys—supervise them

more closely than do the parents of minority youths. The parents do not endorse criminality, claimed Gottfredson and Hirschi; rather, differential patterns of monitoring, recognizing, and correcting evidence of antisocial behavior are at fault, with those practiced within minority families perhaps serving as a primary causal force. . . . Lower self-control levels among non-White children are—along with higher in-group levels of delinquency and analogous behavior—predictable consequences of these putative racial and ethnic differences in parental supervision.

The claim that self-control levels are fixed by early adolescence is viewed by some as a core part of Gottfredson and Hirschi's . . . general theory of crime. . . . If Gottfredson and Hirschi's claims—that age is irrelevant and the propensity and traits are constant through the life span—are without merit, then the theory, which emphasizes the role of poor parenting in creating these propensities, is also suspect.

Exploring the Measurement and Implications of Self-Control's Claim of Invariability

Those researchers exploring the invariability claim have tended to employ two primary analytic approaches. The first approach contrasts low self-control's ability to predict disruptive or law-violating behavior at different ages with the predictive values provided by another theory. For example, Bartusch et al. . . . used longitudinal measures of Moffitt's . . . developmental theory and Gottfredson and Hirschi's . . . general theory. They reported that childhood and adolescent antisocial behavior across the various ages was consistent with Moffitt's predictions that the causes of delinquency vary according to when the individuals begin misbehaving, rather than being constant across the life course as predicted by Gottfredson and Hirschi. Wright et al. . . . examined social selection (self-control theory) and social causation (social bond theory) using the same longitudinal data as Bartusch et al. . . . . They found that low self-control in childhood predicted both disrupted social bonds and criminal conduct later in the lives of the research respondents. Introducing social bonds and adolescent delinquency into the analysis of the respondents' adult crime largely mediated the effects of low self-control. Wright and associates stopped short of claiming that the social-selection process is less important, arguing instead that the joint consideration of both social selection and social causation yields a more complete picture of adolescent and adult offending.

The first approach succeeds in providing unique insights into self-control's longitudinal predictive ability. That is, low levels of self-control during childhood do appear related to misbehavior in adolescence and adulthood. However, as Pratt and Cullen . . . noted in their meta-analysis of Gottfredson and Hirschi's theory, the general predictive value of self-control over time is relatively weak. A second approach, then, explores more directly the question of the stability of self-control measures over time or place. For example, Arneklev et al. . . . examined the claim that the form of self-control "does not change with the age of the individual or context in which the person resides." . . . They compared the conceptualization of low self-control in a group of college students and adults from a different locale and found that the parameter values did not change, suggesting that their unidimensional measure of self-control was invariable across age and place. In a test–retest study among college students, Arneklev, Cochran, and Gainey . . . found relatively stable levels of self-control during a 4-month period.

In perhaps the most comprehensive test of the stability question to date, Turner and Piquero . . . used a national probability sample—the National Longitudinal Survey of Youth (NLSY) child–mother survey—and both attitudinal and behavioral measures of self-control. They created a six-item scale with moderate yet increasing reliability to measure self-control. These items bore some resemblance to the idea contained in Gottfredson and Hirschi's ideas about self-control and contextual similarities to the scales created by Grasmick and associates. . . . Given the ex post facto nature of these items and their small number, the validity of this scale is also suspect. The behavioral measures were parents' or guardians' estimates of how often their children acted in ways that could have been considered to parallel the elements of low self-control (e.g., "acts without thinking" and "bullies or is mean to others"). Turner and Piquero . . . used these statements to create a single composite measure of behavioral self-control. They examined seven waves of the NLSY child–mother survey, restricting their subsample to those NLSY youths who reached the age of 15 by the end of 1994.

Turner and Piquero . . . reported three findings related to the invariability of self-control. First, offenders exhibited significantly lower behavioral and attitudinal measures of self-control than was the case for nonoffenders. Although there was a tendency for nonoffenders to report higher levels of self-control than offenders during childhood and into early adolescence, the reverse was true in late adolescence and early adulthood. Second, they reported mixed results when examining those youths who should have been the lowest in self-control both behaviorally and attitudinally. Finally, sex and race provided mixed results as well. For example, males consistently exhibited lower self-control than females, although the trend was for higher self-control as both sexes age. As for race, non-Whites consistently were lower on self-control in childhood than Whites, a trend that was reversed in late adolescence, although these results were not statistically significant.

Research Questions

Tests that have explored the invariability of self-control over time have suffered from conceptual and methodological shortcomings. Those that looked at the role of age (and aging) generally have failed to reveal whether self-control fluctuated over time; rather, they have emphasized its predictive values compared to or paired with another theory as the respondents aged. Tests that addressed specific self-control measures over time likewise suffer from such shortcomings as no real comparisons over time, too few data points for meaningful comparisons, and operational problems associated with measuring self-control. By using a multisite, multiyear panel of youths, we seek to overcome most of these problems.

We explore a series of questions related to the putative invariability of self-control. First, how stable are the measures of self-control over time irrespective of the respondent's sex or race? Second, do the levels of self-control change over time when we compare offenders to nonoffenders? Third, does stability over time vary depending on the element of self-control employed? Finally, what happens to the stability of self-control measures when we simultaneously consider the respondent's sex, race, and family structure?

The Current Study

Data collected as part of the longitudinal component of the National Evaluation of the Gang Resistance Education and Training program . . . provide the context for testing the stability of self-control theory. The researchers purposively selected students attending 22 middle schools in six cities across the continental United States. More than 3,500 students enrolled in 153 classrooms were eligible for inclusion in the study. Active parental consent was obtained from 2,045 (57%) of these students. The researchers subsequently surveyed the active consent sample during the fall semester for 5 consecutive years (1995–1999). At the outset of the study, the students were in the 6th or 7th grade. During the past year of data collection, those still enrolled in school were in the 10th or 11th grade.

We restricted our analyses to those students who had completed questionnaires during each of the 5 years. This step further reduced our sample to 965 respondents, of whom 445 (46%) were male and 520 (54%) were female. The sample was also racially and ethnically diverse (African Americans comprised 13% of the sample, and Hispanics comprised 18%) and included a mix of offenders and nonoffenders. Compared with the active-consent sample, the complete sample used in the current study included proportionately more White youths and proportionately fewer African Americans and youths of other races, proportionately more youths from intact families (both mother and father present), and proportionately fewer offenders. Youths in the current study were also slightly younger (mean age 12.09 years for the current sample, compared with mean age of 12.14 years for the active-consent sample), and exhibited slightly lower levels of self-control, along with higher impulsivity and risk seeking. Although not substantively large, these differences were statistically significant, suggesting that the sample used in the current study includes slightly lower risk youths than the entire active-consent sample. . . .

The Variables

We derived a series of independent variables from the self-control literature. Respondents' (male or female) race or ethnicity (White/Anglo, non-Hispanic; Black/African American; Hispanic/Latino, American Indian/Native American, Asian/Pacific Islander/Oriental, or other race), family structure (mother only, father only, both mother and father, or other living arrangement), and offending behavior (17 delinquency items, ranging from less serious offenses such as skipping school without an excuse to more serious offenses such as shooting at someone) were collected through self reports. Small numbers of American Indians, Asians, and members of other races led us to recode the respondents' race or ethnicity into four categories (White, African American, Hispanic, and other races) for all analyses. Additionally, we followed Gottfredson and Hirschi's . . . lead by dichotomizing the family structure variable into intact (i.e., residing with both mother and father) and other living arrangement (i.e., residing in any arrangement than both father and mother in the home) for all analyses.

Self-control's unidimensionality is a much-debated topic. . . . As presented by Gottfredson and Hirschi . . . , self-control appears to be a single variable trait. However, in their conceptual and operational processes, Grasmick and associates . . . opened the door to the possibility that self-control is multidimensional. Supporters and detractors have debated this topic nearly since the first application of the scales created by Grasmick and associates. Early evidence supported its unidimensionality . . . ; however, later analyses suggested that the construct of self-control does indeed have multiple dimensions. . . . This debate is far from settled; hence, we elected to use a global self-control measure before performing analyses on the two most prominent and conceptually interesting dimensions of self-control (impulsivity and risk seeking).

At each survey administration, respondents indicated their level of agreement with eight self-control items drawn from Grasmick and associates. . . . Specifically, we created two 4-item scales to measure risk seeking and impulsivity. Scores on each of these items ranged from 1 to 5, with higher scores indicating greater levels of risk seeking and impulsivity (i.e., lower self-control). We also combined the impulsivity and risk seeking scales into a global measure of self-control by summing the values and dividing by the number of indicators. The reliability of the global self-control scale, like the two subscales, was acceptable.

Further examination of the scale, however, raised questions as to whether it was unidimensional. A principal components analysis with varimax rotation conducted with each wave of data produced two factors with eigen values greater than 1.0 for each period. Additionally, there were visible breaks between the second and third factors during each period. We then disaggregated the sample by sex and race and replicated the analyses using each wave of data. The multidimensionality of self-control held for males and females at each temporal period. We observed minimal differences by race or ethnicity, with three factors present for African Americans in 1995 and one factor for Hispanics in 1996 and 1997. For all other comparisons, however, the results were consistent with those conducted on the total sample.

Analyses and Results

The first task was to examine whether levels of self-control remained stable during adolescence. We conducted analyses using both the Statistical Package for the Social Sciences and Stata—Statistical Software for Professionals computer software packages. At each data point, we structured the analyses to examine first a global measure of self-control before separately assessing impulsivity and risk seeking.

STABILITY COEFFICIENTS

We employed stability coefficients to assess preliminarily the relative stability during 5 years of the composite self-control measure and each subcomponent for the entire sample. Over time, risk seeking proved to be more stable than impulsivity. The correlation for impulsivity between 1995 and 1996 was .44, and by 1999 it had dropped to .28. For risk seeking, the correlation between 1995 and 1996 was .59, which dropped to .43 by 1999. The general self-control measure showed similar interyear correlations as those of risk seeking. . . .

Stata provided an estimate of the variability of self-control during the study period through the calculation of the overall mean, which is the average value of the variable during the period examined. The overall mean of the composite low self-control variable was 2.76, impulsivity was 2.66, and risk seeking was 2.86. A visual examination of the score means, however, shows differences in stability between different components of self-control over time. Levels of impulsivity declined steadily during the 5 years (from 2.86 in 1995 to 2.52 in 1999), although levels of risk seeking showed no clear pattern of change. The general self-control measure declined between 1995 and 1996, reached a plateau and remained stable between 1996 and 1997, and declined again between 1997 and 1998.

DIFFERENCES BY SEX AND RACE

A series of *t* tests and analyses of variance (ANOVAs) explored whether levels of self-control differed between males and females and between members of different racial or ethnic groups during each of the survey waves. The sex-specific analyses . . . revealed a consistent pattern of significant differences between males and females on levels of self-control during the adolescent period, with males reporting lower levels of self-control than females. Males reported significantly higher levels of risk seeking than females in each wave and significantly higher levels of impulsivity than females in each of the final three waves. Males also scored significantly higher on the general self-control measure in each of the five periods.

We then used one-way ANOVAs to determine whether there were racial differences in levels of self-control during adolescence (data not shown). Similar to the differences found by sex, the members of the various

racial and ethnic groups had statistically significant differences for risk seeking in each of the five waves, statistically significant differences in impulsivity for the first four waves, and statistically significant differences in the general self-control measure in 1996, 1998, and 1999 ($P < .05$ in all analyses).

Although ANOVAs allow for an examination of whether the group-level means are significantly different, it does not allow for the specification of where those differences exist; however, these differences can be determined from the Bonferroni post hoc procedure. . . . The results of latter analyses showed that Hispanics had significantly higher levels of impulsivity than Whites did during the first 4 years; Hispanics' impulsivity levels were also higher than those reported for the other category, but only in 1998. Examinations of risk seeking also showed differences among racial groups. For example, African Americans reported significantly lower risk taking levels than Whites did during the final four waves and significantly lower levels than Hispanics during 1996, 1997, and 1998. Hispanics reported significantly more self-control than African Americans did in 1996, but the situation was the reverse in 1998. Additionally, Whites reported significantly lower self-control levels than African Americans in 1998 and 1999.

DIFFERENCES BY OFFENDER STATUS

At the next stage in the analysis, we categorized respondents as offenders and nonoffenders depending on their self-reported delinquency during the period immediately prior to the survey administration. For example, we classified respondents who reported at the first administration that they had engaged in each of 17 delinquent activities zero times during the past year as nonoffenders. Conversely, we classified those respondents who indicated that they had engaged in one or more of the delinquent activities one or more times in the prior year as offenders. We used the same method to classify respondents into offender and nonoffender categories during each of the temporal periods, resulting in five groups of offenders and five groups of nonoffenders.

Stata revealed whether group-level differences in impulsivity and risk seeking existed between offenders and nonoffenders. . . . First, two sets of *t* tests were used to determine whether the overall means of impulsivity and risk seeking differed between offenders and nonoffenders. For instance, nonoffenders reported significantly lower mean levels of impulsivity (mean = 2.45), risk seeking (mean = 2.42) and higher levels of general self-control (mean = 2.44) than those reported by offenders (means of 2.77, 3.10, and 2.94, respectively). Additionally, at no time were levels of impulsivity or risk seeking higher for nonoffenders than for offenders; similarly, in no period did general self-control of offenders exceed that of nonoffenders.

To examine the issue further, we restricted analyses to those respondents ranking in the top and bottom quartiles of impulsivity, risk seeking, and general self-control of each of the offender and nonoffender groups. We partitioned respondents into these two groups based on the assumption that those individuals who scored on the extremes of the self-control continuum should be the focus of criminological research. This approach produced a four-tiered typology: (a) nonoffenders with high self-control, (b) nonoffenders with low self-control, (c) offenders with high self-control, and (d) offenders with low self-control. . . .

The observed patterns varied slightly across these four groups. On the general self-control measure, we found different patterns for each of the four groups. Nonoffenders with the highest levels of self-control (i.e., those in the bottom 25% of the low self-control group) showed a sharp decline between Times 1 and 2. The level of general self-control then stabilized. Nonoffenders with the lowest levels of self-control (i.e., those in the top 25% of the low self-control group), however, showed a steady, gradual decline in low self-control during the 5 years of the study. Interestingly, the patterns for offenders with the lowest levels of self-control were quite similar to those for nonoffenders with the lowest levels of self-control. Offenders with the highest levels of self-control, however, illustrated no consistent pattern over time.

The patterns illustrated in the general self-control measure mask important differences in patterns of impulsivity and risk seeking across groups. For nonoffenders in both the top and bottom quartiles, levels of impulsivity and risk seeking declined over time from their Time 1 highs. For low self-control nonoffenders and offenders (i.e., those in the top 25% of impulsivity), levels of impulsivity declined sharply between Times 1 and 2, where they then remained stable for two or three periods before dropping once again. For high self-control offenders and nonoffenders (i.e., those in the bottom 25% of impulsivity), there was no consistent pattern. High self-control nonoffenders showed an initial drop in impulsivity after Time 1, but then showed nearly equal levels at Times 2 and 4 and at Times 3 and 5. Conversely, high self-control offenders showed an increase in impulsivity after Time 1 before showing a steady period of decline between Times 2 through 5. The pattern for risk seeking also varied across groups. For nonoffenders,

regardless of self-control levels, risk seeking dropped between Times 1 and 2 and remained stable thereafter. For offenders in the top 25% of risk seeking, levels of risk seeking remained stable between Times 1 and 3 before beginning to decline. For offenders in the bottom 25% of risk seeking, however, levels of risk seeking dropped slightly between Times 1 and 2, increased between Times 2 and 3, and decreased after Time 3.

We then used t tests to compare group means. The mean levels of impulsivity, risk seeking, and the general self-control measure were significantly higher for offenders in the bottom 25% (when compared with nonoffenders in the bottom 25%) and for offenders in the top 25% (when compared with nonoffenders in the top 25%) at each of the survey administration periods. Equally interesting are the patterns between high self-control offenders and low self-control nonoffenders. Levels of self-control are higher for high self-control offenders (i.e., the bottom 25%) than for low self-control nonoffenders (i.e., the top 25%).

Thus, our analyses suggest that, although the absolute level of self-control may vary somewhat over time, the relative intergroup rankings do not appear to change over time. . . . Our results also suggest that the relationship between self-control and offending is more complex than previously acknowledged. Specifically, there is substantial variation in levels of self-control within offender groupings, leading to high self-control offenders and low self-control nonoffenders, in addition to the commonly acknowledged low self-control offenders and high self-control nonoffenders. Indeed, our results suggest that levels of self-control are higher for a significant portion of offenders compared with nonoffenders.

Multiple Regression Analyses

The one-way generalized least square (GLS) random-effects regression model technique allowed us to examine these factors simultaneously, whereby we ran models separately with general self-control, impulsivity, and risk seeking as dependent variables. . . . GLS models are particularly well suited to handle panel data such as those included in the present study. These analyses allowed examination of stability of self-control over time, although also providing information on variations due to sex, race, family structure, and offence.

In each model, dummy variables were included for sex, race, family structure, offender status, and survey administration period. Results of these analyses showed that females had significantly lower levels of impulsivity, risk seeking, and general low self-control than males, controlling for the effects of race, family structure, offending, and time. Race differences also remained salient. Even after controlling for sex, family structure, offending, and survey period, levels of impulsivity were higher for Hispanics and levels of risk seeking and general low self-control were lower for African Americans when compared with Whites. Family structure, included here as a control variable, exerted no significant effect on the composite self-control measure or its various components.

The regression analyses presented a mixed picture for the stability of self-control over time. Each of the dummy variables representing the survey administration periods was a significant predictor of levels of impulsivity and the general self-control measure, reinforcing the view that levels of impulsivity and general self-control varied over time, even after controlling for the effects of sex, race, family structure, and offending status. For risk seeking, however, only one survey administration period was a significant predictor. This finding suggests that, although levels of risk seeking were relatively consistent, the levels of impulsivity may in fact vary over time. Additionally, using a general self-control measure may mask important differences between various components.

Next, we examined differences between offenders' and nonoffenders' levels of self-control, controlling for the effects of sex, race, family structure, and time. To accomplish this goal, we partitioned the sample by offender status and reran the models. . . .

For both nonoffenders and offenders, general low self-control was lower for females than for males, controlling for the effects of race or ethnicity, family structure, and time. Key differences across nonoffenders and offenders did exist, however, regarding the effects of race or ethnicity and family structure. Controlling for the effects of sex, family status, and time, African-American offenders exhibited significantly higher levels of self-control than White offenders, although we found no racial or ethnic differences for nonoffenders. Similarly, offenders living with both parents exhibited significantly lower levels of self-control than did offenders living in any other arrangement, controlling for the effects of sex, race/ethnicity, and time. For nonoffenders, however, we found no differences in the low self-control levels across living arrangements.

We did find additional differences between nonoffenders and offenders regarding the subcomponents of self-control, controlling for the effects of sex, race/ethnicity, family structure, and time. For nonoffenders, impulsivity varied by sex, race/ethnicity, and time, whereas offenders' impulsivity varied by race/ethnicity and time only. Female nonoffenders exhibited lower levels of impulsivity than males, whereas African Americans and Hispanics exhibited higher levels of impulsivity than White youths. Hispanic offenders also exhibited higher levels of impulsivity than did White offenders. Interestingly, although not statistically significant, impulsivity was lower among African-American offenders than among White offenders, suggesting an important interaction between being African American and offending status. For both offenders and nonoffenders, sex was a significant predictor of risk seeking, with females exhibiting the lower levels of risk seeking. The effect of being African American on risk seeking also varied significantly by offending status, suggesting an important interaction; specifically, African-American offenders exhibited significantly lower levels of risk seeking than White offenders, whereas no significant differences were found between African-American and White nonoffenders.

As for the stability of self-control, we found differences between offenders and nonoffenders and across different manifestations of self-control. . . . Controlling for the effects of sex, race/ethnicity, and family structure, nonoffenders showed significantly lower levels of general low self-control than did offenders at each temporal period. Yet general low self-control showed a more consistent decline in each of the years for offenders than for nonoffenders. Offenders' levels of general low self-control were significantly lower in 1996, 1998, and 1999 than in 1995. By 1999, however, the decrease in offenders' general low self-control was significantly larger than the decrease for nonoffenders. In other words, between 1995 and 1999, both nonoffenders and offenders exhibited decreases in levels of general low self-control, but the difference was more pronounced and consistent for offenders than for nonoffenders.

Examinations of the subcomponents of impulsivity and risk seeking, however, demonstrate that the general low self-control measure may mask important stability differences and that these effects vary for nonoffenders and offenders when controlling for sex, race/ethnicity, and family structure. At each temporal period, levels of both impulsivity and risk seeking were significantly lower for nonoffenders than for offenders. Nonetheless, nonoffenders and offenders showed important differences in their changes in impulsivity and risk seeking over time. For both nonoffenders and offenders, levels of impulsivity were significantly lower in 1996, 1997, 1998, and 1999 than in 1995. The initial drop (between 1995 and 1996) was, however, significantly more pronounced for nonoffenders than for offenders, but the rate of change between nonoffenders and offenders did not differ significantly at any other period. Patterns for risk seeking, however, showed a different pattern. Levels of risk seeking were significantly higher for nonoffenders in 1996, 1997, 1998, and 1999 compared with the baseline level of 1995. Conversely, levels of offenders' risk seeking were not appreciably different between 1995 and 1996 or between 1995 and 1997. In 1998 and 1999, however, offenders' levels of risk seeking were significantly lower than they had been initially. In each year, the changes in risk seeking were significantly different between nonoffenders and offenders.

Summary and Conclusions

Since its introduction, Gottfredson and Hirschi's theory has garnered a great deal of attention from criminologists. Comparative and cross-cultural studies suggest that the theory has some applicability in nations other than the United States, a finding that portends well for its claims as a general theory of crime. . . .

Even when research fails to yield support for all of Gottfredson and Hirschi's contentions concerning the role of self-control in shaping future conduct, the general tendency is to value the theory for its conceptual richness and extension of social causation models. In this regard, consider Wright and associates' . . . mixed selection-causation model or Paternoster and Brame's . . . contention that the data do not support either a pure status/general model or a pure developmental model of crime. Importantly for us, Paternoster and Brame . . . observed the following: "The results of our analysis suggest that an exclusive focus on characteristics of individuals that do not change over time after the beginning of adolescence is inconsistent with the data."

We addressed four questions. Our general findings are, for the most part, unequivocally critical of Gottfredson and Hirschi's orienting assumption (or claim) concerning the unchanging nature of self-control after its establishment in preadolescence. For example, levels of impulsivity declined during the entire 5-year period of the study, and, for its part, risk seeking showed no clear pattern of change, actually increasing slightly between 1995 and 1997 and then declining to levels below those observed in the study's first year. Our findings do not support self-control as an immutable and stable propensity; they also do not support the view that self-control, as operationalized by Grasmick and associates, is unidimensional in nature. At best, our study joins

others that point to possible weaknesses in the operationalization of self-control by Grasmick and his associates; at worst, our work suggests that a unidimensional construct called self-control may not exist. . . .

The findings with respect to sex and race or ethnicity comported well with some of Gottfredson and Hirschi's claims, both in terms of the bivariate year-by-year analyses and multivariate analyses, but less well with others. Males reported higher levels of risk seeking than did females in each wave and higher levels of impulsivity than did females in the latter three waves. Consistently, males had lower self-control levels than did females, controlling for all other factors. The findings for race, however, depend on who and what is involved. For example, African Americans were more prone to report lower levels of risk seeking than were Whites during the final four waves of data collection and lower levels than Hispanics during the middle 3 years. Hispanics reported higher levels of impulsivity than did Whites only for the first 4 years. Again, these findings tend to support a multidimensional view of self-control.

Offender status tended to offer few clarifications of self-control stability or instability. . . . Nonoffenders reported significantly lower levels of impulsivity and risk seeking than offenders, suggesting that nonoffenders have higher levels of self-control than offenders do. Dividing offenders and nonoffenders into the bottom and top quartiles for each element of self-control (i.e., the most and least impulsive and risk-seeking youths) created four groups for comparison purposes. For nonoffenders, the pattern was one of decline for both measures irrespective of whether they were in the group with the most self-control or the one with the least self-control. In the case of impulsivity, these declines were noticeable at two times (between Times 1 and 2 and between Times 4 and 5); however, risk seeking dropped once (between Times 1 and 2) and essentially remained flat for the subsequent surveys. The two offender groups (top and bottom quartiles) also showed declines, although in both cases these declines occurred later than for the nonoffenders. None of these group-specific patterns bodes well for self-control's invariability. However, it is interesting that the relative intergroup rankings for both impulsivity and risk seeking—that is, offenders in the lowest quartile compared with nonoffenders in the lowest quartile and offenders in the highest quartile compared with nonoffenders in the highest quartile—do not change over time.

Finally and significantly, Gottfredson and Hirschi's . . . theory addressed the issue of parenting. They claimed that ineffective childrearing "caused" low self-control. One of the common correlates they conceptually addressed was the single-parent family. After reviewing the literature on this subject—in which children from intact families are described as having lower rates of crime—Gottfredson and Hirschi make the following claim: "The model we are using suggests that, all else being equal, one parent is sufficient. We could substitute 'mother' or 'father' for 'parents' without any obvious loss of child-rearing ability." . . . However, in our study, the intact family made a small but significant impact on the level of risk seeking: Children from what were described initially as intact families had lower levels of risk seeking across all waves of the survey.

Our findings provide more reasons to question the claim that the level of self-control is invariable over time, and they further suggest that we should reexamine the suggestion that self-control is a unidimensional construct. If self-control is truly unidimensional, as some researchers have suggested, then the empirical studies may be measuring something with considerable reliability that is not self-control. Perhaps the predictive validity we report is because of the high conceptual correspondence between central elements of Grasmick and associates' . . . form of self-control and the forms found in other theories. . . .

Indeed, in terms of policy implications, self-control theory suggests a refocusing of attention on at least three related "causal" factors: the absolute level of parental supervision of children prior to age 10, the differential parental supervision of girls versus boys, and the variability in parental supervision found in families of different ethnic and racial backgrounds. Programs such as the current federal initiative to "strengthen families" appear to take into consideration these factors already. . . . Given our findings concerning the changing nature of self-control, especially the various elements of it, such programs need not address only the families of youths less than 10 years of age. Our findings relative to race suggest that Gottfredson and Hirschi's . . . admonition about the misplaced efforts to ascribe differences in misconduct among the races to culture or strain may be correct. Instead, policy analysts and others interested in the disproportionality issue should, in their words, "focus on differential childrearing practices." This may include programs that target the development of parent management and supervision skills, as well as programs such as Olds' Nurse Home Visitation program that emphasize early parenting skills. . . . This focus should facilitate the generation of policies and practices that are sensitive to the needs of a wider range of racial and ethnic groups than are now available.

Questions

1. How do Gottfredson and Hirschi define *self-control* in their general theory of crime?

2. What are the implications of the authors' findings for Gottfredson and Hirschi's theory?

PART VII

LIFE COURSE THEORY

I n part as a rejection of theories that do not account for changes that occur naturally over the life course, Robert Sampson and John Laub developed life course theory, which considers how turning points or significant life events can alter the criminal pathways of career criminals. Based in part on social bonds and the resulting social capital, or positive benefits from those relations, the theory considers how these factors contribute to desistance from and persistence in crime. Using a large sample ($N = 784$) of people sentenced to boot camp, Brent Benda, Nancy Toombs, and Mark Peacock (chap. 25) determine how elements of life course theory influence success in *Distinguishing Graduates From Dropouts and Dismissals: Who Fails Boot Camp?* The authors also consider the roles of social bonds, personal attributes, self-control, drug use, and peer association on boot camp success. Exploring gender differences in the application of life course theory, Marilyn Brown (chap. 26) examines the criminality of women of Hawaiian ancestry in *Gender, Ethnicity, and Offending Over the Life Course: Women's Pathways to Prison in the Aloha State*. She considers how relationships and turning points may affect the criminality of men and women differently.

CHAPTER 25

Distinguishing Graduates From Dropouts and Dismissals

Who Fails Boot Camp?

Brent B. Benda

Nancy J. Toombs

Mark Peacock
University of Arkansas at Little Rock, School of Social Work

Introduction

Boot camps were introduced with great fanfare and expectations by correctional administrators, legislators, and media specialists as an answer to many of the looming exigencies resulting from prison overcrowding and fiscal constraints.... The introduction of these programs was not without controversy. From the outset, critics argued that boot camps were based on military training strategies designed to instill aggression for combat.... Morash and Rucker ... contended that boot camp training reinforced the very attitudes that were associated with the commission of crimes. These programs also were characterized as low-dosage and ill-defined interventions....

More recent critiques were based on empirical evidence.... Some researchers contended that a consensus was emerging in a new era of "evidence-based corrections" that boot camps were siphoning off scarce resources from interventions with demonstrated effectiveness.... In the most comprehensive study to date, MacKenzie, Brame, McDowall, and Souryal ... found that boot camps did not reduce recidivism, whereas programs with more rehabilitation components (e.g., drug treatment, academic education) and programs targeting prison-bound offenders significantly reduced recidivism in comparison with traditional correctional institutions. In a more recent meta-analysis of 44 independent boot camp/comparison sample contrasts, MacKenzie, Wilson, and Kider ... concluded that it was premature to definitely conclude that boot camp programs were ineffective at reducing crime. They maintained that it was possible that the integration of the boot camp model and therapeutic programming may produce a synergy capable of reducing recidivism.

Empirical questions concerning the effectiveness of boot camp programs may well have been a preoccupation of scholars that had limited if any functional relevance to practitioners, policymakers, and legislators.... Boot camps were marketed with extravagant claims based on ideological and political ideas, rather than on empirically established practices.... Conservatives believed boot camps provided a secure facility where inmates were forced to deal with the harsh consequences of crime, and they would learn self-control through regimented military training and hard labor. Liberals believed the same programs offered education and rehabilitation that provided opportunities for conventional living. Boot

Source: "Distinguishing graduates from dropouts and dismissals: Who fails boot camp?" by Benda, B. B., Toombs, N. J., & Peacock, M., (2006), in *Journal of Criminal Justice, 34,* 27–38. Reprinted by permission of Elsevier via Copyright Clearance Center.

camps were sold as the ideal solution to the problem of how to incarcerate a large number of offenders for punishment as well as for rehabilitation. . . .

Purpose of the Present Study

As long as legislators and decision makers in the justice system continue to operate boot camps, it behooves researchers to find out who seems to "succeed" and "fail" in these programs. Success and failure can be variously defined depending on the frame of reference. *Success* was defined as graduation from boot camp, whereas dropping out of and dismissals from the program were considered failures for the purposes of this study. The authors forgo the nuanced discussions that can be presented regarding the fact that some people graduate without benefiting from the program and drop out or are dismissed for reasons that were unrelated to some inability to adapt to boot camp. . . . The purpose of this study was to simply examine what characteristics of inmates differentiate graduates from dropouts and dismissals from the boot camp program. Dropouts are inmates who choose to leave the boot camp program and serve the remainder of their sentence in prison, whereas dismissals are persons who are removed from the program because of infractions. Knowing the characteristics that distinguish among graduates, dropouts, and dismissals is useful to decisions about admission criteria as well as program design. . . .

Aside from identifying which offenders did not seem to be responding to the boot camp program by dropping out or being dismissed, this study also provided clues about promising factors that might be targeted to alter the outcome of graduation versus failure in the program. This investigation had an advantage over many classification studies in using factors that were amenable to planned change, such as self-efficacy or use of drugs. . . .

Conceptual Framework for the Analyses

Factors analyzed in this study were selected based on a theoretical elaboration . . . of life course theory . . . using elements taken from social learning theory. . . . Aspects of peer association—modeling, differential reinforcement, normative definitions, and forming gangs—were used to elaborate on the life course explanation because of their potent explanatory value. . . . Elaboration

involved incorporating propositions from another theory without violating the assumptions of the original explanation. In accordance with the assumptions of life course theory, it was assumed in this study that peer association with individual offenders and gangs facilitated rather than generated unlawful behavior among persons with tenuous bonds to society. . . .

Gangs are considered to be conceptually different than ordinary peer associations. . . . Gangs have more formal rituals, expectations, and sanctions, and they are more organized around criminal behavior than are peer associations, which occur more spontaneously and episodically with little or no organization or expectations about participation. . . . Battin et al. . . . found that gangs had influences on crime in addition to those of peer affiliations. Gang members often sell drugs and regularly carry weapons. . . . Based on prior research and experiential observations, it was hypothesized that gang members who sold drugs and regularly carried weapons would be among those identified as graduates in this study. . . . The reason for this counterintuitive hypothesis was that gang members seemed to be relatively comfortable in the hypermasculine environment . . . of boot camps. . . . They also might be motivated to graduate by the desire to quickly get back to lucrative entrepreneurial enterprises on the street.

Another group hypothesized to graduate was more educated persons who had full-time employment, higher incomes, a spouse, and children. . . . According to life course theory, these assets represented social bonding to society—they were "turning points" in people's life trajectory that signified transitions from criminal and irresponsible behavior to more conventional and responsible choices. . . .

Adults who are making the transition to a more conventional lifestyle are likely to want to expedite their return to family and employment by graduation from a boot camp program that is briefer in duration than prison. Data were not available in this study to examine whether those offenders were "shocked" out of a criminal lifestyle as claimed in ideological arguments advanced in marketing strategies. . . . There was evidence, however, that those offenders were less likely to be recidivists. . . .

Life course theory . . . postulates that social order is based on conventional moral beliefs and values, which are internalized and upheld by society. Attachment to caregivers and involvement in religion . . . facilitate and reinforce the internalization of and commitment to these beliefs and values. Close attachments to caregivers and commitment to religion are posited to facilitate the bonding that leads to transitions from criminal patterns to more conventional approaches to life. . . . Caring attachments along with the meaning and purpose offered in religion are posited to encourage the development of healthy personality traits—such as self-esteem, self-efficacy, and an internal locus of control—that facilitate the transition to conventional pursuits like employment and starting a family. . . . Personality traits increasingly are being reintroduced into criminological theories to achieve more explanatory power. . . . It is hypothesized that attachment and religiosity, together with the personality traits they encourage, will distinguish graduates from dropouts and dismissals from boot camp.

The final group of offenders is of special interest because they are the putative "failures" of the program. Knowing how dropouts and dismissals differ from graduates could prove to be valuable in restructuring boot camp programs for specific offenders to enhance the impact of these programs. Exactly how dropouts and dismissals will differ from graduates cannot be formally hypothesized due to the lack of conceptual and empirical precedence. Based solely on experiential observation, the expectation is that persons who drop out of boot camp will have a greater history of drug treatment and offenses. In contrast, persons who are dismissed from boot camp will likely have emotional problems, including anger, alienation, and suicidal attempts.

Method

Sample

The present study consisted of a sample of 784 male graduates from a boot camp for adults in a southern state. Participation in the boot camp studied was an option to prison offered to eligible inmates. To be officially eligible for boot camp, inmates had to meet five criteria: (a) been a first-time referral to the adult correctional system in this state, (b) been sentenced to ten or less years, (c) had no recorded violent offenses in the adult correctional system, (d) had an IQ above 70, and (e) had no physical or psychological problems, including drug addiction, that would preclude military training. Correctional counselors screened persons at the diagnostic unit for eligibility. . . .

Procedure and Data

A staff psychologist who had eight research associates available to monitor each table of five respondents to clarify wording or to answer questions administered the questionnaire. Research associates were available to interview inmates who could not read the questionnaire. The questionnaire was administered approximately 3 weeks into the 105-day program to allow military discipline to develop, as well as trust in the psychologist who administered the questionnaires, because she also did mental health classes and counseling at this boot camp. While respondents did record their department of correction identification number for a recidivism study, they were assured of confidentiality by telling them that names would not be associated with identification numbers on the questionnaires, and none of the information provided by them was shared with anyone in the department of correction except in aggregate form. Participation in the study was voluntary, and only six persons refused participation during the study period. . . .

Outcome or Dependent Variable

There were three outcomes analyzed in the present study: (a) graduation from the program, (b) inmates could choose to drop out of the program at any time before graduation, and (c) participants could be dismissed from the program because of a flagrant rule violation (e.g., assault on an officer) or series of violations. Dismissals were a formal procedure at the boot camp. This trichotomous outcome served as the criterion variable in this study.

Prediction Measures

Attachment was measured by 4-point scales, ranging from *very little* to *very much*. The same four items were asked of women and men caregivers: (a) how much did you like being with___, (b) how close did you feel to___, (c) how much did you want to be like your___, and (d) how much did you enjoy spending time with ___. . . . Early attachment is theorized to facilitate bonding in later life. . . .

Physical and sexual abuses were each measured with two items (4-point Likert scales ranging from *never* to *more than 10 times*) asking how often respondents had been abused: (a) during the period from birth to 12 years of age, and (b) after 12 years of age. Physical abuse was defined as any physical contact that resulted in severe cuts, bruises, welts, or other marks that took a few days to disappear; concussions or breaking of bones; or scalding or burns. Sexual abuse was defined as any touching of the genitals and oral or anal intercourse that was nonconsensual. Maltreatment early in life can fracture attachment and impede the development of personal assets such as self-efficacy. . . .

Religiosity was measured with six items from Woodroof . . . : (a) church attendance (5-point scale ranging from *once a month or less* to *three times a week*), (b) private prayer (5-point scale ranging from *never* to *daily*), (c) Bible study (5-point scale ranging from *never* to *daily*), (d) financial contributions to religious organizations (5-point scale ranging from *never* to *frequently*), (e) talked about religion with others (5-point scale ranging from *never* to *frequently*), and (f) tried to convert others to faith in God (5-point scale ranging from *never* to *frequently*). Religiosity was theorized to encourage the development of personal assets such as self-esteem and bonding. . . .

Seven items of the self-efficacy scale . . . were also used. The seven items selected (5-point scale ranging from *strongly disagree* to *strongly agree*) included the most salient efficacy items, such as, "I make certain my plans work out" and "I am a self-reliant person." Rosenberg's . . . 10-item self-esteem scale (4-point scale ranging from *strongly disagree* to *strongly agree*) was used, and both of those measures of self-attributes had strong validity. . . . The 28-item internal control index (ICI) . . . , with a 5-point Likert scale, was used to measure locus of control. Persons with an internal locus of control believed outcomes were largely a result of their actions, whereas an external locus of control signified a belief that life was governed by fate, chance, and luck. The ICI had good concurrent validity. . . . Those personal assets were posited to facilitate social bonding and conventional investments. . . .

The central concept of social learning theory was peer association, which was measured with five items (5-point scale ranging from *none* to *more than 10*) asking how many of your best friends: (a) had ever been arrested, (b) used illegal drugs regularly, (c) consumed three or more drinks of alcohol in a day regularly, (d) stole regularly, and (e) had used a weapon on another person. Modeling was measured by four items (4-point scale ranging from *strongly disagree* to *strongly agree*) asking if your friends influenced you to: (a) drink alcohol regularly, (b) use other drugs regularly, (c) steal, and (d) hurt someone in an assault. Four items measured differential reinforcement (same scale as modeling) by asking if the rewards outweighed the costs of: (a) regularly consuming alcohol, (b) using illegal drugs, (c) stealing, and (d) assaulting someone. Normative definitions were measured by two items asking whether each of the following behaviors was okay because (a) no one was seriously harmed, and (b) everyone did it

(same scale as modeling): (a) excessive use of alcohol, (b) used illegal drugs, (c) stole, and (d) assaulted someone when it was needed.

The most common measure of gang membership is a single item asking about whether one is a member of a formal gang. . . . Gang membership in the present study was a single item (coded 0 = no, 1 = yes) that asked whether respondents were members of a formal gang (i.e., a group formally organized for criminal purposes that had a designated hierarchy, name, colors, symbols, graffiti, and allegiance to each other). Because staff members at the boot camp were familiar with the local gangs, only inmates who indicated they were members of known gangs were recorded as gang members. . . . Carrying weapons was measured with two items (5-point scale ranging from *never* to *all the time*) that asked if they: (a) carried a gun most of the time, or (b) carried other weapons such as knives, brass knuckles, chains, shanks, or ball bats most of the time. . . .

Drug use was measured by six items asking inmates how often they had used: (a) barbiturates (chlordiazepoxide, diazepam, glutethimide, meprobamate, methaqualone), (b) amphetamine (other psychostimulate, Methytpheniadate, Ritalin, intravenous Methedrine, Desoxun, diet pills), (c) opiates (heroin, Paregoric, Meperidine, Methadone, Morphine, opium, opium alkaloids and derivatives), (d) cocaine, (e) hallucinogens (LSD, Mescaline, MDA, DMT, PCP, STP, Psilocybin), or (f) solvents. Selling drugs was measured with a single item for each type of drug asking how often inmates had sold the drug. All items asking about drug use and selling illicit drugs had the same 5-point scale (1 = *none*, 2 = *one or two times*, 3 = *three to five times*, 4 = *six to nine times*, and 5 = *10 times or more*). Street names were provided for all drugs to be sure of mutual understanding, such as speed, yellow jackets, crank, pink hearts, and cross-tops for amphetamines.

The addiction severity index (ASI) . . . was administered on a separate day from other measures discussed. The ASI had reports of good reliability and validity. . . . Sociodemographic information taken from the ASI included age, marital status of inmate at the time of the survey (recoded 0 = married, 1 = other), education in years, number of children fathered, annual legal income, annual illegal income, and employment pattern that characterized most of the past 3 years (recoded 0 = full time, 1 = other). Full-time employment was defined as working 40 or more hours a week. A question about race (recoded 0 = White, 1 = person of color) was added to the ASI. Suicidal thoughts in the past year were measured with a single item on the ASI (4-point scale recoded

0 = no, 1 = yes). Agreement between those ASI items and a single item on the other instrument measuring suicidal thoughts was 95%. The same high percentage of agreement was noted for marital status, education, income, and other sociodemographics, suggesting reliability in responses. Regular employment, number of children, higher legal income, marriage, and more education were considered as investments in social bonding in life course theory. . . .

The ASI also provided data about the number of days in substance abuse treatment. A scale was derived from single items on the ASI that asked about whether respondents had real problems in the past 30 days with: (a) depression, (b) tension or anxiety, (c) understanding, concentrating, and remembering, and (d) controlling violence toward others (response options were 0 = no, 1 = yes). This scale was labeled *emotional problems*, and the total scores were standardized to normalize the distribution. Drug use and abuse, along with emotional problems, are theorized to interfere with the development of personal assets and bonding. . . .

An anger/frustration scale was taken from Agnew . . . , which involved five items (5-point scales) asking: (a) lose temper easily, (b) irritated by small things, (c) hold grudges, (d) verbally attack others, and (e) feel like physically assaulting others. An alienation scale asked whether respondents felt unaccepted or very distant from: (a) family, (b) friends, and (c) society (5-point scales used).

Hirschi and Gottfredson . . . argued that the best measures of self-control were based on behavior. Presumably, the behaviors selected were indicative of propensities to engage in risk-taking. These dichotomous (0 = no, 1 = yes) behaviors were selected from the ASI: (a) live with a substance abuser, (b) arrests for disorderly conduct or public intoxication, (c) driving while drunk, (d) major traffic tickets in the past year, (e) car wrecks in the past year, (f) shared needles in the past year, and (g) had unprotected sex with more than one person (the latter two items were added to the ASI). A total score was standardized for analyses. Raw scores, however, were used to calculate the mean and standard deviation for emotional problems and self-control. . . .

Data Analyses

A Pearson product–moment correlation matrix indicated that the only coefficients above 0.40 were between peer association and normative definitions (0.65), self-esteem and self-efficacy (0.56), self-efficacy and locus of control (0.51), self-esteem and locus of control (0.55), and self-efficacy and peer association (–0.54). Tolerance tests and the variance inflation factor indicated that the factors were sufficiently independent of each other. . . .

A maximum likelihood estimation multinomial logistic regression (MLR) . . . was used to identify which factors increase or decrease the likelihood of being a dropout or a dismissal, compared to being a graduate of the boot camp program. . . . The two equations that provided the comparisons of dropouts and dismissals to the reference category (graduates) were computed simultaneously. The estimated betas obtained from MLR gave the magnitude of effect of each factor on being a dropout or being a dismissal in comparison with the reference category. Exponents of the effects were the odds ratio (OR) of being a dropout or a dismissal instead of being a graduate. The OR was the likelihood of change from being a dropout or dismissal instead of a graduate of boot camp with every one-unit increase in a particular factor. All scales and age . . . were standardized (*Z* scores); so one unit change represented one standard deviation. Employment (0 = full time, 1 = other), marital status (0 = married, 1 = other), and race (0 = White, 1 = persons of color) were dichotomous data.

Findings

The MLR . . . analysis is shown in Table 25.1. The spacing among sets of factors shown in that table indicates sets that distinguish among graduates, dropouts, and dismissals from the boot camp program studied. The OR of being a dropout or a dismissal instead of a graduate (reference category) diminish significantly ($\alpha = 0.05$) with increases in the number of children, income, locus of control, self-efficacy, religiosity, self-esteem, education, and age. Full-time employment and marriage also are associated with lower ORs of being a dropout (OR = .32 and .38, respectively) or a dismissal (OR = .40 and .46, respectively). Reciprocal ORs (1/OR) are shown in parentheses in Table 25.1 to facilitate direct comparisons of inverse to positive relationships. These findings offer support for the hypothesized relations derived from life course theory.

Gang membership, selling drugs, illegal income, and regularly carrying a weapon are associated with lower odds of being a dropout or dismissal as well, supporting the experiential observation that there are at least two different types of offenders who graduate from boot camp programs. A discussion of these types of offenders ensues in the next section.

Table 25.1　　　Multinomial Logistic Regression of Being a Dropout or Dismissal Instead of a Graduate From Boot Camp

Variable	Dropout β	OR		Dismissal β	OR	
Attachment	−.22*	.80	(1.25)	−.25	.78	(1.28)
Employment (full time = 0)	−1.14*	.32	(3.13)	−.92*	.40	(2.50)
Number of children	−.87*	.42	(2.38	−.43*	.65	(1.54)
Annual legal income	−.82*	.44	(2.27)	−.58*	.56	(1.79)
Locus of control	−.53*	.59	(1.70)	−.42*	.66	(1.52)
Self-efficacy	−.69*	.50	(2.00)	−.22*	.80	(1.25)
Marital status (married = 0)	−.97*	.38	(2.63)	−.78*	.46	(2.17)
Religiosity	−.56*	.57	(1.75)	−.37	.69	(1.44)
Self-esteem	−.20*	.82	(1.22)	−.60*	.55	(1.82)
Education	−.40*	.67	(1.49)	−.25*	.78	(1.28)
Gang member	−.26*	.77	(1.30)	−.07	.93	(1.08)
Sell drugs	−.45*	.64	(1.56)	−.36*	.70	(1.43)
Annual illegal income	−.73*	.48	(2.08)	−.25*	.78	(1.28)
Carry weapon	−.30*	.74	(1.35)	−.08	.92	(1.09)
Low self-control	.20*	1.22		.02	1.02	
Drug use	.75*	2.12		.18*	1.20	
Days of drug tx	1.10*	3.01		.26*	1.30	
Peer association	.21*	1.23		.06	1.06	
Normative definitions	.44*	1.55		.17*	1.18	
Modeling	.07	1.07		.02	1.02	
Reinforcement	.17	1.19		.04	1.04	
Anger/frustration	.10	1.10		.43*	1.53	
Sexual abuse	.11	1.12		.728	2.02	
Physical abuse	.22*	1.25		.49*	1.63	
Emotional problems	.05	1.05		.67*	1.96	
Suicidal attempts	.26*	1.29		.60*	1.75	
Alienation	.06	1.06		.51*	1.67	
Race	.01	1.01		.03	1.03	
Age	−.82	.44	(2.27)	.43*	.66	(1.52)
−2 log likelihood	1564.14			1543.93		

Note. All data are standardized OR except for employment, marital status, and number of children. OR is the odds ratio of being a dropout or a dismissal instead of a graduate (reference group). The reciprocal OR (1/OR) is shown for inverse relationships for ease of comparison to positive relationships.

*P < .05.

The likelihood of being a dropout is heightened with increases in low self-control, drug use, number of days of drug treatment, peer association with criminals, and use of normative definitions to excuse crime. Dismissals are distinguished by increases in anger, sexual and physical abuses, emotional problems, suicidal attempts, and feelings of alienation.

The likelihood ratio (−2 log likelihood) compares the likelihood function for a model with the effects to the likelihood function for the null hypothesis model that all effects (β), except the intercept, are 0. A chi-square table was used to ascertain the probability of the likelihood ratio, which was beyond .01 in this case. The Nagelkerke... pseudo R^2 was .62, which was the amount of variance in categories accounted for by the factors.

Table 25.2 shows how accurately the 784 cases could be classified into the three outcomes studied. Ninety-three inmates (11.9%) were misclassified. Generally, however, the percentages correctly classified were impressive, with 91.3%, 82.5%, and 73.5%, respectively, of the graduates, dropouts, and dismissals. In fact, 88.5% of the total cases were correctly classified.

Discussion

This investigation of 784 inmates was one of the few studies to examine factors that discriminate among graduates, dropouts, and dismissals from a boot camp program. It was timely because of the controversies swirling around the usage of boot camps as a correctional intervention. Boot camps had been subjected to intense criticism as hypermasculine environments that promote aggression and other antisocial attitudes and offer low-dosage or token treatment. . . . There was no solid evidence that boot camps offer beneficial experiences for any type of offenders or reduce criminal recidivism rates in comparison with other correctional interventions, such as probation and traditional prison. . . .

Despite the lack of empirical evidence for the effectiveness of boot camp programs, legislators and administrators continue to support this correctional intervention based on ideological arguments. . . . Tonry . . . observed that boot camps garner support from several constituencies because of the pervasive acceptance of the belief that military training transforms many immature and wayward youths into responsible adults.

Approximately one quarter (23.5%) of the men who entered boot camp in this study, however, drop out or

were dismissed. This high failure rate did not bode well for the administrative efficiency in choosing intervention options or for the programmatic effectiveness of boot camps. A significant proportion of the inmates were electing to serve out their sentence in prison rather than to finish the briefer boot camp program, or they were dismissed from the program because of various problems in adjusting. This study showed that these dropouts and dismissals could be accurately distinguished from graduates of the program.

Once it is established that dropouts and dismissals can be distinguished from graduates, the question becomes how to use that information administratively and clinically. Use of information always raises the specter of misuse. For example, this classification, in tandem with the findings of previous studies, indicates that inmates who have "personal capital" and form social bonds are likely to graduate from boot camp and live in the community without rearrest or parole violations for at least 5 years. . . . These findings support hypotheses derived from life course theory . . . that these assets and social bonding will promote graduation. Assets—such as self-efficacy, income, and religion—that give people hope and internal and external resources to overcome adversities and achieve are referred to as personal capital . . . , whereas social bonding is signified in life course theory by investments in regular employment, marriage, having children, and education. . . . Religion, for example, can provide a meaning and purpose for life, as well as communal support and a sense of belonging. . . . Full-time employment and a viable income can provide security and a healthy sense of accomplishment that people want to maintain by eschewing unlawful behavior that can jeopardize this investment. . . . This study and prior research . . . also suggested that the offenders who succeeded in boot camp and sustained tenure in the community after graduation from that program were older. . . . [W]ith every increase of three and one-half years in age (standard deviation), the odds of graduation

Table 25.2   Classification Table

		Predicted Group Membership					
Observed Group	No. of Cases	1		2		3	
Graduates 1 (%)	600	548	(91.3)	35	(5.8)	20	(2.9)
Dropouts 2 (%)	120	11	(9.2)	99	(82.5)	10	(8.3)
Dismissals 3 (%)	64	7	(10.9)	10	(15.6)	47	(73.5)
Percentage of cases correctly		88.5					

improved by 2.27 in comparison with dropouts and 1.22 in comparison with dismissals.

Does this mean that older offenders who have investments in conventionality are the best candidates for boot camp and that drug offenders and persons who have emotional problems and a history of being abused should be categorically denied access to these programs? It is tempting to answer this question with a resounding "yes." The classifications were more than 88% accurate. Empirical classifications, however, should not be the sole criteria for making these decisions. These decisions should be informed by evidence on which offenders, if any, are positively affected by the boot camp experience. It is possible that persons who have healthy personal capital and a sense of social bonding . . . experience an awakening to the potential losses in investments they have made by the harsh realities of boot camp. . . . It is equally likely, however, that incarceration and restricted visitation strain and jeopardize social bonds. . . . It is quite possible that a less intrusive intervention, such as intense probation or a community corrections program, would serve as a "wake-up" call to potential losses that crime could present to investments that people have made in social bonding. . . . The preponderance of available evidence on recidivism does not augur well for claims of effectiveness of boot camps. . . . Therefore, instead of automatically assuming that boot camps are an appropriate intervention for men who are forming social bonds, consideration should be given to other correctional options that would enhance bonding mechanisms that seem to deter unlawfulness. This study should inform decision making in concert with clinical and systemic considerations. Decisions regarding appropriate admissions to boot camp have to be made based on services offered in that program and in alternative interventions in a particular department of corrections.

Ironically, another type of offender seems to be successful in graduating boot camp that would likely elicit a different response from decision makers in regard to programming. Older gang members who sell illicit drugs and regularly carry weapons also graduate boot camp in accord with the hypothesis. Gang members may adapt in boot camp because they are accustomed to living with conflict, coercion, and aggression. These offenders, however, have a high recidivism rate . . . , which raises the question of appropriateness of a brief intervention. Certainly, a systemic examination of what precisely is being accomplished with these offenders in boot camp is long overdue. Offering services specifically designed for these offenders in a more extended program might have desirable effects.

The most important use of this study would seem to be in identifying the persons who drop out and are dismissed from the boot camp program. These persons are the putative "failures" of the program, and perhaps there are alternative approaches to intervention for these offenders. The findings regarding dropouts and dismissals supported the hypotheses articulated in the introduction. The profile identified for dropouts included drug use and treatment, low self-control, and criminal peer associations—this profile was identified with more than 80% accuracy. Although it might be true that not all of these offenders needed drug treatment, the odds of being a dropout triple for inmates who were in substance abuse programs before entering boot camp. This evidence strongly suggested that many boot camps might not be a viable program for at least a contingent of drug offenders. It was likely that drug offenders were dropping out of boot camps because most programs currently did not offer comprehensive drug treatment— a few programs did offer meaningful treatments aimed at personal and spiritual well-being, but they were the exceptions. . . . This study suggested that boot camps should provide treatment for drug offenders if they continued to be sent to these facilities. . . .

Dropouts also were identified by low self-control and criminal peer associations. Low self-control was a special concern because many observers . . . believed that the hypermasculine environment of boot camps intensified propensities associated with low self-control. . . . Boot camps were marketed with ideological claims that the regimentation of these programs instilled self-control in persons who led undisciplined lives. . . . The effects of boot camp training on self-control, however, need to be directly measured because it is possible that incarceration in these programs is worsening a personality trait that is strongly associated with crime . . . and recidivism. . . .

This hypermasculine environment may be even more challenging to the persons identified in this study as dismissals. This study identified, with about 73% accuracy . . . , dismissals as persons with a history of being abused—sexually and physically—and emotional problems, including anger, alienation, and suicidal attempts. These offenders were of particular concern because the boot camp environment had been characterized by aggression, humiliation, and intimidation. . . . The verbal and physical abuses likely retraumatize persons who have been victimized as children. . . . Although the adverse conditions in boot camps are especially perilous for persons who have been victimized, they likely intensify emotional problems as well.

Certainly, an atmosphere of intimidation and humiliation is not conducive to treatment and rehabilitation. . . . Experience suggests that these are the very offenders who are often the target of staff and inmates' harassment and abuses. Their emotional problems seem to interfere with timely compliance with staff commands, and their vulnerabilities are regarded with disdain in a hypermasculine environment. Other inmates sense these vulnerabilities and exploit them in various ways to relieve their own anger and frustrations.

The confluence of these personal and environmental forces may well trigger the infractions that eventually lead to dismissal from boot camp. The spiraling pattern of harsh circumstances inciting undesirable behavior that is then punished by dismissal needs to be broken. One approach would be to try to change the program, including hiring staff who are more knowledgeable about how to relate to persons who are having emotional problems and may be suicidal. This approach, however, does not appear compatible with existing boot camp practices and personnel. Programs specifically designed to treat persons with a history of victimization and emotional problems need to be available in departments of correction.

Inferences from this study need to be made cautiously because of its limitations. The more salient limitations included its cross-sectional design and sampling from one site. Multiple measures and sources of information would have strengthened the study. Perhaps the most glaring weakness was the lack of measures of the impact of the program.

In conclusion, a thorough review of the viability of boot camps is long overdue. In an era of "evidence-based corrections" where effective interventions are being identified, a classification that distinguishes graduates from a program from dropouts and dismissals is a useful tool in making programmatic decisions. . . . The statistical accuracy of the classification and its support for theoretical hypotheses offer compelling reasons to believe these distinctions are valid. If the validity is established in other studies, this classification should serve as a basis—not *the* basis—for deciding how boot camps are used. Empirical classifications need to be considered in the context of clinical and administrative realities.

Questions

1. Describe the role of boot camps in the field of corrections.

2. Describe how social bonds differ in those who drop out or are dismissed from boot camp and those who succeed.

CHAPTER 26

Gender, Ethnicity, and Offending Over the Life Course

Women's Pathways to Prison in the Aloha State

Marilyn Brown
University of Hawaii at Hilo

Life Course Development and the Pathways Perspective

Versions of the life course development perspective highlight the links across stages of youthful development, delinquency, and adult crime and their relation to social bonds. Sampson and Laub's *Crime in the Making: Pathways and Turning Points Through Life* (1993) examines the interplay between structural- and individual-level variables over the life course, wherein life events mark processes of continuity and change in patterns of delinquency and offending. This genre examines the effects of social bonds that arise from affiliation with the institutions of family, school, and work and their relationship to human development over the life course. Sampson and Laub . . . see social bonds like marriage or employment as important to explanations of changes in offending behavior. But these events are not separate from the larger influences of culture, political economy, and history. Feminist scholars have adopted concepts from life course development theories to talk about women's pathways to crime and incarceration. Owen and Belknap . . . , Belknap (2001), and Gaarder and Belknap . . . have begun to pull together a pathways framework for understanding the gendered life course events that propel women into delinquency, crime, and ultimate involvement with the criminal processing system.

This chapter is an account of women on parole in the state of Hawaii, examined in the context of change and continuity in a unique penal setting. The state is undergoing a painful transition from a mainly rural plantation-based economy to one based on its identity as a sought-after destination in a globalized visitor market. This transformation has resulted in massive economic, cultural, and social dislocations and accompanying uncertainties that differentially affect segments of Hawaii's population. The impact of these changes has been hardest felt by Native Hawaiian and newer immigrant groups from Asia and elsewhere in the Pacific. Indeed, the colonial transformations that ultimately alienated the indigenous people of Hawaii from their land have been ongoing for more than 200 years. This chapter argues that women's offending is grounded in the larger concerns of culture, society, and history that condition their life course development, a perspective that merits more attention in theories about patterns of women's offending.

The pathways perspective as used in recent feminist research on offending balances attention to macrolevel issues such as race, gender, and class with elements of personal action. . . . This framework pays significant attention to relations of power, arguing that women experience multiple forms of marginality related to delinquency and crime. . . . Women's vulnerabilities—that is, those factors that make them likely to become involved

Source: "Gender, ethnicity, and offending over the life course: Women's pathways to prison in the aloha state," by Brown, M., (2006), *Critical Criminology*, *14*, 137–158. Reprinted by permission of Springer via Copyright Clearance Center.

with the law—are produced by the intertwined effects of race, gender, and class . . . and the effects of personal agency. Studies of incarcerated women have demonstrated the ubiquitous nature of abuse and trauma (especially sexual exploitation and assault), chaotic family lives, personal losses (of family and children), involvement in violent relationships, and drug use in their lives. All of these conditions, highly structured by gender, are central to women's involvement in crime. Male offenders clearly experience many of these problems, but these factors are less clearly related to criminality and offending among males than females. Men's lives are far less likely to be defined by sexual abuse, exploitation, and violent victimization by a loved one. Nor are men's major life events marked to the same extent as women's by pervasive sexism and patriarchal oppression. . . . In the pathways perspective, gendered experiences are considered crucial to explaining the different patterns of offending behavior and the reasons underlying them.

The pathways approach shows that the life events and the social controls shaping outcomes for women are highly gendered, a perspective missing in Sampson and Laub's early work. Maeve, for example, describes how women's sexual victimization and experience of violence "emerge as life-shaping events" in the lives of incarcerated women. . . . In connection with these traumas, Maeve continues, sexual and other forms of self-destructive, risk-taking behaviors follow as sequelae. Chief among these reactions to trauma is using drugs and alcohol to suppress or medicate feelings of anxiety, tension, and sadness.

The family setting and the dynamics of intimate relationships have a special and sometimes paradoxical meaning in the lives of female offenders. Theories that call attention to social control and women's offending have been supported by studies of how conventional families constrain girls' freedom and limit opportunities for delinquency. . . . Chesney-Lind and Shelden . . . argue that a troubled home life plays a more crucial role in producing girls' delinquency than for boys. Family cuts both ways in the lives of girls and women who become involved as offenders in the criminal processing system. Families and intimate relationships can also be crucibles for the formation of addiction, delinquency, and crime. So, rather than affording protection, families may well be the source of victimization and abuse that give rise to offending among women. As stories told by the women in my study show, women are often introduced to drug use and related criminal activities through the significant others in their lives—often the people on whom they are economically or otherwise dependent. . . .

Gender, Culture, and Offending: The Hawaii Context

Hawaii is making the difficult transition from a largely agrarian economy dominated by industrial agriculture to a modern service economy. Hawaii's cultural diversity and residual stratification is the largely the legacy of its plantation past and successive waves of immigration from East Asia, Pacific Islands, Europe, and the Americas. There is also the indigenous population that faces marginalization in its own homeland under the impact of Western (and especially American) colonialism. Therefore, I adopt a more complex view of gender and structure, more in keeping with Elder's work . . . concerning the role that historical and cultural transitions play in shaping the life events of individuals. This perspective, this convergence of social action and structure, resonates with depictions of social transitions described in accounts of deindustrialization of urban centers and consequent dislocations of African-American families by Wilson. . . . The sorts of social, cultural, and economic transformations that have occurred in Hawaii have conditioned the life events of women in this study.

At the end of the 20th century, Hawaii, along with the rest of the nation, saw explosive growth in women's incarceration. Such trends were not initially analyzed to reveal the vulnerabilities of women offenders. The emancipation hypotheses linking the emerging female crime problem with the women's movement were simplistic, ignoring the fact that women were still committing the same types of crimes they had always committed. . . . The beneficiaries of the expanded field of socioeconomic opportunities won by second-wave feminism tended to be White women, not the women of color who make up most inmate populations here in Hawaii and the nation. As my data show, the individual biographies of the female carceral population in Hawaii, 84% of whom are non-White, do not in the least reflect the experiences of the emancipated woman. Rather, the expansion of social, cultural, and economic capital that accompanied the growing equality of opportunity for some women as a result of more expanded educational, economic, and social rights missed this group almost completely. Women offenders in Hawaii were far more affected by the increasingly punitive criminal processing policies and cutbacks in social welfare of the 1980s and 1990s than by legislation that expanded rights and opportunities to other women.

Patterns of Offenses: Current and Previous Offenses

To an extent greater than for men, women's substance abuse is linked to their involvement in the criminal processing system. . . . In looking at the patterns of offending within the aggregate universe of conviction offenses, it is clear that the majority of women in this study were incarcerated for crimes involving property (48%) and drug offenses (44.5%). Few crimes involved violence or crimes against persons (5.6%), and crimes having to do with public order and the like (1.8%) were uncommon. A clear majority (78.5%) of all offenses fall into Hawaii's Felony C category—those offenses resulting in a maximum sentence of 5 years. In terms of serious crime, few conviction offenses (3.5%) were Class A Felonies (involving 20-year sentences), whereas only about 18% involved Class B Felonies. As in other jurisdictions . . . , Hawaiian women offenders involved in drug offenses tend to be low-level users and distributors—indeed, none of their drug-related crimes fell into the Class A Felony category, and only about 8% of such offenses were categorized as intermediate Class B felons.

Half the women in this study had been convicted of an offense (felonies or misdemeanors) prior to their current commitment. The largest single source of previous involvement with the law was in the area of misdemeanor property crimes (35.1%) and in other sorts of misdemeanors (22.9%), such as prostitution and public order offenses. Few women (10.4%) had records for crimes against persons, and most of these were nonserious misdemeanors (7.6%) for issues like making threats (referred to as second-degree terroristic threatening in Hawaii statutes) and minor assaults. Slightly more than one third of the women in the study (36%) had a juvenile record. Although juvenile records are not available for analysis, this pattern of youthful offenses is significant for girls and young women because it often signals traumatic and chaotic home lives, followed by more serious offending as girls attempt to survive on the streets. . . .

Intersections of Family Life and Offending

As in virtually all other jurisdictions, the majority of the women in this study (85%) are mothers. Yet this ubiquitous finding has yet to be integrated into our understandings of offending and the life course. The conventional life course development perspective, which is grounded mainly in the experience of males, suggests that the assumption of adult responsibilities would foster turning points away from crime. Moreover, early attachment to family structures theoretically strengthens self-control. But for many girls in working-class and poor families, responsibilities begin early and do not always protect young women from risks. Women in my study often tell about childhoods that included domestic chores and the care of siblings—routines that continued into adulthood with their own children—that are merged in these narratives with drug use and status offenses. Behavior outside the law, and drug use in particular, does not preclude engagement with conventional gender roles like domestic chores and child care, calling into question the supposed protective role of attachment to the family.

On average, women in this sample who had a previous offense came into the criminal processing system at age 23. Of parenting women in the sample (85%), 71% had already had at least one child at the time they were initially sentenced. These women had a relatively late entry into the criminal processing system, and many had already taken on adult responsibilities for children. These are events that life course theory suggests might spell a cessation to delinquency and offending for males. But for women who continue on the trajectory to prison, childbearing and domestic ties do not seem to preclude continuing drug use or other types of offending.

This is a group for whom motherhood is often a troubled condition. Official records say little about the history and quality of maternal relationships with children, but some serious indications are obvious. The case files contain records of official actions or contacts with Child Protective Services (CPS). Nearly 48 (24%) of the 203 mothers in this study had been involved with CPS. In other words, there were references to such investigations in their case files. In addition, Hawaii or some other state jurisdiction terminated the parental rights of nearly 17% of mothers. These investigative or termination proceedings involved one or more children.

My interviews with women on parole suggest two versions of lifestyle that are important to unraveling these apparent paradoxes. One is that, for some women, drug use begins in adolescence and continues on into adulthood. This pattern converges with most life course theory research, especially the control versions . . . of continuity in offending. It should be noted that these women often ceased their drug use and drinking during pregnancy and during their children's infancy, sometimes resuming the lifestyle as children got older. However, a second group of women explained that their drug abuse began in the context of marriage or relationship with a significant other—often with the father of their children—as adult women. . . .

This pattern of later onset of serious drug use . . . is unusual given that the onset of street drug use tends to precede the adoption of adult roles. But clearly, this later incidence is an important reality for women offenders in my study. Such findings suggest that the pathways approach to women's offending should consider the role of intimate relationships as potential risk factors in the evolution of drug problems and crime for women and that marriage and relationships with intimates may be turning points in the lives of these women toward breaking the law rather than desistance. This may be especially problematic for women who are economically dependent or dependent in other ways and for whom autonomy is a complex issue. Therefore, the pathways perspective also needs to consider the degree of autonomy which women can exercise within relationships that are often marked by dependence, abuse, and victimization.

Education and Employment

Studies of women involved in the criminal processing system routinely find that their subjects are poorly educated and lacking in basic job skills and experience. Hawaii's female offenders share these characteristics, and, in some respects, educational achievement is even worse for these women than in some national studies. Not only do these conditions bode ill for economic survival and family stability, but deficits in these areas may shape the length of time women spend on parole. Continuous full-time employment is a basic requirement for anyone hoping to gain an early discharge from parole in Hawaii. Adequate employment and income are basic to establishing households where women can reunite with their children. As O'Brien notes, inadequate income within a comprehensive parole plan sets a woman up for failure upon leaving prison. Attaining what O'Brien refers to as "environmental sufficiencies" . . . in an environment of diminished social welfare support for women means that ex-inmates will have to depend on themselves for financial resources or on family members who are strapped by the high cost of living in Hawaii.

Women parolees in Hawaii fare less well than women in state prisons as a group when it comes to educational attainment. Although a handful of women in my study had some college prior to incarceration, only two

had college degrees. . . . Nearly 54% of the study group had not graduated from high school, nor had they obtained their General Education Degrees prior to their incarceration. In contrast, the Bureau of Justice Statistics reported in 2001 that 44% of women in state prisons lacked a high school diploma while 39% had a high school diploma or equivalent. About 17% of women in state prisons had at least 1 year of college or more. . . . Fewer than 10% of Hawaii women in this study had any postsecondary education, compared with 17% across the nation. . . .

In addition, I found that educational attainment has a strong relationship to ethnicity among these parolees. Women of Hawaiian descent were less likely to have graduated from high school, compared with other women in this study. In looking at overall educational attainment for women, Hawaii compares favorably with other states, ranking 11th in the nation in 1990. . . . Thus, the educational statistics for women in this sample reflect a departure from this economic indicator for women in our state. The pathways perspective suggests looking at this pattern of early separation from school as another of the turning points in the trajectory of women who get into trouble with the law. Moreover, women of Hawaiian ancestry are even more marginalized in this respect, compared with other women.

Given these dismal educational statistics, the data collected by the Hawaii Paroling Authority as part of their assessment of employment-related skills offer few surprises. In the year before sentencing for their offenses, few women had any substantial employment. The assessments also showed that fewer than 50% had adequate educational or vocational skills. Making a living on parole is crucial to setting up a household and stable living situation. Those of us with secure housing probably take for granted the extent to which our residences, our homes, structure our lives and make access to other resources possible. Our intimate relationships, safe or dangerous, take place in the context of the home. Stable housing is important to children attending school and qualifying for needed services. O'Brien . . . notes that home has both metaphorical and concrete aspects for women offenders leaving prison and that the quality of home in both these regards is crucial to successful reentry into society. Clearly, these subjective and objective factors overlap. Financial instability precludes attaining secure housing, and women's economic dependence increases the potential for living in an unsuitable and even dangerous familial environment. Economic dependency is a common reason that women remain in violent households or in households plagued with family troubles and conflicts. Problems with housing are a primary concern for women leaving prison, but these difficulties frequently existed prior to incarceration for more than a third of the study group according to Hawaii Paroling Authority assessment data.

Economic dependence shapes relationships with intimates. . . . The fates of women on parole and their children are shaped extensively by . . . links to socioeconomic capital, links that often rest on the few tenuous social ties women are able to build with family, friends, and lovers.

Substance Abuse

For the majority of the women in this study, drug and alcohol problems have conditioned their entry into the criminal processing system. The Hawaii Paroling Authority assesses inmates for substance abuse problems, using a scale that differentiates alcohol and drug usage. Data for this population of female parolees indicate that the majority of these group members have experienced significant alcohol and drug problems and that many require substance abuse treatment. Slightly more than two thirds of this population (for whom assessments were available) experienced some disruption or severe disruption of their lives as a result of alcohol use. More than one third of these women had problems so severe that they required alcohol dependence treatment.

In conversations with women in this study, I came to an understanding of their alcohol and drug problems as overlapping, with polydrug patterns of substance use being more typical than not. Pharmaceuticals prescribed by physicians played a role in these accounts as well. Kassebaum and Chandler's . . . study found that polydrug use was the norm for newly sentenced felons in Hawaii prisons. They found nearly universal alcohol and marijuana use, along with extensive use of cocaine, crack, heroin, crystal methamphetamine (ice), and other drugs. Heavy polydrug use was more common among females than the males in their sample. These findings resonate with other studies that find that the link between addiction and property crime is stronger among female than male inmates. . . .

Not surprisingly, serious drug use can be said to be typical of the women in my study, with 80% of those for whom data were available experiencing serious disruption of their lives due to their addiction. Although data are not collected by the Hawaii Paroling Authority on the specific drugs used by parolees, the women I interviewed had patterns of drug use that were similar to those found by Kassebaum and Chandler, with methamphetamine (ice), being especially common. . . .

Violence, Abuse, and Trauma . . .

Gender violence, especially trauma due to childhood sexual assault, has now been established as a precursor to adult drug use and offending among women. . . . Victimization is being recognized as an event in women's lives that accelerates women's trajectories into offending. . . . Macmillan . . . notes that violent victimization has profoundly negative effects over the life course. The socioeconomic status of women places them at risk for violent victimization throughout the life course.

Often the mediating link between histories of abuse and adult offending appear to be drug use and involvement with prostitution. Indeed, as Stein . . . points out in her study of Hawaiian women in an inmate work furlough program, street life and prostitution are associated with ubiquitous violence, "part of the deal." . . . Women who break the law occupy an especially marginalized position that affords them little protection against violence and sexual assaults, nor do they have much recourse when violence occurs.

It is not uncommon for young women from disruptive family backgrounds to enter into adult relationships that are fraught with violence. Betty . . . experienced such a transition from adolescence to adulthood. This mother of four reports that her future husband began hitting her during her first pregnancy. She told me that lots of mental, emotional, and physical abuse followed. There were many trips to the hospital as a result. Her husband threatened her repeatedly, sometimes with a gun. She described what she felt were a number of near-death experiences from this violence. She felt that the continual abuse made her "weaker and weaker." . . .

Living at the margins . . . often precludes getting effective help from the police or other mainstream helping institutions. Indeed, the law often fails to protect women who are leading conventional lives. It is not uncommon for the perpetrators of the violence to be the police.

Trauma related to sexual abuse and violence during childhood and adolescence has begun to be well documented among women offenders. Its link with drug addiction continues to be validated by biographical and life course research on women offenders and addicts. . . . But trauma continues well into adulthood for many of these women, and sometimes it arises as a result of their gendered responsibilities for children. Sometimes a woman's first brush with the authorities arises when she comes under the gaze of CPS and loses a child through court actions—a common problem for incarcerated women. Termination of parental rights, now even more common since the passage of the 1997 Adoption and Safe Families Act, is a singular source of grief for women. Motherhood is extraordinarily powerful as a motivating force in the lives of women, and women offenders are no exception. Their maternal lives are, however, rendered much more complicated by their marginalized statuses, unlawful lifestyles, and incarceration. They often cannot depend on families for help, nor are they particularly successful at securing help from agencies like substance abuse treatment facilities. Of course, there are few facilities that offer treatment services to pregnant or parenting drug addicts along with their young children.

Compared with what is now known about the nexus of abuse, trauma, and addiction, little is known about how the loss of children through the termination of parental rights affects women's trajectories through life. Angela, whose son was born in 1993, viewed her pregnancy as a turning point. She got off the streets and stopped taking drugs for a time. She attributes her descent into addiction, due to the loss of her child, to her mother, who coerced her into giving him up. This loss, she said, "really caused me to bottom out." That event prompted a return to drugs and a cascade of losses, culminating in her arrest. She told me that she used to think that she probably wouldn't have become an addict had it not been for this loss. "Well, at the time," she added, "I didn't understand the disease [of addiction]." Nevertheless, the birth of Angela's child was an important motivator in Angela getting off the street. The loss of the child became an enduring source of pain, one that was linked for her with a return to and an exacerbation of her drug problem.

Ethnicity: Being Hawaiian

The life course perspective emphasizes individual life events and turning points in its causal explanation of delinquency and crime. But there is, in the work of Elder . . . and a number of feminist writers looking at the pathways approach, an understanding of how individuals' life events are positioned by larger structural factors that affect the likelihood of coming before criminal courts. The "triple jeopardy" . . . of race, gender, and class are, of course, cultural and historical outcomes that have an important bearing on women's trajectories into crime— and their fates once they enter the criminal processing

system. Contemporary Hawaii still bears the legacy of its ethnically stratified plantation past, a system that dominated 19th-century society. As a result of its colonial history, *kanaka maoli* (as persons of Native Hawaiian ancestry refer to themselves), and newer immigrant groups from Asia and the Pacific Islands, dominate the ranks of the poorer classes—and populate correctional institutions. . . .

In the 2000 census, about 20% of the population in Hawaii claimed some Native Hawaiian ancestry . . . , but carceral populations routinely reflect the group at present as more than double this rate. Nearly 53% of women parolees in this study are Hawaiian or part Hawaiian. Caucasians, in contrast, at 24% of the overall population, are underrepresented in this group at only 16%. The overrepresentation of Native Hawaiians in the carceral population is consistent from study to study. Stein . . . reported that women of Hawaiian ancestry made up 61% of her sample of inmates at a work-furlough program in Honolulu. Kassebaum and Davidson-Coronado's . . . study of both male and female parolees in Hawaii found that 45% were of Hawaiian ancestry. In July 2000, 33% of Hawaii's 2,319 female probationers were of Native Hawaiian ancestry, as were 40.2% of Hawaii's 542 adult female inmates. Persons of Native Hawaiian ancestry not only make up the largest category of offenders in this study, but are overrepresented in terms of poverty indices, major lifestyle diseases, and a range of other problem categories across the spectrum of social distress. . . . There is considerable consensus among scholars of Hawaiiana that the impact of colonialism, racism, and extensive alienation from aboriginal culture and lands has severely damaged the life chances of the indigenous population. . . .

Like the women in Bloom's study of incarcerated women in California . . . , Hawaii's female offender population is marginalized by race, gender, and class. For women of Hawaiian ancestry, another layer is added to this "triple jeopardy" of vulnerability and marginalization—that of being a colonized indigenous people. Native peoples are present in larger than expected numbers in carceral populations in Canada, the United States, Australia, and other nations where indigenous ties to ancestral lands and ways of life have been interrupted by capitalism and urbanism. Hawaiian cultural capital, with its metaphors of aloha, reciprocity, and respect, was frankly overpowered in a social field dominated by Western models that prioritize economic values and materialist ideologies. . . . The resources that culture provides for individual identity are often difficult to articulate. Kepuhi's story illustrates a particular feeling about cultural identity that can be described as a way of knowing, one that was lost with adulthood:

> But spiritually I've lost that too. It's kind of hard to explain. Say like, I know something or I would feel something or I would sense something and I've lost that. Or see something, nobody else can see it now. You know what I mean?

Kepuhi described two instances of knowing things about people and events that, as a child, she should have had no means of knowing. These intuitive feelings were essential to her Hawaiian identity, giving her a sense of connection to the past and to a reality that Western empiricism denies. She describes these as spiritual gifts linked to being Hawaiian. Accounts of such experiences are met by Westerners with derision, but to native peoples, they are crucial cultural resources that link them to their past and to one another. Looked at in this way, Hawaiian ethnicity and culture are not risk factors for crime. Rather, in the postcolonial context, alienation from indigenous culture and the loss of resources it affords are important and often unanalyzed factors in the overrepresentation of native peoples in corrections populations. . . . The loss of traditional means of subsistence, relationships, spirituality, and identity in modern contexts of poverty and institutional alienation may well be a better explanation for problems like addiction, violence, and the other significant problems that Native Hawaiians face.

Women of Native Hawaiian ancestry are not only more likely to be overrepresented in correctional populations, but their criminal involvement begins earlier. This risk factor for recidivism was found significantly more often for women of Native Hawaiian ancestry in the study compared with others. Additionally, Native Hawaiian women tended to have their first convictions at earlier ages (19 and younger). . . .

Additionally . . . women of Native Hawaiian ancestry were also significantly more likely to have a juvenile arrest record.

Early trouble with the law is strongly related to ethnicity, illustrating that the trajectory to prison begins earlier for these kanaka maoli women.

Finally, women of Hawaiian ancestry, while experiencing problems on parole such as using drugs, domestic violence, and homelessness at rates similar to those of non-Hawaiians, were more likely to be taken into custody or have a warrant issued for their arrest (although this relationship was not statistically significant). Thus, although the burden of parole and continuing personal difficulties affect both groups at equivalent rates, Native Hawaiian women are significantly more likely to have legal repercussions.

Conclusion

The rate of female incarceration has increased exponentially during the latter part of the 20th century. Offending for women is more likely to involve drug and property offenses, rather than crimes against persons. . . . Women's patterns of offending, as my Hawaii data indicate, are deeply embedded in patterns of drug and alcohol use, accompanied by property crimes. The trajectories propelling women into breaking the law are all too often linked to victimization within intimate relationships.

The conventional life course perspective, although powerful, shares an androcentric weakness with other criminological theories, in that it fails to see crime as gendered social action. Nor, regarding female offenders, is sufficient notice taken of unequal power relationships that produce unexpected patterns of criminality among women. Bottcher . . . , for example, notes that events throughout the life course are informed and structured by gendered divisions of labor. She notes that girls take on child-raising responsibilities earlier than boys and usually age out of delinquency earlier than their male peers. . . . The accounts that Hawaiian women give about the onset of their troubles with the law, however, show that the influence of adult relationships, such as the drug addiction of a spouse, can precipitate a late onset into drug use and offending. Traumatic events throughout the life course may propel women into drug use and related types of offending. The loss of a child, especially the termination of parental rights, has been largely unexplored as part of the cascade of losses these women experience as adults. Given that contemporary adoption policies put many incarcerated women in danger of losing their children, the implications for women who are punished a second time (by both imprisonment and the termination of their parental rights) are dire in terms of staying out of prison after release.

The women in my study were far more likely to be imprisoned for low-level property crimes and drug offenses than any other cause. Their major thefts and other property crimes were often in service to sustaining their drug addiction. Their criminality often took place in the confines of relationships where they played highly dependent emotional and economic roles under the influence of abusive, drug-addicted spouses.

Unfortunately for the women in this study and others like them, the dismantling of social welfare policies, with the erosion of entitlement programs that benefit women and children, have been accompanied by more punitive moves in penality. Mandatory minimums for drug offenses, three strikes laws, and reduced judicial discretion have come to dominate late-modern crime control. . . . These trends, coupled with changes in the labor market and other economic sectors, increased the exposure of poor women to criminalization, making them more likely to be incarcerated.

The structural elements that theorists such as Elder . . . find important to shaping life events are embodied in feminist versions of the pathways perspective, but perhaps need to be made even more explicit. I have argued that structural factors, shaped by historical and cultural change, have made it more likely that women of Hawaiian ancestry will come under the gaze of the law. Hawaii's female inmates, more than others in the nation, are likely to have serious educational deficits and to be returned to prison for violations of parole. Merely returning women to their preincarceration state will do little to alter their lives in any significant way. The assumptions underlying rehabilitative ideologies need to be unpacked and assessed against the real lives of women, starting with an understanding of the life events and processes that placed them on their trajectory to prison as well as how their biographies intersect with various forms of marginality.

Questions

1. How do typical life events and social controls differ for males and females?

2. How has the changing Hawaiian culture contributed to female criminality according to the author?

PART VIII

CULTURAL CRIMINOLOGY

Cultural criminology is a perspective that incorporates labeling and Marxist theories in a critical assessment of society, specifically crime and justice and how they are represented in the media. In *Cultural Criminology and Kryptonite*: *Apocalyptic and Retributive Constructions of Crime and Justice in Comic Books*, Nickie Phillips and Staci Strobl (chap. 27) use a content analysis methodology to provide a cultural criminological analysis of the principles of justice portrayed in contemporary American comic books. In *Framing Homicide Narratives in Newspapers: Mediated Witness and the Construction of Virtual Victimhood*, Moira Peelo (chap. 28) identifies how newspapers get readers to identify with crime victims. The author calls attention to how these newspaper articles serve as and create what the general public comes to think about crime and victimization.

CHAPTER 27

Cultural Criminology and Kryptonite

*Apocalyptic and Retributive Constructions
of Crime and Justice in Comic Books*

Nickie D. Phillips

St. Francis College, Brooklyn, NY

Staci Strobl

City University of New York, John Jay College of Criminal Justice

Although various media studies have focused on portrayals of crime depicted in TV, literature, film, and music, comic books have traditionally been neglected. . . . The recent resurgence in popular interest in comic books has led to a handful of studies by criminologists that focus narrowly on criminal justice depictions related to particular comic books, characters, themes, or historical periods. . . . However, understanding the medium's criminal justice themes holistically represents a new frontier. Using a cultural criminology framework, this study examines a wide cross-section of representations of criminal justice in contemporary American comic books.

Literature Review

SHAZAM! THE RESURGENCE OF INTEREST IN COMIC BOOKS

Comic books are a highly regarded art form rich with representations of crime and justice. . . . Since the first issue of *Action Comics* in 1938 featuring Superman, comic books have penetrated American consciousness. Even those who have never read a comic book are familiar with American superheroes such as Spider-Man, Captain America, Batman, and Wonder Woman, and they understand that such heroes are devoted to fighting crime, punishing the bad guys, and, ultimately, establishing a sense of justice.

In addition to mainstream popularity, comic books have received critical acclaim. Various comics' creators have earned the highest literary awards for their comics. For example, Art Spiegelman received a Pulitzer Prize in 1992 for *Maus*, Neil Gaiman and Charles Vess were awarded the 1991 World Fantasy Award for *The Sandman's A Midsummer Night's Dream*, and Alan Moore and Dave Gibbons received the Hugo Award in 1988 for *The Watchmen*.

Although some argue that comic books occupy merely a subcultural niche of the mass media, comic books have been the inspiration for countless Hollywood movies. In fact, comic book justice is increasingly influential for mass movie-going audiences. For example, according to the *Rough Guide to Superheroes*, movies based on comic books averaged approximately two per year between 1990 and 2002, but there were seven such movies in 2003 and six in 2004. . . . Recent comic book-related commercial successes include *Sin City*, *Spider-Man 2*, and *Constantine*. Additionally, comic books have inspired

Source: "Cultural criminology and kryptonite: Apocalyptic and retributive constructions of crime and justice in comic books," by Phillips, N. D., & Strobl, S., (2006), *Crime, Media, Culture, 2,* 304–331. Reprinted by permission of Sage Publications, Ltd.

countless video and console games from *Spider-Man* to the *Fantastic Four*, with video games alone grossing nearly $10 billion in 2004. . . .

CULTURAL CRIMINOLOGY CONFRONTS POPULAR MEDIA

The current study examines representations of crime and justice in American comic books through the lens of cultural criminology. Cultural criminology is influenced by a variety of perspectives, including postmodernism, labeling, and Marxism, among others. . . . Importantly, cultural criminology rejects the positivist notion of objectivity in favor of a focus on the meanings of symbols and styles within particular cultural and subcultural frameworks. This study falls within the burgeoning field of cultural criminological explorations of media.

The influence of postmodernist thought on cultural criminology is apparent as the reality of the crime problem is constantly questioned. Cultural criminologists question media representations of crime and justice, specifically, any overreliance on official data derived from government sources. . . . Media studies have shown the importance of the ways in which media frame issues of crime and justice and, in turn, influence public discourse. . . . From a postmodern perspective, the media do not merely reflect social reality, but, in a media-saturated world, increasingly constitute the social reality. . . . Justice and representations of justice, therefore, can be seen as resonating in a "vast hall of mirrors" . . . , thereby producing a dialectic of reflections on and constructions of justice.

Cultural criminology also focuses attention on the role of power and social inequality. Through a critical eye, cultural criminologists note the crucial connection between media and legal authority. . . . Specifically, cultural criminologists have described how media may influence public perception of social problems, such as the creation of moral panics, and may, in turn, influence criminal justice policy. . . .

Indeed, cultural criminologists have turned their gaze toward the media's extensive use of the criminal justice system as the source for popular images and storytelling, which in turn may contribute to public support for tough-on-crime agendas by "entertaining the crisis" of crime in society. . . .

For example, Epstein . . . shows how serial killer themes have emerged as intensely popular themes with the movie-going public. Typically, the serial killer is portrayed as a mythic monster, often evil incarnate, with superhuman powers. Epstein . . . notes that one potential effect of this cultural obsession is that "police have been known to release serial killers because they did not fit the mythic persona created by the media." . . . The investigation into the DC snipers was hindered by the use of the stereotypic, lonely White male serial-killer profile—a profile that had taken on its own reality through the media's obsession with it. . . . Likewise, Ferrell . . . writes of the influence of fictional programming: "Contemporary policing can in fact hardly be understood apart from its interpenetration with media at all levels, including . . . television programs shap[ing] public perceptions of policing and serv[ing] as controversial tools of officer recruitment." . . .

IMAGINING CRIMINAL JUSTICE: TRUTH, JUSTICE, AND THE AMERICAN WAY

Like other fictional media, comic books provide an alternate social reality for the characters to occupy, which may mirror broader society. But their impact extends deeper than mere reflection because they also provide an entertaining vehicle for readers to symbolically and vicariously experience the moral and philosophical questions sparked by criminal justice themes. Comic books seduce readers into a dominant narrative of good triumphing over evil while allowing them to experience criminal transgressions voyeuristically from a safe distance. . . . As Katz . . . suggested, reading about crime serves as a ritual moral exercise, in which people can work out their own moral unease without having to engage in anything more than passive consumption. Yet under this phenomenological understanding, crime media and entertainment—including comic books—become spaces in public life where the meaning of crime and punishment is created, consumed, and re-created. Consumption of media that appears passive may have an active role in shaping public consciousness. Examinations of crime and justice representations, then, become important for understanding the cultural raw material that interacts with and feeds into public attitudes and perspectives.

In a postmodern world of infinite mirrors, media involvement with crime themes reflects the political climate and vice versa. Sanders and Lyon . . . state that one way in which "media misrepresent illegal behavior is by focusing on crimes as simple and direct individual acts rather than as sophisticated activities engaged in by established groups." Fictional depictions of law enforcement and their response to criminals favor "individualistic etiological explanations" and "are dominant and often become the foundation for agency approaches." . . . Likewise, Beckett . . . found that public concern regarding the crime and drug problem is related to "levels of prior political initiative" and media coverage of the issues rather than actual crime rates. . . .

American criminal justice policy emphasizes individual motivation and responsibility for criminal behavior and deemphasizes pointing the finger at social structural causes. As in Reagan's 1985 inaugural address and later repackaged in *Contract With America* . . . , crime is envisioned as a threat to the larger population by those who should be held individually responsible for their behavior. The tough-on-crime approach crossed party lines when Clinton enacted the 1994 Crime Control Act. These recent political and ideological tendencies represent a neoclassical approach to crime and justice, underpinned by the Enlightenment notions of free will and responsibility that have long characterized American philosophical thought. Despite social-scientific data on the socioeconomic etiology of crime, the political climate in America remains one loyal to notions of individual culpability and responsibility. . . .

DOMINANT NOTIONS OF JUSTICE

Constructions of justice in comic books frequently manifest in story arcs that reproduce the existing power structures of larger society. Wright . . . describes major comic book publishers DC, Dell, and Charlton as affirming "all the basic assumptions of an American Cold War consensus . . . none questioned the state of American society or the meaningful place of individuals within it." . . . As Fingeroth . . . explains, the superhero mass market craves comics that embody the old *Superman* TV slogan, "Truth, justice and the American way." . . . Patriotic story lines in comic books, reinforcing the political status quo, were common during World War I and the cold war, imagining justice as a form of community redemption that rejects foreigners as the evil enemy. . . .

Since 9/11, the George W. Bush administration has steadily worked to reinvigorate a sense of nationalism using rhetoric based on fear. . . . Specifically, understanding of the social world has been sharply divided and recast as *pre-* and *post-*9/11, in which danger lurks at every corner and threats are graver than ever before. . . . The solution is simply to rid the world of the "evildoers." . . . Although simplistic, the nationalistic rhetoric resonated with citizens as Bush's approval ratings soared above 80%. . . . One way in which comic book creators responded to the events of 9/11 was by issuing numerous special issues such as Marvel's *Heroes* and 9–11: *Artists Respond*, in which traditional superheroes saluted the

"true" heroes such as law enforcement officers, firefighters, and other rescue personnel.

NOSTALGIA FOR A DESIRED SOCIAL ORDER

Patriotic themes are presented as a form of nostalgia in many comic books. Anderson . . . potently theorizes the deep relationship between nostalgia and nationalism through his elucidation of imagined communities. National story lines based on nostalgic cultural symbols such as poetry, myth, and legend become ideological tools employed by governments that construct an idealized past as a model for a hopeful future.

Comic creators appear to be expressing a similar political and social longing through nostalgic reveries that ultimately uphold conservative American values. In comic books, the desired social order the protagonist strives to achieve is the mythic return of better days, allegedly characterized by infrequent crime and just punishment. In this imagined social order, individuals who threaten the peace are identified as the "other" and swiftly neutralized. The archetypal setting for comics is a tranquil community, with strong family values, enviable social capital, and equality—all threatened by overwhelming evil, usually in the form of criminal violence—which has destroyed a peaceful, historic status quo. . . . Only through the cleansing of criminality by the protagonist can the desired status quo return, much like the retributive end of days in Christian eschatology, where the chosen good are saved at the expense of those defined as unworthy by their evil deeds. As one online Christian magazine writer observed, "The great Bible stories—such as Samson in the book of Judges—are packed with the epic visions and good-versus evil absolutes that fill the pages of classic comics and their modern, supercharged siblings known as 'graphic novels'." . . . Themes of the community redemption through the hero's crusade to justice are often overtly Christian. For example, Nightcrawler, in the *X-Men* series, often quotes the Bible and pontificates about sin, penance, and righteousness while engaged in his fight for justice.

RETRIBUTION

According to Fingeroth . . . , comic books, like other media, invoke a populist notion of punishment—that which is morally satisfactory to the majority of community members. . . . Retribution as a philosophy of punishment has often been associated with populism because of its appeal to the larger public as a ritual that symbolically returns society to its original order. . . .

Retribution differs from the policy aims of deterrence, which promotes crime prevention as its main objective; rehabilitation, which focuses on crime as a disease and corrective treatment as the response; and incapacitation, which banishes the offender to prison. Retribution's function rests on a Western, philosophical notion of moral symmetry, in which offenders get what is deserved—their "just deserts."...

Oldenquist . . . argues that a community cannot achieve its full humanity without the rituals associated with holding others morally accountable for their actions. Retribution is justified, therefore, because it benefits the society psychologically. This echoes the Nietzschean notion that rituals of punishment are deeply embedded in the essence of human nature. Nozick . . . argues that retribution satisfies the community's need to communicate to offenders that what they did was wrong. The punishment is designed to send the message of just how wrong the offense was and becomes a means to reconnect the offender to the moral norms of the society: "When [the offender] undergoes punishment . . . correct values are not totally without effect in his life (even though he does not follow them) because we hit him over the head with them."...

Retribution, as a cleansing social ritual for the community and a means of communicating moral norms to the offender, has been immensely popular with the American public and conceivably forms a crucial part of the "ritual moral exercise" of crime and justice in modern times. . . . Retribution-style rhetoric has often been invoked by lawmakers and politicians who have long realized the political value of being perceived as "tough-on-crime."...

For example, the success of Bush's rhetoric mobilizing public support for the War on Terror arguably was based on his ability to conjure up nostalgic imaginings of crime and justice that symbolically resonated with the public, even if the facts on the ground were something else altogether. In response to the terrorist attacks in 2001, Bush invoked sound bites such as, "I want justice, and there's an old poster out West . . . I recall, that said, 'Wanted, Dead or Alive'." . . . A year later, Bush succinctly described the foreign policy approach toward the accused terrorists as an effort to "smoke 'em out." . . . Such rhetoric richly imagines terrorists and those who fight them as Old West villains and their vigilante cowboy protagonists. Implied here is a nostalgic yearning for the strong-arm, extralegal tactics that in the Old West were justified by the absence of legitimate law enforcement, a theme that also strongly resonates in fictional media like comic books.

Doing Retribution

According to the literature on comic books, retribution and restoration of the desired social order may be accomplished by the comic book protagonist through both legal and/or extralegal means (i.e., taking the law into one's hands). Legal approaches include story lines—often influenced or funded by the U.S. government—that depict the effectiveness of legitimate law enforcement agencies and/or officials in combating crime. For example, during the 1930s, J. Edgar Hoover influenced the comic strip *War on Crime*, which depicted "real-life tales of the FBI" and portrayed a favorable view of law enforcement. . . . In 1971, the Department of Health, Education, and Welfare approached the creator of *Spider-Man* to write a story arc illustrating the dangers of drug use. . . . In 1990, the government enlisted Captain America as a soldier in the drug war in the government-inspired special issue entitled *Captain America Goes to War Against Drugs*. More recently, in 1998, the government provided Marvel Comics with $2.5 million to portray the dangers of marijuana use. . . .

More often, extralegal responses to crime are portrayed in comics as necessary adjuncts to legitimate enforcement to be used in times of crisis. . . . Comic book plots move inevitably toward the position of last resort: retaliatory, technically illegal actions that must be tolerated in a time of crisis. The inadequacy of legitimate law enforcement is often a critical component of the crisis, thus freeing protagonists—both superhero and non-superheroes—to resort to illegitimate avenues to restore justice. In fact, Newman . . . described the 1990 *Batman* movie's overarching message as one in which "Law Enforcement may call on Batman at any time to do violence to criminals which the established law enforcement machinery seems unable to carry out." . . . Other characters such as The Punisher and Daredevil also resort to vigilante violence to avenge injustice. . . . Vigilante-related plots are enthusiastically embraced by readers. Mike Baron, Editor and writer of *Punisher: War Journals*, attributed the popularity of *Punisher* to "the average citizen's outrage at the failure of society to punish evil."...

Despite the dominance of a conservative effort to restore the status quo, the pendulum briefly swung in a more liberal direction in the 1960s. During this era, story arcs reflected the social upheaval apparent in society and explicitly questioned authority. *Green Lantern*, for example, was portrayed as a radical leftist tackling social issues such as racism, poverty, and corruption with special issues devoted to the assassinations of Martin

Luther King, Jr., and Robert Kennedy.... However, incorporating social issues, such as the civil rights movement, into comics was dismissed as "well-meaning, but clumsy"..., and the old plots returned.

This research contributes to the literature by positioning comic books and their overwhelming emphasis on crime and justice as a cultural medium worthy of analysis. We examine the type of crimes depicted in comic books, the desired social order in the comic books' imagined community, the style of justice employed by the protagonist (legal or extralegal), and whether the depiction implies a retributive policy message, thereby reproducing dominant American notions of justice.

Methodology

To the Batcave!

Kane ... describes media studies within the framework of cultural criminology as "an experimental ethnographic space" in which culture can be explored through the characters as "virtual inhabitants." ... Such an approach links social reality to the social artifacts analyzed and takes into consideration what Hayward and Young ... refer to as the deep interplay of media and reality in postmodernism.

In our study, a purposive sample of 20 titles was drawn from the top 210 best-selling comic books and trade paperbacks released in December 2003 as recorded by ICv2. Each monthly comic book has an issue number and often a story arc or episode that extends over several issues. To sample entire story arcs, we followed the selected issues forward and/or backward in time, from December 2003, to include the entire arc in our analysis. Trade paperbacks are compilation books of all the issues in a particular story arc and thus are relatively self-contained sagas.

The selection of monthlies involved separating the top best sellers into ranked groups of 15 titles. Within each group, we purposively selected a comic book. Purposive sampling allowed for the avoidance of children's books, such as *Archie* and *Daffy Duck*. The sample also contains a mixture of superhero and non-superhero titles. By spanning the top 200 best-selling comic books and selecting one title from the ranked groups, we included in our sample the most popular comic books, as well as those published by alternative or independent publishers located further down the list. Titles included *Ultimate Spider-Man*, *Justice League of America* (*JLA*), *Punisher*, *Wonder Woman*, *100 Bullets*, and *Lucifer*. See Table 27.1 for a complete list of sampled monthly titles.

Trade paperbacks were chosen from the ranked list of the top 30 best sellers. The list was divided into ranked groups of 10, from which 2 books were selected from each. The sample included *Dark Knight Strikes Again*, *Powers: Anarchy*, *Wolverine: The Brotherhood*, *Heaven's War*, *Violent Cases*, and *Sleeper: Out in the Cold*. Titles represented both superhero and nonsuperhero genres, and children's books were avoided. See Table 27.1 for the list of sampled trade paperbacks.

Qualitative analyses can suffer from the validity problem of selection bias because they involve researchers selecting a sample in a nonrandom fashion to prove or disprove an a priori hypothesis.... Several measures were taken to counterbalance the selection bias associated with a purposive sample, including the use of a relatively large sample size, the selection of titles across the spectrum of top sellers, and the inclusion of superhero and nonsuperhero genres. As the historian Lustick ... reminds qualitative researchers, selection of sources should be a self-conscious endeavor that recognizes the variance of information within a "normal distribution of implicit theoretical commitments." ... Thus, patterns can be discerned without ignoring competing narratives, and confidence in results is increased as the size and narrative scope of a sample increase.

Comic books, unlike other literary media, provide juxtapositions between what is seen and what is read, offering more possibilities for interpretation. Identifying manifest or surface content involved noting the explicit behavior of the characters and the social environment they occupy by following the interaction between the language and graphics. As McCloud ... notes, most American comic books play on the differences between words and pictures, both of which contribute to the comic book's "vocabulary." ... Although graphic depictions have become increasingly realistic with the advent of computer animation, comics still operate iconically— using pictures that are simpler than reality as symbolic cues for interpretation—which, when coupled with well-crafted, yet sparse narrative or dialogue, can convey worlds of plot development in only a few frames.

If we dig deeper, we find that the juxtaposition of words and pictures also contributes to latent or underlying content, which is more relevant for answering the policy questions implied by the depictions of justice in the comic book. Denisoff ... cautions that social scientists conducting content analysis may find meaning that

Table 27.1   Comic Books Selected

Monthly Title	Issues	Publisher	Rank	Distribution*
Ultimate Spider-Man	51, 52, 53, 54	Marvel	9	97
JLA	91, 92, 93	DC	21	58
Punisher	33, 34, 35, 36, 37	Marvel	43	38
Batman DC	788, 789	DC	50	36
Wonder Woman	197, 198, 199, 200	DC	67	29
Fables	19, 20, 21, 23	DC	80	25
Rose & Thorn	1, 2, 3, 4, 5, 6	DC	92	22
Superman Kansas Sighting	1, 2	DC	120	18
100 Bullets	47, 48, 49	DC	128	17
Lucifer	141	DC	141	13
Losers	7, 8	DC	154	12
Route 666	19	CrossGen	177	10
Sam & Twitch	1, 2, 3, 4, 5, 6	Image	186	9
Queen & Country	21, 22, 23, 24, 25	Oni Press	207	6
Trade Paperback Title	Issues	Publisher	Rank	Distribution*
Dark Knight Strikes Again	—	DC	3	5.1
Powers Volume V: Anarchy	—	Image	5	5.1
Wolverine: Brotherhood	—	Marvel	14	3
Heaven's War	—	Image	17	2.8
Violent Cases	—	Dark Horse	22	2.4
Sleeper: Out in the Cold	—	DC	25	2.3

Source: ICV2 sales estimates based on January 13, 2004, data from Diamond Publisher (2004) comics distributors.

*Distribution is represented in thousands of copies.

the author neither intended nor the reading public perceived. Regardless, such underlying meaning arguably exists to be discovered provided that it has a foundation in the more obvious surface content. Interrater reliability in discovering latent content was accomplished by having two readers approach each comic book in the sample independently before joining forces in the analysis. On all but two comic books, there was agreement on the themes represented. Regarding the two disagreements, further discussion settled the discrepancies.

Once the sample was compiled, a content analysis was conducted to systematically understand the crime and justice themes contained in the comics as social artifacts. Content analysis involves the study of messages and the meaning they convey. . . . To examine the extent to which contemporary comic books reproduce dominant notions of justice, four main research questions were developed:

- What is the crime problem addressed in the comic book?
- What is the desired social order in the community of the comic book?
- How is justice achieved, legally or extralegally?
- What is the implied policy message of the comic book?

To ascertain the dominant notions of justice revealed in the comic books, we must first address the crime problem depicted in the comic book. Based on the literature about comic books we examined, it is expected that the most frequent crime problem depicted in the comic books will be street crimes. As such, individual criminal intent, motivations, and pathologies will be highlighted by the comic books with little concern for the social forces propelling the actor. . . .

Moreover, as has historically occurred in American comics . . . , it is expected that contemporary comic book story arcs will imagine nostalgic communities characterized by a desired social order that values a nostalgic patriotism and retributivism. These dominant notions of justice will be addressed by examining the responses to the crime problem and implied policy messages. Based on previous literature . . . , it is expected that protagonists will resort to extralegal approaches to reassert the desired social order. Therefore, we hypothesize that these comic books explicitly or implicitly endorse retributive criminal justice policies.

Results

HOLY CRIME PROBLEM, BATMAN!

Crime themes were separated into three categories: dominant crime problems, secondary crime problems, and social problems. . . . The dominant crime problem represents the primary problem that the protagonist faces in terms of criminal behavior and acts as the focus of the plot development. Secondary crime problems are depictions of crimes that happen along the way as the protagonist responds to the dominant crime problem. In essence, these are crime-related subplots. The social problems category relates to portrayals of social, but not necessarily criminal, ills such as environmental destruction and homophobia.

The crime themes that emerged from the sample included organized crime, government corruption, terrorism, violent street crime, domestic violence, and war crimes, among others. In contrast to the expectation that street crime would be the dominant crime problem, organized crime was found most frequently. In *Violent Cases*, for example, a retelling of the Al Capone stories is juxtaposed with the protagonist's reflection on his boyhood loss of innocence. He comes to realize the scope of human depravity in the world through hearing stories of mob violence from Capone's former osteopath. Organized crime also comes to the forefront in *Fables*, *Ultimate Spider-Man*, *Wonder Woman*, and *Sleeper*.

Government corruption is often depicted as a dominant and secondary crime theme. For example, *The Losers* are a group of rogue CIA agents who are betrayed and left for dead by an unknown operative. The group, determined to identify the mastermind and avenge their betrayal, recalls numerous historical instances of corruption perpetrated by the U.S. government.

Another dominant crime problem is terrorism. *Queen & Country*, a British spy book, depicts an M16-like operations chief lamenting the complications of "the endless inquiries into off-shore accounts and wire transfers" that the War on Terror has spawned. . . . The image shows the operations chief swishing his wine glass in a show of power and cool sophistication that could only come from a veteran of the most secret intelligence operations. Yet the image also implies that even the most sophisticated spies are becoming increasingly challenged by the complexity of the new age of terrorism, which is worthy of a deep sigh.

A less frequent dominant crime problem is psychopathic criminality, referring to plots featuring a villain whose primary motivation is a psychological need brought on by some sort of psychosis to hurt others. Of note is the world of *Sam & Twitch*, in which the detectives combat such offenders as pedophile clowns, vengeful "Frankenwomen," and other criminals described as "monsters." . . .

Violent street crime emerges as the most prevalent secondary crime theme. For example, in *Sam & Twitch*, Twitch's daughter is kidnapped off the street by a criminal seeking revenge on Twitch, the detective who caught him after a prior offense. . . . These panels evoke every parent's worst nightmare. The disguised predator lies in wait, dressed as a helpless elderly lady, as the young girl approaches. The attire of the young girl, her cheerleading skirt and turtleneck, portrays her innocence. Quickly, the predator violently abducts her and forces her into the trunk of his car.

Finally, several comic books illustrate social problems, but in general these problems provide background or subplot material. Global economic inequality is touched on in *JLA*. *Queen & Country* explores homophobia in military institutions while *Wonder Woman* exhibits concern about the environment.

RETURNING TO SMALLVILLE: COMMUNITY REDEMPTION

The crime problem represents a crisis for the community, or other idealized entity, in the form of a nation, planet, or universe. In the sampled comics, the following imagined social orders were identified: American hegemony, transnationalism/globalism, cosmic order, small-town America, intergalactic cooperation, and traditional England.

Most often the comics reflect a need to maintain American hegemony, expressed as a longing for America as a bastion of freedom and democracy and as a super-power leading the world. This occurs in *Batman Detective Comics, Ultimate Spider-Man, Powers, 100 Bullets, Sam & Twitch, Route 666, Punisher,* and *Rose & Thorn*. In *Route 666*, for instance, the cold war is revisited, and Cassie, the protagonist, has the superhuman ability to see the communists for who they are: demons. Cassie must appeal to the government of Empyrean, a thinly disguised America, to prevent the demons from taking over the country. As one of her allies states, "If Cassie can make someone see one of these creatures the way she made us see 'em, then maybe we can organize a decent counterattack!"...

Transnationalism or globalism is idealized in several crime books, including *JLA, The Losers, Queen & Country, Sleeper,* and *Dark Knight*. This category embodies the goal of international cooperation and the use of transnational governing bodies, similar to the United Nations, as a means of maintaining order. In *JLA*, Superman is called away from his post as a representative at the United Nations (UN) in order to respond, with his superhero sidekicks, to an alien invasion. Although this comic book has an interplanetary setting, the superheroes seek order among nations on planet Earth and do not generally cooperate with aliens. In addition, *Wonder Woman* works toward maintaining international balance as the UN representative of her Amazon island nation.

Small-town America is imagined in *Superman: Kansas Sighting*, in which Superman returns to his midwestern American roots in Smallville. Small-town America is also idealized in *Wolverine: The Brotherhood*. In this story arc, Wolverine is avenging the murder of a small-town girl who escaped from a terrorist militia (which also operates as a female sex slavery cult) only to be hunted down and killed by the militia leaders. As Wolverine states during a denouement moment with his friend Elf (a.k.a. Nightcrawler), "They were a cult. They'd broken a town. Made it afraid. They kidnapped women. Girls. And they used them up."... Exiled to New York City, the characters in *Fables* long for a return to their bucolic place of origin, Fabletown, a pseudo-America with democratic elections and a criminal justice system complete with rules of evidence and due process protections.

The cosmic battle of good versus evil reigns in *Lucifer* and *Heaven's War*. These plots imagine a community whose citizens always choose good over evil and fight against moral relativism and Satanism. The worldview in both comic books reflects a need to restore Heaven and Hell to their proper cosmic positions with the eventual defeat of Hell in an apocalyptic age. By contrast, despite the focus on good and evil, *Violent Cases* reminisces about traditional England; the main character recalls his childhood in Portsmouth living with his maternal grandparents. Remembrances of custom-made tweed coats, a fifth birthday party at the Queen's hotel, adults drinking sherry, and grimy rain-soaked streets are juxtaposed with instances of probable child abuse and stories of gangsters from Capone's former osteopath. *Violent Cases* ends with the protagonist commenting that "Nobody seems to wear a hat these days."

Gee Whiz! The Authorities Cannot Protect Us

Unfortunately, in the world of comic books, those entrusted with the job of maintaining an ordered community through public security are largely unsuccessful. The majority of the comic books depicted government and law enforcement as ineffective in the fight against crime. Often the police were characterized as either dimwitted or lacking the resources to wage the battle against the crime problem. In *Route 666*, the police are seen reclining in their station reading the crime news in a tabloid newspaper, ignorant of a dangerous plot brewing. In *Fables*, the mayor, Old King Cole, and the Wolf from Little Red Riding, who works as Fabletown's detective, argue about being unable to gain a conviction of Prince Charming for the murder of Bluebeard.... Old King Cole blames it on the detective's inability to gather admissible evidence, but the detective faults Fabletown's convoluted rules of evidence and due process requirements.

Government and law enforcement corruption occurred in the plots of a majority of comic books, many of which paired corruption and ineffectiveness themes. In *Wolverine: The Brotherhood*, an ATF agent brutalizes a suspect in interrogation as a necessary means of gaining information about a dangerous right-wing cult. In *Dark Knight Strikes Again, The Losers* and *Rose & Thorn*, the original dominant crime problem involves government corruption, which further complicates the response to crime. In these stories, the protagonists find that the authorities have created the crime problem. *Dark Knight Strikes Again* is set in a society that has deteriorated into a police state, with a holographic president, news merging into entertainment, and Congress passing the "Freedom From Information Act." One of the superheroes' arch-nemeses has gained control of the world and has, at least temporarily, suppressed all superheroes.

THIS LOOKS LIKE A JOB FOR SUPERMAN: EXTRALEGAL JUSTICE

The primary path to justice reflects extralegal responses to crime or taking the law into one's own hands. The plots reveal a continuum of support for extralegal or vigilante paths to achieve justice. *Lucifer, Heaven's War,* and the *Punisher* represent the most extreme abandonment of the rule of law in favor of extralegal moral crusading. The Punisher, for example, never attempts to work within the legal system and immediately embarks on his vigilante mission in the opening pages of the story arc. Necessitated by the confluence of the geopolitical forces inciting organized and transnational crime and the inadequate and/or corrupt law enforcement responses, the plot inevitably moves toward the position of last resort: retaliatory, technically illegal actions that must be tolerated in a time of crisis. The narrator in the *Punisher* explains, "He judges them, he passes sentence, then he blows them away. Justice happens in the time it takes to pull the trigger."...

Along the path to extralegal justice, several additional themes emerged that suggest an apparent formula in comic books: justifications for the use of violence, framing the world starkly as good versus evil, building and cooperating as a team, responding to broken treaties, taking control of the media, and soul-searching about the role of superheroes.

A majority of the titles highlighted the crisis justification for violence: Disorder has gotten so out of hand that the protagonist must resort to violent solutions outside the law. For instance, in *Punisher,* although Spider-Man and Daredevil take issue with the extreme vigilantism, their perspective is drowned out by the triumphant extralegal violence. In *Dark Knight Strikes Again,* Batman swoops down to save the citizens of Gotham only after legitimate law enforcement and other superheroes have failed to bring justice. In the context of the greater evil of the destruction of values such as public safety, democracy, and individual freedom, violence outside the law for social good is depicted as a justifiable response.

In most of the comic books sampled, good and evil are visually depicted with no shading in between. For example, in *Rose & Thorn,* the neighborhoods that form the backdrop to the story are either an idealized urban park landscape with technocolor foliage or a seedy, socially disorganized part of the city where crime is rampant. This mirrors the duality of the Dr. Jekyll/Mr. Hyde-like main character. As Rose, she is a sweet, law-abiding woman with bright blue eyes, but when she is Thorn, she is a green-eyed, dangerous, arbitrarily violent, and hypersexualized psychopath....

Other comic books are more ambiguous regarding the theme of good versus evil. For example, in *The Losers,* the U.S. government has clearly betrayed a team of CIA agents, yet when the characters are reflecting on the litany of corruptive behaviors perpetrated by the government throughout history, the scenes are portrayed in a hazy blue/gray color, graphically revealing the shades of gray surrounding the conduct. Additionally, in over half of the comic books sampled, the protagonist assembles a team of allies to fight for justice. *The Losers* are a rag-tag team of rogue CIA agents working together to understand why they were betrayed by the government. *JLA* revolves around a cooperative theme in which Superman is called away from a UN meeting by Plastic Man to meet with team members about an alien invasion....

Half of the titles explored the theme of broken treaties among rivals and broken contracts among partners. In the world of comic books, heroes and villains battle according to rules previously agreed on by participants. The challenge for protagonists comes when either allies or enemies begin to play outside the rules. Antagonists often betray prior contracts, thus freeing up the hero(es) to also play dirty and become vigilantes. For instance, in *Lucifer,* the delegates of Hell explicitly broke the rules established by Lucifer when they inhabited the body of the protagonist, thus disturbing the balance between good versus evil and necessitating a cosmic battle.

Justice is also achieved by using the media to one's advantage. Avenues include utilizing cable talk shows (*Sam & Twitch*), penning a tell-all best seller (*Wonder Woman*), and releasing surveillance footage to news programs (*Powers: Anarchy*). In fact, Miss Misery directly addresses the importance of media to her partner and states, "Pop culture is just another way to control the masses" (*Sleeper: Out in the Cold*).

Finally, over half the titles belonging to the superhero genre featured soul-searching moments during which the hero reflects on his or her role in society. Historically, the classic thoughtful and perhaps reluctant hero was Spider-Man. True to form, the *Ultimate Spider-Man* story arc shows a superhero ready to leave the hero circuit for a calm and settled life with Mary Jane. *Wolverine: The Brotherhood* follows the hero as he is plagued by the thought that, by killing 27 people during his revenge sequence, he may have turned into a mere animal. His friend Elf (a.k.a. Nightcrawler) consoles him: "Were those men evil? Without question. By killing them in your rage are you evil? You are unique [Wolverine].

And I do not speak of what has been done to you. Is the wolf evil when it culls the sickness from the herd?" . . .

DEATHWORTHINESS: IT'S CLOBBERIN' TIME

Frequently, antagonists and even peripheral characters are killed as the protagonist travels the path to justice. However, not every character is morally "deathworthy" in the eyes of the protagonist. In fact, three levels of deathworthiness, or justifiable victims the hero kills, were observed.

Most frequently, protagonists will only kill characters explicitly responsible for harms done to themselves or their family members. In *Batman Detective Comics*, a suspect falsely accused of a murder rampage turns murderously violent to avenge the wrongs done to him by the criminal justice system. The narrator states, "Wrongly accused, wrongly imprisoned, Eddie Hurst's sudden madness, surely, was forgivable." As the story arc unfolds, Batman openly sympathizes with the suspect's need for personal revenge. In *Sam & Twitch*, Twitch resorts to murder to avenge a crime against his daughter. The message of the story arc is that seeking revenge for crimes against one's family is a moral obligation and may be rewarded rather than punished.

Furthermore, some protagonists kill anyone morally depraved, for any reason, whom they encounter during their fight for justice. Even criminals guilty of minor offenses may warrant an unofficial death penalty. For example, a street junkie is blown away after informing the Punisher of the whereabouts of a sought-after criminal. . . . As a street junkie, the informer is death-eligible under the Punisher's paradigm of ridding the community of all criminals, big and small.

Finally, in a minority of the comic books sampled, even innocents are eligible for death as part of a cosmic battle between good and evil. In *Lucifer*, a morally laudable John is nonetheless demonically possessed and ultimately killed as part of a larger battle between Heaven and Hell. When John asks the demon possessing him why he deserved his fate, the demon replies that it isn't deserved: "You were just neutral ground, John," the demon says. . . .

Discussion

Cultural criminology suggests that media reflect and reproduce social reality. Popular media are replete with representations of crime and justice, and comic books are no exception. The extent to which comic books reflect dominant notions of justice is evident in the crime problems faced by protagonists, the imagined communities that promote American hegemony, the preference for retribution, and the tacit approval of extralegal means of achieving justice.

Our analysis revealed that contemporary comic books focus on organized crime and terrorism, rather than on street crime and psychopathic criminality. The crime problems depicted in this sample are complex affairs involving multiple entities, often legitimate institutions gone bad, that operate in a variety of contexts transnationally, intergalactically, and across cosmic dimensions. However, at the same time, when considering subplots, street crime is quite prevalent.

That the crime problem extends beyond the borders of the United States is most likely a reflection of the increasing awareness and concern regarding global issues in a post-9/11 world. Terrorism and organized crime networks operating on a variety of fronts in a geopolitical struggle for power and control reflect current political dynamics. Further, the crime problem presents a formidable crisis for those who imagine their community otherwise. A plurality of comic books sampled seeks to maintain an imagined community of perfect order and safety in the context of an American, hegemonic, yet democratic, political entity. The imagined community is focused on an urban core hoped to be swept of the dark vices that blight it, such as is the case with Batman's Gotham City. A notable minority of the comic books exhibit utopian yearnings for small-town America, like Superman's Smallville, and a remembered traditional England. These three categories together reflect a status quo-oriented goal for the protagonist who aims to achieve not a revolutionary new world, but a reactionary old order.

As expected, legitimate criminal justice institutions are either too corrupt or too ineffective—or both—to adequately respond to the challenges posed by the crime problem. Positive portrayals of legitimate authorities are rare, thus necessitating revenge-oriented, extralegal justice. This represents a uniquely comic book-related theme that can be appreciated in contrast to popular American TV crime dramas. In *CSI*, *Law & Order*, *24*, and *NYPD Blue*, to name only a few, legitimate authorities are largely shown as sexy, clever, and morally justified as they use their logical, physical, and technological talents to bring down all manner of crime. Corrupt authorities surface in particular episodes, but they are eventually rooted out in these time-honored morality plays.

Retribution and revenge policy messages appear to dominate the comic book landscape. The message in

Ultimate Spider-Man resonates within nearly half of the sample: The hero must be on the right side of the moral equation, but not necessarily on the right side of the law. Frequently, and ironically, the rule of law can only be defended by acting outside the law to restore an out-of-control world to balance. Extralegality, then, gains a veneer of legality....

The irony of comic books as a revenge fantasy is that evil is employed against evil in hopes of giving birth to good, a uniquely Judeo-Christian notion of apocalyptic redemption....

Much like the book of Revelation and earlier prophetic narratives depict a symbolic return to the Kingdom of God lost to humans after the Original Sin, so too do comic books reflect violence as a hope-and-redemption strategy in the American cultural consciousness....

Our analysis indicates that for a return to paradise lost any number of revenge killings can be undertaken and a curious balance sheet ensues. To avenge one person's murder, Wolverine kills an additional 27 people. As the analysis of death-worthiness reveals, some characters' lives are just not as valuable as others. If the 27 people are morally depraved, then no harm in the larger sense has occurred. Victims of revenge violence are not the chosen ones during the apocalyptic battle against crime, and thus their demise in the metaphoric Lake of Fire restores balance even if the number of people killed by the hero reflects a numeric imbalance. Indeed, retribution extends beyond utilitarian thinking. (Notably, there are a few indications of utilitarian-style deterrence policy messages in the sample.) Retribution as a policy goal seeks what is deserved.... In comic books, such a symmetrical response frequently involves numerous death-worthy characters whose lives are fundamentally devalued due to the characters.

In fact, loss of life is easier to tolerate when the loss is considered inevitable, as a necessary consequence of action. During wartime, the death-worthiness of innocent civilians is referred to as "collateral damage."... In a December 2006 press conference, Bush indicated that he believed about 30,000 deaths of military troops and civilians had resulted from the War in Iraq. He then commented about the decision to go to war: "Knowing what I know today, I'd make the decision again."... In response to a question regarding the loss of civilian lives as a result of the War on Terror, Paul Wolfowitz, Deputy Secretary of Defense, stated simply that "bad things happen in combat zones."... The political climate reflects the justification of mass violence that stems from the clear delineation of good and evil and granting oneself as the moral executor of the abolishment of evil. Comic book protagonists are depicted as holding themselves similarly responsible for the moral and spiritual fate of the world....

Likewise, Bush called the War in Iraq the "moral equivalent" of the Second World War and likened the Iraqi insurgents to the German and Japanese in that conflict.... The nostalgia for the widely considered just-war actions of the Allies in the Second World War is utilized to garner support for the War in Iraq as a moral quest where the enemy is clearly evil and the motivations of Allied forces are morally necessary. Likewise, the nostalgia for the Second World War and the cold war are palpable in the American hegemony themes in the comic books sampled, most notably in *Route 666* and *Heaven's War*.

In contrast, nearly a half-dozen of the comic books reflect a deep sense of futility, in which justice is completely outside the control of most humans and superhumans. According to the worldview depicted in *Sleeper: Out in the Cold*, oligarchic elites control all aspects of the political and social order, and most humans are mere pawns in the game. The protagonist exhibits no hope that the social and political order can be changed, and thus a fundamental injustice is the normative state. In *JLA*, terrorists, insurgents, and fundamentalists are seen as ultimately unstoppable because there can be no criminal justice policy response for criminal acts of desperation. This particularly nihilistic view of the world is constructed in a minority of comic books and suggests one way that the medium in some cases reflects an anti- or postapocalyptic consciousness.

Rehabilitation and Peacemaking: With Great Power Comes Great Responsibility

Our sample indicated that paths to justice exist on a broad continuum, and alternatives to vigilantism and retribution—such as restorative justice/diplomacy and rehabilitation—are also depicted. As Williams . . . discussed in an analysis of seven comic books, although it is tempting to make vast generalizations about comic books, there is enough variation in themes to warrant a more muted conclusion. Employing a Gramscian framework to discuss comic books as sites of hegemonic and counterhegemonic discourse, smaller, independent comic books can be vehicles for counterhegemonic themes of social justice.... This study indicates, however, that a not-so-silent minority of top-selling comic books describe alternatives to extralegal justice, including main staples like *Wonder Woman* and *100 Bullets*.

For example, peacemaking criminology is reflected in *Wonder Woman*. Wonder Woman prefers to talk through issues with her enemies whenever possible to restore order. As a representative of her home country in a transnational governing body, Wonder Woman envisions a kinder, gentler world. Rehabilitation is suggested by *100 Bullets* in a storyline in which criminals are likened to animals in cages; as the protagonist ceases his drug habit, he is shown freeing a tiger from a cage. The tiger leaves only a trace of footprints in the sand.

LIMITATIONS OF THE STUDY

As a starting point for the holistic study of comic books across genres, we took a broad approach that sought to underscore the basic constructions of crime and justice. As a result, a detailed analysis of the interaction between themes of crime and justice and portrayals of gender, class, and race was beyond the scope of this study. Questions for future research include whether Wonder Woman's peacemaking ideology is acceptable to readers because she is female. Are stereotypes of women as nurturing and nonviolent playing into her construction as the superheroic diplomat? Another red flag is raised in regards to race and death-worthiness. Is it a coincidence that the morally depraved street junkie, death-worthy under the logic of the Punisher, is Black? Is there a working-class logic underlying mainstream comics, in which street justice is the avenue of the economically powerless, disenfranchised from the halls of political power?

Conclusion

Although there are notable exceptions, contemporary mainstream comic books tend to fit into formulaic revenge fantasy plots, in which protagonists respond to crime as a larger-than-life global or cosmic phenomenon. They are willing to act violently outside the law to restore the rule of law in a utopian American-style democracy. Retribution, and valuing some people's lives over others based on a Judeo-Christian moral balance sheet, is the underlying policy message conveyed by the medium.

Overly positivistic hype over the effects of comic books has created moral panics in the past, suggesting that comic books directly influence readers' behavior, causing juvenile delinquency . . . and a retreat from Christianity. . . . However, our results show that mainstream comics push American values to their extreme in defense of status quo notions of preserving public safety in democracies and maintaining a Christian dualistic worldview. Comic books may not directly influence behavior, but they are a cultural resting place—perhaps a cultural sleeper cell—for an extreme paranoia about crime, fantasies about violent revenge, and longings for a utopian American hegemony. Given the current rise of fundamentalist Christian ideology in mainstream politics and the suppression of the rule of law in a time of paranoia, it is no surprise that an increase in comic book-inspired Hollywood movies and interest in graphic novels is simultaneously palpable. Best-selling comic books are a cultural touchstone for conservative, reactionary values, such as criminal punishment as retribution, and reinforce the status quo with seductive and exciting storylines.

Questions

1. How do cultural criminologists regard media representations of crime and justice?

2. Comic books send what message regarding criminal justice?

CHAPTER 28

Framing Homicide Narratives in Newspapers

Mediated Witness and the Construction of Virtual Victimhood

Moira Peelo

University of Lancaster, UK

Introduction

This chapter explores some of the ways in which sensational newspaper reporting contributes to the construction of public narratives about homicide. It is argued that to make sense of the construction and role of public narratives, researchers need to explore the nature of the reader–newspaper dialogue at a microlevel. Most particularly, "mediated witness" is presented as one means by which the newspaper reader is invited to take sides not just about the human interest story surrounding the brutal events, but in the social commentary that attaches to such killing. Mediated witness is presented as a stylized dialogue made up of a collection of authorial techniques that attempt to align the reader emotionally with victimhood; this *virtual* victimhood is distinguished here from the real experience of families, friends, and acquaintances of *actual* victims. The examples of defamiliarization and the process of objectifying victims of homicide are used to illustrate how mediated witness both allows readers to consume crime yet, as a part of society, distance ourselves from the actuality of events.

Newspapers express emotions surrounding major events and, it is argued, that what have been identified as "megacases" of homicide. . . . can bring to the surface social divisions and tensions that are difficult for a society to manage. Megamedia stories on homicide are unusual cases that particularly offend society; some are *repeatedly* reported, transforming them into a point of reference that can help us to interpret later killings. . . . Megacases are often framed to appear most supportive of those immediately hurt by killing. Yet this alignment is really a point of entry to a social commentary by which newspapers and their readers can restore a sense of control by confirming a viewpoint of society and its ills and neutralize anguish by objectifying victims of homicide who have become, therein, public property. It is precisely for these two reasons that the gulf between virtual victimhood and the actual experience of victimhood needs to be emphasized. This social commentary echoes Katz's . . . thesis that reading crime stories is a form of moral workout, in which readers "work out individual perspectives on moral questions of a quite general yet eminently personal relevance."

At one level, megakillings can be seen as an example of a moral panic. In particular are the three core ingredients that Cohen . . . outlines: a suitable enemy (murderers), a suitable victim, and agreement that the homicide is part of a wider social malaise . . . about which action should be taken. Here it is argued that this gives us only a partial explanation and that, although relevant, much is missed by settling too rapidly for the concept of moral panic alone to explain all examples of newspaper–reader emotionality and intense media activity. Recently, Innes

Source: "Framing homicide narratives in newspapers," by Peelo, M., (2006), *Crime, Media, Culture, 2,* 159–175. Reprinted by permission of Sage Publications, Ltd.

... commented that the "analytic purchase of the concept has been loosened" by its *loose* application in many situations. In relation to public narratives, Peelo ... has argued that these are both contested and based on cumulative knowledge over time, unlike the short-term frenzy of moral panics. To understand, for example, virtual victimhood and the objectification of homicide cases, additional (and more specific) analysis is needed to understand how the reporting of serious crime is constructed in newspapers over time.

Megamurders would undoubtedly figure as what Innes ... describes as signal crime. They would be one of the few major crimes repeatedly and widely covered that ... :

> involves a crime incident being constructed by journalists through their use of particular representational and rhetorical techniques, and interpreted by audiences, as an index of the state of society and social order. ...

What is argued here, however, is that, although representational and rhetorical techniques are an essential part of deconstructing public narratives around major homicides, there is a dynamic process at work: After the experience of consumption via virtual victimhood, the process moves to one of distancing via objectification and restoration of one's view of society within a contested narrative.

The concept of signal crimes illustrates the ways in which the emotionality surrounding crime debates has moved up criminology's agenda. Traditionally, concerns about social emotions have been raised in relation to the role of the media in promoting fear of and about crime. ... The range of other possible emotions—in addition to fear and anxiety—that surround crime have become, of themselves, a focus for criminology. So, for example, Presdee ... explores the pleasure associated with transgression as part of a wider approach to cultural criminology. Emotional experience is not just a personal response, but one that has the potential for collectivity; hence, the symbolism of crime reporting in society is closely linked to emotionality. ... Transcending these debates about the types of emotion surrounding crime is a concern as to whether media representation of crime is an active ingredient in the criminal justice process. The study from which this chapter is drawn was not based on expectations of simple cause-and-effect relationships, with an assumption that reporting leads to a specific social outcome. But I do argue that media representation can actively contribute to a society's construction of

crime and therefore requires examination; megakillings, in particular, occupy a powerful, symbolic place in our collective, cultural history. Even if it is not possible to assess the impact of reporting on each individual reader, newspapers are, nonetheless, powerful voices contributing to the public narratives within which societies make sense of crime. This chapter is based on an expectation that researchers wish to deconstruct this process at a micro- as well as a macrolevel.

Mediated Witness: Dialogue, Representation, and Objectification

Reiner ... has argued that news organizations use a variety of sources. This is illustrated time and again in homicide reporting, in which the voices of victims' families, friends, and police are used frequently, and often these various voices are used to critical effect. Yet although writers such as Ericson et al. ... have developed a sophisticated framework within which to interpret and understand the interrelations of reporting and authority, with all their layers of complexity, it is still possible for the emphasis in analyses to cast journalists as separate from readerships. It is this balance that Wykes ... redresses when she places journalists in their wider world, sharing social values with their readers. How then do we understand Reiner's ... comment that news media "reproduce order in the process of representing it" ... if we cannot depend on a model of journalism that casts journalists as separate from the world and newspaper production simply as a channel for the views of the powerful? The resolving of this apparent paradox lies, in part, in the recognition by researchers of a need for a microanalysis of text that goes beyond the traditional counting of column inches or analysis of the story production-selection processes.

STYLIZED DIALOGUE

Repetition is one of the key techniques that turns homicide stories into megastories, both repetition around the time of the case and its trial and, in some cases, repetition over many years. Repetition is part of the stylized dialogue that constitutes reader–newspaper reciprocity ... , a reciprocity that lies in the actual medium of communication.

In this chapter, the megacases I draw on for illustration are the James Bulger killing, the Moors Murders, and the Gloucestershire killings ... , and I consider in more detail the newspaper response to the killing of Philip Lawrence. Some of these megacases have become part of a general background knowledge of murder: They have achieved this status either by being repeatedly reactivated as part of the story of another killing or because some new event has allowed repetition of a shocking homicide story. . . . In these ways, they are sometimes used as a measure against which other cases are tacitly weighed, hence they can contribute to the knowledge that helps us interpret new stories. They are reviewed, mentioned, and brought out again regularly. In this way, megastories can remain an active ingredient in the construction of the public narratives by which society makes sense of major crime long after the events. . . .

The dialogue between readers and newspapers is a curious one: It can be seen as both influencing opinion and as struggling to reflect readers' viewpoints. Berger . . . writes that "narratives rely on their readers having stores of information that make it possible to understand what is going on" . . . and succinctly summarizes "reader-response theorists" or "reception theorists" as arguing that most texts "require readers to fill in a lot of blank areas." . . . Readers are an active part of the equation; although newspapers and their readerships may fit each other only approximately, they nonetheless share and *recognize* aspects of each other's viewpoints (even if one cannot be sure that they *share* that viewpoint in all its details).

So, for example, in the general reporting of homicide (as opposed to the megacases), different newspapers select different killings to report (although their criteria for selection remain similar), engaging in a subtly different set of dialogues with their own readerships. Yet although newspapers are anticipating subtly different stores of information and reception contexts to each other, these separate readership–newspaper dialogues share family relationships across papers and similarities of distortion in the representation of homicide, albeit illustrated by different cases. . . . The family relationship that is distinct in terms of device—even where choice of story, language, and presentation is quite different—is that the narrative engages the reader in relation to close witness of victimhood. Hence, in this chapter, I argue that megacases have not only the potential to form a part of the store of knowledge that we bring to understanding homicide, but their narrative style is part of the history that has sensitized readers to respond and to fill in the blanks in distinct ways.

To interact with readers requires newspapers to use shorthand symbols, making it easier for readers to know when to hiss and boo as the villain appears and when to

identify with the good and worthy. Symbolically, all murders—indeed all serious crimes—have roles in the drama assigned to victims and to perpetrators; they are investigated and prosecuted by an additional cast of players. These roles can become easily recognized by depiction in stereotypical ways. . . . Mediated witness is the paradoxical phenomenon of *virtual* experience in which detail about a homicide is communicated in a way that engages us personally and emotionally on the side of those who are hurt. As witnesses to the drama, we are invited to focus our attention on and emotionally align ourselves with victims, covictims, and survivors of homicide.

REPRESENTATION AND MEDIATED WITNESS

A difference between the realities of narrative and life needs to be acknowledged because public discussion of homicide can sound strangely divorced from the serious and profound disruption caused. Reality is perhaps too naive a word to describe the gulf between virtual representations and the substantive materiality of life experience. Further, analysis of the reporting of megacases is especially unsettling: Not only does it remind us of unhappy events, but the history of reporting turns these cases into social property, leaving them shorn of the personal meaning arising from direct experience. It needs to be said when discussing homicide that illegal killing is an act of great violence and social disquiet. Killing is an event that disturbs greatly—the families of victims, the families of killers and their surrounding society, and those professionals who work with homicide cases. Indeed, one of the distinctions between megacases and most other homicides lies in the scale of social disturbance.

Hence, in this chapter, I distinguish between the nature of the actual, personal experience of losing a family member, friend, or acquaintance through illegal killing and the representation of emotionality stirred in readerships by the techniques of mediated witness.

Defamiliarization. The devices of mediated witness stir us emotionally as readers and as viewers and, thereby, cause us to feel more fully involved in the actual event (or events) than has been the case. The study by Peelo et al. . . ., like others, has shown that the profile of actual homicides is, in reality, quite different *from* those reported. What makes a megakilling especially newsworthy is the exceptional quality of its horror, its oddness. Yet, paradoxically, a part of what *turns* a murder into entertainment is the shock of ordinariness invaded by the brutal or the corrupt. Berger . . . refers to Victor Shlovsky's . . . notion of how art defamiliarizes what is known by presenting it back in unusual ways. Katz . . . has described this phenomenon as one that helps to spur the readers' outraged reaction because they "can see the event as potentially within his or her own experience." . . . Getzel and Masters . . . have discussed how one casualty of illegal killings for covictims and survivors is a loss of trust in the world and assumptions or beliefs about how society operates. It is an echo of this loss of trust, at a different level, that also shocks the rest of society: Killing is a threat to social agreements and understandings about how ordinary, everyday life functions. The known becomes strangely unknown via apparent moments of communication.

The shock to society of a killing is greater according to its invasion into homely coziness; the greater the shock, the harder it becomes to regroup our sense of social order. Mediated witness brings homicide closer to personal experience through the reporting of moments and objects of familiarity, which, thereby, become grotesque by a process of defamiliarization, and this brings us closer to the chaos and disorder that we fear. For a period of time, what is safe and home is transmuted by shock into alien, strange, and hostile otherness. . . . Topping . . . describes . . . such [a] moment when, as a police officer, he was investigating the Moors Murders case. This was a series of child murders that took place in the 1960s, named after Saddleworth Moors, where the children were buried by murderers Ian Brady and Myra Hindley. When interviewing Brady, a moment of ordinary domesticity from his own life was reproduced in extraordinary circumstances. In 1963, Brady and Hindley hired a car from a particular Manchester garage:

> In the event her licence did not arrive in time and it was not until Saturday 23rd that they picked up the two-door white Anglia they had booked. (As she told me this I was startled by the memory of having hired a white Anglia from Warren's Autos myself in the 1960s and of taking my young family on holiday in it.) . . .

Shocking Events Distort the Ordinariness of Lives and Its Meanings to People

Not only do mediating instruments bring horror nearer, but they also interpret, contaminate, and contribute to the construction of our experience—hence, *mediation*. They are not neutral, but contribute a part to our understanding. Defamiliarization is a strong technique through which the ordinary is reconstructed and

presented back to us. . . . It is in these small ways that crime threatens society as much as the larger ways. Similarly, the West case overturned familiar notions of family life, its safety, and ordinariness. The Gloucestershire serial killings were named after the county in which they took place from 1967 onward (although the bodies were not discovered until 1994). Fred West seemed to be accepted by neighbors as endlessly engaged in "do it yourself" work around the home—a current sign of familial respectability. More recently, the case of family doctor Harold Shipman, convicted in January 2000 of the murder of 15 of his patients, has undermined safe notions about old-style family doctors working to provide personal care and involvement with families within a community.

The cases that make it into the megagroup contain ingredients that shock us all, somehow or in some way, more than illegal killing alone would usually do. Exceptional crimes receive exceptional levels and styles of media attention. Outrage is a complex mixture of the ordinariness of life invaded by brutal events, sometimes the worthiness of the life lost, and the perceived innocence or vulnerability of the victim(s). The ordinary, the worthy, and the innocent may all combine in representing social responsibility, such as the role of protecting children or caring for the elderly. Katz . . . refers to crime stories that appear to pose "threats to the sacred centres of society" as interesting because they trigger readers "to define moral perspectives on questions about elusive collective entities." . . . In identifying the characteristics of the victim, we learn not just about the seriousness of the killing, but about the readership of a newspaper and what responsibilities they are assumed to recognize. In socially constructed victimhood, offenses can be more abstract than physical damage alone, such as disturbing acknowledged understandings of family or of childhood.

Objectification

In effect, different groups within society both share an understanding of killing and contain its horror by reconstructing it in the light of their view of social reality, particularly in response to megacases. This route is not easily available to survivors of homicide because . . . their understanding of society is shaken and altered by the experience of bereavement through killing. Survivors of homicide may feel their lives have been changed forever, but the rest of society will move on and probably quite swiftly. The objectification of homicide victims, even as heroes and angels, is part of a social process of neutralizing anguish. This route to neutralizing anguish can never be open to covictims and survivors of homicide. Although families may engage in campaigns relating closely to their loss, newspaper reporting allows society to focus emotional energy on confirming the rightness of our existing viewpoint about the wider world.

In this section, I explore the comments arising from the reporting of Philip Lawrence's death and how it gave rise to a wider social commentary beyond the murder. This case was chosen to be illustrative of the techniques used, rather than to be seen as the definitive account. By their nature, megacases tend to summarize the elements that make a crime headline grabbing, and yet each is fundamentally exceptional in some way. . . .

Philip Lawrence was a headmaster who was stabbed to death by a 15-year-old boy, a member of a gang preparing to attack pupils at the school. The killing took place outside his school in Maida Vale, London, on December 8, 1995. After Philip Lawrence's death, there was much media debate around morality in contemporary society, and a campaign was set up to ban knives. The killing—although tragic—raised the spectre of an ordinary event made sinister: that of children coming out of school. The response of newspapers, in expressing social emotion about society and its values, expresses, reflects, and reinforces the public turmoil resulting from this horror. Reports moved rapidly through (a) reflecting parents' fears, to (b) accounts of social disintegration, and then to (c) defining *otherness* and *bad* in the world at large. Hence, the tragedy of one person's brutal killing becomes strangely depersonalized and held to represent a mass of social discontent.

The first stage of reflecting parents' understandable fears quickly becomes evident. Although Philip Lawrence is presented as a fatherly figure, taking responsibility for all of society's children, the readers of the *Daily Mirror* . . . were assumed to be on the side of good parents. This identification with good parents' viewpoints (as opposed to the parents of gang members) was spelled out in one column, where drugs and gangs are seen as part of the larger social malaise:

> Like millions of other families, my children will be entering the secondary system in a few years. Drugs apparently now exist in some form in every upper school in the country, private or State, posh or poor. Gangs that hang around school gates don't just exist in London. . . .

The three British daily newspapers studied (*The Times*, *Daily Mirror*, and *Daily Mail*) and their Sunday counterparts were clear that the killing represented all that is wrong in our society. Most particularly, Philip

Lawrence was presented as holding the line against a violent and disintegrating society. Each readership is invited in as a member of the group that is the last bastion of commonsense in an evil world. The tone varied, but each of the three newspapers represented this as more than the tragic, mindless loss of one outstanding man, but as a symbol for all that has gone wrong. The immediate issues were much discussed: of school and teacher safety, the activities of street gangs in London, and all the problems surrounding young people carrying knives. As a social issue, then, it gave rise to a *Mirror* campaign against carrying knives and subsequent amnesty in major cities, allowing knives to be handed in at police stations.

However, the social issues identified were much more wide ranging than being just about the immediate practicalities of knives, gangs, and teacher safety, important though these are. Hence, in the immediate aftermath of the murder, each paper identified subtly different social dangers that have brought us to this point of apparent national fragmentation and disintegration, pointing out how we should identify other and badness and how to identify goodness. In so doing, the exploration of the shocking had, within it, both the seeds of restoring a sense of order—for the explanations of badness confirm existing (and wide-ranging beliefs) about the ordering of society—and the expression of a sense of despair at the extent of society's ills.

A *Mail on Sunday* . . . article illustrates the extent to which one death can symbolize social disintegration:

> It has become fun to mock anyone in authority, to sneer at teachers, disparage politicians, guffaw at the Royal Family and undermine the police. Alongside the collapse of family life in many of our inner city estates and the appalling rise of drug and me-first cultures, we are raising a breed of youngsters who seem to know no rules. . . .

We were made aware, in the same article, that there are bad elements to blame in society beyond the killers (in the form of assorted apologists) who do not recognize the danger and, rather than punish gangs, have wailed excuses on behalf of gangs. In a commentary piece, the author described many schools as being dominated "by the righton educational fashions of the Sixties; schools where discipline amounts to little more than indulging the trouble-makers; schools dominated by politically-correct idealogues in the local education authority." However, the same writer assured us that "the pernicious and permissive doctrines preached at so many training colleges are on their way out." . . .

The Times . . . invited readers to identify with the questions of "all decent people" and called into the frame the "decline of the stable nuclear family, of the old-fashioned neighbourhood and of the Church's parochial structure." The same article explained that schools are not equal to the responsibility resulting from such shifts, comprehensive schools having apparently embraced a progressive ideology that marginalized discipline. We were assured, however, that this tide is turning as schools cease to be "branch offices of a town hall education system." . . . This essentially party political commentary went beyond education policy, and the leader of the Labour Party (then in opposition) was quoted as commenting on a lack of moral purpose and direction in the whole of national life. . . . It was a time in politics where probity in the lives of, particularly, Conservative politicians was under question.

The Times . . . extended the accusatory frame still further: The moral relativism of "Freddie Ayer [Frederick Ayer, erstwhile philosopher at Oxford University] is the dominant creed of the life peers, of the former vice-chancellors, the former ministers, the bishops, even many of the judges." For moral definition, he argued, one must look to the aristocracy, "to those who were not so highly educated as to suppose that there is no such thing as sin or to get into one of the new universities of the 1960s." . . . The list went on to include modern government, education, and broadcasting.

Although all three newspapers might be described as reflecting public fears and views, the *Mirror* most clearly gave its readers the possibility of channeling fear into social action through a Save Our Schools campaign and promoted the Bin a Knife amnesty for those possessing knives. However, badness is conceptualized as a foreign import as well as a practical problem in our midst: At the time of the murder, they quoted an American describing the violence in American schools as "a microcosm of our own sick society." . . . In America, we were told, "murder and mayhem have been on the timetable for years." . . . Although the *Mirror's* social analysis kept most closely to the facts of the case (out-of-control youth, carrying knives), their concern about foreign imports was clear. Hence, gang culture in London was linked to organized crime through Chinese Triads (likened to the Sicilian Mafia and Japanese Yakuza). . . .

The politicians of the time linked in again and again to the case as discussions of knife amnesties, appropriate punishments, effectiveness of the justice system, and teachers' safety were discussed. But as part of the wider social malaise argument, the *Mirror* . . . explicitly linked the case to current politicians' activities: "It is all very well for John Major to praise Mrs. Lawrence when she condemns the 'me culture.' But will John Major act to curb this culture that promotes so much sleaze and greed?" . . . So the tragic death of one individual has evolved from social outrage to being a symbol in which the actuality of death is eclipsed by the range of current and past political ills, which it is held to represent.

Conclusion

Newspapers develop the "victim" role in major crimes by inviting us to witness and take part on the side of those closely affected by a killing—the reader is invited to focus on the side of the offended against and is encouraged to feel hurt; this invitation is embedded at a microlevel in the authorial techniques of the crime-reporting genre. But individually and as members of the larger society, our sense of outrage is necessarily different from those who have actually been bereaved. One of the consequences of mediated witness is that megakillings enter cultural and social awareness, in part, due to the nature of coverage and mediation. One further consequence of this collection of techniques is the construction of a contested framework (public narrative) within which the struggle for control of the crime agenda takes place.

Public narrative is both a historical artifact and a heuristic device that helps to explore particular issues. It refers to a slower, cumulative process over a longer time period than is the case with moral panics. Some mega-cases will be returned to many times, but over a time span more drawn out and episodic than one would expect with a classic moral panic. . . . Likewise, although signal crime encapsulates the moments of shock and social reflection, the public narratives surrounding megahomicides encompass the entire process through to distancing and restoring a sense of social order via a framework of contested social perspectives. The nature of the public memory is different from that of the private one because the public one allows restoration of some sense of order.

Entry into long-term cultural and social consciousness lies, in part, in the amount of coverage and shock factor of the crime, but also, in part, in the nature and style of that coverage. As a consumer item, a megakilling is a matter of vicarious experience, and its exploitation is essential in the genre of infotainment . . . ; the authorial techniques of mediated witness contribute to its eventual iconic status. Repeated telling, as with fairy tales, helps pin a historical megakilling in the public memory. Microlevel analysis is, then, an essential ingredient in helping to unravel how signal crimes transmute into long-term social consciousness.

The rich layers of varied response under the heading "victimhood" hold much importance for criminologists, not least because making decisions about victims—their worthiness or otherwise—has traditionally been a central part of how society estimates the degree of badness in serious crime. In the case of homicide, there are many questions to be answered about how this sits alongside the long tradition of entertainment in the reporting of exceptional cases. As consumers of media crime, we are as bystanders. One of the chief emotional distinctions between virtual and actual victimhood is that virtual experience allows us still to be entertained by crime, which must seem grotesque to those bereaved by homicide. Major crime touches us all as members of the community, yet provides us, as individuals, with a source of entertainment, thrills, and fear. Whatever moral high ground is claimed, one must never forget that newspapers need readers and violent crime has long helped to sell papers. The translation of public emotional responses into "something must be done" is, at one level, an expiation of mediated witness—no longer bystanders, we take action to ensure that we will not be caught out the same way again. Although families, friends, and survivors of real homicide victims may engage in campaigning activities, this cannot take away their experience of the crime. Hence, our apparent unanimity and empathy with survivors of major crime is illusory.

Similarly, Breithaupt . . . has charted the media construction of trauma, which he separates out from the actual suffering of people affected. . . . The attacks on the World Trade Center, in particular, appeared on TV as an attack on America in the traditional way of old-style wars: by air. Hence, unlike most megakillings, America could watch and view itself under attack; by comparison, the artifacts of murder are usually seen retrospectively. Nonetheless, there are links between the two, especially in the way Breithaupt shows us how the media channel not only the experience of crime, but notions of healing and recovery. The style of channelling public response is one that also tells us how we might move away from the event, and this is clearly evident in the highly politicized social commentary surrounding Philip Lawrence's death.

In addition to the long-standing role of violent crime as a source of entertainment, some argue that crime has become increasingly politicized in recent years. Downes and Morgan . . . have charted the move to political center stage of all matters related to law and order, particularly since 1979. There has also been a shift in emphasis in the public framing of crime: Where Katz . . . comments that the moral symbolism of reading crime news was linked to its emphasis on the criminal, Garland . . . argues that victimhood is central to the new politicization of crime control. It is not, then, surprising that newspapers both echo and shape this aspect of the public narrative regardless of the experience of actual victims. Indeed, Garland argues: "The symbolic figure of the victim has taken on a life of its own, and plays a role in political debate and policy argument that is often quite detached from the claims of the organized victims movement, or the aggregated opinions of surveyed victims." . . .

Exploitation and ownership of victimhood, within this framework, are far removed from the experience of actual victims. Rather, we turn away from the pain of the bereaved and focus instead on conflicting claims as to how society should be run. Karstedt . . . has raised the question as to whether emotions should be the basis for moral principles. Here I argue further that our social commentary is shaped by *virtual* emotions arising out of a manufactured victimhood. How, then, do criminologists balance the symbolism of public narratives about violent crime against the consumption of crime as entertainment in a time when engagement with the emotionality surrounding crime is a route to political one-upmanship?

One of the potential consequences for those immediately affected by illegal killing in their own lives is to distance them further from the rest of society at precisely the moment we seem to be communicating most clearly about their experience. Spungen . . . offers the concept of the "second wound," whereby survivors are victimized after the homicide. She includes media intrusions along with those of the defendant, the police, the justice system, would-be helpers, and family and friends as sources of this subsequent victimization. She recognizes, however, that, although the media can hurt, so can they help: Public media can help solve crimes, and celebrity can allow covictims to speak out on social, family, and criminal justice issues and achieve positive effects. However, Spungen questions whether the price can be too high for the individuals concerned. . . . For supporters of covictims, she stresses the need for all to understand that the media have different processes and agendas to those of the victims.

Public consumption of crime, through media representation, is now framed within a period that has politicized criminological problems. Crime is a site of contest between competing groups with competing worldviews concerning how society should be run, and control of crime agendas is about social and political power. Working only within existing theoretical frameworks, such as moral panics, can mean settling for a partial explanation of the rich range of public and private emotions surrounding crime and victimhood—emotional phenomena that contribute to the construction of the highly politicized public narratives surrounding homicide. The complex uses and abuses of the emotionality surrounding crime have become, thereby, a matter of even greater importance to criminology, requiring a level of microanalysis from researchers to deconstruct the precise ways in which emotionality is framed publicly.

Questions

1. Describe how news organizations shape the public's definition of crime.

2. The research findings are based on data from Britain; how applicable are they to the U.S.?

PART IX

CRIME POLICY

Criminal justice is a practical topic of study of the direct impact the system has on millions of people in the country. Ideally, the criminal justice system would incorporate what is known about criminality based on the findings of criminological research. Much to the chagrin of criminologists everywhere, however, this is not the case. In the United States, criminal justice policy is shaped by politics and is largely fear-driven. In *Contextualizing the Criminal Justice Policymaking Process*, Karim Ismaili (chap. 29) outlines the complexity of the environment in which policy is developed.

CHAPTER 29

Contextualizing the Criminal Justice Policymaking Process

Karim Ismaili

St. John's University, New York

In 2002, British criminologists Trevor Jones and Tim Newburn lamented that "we still know very little about how penal policy comes to be the way it is." . . . According to Jones and Newburn, this lack of knowledge can be attributed to two factors. First, criminologists have tended to focus their empirical research on the effects of policies, rather than on their origins. Second, political science, the discipline most often engaged in studies of the policy process, has largely neglected the field of crime control. The observation that the criminal justice policymaking process has been neglected is not a new one. Indeed, this same knowledge gap was identified in 1981 by the Canadian political scientist Peter Solomon. . . . Solomon argued that it was important for researchers to study the policy process in criminal justice to facilitate an understanding of how the political process negotiates change, to explore the constraints the process places on the translation of ideas and analysis into action, to describe the degree to which various actors influence the movement of criminal justice proposals through the policy process, and, ultimately, to provide insight into how politics determines what is and can be implemented. . . . Solomon believed that research of this kind would shed light on how criminal justice policy differs from other policy realms, uncover whether crime policy tends to change more slowly than others, provide insight into whether there are greater obstacles to innovation in criminal justice, and describe how political structure and cultural traditions affect the policy process and account for variations between nations.

In the years following the publication of Solomon's . . . article, criminal justice policy has matured into a separate subfield within criminology. Journals devoted to crime policy have been founded, conferences regularly feature panels on policy issues, and university criminology and criminal justice programs have designed courses and hired faculty based on the interest in and growth of this subfield. This intellectual and financial investment has generated a corresponding proliferation of research on a broad range of substantive policy issues. Yet when it comes to whether our knowledge of the criminal justice policymaking process has evolved, the results have been disappointing. Although a few notable contributions have been made to this literature . . . , Solomon's observation, like Jones and Newburn's . . . two decades later, remains a feature of the subfield: The policymaking process continues to be neglected in studies of crime policy.

It is my contention that building a theoretical infrastructure that supports the accumulation of knowledge about the criminal justice policymaking process is especially important at this time. Not only would it open up an important field of inquiry, it would also help researchers better understand the dynamics that have contributed to the politicization of crime. It might also reverse the decline in influence experienced by criminologists during this highly politicized era. . . . Gilsinan . . . has noted that criminology has been preoccupied with policy relevance since its inception. It is therefore noteworthy that the historical pattern of criminological

Source: "Contextualizing the criminal justice policy-making process," by Ismaili, K., (2006), *Criminal Justice Policy Review, 17*, 255–269. Reprinted by permission of Sage Publications, Inc.

expertise contributing to the development of crime policy has been displaced in the past two decades. Haggerty . . . argues that broad social transformations in governance (the rise of neoliberalism), politics (the emergence of a highly charged symbolic discourse about crime), and criminal justice (the transformation of the criminal justice system by technologies emphasizing detection, capture, and monitoring) have conspired to alter criminology's policy influence. Zajac . . . has observed that academics and policymakers or practitioners do not appreciate one another because they tend to operate largely within their own communities. This, in turn, further erodes the significance of criminology in the policy process. It is increasingly the case that empirical research about crime has an uneasy relationship with the values and needs that often dominate the world of politics and policy. . . . This is especially true in the realm of crime policy, where the subject matter of crime is socially and politically defined. In this sense, criminal justice policy "can . . . only be fully understood in this wider context—and with due respect to an historical understanding of the relationship between perceptions of crime and the various strategies that have been employed in the attempts to control it." . . .

John Laub . . . recently noted that the belief that "scholarly knowledge and this knowledge alone should determine policy outcomes is naïve." . . . Indeed, if there is one lesson to be learned from the decline of criminological influence in the contemporary period, it is that pure reason competes with politics in shaping state responses to the crime "problem." . . . Put another way, both the process and environment of policymaking play a significant role in shaping policy outcomes. . . .

At a time when the U.S. prison population has reached 2.2 million, urban crime rates have declined dramatically, and nations are forced to consider how to ensure safety and security in a post-9/11 world, criminologists must strive to reclaim and reassert their roles as important contributors to the public dialogue on all of these matters. But precisely because relatively little attention has been devoted to understanding the policy making environment in which claims, counterclaims, and policy options are negotiated, the "messiness of real-world decision making" remains largely unknown. The result is that an important dimension of policymaking—one that could benefit from the cultivation of criminological expertise—has instead become an unfortunate blind spot.

This chapter is an attempt at improving our knowledge base on the criminal justice policymaking process. As the criminological subfield of crime policy leads more

criminologists to engage in some form of policy analysis, understanding the policymaking environment in all of its complexity becomes more central to the enterprise of criminology. This, in turn, becomes an important step toward theorizing about the policy process. To advance this enterprise, policy-oriented criminologists might look to theoretical and conceptual frameworks that have established histories in the political and policy sciences. Indeed, one of the central objectives of this chapter is to demonstrate the benefits that can be accrued by incorporating such scholarship into criminology. In the pages that follow, I present a contextual approach to examine the criminal justice policymaking environment and its accompanying policymaking process. But what exactly is a contextual approach? Why is it better suited to this task than are other approaches? As we see, one of the principal benefits of this approach is its emphasis on addressing the complexity inherent to policy contexts. For research on the policy process to advance, contextually sensitive methods of policy inquiry must be formulated. Those methods should illuminate the social reality of criminal justice policymaking through the accumulation of knowledge both *of* and *in* the policy process. . . .

Constructing a Framework for Analysis

Within the literature of policy studies, numerous models have been developed to make sense of the policymaking process. . . . Early models, influenced by the technocratic orientation of decision-making theory, portrayed the policymaking process as a rational enterprise that unfolds in a series of clearly defined steps. Deborah Stone . . . summarizes these steps in the following manner: "Identify objectives; identify alternative courses of action for achieving objectives; predict and evaluate the possible consequences of each alternative; select the alternative that maximizes the attainment of objectives." . . . Although this rational, sequential, and mechanistic depiction of the policy process remains powerful today, it has been challenged by alternative models that emphasize the "somewhat anarchic" . . . nature of policymaking. Far from being rational enterprises, these models point to the volatility that is characteristic of the everyday policymaking process. Value differences, the roles of interest groups, shifts in public moods, and institutional constraints are only a few of the many challenges encountered in contemporary policy environments. Critics of the rational perspective contend that such forces serve to militate against wholly rational policy action.

It is clear that the framework that a policy analyst selects and/or constructs to investigate and understand public policy will have a significant effect on what is found. According to David Bobrow and John Dryzek . . . , this environment often features dynamic, intertwined policy problems and multiple, conflicting values. The more complex a case, Bobrow and Dryzek assert, the greater the number of plausible interpretations of it, and the harder it becomes to adjudicate among them. Significantly, this holds true both within structures of government and in the wider society where claims to action are often shaped. Adding to this spiral of complexity is the fact that policy analysts are not value-free; they are predisposed to particular methodological and ideological orientations based on a range of interacting personal and professional life experiences. Considering these complex processes, it would appear that the development and application of a broadly based policy approach is essential to consider for any analyst attempting to understand or develop public policy. . . .

An early proponent of this contextual orientation to public policy analysis was the political sociologist Harold Laswell. Laswell, who spent the bulk of his career at the University of Chicago and at Yale Law School, is perhaps best known for his definition of *politics* as "who gets what, when, how." . . . Laswell believed that policy research should attempt to influence policymakers as well as "understand the problems thrust upon them, to appreciate their motives as human beings, and to clarify the options realistically open to them." . . . He argued that whatever solutions to policy problems are possible must arise from the forces within the contextual arena being studied. Within this arena, policy researchers should "expect to find various participants with distinctive perspectives . . . where they use their base-value resources according to consciously adopted strategies in their efforts to control the distribution of value outcomes and to prevent other systemic effects." . . .

[T]he scope of Laswell's . . . conception of context is at once broad, ambitious, and evolutionary (seeking knowledge of the whole), although ultimately it remains modest (recognizing that complete success is impossible). . . . It acknowledges that most errors of policy analysis stem from important elements of the context being overlooked or misconstrued in the analyst's attempt to make policy issues tractable for analysis. . . . It also acknowledges the complexity of public policy and demands that the analyst immerse him or herself in that complexity. In this sense, complexity and context are inextricably connected. The purpose of inquiry is not to discover universal laws. It is to enable the policy analyst and decision maker to find their ways through the complexities of the social situation in which they find themselves, "to come to terms with an inexhaustibly complex and constantly shifting universe by grasping it both as an objective configuration and as a context to be penetrated by the subject." . . .

The contextual approach to policy research and analysis has embraced Laswell's . . . notion of creativity. Its primary objective is the development of contextually sensitive methods of inquiry that will enhance the development and analysis of public policy. Descriptions of the policy context influenced by Laswell have ranged from those that are general and theoretical to formulations that are specific and almost prescriptive. . . .

A . . . specific formulation of the issues to be considered in a contextual analysis of public policy formation is offered by Fisher and Forester. . . . Their perspective emphasizes

the context-specific character of analytical practices—the ways the symbolism of their language matters, the ways the consideration of their audience matters, the ways they construct problems before solving them. In political terms . . . [it teaches] us about the ways policy and planning arguments are intimately involved with relations of power and the exercise of power, including the concerns of some and excluding others, distributing responsibility as well as causality, imputing blame as well as efficacy, and employing particular strategies and problem framing and not others. . . .

A contextual analysis of public policy must include a combination of these various levels of analysis. It is a melding of Fischer and Forester's . . . broad "appreciation of what constitutes policy research and makes it effective regarding matters of context, process, and client" . . . with Sabatier's . . . reminder of the significance of and richness and complexity inherent to substantive policy communities. It "points towards an explicit inclusion of a *normative* or *value-critical* policy analysis completely cognizant of the hurly-burly and ultimately decisive role that politics imposes on the art and craft of policy analysis and policy-making." . . . It is the principle of contextuality that will guide this incursion into the environment of criminal justice policymaking. The significant features of this environment are introduced shortly. In the meantime, I explore some of the peculiarities associated with this particular policy field.

Contextualizing Criminal Justice Policy

Understanding the evolution of public policy requires researchers to pay special attention to the policymaking process, to the actors involved in that process—the public, professionals, and politicians—and to the sites where participants interact and policy decisions are made. Observers of criminal justice policymaking have noted some peculiarities to the field that frustrate conventional forms of analysis. Briefly, they include institutional fragmentation and the symbolic dimension of criminal justice policy and criminal law. . . . Although these peculiarities are found in the criminal justice sectors of most liberal democracies, the degree to which they influence public policy varies from jurisdiction to jurisdiction.

An ongoing debate within the criminal justice literature involves the degree to which the state agencies and departments of the criminal justice process act as a coherent and unified system. Critics argue that the major components of the system—policing, courts, and corrections— carry out their respective mandates independently, generating systemic or institutional fragmentation. Diverse organizational objectives and differences in the use of discretionary powers exacerbate the fragmentation. This has led many to view the criminal justice system as "a network of interrelated, yet independent, individuals and agencies, rather than as a system *per se.*" . . . In such an environment, the development of coherent criminal justice policy that reflects the needs and expectations of each component of the system becomes a significant challenge. In situations where a degree of consensus on policy is secured, difficulties can often arise at the implementation phase.

Nagel and his associates . . . contend that institutional fragmentation is the result of differences in training, status, and ideology among police, courts, and corrections personnel. . . . It is worth noting that institutional fragmentation can also exist within subsystem organizations. For example, it is not uncommon to find executive and rank-and-file police officers, or prosecutors and defense lawyers, holding contrasting views on important policy issues.

Because the criminal law and criminal justice policy are expected to embody fundamental principles of society, a distinctive characteristic of research in the area has been the attention devoted to analyzing the symbolic quality of crime and criminal justice. . . . Crime and criminal justice are condensation symbols that have the potential to arouse, widen, and deepen public interest by appealing to ideological or moral concerns. . . . They condense a number of stresses that people experience in their day-to-day lives and are powerful because they relate to the moral, ethical, and cultural concerns of the social order. . . . The subject matter of crime and criminal justice is a significant source of complexity. The potential of evoking strong responses suggests that crime and criminal justice symbols are especially vulnerable to transformation for strategic purposes. . . . The variability of both the meaning of criminal justice and the symbols underlying that meaning compels an analysis of the evolving material basis of the symbol and the shifting sociopolitical environment in which it is lodged. . . .

The preceding discussion serves as a reminder of the complexity inherent to both the policy environment and the policymaking process in criminal justice (see Figure 29.1). It is not, however, a complete description of the various forces that influence the shape and direction of criminal justice policy. To enhance our understanding of this environment, it is important to organize for analysis the various institutions, groups, and individuals that participate in the policymaking process. Political scientists have developed just such an organizational framework—the policy community—that captures the constellation of forces that influence the development of public policy in a variety of sectors. As I describe next, it is a framework that can be used to further contextualize the development of criminal justice policy.

- Political Culture
  - Socioeconomic Characteristics
  - Political Parties, Partisanship, and Ideology
  - Checks and Balances/Federalism

- Politicization of Crime
  - Symbolic Dimension of Crime and Criminal Justice
  - The Definition and Construction of Policy "Problems"
  - Campaigns and Elections
  - Public Opinion
  - Policy Networks Within the Policy Community (see Figure 29.2)
  - Policy Trends in Other Policy Sectors and in Other Jurisdictions

- Institutional (Criminal Justice System) Cohesiveness/Fragmentation

---

Figure 29.1   Contextual Features of the Policy Environment

Mapping the Environment: The Criminal Justice Policy Community

A policy community . . . includes all actors or potential actors with a direct interest in the particular policy field, along with those who attempt to influence it—government agencies, pressure groups, media people, and individuals including academics, consultants, and other "experts." . . .

The policy community subdivides into two segments: the subgovernment and the attentive public. The subgovernment is composed of government agencies and institutionalized associations that actually make policy within the sector. . . . It normally consists of a small group of people who work at the core of the policy community. The attentive public, in contrast, is less tightly knit and more loosely defined. Its composition varies, but it usually contains important, although less central, government agencies, private institutions, pressure groups, specific interests, and individuals. As Pross . . . states, "The attentive public lacks the power of the subgovernment but still plays a vital role in policy development." . . .

Research has demonstrated that the structure and functions of policy communities vary from policy field to policy field. . . . Similarly, the relationships among actors in policy communities also vary. This reality has been captured in the concept of "policy network." It refers to the relationships that emerge among both organizations and individuals who are in frequent contact with one another around issues of importance to the policy community. . . . Atkinson and Coleman . . . have commented that policy community and policy network "appear to possess the required elasticity" . . . to stretch across a variety of policy sectors. They are "encompassing and discriminating: encompassing because they refer to actors and relationships in the policy process that take us beyond political-bureaucratic relationships; discriminating because they suggest the presence of many communities and different types of networks." . . .

Nancy Marion . . . has developed a useful way to organize the various actors and significant forces that shape the criminal justice policy community. Her discussion begins with the observation that both the states and the federal government develop criminal justice policy in the United States. This concurrent power effectively means that "all levels of government have the right to act to control criminal behavior and create a safe society for its citizens." . . . With this in mind, it is more precise to state that 51 criminal justice policy communities coexist, each reflecting differences with respect to participants, cultural traditions, and political dynamics. As a system of government, federalism implies that intergovernmental relations represent a significant feature of the policy field, especially where crime control responsibilities overlap between the federal and state governments or when the federal government attempts to create national criminal justice policy through its so-called power of the purse. Although federalism represents a significant source of complexity for the criminal justice policy community, it is important to note that traits and experiences shared across jurisdictional and geographic boundaries can also serve to unite its diverse elements. As we see, all criminal justice policy communities are encountering policy environments with increasingly diverse and rapidly maturing interest groups. All contain subgovernments dominated by a hierarchy of professional interests. All are experiencing the pressures of an expanding attentive public.

ELECTED OFFICIALS

Just as federalism provides an institutional context through which one can understand the development of criminal justice policy, so too does the system of checks and balances. Many elected officials of each branch of government are deeply involved in the criminal justice policymaking process; some are de facto members of the subgovernment. The executive branch actors of primary significance include the president (federal level), governors (state level), and mayors (local level . . .). Elected members of the legislative branch, especially those serving on criminal justice legislative committees, can also be viewed as being important members of the criminal justice policy community subgovernment. These include elected members of congress, state legislatures, and town and city councils. . . . Finally, whether elected, as they are in 38 states . . . , or appointed, judges shape criminal justice policy through the application, review, and interpretation of law. Often underexamined, judicial actors exert both a strong and steady influence on the work of the subgovernment. Although not active participants in the policymaking work of the subgovernment in a conventional sense, they are nonetheless of central importance to the criminal justice policy community.

UNELECTED ACTORS

Directly responsible for translating the political priorities of elected officials into public policy, appointed heads of criminal justice government departments and agencies are central participants in the policy community subgovernment. Also active in the initiation and screening of proposals for change in criminal justice policy are bureaucrats at all levels of government who have no operational responsibilities, but who concern themselves with monitoring policies and advising elected officials. . . . Although not part of the formal criminal justice system, government departments and individual bureaucrats (or policymakers) are important to consider in terms of their efforts to reduce institutional fragmentation. The relationships that are struck among government policymaking agencies and the various components of the justice system are essential to its smooth functioning. Bureaucrats thus engage in a precarious balancing act, at once trying to accommodate the diverse needs and demands of the various system components, along with those of politicians, interest groups, and other interested members of the public.

The criminal justice policy community is also populated by a wide range of interest groups. Each group is committed to influencing the outcome of public policy, although the degree to which they are ultimately successful is subject to considerable variation. Stolz . . . has identified eight distinct types of interest groups that attempt to influence criminal justice policy. Professional-, business-, social welfare-, civic-, ad hoc-, victim-, ex-offender-, and offender-oriented interest groups mobilize resources and press their respective positions at various decision points in the policy process.

The interest groups that have traditionally had the most influence on criminal justice policy are those that represent professionals and other officials involved in the operation of the criminal justice system—police associations, bar associations, judicial organizations, and correctional associations. . . . As active members of the policy community subgovernment, these interest groups represent professions with institutionalized stakes in the operation of the criminal law and the criminal justice system. . . . Their influence is enhanced by the high degree of public deference accorded them, especially on policy matters concerning the day-to-day operation of the criminal justice system.

According to Nagel et al. . . . , the power of various professional groups reduces the influence of criminal justice clients (i.e., the accused, the convicted, and the victims of crime) on the development of public policy. The largely closed, expert-driven criminal justice system, characterized by complicated laws and regulations,

serves to frustrate and disempower clients who often end up turning to underfunded and overworked third parties to represent their interests in the policy process. Considering the marginalization that the clients of criminal justice experience in the system and in the wider society, it is not surprising that civil libertarian groups, prisoner advocacy groups, and other client-focused groups face uphill battles in their attempts to influence the policy process. In such an environment, criminal justice policy often reflects little more than the bargaining and compromise of system players on matters of self-interest. . . .

The relationships that develop between institutionalized interests and governments are considered crucial to the policymaking process. They are relationships based on a principle of reciprocal return. Governments, for example, can ill afford to develop policy that will be met with criticism from professionals. Close ties with professional groups are cultivated to preclude such occurrences. Views are solicited and perspectives shared. Their opinions are considered vital and their support essential. . . . Similarly, professional organizations exist to ensure that their positions on issues are represented at various stages of the policy process. Their involvement goes a long way toward ensuring that that objective is met. It is this close and privileged access to the policy development process that often distinguishes the influence of professionally oriented groups from other interests in the criminal justice policy community.

In cases where a crime or criminal justice issue is in the public spotlight, elected officials are particularly responsive to public concerns and pay correspondingly less attention to views of policy professionals, including criminologists. It is therefore inaccurate to state that nonprofessional interest groups are completely shut out from the subgovernment in the criminal justice policy community. The views of a number of reform-oriented interest groups are considered vital and essential to the policy process, particularly those with an established presence in the policy community. Indeed, if there is one trend that has characterized the policy community during the past two decades, it is the increasing number of maturing interests that have developed around issues of criminal justice: Institutionalized victims' groups, groups working toward the elimination of violence against women, and other groups focused on the needs of minorities are proliferating. All are seeking to influence the shape and direction of public policy.

The attentive public in the criminal justice policy community is also expanding: "Matters of criminal law go to the heart of questions about governmental legitimacy, state authority, and other popular conceptions of right and wrong, and are thus of closer concern to many individuals than are most other legislative issues." . . . This explains, in large part, the increase in the number of ad hoc and single-issue reform interests that have recently been created around various criminal justice issues.

The attentive public obtains much of its information about crime and the criminal justice system from the media. Katherine Beckett . . . has noted that for 90% of those polled, the media represents the principle source of information about crime. . . . Because the coverage of crime is so prominent in "all means of mass communications, including daily and weekly newspapers, television, radio, news magazines, and so on" . . . , both the quantity and nature of media imagery can have a significant influence on how crime is perceived and, ultimately, on which criminal justice policies are pursued. As Beckett has argued, the coverage of crime in the media may influence the actions of both elected and unelected actors in the policy community independent of any effect on public opinion. This is manifested when policymakers interpret heightened media coverage as an indication of public concern warranting public action or as an opportunity for political exposure and/or direct political gain. . . . Viewed in this light, the manner in which crime and criminal justice issues are framed by the mainstream media becomes a significant contextual feature of the policy community. . . . Perceptions are, by their nature, malleable. As I have argued here, when those perceptions relate to crime, they are rarely grounded on sound, accurate information. What remains is an apparent gulf between two related, but independent, domains: attitudes about crime and knowledge about crime. . . . It is difficult to narrow this gulf in a policy sector where political reaction to the public's anxiety over crime is commonplace. This is especially troubling because it is these reactions that often serve to reinforce and perpetuate the inaccurate perceptions held by a large segment of the population.

Figure 29.2 summarizes the criminal justice policy community described previously. It should be emphasized that the policy community is a dynamic entity constantly shifting and evolving to meet the needs and expectations of diverse groups and individuals with interests in both the process and substance of criminal justice policy.

The Subgovernment

- Elected (Executive) Actors
  o President, Governors, Mayors
- Key Elected Legislative Actors
  o Senators, Representatives
- Major Interest/Pressure Groups
- Appointed Heads of Government Departments and Agencies
  o Cabinet Secretaries (U.S.)
- Key Judicial Actors (not active participants in the work of the subgovernment, but a major influence on the product of that work)

The Attentive Public

- The Media
- Less Central Government Agencies
- Experts, Academics and Consultants
- Interest/Pressure Groups
- Elected Officials
- Interested Members of the Public
- Private Institutions and NGOs
- Judicial Actors

Figure 29.2   The Criminal Justice Policy Community

Conclusion

This chapter began with the observation that the policymaking process has been largely neglected in studies of crime policy. It has argued that, for a truly policy-oriented criminology to advance, it is vital that this process be explored in all of its complexity. Drawing on Laswell's . . . call for policy researchers to come to terms with the entire complex, shifting policy universe, this chapter has proposed a contextual approach to criminal justice policy analysis. It is a form of policy analysis that insists that the researcher grapple with the complexity inherent to the criminal justice policymaking process to accumulate knowledge both *of* and *in* the policy process. For those interested in the criminal justice policymaking process, this complexity is both an attraction and a significant challenge. Three steps have been identified to meet this challenge. The first step entails the identification of the various contextual features that are more or less unique to the criminal justice policy environment. The second step involves organizing this environment into a policy community with a subgovernment and an attentive public. This not only provides shape to the policy sector, it also helps to expose patterns of power and influence. The final step requires the researcher to uncover the networks and relationships that evolve within the policy community and consider the implications of these patterns for the development of policy. As the subfield of criminal justice policy matures, so too must its theoretical frameworks and conceptual tools. With the potential of significantly enhancing our understanding of democracy in action, the contextual approach presented here is a reflection of and response to this maturation.

Questions

1. Describe the concept of a policy community.

2. What groups are part of the attentive public?

PART X

THE FUTURE OF CRIMINOLOGY

I t is impossible to predict the future of the field of criminology. In *Criminalizing War: Criminology as Ceasefire* (chap. 30), Vincenzo Ruggiero argues that the field has largely ignored war. He suggests that a sociological-criminological analysis of war would inevitably lead to war's criminalization. Given the presence of war in our contemporary society, the author's ideas certainly deserve consideration.

CHAPTER 30

CRIMINALIZING WAR

Criminology as Ceasefire

Vincenzo Ruggiero

Middlesex University, UK, and University of Psa, Italy

In a novel by Stefan Zweig . . . , war is a chess game that turns into vulgar business engaging passionate, noble individuals who regularly lose against coarse, inhuman beings endowed with purely mechanic abilities. Similarly, Ernst Jünger . . . identifies in the bloody mud of World War I the end of heroic wars and the inception of mechanic, industrial, productive armed conflicts where human work is finally subsumed in violence: War is an industry. Whereas the former develops a type of radical pacifism and, after fleeing Germany with a sense of tragic defeat, commits suicide, the latter elaborates, along with a critique of modern wars, a notion of war as value: The reason that we fight is irrelevant, what is important is that we do.

Zweig and Jünger exemplify the two extreme reactions to war—namely, total rejection through self-obliteration, on the one hand, and acceptance through ideological revaluation, on the other hand. This chapter attempts to shun defeatism and impotence while arguing that the notion of "war as value" has enjoyed unmerited longevity, and that a sociological-criminological analysis of war may today lead to its unconditional criminalization. Before presenting the criminalization argument, however, a brief analysis of how mainstream criminology has failed to address war and the recent development of a new criminology of war is provided.

War and Identities

Conventional criminologists have long shied away from the study of war, as they have from legitimate behavior.

Little curiosity, in this respect, has also provoked the evidence that legitimate behavior may be extremely harmful to people and property, that institutional and cultural processes determine what is to be regarded as legitimate, and, finally, that legitimate power is always accompanied by illegitimate opportunities for its constant reinforcement. However, the study of white-collar crime has partly changed this, for example, by revealing how official occupational roles are intertwined with criminal opportunities and how illegal techniques are transmitted along with rationalizations making crime "during the course of one's occupation" a widespread phenomenon. . . . Labeling theory, in its turn, has questioned ontological definitions of crime . . . and even disputed the deviant nature of killing:

> Homicide is a way of categorizing the act of killing, such that taking another's life is viewed as totally reprehensible and devoid of any redeeming social justification. [However], some types of killing are categorized as homicide. Others are not. . . .

The reference to war is obvious here. Finally, students of state crime have shown that legitimate authority is far from being the embodiment of the law and that legality and illegality are constantly maneuvered in the practical exercise of authority . . . .

Despite these unequivocal pointers, war has miraculously escaped attention; when faced with the millions of legitimate killings perpetrated, for example, during

Source: "Criminalizing war: Criminology as ceasefire," by Ruggiero, V., (2005), *Social and Legal Studies, 14,* 239–257. Reprinted by permission of Sage Publications, Ltd.

the wars of the 20th century, most conventional criminologists refuse to consider that many of those killings
were, in fact, illegitimate, let alone consider that the legitimacy of those wars might be challenged. There is a bur-
densome legacy favoring such refusal, one that is found
in the traditional notion that war is a great foundational
event, replete with positive values, capable of marking
the difference between barbarianism and civilization.
War is assumed to establish just hierarchies and allocate
deserved ranks: A necessary evil, it is a regenerative
event nonetheless, shaping the world and triggering
transformation. . . . Moreover, war appears to belong to
the divine sphere because it generates social and institutional forms through a sort of theomachy, a sacred fight
that brings destruction while creating something new. In
brief, war is the expression of supreme forms of interaction and a crucial factor for the constitution of identities.

Similar notions are somehow absorbed by functionalist criminology through the espousal of Durkheimian
concerns around solidarity, consensus, and integration.
The perceived loosening of social bonds under the
conditions of urban and industrial life has favored the
appreciation of war as a crucial artifice for the production of collective identities, solidarity, and supreme integration. . . . As Durkheim . . . suggests, when individual
minds are not isolated, but enter into close relation with,
and work upon, each other, a new kind of psychic life
takes shape, a synthesis of superior energy and intensity.
This synthesis, which allows for personal interests to
be temporarily set aside, can express itself in the form of
uncontrollable force, an overflow of strength and senti-
ments as the inevitable effects of collective ferment. This
force can translate into "stupid destructive violence" or
"heroic folly," but its main function is to generate
moments of higher forms of life, and its intensity and
exclusiveness "monopolizes all minds to the more or less
complete exclusion of egoism and the commonplace." A
society is not a mere organized body of vital functions
and cannot be constituted without creating ideals: "This
body has a soul which is the composition of collective
ideals." Ideals, in turn, are not abstractions, cold intellectual concepts lacking purposeful power. They are essentially dynamic because behind them "are the powerful
forces of the collective." "They are collective forces—that
is, natural but at the same time moral forces, comparable
to the other forces of the universe." . . .

War, as a supreme act of collective force, brings the
ideal close to the real, but, more important, leaves in the
collective memory a powerful legacy of solidarity, organized unity, and integration. Why should criminology

engage in the study of solidarity, unity, and integration?
A criminology concerned, on the contrary, with egoism,
disorder, and disorganization may find it inappropriate
to include war among its objects of study, as the central
question it poses is why some people commit crimes, not
why most do not.

Solidarity and Innateness

. . . The notion that war is intimately irrational established itself in relatively recent times, particularly after
the two world wars and as an effect of the nuclear threat.
This irrationality shares many components with the
innate violence possessed by Nietzsche's . . . "blonde
beast," the wild animal lying inside the human race, the
magnificent, wandering beast avid of prey and victory.
Its rapacity is bound to manifest itself every now and
then and cannot be suppressed by civilization, let alone
by the State. In much Greek philosophy, war is the original principle of the State because it marks the passage
from the primitive "state of the pigs" to the advanced
state of luxury. A constant element of humankind, the
instinct of pugnacity is not a survival from brutal ancestry and cannot be eradicated. In fact, its operation is far
from being wholly injurious; on the contrary, it is one of
the essential factors in the evolution of higher forms of
social organization. . . .

In a letter addressed to Albert Einstein, who poses
the question of whether it is possible to free humankind
from the menace of war, Sigmund Freud . . . starts off by
examining, as he is required, the relationship between
might and right. He replaces the term *might* with the
more telling word *violence* and remarks that, although in
right and violence many may see an obvious antinomy,
a proper enquiry would prove that the former evolved
from the latter. Original violence is, in his view, the force
of a community expressed in its law. Conflicts among
humans have always been resolved by the recourse to
violence, and brute force is the deciding factor of property ownership and the establishment of the prevailing
will. Freud notes, however, that physical force is increasingly replaced by the use of various mechanic adjuncts,
whereby the victors prove to be those whose weapon is
more effective or handled more skillfully. With the coming of weapons, superior brains begin to oust brute force,
but the object of the conflict remains the same: One
party has to be constrained, by injury or impairment, to
retract a claim or refusal. This objective is fully achieved
when the opponent is definitively put out of action—in

other words, is killed. This procedure, Freud continues, has two advantages: First, enemies cannot renew hostilities, and, second, their fate deters others from following their example. Moreover, the slaughter of a foe gratifies an instinctive human craving.

War, in brief, is the result of an active instinct for hatred and destruction, an instinct cohabiting in humans together with its opposite, namely "eros," which aims at conserving and unifying. Love and hate are akin to those eternal polarities—attraction and repulsion—which fall within the field of study of the physical sciences, and Freud concludes that both instincts are indispensable: All the phenomena of life derive from their activity; whether they work in concert or opposition, each is blended with a certain dosage of its opposite.

Classical sociology deals with the issue of "war as an expression of innateness" by adopting an optimistic, evolutionist perspective. The example of August Comte . . . is, in this respect, significant. Military societies and industrial societies are said to represent two fundamentally different types of social organization. The predominance of the second type is destined to diminish warfare, which is essentially connected with the predominance of the first. The argument is put forward that there is a fundamental antithesis between military civilization and the civilization of labor, between the spirit of conquest and industry. In an ideal evolution, first, industry is seen as being in the service of war, then war is regarded as being in the service of industry, and, finally, in the ultimate form of society, peace is deemed the inevitable outcome of industry . . . . True, Comte was proved wrong in his prediction that the last century would be free from war, but it is controversial whether he is equally wrong in foreseeing that in the only kind of conceivable future war is that which aims to establish directly the material "preponderence of more advanced over less advanced populations." . . .

Political scientists such as Gaetano Mosca . . . regard attempts to introduce Darwin's doctrine of evolution of the species into the social sciences as based on a fundamental confusion. These attempts are said to identify the struggle for existence, which is characteristic of the lower animals, with the struggle for preeminence, which is characteristically human and a constant phenomenon that arises in all human societies. Conversely, mainstream criminologists who may even have rejected innateness in respect of crime have failed to extend such rejection to the notion that war is an innate need of humans. Traditional criminological analysis, at most, has considered crime caused by war situations. Bonger . . . , for example, argues that war drives up to the top all the

factors that may lead to crime: Family life is ripped apart, children are neglected, destitution spreads, and scarcity of goods generates theft and begets illicit markets. Crime is also caused by a general demoralization, and violent behavior increases as a mimetic outcome of the spectacle of "killing, maiming and terrible destruction." Crime statistics swell despite the fact that a large part of the male population, in the age range of the most represented offenders' group, is sometimes in military service, and thereby outside the jurisdiction of the ordinary courts. The dark figure of crime, in its turn, is assumed to increase due to the weakening of institutional agencies, such as the police and the judiciary. War is, therefore, criminogenic for those who do not fight, but, as Bonger suggests, it also pushes the individuals who fight to commit a variety of offenses, although "the figures of the crimes committed in the field will probably never be published." . . .

This perspective overturns the analysis of Durkheim: War is described less as an event encouraging supreme integration and solidarity than as a normless condition conducive to egoism and to the dangerous weakening of social bonds. A further critique of war as crime (rather than simply as criminogenic) does not come from criminology, but from anthropology. More specifically, it is scholars like Margaret Mead . . . and colleagues from her entourage who take issue with the innateness or atavistic thesis put forward by Freud. War is an invention, and traditional or advanced societies, mild or violent peoples, assertive or shy communities will go to war if that invention is part of their cultural repertoire: "Just like those peoples who have the custom of duelling will have duels and peoples who have the pattern of vendetta will indulge in vendetta." . . . That invention is seen by Mead as fit for certain types of personality and consistent with the needs of autocrats, the expansionist desires of crowded countries, and "the desire for plunder and rape and loot which is engendered by a dull and frustrating life." There is no place for heroism in her analysis of war, nor is there any appreciation of how victory or conquest may forge national identities. Her plea for the supersedure of the invention of war leads her to draw a parallel with other barbaric inventions that were eventually superseded . . . . The conclusion seems obvious: To get rid of war, "we need a new social invention," replacing it because a form of behavior becomes out of date only when something else takes its place: in order to invent forms of behaviour which will make war obsolete, it is a first requirement to believe that an invention is possible." . . .

Margaret Mead's argument appears to have followers among some radical penal reformers of the abolitionist school, who similarly remark that imprisonment may well be equated to an obsolete invention and that new inventions are needed to deal with the problematic situations that we call crime.

Legitimacy and the Carnival of War

The contribution of the Chicago sociologists on the subject matter is ambivalent, and it remains obscure why their particular sensitivity with respect to social exclusion and their active intervention in communities and ghettos are not translated into a similar degree of sensitivity vis-à-vis international matters. Park . . . likens war to its ancestors, namely the judicial procedure known as trial by combat or the duel, although he is unsure whether to regard it as a social institution or a biological necessity. The latter hypothesis seems to be validated if one considers that war has always been one of the available ways of making claims and settling disputes. War must, therefore, be an innate human enterprise if it still constitutes a form of litigation by which states make their claims valid. Park notes, however, that limits need to be imposed on such an innate behavior and finds a response to this need in the technical limits drawn by international agencies trying to make war more consistent with "the requirements of humanity" and develop an understanding of the consequences of unrestricted warfare. However, he argues that all attempts to regulate wars and govern military conducts may simply result in the legitimization of both and in conferring a respectable institutional character on them. Legitimacy, moreover, belongs to authorities and institutions whose actions and their effects are predictable, whereas "we do not know what to expect of war anymore." . . . In a final attempt to identify the nature of war and its function, Park reiterates the adage that war is politics in its original form, through which the belligerent states or parties seek to extend the territorial limits of their sovereignty and to establish their own political and economic order. The victorious party will, of course, impose its own racial or national interests and attempt to build up an ideology that rationalizes the acceptance of its superiority and the social order imposed on the vanquished.

Park's critical remarks express a sense of impotence and inevitability in the face of processes leading advanced socioeconomic orders to impose themselves on other systems. He is faced with the Comtean dilemma of whether the potential wars waged by more mature systems, although condemnable, are perhaps destined to perennially loom as threats during the course of human evolution. Because unequal development is a permanent feature of the history of the international community, and given that aggression by more developed nations is always a possibility, does this mean that war is indeed an immutable trait of human behavior? War, in this way, becomes the price to be paid for global development and its alleged corollary of generalized social advancement.

It is true that war possesses an aura of sacredness, and its rejection, apart from signalling lack of virility, appears as a form of atheism. . . . But the argument developed earlier indicates that rejecting war also amounts to refusing the evolutionary mechanisms of human societies at large. It is the sacredness of development and the surrounding advanced societies and states that give war its sense of a civilizing mission. Establishing an advanced social order in traditional societies, albeit through war, is an inescapable burden of developed societies, which have a duty to drag low-achieving societies along their path. War, in this perspective, is not only the most intense manifestation of a collective endeavor binding a national community and strengthening its identity, but it is also a way of bringing the international community together and establishing cultural and material uniformity in it. In this way, "permanent massacre becomes an element of universal harmony." . . .

War is also equated to an immense party, a massive celebration in which social roles are challenged and transgression encouraged. A return to chaos, war is an allegory of child delivery, equally bloody and painful, but a natural manifestation of fecundity. War is also a regenerative rite, like a carnival where conventions are defied and, through temporary collective deviance, the official order is then restored and celebrated. Recent contributions in criminology do consider these aspects of collective behavior, when, for instance, the examination is offered of "the world of excess, obscenity and degradation" as "the only true site for the expression of one's true feeling for life. . . . The expression of the second life of the people is performed and brought to life through carnival, which becomes for rational society understood as no more or less than the carnival of crime."

But this type of analysis, although unveiling some mechanisms that trigger moral panics and advocating tolerance toward transgression, stops short of examining the supreme form of collective celebration of "the second life." Also "war as carnival," in fact, allows for moral imperatives to be overturned. War allows people to kill and steal; in war, it becomes "obligatory to behave in a dissolute and criminal way." Wars are "prolonged orgies creating a climate favourable to excesses, where rules are temporarily suspended: rape, obscenity, and atrocity become the norm." . . . War as carnival, in other words, is not a defiance of conventions causing moral panics, but the most extreme manifestation of conventional power relations. As such, war is highly criminogenic, and it is on this aspect that the recent development of a new criminology of war is centered.

A New Criminology of War

War offers a variety of empirical and theoretical areas to criminological analysis, not least because of the disproportionate character and magnifying effect that it confers on human conflict, social interaction, and state responses. Violence, predation, social control, and state action, despite attempts to publicly sanitize their manifestations, are engaged in one, central, obsessive task—namely, killing. This task is one with its opposite—that is, surviving—which signifies triumph over death while inflicting it on others. Those involved lose all sense of proportion because fear is kept at bay by the satisfaction of causing fear in the enemy, while even the terror associated with death is tempered by the joy of not being dead oneself. The extremity of war situations induces the adoption of the lowest forms of survival and includes killing among them. . . . Killing, in its turn, grants the sensation of immortality because it allows one to survive, and "enthusiasm for survival is a destructive social power." . . .

Calls for students of crime to be attentive to the conditions shaping the relationship between war and crime are prompted by the "incidence and ferocity of wars and ethnic conflicts which show no sign of abating." . . . A criminology of war, therefore, focuses on mass, devastating victimization, violations of human rights, and other forms of state crime; moreover "states of emergency usher in massive increases in social regulation, punishment and ideological control, new techniques of surveillance and, with that, a corresponding derogation of civil rights." . . .

"Crimes in war" and "war crimes" are central areas of investigation. Although the former are exemplified by conventional predatory offenses, interpersonal violence, and illicit market operations, the latter tend to be included under the rubric of state crime. . . . Examples of crimes in war are provided by Nikolic-Ristanovic . . . , who describes how in the former Yugoslavia, as in other wars, people who had never been involved in crime

before turned to predatory or violent acts "under the influence of dire necessity and the breaking down of inhibitions." . . . War zones, she adds, became business areas for organized criminal groups that provided goods such as smuggled fuel, illicit drugs, and weapons. Examples falling in areas of both crimes in war and war crimes focus on arbitrary arrests, violent and property crimes committed by police and paramilitary forces. Both forces, in the former Yugoslavia, recruited "obsessed soccer fans, criminals and alcoholics, and one in five volunteers had committed serious offences, some going to battle directly after serving their time." . . . Social disorganization is invoked to explain the dramatic, pervasive increase in criminal activity, especially in situations of civil war, when it is hard to distinguish between the police, the army, and criminals: All of these become components of social control agencies, and crime is encouraged as one of the forms of war.

Although scarcity may account for the growth of grey or hidden economies, the inflationary effect of violence, in war situations in general, may be mobilized to explain an increase in interpersonal violent conducts. Once made legitimate, it is argued, violence may also come to be viewed as the only effective tool for the protection of one's well-being, the achievement of one's goals, or the solution of personal differences. . . . Based on learning theories of crime, such explanations posit the magnifying effect of institutionalized violence on social interactions, leading to the devaluation of human life, both during and immediately after war periods. Belonging to the same family of explanations are contributions highlighting the transgressive nature of crimes committed by marginalized youth, whose violent behavior is said to assume similar etiologies and characteristics as violence in war and terrorism . . . .

It is on the related analysis of the metaphor of war that this new branch of criminology has expressed its major strength. The metaphor of *war* is attributed a central place in hegemonic thought, invading the public discourse in many internal and international affairs. Law and order do not escape this, as responses to crime take on the strong emotions triggered by war, whereby "the metaphor creates pressure for unity, solidarity, mobilisation of people and resources for the common good (against the foe)." . . . The line between warfare and police work becomes blurred while policing as conflict regulation is supplanted by an escalation of hostilities, against internal as well as external enemies. . . . The metaphor of war is applied to crime as group conflict, generating mass arrests, aggressive surveillance, curfews, summary punishments, and mass deportation.

As for war crimes, techniques of neutralization are invoked as explanatory devices, whereby atrocities committed are psychologically removed. The celebrated analysis of Sykes and Matza . . . is applied to torture and other war excesses so that the worst political atrocities, like mundane and trivial delinquency, are viewed as relying on similar vocabularies that mitigate responsibility when behavior is questioned. Denying responsibility for the injury caused, denying that an injury has indeed been caused, denying the human worth of the victim, or appealing to higher loyalties, for example, all constitute recognizable devices to evade conventional judgment. . . .

It is recognized, however, that conventional law breakers may use these techniques as ex-post justifications for their behavior that they themselves, at heart, cannot inscribe in an alternative repertoire of values and conducts. In other words, neutralization vocabularies may work to protect from self-blame and blame from others when perpetrators possess a form of allegiance, if weak and contorted, to the official norms that they nevertheless breach. In war, on the contrary, it is not necessary to mobilize techniques of neutralization, the violence deployed being not only legitimate, but associated with virtuous, patriotic, qualities, and, ultimately, with a supreme form of citizenship. Participating in a war grants the definitive seal of national, ethnic, or political identification. "'I was just following orders' may be offered as an excuse (denial of responsibility) or as an affirmation of higher allegiance to values such as patriotism and obedience to legitimate authority." . . . Techniques of neutralization, on the contrary, are required when individuals refuse to participate in wars—namely, when they find alternative sets of values and conducts that justify their objection to following orders. War is the supreme expression of conventionality, and soldiers do not have to excuse themselves for anything unless they refuse to kill.

In short, the new criminology of war, so defined in this brief overview, has mainly dealt with war as criminogenic and with war crimes, in my view providing the background for a logical extension of its own arguments—namely, for a definitive criminalization of war itself.

Criminalizing War

In this final section, a brief thematic manifesto for pacifist criminology is presented. It is suggested that some key criminological concepts, although at times radically overturned, may work as indictments of war and as a notional ceasefire.

War as Cancer

We have seen that functionalism, as commonly applied by conventional criminology, may lead to the acceptance or even the glorification of war as the most intense expression of solidarity, collective identity, and integration. Alleged to offer individuals the opportunity to set their particularistic interests aside, war is regarded as an exemplar event that will find space in the collective memory, providing citizens with a sense of unity and strong feelings of shared achievement or suffering. Collective memory, in brief, may become an important propellant for war, granting people excessively cemented identities in the form of nationalism. National psychologies activate remote meanings and cultures, and under certain circumstances, as Jung . . . suggests, the collectivity is persuaded that such meanings and cultures are under threat and must be defended or restored. Collective psychologies and memories are more primordial than individual ones, and Jung fears that their impact may be ungovernable. Against these excessive forms of memory, a proper degree of oblivion may temper the desire to engage in wars. Moreover, an alternative use of the functionalist tradition would emphasize that some forms of collective action are the negation of solidarity and, like cancer and tuberculosis, cause damage beyond the functional threshold. Durkheim . . . is adamant on this point when he stresses, for example, that there are some functionally incompatible forms of behavior that are antisocial and, instead of bringing vital forces together, cause disintegration, like microbes and, indeed, cancer. Criminology as ceasefire would simultaneously dilute excessive forms of memory through oblivion and pursue this alternative use of the functionalist tradition.

Pacifist Entrepreneurs

Helpful support for the criminalization of war may come from labeling theory, not only for its questioning of the ontological difference between killing and killing at war, but also for its focus on moral entrepreneurs contributing to the inclusion of certain conducts within the realm of the criminal justice process. Crime and deviance are the result of enterprise; although a conduct is objectively harmful, the harm needs to be discovered and pointed out. . . .

Becker argues that new types of offenders have to be identified and noted as different or stigmatized for their nonconformity so that the rule may be applied to particular people or a class of outsiders. . . . His notion of moral entrepreneurs . . . may well be utilized by pacifist criminologists to identify the harmful conduct of those supporting and waging war and, in a similar fashion, to stigmatize them as outsiders. War as an unacceptable deviance and the outsiders who personify that deviance, as Becker would put it, will be the target of an abstract conception and, indeed, the product "of a process of interaction between people." Yet in our case, those applying the stigma will serve general, human, collective interests, whereas those receiving it will be singled out and shamed for being at the service of their own limited interests.

Labeling as Civilization

Pacifist entrepreneurship is inscribed in "processes of civilization," . . . which have allowed for the criminalization of other, previously accepted, conducts, for example, domestic violence, child abuse, and environmental crime. It may be true that civilization and barbarism are peculiarly interlinked and that the latter is not an occasional setback or a temporary lapse within an otherwise smooth development leading to the control of primitive instincts and cruelty. It may also be true that civilization creates the conditions for its own collapse. "Modern science was bound to invent the nuclear bomb. State bureaucracy was bound to be transformed into the practice of genocide as a public service." . . . Finally, it may be argued that the Holocaust is a genuine product of the development of bureaucratic rationality in the modern world . . . and that the idea of civilization serves to justify all forms of violent excess. However, even if violence and cruelty are deemed invariable aspects of human history, societies have always attempted to restrain them. The use of the symbolic function of the law, when applied, for example, against domestic violence or the crimes of the powerful, is not to be associated with optimistic views of civilizing processes, whereby such crimes are alleged to progressively disappear. The law is applied when prohibitions are identified as the result of conflicting interests in society, as the establishment of collective, prevailing, priorities, ultimately as examples of sensibilities gaining partial hegemony in specific social settings. In this respect, parts of Freud's analysis may be of help.

Conflicting social interests, in Freud, are translated into inner psychological conflicts engaging the desire to annihilate and that to conserve. In his view, however, cultural change is accompanied by striking psychic changes, whereby norms and regulations may produce a "progressive rejection of instinctive ends and a scaling down of instinctive reactions." "Criminology as ceasefire" might introduce cultural change so that conducts "which delighted our forefathers" will become "unbearable to us." The exposure of other, previously unnoticed, harmful acts proved instrumental in triggering this sort of cultural change, and war may well be included among such acts. . . .

War as Crimes of the Powerful

State and corporate crime are central areas of concern for criminology, especially since the pioneering work of Sutherland . . . challenged the assumption that crime is the exclusive reserve of individuals and groups characterized by economic disadvantage and social marginalization. His is an example of how cultural change may fruitfully lead to the identification of new areas of social injustice. Learning processes in place among people endowed with power and resources may lead to criminal conduct and, in some cases, to forms of recidivism akin to those of professional, career criminals. The crimes of the powerful are said to occur in contexts in which the growth of corporate actors causes a structural change in society, whereby natural persons play an increasingly insignificant role. In such contexts, interactions become largely asymmetric, in that corporate actors are in the position to control the conditions in which their relationships with natural actors take place. The former hold more information regarding the nature of their relationship and the way in which this can be altered. . . . War can be equated to state and corporate crime for the similar asymmetric position that decision-making groups occupy vis-à-vis natural persons, who become victims even when they are unaware of having been victimized and even when victimization is disguised under heroism and patriotism.

Invisibility of the victim, commonly listed among the characteristics of corporate crime, can be extended to the victims of war, their invisibility being the result of our lack of imagination and empathy. Criminology as ceasefire will see in wretched, hollow-eyed soldiers not only the denial of militarism, but also young men who, while "doing their unpleasant, ennobling duty" . . . , are being victimized by state and corporate actors. Moreover, the criminalization of war may be likened to the criminalization of police malpractice and abuse, contemporary wars being increasingly akin to improper, illegitimate, international policing. . . . Finally, criminalization may be invoked because war is also a specific form of crime against women. Throughout the 20th century, wars have increasingly targeted civil populations. In some cases, armies have avoided fighting one another, going straight for the cities and their inhabitants, "raping, destroying the achievements of the daily civilising work of women." . . . In countries at war, medical conditions that had virtually disappeared return, particularly those affecting women who have been raped: They epitomize "war against women." This leads us to appreciate yet another distinctive feature of contemporary wars.

War as Asymmetric Conflict

Conflict theory in criminology could be used as an analytical legitimation of war, in that groups (i.e., nations) can be seen as engaged in permanent confrontation in search of power and resources. Conflict, including war, may therefore be deemed an essential component of the continuous functioning of the world system. . . . In this perspective, no possibility is given to groups and nations to establish limits to their action because the pursuit of one's interest appears to form an essential part of one's socialization. However, although some conflicts may describe situations in which resources are contested and group or national interests pursued with a view to fair distribution, recent wars occur in conditions whose enormous asymmetry renders such contestation and pursuit unrealistic. I am thinking of largely asymmetric wars in which one country or coalition can attack another on its own territory while the country attacked cannot respond in kind. Asymmetric wars inevitably result in massacre. . . . In the typology proposed by Tilly, this type of war is not a deadly contest where two groups inflict mutual harm to reduce the other's capacity to inflict harm. Rather, it is a "campaign of annihilation," in which one contestant wields overwhelming force against the other. Contemporary wars have taken on these features, and their outcomes include "collective survival, on one side, and recognition as the sole party with the right to territorial control, on the other."

Criminology as ceasefire would focus on this inequality. Victimology, rather than conflict theory, may help in this respect, particularly its attempts to unveil the dark figure of crime suffered by weaker actors and its efforts to empower those victimized. The criminalization of war, in this sense, echoes Aron's . . . argument for peace. His pacifist sociology identifies two conditions for ceasefire: (a) the diminution of the gulf between the privileged minority and the mass of humanity that remains sunk in poverty, and (b) the constitution of nations ready to accept each other within an international community (the lowering of barriers between nations, demilitarization, and the transfer of some state powers to a supranational organization). The first condition can be found within the criminological tradition—for example, in the efforts made by Chicago sociologists to empower and regenerate destitute communities. An internationalization of such efforts would be a crucial component of pacifist criminology.

Criminology as Perpetual Peace

In his philosophical manifesto for peace, Emmanuel Kant . . . stresses that perpetual "peace means an end to all hostilities . . . a conclusion that nullifies all existing reasons for a future war, even is they are not yet known to the contracting parties." . . .

Kant sees war as commodification of countries and persons and perpetual peace as collective rights for the former and individual, human rights for the latter. Criminology as ceasefire may find inspiration from this view and expand its concerns with rights to include peace as a supreme, ultimate human right. War as a policy for adjudicating national differences, in contrast, is utterly discredited because if logically pursued it leaves nothing to be adjudicated, not even the enemy nations. . . . Finally, a war of punishment (*bellum punitivum*) between states is inconceivable because it is difficult to establish who should punish whom, whereas war as extermination "would allow perpetual peace only on the vast graveyard of the human race." . . .

Kant's perpetual peace resonates with the notion of the unfinished in criminology—namely, the pursuit of alternative ways of dealing with crime that are "not yet fully existing." . . . As Kant . . . warns, it is not a question of whether perpetual peace is really possible; "we must simply act as if it could really come about and turn our efforts towards realizing it." . . . Similarly, prison reform, for example, may become possible if efforts toward unfinished alternatives are made and continuously pursued, as if the final abolition of prison could really come about.

Abolitionism Against War

Dealing with aggression is among the crucial issues engaging criminology. Although conventional scholars may favor violent, institutional responses to violent behavior, abolitionists have long attempted to provide alternative responses. Criminology as ceasefire would reject the notion of just wars as abolitionists reject the idea of just desert; it would refuse the logic of killing the killers, imprisoning them or harming them in other ways . . . .

Recent wars (Kosovo, Iraq) were waged before "mediation leading towards peacemaking" had been given a chance, and peace observers, inspectors, and international mediation and arbitration agencies were impeded, silenced, and hampered in all possible ways: "They were withdrawn so that the bombing might commence." . . . International tribunals, in their turn, are an extension of successful bombings because they are established by the winners, who refrain from passing judgment on their own atrocities and unprovoked aggression. Negotiation and conversation may provide a better protection than bombs.

As abolitionism tries to civilize our responses to crime, criminology as ceasefire will attempt to civilize war, applying restorative and reparative philosophies, rather than retribution. Aggressors may be impeded long before their act of aggression is implemented and prior to the use of violent responses, which usually turns threats into a full-blown attack. By focusing on relational dynamics, peacekeeping will defuse potential aggressors through negotiation and, in extreme cases, with quarantine and sanctuary. "We should reintroduce sanctuaries in our societies," places of refuge, endowed with the right of immunity, under international control, where aggressors are granted asylum until they are willing to open negotiations. . . .

CRIMINOLOGY AS WAR PREVENTION

Sociological attempts have been made to indicate processes leading to a world in which war is effectively ruled out. The study of organizations, for example, would suggest that the more employees view their employers as father figures, the more likely they are to justify the profits the latter make. "Abstractly stated, we might say that the more low-ranking members of an organisation identify with those higher in rank, the more likely they are to view the goals of the organisation as legitimate." . . . If we apply this proposition to the army, we would expect that the more soldiers view their officers as father figures, the more likely they are to view the war effort as a just one. Encouraging soldiers to expose the malpractice or the gratuitous violence of officers amounts, in criminology, to supporting whistleblowers who expose corrupt senior staff in organizations.

Criminologists indicating ways of curbing interpersonal violence would agree that strong social bonds reduce violations of the peace and that violence is negatively associated with integration. . . . Ideal nonviolent societies would show a high degree of socialization to a common set of values, social control mechanisms to reinforce bonds, and mechanisms to arbitrate differences among actors. These notions are normally invoked when the limitation of conflict among groups is discussed. Criminology as ceasefire would extend the application of these notions to the world system. Strong social bonds, in contrast, are more likely to be established if a fair reallocation of assets is consistently pursued. . . .

On the contrary, by tolerating that survival becomes impossible in so many areas of the world, developed countries devalue the life of millions of individuals, "bringing up a generation of young people who have already sacrificed their life, long before they make their body the instrument for the death of others." . . .

Criminology regards the reallocation of wealth as a primary precondition for crime prevention, a view that criminology as ceasefire would have to extend to the international level.

Conclusion

In "The Disasters of War," his great series of etchings, Goya documents with realism the machine-like efficiency of war as oppression. Those etchings seem to state: "I saw it." There is no glory, but only pity and cruel loss: One can see it, but cannot look at it. . . . Mainstream criminology avoids looking at war perhaps because, as legitimate violent behavior, war is seen as part of the necessary running of state interests, akin to bureaucratic rationalism and law enforcement—or perhaps because it accepts that the exclusive domain of criminological analysis pertains to state-defined harmful acts. When concerned with international violent conflicts, criminologists have mainly focused on how such conflicts are criminogenic—namely, how they produce widespread social disorganization, leading to the proliferation of conventional criminality. This chapter suggested that some theoretical tools belonging to the criminological tradition may be expanded and utilized for the criminalization of war.

Political scientists and international relations experts use their own tools of analysis for a similar purpose. Faced with new types of organized violence, some commentators, for example, see in contemporary conflicts a blurring of the distinctions among war, organized crime, and large-scale violations of human rights.

Cosmopolitan or humane governance is advocated based on an alliance between islands of civility and transnational institutions. . . . Other commentators argue for the elimination of conflict through the use of international law, disarmament, the promotion of international well-being, and education for peace, conflict resolution, and other symbolic and material resources. . . . In this chapter, functionalism, labeling, conflict theory, abolitionism, ideas of corporate and state crime, as well as social disadvantage, in the form of international relative deprivation, have been discussed with a view toward determining whether within criminology analogous, pacifist, resources can be found.

Questions

1. How has conventional criminology regarded war?

2. What is a pacifist criminology?

---------- \\\\ ----------

PART XI

CRIME TYPOLOGIES

Just as there are a variety of explanations for crimes, so, too, are there a variety of types of crimes. The major categories include violent crime and terrorism, property crimes, white-collar crimes, and public order crimes.

Violent Crime and Terrorism

A little known criminal justice policy, the felony murder statute, holds a nonviolent accomplice to a murder that occurs during a felony as being as accountable as the actual killer, as outlined in *Serving Life for Providing Car to Killers* (chap. 31). Although the general public fears violent crime, law enforcement officers are increasingly being killed in the line of duty according to *Police Fatalities on the Rise in '07* (chap. 32). After a crime occurs, it becomes a priority to catch the perpetrator, but as *With Witnesses at Risk, Murder Suspects Go Free* (chap. 33) describes, witness intimidation is increasingly a barrier to solving crimes.

Property Crime

More common than violent crime is property crime, and *Dragnet That Ensnares Good Samaritans, Too* (chap. 34) describes a disputable tactic used by law enforcement officers to catch potential per-petrators. When property is stolen, it generally needs to be resold for the perpetrator to profit from the theft. But as *Where Have All the Hot Goods Gone? The Role of Pawnshops* (chap. 35) describes, pawnshops are not necessary for the sale of stolen merchandise—the demand for stolen goods remains high.

White-Collar and Organized Crime

As white-collar and organized crime have gained more attention in the past decade, it should come as no surprise that corruption is an international phenomenon, as described in *Nonstop Theft and*

Bribery Stagger Iraq (chap. 36). Also a challenge for law enforcement beyond domestic borders is the mafia, as outlined in *As One Mafia Fades, Italy Faces Another* (chap. 37).

Public Order Crimes

Morality and law meet when a society defines public order crimes. *As Prostitutes Turn to Craigslist, Law Takes Notice* (chap. 38) discusses how the Internet is not only increasingly being used as a forum for people to meet others, but also for law enforcement to catch those trading sex for money. As with other so-called therapeutic jurisprudence tactics, including those aimed at people with mental illness and drug addiction, *New York Gambling Treatment Court Stresses Help* (chap. 39) describes a recent attempt to offer counseling and treatment as an alternative to incarceration for those addicted to gambling.

CHAPTER 31

Serving Life for Providing Car to Killers

Adam Liptak

The New York Times

Murder, Once Removed

CRAWFORDVILLE, Fla. — Early in the morning of March 10, 2003, after a raucous party that lasted into the small hours, a groggy and hungover 20-year-old named Ryan Holle lent his Chevrolet Metro to a friend. That decision, prosecutors later said, was tantamount to murder.

The friend used the car to drive three men to the Pensacola home of a marijuana dealer, aiming to steal a safe. The burglary turned violent, and one of the men killed the dealer's 18-year-old daughter by beating her head in with a shotgun he found in the home.

Mr. Holle was a mile and a half away, but that did not matter.

He was convicted of murder under a distinctively American legal doctrine that makes accomplices as liable as the actual killer for murders committed during felonies like burglaries, rapes, and robberies.

Mr. Holle, who had given the police a series of statements in which he seemed to admit knowing about the burglary, was convicted of first-degree murder. He is serving a sentence of life without the possibility of parole at the Wakulla Correctional Institution here, 20 miles southwest of Tallahassee.

A prosecutor explained the theory to the jury at Mr. Holle's trial in Pensacola in 2004. "No car, no crime," said the prosecutor, David Rimmer. "No car, no consequences. No car, no murder."

Most scholars trace the doctrine, which is an aspect of the felony murder rule, to English common law, but Parliament abolished it in 1957. The felony murder rule, which has many variations, generally broadens murder liability for participants in violent felonies in two ways. An unintended killing during a felony is considered murder under the rule. So is, as Mr. Holle learned, a killing by an accomplice.

India and other common law countries have followed England in abolishing the doctrine. In 1990, the Canadian Supreme Court did away with felony murder liability for accomplices, saying it violated "the principle that punishment must be proportionate to the moral blameworthiness of the offender."

Countries outside the common law tradition agree. "The view in Europe," said James Q. Whitman, a professor of comparative law at Yale, "is that we hold people responsible for their own acts and not the acts of others."

But prosecutors and victims' rights groups in the United States say that punishing accomplices as though they had been the actual killers is perfectly appropriate.

"The felony murder rule serves important interests," said Mr. Rimmer, the prosecutor in the Holle case, "because it holds all persons responsible for the actions of each other if they are all participating in the same crime."

Kent Scheidegger, the legal director of the Criminal Justice Legal Foundation, a victims' rights group, said "all perpetrators of the underlying felony, not just the one who pulls the trigger" should be held accountable for murder.

"A person who has chosen to commit armed robbery, rape or kidnapping has chosen to do something with a strong possibility of causing the death of an innocent person," Mr. Scheidegger said. "That choice makes it morally justified to convict the person of murder when that possibility happens."

About 16% of homicides in 2006 occurred during felonies, according to the Federal Bureau of Investigation

(FBI). Statistics concerning how many of those killings led to the murder prosecutions of accomplices are not available, but legal experts say such prosecutions are relatively common in the more than 30 states that allow them. About 80 people have been sentenced to death in the last three decades for participating in a felony that led to a murder although they did not kill anyone.

Terry Snyder, whose daughter Jessica was the victim in Mr. Holle's case, said Mr. Holle's conduct was as blameworthy as that of the man who shattered her skull.

"It never would have happened unless Ryan Holle had lent the car," Mr. Snyder said. "It was as good as if he was there."

Prosecutors sometimes also justify the doctrine on the ground that it deters murders. Criminals who know they will face harsh punishment if someone dies in the course of a felony, supporters of the felony murder rule say, may plan their crimes with more care, may leave deadly weapons at home, and may decide not to commit the underlying felony at all.

But the evidence of a deterrent effect is thin. An unpublished analysis of FBI crime data from 1970 to 1998 by Anup Malani, a law professor at the University of Chicago, found that the presence of the felony murder rule had a relatively small effect on criminal behavior, reducing the number of deaths during burglaries and car thefts slightly, not affecting deaths during rapes, and, perversely, increasing the number of deaths during robberies. That last finding, the study said, "is hard to explain" and "warrants further exploration."

The felony murder rule's defenders acknowledge that it can be counterintuitive.

"It may not make any sense to you," Mr. Rimmer, the prosecutor in Mr. Holle's case, told the jury. "He has to be treated just as if he had done all the things the other four people did."

Prosecutors sought the death penalty for Charles Miller, Jr., the man who actually killed Jessica Snyder, but he was sentenced to life without parole. So were the men who entered the Snyders' home with him, Donnie Williams and Jermond Thomas. So was William Allen, Jr., who drove the car. So was Mr. Holle.

Mr. Holle had no criminal record. He had lent his car to Mr. Allen, a housemate, countless times before.

"All he did was go say, 'Use the car,'" Mr. Allen said of Mr. Holle in a pretrial deposition. "I mean, nobody really knew that girl was going to get killed. It was not in the plans to go kill somebody, you know."

But Mr. Holle did testify that he had been told it might be necessary to "knock out" Jessica Snyder.

Mr. Holle is 25 now, a tall, lean, and lively man with a rueful sense of humor, alert brown eyes, and an unusually deep voice. In a spare office at the prison here, he said that he had not taken the talk of a burglary seriously.

"I honestly thought they were going to get food," he said of the men who used his car, all of whom had attended the night-long party at Mr. Holle's house, as had Jessica Snyder.

"When they actually mentioned what was going on, I thought it was a joke," Mr. Holle added, referring to the plan to steal the Snyders' safe. "I thought they were just playing around. I was just very naïve. Plus from being drinking that night, I just didn't understand what was going on."

Mr. Holle's trial lawyer, Sharon K. Wilson, said the statements he had given to the police were the key to the case, given the felony murder rule.

"It's just draconian," Ms. Wilson said. "The worst thing he was guilty of was partying too much and not being discriminating enough in who he was partying with."

Mr. Holle's trial took 1 day. "It was done, probably, by 5 o'clock," Mr. Holle said. "That's with the deliberations and the verdict and the sentence."

Witnesses described the horror of the crime. Christine Snyder, for instance, recalled finding her daughter, her head bashed in and her teeth knocked out.

"Then what did you do?" the prosecutor asked her.

"I went screaming out of the home saying they blew my baby's face off," Ms. Snyder said.

The safe had belonged to Christine Snyder. The police found a pound of marijuana in it, and, after her daughter's funeral, she was sentenced to 3 years in prison for possessing it.

Not every state's version of the felony murder rule is as strict as Florida's, and a few states, including Hawaii, Kentucky, and Michigan, have abolished it entirely.

"The felony-murder rule completely ignores the concept of determination of guilt on the basis of individual misconduct," the Michigan Supreme Court wrote in 1980.

The vast majority of states retain it in various forms, but courts and officials have taken occasional steps to limit its harshest applications.

In August, for instance, Gov. Rick Perry of Texas commuted the death sentence of Kenneth Foster, the driver of a getaway car in a robbery spree that ended in a murder.

Mr. Holle was the only one of the five men charged with murdering Jessica Snyder who was offered a plea bargain, one that might have led to 10 years in prison.

"I did so because he was not as culpable as the others," said Mr. Rimmer, the prosecutor.

Mr. Holle, who rejected the deal, has spent some time thinking about the felony murder rule.

"The laws that they use to convict people are just— they have to revise them," he said. "Just because I lent these guys my car, why should I be convicted the same as these people that actually went to the scene of the crime and actually committed the crime?"

Mr. Rimmer sounded ambivalent on this point.

"Whether or not the felony murder rule can result in disproportionate justice is a matter of opinion," Mr. Rimmer said. "The father of Jessica Snyder does not think so."

Question

1. Is the felony murder law just for the nonviolent participants of a crime? Why?

CHAPTER 32

Police Fatalities on the Rise in 2007

Patrik Jonsson

The Christian Science Monitor

The shooting of four police officers, one of them fatally, near Miami on Thursday became another dark day in what is already a tough year for America's 800,000 police officers.

Coming only a few days after a shootout in Odessa, Texas, that killed three officers, the Miami incident became part of a troubling phenomenon for 2007: a spike in the number of police officers who died in the line of duty to a level not seen since 1978.

Of the 132 officers to die so far this year, 54 were shot. The number of shootings represents a 59 percent increase over the same period in 2006, according to the National Law Enforcement Officers Memorial Fund in Washington.

After years of watching these figures decline or hold steady, experts are not prepared to say whether this year's increase is a trend or an aberration.

Still, "the figures this year are nothing short of alarming," says Craig Floyd, chairman of the officers' memorial fund.

Police offer several possible explanations for the high losses, including an uptick in violent crime around the country. Some experts suggest that community empathy for police, which rose after 9/11, may be waning now, especially in places where tensions exist between poor minority residents and police forces, or where transiency is relatively high, as in Miami or New Orleans.

The '07 trend line, while distressing, does not signal a danger level akin to that of the social upheaval of the 1960s and '70s, or of the "crack wars" of the late 1980s, experts say.

"It is a different time today and [there is] less of a generalized adversarial relationship between the citizenry and the cops," says Laurence Miller, a psychologist who works with the West Palm Beach Police Department in Florida. "The hard cases [in the 1960s and '70s] were a large group of criminals who politicized their criminality as rebellion. Some were sincere rebels with or without a cause, and some were petty criminals who said it was OK to take their anger out on cops."

Between the afterglow of 9/11 and TV shows such as "Cops," which usually depict police officers as tough-guy professionals who exude gritty determination in the face of criminality, law-enforcement officers today enjoy relatively high standing in society at large.

Police Losses Much Higher in Early 1970s

Those attitudes can affect the police fatality rate. Back in 1973, when there were about 210 officers for every 100,000 Americans, 134 police were feloniously killed, according to statistics from the US Department of Justice. In 2005, the last year for which the DOJ has figures, 55 police officers were feloniously killed and there were about 250 police officers for every 100,000 residents.

(On the other side of the coin, the Justice Department counts an average of 350 "felons justifiably killed by police" in recent years, down from a peak of about 400 in 1994.)

The recent officer deaths from shootings have raised awareness and tension in station houses across the US.

In Florida, 10 police officers have been killed this year. But big metro areas and sprawling, transient suburbs are not the only places affected. Veteran cop Bruce McKay was shot and killed in rural Franconia, N.H., in May.

In the Miami incident, police caught up with the suspect, Shawn Sherwin Labeet, Thursday night at an apartment complex, where he was shot and killed. Police say he was armed and armored, and they have arrested six others for helping him flee or for giving false information. Miami-Dade officer Jose Somohano died in the shootout earlier that day, one officer is hospitalized, and two were treated and released.

"It's gut-wrenching," said Miami-Dade County Mayor Carlos Alvarez on Thursday before the suspect was found. "It's a sad day."

The suspect had used a powerful semiautomatic weapon to shoot the four officers, police say. Dangers of police work remain high Nationwide, six incidents this year resulted in multiple officer deaths, from Moncks Corner, S.C., to New York City.

The fact that cops are backed up by tough laws, improved armor, and better training should not lull anyone into complacency about the danger of police work, says Terry Lynn, a professor at Endicott College in Beverly, Mass., and a former police officer who was wounded in action in Boston in 1993.

"When good intersects with the bad, we hope that good is always going to result, and that's not always the end result," says Mr. Lynn.

Despite tragic incidents, police work is safer than many people might think. Policing is ranked eighth—below convenience store clerks, construction workers, and Bering Sea crabbers—when it comes to dangerous jobs.

Mr. Floyd of the officers' memorial fund allows, too, that recent events could be aberrations. Between 2005 and 2006, he says, North Carolina went from zero officer deaths to 10. A similar thing happened in Virginia the year before. "It's hard to explain that," he says.

Questions

1. Should a person who kills a law enforcement officer in the line of duty be punished differently from a person who kills a civilian? Why?

CHAPTER 33

With Witnesses at Risk, Murder Suspects Go Free

David Kocieniewski

The New York Times

NEWARK, Feb. 27—When Yusef Johnson, a 15-year-old honors student, was killed outside an apartment complex here so gang-infested it is known as Crazyville, a witness came forward within days and told the police she knew the man she had seen fire the fatal shots.

In another case three months later, in November 2005, officers found two people who identified a street gang leader as the man they saw kill a marijuana dealer named Valterez Coley during a dispute over a woman.

And when Isaiah Stewart, a 17-year-old wearing an electronic monitoring bracelet from a recent brush with the law, was gunned down that December, another Newark teenager sketched a diagram of the crime scene, correctly identified the murder weapon and named a former classmate as the person he had watched commit the crime.

They seem like slam-dunk cases, but none of the three suspects have been arrested. It is not that detectives are unsure of their identity or cannot find them. Rather, it is because so many recent cases here have been scuttled when witnesses were scared silent that the Essex County prosecutor has established an unwritten rule discouraging pursuit of cases that rely on a single witness, and those in which witness statements are not extensively corroborated by forensic evidence.

The 3 are among at least 14 recent murders in Newark in which witnesses have clearly identified the killers but no charges have been filed, infuriating local police commanders and victims' relatives.

In 8 of the 14 cases, according to court documents and police reports, there was more than one witness; in two of them, off-duty police officers were among those identifying the suspects. But in a DNA era, these are cases with little or no physical evidence, and they often involve witnesses whose credibility could be compromised by criminal history or drug problems, or both.

"No one wants to solve these cases and lock up the killers in these cases more than we do," the county prosecutor, Paula T. Dow, said in a recent interview. "But we have to weigh the evidence and move forward only if we believe that the witnesses are credible and that they'll be there to testify at trial."

The tension between the police and prosecutors here over the evolving standards of evidence required to authorize arrest warrants is a stark example of the profound effect witness intimidation is having on the criminal justice system in New Jersey and across the country.

Surveys conducted by the National Youth Gang Center, which is financed by the federal Department of Justice, have found that 88 percent of urban prosecutors describe witness intimidation as a serious problem.

In both Baltimore and Boston, where "stop snitching" campaigns by rap artists and gang leaders have urged city residents not to cooperate with the authorities, prosecutors estimate that witnesses face some sort of intimidation in 80 percent of all homicide cases.

In Essex County, prosecutors report that witnesses in two-thirds of their homicides receive overt threats not to testify, with defendants and their supporters sometimes canvassing witnesses' neighborhoods wearing T-shirts printed with the witnesses' photographs or distributing copies of their statements to the police.

Dozens of New Jersey murder cases have been undone over the past five years after witnesses were killed, disappeared before trial or changed their stories.

In 2004, the Newark police determined that four people found dead in a vacant lot had been killed to silence a witness to a murder; a witness to that quadruple homicide was later shot to death as well.

Ms. Dow, who was appointed in 2003 amid criticism of county prosecutors' ability to close cases, said she was simply adapting to the evolving code on the streets, where gang violence and widespread distrust of law enforcement have deprived prosecutors of one of the legal system's most crucial components: dependable witnesses.

The state's attorney in Baltimore, where witness intimidation is a notorious problem, has taken an even more rigid stand, refusing to file charges in any single-witness case without extensive forensic corroboration.

But that approach differs sharply from those of prosecutors in many other urban areas, like Brooklyn, where the district attorney, Charles J. Hynes, has in recent years taken to reviewing all single-witness cases personally.

In Newark, where the homicide rate has risen in the past few years, the police, local politicians and victims' relatives are all questioning why prosecutors are holding detectives to a higher standard than the law requires—and letting dangerous criminals remain on the streets.

"How can they leave him out there?" asked Yusef's mother, Tosha Braswell, referring to the man who shot him. "Are they waiting for him to kill someone else's son?"

Tension Between Officials

Newark's mayor, Cory A. Booker, who was elected last year on a promise to reduce crime in the city, recently met with Ms. Dow to ask her to be more aggressive in filing charges. In recent years Newark police officials have accused the prosecutor of being reluctant to take on cases that could be difficult to win because her office was criticized after losing a succession of high-profile trials.

The police director, Garry F. McCarthy, worries that the prosecutor's approach undermines his crime-fighting strategy of focusing on the small group of criminals responsible for a disproportionate amount of crime.

"The law states the standard for arrest is probable cause, which is different than what is required for conviction beyond a reasonable doubt," Mr. McCarthy said. "Our goal is to arrest quickly to avoid the potential for additional crime. An arrest does not prevent an ongoing investigation from proceeding."

Ms. Dow declined to discuss details of any open cases. But she said that she was proud of her office's

performance, and that she hoped her rigorous standards for filing charges would lead investigators to work harder at getting corroboration.

"It's easy for the police to point fingers when they haven't done enough detective work to get a conviction," she said.

In Essex County, the conviction rate for homicides, which includes plea agreements, was 79 percent in 2006, up from 74 percent when Ms. Dow took over three years earlier (but down from 86 percent in 2005 and 83 percent in 2004).

In Baltimore, prosecutors under Patricia C. Jessamy, the state's attorney, obtained convictions in 65 percent of homicide cases last year, up from 59 percent in 2005 and 52 percent in 2004.

While prosecutors are often measured by such conviction rates, it is difficult to tell through statistics whether they are shying from hard-to-win cases.

What most irks the police is the failure to even file charges in cases in which witnesses have solidly identified a suspect, like the 14 here in Newark over the past three years in which Ms. Dow has declined to authorize arrest warrants. Six of these cases rely on a single witness, including the slayings of Yusef Johnson and Valterez Coley.

Yusef was a football star with a 3.7 grade-point average before he was killed in August 2005. According to police reports, a woman told detectives she had seen the shooting from 30 feet away and was well acquainted with the gunman, a member of the Crips street gang, because he frequently sold cocaine to her.

The case helps illustrate why prosecutors may shy away from single-witness cases: Given the suspect's status as both a gang member and the witness's drug supplier, even detectives have their doubts about whether the woman would ultimately testify at trial—or be believed.

On the night Mr. Coley was gunned down near a porch in Newark's Central Ward, two men told the police they had seen the gunman, whom they identified as a leader of the 252 Bloods street gang. The witnesses said the gunman was looking to settle a score with a young man who had a relationship with his girlfriend, and mistook Mr. Coley for his rival.

But one of the men soon fled the state, leaving the police with a lone witness—and thus no charges have been brought.

Danger in Cooperation

Gregory DeMattia, chief of the Essex County prosecutor's homicide division, said his investigators saw fallout from witness intimidation every day. When they arrive at a crime scene, he said, bystanders scatter so neighbors will not think they are cooperating with the police.

Those who do help often do so surreptitiously—leaving detectives a note in a trash can or asking to be taken away in handcuffs "so that neighbors will think they're in trouble with the police and not cooperating," Mr. DeMattia said.

Prosecutors in other cities tell similar stories about their witnesses being pressured, and say they are cautious about pursuing cases based on lone witnesses because of worries about faulty memory, ulterior motives and, as in the Yusef Johnson case, credibility.

That is part of why Ms. Jessamy, in Baltimore, has all but refused to file charges in single-witness situations.

But across Maryland in Prince George's County, where there is also a serious gang problem, State's Attorney Glenn F. Ivey has taken the opposite tack. He insists on pursuing single-witness cases even though he was criticized publicly for losing 4 of them in 13 months.

"If you have a single witness and you believe their story, I believe you've got to go forward, even if it's a case you might lose," said Mr. Ivey, whose office's conviction rate on homicides is more than 80 percent. "I'm not going to give the gang members, the murderers and the rapists an easy out. And if they know that all they have to do is get your case down to one witness, I think it would encourage them to use even more intimidation." Here in Newark, even in cases with multiple witnesses—and occasionally even when one of those witnesses is a police officer—the prosecutor has sometimes been unwilling to authorize arrests.

Take the case of Lloyd Shears, an Army veteran killed during a robbery in December. A man told the police he had seen his neighbor fire the fatal shots. A woman who had been standing next to him told detectives she heard the shots, and then turned to see the neighbor running from the scene. But the neighbor has not been charged.

Or consider the killing of Shamid Wallace, an 18-year-old found face down in the street last August with several gunshot wounds in his torso. Detectives found two witnesses who identified the man they said they saw kill Mr. Wallace. An off-duty Newark police officer heard the gunshots, saw a man fleeing with a gun and later picked the suspect out of a photo array. The suspect has not been arrested.

Then there is Farad Muhammad, who was stabbed to death last July. One witness told the police she had seen someone she knew running away from Mr. Muhammad's body. An off-duty police officer from neighboring East Orange identified the same man, saying he had seen the suspect chasing Mr. Muhammad with a knife. Again, no charges were filed.

Yusef's parents, who keep a shrine of photographs surrounding his school sports trophies, still hope that his suspected killer will be arrested soon.

"It's like they don't care enough," said his father, Scottie Edwards, a delivery truck driver.

Wielding Fear Like a Weapon

But to those who suggest Ms. Dow is overreacting to the problem of witness intimidation, her supporters point to the death of Steven Edwards, who was shot and killed in a car on South Eighth Street in January 2006. Within a month, detectives had three witnesses identifying the gunman.

One of the witnesses, a gang member, quickly announced he would never testify for fear he would be ostracized for helping the police—or wind up murdered himself. Six months later, another witness was himself charged in two homicides, shattering any credibility.

The third witness picked the suspect out of a photo array, but immediately began to waver when asked about testifying in open court.

"She would not say she was 100 percent sure," said a police report on the case, "because she was afraid of retaliation."

Question

1. What does the so-called hip-hop culture's 'no snitchin' philosophy contribute to the phenomenon of witness intimidation?

CHAPTER 34

Dragnet That Ensnares Good Samaritans, Too

Jim Dwyer

The New York Times

About New York

At first, an epidemic of absent-mindedness seemed to have broken out.

One purse was found just sitting on a display shelf in the shoe department at Macy's. Another one turned up downstairs, in Macy's Cellar. Yet another rested on a chair in a Midtown McDonald's, left by a woman who had stepped into the restroom.

In fact, all three items had been planted by police officers in plainclothes during the previous six weeks. And the three people who picked them up were arrested, and now face indictment on charges that could land them in state prison.

Nine months ago, a similar police decoy program called Operation Lucky Bag was effectively shut down by prosecutors and judges who were concerned that it was sweeping up the civic-minded alongside those bent on larceny. Shopping bags, backpacks and purses were left around the subway system, then stealthily watched by undercover officers. They arrested anyone who took the items and walked past a police officer in uniform without reporting the discovery.

Now, a new version of the operation has started to catch people in public places outside the subways, and at much higher stakes, Criminal Court records show.

Unlike the initial program, in which the props were worth at most a few hundred dollars, the bags are now salted with real American Express cards, issued under pseudonyms to the Police Department.

Because the theft of a credit card is grand larceny, a Class E felony, those convicted could face sentences of up to four years. The charges in the first round of Operation Lucky Bag were nearly all petty larceny, a misdemeanor, with a maximum penalty of one year in jail.

Over the years, decoy operations have proved to be very effective in flushing out criminals lurking in public places. They also have a history of misfires involving innocent people who stumbled into a piece of theater in the routine drama of city life.

When Lucky Bag began in February 2006, among its first 220 arrests were about 100 people who had prior charges and convictions. Police officials said those arrests helped drive down crime in the subways by about 13 percent.

However, more than half of those 220 involved people with no prior criminal record. In dismissing one case, a Brooklyn judge noted that the law gives people 10 days to turn in property they find, and suggested the city had enough real crime for the police to fight without any need to provide fresh temptations. The penal law also does not require that found items be turned over to a police officer. The Manhattan District Attorney's Office began to dismiss Lucky Bag charges.

"We spoke with N.Y.P.D.'s legal division and the transit bureau so they would understand the essentials needed for prosecution, because the early arrests were being made on faulty premises," said Barbara Thompson, a spokeswoman for the office. "There must be evidence that the taker did not intend to return the property."

Sneaky behavior—like trying to hide a found wallet, or slipping money out and leaving a purse behind—could show that the person meant to steal the valuables. Those instructions were added to a prosecutors' handbook.

In February, Aquarius Cheers, a 31-year-old Manhattan man who said he was on a shopping expedition with his wife, spotted a Verizon shopping bag with a cell phone and iPod inside at the 59th Street station of the No. 1 train.

As he was looking in the bag, a train arrived. Mr. Cheers said he and his wife boarded, rushed past a uniformed officer, bringing along the bag with the intention of looking for a receipt. Undercover officers then grabbed him. After his case was reported by NY1, the prosecutors vacated the charges.

A spokesman for the Police Department took questions yesterday about the revived decoy operations, but did not provide any answers.

So far, lawyers at the Legal Aid Society have identified four pending felony cases arising from the decoys. The police complaints describe suspicious behavior. For instance, after a 50-year-old man picked up the purse left in the Macy's shoe department, he put it in a shoe box and carried it to the other side of the store, a complaint said. Then he took the wallet out of the purse, put it in his pocket, and left the shoe box and purse behind, according to the police. That case is pending.

"We want to make sure these are not people intending to return wallets or found property," Ms. Thompson said.

Question

1. How is the tactic described in this article different from when law enforcement officers serve as decoys in undercover operations, such as posing as tourists to catch muggers?

CHAPTER 35

Where Have All The Hot Goods Gone? The Role of Pawnshops

Simon M. Fass

Janice Francis
University of Texas at Dallas

Recent improvements in public understanding of markets for stolen goods have led some researchers, Clarke . . . ; Kock, Kemp, and Rix . . . ; and Sutton . . . , for example, to conclude that these markets, because they facilitate disposal, act as incentives to steal. From this they argue that police and criminologists focus too much on thieves and not enough on reducing demand for hot goods. They then urge more research on the markets and on methods of disruption, such as encouraging stores that do not want illicit merchandise to install closed-circuit TVs, photograph sellers, and post signs announcing participation in crime prevention programs. . . .

More research is certainly warranted. But a shift in focus from thieves to disrupting demand seems premature. As Freiberg . . . highlights, all studies to date merely hint at the size and other features of the market. They offer no basis to justify diverting attention or for expecting that the markets can be upset in meaningful ways. Indeed, Freiberg stresses, "public knowledge of [the] market [for stolen goods] and its dynamics . . . is so impoverished as to border on the scandalous. Good policy cannot be developed on the foundations of ignorance." . . .

A glaring sign of this poverty is scarcity of research on pawnshops (i.e., pawnbrokers who make loans as main businesses or sidelines to other enterprises). Rarely arrested, these brokers have long been suspected of illicit trade. Scholars recurrently point fingers at them. Interviews with burglars show their importance for

quick disposal, and everywhere there are pawnshop laws that, among other objectives, aim to reduce traffic in stolen goods.

What makes the dearth of research especially dismaying is that, although denunciation of pawnshops and efforts to halt illegal trade have recurred for a long time, the few empirical studies done on them, mainly by economists . . . , legal analysts . . . , and others . . . , ignore or downplay their involvement. Although these scholars act as deliberate or inadvertent pawnbroker defenders, adversaries, such as Glover and Larubbia . . . and other investigative journalists, continue to underscore close connections between brokers and stolen merchandise.

Missing from this arena is dispassionate inquiry that might help estimate pawnbrokers' share of the market and also answer the question of whether new attempts to reduce that share could prove more effective than past attempts. This question is important because if the answer to it is no, then prospects for disrupting other, less visible and less regulated markets for stolen merchandise are remote. There would then be little reason for attention to shift from thieves to markets.

Following a brief look at pawnbroking in the United States, we move toward answering the question with a review of what has been alleged about the link between brokers and stolen goods. With data for Dallas, Texas, we then show that the pawnshop customer base holds a small group of prolific pawners. Containing many people with arrests for thievery, this group is responsible for

Source: "Where have all the hot goods gone? The role of pawnshops," (2004) by Fass, S. M., & Francis, J., in *Journal of Research in Crime and Delinquency, 41,* 156–179. Reprinted by permission of Sage Publications, Inc.

a disproportionate number of transactions that, we suspect, involve hot items. These data also show that even if the items are but a fraction of all things passing through shops, that fraction represents a significant portion of broker revenue and a nontrivial share of the estimated $40 to $45 billion of goods that we estimate are stolen every year. . . .

Pawnbroking in the United States

Pawnbroking is the business of lending cash for a fixed term against the security of a deposit, or pledge, of personal property. The loan is typically 30% to 75% of the market value of the pledge. If borrowers repay the loan on time together with interest and other fees, the broker returns the goods. If obligations are not paid, then borrowers forfeit their property. The broker earns revenue from interest and fees or from the sale of the forfeited items.

The business has almost always been associated with exorbitant interest rates and the facilitation of traffic in stolen goods. As a result, pawnshops are everywhere subject to specific state and local regulation. Some laws set maximum limits, or ceilings, on nominal (i.e., official) interest rates and on storage and other administrative fees that brokers use to push effective rates that customers pay to levels higher than nominal rates. In addition to licensing, bond, land use zoning, and like requirements, other regulations focus mainly on identifying stolen goods and limiting their flow through shops. Among other things, these require that brokers submit records of all transactions to police in a timely manner, that the records describe every item pawned, and that borrowers supply personal identification, at times including fingerprints or photographs.

Laws were highly restrictive during the first half of the 20th century, dampening growth of pawnbroking, or at least that of visible, licensed shops. Levine . . . counted 1,976 of them in 1911, after which the number dropped to 1,509 in 1929 and 1,374 in 1948. . . .As they still do, laws also varied greatly across states. With profitability harder in some places than in others, this variation contributed to big differences in spatial distribution, for example, from 2.6 shops per 100,000 urban population in Kentucky to 17.9 in Florida. . . .

Numbers exploded during the second half of the century, due in part to regulatory reform, especially liberalization of interest ceilings . . ., and in part to rapid growth in demand for used merchandise. Based on a count of telephone directory listings, Caskey . . . estimates that the number of shops jumped from 4,850 in 1985 to near 10,000 in 1994. We count 12,300 unduplicated listings in 2002. With allowance for those that do not list themselves, this suggests the presence of perhaps 15,000 brokers. . . .[P]awnshops have become as convenient to their customers, be they borrowers or criminals, as the 12,500 McDonald's fast-food restaurants are to their hungry patrons.

Another change, in recent years especially, is the structure of the industry. Independent outlets have been absorbed or displaced by regional and national firms, such as Cash America, which in 1987 became the first publicly traded pawnshop corporation in the country . . . , and EZCorp, Express Cash, and First Cash, which traded on Wall Street a few years later. . . .

These corporate players have moved aggressively to acquire merchandising respect to replace the pawnbroker's disreputable image with that of virtuous entrepreneurship. . . . Some efforts focus on transforming seedy shops into smart-looking retail stores. . . . Others involve strategic use of advertising in local media and encouraging these media to report positive trends in the industry, notably the move of brokers into suburbia and corresponding widening of the customer base to include more middle- and higher income individuals. . . .

What Scholars and Journalists Say About Pawnshops and Stolen Goods

These exertions may have succeeded in removing some of the stigma attached to use of pawnbrokers, especially in higher income strata. But they have yet to undermine the widely held conviction that shops serve what Glover and Larrubia . . . call the modern thief's automatic cash machine. The perceived link between theft and pawnbrokering, as mentioned earlier, is views of 30 apprehended burglars in Texas showing that 18% used pawnshops as a primary method of disposal, whereas others used them irregularly. Our analysis of transcripts from interviews by Richard and Decker . . . of 100 burglars in Missouri suggests that, although required to have their picture taken, 42% used pawnshops for goods disposal, half of them regularly.

More commonly, the perception is sustained by recurrent newspaper articles concerning pawnshop crackdowns, arrest of operators, proposals to computerize pawn records, and the like. . . . Grounded or not, belief that shops attract criminals continues to fuel opposition to their presence in residential areas. . . .

Pawnbrokers insist that this is misperception, countering that shops are in fact good neighbors serving the needs of cash-strapped populations. They illustrate this with genial stories in the media of the benefits obtained by individual borrowers in financial distress.... They claim, furthermore, that most, if not all, pawnbrokers are honest, hard-working individuals who try to reduce the risk of receiving stolen property by working closely with police.... As a result, they say, pawnshops accept few stolen items.

Some data seem to bolster this assertion. A review of 150,000 pawn transactions by Cash America found only 34 stolen items, or 0.02% of the total.... A 1991 check of 65,000 transactions in Dallas County, Texas, found 250 stolen items, or 0.4%.... In Oklahoma, 873 of more than 1.5 million items pawned in 1995, or less than 0.1%, were identified as stolen.... Police in Los Angeles, California, recover about $700,000 a year in stolen property, also a tiny share of all transactions. Similar figures, .01% and .07%, respectively, are reported in Florida for Collier and Palm Beach counties....

But these data are not convincing. They stem from efforts to match goods in pawn against lists of stolen items with serial numbers, engraved ownership markings, or other unique identifying features that victims report to police. Most stolen goods do not have such unique features....

Pawnbrokers also find support from scholars studying the business. Caskey..., after interviewing six brokers, argues that they do not traffic in stolen goods because, risking arrest or suspension of their licenses, it would be foolish for them to do so. Nickles and Adams ..., to buttress their argument that possession of property by pawnbrokers should imply legal right to the property, claim that virtually all pawned goods involve true owners. Oeltjen..., reacting to a broker's claim in court that 5% of transactions involve stolen goods, tries to discredit the assertion in a footnote by saying, disingenuously, that it is not substantiated by fact.

Evidence to challenge the idea that hot goods are an insignificant share of all pawned items is often just as anecdotal as that which supports it. Much of this evidence flows from ad hoc law enforcement actions, such as a sting operation by police in Manatee County, Florida, that was filmed and then broadcast on national TV during the NBC network's *Dateline* program on May 11, 1999.... Here, undercover officers created a pawnshop to investigate the extent to which thieves would use this type of facility. Hidden cameras then recorded how several frequent pawners came in to fence wares that were obviously hot, a few even revealing how they burgled homes and businesses. The state requirement that pawners leave a thumb print at every transaction did not deter these individuals.

An earlier undercover operation in Fort Lauderdale, Florida, filmed and then aired on December 21, 1997, during the CBS network's *60 Minutes* program, involved detectives posing as homeless people trying to pawn computer equipment with stickers indicating that they belonged to a prominent local business.... Notwithstanding overt signs that the goods might be hot, staff at three of five shops accepted them, one even asking for computer monitors the next time.

Luring CBS to Fort Lauderdale was a series of investigative reports by Glover and Larrubia... in a local newspaper claiming that city pawnshops routinely accepted suspect merchandise. After sorting through 70,000 pawn tickets to identify and examine backgrounds of the 50 most prolific pawners, the journalists found three common characteristics: Most were unemployed, 78% had arrest records (half of them for property crimes, most others for drug offenses), and all possessed a seemingly endless supply of things to pawn. A police survey of frequent pawners produced like findings in Portland, Oregon. It noted that 90% were chronic drug users with long criminal records and most were unemployed....

The combination of high arrest and unemployment rates among prolific pawners implies that pawnbrokers have a correspondingly high probability of receiving stolen goods from such people. However, without an indication of the proportion of prolific pawners in the whole population of customers or of the share of their goods relative to all pawned items, it is hard to gauge the significance of Fort Lauderdale and Portland findings. Johnson and Johnson..., for example, make clear that frequent pawners are not representative of the general clientele. Their interviews with 1,100 randomly selected borrowers in 1997 show that most are employed males, usually high school graduates, without bank accounts....

In general, research by scholars and journalists suggests three things. First, pawnbrokers do have some role in recycling stolen goods. Second, frequent pawners present the highest likelihood of acting as main agents through which pawnshops acquire hot goods. Third, the volume and value of these goods may be substantially greater than the tiny fractions that have been proposed. Pawn data from Dallas, Texas, provide circumstantial evidence to support these suggestions.

Data From Dallas, Texas

In addition to data from interviews with nine imprisoned property offenders, . . . 11 pawnshop managers, and a dozen police officers in pawn units in Dallas and surrounding municipalities, these data comprise three related components. First is a primary database of all pawn transactions recorded by the Dallas Police Department (DPD) during the 6-year period from January 1, 1991, through December 31, 1996. Each transaction shows a pawn ticket number, a pawner identification number, shop identification number, transaction date, and classification code for items pawned.

The second component, devised to help us calculate transaction values, comprises 1,000 randomly selected pawn tickets issued by 102 pawnbrokers during the first half of 1993. In addition to items in the primary database, each ticket shows the pawner's zip code address, age, sex, and race; the loan period, amount of loan, finance charge, description and quantity of items pawned; and whether the transaction invokes a loan or sale. With these data, we estimate mean dollar values for 21 items that together represent almost 70% of all pawned goods.

The third data component, designed to examine arrest histories, is sample data on 2,000 pawners. These show pawner identification number, street address, age, race, gender, and state arrest record, if any. To create the sample, we stratified the primary database into 10 frequency-of-transaction classes (i.e., one pawn transaction during 1991-1996, two transactions, etc.) and then randomly selected 200 individuals from each category. The selection provided a list of identification numbers that we then used to search through state and county public records for individual arrest information. Glover and Larrubia . . . used a similar method. The difference between the two approaches is that we cover all pawners for 6 years, not just the prolific ones for 1 year.

The Evidence Connecting Pawnshops and Stolen Goods

These data show that Dallas pawnshops received more than 5.5 million items in pledge during the 6-year period or a daily average of 23 items per shop. . . . [A]bout two dozen items made up more than 70% of the total, most in the categories of jewelry, electronics, tools, office equipment, and firearms. This distribution pattern is roughly similar to that reported by Caskey and Zikmund. . . .

This similarity between types of items pawned and stolen is expected because the features that make some things better candidates for theft than others (i.e., easily concealed, removable, valuable, enjoyable, and disposable . . .) also make them good things to pawn.

The 5.5 million items were pledged by 523,000 different individuals during the course of nearly 2.9 million transactions. . . . We estimate the total loan value of these transactions at about $208 million in 1999 dollar terms or an average of $73 per transaction. This is near the $70 that Johnson and Johnson . . . report for 1.2 million pawn tickets reviewed by the National Association of Pawnbrokers in 1997 and the $75 for 1.6 million tickets issued in Illinois in 1998 and 1999. . . .

Frequent pawners generated a disproportionate share of this activity. The 14,500 people pawning 30 times or more, although only 2.7% of the total, were responsible for 29% of all transactions and goods and 24% of total loan value. This group, as in Ft. Lauderdale and Portland, also held a higher proportion of individuals with arrest records. Its members were two to three times more likely to have been convicted for theft, larceny, burglary, or robbery than those who pawned once or twice. Nearly two thirds of the 1,100 individuals within the group who pawned more than 100 times had arrest records, more than half of them for some kind of stealing.

Looking at the most prolific pawners, [of] the top 100 individuals who each pawned more than 250 times . . . 83 [had] arrest records. Of these, 58 had accumulated 300 convictions for property as well as other offenses, or an average of 5.2 arrests per individual. Most property crime arrests (74%) were for theft, 11% for burglary of vehicles, 7% for burglary of homes or businesses, 5% for robbery, and the rest for forgery and car theft. Other infractions mainly involved drug possession (23%) or driving without a license (23%).

Among the 42 persons not apprehended for property crimes, 17 had no records, whereas 25 had 49 convictions for nontheft infractions, or an average of two arrests per person. Similar to the previous group in age, sex, and race composition, arrests here were mainly for drug possession (40%) and driving without a license (14%). But it would be premature to assume that these people committed no property offenses . . . [N]early three fourths of thefts from households, half of burglaries, and a third of robberies were not reported in 1999. Employee theft, a prime source of stolen goods, usually goes unreported, too. For reported crimes, clearance rates are low in large cities: 15% for theft, 12% for burglary, and 23% for robbery. . . . That is, 85% to 95% of property crimes are not solved. This suggests that many thieves are able to evade arrest, a fair share of them are likely to be in the group of frequent pawners that do not have property-related arrest records, and a goodly proportion of things pledged by members of this group are unlikely to be their own property.

By the same token, however, it is equally premature to presume that all frequent pawners, or even just those with property arrests, systematically dispose of stolen goods through pawnshops. Although reliance on pawnbroker loans is an expensive method of personal finance, individuals may confront situations where this is the best source available to them. What our observations suggest is that, although research by those who look only at the most prolific pawners may inflate the role of pawnbrokers in disposal of hot goods, evidence still indicates that more of these goods flow through shops than scholarly research has acknowledged. The amount may not be as high as 25% of total value, but it is certainly greater than the fractions of 1% noted earlier.

The DPD, for example, reports recovery of $23 million in stolen property from pawnshops in 1997. This represents about 3.5% of the average annual value of transactions during 1991 to 1996. Given that police recover only goods with unambiguous markings that determine true ownership, it seems likely that the share of stolen goods is much greater, greater even than the 5% dismissed by Oeltjen. . . .

What that higher share might be is uncertain. Caskey and Zikmund . . . report pledge forfeit rates in three states ranging from 14% to 22% of loans and from 10% to 20% of loan value. Our interviews with brokers suggest 20% to 25% of loans. Johnson and Johnson . . . indicate that 29% of pawners forfeited at least once during the year. Of more interest, they also report that, although 23% of individuals who pawned only once lost their pledges, 34% of those pawning four times or more forfeited at least once, 20% at least twice. In other words, as might be expected, if one suspects that the frequent pawner population contains many thieves, prolific pawners are much more likely to walk away from their goods than infrequent pawners.

Given the many legitimate reasons that people might have to forfeit, it seems unlikely that hot goods constitute as much as 20% of all things pawned. By the same token, high reported rates of forfeiture make it equally unlikely that they represent less than 5%—especially when 15% to 20% of transactions are straightforward sales of goods, not loans. The actual proportion

seems likely to lie somewhere in between. If it is in the vicinity of, say, 10%, then the annual value of stolen goods at second-hand market prices might average about $64,000 per pawnshop. Extrapolated to the universe of 15,000 brokers, the total approaches $1 billion.

This is substantial in relation to pawnshop turnover because brokers make nearly as much money selling forfeited goods as they do collecting interest. Income from interest and fees averaged $145,000 per pawnshop in 1997 or, extrapolating to 15,000 shops, a total of about $2.2 billion. . . . Sale of forfeit property produced an average of $253,400 per shop, suggesting a net revenue of around $126,700 after deducting loss of capital. For all shops, these figures imply a gross income of $3.8 billion and a net of $1.9 billion from sale of merchandise. That is, $1 billion may represent more than a quarter of the pawnbroking industry's gross and more than half of its net proceeds from sale of property.

At the same time, if the total value of pilfered merchandise is close to our estimate of $40 to $45 billion per year, then this $1 billion also represents 2.0% to 2.5% of all stolen goods. If, say, half the items are retained by the people who steal them, it represents 4% to 5% of all goods disposed. This is a modest share of the whole market. But pawnshops are only one component of used merchandise trade. Excluding repair and other shops selling second-hand items as sidelines, the census counted an additional 105,000 used merchandise stores with gross sales of $8.3 billion in 1997. . . . If stolen goods comprised a quarter of these sales as well, then one could account for another $2.1 billion and thus another 8% to 10% of the market for stolen goods. The entire used merchandise sector, including pawnshops, might then be handling $3.1 billion per year, or 12% to 16% of the market for hot goods.

Conclusions

Although our estimates may eventually prove inaccurate, there seems no way to circumvent a few essential facts. One is that pawnbrokers, as omnipresent today as McDonald's restaurants, offer thieves a potentially convenient method of disposing of merchandise, especially items with no obvious markings. Another fact, found in our data and by journalists in Fort Lauderdale and police in Portland, is that the population of prolific pawners contains a large segment of people with robust arrest records. Combined with findings from burglar interviews, this strongly intimates that the population contains a substantial corps of habitual thieves who actually do rely on pawnbrokers for their recurrent service needs. A third fact, as we have tried to show, is that a modest percentage of the total value of pawnbroker transactions is sufficient to constitute a noteworthy share of our estimated $40 to $45 billion per year in stolen property. Even if our numbers are wrong, there is enough circumstantial evidence here to warrant much more scholarly research, the quantitative sort especially, on connections between pawnbroking (and other components of the used merchandise retail sector) and hot goods. This is our first conclusion.

Our second conclusion is that the idea of deliberately disrupting markets for stolen goods does not seem well founded. In the case of pawnshops, Sutton's . . . notion that businesses can avoid buying such goods by use of closed-circuit TVs, photographs and/or signs is not convincing because these actions are the same or similar (e.g., fingerprints) to measures that most pawnbrokers undertake routinely. Such tactics and police oversight may have reduced the flow of stolen goods through pawnshops at different times, but there is no evidence to confirm this. More likely, given the criminal records of prolific pawners, is that they have not dissuaded thieves from availing themselves of pawnbrokers. One reason, proposed by Hall . . . , may be that enforcement of pawnshop regulations is too perfunctory to interfere with receipt and disposal of stolen goods. Another is that enforcement has been effective, but only to the extent of displacing part of the trade to other, less regulated enterprises, such as second-hand, precious metal and antique dealers or, where these are also under perpetual scrutiny (e.g., Illinois, Washington), flea markets and the like. A third possibility, the most plausible, is that most stolen goods are not identifiable as such.

There are several dimensions to this issue. As discussed by Clarke . . . and Sutton . . . , one is technical. Most stolen items are not unique; do not have serial numbers, engraved codes, or other property identifiers; or else have markings that are easy to remove. Another dimension is social. Most households neither record serial numbers of what they buy nor engrave them, and, together with firms, do not report their loss to police.

The third aspect, the most important, is economic. Because the annual volume of hot goods is large, perhaps measuring in the hundreds of millions of items, the societal outlay required to create a record for each reported item and, at the same time, a reference base for the billions of things that businesses buy legitimately is larger. It is for the moment prohibitive. In other words, stolen goods are not identifiable largely because it costs too much to identify them. They are, as a result, invisible in the daily exchange of millions of second-hand items between sellers and buyers.

Viewed in this context, the claim that markets for stolen goods act as underlying incentives to steal makes sense only if one subscribes to the notion that these markets are clearly separate or separable from retail trade in general and used merchandise trade in particular. Because they are neither clearly separate nor separable, because it is usually impossible to know what is or is not stolen, a recommendation to deliberately disrupt demand for hot goods is a recommendation to deliberately disrupt demand for second-hand goods in general. This is unwise counsel.

From this, our third and final conclusion is that wiser would be support of actions to render more efficient the monitoring of people and things circulating through pawnshops, second-hand stores, and similar establishments. The premise here is that identification and apprehension of thieves need to remain the focus of police and criminologist attention. More efficient monitoring of suspicious pawners and goods, achieved through strengthened pawn details, speedier transfer of transaction records from pawnshops to police computers, accelerated analysis of the data, and similar means can help in this. To the extent that pawnbrokers cooperate with police in improvement of monitoring, these actions may also protect the interests of firms that prefer to shun hot goods.

The problem, now and in the past, is that pawn units (called *details* or *squads* sometimes) are relatively understaffed partly because police departments are asked to concentrate on crimes against persons, partly because policymakers do not see gain from spending on data collection, and partly because most pawnbrokers object to the extra cost and intrusion into their affairs. The units, as consequence, are usually behind in data entry. Fort Lauderdale's pawn unit recorded less than 50% of the pawn information it received during 1995. . . . Dallas police recorded 100% of all information for only one continuous 12-month span during 1991 to 1996, managing an average completion rate of 70% to 80% through the period. Consequently, items were often identified as hot after pawnbrokers disposed of them, and transaction trails that could justify surveillance of suspicious pawners were often identified after they ran cold.

Benefits of improved monitoring have already shown themselves through increased recovery and apprehension. Murray . . . , for example, reports that police in

Atlanta, Georgia, entered only 25% of transaction data in 1996. A year later, after the installation of a computer system with electronic data transfer from brokers, police entered 100% of pawn information, reduced processing time from several weeks to 24 hours, and increased recovery rates from 12 to 42 items per month. . . . In Florida, similarly, Perez . . . reports a rise in recovery after the Broward County Sheriff established an automated pawn-tracking database. The new system also helped catch 175 parole violators and 110 felons pawning firearms in 1998. By 2000, some 50 state and local agencies were using similar tracking systems, including the Florida Department of Law Enforcement (FDLE), which initiated a project to install a statewide database in that year.

In addition to property recovery and apprehension of criminals, there is also the prospect of using transaction data to map suspicious behavior in "real" time. People pawning 20 diamond rings or watches or electric tools or city street directories or anything else of value within a relatively short period, especially if encumbered with interesting criminal histories, earn immediate suspicion of stealing or of receiving hot goods. If the items are not reported stolen or if they lack markings, then arrest is not possible. But it is possible to conduct surveillance to determine whether initial suspicions are justified, whether there are networks of accomplices warranting police attention, or whether there are other ways to identify and maybe apprehend there or other thieves.

The prime obstacle to improved tracking is pawnbroker resistance. Rarely conceding the utility of anything but "article only" tracking to help identify stolen goods, brokers habitually oppose collection of personal information that might reduce the flow of patrons. In 2001, for instance, the Florida Pawnbrokers Association responded to the introduction of automated tracking by threatening to initiate legislation that would delete all customer data from pawn unit computer systems. The association did not achieve this goal, but it convinced the legislature to reduce funding for FDLE's statewide database project from $1 million in 2000 to $275,000 in 2001, and then to zero in 2002.

Pawnbrokers are nowhere strong enough to eliminate policy scrutiny. But as the industry organizes for common cause, strength such as that shown in Florida may spread. Helping in this is the ability of brokers to propagate image-enhancing media stores containing references to academic studies that point to minuscule quantities of stolen goods in their merchandise. Scarcity of proper research on the role of pawnshops and other second-hand stores in hot goods trade thus makes it easier for brokers to thwart efforts at improved tracking. Accordingly, the first conclusion put forward above, about the need for more scholarly research, is, in our opinion, the most important.

Question

1. What is the allure of buying stolen property?

CHAPTER 36

Nonstop Theft and Bribery Stagger Iraq

Damien Cave

The New York Times

BAGHDAD, Dec. 1—Jobless men pay $500 bribes to join the police. Families build houses illegally on government land, carwashes steal water from public pipes, and nearly everything the government buys or sells can now be found on the black market.

Painkillers for cancer (from the Ministry of Health) cost $80 for a few capsules; electricity meters (from the Ministry of Electricity) go for $200 each, and even third-grade textbooks (stolen from the Ministry of Education) must be bought at bookstores for three times what schools once charged.

"Everyone is stealing from the state," said Adel Adel al-Subihawi, a prominent Shiite tribal leader in Sadr City, throwing up his hands in disgust. "It's a very large meal, and everyone wants to eat."

Corruption and theft are not new to Iraq, and government officials have promised to address the problem. But as Iraqis and American officials assess the effects of this year's American troop increase, there is a growing sense that, even as security has improved, Iraq has slipped to new depths of lawlessness.

One recent independent analysis ranked Iraq the third most corrupt country in the world. Of 180 countries surveyed, only Somalia and Myanmar were worse, according to Transparency International, a Berlin-based group that publishes the index annually.

And the extent of the theft is staggering. Some American officials estimate that as much as a third of what they spend on Iraqi contracts and grants ends up unaccounted for or stolen, with a portion going to Shiite or Sunni militias. In addition, Iraq's top anticorruption

official estimated this fall—before resigning and fleeing the country after 31 of his agency's employees were killed over a three-year period—that $18 billion in Iraqi government money had been lost to various stealing schemes since 2004.

The collective filching undermines Iraq's ability to provide essential services, a key to sustaining recent security gains, according to American military commanders. It also sows a corrosive distrust of democracy and hinders reconciliation as entrenched groups in the Shiite-led government resist reforms that would cut into reliable cash flows.

In interviews across Baghdad, though, Iraqis said the widespread thieving affected them at least as powerfully on an emotional and moral level. The Koran is very clear on stealing: "God does not love the corrupters," one verse says. And for average Iraqis, those ashamed of the looting that took place immediately after the fall of Saddam Hussein, the current era of anything-goes is particularly crushing because almost no one can avoid its taint.

For many, it is not a question of getting rich. Theft and corruption have become survival tools, creating a spiral of dishonest transactions that leave nearly everyone feeling dirty.

Abu Ali is a 23-year-old Sunni with a soft middle and a common tale. Identifying himself by only a nickname, which means father of Ali, he said that he, his wife, his elderly mother and six relatives fled their home in eastern Baghdad last year after receiving death threats from Shiite militias. First they rushed to Diyala Province, and when that turned violent, they moved back to a safer area of Baghdad—broke and desperate.

A major breadwinner for his family, Abu Ali needed a job. And like many Iraqis, he saw only one employer hiring: the government. A neighbor who was a police officer suggested joining the force. Abu Ali asked how, noting that recruits outnumbered positions. The answer was simple: a $500 bribe.

Abu Ali borrowed the money a few months ago and found his way to a cellphone shop downtown, where, he said, a man in his late 20s welcomed him inside. The man identified himself as a police captain and seemed at ease with the transaction. His wealth sparkled all around.

"He had a silver Mercedes," Abu Ali said. "He was wearing a thick gold chain and a gold watch."

Abu Ali tried to bargain for a lower fee, but failed, handing over the cash and filling out official forms. In return, he said, he received a blue card stamped "Ministry of the Interior," which declared him an accepted member of the police force. The man with the gold chain told him to watch for an announcement in the local paper that listed the names of newly accepted recruits, and to bring the card to his first day of training.

"How do I know I'll really get the job?" Abu Ali said he asked. "He told me, 'I've put in 70 or 80 people already. Don't worry about it.'"

Five months later, Abu Ali's name appeared in the newspaper. At the police academy in September, he said, he discovered that most of his class was from Sadr City and that everyone paid $400 to $800 to join.

"There's not a single person among the 850 people in my class who joined for free," he said.

His commanders, he added, also now collect the salaries of recruits who quit, a payout of more than $100,000 a month. "No one can stop it," Abu Ali said. "Corruption runs from top to bottom."

The details of Abu Ali's story could not be independently verified, but they fit a pattern of bribes and payroll schemes found in nearly every nook of Iraq's government, according to government workers, Iraqi lawmakers and some American officials.

Many Iraqis speak from personal experience.

Mr. Subihawi, the Shiite tribal leader in Sadr City, said that when he recently tried to find a job for a young member of his tribe, he was told by local government officials that there was nothing available unless he was willing to pay.

Other Iraqis, in interviews, described similar encounters.

Cash is also often what leads to promotions—with the help of a fake college degree, purchased for about $40—and theft is no less common. One government worker, who goes by the name Abu Muhammad, said a senior administrator at the ministry where he worked recently sold off computers, laser printers, office furniture and other supplies that appeared to have been paid for with American aid. The official was never caught or prosecuted, he said.

Haider Abu Laith, an engineer at the Ministry of Culture, said a close friend and fellow engineer at a government agricultural agency recently told him he was being pressured to inflate the cost of equipment purchased abroad so that senior officials could skim the surplus.

He said his friend quit, fearing that he would be killed if he refused.

And at the Ministry of Health's main warehouse in Baghdad, American troops discovered this summer that two trucks full of medicines and medical equipment had disappeared while several guards on duty—young men in acid-washed jeans, with gel in their hair—said they saw nothing.

Even some Iraqi lawmakers admit that the free-for-all has become too extensive to stop easily. "The size of the corruption exceeds the imagination," said Shatha Munthir Abdul Razzaq, a member of Parliament's largest Sunni bloc. "Because there are no tough laws, no penalties for those who steal."

Stuart W. Bowen Jr., who runs the Office of the Special Inspector General for Iraq Reconstruction, said Prime Minister Nuri Kamal al-Maliki actually undercut anticorruption efforts this year by requiring that investigators get permission from his office before pursuing ministers or former ministers on corruption charges.

Mr. Maliki has also not rescinded a law, opposed by the Americans, that lets ministers exempt their employees from investigation. "Those two legal positions within the fledgling Iraqi government are incompatible with democracy," Mr. Bowen said in an interview. "My concerns about the corruption problem have risen."

Ali al-Dabbagh, the prime minister's spokesman, has said the government is determined to fight corruption. And at some gas stations, especially where American troops have concentrated their efforts, Iraqis report fewer demands for the bribes that once tripled or quadrupled the price of gas.

But for a large number of people, survival still depends on taking what they can, when they can. Some estimates put unemployment at 40 percent. For many Iraqis, minor theft seems justified because others take so much and because daily life in Iraq still feels precarious— a crust of calm resting on currents of sectarianism, poverty and anger.

Baghdad, in particular, is still marked by desperation, with more women begging at intersections and with many Iraqis barely getting by, even with a little cheating.

These are people like Sattar Alwan, 41, a taxi driver with a dark mustache who lives with nearly a dozen relatives in a makeshift, illegal house on government land in eastern Baghdad. He said his family built the squat brick structure because gunmen pushed them out of their own home and they had nowhere else to go.

Or Abbas Wadi Kadhim, 42, who uses a raspy air compressor to extract city water from broken pipes so he can earn money washing cars.

Mr. Kadhim acknowledges that he does not pay for the water, nor does he pay rent at the abandoned government building a few hundred yards away, where he often sleeps so he can be ready when customers arrive at 7 a.m.

He figures his government owes him. He was imprisoned by Mr. Hussein's government and disabled in the Iran-Iraq war. His left forearm is as thin as a child's, and crooked at the wrist.

"I have six kids," he said, spraying down a silver sedan last week, "and all I get is 150,000 Iraqi dinar," about $120 a month in disability payments. "It's not enough."

Mr. Kadhim said he was from Sadr City, a sprawling public housing project dominated by the Mahdi Army, Iraq's most prominent Shiite militia. He suggested that he could make more money if he were less religious.

"The forbidden work is far away from us, as far away as the seven seas," he said, looking east toward his old neighborhood.

He sounded proud. He spends long hours scrubbing cars for $4 each in an empty lot with a clear view of Baghdad's main soccer stadium. His customers praise him for being thorough. But like many Iraqis who have made a choice to bend the rules, he seems still unsure of his moral footing: a little bit ashamed, a touch defensive.

"This job is better for us than doing things that are forbidden," he said, his voice getting louder. "It's better than stealing or using people. The more honest the job is and the harder we work, the better."

Reporting was contributed by Anwar J. Ali, Diana Oliva Cave, Hosham Hussein, Qais Mizher, and Abeer Mohammad.

Question

1. What might the corruption taking place during the rebuilding of Iraq tell us about human nature and the opportunity to profit?

CHAPTER 37

As One Mafia Fades, Italy Faces Another

Bruce Livesey

The Christian Science Monitor

Rome

This past August, the fatal shooting of six Italian men exiting a restaurant in Duisburg, Germany, informed the world of what Italian authorities already knew: Italy's 'Ndrangheta crime syndicate had come of age as an international force.

The Cosa Nostra, Italy's Sicilian mafia, used to be the country's most notorious and feared organization. But the capture this week of Salvatore Lo Piccolo showed how far they have fallen: For the second time in less than two years, their top boss was arrested.

As the Cosa Nostra wilted under the focused efforts of Italy's antimafia forces, however, the 'Ndrangheta quietly flourished. But after the assassination of a politician in the 'Ndrangheta's home province in 2005, the government vowed to crack down on the syndicate. An antimafia youth group—Ammazzateci Tutti—also rose up, vowing to hold the government to its promise.

"It was a mistake, because the state should investigate all criminal organizations," says Giuseppe Lumia, vice president of Italy's antimafia parliamentary commission. "If we were to use a sports metaphor, the state is recuperating, is training with its best players, but has not yet formed a team that is able to win the championship."

Europe's Biggest Cocaine Player

Based in Calabria, the southernmost province of Italy's mainland, the 'Ndrangheta was once largely limited to shaking down small-town merchants and kidnapping for ransom.

Today, the 'Ndrangheta has formed close ties with Colombia's Medellin drug cartel and become the biggest player in Europe's cocaine market, says Alberto Cisterna, a magistrate with Italy's National Antimafia Directorate in Rome.

Italian officials and experts estimate that 80 percent of Europe's imports come through the Calabrian port of Gioia Touro, which local police say is controlled by the syndicate.

Prosecutors estimate that the 'Ndrangheta's operation generates €36 billion ($52 billion) a year in revenues. According to a 2005 report by the Italian social research institute Eurispes, drug trafficking accounted for €22.3 billion, with extortion, arms trafficking, and loan sharking also bringing substantial revenues.

The syndicate has used its proceeds to invest in northern Italy and the rest of Europe, says Nicola Gratteri, Calabria's senior magistrate, who has battled the 'Ndrangheta for nearly 20 years—doing everything from ordering wiretaps to prosecuting court cases. The Italian and German press, including Panorama and Stern magazines, have reported money-laundering schemes by the 'Ndrangheta across Europe.

According to a report presented by Italian Prime Minister Romano Prodi's office in August, the syndicate has "a sizable presence" in Germany, France, Belgium, the Netherlands, the Balkans, Eastern Europe, and South America.

Virtually Impervious Family Ties

With members recruited on the basis of family ties, the 'Ndrangheta is virtually impervious to police infiltration. "Every *locali*, or cell, is composed of people who belong to family, and this is why there are no justice collaborators," says Mr. Gratteri, adding that only 42 turncoats have come from the 'Ndrangheta, compared with 700 to 1,000 from the Cosa Nostra and 2,000 from the Camorra.

Yet the 'Ndrangheta's clans can be quarrelsome—with fatal results. The killings in Duisburg last summer are rooted in such an internecine dispute, says Mr. Gratteri, who is overseeing the investigation into the origins of the attack.

One of the men shot in Duisburg, Marco Marmo, was wanted by authorities for involvement in the December 2006 murder of the 'Ndrangheta leader's wife in the Calabrian village of San Luca. Gratteri refused to discuss the details of the investigation under way, but the Italian press has speculated that Marmo was the reason an 'Ndrangheta clan executed the Duisburg attack.

Mr. Lumia of Italy's antimafia parliamentary commission says this conflict "has become a clash for financial and territorial control of San Luca . . . [which] becomes control on an international level."

In order to bring down the 'Ndrangheta, Gratteri contends, new legislation is needed. "We have no laws that are proportional to the force of the 'Ndrangheta," he says, explaining that well-behaved convicts can leave prison after five years. "I would like . . . [them] not to be released before 30 years."

Youths' Challenge to Italy: Rise Up

For magistrates battling the 'Ndrangheta, a welcome ally has been Ammazzateci Tutti—formed two years ago by fed-up young people. "The 'Ndrangheta is an octopus which tries to control everything and to kill all of the fish," says Bruno Marino, a student whose father was killed by the group.

Since its founding, Ammazzateci Tutti has held regular demonstrations designed to pressure the Italian state into taking action against the 'Ndrangheta.

Last February, a protest in Reggio di Calabria drew thousands into the streets. In recent weeks, the group has staged regular protests against the government's pending transfer of Luigi De Magistris, an antimafia magistrate investigating links between politicians and the 'Ndrangheta.

"The 'Ndrangheta . . . is infiltrating the political system," says Aldo Pecora, a law student and spokesman for Ammazzateci Tutti, whose taunting title means, "Now Kill Us All."

"Ammazzateci Tutti is a message that expresses both hope and challenge to the 'Ndrangheta, saying 'See if you have enough lead to kill us all,'" explains Mr. Pecora. "It's also a challenge to normal people to rebel against the 'Ndrangheta."

Pecora says the group continues to form chapters across both Calabria and throughout Italy, their message spreading via the Internet, which he credits with helping them to become a national organization.

Still, he concedes that they don't yet pose a serious threat to the 'Ndrangheta, but are rather "bothering" those who want to control Calabria.

He hopes to one day become an antimafia magistrate, and says he's put Ammazzateci Tutti "before everything, before my family and my studies, because I am not wasting time. I am doing something for my children, if I ever have any. There is nothing to lose and only the future to gain."

Question

1. Can the mafia ever be completely wiped out in a country? Why?

CHAPTER 38

As Prostitutes Turn to Craigslist, Law Takes Notice

Bruce Lambert

The New York Times

GARDEN CITY, N.Y., Sept. 4—The eight women visited Long Island this summer along with vacationing families and other business travelers, staying in hotels and motels in commercial strips in middle-class suburbs like East Garden City, Hicksville and Woodbury. Their ages ranged from 20 to 32.

Three had come all the way from the San Francisco Bay area, one from Miami. Two lived less than 60 miles away, in Newark and Elizabeth, N.J. and two even closer, in Brooklyn.

All eight were arrested on prostitution charges here, snared in a new sting operation by the Nassau County police that focuses on Craigslist.org, the ubiquitous Web site best known for its employment and for-sale advertisements but which law enforcement officials say is increasingly also used to trade sex for money.

Nassau County has made more than 70 arrests since it began focusing on Craigslist last year, one of numerous crackdowns by vice squads from Hawaii to New Hampshire that have lately been monitoring the Web site closely, sometimes placing decoy ads to catch would-be customers.

"Craigslist has become the high-tech 42nd Street, where much of the solicitation takes place now," said Richard McGuire, Nassau's assistant chief of detectives. "Technology has worked its way into every profession, including the oldest."

Augmenting traditional surveillance of street walkers, massage parlors, brothels and escort services, investigators are now hunching over computer screens to scroll through provocative cyber-ads in search of solicitors.

In July raids, the sheriff of Cook County, Ill., rounded up 43 women working on the streets—and 60 who advertised on Craigslist. In Seattle, a covert police ad on Craigslist in November resulted in the arrests of 71 men, including a bank officer, a construction worker and a surgeon.

And in Jacksonville, Fla., a single ad the police posted for three days in August netted 33 men, among them a teacher and a firefighter. "We got hundreds and hundreds and hundreds of hits" in phone calls and e-mail messages, said John P. Hartley, the assistant chief sheriff there.

Sex and the Internet have been intertwined almost since the first Web site, but the authorities say that prostitution is flourishing online as never before. And while prostitutes also advertise on other sites, the police here and across the country say Craigslist is by far the favorite. On one recent day, for example, some 9,000 listings were added to the site's "Erotic Services" category in the New York region alone: Most offered massage and escorts, often hinting at more.

Law enforcement officials have accused Craigslist of enabling prostitution. But the company's president, Jim Buckmaster, said its 24-member staff cannot patrol the multitude of constantly changing listings—some 20 million per month—and counts on viewers to flag objectionable ads, which are promptly removed.

"We do not want illegal activity on the site," he said. Asked whether the company supported the police's placing decoy ads on Craigslist, Mr. Buckmaster said: "We don't comment on the specifics" of law enforcement.

Craig Newmark, the site's founder and chairman, deferred all questions to Mr. Buckmaster.

The police have also occasionally turned to Craigslist to trace stolen goods offered for sale or make drug arrests. In June, in Nassau, spotting code words like "snow" or "skiing" to refer to cocaine, they set up a sting with an undercover officer to arrest a man who advertised cocaine for sex.

Experts say that under the federal Communications Decency Act of 1996, the ads are legal and Web site owners are exempt from responsibility for content posted by users. Craigslist, for example, last fall won dismissal of a suit that alleged housing discrimination in ads posted on its Web site. "You hold the speaker liable, not the soapbox," explained Kurt B. Opsahl, senior staff attorney for the Electronic Frontier Foundation, a digital civil liberties group based in San Francisco.

While Mr. Buckmaster said Craigslist was no different from old-media publications that have long carried sex-oriented ads, law enforcement officials say its scope and format are especially useful to the sex industry. With listings for some 450 cities around the world, Craigslist claims to have 25 million users and 8 billion page views a month. Posting advertisements, except those in the employment and some housing categories, is free, as is responding to them by e-mail.

"The Internet has allowed people to make contact in a way not possible before," said Ronald Weitzer, a sociology professor at George Washington University and a researcher on prostitution. "Ten years ago this was not happening at all."

As Nassau's district attorney, Kathleen Rice, said of Craigslist: "It's as easy as it gets."

Tracy Quan, a member of the advocacy group Prostitutes of New York and author of the autobiographical novel "Diary of a Married Call Girl" (Harper Perennial, 2006), acknowledged that "the Internet became a virtual street for people in the sex industry," but said that "the police are as inventive and as wily as sex workers are." She said that the stings amounted to entrapment of consenting adults, and that "it seems like an enormous waste of time resources by authoritarian busybodies."

The police say that Craigslist has changed prostitution's patterns, with people roaming the country, setting up shop for a week or two in hotels—often near airports—where they use laptop computers and cell phones to arrange encounters for hundreds of dollars, then moving on to their next location.

"They like to move around, that's for sure," said Assistant Chief McGuire. "They're flying in from out of state because there is money here" on Long Island.

In Westchester County this spring, the police in Greenburgh, Rye, Rye Brook and Elmsford formed a joint task force to investigate ads on Craigslist, resulting in 30 arrests. Some of those arrested were out-of-town prostitutes who booked numerous dates in advance, then whisked in for a busy couple of days, the police said.

In Sandpoint, Idaho, population 8,105, R. Mark Lockwood, the police chief, said that an arrest this summer involving Craigslist "was probably our first prostitution case since World War II."

Amid the police crackdown, in a game of electronic cat-and-mouse, the authorities say that Web site users who get wind of enforcement sometimes post warnings to thwart investigators.

The Craigslist modus operandi provides mobility, helping prostitutes keep a few steps ahead of the law, law enforcement officials say. It also affords a degree of anonymity—if they are caught, being away from home makes an arrest less embarrassing.

Pimps have also adapted to the computer age, the police say. Among those arrested here in August, on charges of promoting prostitution, was Victor Teixeira, 31, of Mineola. "He was managing the technology of it," said Assistant Chief McGuire. "He recruited the women on the Internet. He put different ads up sometimes three times a day. He would screen the calls and make the appointments."

Mr. Teixeira pleaded not guilty; he could not be reached for comment.

Most of the arrests are on misdemeanor charges, with convictions resulting in fines of a few hundred dollars; only repeat offenders risk jail time. The real penalties are the disruption of business, the cost of lawyers and the seizures of computers and cash—as much as several thousand dollars at a time. The police say the focus on such misconduct is worthwhile because prostitution is often linked to other crimes involving drugs, weapons, physical abuse and exploitation of minors and immigrants.

Law enforcement officials ask why Craigslist even includes Erotic Services among its 191 categories. Mr. Buckmaster, the company president, said the site created that category "at the request of our users" for legitimate massage, escorts and exotic dancers. In an e-mail interview, he said that the police had praised the company's cooperation, though he did not give examples.

Despite police complaints that Craigslist facilitates prostitution, some experts say the Web site also aids enforcement.

"Craigslist is a very open site, and it leaves digital footprints," said Leslie A. Harris, president of the nonprofit Center for Democracy and Technology. "It makes it easier for the police."

Question

1. How has Craigslist changed how people interact with each other?

CHAPTER 39

New York Gambling Treatment Court Stresses Help

Ken Belson

The New York Times

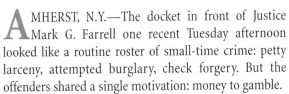

AMHERST, N.Y.—The docket in front of Justice Mark G. Farrell one recent Tuesday afternoon looked like a routine roster of small-time crime: petty larceny, attempted burglary, check forgery. But the offenders shared a single motivation: money to gamble.

Such is the criminal parade in the country's first and only gambling treatment court. Following the model of about 2,000 "therapy courts" devoted to drugs and spousal abuse that have opened nationwide in the last two decades, the setup here allows defendants to avoid jail time if they follow a court-supervised program that includes counseling sessions, credit checks and twice-monthly meetings with Justice Farrell.

"I realize this is demanding," the judge said the other day as he ordered Andrew Hallett, 19, who forged his father's checks to feed a bingo and lottery addiction, to attend Gamblers Anonymous meetings twice a week. "If you continue to apply yourself to the program, and you continue to go to the self-helps, we'll get you through it."

Mirroring the rise in gambling nationally and the opening of two new casinos near this suburb of Buffalo, the court's caseload has grown steadily since it opened in 2001, to several dozen cases a year from a handful. And as gambling has become more popular, with the growth of online poker and with New York State lottery revenues nearly doubling to $6.8 billion over the past six years, Justice Farrell's docket includes middle-aged parents with college degrees and steady jobs as well as young drug users with criminal records.

"Gambling has become almost a genre in our society," said Justice Farrell, who lectures defendants with a stern voice and a no-nonsense tone. A majority of the gamblers he sees can hold their own, he said, "but it's the 5 percent that have problems, and we're seeing an expression of it in gambling court."

The gambling court is too small and too young to show statistically significant results, but its staff members say that more than half the 100-plus defendants so far have completed the treatment program, and only one has been arrested again—on an offense not connected to gambling. But drug courts have shown some impressive results: a 2003 study in Washington State found that participants were 13 percent less likely to become repeat offenders than defendants who went through the regular criminal system, saving $3,759 per participant in potential administrative costs and $3,020 in costs to victims.

The idea of expanding therapeutic courts to problem gamblers seems to be gaining momentum. Judges and lawyers in Buffalo have recently started steering gambling-related cases toward Amherst, and Justice Farrell has been in demand on the speaking circuit, talking about the program to prosecutors, counselors and other officials in 15 states since 2002.

Don E. Dutton, commissioner of the New Mexico Gaming Control Board, said a statewide task force there plans to recommend the start of such a diversion program by year's end.

Jeffrey J. Marotta, who manages the Oregon Problem Gambling Services in that state's Department of Human Services, said his agency expects to start a pilot program soon.

And in Louisiana, the state attorney general in 2004 set up a diversion program in which gamblers charged with nonviolent crimes can avoid trial if they get treatment.

Keith S. Whyte, executive director of the National Council on Problem Gambling, said California and Illinois have expressed interest in starting gambling courts. Also, Arizona trains its probation officers to watch for problem gamblers.

Justice Farrell, a 59-year-old lawyer, has spent about 35 hours a week since 1994 running Amherst Town Court. With 43,000 cases a year, it is one of the larger of New York's approximately 1,250 town and village courts, which handle two million criminal, domestic-violence, landlord-tenant, traffic and other cases each year. Justice Farrell started a diversion program from drug crimes in 1996, and for domestic violence in 1999.

Justice Farrell, who said he will visit local casinos a few times a year, "lose $100 and figure out what kind of idiot I was," noticed the spike in gambling-related crime by looking for warning signs similar to those he saw with drug addiction and domestic violence.

In a two-and-a-half-week span a few years ago, he said, he saw a dozen cases of car theft, larceny and other crimes committed by otherwise unlikely suspects, and called in experts who determined that gambling was the common theme. Soon, the gambling court was born.

As with drugs and domestic violence, the gambling defendants must plead guilty to be eligible for the diversion program, which gives Justice Farrell broad discretion to defer punishment for up to a year and dismiss charges for those who complete the prescribed treatment regimen. But he said gambling can be more complicated, because the connections to the crimes are indirect. For example, there is no urine test to identify gamblers, and society generally treats addiction to cards or dice as a character flaw rather than a psychological disorder.

"People are more likely to admit they are a heroin addict than a gambling addict," Justice Farrell said.

So the judge and his staff members screen defendants after arraignments by asking those accused of, say, check forgery, why they needed the money. Court-appointed counselors look for signs of impulsiveness and weak self-control.

The gambling court meets every other Tuesday for an hour—just before the much busier drug court session—and on one recent afternoon it started by distributing leaflets on gambling addiction to all the defendants. Then the defendants heard from Karreen Kelly, a graduate of the drug court program after an arrest for driving while intoxicated, who said she spent "two years drinking in my bedroom" to deal with her husband's compulsive betting.

Mrs. Kelly, who is 45 and works in retailing, said that constant calls from loan sharks and credit-card companies, and the loss of more than $160,000, led her to consider suicide with a bottle of tranquilizers and a 12-pack of beer.

"When he started gambling, I didn't think anything of it," she said between sobs. "I had no time because I was working and with kids."

Over the hour-long session, a young woman numbly admitted that she had relapsed, both using drugs and buying daily scratch-off lottery tickets. A man in sweat pants told a story about "replacing one addiction with another," explaining that he had recently been in jail and found himself losing $400 gambling with cellmates.

In another case, a man whose habits included sports betting, dice and animal fights had missed a scheduled counseling session.

"You need to be where you're scheduled to be," Justice Farrell warned him. "You play ball with me, I'll play ball with you."

Mr. Hallett, pencil-thin under a puffy ski jacket, started playing bingo at church before he turned 12, experimented with slot machines while on a cruise and soon was buying 15 to 20 lottery tickets at a time while also sneaking out for bingo.

"It was like a rush of adrenaline," he recalled. "You're hooked on that feeling."

Mr. Hallett said he drained his bank account, then manipulated accounts at the doctor's office where he worked, to keep finding the money to gamble. When he was fired, he took a job at Target and soon was caught stealing gift cards. He sold his stepsister's DVDs, prompting his father to put locks on the bedroom doors.

Then his father had him arrested this year for forging checks.

Judith Munzi, a gambling recovery counselor at Jewish Family Service of Buffalo and Erie County, stood with Mr. Hallett in court and told Justice Farrell that the young man was a motivated patient, but that he suffers from attention-deficit hyperactivity disorder and may need to change his medication.

"The judge makes you not want to do something," Mr. Hallett said afterward, vowing to stay out of trouble.

The three therapeutic courts, run under the broader auspices of the town court system, which pays the judge's

$69,500 annual salary, receive about $50,000 a year in grants and donations to cover the cost of urine tests, educational materials, computers, travel expenses and overtime for police officers who search for defendants with outstanding warrants. Treatment costs are separate.

While Justice Farrell's court handles only misdemeanors involving $1,000 or less, or felonies in which charges were reduced through plea bargains, the authorities here have also seen a rise in more serious offenses rooted in gambling.

John C. Doscher, chief of the white-collar crime bureau in the Erie County district attorney's office, said his group has convicted nine people of stealing $100,000 or more in gambling-related crimes since 2005.

Among them was Judith Ann Scheitheir, who pleaded guilty in January to stealing $350,000 from the plant nursery where she worked to cover her credit-card debts and losses at casinos in Niagara Falls and Ontario. And Kenneth Mangione, chief financial officer at a boarding school for troubled children, was sentenced in March to six months in jail and ordered to repay $50,000 after he confessed to stealing almost $200,000 from the school to cover gambling losses.

When asked where the stolen money was, Mr. Doscher recalled that Mr. Mangione told prosecutors, "It's at the casino."

In gambling court, where Justice Farrell presides in front of a floor-to-ceiling mural that includes the American flag and a bald eagle, the numbers are smaller, but the stories are similar.

Experts said that therapeutic courts remain a rarity because many judges consider them an administrative burden, lawyers are often wary of letting their clients admit to an addiction on top of any particular crime, and financing is scarce.

"The easier thing to do is to sit back and see if it works elsewhere," said Carson Fox, director of operations at the National Association of Drug Court Professionals.

It seems to be working for an up-and-coming boxer identified in court as Leslie R. After being arrested for petty larceny, he recently completed a year of treatment.

Justice Farrell gave the boxer a certificate and a key chain with the inscription, "Amherst Court: Where Treatment and Justice Meet," along with a copy of "The Little Engine That Could," the classic children's book.

"I think Judge Farrell is very strict, but he's fair," Leslie R. said. "I don't plan to be back here again."

Questions

1. What are some prosocial activities a community could put in place to occupy the spare time of its young people?

2. Should people with an addiction to gambling be given the opportunity to receive treatment rather than punishment as some drug offenders and people with mental illness? Why?

INTERNET RESOURCES

Part I. Introduction

http://www.worldsocietyofvictimology.org/

The World Society of Victimology is a non-profit organization dedicated to advancing research, services, and awareness of victims around the world.

http://www.ndvh.org/

The National Domestic Violence Hotline is a 24-hour per day call center able to provide referrals and information regarding the services available in all 50 states, Puerto Rico, and the Virgin Islands.

http://www.ncadv.org

The National Coalition against Domestic Violence website is a clearinghouse of information regarding ways to get involved in domestic violence advocacy, available programs and resources, and other ways to get involved with this issue.

http://www.ojp.usdoj.gov/bjs/cvict.htm

The website for the U.S. Department of Justice's Office of Justice Programs, Bureau of Justice Statistics makes available statistics collected by the National Crime Victimization Survey and the National Incident-Based Reporting System.

Part II. Classical Criminology

http://www.securityoncampus.org

Security on Campus, Inc. is a non-profit organization started by the parents of Jeanne Clery, a college student murdered in her dorm room in 1986 and whose name has been incorporated into the legislation passed in 1990 that mandates colleges and universities collect and make available campus crime statistics.

http://www.fbi.gov/ucr/ucr.htm

The Federal Bureau of Investigation's website with Uniform Crime Reports data as well as general information about the work of the FBI. Statistics on Index crimes and hate crimes going back to 1995 are available.

http://www.cybercrime.gov

The Department of Justice's Computer Crime and Intellectual Property Section website. Includes information on agency efforts to control and prevent computer crimes, as well as federal court cases the division has prosecuted.

III. Positivism

http://www.victorianweb.org/science/phrenology/phrenologyov.html

Part of a larger website about life during the Victorian age, this section provides an overview of phrenology, a historical chronology of the approach, and terms and definitions of concepts related to phrenology.

http://www.socialresearchmethods.net/kb/desexper.php

A website devoted to the research methods used by the social sciences that accessibly describes various research designs including the various types of experimental designs as well as quasi-experimental designs.

IV. Psychological Theories

http://www.psychopathology.org

The official website of the Society for Research in Psychopathology includes a resource library and information regarding the organization's annual meeting.

http://www.rand.org/ise/security/

RAND is a non-profit organization that conducts research on a variety of social issues. This is the home page for the Homeland Security program, part of the Infrastructure, Safety, and Environment Division.

http://www.dhs.gov/index.shtm

The official website of the federal Department of Homeland Security. Includes information about travel security and procedures, as well as prevention and protection efforts.

V. Social Structure Perspective

Strain

http://www.ojjdp.ncjrs.org

The website of the U.S. Department of Justice's Office of Juvenile Justice and Delinquency Prevention includes information regarding the agency's programs designed to prevent juvenile delinquency.

Disorganization

http://www.usaonwatch.org

The National Neighborhood Watch Program is sponsored by the National Sheriffs' Association. The website provides information about starting a neighborhood watch and how to find an established local watch.

Subculture

http://www.iir.com

The Institute for Intergovernmental Research supports several law enforcement training and research programs, including the national Youth Gang Center.

VI. Social Process Perspective

Social Learning

http://sitemason.vanderbilt.edu/files/l/l3Bguk/Empirical%20Status%20of%20Social%20Learning%20Theory%20of%20Crime%20and%20Deviance.pdf

A link to a paper entitled, "Empirical status of social learning theory of crime and deviance: The past, present, and future," written by Ronald Akers and Gary Jensen.

Labeling and Reintegrative Shaming

http://www.voma.org

The website of the Victim Offender Mediation Association, an international organization that promotes restorative justice practices.

Social Control/Bond

http://www.uscourts.gov/misc/propretrial.html

The federal court's information page about probation and pretrial services.

Self-Control

http://www.plagiarism.org

The website of The Learning Center is designed to aid teachers and students better understand what plagiarism is and how to prevent it.

VII. Life Course Theory

http://www.aapss.org/uploads/Annals_Nov_2005_Sampson_Laub.pdf

A link to a paper authored by the founders of life course theory, Robert Sampson and John Laub, entitled 'A Life-course view of the development of crime.'

VIII. Cultural Criminology

http://www.critcrim.org

The official website of the Division of Critical Criminology of the American Society of Criminology, it includes access to the division newsletter and links to other critical criminology websites.

IX. Crime Policy

http://www.ncjrs.gov

The National Criminal Justice Reference Service is a clearinghouse of information and research results on a wide range of criminal justice and substance abuse issues.

http://www.criminologycenter.fsu.edu

The Center for Criminology and Public Policy based at Florida State University conducts research with criminal justice policy implications.

X. The Future of Criminology

http://www.hrw.org

Human Rights Watch is an organization dedicated to monitoring human rights and abuses around the world.

XI. Crime Typologies

Violent Crime and Terrorism

http://www.ncjrs.gov/pdffiles1/bja/213930.pdf

U.S. Department of Justice, Office of Justice Programs, Bureau of Justice Statistics; a document about how to protect judicial officials from threat in the line of duty.

http://www.policeforum.org/index.asp

Police Executive Research Forum, an organization of police executives from the largest agencies that serves to produce research and provide training in the latest law enforcement strategies.

Property Crime

http://www.ojp.usdoj.gov/bjs/abstract/cv06.htm

Criminal victimization rates for personal and property crime in 2006.

White-Collar and Organized Crime

http://www.fbi.gov/hq/cid/orgcrime/ocshome.htm

The Federal Bureau of Investigation's Organized Crime Division; research and resources about organized crime domestically and internationally.

Public Order Crimes

http://ojjdp.ncjrs.gov/programs/ProgSummary.asp?pi=19&ti=&si=&kw=&PreviousPage=ProgResults

U.S. Department of Justice, Office of Justice Programs, Office of Juvenile Justice and Delinquency Prevention; Program of Research on the Causes and Correlates of Delinquency.

http://www.law.arizona.edu/depts/upr-intj/

International Network on Therapeutic Jurisprudence; home page of an international clearinghouse and resource center regarding developments in therapeutic jurisprudence.

http://www.cybercrime.gov/

U.S. Department of Justice, Computer Crime and Intellectual Property Section, describes the work and research of this agency.

INDEX

ABOUT THE EDITOR

Gennifer Furst is currently an assistant professor in the Sociology Department at William Paterson University in New Jersey. She received her doctorate in Criminal Justice from CUNY Graduate Center/John Jay College. Dr. Furst's research interests focus on issues of incarceration. She published the first national survey of prison-based animal programs in the United States. Additionally, she is interested in race and the administration of justice, capital punishment, and drugs and crime.